Greenwich Readers: 7

The Black Experience 1865–1978

The Black Experience 1865–1978

A Documentary Reader

edited by

ANTHONY J. COOPER

SCHOOL OF HUMANITIES
UNIVERSITY OF GREENWICH

First published in 1995 by
Greenwich University Press
Unit 42
Dartford Trade Park
Hawley Road
Dartford
Kent DA1 1PF
United Kingdom

British Library Cataloguing-in-Publication Data
A CIP catalogue record for this book is available from the British Library

ISBN 1 874529 51 5

Designed and produced for Greenwich University Press by
Angela Allwright and Kirsten Brown.

Printed in Great Britain by The Bath Press, Avon.

Contents

Introduction

This collection of documents has its origins in a course on black history and experience since the American Civil War, which has been offered for several years as an option in American Studies in the Humanities Degree of the School of Humanities at the University of Greenwich. The course is grounded in contemporary materials and in those secondary commentaries and interpretations which have, over the years, themselves become source materials for the study of this area. It aims to present students with a historical understanding of the black experience in the United States since 1865, but also with the interaction between historical events and experience and theoretical analyses and explanations of social behaviour which bear upon race relations. In the course, students gain some insight into the nature and reliability of the sources available to them, and also into the social, economic and political context in which the documents have been generated, whether primary or secondary.

The range of extant original materials for the study of black life and history in the United States is extremely rich, as is evidenced by the many collections (now largely out of print) which have been previously produced on different aspects, and on which this present Reader has partly drawn. This collection represents the editor's chosen amalgam of sources for the pursuit of a particular historical trail, but one which is related to relevant theoretical analyses and which reflects a long-standing debate about the status and treatment of Black Americans.

The starting point of the Reader is the end of the Civil War and the emancipation of the previously enslaved black population in the South. Over a period of more than a hundred years, the documents illustrate and explore the attempts by black Americans to gain a recognised economic and political status in the United States, and the reasons why this has taken so long and is arguably still incomplete. They exemplify the different ways forward advocated by a variety of black leaders and thinkers; and they explore the background to white prejudice against black Americans, and the consequent reluctance of whites, and, in particular, Southern whites, to accord equal political and economic rights and opportunities to a racially distinct group forming between 10 – 12% of the total population.

The documents illustrate a number of themes in the black experience which are recurrent for much of the period which is covered:

(i) the resistance of the white South to the abandonment of the social control of the black population as well as to the loss of a captive labour force, both of which were features of the ante-bellum slave system;

(ii) the consequences of the failure of the United States government to provide grants of land for ex-slaves, which hindered their ability to build a sound economic future in the South;

(iii) the systematic denial of political rights to the black population in the South, which limited their opportunity for effective influence nationally, just as the denial of participation in organised labour and skilled work limited their opportunities for employment outside the rural South;

(iv) the stress which all black leaders placed on education, personal effort and entrepreneurial activity – the pursuit of the "Protestant work ethic", in fact, – which typified so many immigrant groups, even if the rewards for Afro-Americans were less apparent than with other groups;

(v) the existence of racism throughout the country even if its most dramatic manifestations tended to be located in the South;

(vi) the continued tension between the accommodationist approach advocated by some black leaders and the more confrontational style adopted by others; and between the divergent aims of segregation or integration for the black population in the pursuit of progress and recognition;

(vii) the difficulty of reconciling different explanations for the experience of race relations in the United States based on economic/capitalistic/class exploitation, white racism, or other social/psychological factors.

From the perspective of the 1990s, it seems that many of the social and political advances to which Gunnar Myrdal looked forward in An American Dilemma have been achieved: the American Creed has ultimately delivered. Nevertheless, problems still abound for the black community in the United States – problems of economic status, opportunity, and valuation by the white society and culture. Such problems are less easily resolved by legislation and the democratic spirit, and are likely to have to wait upon time, persistence and the development of the melting pot.

In the preparation of this Reader, the editor has been greatly supported by Iain Moir and Clive Seymour of Greenwich University Press.

Anthony J. Cooper
June 1995

Bibliographic sources

Brotz, H. (ed.), *Negro Social and Political Thought, 1850-1920: Representative Texts* (New York: Basic Books, 1966).

Commager, H.S. (ed.), *Documents of American History*, 10th edn (Englewood Cliffs: Prentice-Hall, Inc., 1988; originally published by F.S. Crofts & Co, Inc., 1934).

Cox, L. and Cox, J.H. (eds.), *Reconstruction, the Negro, and the New South* (New York: Harper Torchbook, 1973).

Cox, O.C., *Caste, Class & Race* (New York: Monthly Review Press, 1970; originally published by Doubleday & Co, Inc., 1948).

Dollard, J.H., *Caste and Class in a Southern Town*, 4th edn (Madison: University of Wisconsin Press, 1989; originally published by Harper & Brothers, 1937).

Fishel, L.H. and Quarles, B. (eds.), *The Black American: A Documentary History*, 3rd edn (Glenview: Scott, Foresman & Co, c. 1976; originally published in 1967 and 1968 under the title: *The Negro American*).

Fisher, S., *Power and the Black Community: A Reader on Racial Subordination in the United States* (New York: Random House, 1970).

Foner, P.S. and Lewis, R.L. (eds.), *The Black Worker: A Documentary History from Colonial Times to the Present*, Vols I-IV (Philadelphia: Temple University Press).

Meier, A., Rudwick, E. and Broderick, F.L. (eds.), *Black Protest Thought in the Twentieth Century* (Macmillan, 1971; originally published by Bobbs Merrill, 1971).

Myrdal, G., *An American Dilemma: The Negro Problem and Modern Democracy* (Harper Torchbook, 1969; originally published by Harper & Row, 1944).

Osofsky, G., *The Burden of Race: A Documentary History of Negro-White Relations in America* (Harper & Row, 1968).

Park, R.E., *Race and Culture: Essays in the Sociology of Contemporary Man* (New York: The Free Press, 1964; originally published by The Free Press in 1950 as Vol. I of *The Collected Papers of Robert Ezra Park*, edited by Everett Cherrington Hughes, Charles S. Johnson, Jitsuichi Masuoka, Robert Redfield, and Louis Wirth.

Ransom, R. and Sutch, R., *One Kind of Freedom: The Economic Consequences of Emancipation* (Cambridge: Cambridge University Press, 1977).

The New York Times

Van Noppen, I., *The South: A Documentary History* (D. Van Nostrand Company, Inc., 1958).

Publisher's note

The readings in this anthology have been reproduced exactly as they appear in the publications from which they are taken. In the majority of cases footnotes and bibliographic material are included, the exceptions being where they are of excessive length. Photographs have not been reproduced.

The Era of Reconstruction

1.1 Freedmen's Bureau Report, 1865

Established by Congress in 1865 as part of the War Department, the Bureau of Refugees, Freedmen and Abandoned Lands was intended to make provision for the many thousands of former slaves made destitute by the breakdown of the plantation system in the course of the Civil War. The Bureau operated through the occupying Federal armies in the states of the Confederacy and was authorised to make available 40 acre plots to the landless Freedmen from the lands confiscated from rebel owners. The availability of such lands rapidly declined when President Andrew Johnson granted pardons in the summer of 1865 to many rebel owners who were then able to reclaim their property. The following is a summary report submitted by Colonel E. Whittlesey, assistant commissioner for the Bureau in North Carolina, in October 1865.

On the 22nd of June I arrived at Raleigh with instructions from you to take the control of all subjects relating to "refugees, freedmen, and the abandoned lands" within this State. I found these subjects in much confusion. Hundreds of white refugees and thousands of blacks were collected about this and other towns, occupying every hovel and shanty, living upon government rations, without employment and without comfort, many dying for want of proper food and medical supplies. A much larger number, both white and black, were crowding into the towns, and literally swarming about every depot of supplies to receive their rations. My first effort was to reduce this class of suffering and idle humanity to order, and to discover how large a proportion of these applicants were really deserving of help. The whites, excepting "loyal refugees", were referred to the military authorities. To investigate the condition of refugees and freedmen and minister to the wants of the destitute, I saw at once would require the services of a large number of efficient officers. As fast as suitable persons could be selected, application was made to the department and district commanders for their detail, in accordance with General Order No. 102, War Department, May 31, 1865. In many cases these applications were unsuccessful, because the officers asked for could not be spared. The difficulties and delays experienced in obtaining the help needed for a proper organization of my work will be seen from the fact that upon thirty-four written requests, in due form, only eleven officers have been detailed by the department and district commanders. . . .

With this brief history of my efforts to organize the bureau, I proceed to state

The design and work proposed

In my circulars Nos. 1 and 2 (copies of which are herewith enclosed) the objects to be attained are fully stated. All officers of the bureau are instructed –

1. To aid the destitutes, yet in such a way as not to encourage dependence.
2. To protect freedmen from injustice.
3. To assist freedmen in obtaining employment and fair wages for their labor.
4. To encourage education, intellectual and moral.

Under these four divisions the operations of the bureau can best be presented.

Relief afforded

It was evident at the outset that large numbers were drawing rations who might support themselves. The street in front of the post commissary's office was blocked up with vehicles of all the descriptions peculiar to North Carolina, and with people who had come from the country around, in some instances from a distance of sixty miles, for government rations. These were destitute whites, and were supplied by order of the department commander. Our own headquarters, and every office of the bureau, was besieged from morning till night by freedmen, some coming many miles on foot, others in wagons and carts. The rations issued would scarcely last till they reached home, and in many instances they were sold before leaving the town, in exchange for luxuries. To correct these evils, orders were issued that no able-bodied man or woman should receive supplies, except such as were known to be industrious, and to be entirely destitute. Great care was needed to protect the bureau from imposition, and at the same time to relieve the really deserving. By constant inquiry and effort the throng of beggars was gradually removed. The homeless and helpless were gathered in camps, where shelter and food could be furnished, and the sick collected in hospitals, where they could receive proper care . . . .

Protection

Regarding this bureau as the appointed instrument for redeeming the solemn pledge of the nation, through its Chief Magistrate, to secure the rights of freedmen, I have made every effort to protect them from wrong. Suddenly set free, they were at first exhilarated by the air of liberty, and committed some excesses. To be sure of their freedom, many thought they must leave the old scenes of oppression and seek new homes. Others regarded the property accumulated by their labor as in part their own, and demanded a share of it. On the other hand, the former masters, suddenly stripped of their wealth, at first looked upon the freedmen with a mixture of hate and fear. In these circumstances some collisions were inevitable. The negroes were complained of as idle, insolent, and dishonest; while they complained that they were treated with more cruelty than when they were slaves. Some were tied up and whipped without trial; some were driven from their homes without pay for their labor, without clothing or means of support; others were forbidden to leave on pain of death, and a few were shot or otherwise murdered. All officers of the bureau were directed, in accordance with your circular No.5. to investigate these difficulties between the two classes, to settle them by counsel and arbitration as far as possible, to punish light offences by fines or otherwise, and to report more serious cases of crime to the military authorities for trial. The exact number of cases heard and decided cannot be given; they have been so numerous that no complete record could be kept; one officer reported that he had heard and disposed of as many as 180 complaints in a single day.

Industry

Contrary to the fears and predictions of many, the great mass of colored people have remained quietly at work upon the plantations of their former masters during the entire summer. The crowds seen about the towns in the early part of the season had followed in the wake of the Union army, to escape from slavery. After hostilities ceased these refugees returned to their homes, so that but few vagrants can now be found. In truth, a much larger amount of vagrancy exists among the whites than among the blacks. It is the almost uniform report of officers of the bureau that freedmen are industrious.

The report is confirmed by the fact that out of a colored population of nearly 350,000 in the State, only about 5,000 are now receiving support from the government. Probably some others are receiving aid from kindhearted men who have enjoyed the benefit of their services from childhood. To the general quiet and industry of this people there can be no doubt that the efforts of the bureau have contributed greatly. I have visited some of the larger towns, as Wilmington, Newbern, Goldsborough, and both by public addresses and private instructions counselled the freedmen to secure employment and maintain themselves. Captain James has made an extensive tour through the eastern district for the same purpose, and has exerted a most happy influence. Lieutenant Colonel Clapp has spent much of his time in visiting the county seats of the central district, and everywhere been listened to by all classes with deep interest. Other officers have done much good in this way. They have visited plantations, explained the differences between slave and free labor, the nature and the solemn obligation of contracts. The chief difficulty met with has been a want of confidence between the two parties. The employer, accustomed only to the system of compulsory labor, is slow to believe that he can secure fruitful services by the stimulus of wages. The laborer is unwilling to trust the promises of those for whom he had toiled all his days without pay; hence but few contracts for long periods have been effected. The bargains for the present year are generally vague, and their settlement as the crops are gathered in requires much labor. In a great majority of cases the landowners seem disposed to do justly, and even generously; and when this year's work is done, and the proceeds divided, it is hoped that a large number of freedmen will enter into contracts for the coming year. They will, however, labor much more cheerfully for money, with prompt and frequent payments, than for a share of the crop, for which they must wait twelve months. A large farmer in Pitt county hires hands by the job, and states that he never saw negroes work so well. Another in Lenoir county pays monthly, and is satisfied so far with the experiment of free labor. *Another obstacle to long contracts was found in the impression which had become prevalent to some degree, i.e., that lands were to be given to freedmen by the government*. To correct this false impression I published a circular, No.3. and directed all officers of the bureau to make it as widely known as possible. From the statistical reports enclosed, it will be seen that during the quarter 257 written contracts for labor have been prepared and witnessed; that the average rate of wages, when paid in money, is from $8 to $10 per month; that 128 farms are under the control of the bureau and cultivated for the benefit of freedmen; that 8,540 acres are under cultivation, and 6,102 are employed. Many of the farms were rented by agents of the treasury as abandoned lands, previous to the establishing of this bureau , and were transferred to us with the leases upon them. Nearly all have been restored to their owners, under the President's proclamation of amnesty, and our tenure of the few that remain is so uncertain that I have not deemed it prudent to set apart any for use of refugees and freedmen, in accordance with the act of Congress approved March 3, 1865. But many freedmen are taking this matter into their own hands, and renting lands from the owners for one or more years. . .

Source: *Report of the Joint Committee on Reconstruction*, Washington, 1866.

1.2 The Black Codes, 1865

These laws were passed in the period of Presidential Reconstruction by state governments dominated by planters, ex-Confederates and ante-bellum politicians. Their aims were to control the activities of the free black population in the states of the South, and to preserve a captive labour force for the plantations. Their provisions hark back to the previous slave codes. The Black Codes remained in force only until military rule was established by Congress in the states of the former Confederacy and the passage of the Civil Rights Act of 1866 and the Fourteenth Amendment.

BLACK CODE OF MISSISSIPPI 1865

1. Civil Rights of Freedmen in Mississippi

Sec. 1. *Be it enacted,* . . . That all freedmen, free negroes, and mulattoes may sue and be sued, implead and be impleaded, in all the courts of law and equity of this State, and may acquire personal property, and choses in action, by descent or purchase, and may dispose of the same in the same manner and to the same extent that white persons may: *Provided,* That the provisions of this section shall not be so construed as to allow any freedman, free negro, or mulatto to rent or lease any lands or tenements except in incorporated cities or towns, in which places the corporate authorities shall control the same . . .

Sec. 3. . . . All freedmen, free negroes, or mulattoes who do now and have herebefore lived and cohabited together as husband and wife shall be taken and held in law as legally married, and the issue shall be taken and held as legitimate for all purposes; that it shall not be lawful for any freedman, free negro, or mulatto to intermarry with any white person; nor for any white person to intermarry with any freedman, free negro, or mulatto; and any person who shall so intermarry, shall be deemed guilty of felony, and on conviction, thereof shall be confined in the State penitentiary for life; and those shall be deemed freedmen, free negroes, and mulattoes who are of pure negro blood, and those descended from a negro to the third generation, inclusive, though one ancestor in each generation may have been a white person.

Sec. 4. . . . In addition to cases in which freedmen, free negroes, and mulattoes are now by law competent witnesses, freedmen, free negroes, or mulattoes shall be competent in civil cases, when a party or parties to the suit, either plaintiff or plaintiffs, defendant or defendants, and a white person or white persons, is or are the opposing party or parties, plaintiff or plaintiffs, defendant or defendants. They shall also be competent witnesses in all criminal prosecutions where the crime charged is alleged to have been committed by a white person upon or against the person or property of a freedman, free negro, or mulatto: *Provided,* that in all cases said witnesses shall be examined in open court, on the stand; except, however, they may be examined before the grand jury, and shall in all cases be subject to the rules and tests of the common law as to competency and credibility. . . .

Sec. 6. . . . All contracts for labor made with freedmen, free negroes, and mulattoes for a longer period than one month shall be in writing, and in duplicate, attested and read to said freedman, free negro, or mulatto by a beat, city or county officer, or two disinterested white persons of the county in which the labor is to be performed, of which each party shall have one; and said contracts shall be taken and held as entire contracts, and if the laborer shall quit the service of the employer before the expiration of his term of service without good cause, he shall forfeit his wages for that year up to the time of quitting.

Sec. 7. . . .Every civil officer shall, and every person may, arrest and carry back to his or her legal employer any freedman, free negro, or mulatto who shall have quit the service of his or her employer before the expiration of his or her term of service without good cause; and said officer and person shall be entitled to receive for arresting and carrying back every deserting employee aforesaid the sum of five dollars, and ten cents per mile from the place of arrest to the place of delivery; and the same shall be paid by the employer, and held as a set-off for so much against the wages of said deserting employee: *Provided*, that said arrested party, after being so returned, may appeal to the justice of the peace or member of the board of police of the county, who, on notice to the alleged employer, shall try summarily whether said appellant is legally employed by the alleged employer, and has good cause to quit said employer; either party shall have the right to appeal to the county court, pending which the alleged deserter shall be remanded to the alleged employer or otherwise disposed of, as shall be right and just; and the decision of the county court shall be final . . . .

Sec. 9. . . . If any person shall persuade or attempt to persuade, entice, or cause any freedman, free negro, or mulatto to desert from the legal employment of any person before the expiration of his or her term of service, or shall knowingly employ any such deserting freedman, free negro, or mulatto, or shall knowingly give or sell to any such deserting freedman, free negro, or mulatto, any food, raiment, or other thing, he or she shall be guilty of a misdemeanor, and upon conviction, shall be fined not less than twenty-five dollars and not more than two hundred dollars and the costs; and if said fine and costs shall not be immediately paid, the court shall sentence said convict to not exceeding two months' imprisonment in the county jail, and he or she shall moreover be liable to the party injured in damages: *Provided,* if any person shall, or shall attempt to, persuade, entice, or cause any freedman, free negro, or mulatto to desert from any legal employment of any person, with the view to employ said freedman, free negro, or mulatto without the limits of this State, such person, on conviction, shall be fined not less than fifty dollars, and not more than five hundred dollars and costs; and if said fine and costs shall not be immediately paid, the court shall sentence said convict to not exceeding six months imprisonment in the county jail.

2. Mississippi Apprentice Law

Sec. 1. . . . It shall be the duty of all sheriffs, justices of the peace, and other civil officers of the several counties in this State, to report to the probate courts of their respective counties semi-annually, at the January and July terms of said courts, all freedmen, free negroes, and mulattoes, under the age of eighteen, in their respective counties, beats or districts, who are orphans, or whose parent or parents have not the means or who refuse to provide for and support said minors; and thereupon it shall be duty of said probate court to order the clerk of said court to apprentice said minors to some competent and suitable person, on such terms as the court may direct, having a particular care to the interest of said minor: *Provided,* that the former owner of said minors shall have the preference when, in the opinion of the court, he or she shall be a suitable person for that purpose.

Sec. 2. . . . The said court shall be fully satisfied that the person or persons to whom said minor shall be apprenticed shall be a suitable person to have the charge and care of said minor, and fully to protect the interest of said minor. The said court shall require the said master or mistress to execute bond and security, payable to the State of Mississippi, conditioned that he or she shall furnish said minor with sufficient food and clothing; to treat said minor humanely; furnish medical attention in case of sickness; teach, or cause to be taught, him or her to read and write, if under fifteen years old, and will conform to any law that may be hereafter passed for the regulation of the duties and relation of master and apprentice . . . .

Sec. 3. . . . In the management and control of said apprentice, said master or mistress shall have the power to inflict such moderate corporal chastisement as a father, or guardian is allowed to inflict on his or her child or ward at common law: *Provided,* that in no case shall cruel or inhuman punishment be inflicted.

Sec. 4. . . . If any apprentice shall leave the employment of his or her master or mistress, without his or her consent, said master or mistress may pursue and recapture said apprentice, and bring him or her before any justice of the peace of the county, whose duty it shall be to remand said apprentice to the service of his or her master or mistress; and in the event of a refusal on the part of said apprentice so to return, then said justice shall commit said apprentice to the jail of said county, on failure to give bond, to the next term of the county court; and it shall be the duty of said court at the first term thereafter to investigate said case, and if the court shall be of opinion that said apprentice left the employment of his or her master or mistress without good cause, to order him or her to be punished, as provided for the punishment of hired freedmen, as may be from time to time provided for by law for desertion, until he or she shall agree to return to the service of his or her master or mistress. . . if the court shall believe that said apprentice had good cause to quit his said master or mistress, the court shall discharge said apprentice from said indenture, and also enter a judgement against the master or mistress for not more than one hundred dollars, for the use and benefit of said apprentice. . .

3. Mississippi Vagrant Law

Sec. 1. *Be it enacted,* etc., . . . That all rogues and vagabonds, idle and dissipated persons, beggars, jugglers, or persons practicing unlawful games or plays, runaways, common drunkards, common night-walkers, pilferers, lewd, wanton, or lascivious persons, in speech or behavior, common railers and brawlers, persons who neglect their calling or employment, misspend what they earn, or do not provide for the support of themselves or their families, or dependents, and all other idle and disorderly persons, including all who neglect all lawful business, habitually mis-spend their time by frequenting houses of ill-fame, gaming-houses, or tippling shops, shall be deemed and considered vagrants, under the provisions of this act, and upon conviction thereof shall be fined not exceeding one hundred dollars, with all accruing costs, and be imprisoned at the discretion of the court, not exceeding ten days.

Sec. 2. . . . All freedmen, free negroes and mulattoes in this State, over the age of eighteen years, found on the second Monday in January, 1866, or thereafter, with no lawful employment or business, or found unlawfully assembling themselves together, either in the day or night time, and all white persons so assembling themselves with freedmen, free negroes or mulattoes, or usually associating with freedmen, free negroes or mulattoes on terms of equality, or living in adultery or fornication with a freed woman, free negro or mulatto, shall be deemed vagrants, and on conviction thereof shall be fined in a sum not exceeding, in the case of a freedman, free negro or mulatto, fifty dollars, and a white man two hundred dollars, and imprisoned at the discretion of the court, the free negro not exceeding ten days, and the white man not exceeding six months . . .

Sec. 7. . . If any freedman, free negro, or mulatto shall fail or refuse to pay any tax levied according to the provisions of the sixth section of this act, it shall be *prima facie* evidence of vagrancy, and it shall be the duty of the sheriff to arrest such freedman, free negro, or mulatto or such person refusing or neglecting to pay such tax, and proceed at once to hire for the shortest time such delinquent tax-payer to any one who will pay the said tax, with accruing costs, giving preference to the employer, if there be one . . .

4. Penal Laws of Mississippi

Sec. 1. *Be it enacted,* . . . That no freedman, free negro or mulatto, not in the military service of the United States government, and not licensed so to do by the board of police of his or her county, shall keep or carry fire-arms of any kind, or any ammunition, dirk or bowie knife, and on conviction thereof in the county court shall be punished by fine, not exceeding ten dollars, and pay the costs of such proceedings, and all such arms or ammunition shall be forfeited to the informer; and it shall be the duty of every civil and military officer to arrest any freedman, free negro or mulatto found with any such arms or ammunition, and cause him or her to be committed to trial in default of bail.

Sec. 2. . . . Any freedman, free negro, or mulatto committing riots, routs, affrays, trespasses, malicious mischief, cruel treatment to animals, seditious speeches, insulting gestures, language, or acts, or assaults on any person, disturbance of the peace, exercising the function of a minister of the Gospel without a license from some regularly organized church, vending spirituous or intoxicating liquors, or committing any other misdemeanor, the punishment of which is not specifically provided for by law, shall, upon conviction thereof in the county court, be fined not less than ten dollars, and not more than one hundred dollars, and may be imprisoned at the discretion of the court, not exceeding thirty days.

Sec. 3. . . . If any white person shall sell, lend, or give to any freedman, free negro, or mulatto any fire-arms, dirk or bowie knife, or ammunition, or any spirituous or intoxicating liquors, such person or persons so offending, upon conviction thereof in the county court of his or her county, shall be fined not exceeding fifty dollars, and may be imprisoned, at the discretion of the court, not exceeding thirty days. . .

Sec. 5. . . . If any freedman, free negro, or mulatto, convicted of any of the misdemeanors provided against in this act, shall fail or refuse for the space of five days, after conviction, to pay the fine and costs imposed, such person shall be hired out by the sheriff or other officer, at public outcry, to any white person who will pay said fine and all costs, and take said convict for the shortest time.

Source: *Laws of Mississippi*, 1865, p. 82ff; p. 86; p. 90; p. 165.

BLACK CODE OF LOUISIANA 1865

1. An Act to Provide for and Regulate Labor Contracts for Agricultural Pursuits

Sec. 1. Be it enacted by the Senate and House of Representatives of the State of Louisiana in general assembly convened, That all persons employed as laborers in agricultural pursuits shall be required, during the first ten days of the month of January of each year, to make contracts for labor for the then ensuing year, or for the year next ensuing the termination of their present contracts. All contracts for labor for agriculture purposes shall be made in writing, signed by the employer, and shall be made in the presence of a Justice of the Peace and two disinterested witnesses, in whose presence the contract shall be read to the laborer, and when assented to and signed by the latter, shall be considered as binding for the time prescribed. . .

Sec. 2. Every laborer shall have full and perfect liberty to choose his employer, but, when once chosen, he shall not be allowed to leave his place of employment until the fulfillment of his contract . . . and if they do so leave, without cause or permission, they shall forfeit all wages earned to the time of abandonment. . .

Sec. 7. All employers failing to comply with their contracts, shall, upon conviction, be fined an amount double that due the laborer . . . to be paid to the laborer; and any inhumanity, cruelty, or neglect of duty on the part of the employer shall be summarily punished by fines . . . to be paid to the injured party . . .

Sec. 8. Be it further enacted, &c., That in case of sickness of the laborer, wages for the time lost shall be deducted, and where the sickness is feigned for purposes of idleness, and also on refusal to work according to contract, double the amount of wages shall be deducted for the time lost; and also where rations have been furnished; and should the refusal to work continue beyond three days the offender shall be reported to a Justice of the Peace, and shall be forced to labor on roads, levees, and other public works, without pay, until the offender consents to return to his labor.

Sec. 9. Be it further enacted, &c., That, when in health, the laborer shall work ten hours during the day in summer, and nine hours during the day in winter, unless otherwise stipulated in the labor contract; he shall obey all proper orders of his employer or his agent; take proper care of his work-mules, horses, oxen, stock; also of all agricultural implements; and employers shall have the right to make a reasonable deduction from the laborer's wages for injuries done to animals or agricultural implements committed to his care, or for bad or negligent work. Bad work shall not be allowed. Failing to obey reasonable orders, neglect of duty, and leaving home without permission will be deemed disobedience; impudence, swearing, or indecent language to or in the presence of the employer, his family, or agent, or quarreling and fighting with one another, shall be deemed disobedience. For any disobedience a fine of one dollar shall be imposed on and paid by the offender. For all lost time from work-hours, unless in case of sickness, the laborer shall be fined twenty-five cents per hour. For all absence from home without leave he will be fined at the rate of two dollars per day. Laborers will not be required to labor on the Sabbath unless by special contract. For all thefts of the laborer from the employer of agricultural products, hogs, sheep, poultry, or any other property of the employer, or willful destruction of property or injury, the laborer shall pay the employer double the amount of the value of the property stolen, destroyed, or injured, one-half to be paid to the employer and the other half to be placed in the general fund provided for in this section. No live stock shall be allowed to laborers without the permission of the employer. Laborers shall not receive visitors during work-hours. All difficulties arising between the employers and laborers, under this section, shall be settled by the former; if not satisfactory to the laborers, an appeal may be had to the nearest Justice of the Peace and two freeholders, citizens, one of said citizens to be selected by the employer and the other by the laborer, and all fines imposed and collected under this section shall be deducted from wages due, and shall be placed in a common fund, to be divided among the other laborers on the plantation, except as provided for above . . .

Sec. 10. Be it further enacted, &c., That for gross misconduct on the part of the laborer, such as insubordination, habitual laziness, frequent acts of violation of his contract or the laws of the State, he may be dismissed by his employer; nevertheless, the laborer shall have the right to resist his dismissal and to a redress of his wrongs by an appeal to a Justice of the Peace and two freeholders, citizens of the parish, one of the freeholders to be selected by himself and the other by his employer.

2. An Act Relative to Apprentices and Indentured Servants

Sec. 1. Be it enacted . . . That it shall be the duty of Sheriffs, Justices of the Peace, and other Civil officers of this State, to report . . . for each and every year, all persons under the age of eighteen years, if females, and twenty-one, if males, who are orphans, or whose parents, . . . have not the means, or who refuse to provide for and maintain said minors; and thereupon it shall be the duty of the Clerk of the District Courts . . . to examine whether the party or parties so reported from time to time, come within the purview and meaning of this Act, and, if so, to apprentice said minor or minors, in manner and form as prescribed by the Civil Code . . .

Sec. 2. That persons, who have attained the age of majority, . . . may bind themselves to services to be performed in this State, for the term of five years, on such terms as they may stipulate, as domestic servants, and to work on farms, plantations, or in manufacturing establishments.

Source: Acts of the General Assembly of Louisiana Regulating Labor. Extra Session, 1865, p. 3. ff.

1.3 The Fourteenth Amendment, 1868

Rejected by most of the states of the South in the period of Presidential Reconstruction, ratification of the Fourteenth Amendment was made a condition of their readmission to the Union by Congress. The Amendment defined citizenship for the first time, and gave Federal protection against any infringements of the rights of citizenship by state governments. Also for the first time, the right to vote was specifically reserved to the male inhabitants of a state.

Art. XIV

Sec. 1. All persons born or naturalized in the United States, and subject to the jurisdiction thereof, are citizens of the United States and of the State wherein they reside. No State shall make or enforce any law which shall abridge the privileges or immunities of citizens of the United States; nor shall any State deprive any person of life, liberty, or property, without due process of law; nor deny to any person within its jurisdiction the equal protection of the laws.

Sec. 2. Representatives shall be apportioned among the several States according to their respective numbers, counting the whole number of persons in each State, excluding Indians not taxed. But when the right to vote at any election for the choice of electors for President and Vice-President of the United States, Representatives in Congress, the Executive and Judicial officers of a State, or the members of the Legislature thereof, is denied to any of the male inhabitants of such State, being twenty-one years of age, and citizens of the United States, or in any way abridged, except for participation in rebellion, or other crime, the basis of representation therein shall be reduced in the proportion which the number of such male citizens shall bear to the whole number of male citizens twenty-one years of age in such State.

Sec. 3. No person shall be a Senator or Representative in Congress, or elector of President and Vice-President, or hold any office, civil or military, under the United States, or under any State, who, having previously taken an oath, as a member of Congress, or as an officer of the United States, or as a member of any State legislature, or as an executive or judicial officer of any State, to support the Constitution of the United States, shall have engaged in insurrection or rebellion against the same, or given aid or comfort to the enemies thereof. But Congress may by a vote of two-thirds of each House, remove such disability.

Sec. 4. The validity of the public debt of the United States, authorized by law, including debts incurred for payment of pensions and bounties for services in suppressing insurrection or rebellion, shall not be questioned. But neither the United States nor any State shall assume or pay any debt or obligation incurred in aid of insurrection or rebellion against the United States, or any claim for the loss or emancipation of any slave; but all such debts, obligations and claims shall be held illegal and void.

Sec. 5. The Congress shall have power to enforce, by appropriate legislation, the provisions of this article.

Source: Constitution of the United States, Article XIV, 28 July 1868.

1.4 Negro Suffrage, 1867

Thaddeus Stevens was a leading Radical Republican in the House of Representatives. In the light of the initial establishment of Confederate-dominated state governments in the South at the end of the Civil War, he advocated giving the vote to the black population in the South (and, by extension, throughout the country), first, to build up the strength of the Union/Republican Party in the South, and second, to guarantee the continuance of the Congressional reforms there.

UNLESS THE REBEL States, before admission should be made republican in spirit, and placed under the guardianship of loyal men, all our blood and treasure will have been spent in vain. I waive now the question of punishment which, if we are wise, will still be inflicted by moderate confiscations . . . Having these States . . . entirely within the power of Congress, it is our duty to take care that no injustice shall remain in their organic laws. Holding them "like clay in the hands of the potter," we must see that no vessel is made for destruction. Having now no governments, they must have enabling acts. The law of last session with regard to Territories settled the principles of such acts. Impartial suffrage, both in electing the delegates and ratifying their proceedings, is now the fixed rule. There is more reason why colored voters should be admitted in the rebel States than in the Territories. In the States they form the great mass of the loyal men. Possibly with their aid loyal governments may be established in most of those States. Without it all are sure to be ruled by traitors; and loyal men, black and white, will be oppressed, exiled, or murdered. There are several good reasons for the passage of this bill. In the first place, it is just. I am now confining my argument to negro suffrage in the rebel States. Have not loyal blacks quite as good a right to choose rulers and make laws as rebel whites? In the second place, it is a necessity in order to protect the loyal white men in the seceded States. The white Union men are in a great minority in each of those States. With them the blacks would act in a body; and it is believed that in each of said States, except one, the two united would form a majority, control the States and protect themselves. Now they are the victims of daily murder. They must suffer constant persecution or be exiled . . .

Another good reason is, it would insure the ascendency of the Union party . . . I believe . . . that on the continued ascendency of that party depends the safety of this great nation. If impartial suffrage is excluded in the rebel States, then every one of them is sure to send a solid rebel representative delegation to Congress, and cast a solid rebel electoral vote. They, with their kindred Copperheads of the North, would always elect the President and control Congress. While slavery sat upon her defiant throne, and insulted and intimidated the trembling North, the South frequently divided on questions of policy between Whigs and Democrats, and gave victory alternately to the sections. Now, you must divide them between loyalists, without regard to color, and disloyalists, or you will be the perpetual vassals of the free-trade, irritated, revengeful South . . . I am for negro suffrage in every rebel State. If it be just, it should not be denied; if it be necessary, it should be adopted; if it be a punishment to traitors, they deserve it.

Source: *Congressional Globe*, January 1867.

1.5 Redistribution of Confiscated Confederate Lands to Freedmen, 1865

In order to change "the whole fabric of Southern society", Thaddeus Stevens had advocated the confiscation of the estates of substantial Confederates and their redistribution to freedmen. This proved impossible as a result of President Johnson's decision to allow leading rebels to sue for pardon and to regain their lands, and the landless situation of the freedmen remained an economic and political issue for the future.

. . . Four years of bloody and expensive war waged against the United States by eleven States, under a government called the "Confederate States of America" to which they acknowledged allegiance, have overthrown all governments within those States, which could be acknowledged as legitimate by the Union. The armies of the Confederate States having been conquered and subdued, and their territories possessed by the United States, it becomes necessary to establish governments therein, which shall be republican in "form and principles, and form a more perfect union" with the parent government. . . . We hold it to be the duty of the Government to inflict condign punishment on the rebel belligerents, and so weaken their hands that they can never again endanger the Union; and so reform their municipal institutions as to make them republican in spirit as well as in name.

We especially insist that the property of the chief rebels should be seized and appropriated to the payment of the National debt, caused by the unjust and wicked war which they instigated.

How can such punishments be inflicted and such forfeitures produced without doing violence to established principles.

Two positions have been suggested

1st – To treat those States as never having been out of the Union. . . .

2nd – To accept the position in which they placed themselves as severed from the Union, an independent government *de facto*, and an enemy alien to be dealt with according to the laws of war . . .

In reconstruction . . . no reform can be effected in the Southern States if they have never left the Union. But reformation *must* be effected; the foundation of their institutions, both political, municipal and social *must* be broken up and *relaid*, or all our blood and treasure have been spent in vain. This can only be done by treating and holding them as a conquered people. Then all things which we can desire to do, follow with logical and legitimate authority. As conquered territory Congress would have full power to legislate for them. . . They would be held in a territorial condition until they are fit to form State Constitutions, republican in fact not in form only, and ask admission into the Union as new States . . .

We propose to confiscate all the estate of every rebel belligerent whose estate was worth $10,000, or whose land exceeded two hundred acres in quantity. Policy if not justice would require that the poor, the ignorant, and the coerced should be forgiven. They followed the example of their wealthy and intelligent neighbors. The rebellion would never have originated with them. Fortunately those who would thus escape form a large majority of the people, though possessing but a small portion of the wealth. The proportion of those exempt compared with the punished would be I believe about nine tenths.

There are about six millions of freemen in the South. The number of acres of land is 465,000,000. Of this those who own above two hundred acres each, number about 70,000 persons, holding in the aggregate (together with the States) about 394,000,000 acres, leaving for all others below 200 each about 71,000,000 of acres. By thus forfeiting the estates of the leading rebels, the Government would have 394,000,000 of acres . . . ., yet nine tenths of the people would remain untouched. Divide this land into convenient farms. Give if you please forty acres to each adult male freed man . . .

The whole fabric of southern society must be changed, and never can it be done if this opportunity is lost. Without this, this Government can never be, as it never has been, a true republic. Heretofore it has had more the features of aristocracy than of democracy. . . .

Let us forget all parties, and build on the broad platform of reconstructing the Government out of the conquered territory, converted into new and free states, and admitted into the Union by the sovereign power of Congress, with another plank, – *the property of the rebels shall pay our national debt, and indemnify freed-men and loyal sufferers* . . . .

Let all who approve of these principles tarry with us. Let all others go with Copperheads and rebels. Those will be the opposing parties. Young men, this duty devolves on you. Would to God, if only for that, that I were still in the prime of life, that I might aid you to fight through this last and greatest battle of Freedom.

Source: Speech by Thaddeus Stevens, 1865.

1.6 Landownership in the South, 1880

Land ownership by blacks in the South, although increasing, remained pitifully small throughout the period of Reconstruction and after, as the example of Georgia indicates.

Distribution of farms and farmland, by race of farm operator and form of land tenure and farm class, Cotton South: 1880

	Percent distribution of farms		Percent of all land in each class		Percent of all acres reported in crops in each class[b]	
Type of farm[a]	White	Black	White	Black	White	Black
Small family farms	40.2	29.6	29.0	8.4	24.2	16.8
Owned	23.6	4.8	23.1	2.3	15.0	2.5
Tenanted	16.6	24.8	5.9	6.1	9.2	14.3
Rented	3.2	7.9	1.5	2.0	2.0	4.6
Sharecropped	13.4	17.0	4.4	4.1	7.2	9.8
Other small farms	5.9	2.6	7.5	1.0	4.4	1.7
Owned	4.4	0.3[c]	6.3	0.2[c]	3.3	0.2[c]
Tenanted	1.5	2.2	1.2	0.8	1.1	1.5
Rented	0.3[c]	0.6[c]	0.5[c]	0.1[c]	0.2[c]	0.4[c]
Sharecropped	1.2[c]	1.6	0.7[c]	0.7	0.8[c]	1.1
Medium-scale farms	12.3	4.2	29.2	4.2	19.9	6.6
Owned	9.4	1.4	25.1	1.5	15.2	2.2
Tenanted	2.9	2.8	4.2	2.7	4.8	4.4
Rented	1.0	1.1	2.0	1.2	1.7	1.8
Sharecropped	1.9	1.7	2.2	1.5	3.1	2.6
Plantations	0.8	0.1[c]	6.2	0.6[c]	7.7	1.2[c]
Owned	0.8[c]	0.1[c]	5.9[c]	0.6[c]	7.2[c]	1.2[c]
Tenanted	0.1[c]	0.0[c]	0.3[c]	0.0[c]	0.5[c]	0.0[c]
Other large farms	3.5	0.9[c]	11.4	2.5[c]	13.2	4.2[c]
Owned	3.1	0.7[c]	9.5	2.1[c]	10.4	3.7[c]
Tenanted	0.4[c]	0.2[c]	1.9[c]	0.4[c]	2.8[c]	0.5[c]
All farms	62.7	37.3	83.2	16.8	69.5	30.5
Owned	41.3	7.3	69.8	6.7	51.0	9.8
Tenanted	21.5	29.9	13.4	10.0	18.5	20.7
Rented	4.8	9.6	5.8	3.4	6.7	6.9
Sharecropped	16.6	20.3	7.6	6.7	14.8	13.8

[a] Definition of farm type is as follows: *small family farms*, farms reporting 50 acres or less in crops and 26 weeks or less of hired labor; *other small farms*, farms reporting 50 acres or less in crops and more than 26 weeks of hired labor; *medium-scale farms*, farms reporting more than 50 acres but 100 acres or less in crops; *plantations*, farms reporting 200 acres or more in crops, greater than 98 weeks of hired labor, and relying on hired labor for at least 60 percent of their requirements; *other large farms*, all farms not included in one of the above categories.

[b] Acres reported in crops are total acres harvested in 1879 planted with the following crops: rice, barley, buckwheat, Indian corn, oats, rye, wheat, cotton, flax, hemp, sugar cane, sorghum, tobacco, apples and peaches.

[c] Figure reported is based on fewer than forty sample farms.

Source: Computed from a sample of farms from the 1880 Census of Agriculture.

Landownership by race in Georgia: 1874, 1876, 1880

	Acres of land owned by		Percent of
Year	Whites	Blacks	total acreage owned by blacks
1874	34,196,870	338,769	1.0
1876	35,313,351	457,635	1.3
1880[a]	36,792,243	586,664	1.6

[a] The 1880 figures exclude Camden County. Apparently the county tax receiver did not report to the state in time for publication.

Source: Georgia, Office of the Comptroller General, *Report of the Comptroller General of the State of Georgia* for the years given as follows: *1874*: (Savannah: J. H. Estill, 1875), Tables 5, 13, pp. 14-17, 58-62. *1876*: (Atlanta: H. G. Wright, 1877), Tables 6, 7, 12, pp. 16-25, 46-50. *1880*: (Atlanta: Constitution Publishing Company, 1880) Tables 10, 16, pp. 123-127, 153-157.

Value of assets held in rural counties of Georgia, by race: 1876 [a]

	Whites		Blacks	
Asset class	Value (thousands of dollars)	Percent of all assets held	Value (thousands of dollars)	Percent of all assets held
Land	84,613	50.1	922	21.6
City and town property	15,906	9.4	441	10.4
Money and liquid assets	21,335	12.6	84	2.0
Kitchen and household furniture	8,279	4.9	450	10.6
Horses, mules, hogs, etc.	21,086	12.5	238	5.6
Plantation and mechanical tools	2,337	1.4	121	2.8
All other property	15,314	9.1	2,003	47.0
Aggregate taxable wealth	168,870	100.0	4,259	100.0

[a] "Rural counties" include all counties reporting to the comptroller that did not contain a city with 4,000 or more inhabitants in 1880.

Source: Georgia, Office of the Comptroller General, *Fourth Annual Report . . . for the Year 1876* (Atlanta: H. G. Wright, 1877), Table 6, pp. 16-20; Table 8, pp. 26-30; Table 9, pp. 31-35; Table 11, pp. 41-45; Table 12, pp. 46-50.

1.7 Black Labour in Agriculture after Emancipation

During Reconstruction, Southern agriculture was slow to return to the levels of production and prices which were current in the later 1850s, e.g., cotton, which did not match the output of 1860 till 1875, and which temporarily commanded vastly inflated, if declining, prices. The reasons are generally ascribed to the devastation and other effects of the Civil War, but the following interpretation suggests that the ending of slave labour was a more likely cause.

According to some accounts, the southern supply of agricultural capital, particularly working stock, was substantially reduced. This decline in the supply of labor and these capital losses would explain the decline in agricultural output, and the South's slow recovery could be understood as a consequence of the difficulties in restoring the depleted stock of inputs.

This interpretation seems to us unfounded. It can be established fairly conclusively that the destructive impact of the Civil War on southern agriculture has been greatly distorted and exaggerated. The failure of the southern economy to return rapidly to its pre-war potential cannot be adequately explained by the loss of capital, work stock, or transportation facilities. As we shall show, the failure of per capita output to recover its pre-war level by the end of the century is explained by the withdrawal of black labor and not by the physical damage wrought by the war.

The withdrawal of black labor

Emancipation gave the ex-slave the freedom to lighten his burden and, for the first time, reserve a portion of his time for himself. The slave was literally worked to the limit of his economic capacity. Once free, he quite naturally chose to work less, so that he might reserve a portion of each day within which to enjoy the fruits of his labor, fruits that had previously been taken from him by his master. The result was that the amount of labor offered by each freedman and his family was substantially less than when slavery forced every man, woman, and child to work long hours throughout the year. Rather than work like slaves, the freedmen chose to offer an amount of labor comparable to the standard for free laborers of the time.

To indicate how substantial this decline in the labor supply was, we have constructed a conjectural estimate of the decline in the man-hours per capita supplied by the black population to agriculture. We have tried to make a conservative estimate, one that can be considered a lower limit to the actual decline. Our estimate takes account of the reduction in labor force participation (particularly noticeable among women and children) and the general declines in both the number of days of work and the number of hours worked each day. We made no attempt to estimate the reduction in the intensity of work performed each hour. While the estimate is conjectural, it is nevertheless solidly based on an extensive review of contemporary commentary as well as census samples and contemporary agricultural surveys. Our estimates are summarized in Figure 1, which contrasts the number of hours worked per year before and after emancipation separately for men, women, and children. In each case both a high and a low estimate is offered.

Percent decline in man-hours per capita offered by the rural black population as a consequence of emancipation

	Low estimate	High estimate
1. Fraction of rural population employed in agricultural occupations	17	24
2. Average number of days worked per year	8	11
3. Average number of hours worked per day	9	10
Cumulative effect of 1 through 3	28.3	37.2

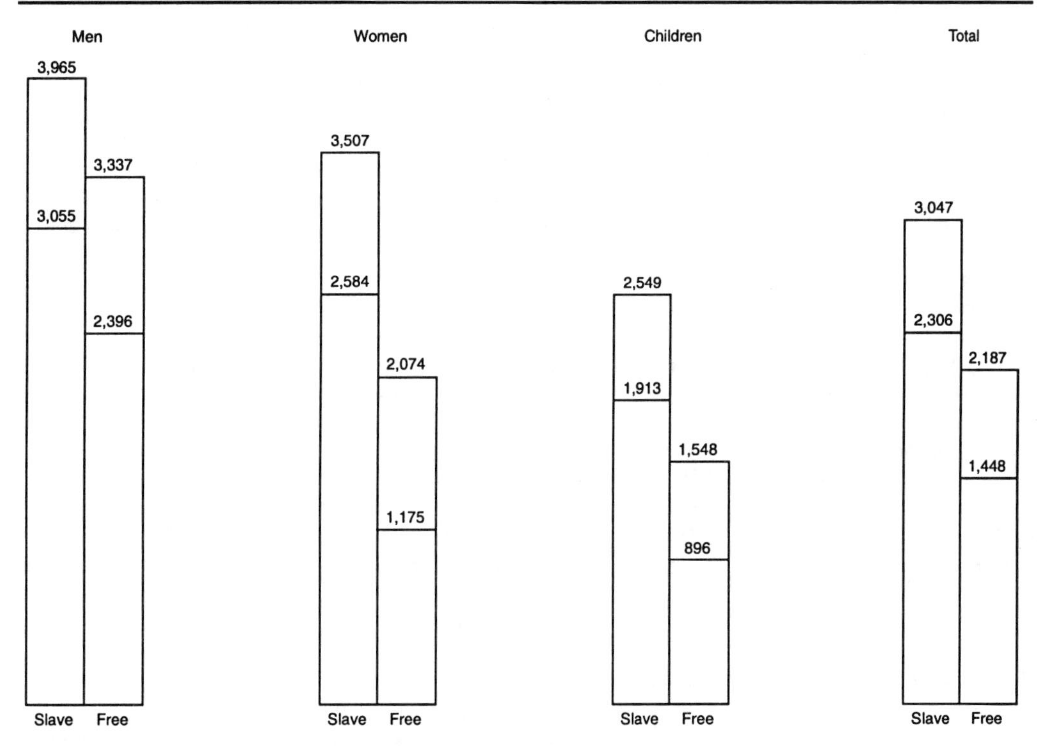

Figure 1. Maximum and minimum estimates of the number of hours worked per year by the black population over ten; as slaves in 1850s and freedmen in 1870s. Total presented is the male-equivalent hours supplied per person ten years old or older.

Source: Roger L. Ransom and Richard Sutch: *One Kind of Freedom: The Economic Consequences of Emancipation* (Cambridge University Press, 1977). Figure 3.1, pp. 44-45.

1.8 Black Occupations in the South, 1890

The occupations of males, – overwhelmingly concerned with farming and agriculture – and of females – largely involved in agriculture and domestic service – in the states of the South.

Occupations of males, ten years old and older, Five Cotton States: 1980

Occupation	Number occupied	Comments
Laborer	805,080	
Agriculture	594,700	
Not specified	132,417	
Railroad employee	34,099	
Teamster	17,167	Includes draymen and hackmen
Lumberman	9,333	Includes woodchoppers and raftsmen
Other	17,364	Includes miners in Alabama, Georgia, and South Carolina; quarrymen in Alabama; dairymen in Louisiana; and sailors, boatmen, canal men, pilots, fishermen, and oystermen in all states but Georgia
Service	36,262	
Servant	23,336	
Porter	5,985	Includes messengers and packers
Gardener	3,566	Includes florists, nurserymen, and vinegrowers
Barber	3,475	Includes hairdressers
Factory operative	32,088	
Saw mill	13,197	Includes planing mill employees
Cotton mill	12,326	Includes woolen and other textile mill operatives
Iron and steel mill	4,487	In Alabama, Georgia, and Louisiana only
Other	2,078	Includes charcoal, coke, and lime burners in Alabama and Mississippi; and tobacco and cigar factory operatives in Louisiana
Skilled labor	95,982	
Carpenter	32,781	Includes joiners and woodworkers in Georgia and Mississippi; and cabinet makers and upholsterers in Louisiana
Blacksmith	10,769	Includes wheelwrights
Mason	7,503	Includes marble and stone cutters
Painter	6,663	Includes glaziers, varnishers, and in Alabama and Georgia plasterers
Engineer, and fireman	6,105	Excludes steam railroad employees
Machinist	4,947	
Shoemaker	4,463	Includes bootmakers and boot and shoe repairers
Printer	3,557	Includes engravers and bookbinders
Butcher	3,433	

(cont.) Occupation	Number occupied	Comments
Miller (flour, grist)	3,310	Excludes millers in Louisiana; probably includes millwrights
Other	12,451	Includes brick makers, potters, mechanics, and telegraph and telephone operators (except in Louisiana); coopers in Georgia, Louisiana, and South Carolina; tailors and bakers in Louisiana and South Carolina; and tinners and tinware makers in Louisiana and Mississippi
Farm operator	707,811	Includes farmers, planters, sharecroppers, tenant farmers, agricultural overseers, and farm managers
Managerial, commercial	117,313	
Merchandiser	59,730	Includes merchants, dealers, peddlers, agents, salesmen, collectors, and commercial travelers
Bookkeeper, clerk	35,002	
Hotel, stable, saloon keepers	8,494	Includes restaurant and boardinghouse keepers, bartenders, and hostlers, coverage of all categories is complete only for Mississippi; excludes restaurant and saloon keepers in Alabama and South Carolina, bartenders in South Carolina; and hotel and boardinghouse keepers in Georgia, Louisiana, and South Carolina
Foreman, watchman	5,877	Includes policemen, detectives, and nonagricultural overseers; excludes foremen and overseers in Louisiana
Government official	4,837	
Banker	3,373	Includes officials of banks and brokers
Professional	37,695	
Clergyman	8,952	
Physician, surgeon	8,246	
Teacher, professor	8,049	
Lawyer	5,780	
Manufacturer	5,455	Includes publishers
Surveyor	1,213	Excludes Georgia and Mississippi; includes civil, mechanical, and mining engineers in the other states
Total specified	1,832,231	
Other	51,833	Computed as a residual
Total gainfully occupied	1,844,064	

Source: U.S. Census Office [1890], *Report on the Population . . . 1890*, Part 2 (Washington: GPO, 1897), pp. 530, 548, 562, 574, 606.

Occupations of females, ten years old and older, Five Cotton States: 1890

Occupation	Number occupied	Comments
Laborer	354,352	
Agriculture	327,820	
Not specified	26,319	
Other	213	Includes dairymaids in Georgia, Louisiana, and Mississippi; and employees of steam railroad companies in South Carolina
Service	174,801	
Servant	109,880	Includes stewardesses and professional housekeepers
Laundress	64,656	
Other	265	Includes gardeners (except in Mississippi) and barbers and hairdressers in Louisiana
Factory operative	11,787	
Cotton mill	11,374	Includes woolen and other textile mill operatives
Other	413	Includes tobacco and cigar factory operatives in Louisiana and basket makers in Mississippi
Skilled Labor	27,413	
Seamstress	26,752	Includes dressmakers, tailoresses, and milliners
Other	661	Includes bakers in Louisiana and South Carolina; printers, engravers, and bookbinders (except in Louisiana); and telegraph and telephone operators in Alabama and Georgia
Farm operator	56,195	Includes sharecroppers, tenant farmers, planters, and overseers
Managerial, commercial	8,782	
Merchandiser	3,404	Includes merchants, dealers, peddlers, and saleswomen
Hotel, saloon keeper	3,101	Includes boardinghouse, lodginghouse, and restaurant keepers
Clerk, bookkeeper	1,916	Includes copyists, stenographers, typists, and accountants
Government official	361	
Professional	16,809	
Teacher	14,383	Includes artists, musicians, and teachers of art and music (except in Louisiana)
Nurse, midwife	2,426	
Total specified	650,139	
Other	2,770	Computed as a residual
Total gainfully occupied	652,909	

Source: U.S. Census Office, Eleventh Census [1890], *Report on the Population . . . 1890*, Part 2 (Washington: GPO, 1897), pp. 530, 548, 562, 574, 606. Both the above tables are to be found in Roger L. Ransom and Richard Sutch: *One Kind of Freedom: The Economic Consequences of Emancipation* (Cambridge University Press, 1977). Tables B.6 and B.7, pp. 228-230.

1.9 Black Labour in the South, 1870s

With the black labouring population released from slavery and needing to compete with white labour, there was a demand for access to training for skilled occupations and for admission to union organisation. In each case, there was a fear of exclusion: from training, which would result in the de-skilling of the black working population that had once commanded a variety of skills on the plantation; and from unions, in which white workers were unwilling to enrol black competition. Most black workers in the South continued to work on plantations on the basis of share-cropping or leasing land; whatever the system, the workers were exposed to exploitation and fraud.

Proceedings of the (Colored) National Labor Union Convention

The Convention was called to order by Isaac Myers, Esq., of Maryland, who read the call for the Convention; after which he nominated George T. Downing, of Rhode Island, temporary Chairman, who was unanimously chosen. Mr. Downing, on taking the chair, addressed the Convention:

FELLOW DELEGATES. – Accept my acknowledgement of an appreciation of the honor you have conferred on me, in selecting me to fill the responsible and honorable position of temporary chairman of this important gathering; be assured I shall strive to merit the implied confidence, by being strictly impartial in discharging the duties of the office. I shall know no one personally, but you all as equal delegates.

This convention bears the title "National Labor Convention"; I desire that it shall not falsify its name; that it be a "labor convention;" in a word that it shall labor, that it bring forth something. Much is expected of it; the eyes of every intelligent laborer of the land, without regard to color, are fixed on it; its doings will be eagerly caught up and canvassed by the laborers of Europe, now banding together to the end of causing labor to be respected, and of enjoying its just rewards.

That the colored, as well as the white laborers of the United States, are not satisfied as to the estimate that is placed on their labor, as to their opportunities, as to the remuneration for their labor, the call for this convention, and the very general and highly intelligent response which I gaze on in you, my fellow delegates, attest. No other class of men would be satisfied under the circumstances; why should we be?

The Republican party has been made an effective agent under God in liberating us from unrequited toil, from chattel thraldom – all of my class have been slaves by virtue of prescriptive laws, and still worse, the greater portion have been slaves by positive enactment, been deemed, declared, created and adjudged slaves to all intents and purposes. We owe that party respect and support, in view of its agency in freeing us from that degradation. We think that it should have been more consistent, more positive in its dealings with our and the country's enemies; that it should not have set us free, but that it should have been with us in the wilderness; that should have fed us during our pilgrimage; that it should have given us quails and manna, homes and the letter, the latter, a fitting office of government. We should be secured in the soil, which we have enriched by our toil and blood, to which we have a double entitlement.

When the ratification of the proposed fifteenth amendment to the Constitution shall have been effected, with what has already been accomplished in the same direction, much of the adhesive element which has made the composite Republican party a unit have disappeared; for it to hold together, it must have attractive elements. Let the party have a wise financial policy. Let it be mindful of the fact, that the masses are becoming more and more intelligent; that the laboring man thinks, and is, therefore, restive; the mass are becoming so; they expect and will demand some legislation in their behalf; they realize that by being united, they can be an influence equal to capital. That which is known as the labor movement is growing in strength. I beseech our friends to be mindful of the same, to take such action in the premises as will draw to their party, away from a corrupt dishonorable influence that is striving to ally itself with the labor movement, the honest and intelligent agitators for reform in the matter of labor; they, with the colored laborers and voters, will be a host for the right.

The colored man's struggle until now has been for naked existence, for the right of life and liberty; with the fifteenth amendment, henceforth his struggle will be in pursuit of happiness; in this instance, it is to turn his labor to the most effective account, to be respected therein; this is a great problem; it is racking the brains of the ablest economists; the most we can hope to effect, at this gathering, is a crude organization; the formation of a labor bureau to send out agents, to organize colored labor throughout the land, to effect a union with laborers without regard to color.

Good has come out of Nazareth. Slavery, when it existed, shut out the light to the end of shutting out the right; it had, however, to have some light for its own purposes. It did not permit the educated white mechanic and laborer from the North and abroad to come within its darkened abode; to have done so would have jeopardised its existence; hence, it had to and did teach its subjects, the slaves, mechanical arts; they now have those arts as freemen. In the North, from selfish motives, from prejudice, to serve their then Southern masters, they would not teach or encourage the colored man in mechanism; so that, whatever mechanical acquirements, with some exceptions, exist among colored men in the country, are to be found in the South. They are crying for organization. We desire Union with the white laborer for a common interest; it is the interest of both parties, that such a union should exist, with a fair, open, and unconcealed intent; with no aim to destroy any organization, political or otherwise; with no thought of fostering dishonor, whether in the nation or in individuals; repudiating all attempts to weaken obligations engaged in openly, seriously, with a full knowledge of the same; with an intent to share honorably all obligations "as nominated in the bond." I think that I may say, in behalf of the delegates here assembled, that they stand ready to extend an earnest hand of welcome to every effort, associated or otherwise, that looks to the dignity of labor, to its enjoyment of full remuneration and protection, and which shall manifest a spirit to be in harmony with capital in every instance, when capital shall be properly mindful of its true interest in harmonizing with labor.

Trades for our Boys

To the Editor of the New National Era:

I wish to call your attention to the importance of some movement whereby trades, &c., may be secured to our boys. There are hundreds of boys in this city alone who, after having exhausted every effort to secure employment, from the fact that paper-peddling, boot-blacking, driving, waiting, and choosing, have more than their quota of employees, resort, to petty crimes; thence, through successive stages, to bolder schemes against the peace and security of society, and thus swell the number of criminals and vagrants, and prey upon the community, because an uprighteous public sentiment excludes them from the workshops, and religion, philanthropy, patriotism, have not a word to say in condemnation of the anti-American policy.

To the son of the German, the Irishman, the Canadian, Scotchman, the far off Pagan Japanese, the doors of your manufactories open wide, the next day after arrival even before one word of the language has been uttered, while against the native-born youth, with the same aspirations as a white American, to appropriate and apply mechanical knowledge, and to improve upon it, by application and invention, the doors are not only closed by individual bosses, but society combines to supplement the injustice by voting exclusion.

We have in this city, colored mechanics whose work upon inspection equals the very best done by the fairest American or foreigner; these men take colored boys to be taught, but the hand of God is upon them in that he gave them a color which suited Him, so that the large number are so poorly patronized that but a limited number are now instructed.

The condition of colored youth in this city and District is true of them throughout the country. But the opposition by Americans is not the only cause of this sorry state of things, though mainly so; indifference on the part of leading colored men, and the death-like silence of colored women, contribute to it. A people whose leaders seek to learn the tortuous ways of speculation, and whose women are awed into silence upon vital questions, must for the time take back seats among the people. The white men of this and other countries deal vigorously now with every issue for the good of their youth, and white women are to the front with them in the work as having a common mission; they even unite in our exclusion and mutual congratulations, the result, are neither few nor whispered. Our women must speak out; the boys must have trades. What the crowned heads of Europe, and the poorest of white Americans do for their sons, we cannot afford to neglect.

I have a boy who must and shall have a trade, (D.V.) and yet where may he learn it, or where exercised it when learned?

To begin at headquarters, not under Government patronage surely, for there, should a colored lad upon examination distance competitors, let but a persistent Southern rebel, a clamorous foreigner, or a Canadian rebel, seek the position also, and even after given, the well-known out-cry, "reduction of force" is made, which, by interpretation, means change of base, and down comes the headsman's axe upon apprentice, mechanic, clerk, and into his place goes the anti-Government aspirant.

Where then exercise? The people exclude him. Clannish they worship their kind. As much as may be said about race ostracism by whites, and how much may not be, too much cannot be said against indifference among ourselves. I want our poor tongue-tied, hoppled, and "scart" colored women – "black ladies" as Faith Lichen had the bravery to call them in her Mary-Clemmer-Ames-i-ades – to let the nation know how they stand. White women are getting to be a power in the land, and colored women cannot any longer afford to be neutrals. Never fear the ward-meetings; get the boys started properly in life, and the ward-meetings will come right.

I want to see the colored preacher canonized, who looking after the great interests of the Master's flock, will, Beecher-like, cry out on Sunday against this sin of keeping our boys from trades, to the fostering of iniquity and the ruin of our souls.

Your millions of "laborers" in the midst of thirty millions of active, energetic people with arts, science, and commerce in their hands, and the love of domination a cardinal point in their creed – four millions that chain to this dank and hoary "labor" carcass – are as certain of subjugation, ultimately, as were the Helots; and this should arouse to action the entire force among the people. I know we have resolutions of conference and of conventions, and have had for a generation; and that each convention is the greatest ever held; but the people know comparatively little about them or their resolutions. We want then, an arousing of the people, and the pulpit must help in the work.

We have no theatres, beer-gardens, opera, nor grand lecture amphitheatres, wherein such questions may be discussed, reshapen, dramatized, made vital issues; the church – the pulpit stands to us in this stead; our preachers, as they should be, are politicians, and do use their churches often as places in which blessed white christians help them to adjust, arrange, and work party laws. No greater party work than this for our boys can they do.

I have not forgotten that we have a few live members of Congress, though I believe no one has as yet got around to trades; and although we must have Civil Rights, I look upon trades exclusion as meanly and wickedly beyond even the reach of that. In parenthesis, another of the many weak places in "your armor", so be it.

I know that we have members of State Legislatures and from whom more may be expected than from even Congress; also, attaches of the learned professions, and aspirants in the field of letters, all of which is enjoyably rose-tinted and gilded as compared with the past, but we, no more than others, can afford to build at the top of the house only. Ill-timed and unseemly as it may appear, the craftsmen, the architect, the civil engineer, the manufacturer, the thoroughly equipped citizen, must all come, though silently, surely through the door opened to us by the mechanic. So agitate for the boys!

Mary A. Shadd Cary

New National Era, March 21, 1872.

Colored Labor

The condition of the negro as a slave, and the moral and economical effects of slavery, has been discussed by the press, from the public rostrum, and, the halls of congress for sessions, with energy and zeal; what shall or ought to be his status as a freeman is at present a matter of no less national anxiety. But aside from this, his interest as a workingman, and especially the part he is to take in advancing the cause of labor have as yet received from those most deeply interested but little consideration. It is in this last respect exclusively that the question has a vital interest for the friends of labor reform; an interest of such importance that, delicate as the question may be, and not withstanding the impossibility of expressing an opinion in reference to it, which would meet with the universal approval of workingmen in general, the principle involved and its growing importance demand that the truth should be fearlessly expressed no matter at what cost.

The primary object to be accomplished before we can hope for any great results is the thorough organization of all the departments of labor. This work, though its beginning is of comparatively recent date, has progressed with amazing rapidity. Leagues, labor unions, granges, and trades associations exist in all our large towns and cities, and in thousands of villages and county districts. There are central organizations in many of the States, and a National Industrial Congress, the result of whose deliberations on the future welfare of the county can scarcely be overestimated. In this connection we cannot overlook the important position now assigned to the colored race in this contest. Unpalatable as the truth may be to many, it is needless to disguise the fact that they are destined to occupy a different position in the future to what they have in the past; that they must necessarily become, aye, have become in their new relationship an element of strength or an element of weakness, and it is for the workingmen of America to decide whether that position shall be that of an enemy or that of an ally.

The systematic organization and consolidation of labor must hereafter be the watchword of the race reformer. To accomplish this the co-operation of the African race in America must be secured. If those most deeply interested fail to perform their duties, others will avail themselves of it to their injury. What is wanted, then, is for every union to inculcate the grand, ennobling idea that the interests of labor are one; that there should be no distinction of race or nationality; no classification of Jew or Gentile, Christian or Infidel; that there is but one dividing line – that which separates mankind into two great classes, the class that labors and the class that live by others' labors. This, in our opinion, is the true course for workingmen to pursue. The interests of all on one side of the line is the same, and should they be so far misled by prejudice or passion as to refuse to aid the spread of union principles among any of their fellow toilers, they must prove untrue to themselves and the great cause which they profess to have at heart.

But aside from all this the workingmen of the United States have a special interest in seeking their co-operation. This race is being rapidly educated, and has already been admitted to all the privileges and franchises of citizenship. That it will neither die out nor be exterminated, is now recognized as a settled fact. They are here to live amongst us, and the question to be decided is, shall they make them their friends or shall capital be allowed to turn them as an engine against them? They number four million strong, and a greater proportion of them labor with their hands than can be counted from among the same number of any other people on earth. Their moral influence and their strength at the ballot box would be of incalculable value to the cause of labor. Can they afford to reject their proposed co-operation and make them enemies? By committing such an act of folly they would inflict greater injury upon the cause of Labor Reform than the combined efforts of labor could accomplish. Their cherished idea of an antagonism between capital and labor would be realized, and as Austrian despotism makes use of the hostility between the different races, which compose the empire, to maintain her existence and balance, so capitalists, North and South, would foment discord between the white and colored race, and hurl the one against the other, as interest or occasion may require, to maintain their ascendency, and continue the reign of oppression. Lamentable spectacle! Labor waring against labor, and capital smiling and reaping the fruits of the mad contest.

Taking this view of the question we are of the opinion that the interests of labor demand that all workingmen shall be included within its ranks, without regard to race or nationality; and that the interests of the workingmen of America especially requires that the formation of trades unions and other labor organizations should be encouraged among the colored race; that they be instructed in the true principles of Labor Reform, and that they be invited to co-operate with their white co-laborers in the general labor undertaking. The time when such co-operation should take effect has already arrived, and we believe a recognition of this fact by our representative organizations will redound to the best and most lasting interests of all concerned.

Workingman's Advocate, February 7, 1874

Emigration: Richard H. Cain to Hon. Wm. Coppinger

January 25, 1877

Dear Sir, The deep and growing interest taken by the Colored people, in the south in the subject of Emigration, prompts me to write you, requesting information as to whether the society will send a vessel this spring to Liberia, and if so about what month, and what are the arrangements for the passage. There are thousands who are willing and ready to leave, South Carolina, Georgia, Florida and, North Carolina, but are not able to pay their way; Many are willing to do so. Will you be kind enough to send me any information on the subject. What vessel the society has now employed? Could not some shipowner be induced to put a couple of vessels on a line regularly from this country to Africa? Putting the passage at a low rate; if so there are fifty thousand people who would lease and pay their own passage and a brisk trade, could be established between the two countries. And would pay the owner well. The Colored people of the south, are tired of the constant struggle for life and Liberty with such results as the *'Missippi Plan'* (sic) and prefer going where no such obstacles are in their way of enjoying their Liberty.

An early reply will greatly oblige yours Respectfully,

Richard H. Cain.

American Colonization Society Records, Container 227, Series I, Library of Congress.

The Labor Question South

The recent discussion regarding the relative prosperity of cotton factories North and South have developed the fact that during the twelve years since the war, under a system of free labor, there were produced in this country 2,772,371 bales of cotton more than during the twelve years before the war under the old system of slave labor. The planters are more independent than they ever were then, their crops are seldom mortgaged as they were formerly, and instead of being dependent upon the farmers of the West for their supplies, they grow a great part of their corn and bacon at home. That the emancipation of the slaves has been the first great cause of this result there can be no doubt. The free colored man, having more self-respect, a greater feeling of responsibility, more knowledge, and from the necessities of the case being more industrious and faithful, is much more valuable as a laborer than was the negro slave. Unfortunately, there is a very large class of persons in the South who are not willing to acknowledge these facts, or who are so blinded by prejudice that they cannot regard them as do practical business men in other parts of the country. There are, indeed, in several of the cotton States, notably in South Carolina, Alabama, and Louisiana, a number of so-called leaders who freely express the belief that the negro, to be made useful must be kept in a state little better than bondage, in short, as nearly in a condition of slavery as is possible under the law.

To bring about this result, the Rifle Clubs of South Carolina and a number of the most prominent Democrats in Alabama and Louisiana are engaged in a determined effort to reorganize the old Labor League, and secure such legislative enactments as will place the unfortunate black laborer absolutely under their control. The demands made by the promoters of the movement are not exactly calculated to find favor in the eyes of the men who call themselves citizens of a free country. They ask, in the first place, that agricultural labor of all kinds shall be performed under contracts to be drawn by individual employers, or drawn by them and approved by the Labor Leagues. The share system, by which the negro receives bacon meal and implements, and in return gives the white landowner one-half or two-thirds of the entire crop raised by himself and family, is to be continued, but under the laws which it is hoped may be passed every violation by a colored man of such a contract would be considered a misdemeanor, to be punished by imprisonment, forfeiture of crops, or, as is proposed in Edgefield and other White League strongholds, by the lash. Further than this, it is proposed that all colored men found out of employment or trespassng upon the lands of the whites shall be regarded as vagrants, and punished accordingly. Should such laws go into effect, and their advocacy by the powerful Labor Leagues of South Carolina and the secret organization known as the State Grange of Louisiana leaves no doubt that there is grave danger of this being the case, the Southern black men would be almost as completely at the mercy of their white masters as they were twenty years ago. Even under Republican Governments, where the State, county, and Judicial officers were all pledged to do full justice to every class of citizens, the negro laborers who worked on the share system with the landowners were frequently defrauded out of all their earnings. The white men were quickwitted and greedy of gain; the negroes ignorant and easily satisfied; and so at the end of the season, when the crops were harvested and the accounts made up, they were only too often obliged to repeat that verse familiar to all the laborers of the Black Belt:

"Nought's a nought, figure's a figure
All for de white men –
None for de nigger."

Still the negroes did not complain; their wants were easily supplied, and if they had enough to eat and a cabin to shelter them, they went on with their work without a murmur. That they should rest quietly under such laws as those proposed, however, is not to be expected. Indeed, we have no doubt that in this new movement of the Labor Leagues is to be found the secret spring which impels so many of the freedmen to listen to the glowing and, as the result has proved, the delusive, promises of the Liberian emigration swindlers. They certainly have every reason to be alarmed at the prospect before them, for even should the law-makers, who are being appealed to, have the good sense to refuse the demands of the land-owners, the Labor Leagues threaten, as a last resort, to openly take the law into their own hands, as they have already substantially done in secret, and agree among themselves not to rent land or give work to any laborer without the consent of his former master, or to buy corn, cotton, or produce of any kind from any employee without the consent of the proprietor of the land upon which it has been raised. In the same way, that is by an agreement among themselves, it will be a very easy matter for the Labor Leagues to determine what rates of wages they will pay their laborers. It will thus be said that under the new reconciliation plan, which has so effectually broken down the color line, the outlook for the black man is not exactly the rosy one that gentlemen of the Stanley Matthews school of politics would have the country believe.

New York Times, January 14, 1878.

Labour in the far South: How colored workmen are defrauded

It has from time to time been fully proved in these columns that the colored men of the South were not regarded as equals before the law; that they were not permitted freely to exercise the rights of suffrage conferred upon them by the national Constitution, and that the Democratic State and local Governments gave them next to no opportunity of educating their children. But these are not the only wrongs of which the freemen have to complain. From a number of facts which I obtained during a recent visit to the Gulf States – facts which will not be successfully disputed – it is evident that in every material relation the negroes are cheated and taken advantage of by the whites. From year's end to year's end they have been made to work for the profit of the land-owners, and each year they have found themselves growing poorer and poorer. Of course, there are isolated exceptions to this general rule. Here and there may be found a black man who, by dint of hard work and close economy, coupled with circumstances of a peculiarly fortuitous character, has gathered together enough money to buy a small farm, and who has a few thousand dollars in good securities. But such cases are very rare, so rare, in fact, that when one of them is discovered the Southern newspapers have much more to say about it than they would about half a dozen murders. In the great majority of cases the negroes are living actually from hand to mouth. They and their families are kept alive very much as they were in the days of slavery. That they are in any of their material relations more independent than they were during those days there is very little evidence. Since the results of the war made them free all sorts of means have been resorted to by the whites, who had and have all the money, to keep them from bettering their financial condition, and thereby placing themselves in a position to make more favorable terms with their former owners. One of the earliest of these devices was known as "the share system." Under its provisions the white capitalists supplied the land, provisions, seeds, and implements, the negroes, with their wives and children, gave their labor, and it was understood that at the end of the year the profits of the crops which were obtained should be divided between all those engaged in raising them. When the time for a division came, however, it was almost invariably found that all the money which had been made was by one means or another placed in the pockets of the land-owners, while the black laborers were declared to be in debt for extra supplies, to provide for which they were coolly required to give a lien on the share of the next year's crop which was supposed to be theirs. For a time this pretty little scheme worked admirably and to the very great advantage of the capitalists. But by degrees the negroes began to see that they were being systematically cheated out of their hard earnings, that, indeed, for all practical purposes, they might just as well be slaves as freemen. Knowing this, they ceased to take any interest in their work under "the share system" which never brought any "share" to them. They neglected the fields, and after a time convinced the land-owners that some new and less transparent means of defrauding them would have to be devised. To a very great extent the latter have succeeded.

In the far South, but particularly in Mississippi, the "share system" has now given place to what is known as the "lease system" and the "hire system". Under both of them the whites continue to get very much the best of the bargains which are made with the colored men. For instance, under the so-called hire plan the land-owner usually contracts to pay an able-bodied and experienced farm-hand, who is aided by a wife and perhaps by children, $16 a month, or a total of $192 a year. It is also understood that the negro is to be supplied with a "furnish", which consists of certain stipulated quantities of meal, port, sugar and coffee, and which is to be given at certain stated periods in the year. This "furnish" costs the capitalist $85. One mule and the farming implements necessary for the use of the negro, the ownership of which rests with the land proprietor, costs him about $200. The wear and tear of mule and implements, at a very liberal estimate, is $50 a year. These are the usual expenses which have to be borne by the landowner under the "hire plan." It will be seen that they foot up a total of $327 a year; but, to be on the safe side, and to include a liberal sum on account of interest on the capital invested by the owner, let be assumed that the total expense to him is $400 a year. On the other hand, what are his profits from the negro, the mule, the implements, and the land upon which he is supposed to expend this sum? It is always expected that the negro and mule will cultivate during the year 12 acres of ground. It is usual in Mississippi to plant nine acres of this in cotton and three in corn. In a reasonably good year nine acres of the rich bottom lands of the Mississippi, to which the figures given are applied, yield 12 bales weighing 500 pounds each. At 10 cents a pound, the total derived from the sale of this product would be

$600. From the corn land 60 bushels are usually expected from the acre. From three acres the yield at this rate would, of course, be 180 bushels, which, if sold at the average price of 70 cents a bushel, would bring $126. From these figures it will readily be seen that the total yield in money from the 12 acres would be $726. If the $400 which was allowed for expenses be deducted from this sum, it will be found that the land-owner has realized from his 12 acres the handsome profit of $326. And the majority of them are not content with these returns. By every conceivable trick, by extortionate charges for extra provisions which they may or may not have supplied to the negroes, they continue to evade payment of a large portion of the wages which it was agreed should be given to the laborer and the blacks in ninety-nine cases out of a hundred at the end of the year find themselves precisely where they commenced – that is to say, penniless and entirely dependent upon the white land-owner for the food which keeps them from starvation and the miserable cabin which gives them but scant protection from the elements.

Still bad as it is, many of the negroes with whom I talked on the subject said that they preferred the hire to the lease system. On the surface there is no good reason why this should be so. The inquiring stranger is always told that the negroes can lease land at $8 an acre, or $96 a year, for 12 acres, which in many cases is true. It is also stated to those who make such inquiry that a negro can feed and clothe himself for $100 a year, get a mule for $110, farming tools for $50, a wagon for $75, and that all other expenses for himself and a small family could be covered for $100, or a total of $536 a year. On this basis his crop should yield him $190 clear profit the first year, and subsequently, when he need make no expenditures for mule or implements, such profit should be largely increased. But, unfortunately for the negro, the figures given are only superficial ones. Close inquiry reveals the fact that there is one set of prices for a black man in the far South and another set for the whites. It being always assumed that the negro buys on credit, he is obliged on an average to pay $160 for the mule which costs the white man $110, $110 for the wagon, $75 for the farming implements, and for meal, bacon, sugar, coffee, calico, and everything else in the same proportion. The plantation storekeepers who charge him these prices are, in nearly every instance, in partnership with the land-owners, and divide with them the profits. In addition to everything else, the negro debtor is charged by these all-powerful oppressors interest on all his purchases at the average rate of 18 per cent. To secure payment of their advances made on these outrageous terms the storekeepers in every case exact from the negroes a deed in trust on the mule and all implements furnished, and also on all growing crops which may be raised by their use. So, at the end of the year the unfortunate Mississippi "freedman" who has been bold enough to venture upon farming under the lease system is lucky if he escapes from his creditors with the clothes on his back. And for these wrongs there is next to no redress before the Democratic courts. In the great majority of the counties in Mississippi it is impossible to find record of a case in which a negro has successfully sued a white man. Their only escape from oppression seems to be in leaving their old homes and emigrating to other States. This, they have already done to a greater extent than is generally supposed. In all parts of Louisiana and Mississippi there is a growing complaint of a scarcity of labor. To such an extent is this true that the planters in the Teche country have been making earnest effort to get Chinese from Cuba to move their sugar crops, and at this moment the steamboat men at New Orleans, Vicksburg, and Memphis are not able to get men sufficient to handle their cargoes, and this is the case despite the fact that they are offering prices to this class of laborers which three years ago would have been looked upon as little short of fabulous. The land-owners and capitalists of the South should be warned in time. When it is too late they may be only too forcibly reminded of the fact that they killed the goose which for generations has laid their golden eggs.

H.C.

New York Times, November 26, 1880.

Sources: Various journals as indicated, 1869-80

1.10 The Condition of the Black Population in the South, 1883

Editor of the New York Globe, *and founder of the Afro-American League (a forerunner of the Niagara Movement and the NAACP), T. Thomas Fortune gave evidence on the condition of the black population in the South to the Senate Committee upon the Relations between Labor and Capital.*

New York, September 17, 1883.

T. Thomas fortune sown and examined

By the Chairman:

Question. Where do you reside? – Answer. In the city of New York.
Q. What is your occupation? – A. I am a journalist.
Q. What is your connection with the press? – A. Editor and proprietor.
Q. Of what paper? – A. The New York Globe.
Q. To what special interests is that paper devoted? – A. It is devoted especially to the interests of the colored population.
Q. It is the organ of the colored interests of the North, or of this city? – A. Well, it was intended to be a newspaper devoted to the interests of the citizens of New York, but it has so extended that it may be said to cover the whole ground of the United States; so that it may be said to have no legal habitation, but to be rather national in its character.
Q. You have seen the resolution under which the committee is acting? – A. Yes, sir.
Q. Will you now, in your own way, make such statements of fact and such suggestions as seem to you pertinent, bearing upon the condition and the improvement of the condition of the colored population of the country, and also in regard to its relations to the white population with which it is thrown in contact?

The colored population

THE WITNESS. According to the census of 1880 there were in the country 6,580,793 people of African ancestry. In 1790, according to the first census, there were only

757,208. The increase of population from 1850 to 1860, under the slave régime, was 22.1 per cent; from 1870 to 1880, 34.8 per cent. The increase is and will continue to be healthy in the state of freedom, since human effort and propagation have their greatest expansion in a state of freedom from all tyranny and narrowness. If we were freer our growth and propagation would be vastly greater. As it is, we are fettered by the State and repressed by individuals and corporations. We are not free as other men to come and go, to make and spend, to enjoy the protection of the laws equally, or to share as other men the rights and immunities of Government. Like the Irish subjects of Great Britain, we have received everything from our Government except justice in equal degree with others of our fellow-citizens. This she has always denied and still denies to us.

This large body of our population has, since the foundation of our Republic, been a subject of the gravest moment, of the most earnest contention in the home, in the halls of legislation, and on the field of battle. But in all the conflict the negro has never received full justice at the hands of the Government, State or Federal, and he does not receive it to-day in any portion of our vast territory.

At the close of the great rebellion the negro population of the country was thrown upon its own resources, so to speak; made men and citizens at one stroke of the pen. These men were poor, ignorant beyond conjecture, cowed and debaunched by the foul iniquity of human slavery, and surrounded by a hostile public sentiment which vented itself in all sorts of intolerance, in assassination, intimidation, and open robbery. Assassination for political causes has ceased because no longer necessary; but intimidation and robbery remain; so that the negro population of the South is today, as it was thirty years ago, a disturbing element, requiring a wise statesmanship to properly adjust it. But instead of attempting to honestly adjust, the people and the press of the country constantly talk of eliminating it from political consideration and discussion, as if it were possible to heal a cancer by leaving it severely alone.

The greatest misfortune which the Government inflicted upon us up to the close of the war was the almost universal illiteracy of the masses – illiteracy which was designed and made irrevocable by the most stringent of statutory enactments. Our intellectual and material poverty, absolute bankruptcy, was caused by the Government, which closed the book of knowledge to us and denied us the common right to accumulate. We are not responsible even to-day for the widespread poverty which obtains among us. We have not the facilities and aptitude to amass large fortunes by speculation and peculation, but we are learning to emulate the virtuous example of our white fellow-citizens in this regard.

Considering honestly our lowly beginning, the following facts are of interest. From the Bureau of Statistics we find –

School attendence of colored children

Enrollment of colored youths, as far as reported by the State school officers for the year 1880, 784,709; per cent. of colored youth of school age enrolled, about 48.
Colored school teachers in the United States: males, 10,520; females, 5,314; total 15,834.

Normal schools for colored youth, 44; teachers, 227; pupils, 7,408.
High schools, or academic, 36; teachers, 120, pupils, 5,327.
Universities and colleges, 15; teachers, 119; students, 1,717
Schools of theology, 22; teachers, 65; pupils reported, 880.
Schools of law, 3; teachers, 10; pupils, 33.
Schools of medicine, 2, with 17 teachers and 87 pupils.

State appropriations for colored schools

According to the census of 1880, there is in the South a total school population of 5,426,890–3,758,480 being white, and 1,668,410 being colored; enrolled, white, 2,013,684; colored, 685,942. The total appropriation for school purposes by these States is set down at $12,181,602, being the beggarly pittance of $2.26 per capita. Only 31 per cent. of the white, and 26 per cent. of the colored children of Louisiana availed themselves of the advantages of the public schools, while the State appropriates the munificent sum of $529,065 for educational purposes, being $1.94 per capita; while the city of New York alone expends more than $3,000,000 per annum for the education of her youth. Four and two-tenths per cent. of the school population of New York State can't read, and 5.5. cannot write, while in Louisiana 45.8 cannot read, and 49.1 cannot write. Florida, with a school population of 82,606, appropriates only $134,880 for school purposes, being $1.63 per capita. The District of Columbia, with a school population of 38,800, appropriates $368,343, and 61 per cent. of the white and 73 per cent. of the colored school population are enrolled, the per capita being $9.49. In the District of Columbia, 5.7 per cent. of the school population cannot read, and 18.8 per cent. cannot write, while in Florida 38 per cent. cannot read, and 43.4 per cent. cannot write. These facts are suggestive.

Inadequacy of such appropriations

Aside from the vastly inadequate work being done in the South by the States, it should not be omitted here that Northern churches and organizations and individuals contribute annually to the education of the freedman quite as much as the States; but the contributions from these sources are uncertain and fluctuating. Yet, after all that is done is considered, it must be conceded that ignorance is growing in the South as rank as the weeds that choke her corn and cotton. Whether it be the poverty of the people of the States, or disinclination of the people to tax themselves for the rooting out of illiteracy and the vices it breeds, I am not prepared to say; but that the evil is vast and menancing, all must concede. The rural journals of the South, which are usually ignorant of the first principles of political economy, object to popular education, on the ground that the blacks pay no taxes, supremely oblivious that the laboring classes of every country always create capital, and pay in rental the taxes of the land-owner, who has no more inherent right in ownership of the soil than the laborer. What the State refuses to pay for education it gladly pays for penitentiaries, preferring a pound of remedy to an ounce of cure.

It must not be forgotten that the teachers employed in the South labor under many disadvantages, which react with fearful effect upon the pupils. Because of the miserable compensation and the shortness of the school term, together with social isolation and political intolerance of the South, competent teachers cannot and are not always secured. The school term in the South does not average more than four months of the year, and I doubt much if the salaries paid will average $30 per month, subject to further reduction on school warrants by regular scalpers, merchants, and others. At least, such was my unfortunate experience in Florida as a teacher. And, then, these school teachers are subjected to every species of persecution from school superintendents, trustees, and the white braggarts of the town. The position of a colored school teacher in the South is not a desirable one from any standpoint. Before I would teach again in the South I would drive a dray on the streets.

I do not believe in centralization of government. I know the evils which come upon the people by merging into the hands of the few men, who must of necessity administer government, more power than they should control, and yet I am thoroughly convinced that the education of the people is a legitimate function of government – not in any sense a measure of centralization, but eminently one of self-preservation. We make lavish appropriations for harbors, forts, the Navy, and the Army, for the common defense, but illiteracy is a far more insidious foe from within than any that can or will assail us from without.

A national board of education wanted

I would advocate the creation of a board of education, with four commissioners (one for each section), and I would advocate an annual appropriation of $25,000,000 to $30,000,000, to be applied according to the ratio of illiteracy. It could be applied through the superintendents of education of the several States, subject to the approval of the commissioner or commissioners, or by some other more effective and satisfactory method.

The desire of the black race of the South to take advantage of educational opportunities is too well known and too conclusively demonstrated by statistics to require more than a passing notice.

It may be pertinent to remark here that there are in this country 7,646 colored ministers of all denominations, and a church membership of nearly 2,000,000 souls.

Slave labor and free labor contrasted

It is often charged that the race is lazy, but I think the charge is absurd. If it is lazy now, what must it have been under the system of slavery? It is undeniable that the negroes of Georgia own 680,000 acres of land, cut up into small farms, and in the cotton States they own and cultivate 2,680,000 acres. Dr. Alexander Crummell, in his thoughtful reply to the misrepresentations of Dr. Tucker, of Mississippi, says, basing his statement upon accepted data, "Let us put the figures as low as 400,000 acres for each (meaning Southern) State – for the purchase of farm lands has been everywhere a passion with the freedmen – this 400,000 acres, multiplied into 14, i.e., the number of the chief Southern States, shows an aggregate of 5,600,000 acres of land, the acquisition of the black race in less than twenty years. Again, I find that the Freedman's Bank, which opened in 1865 and closed in 1874, had no less than 61,000 black depositors, the aggregate of whose deposits was $56,000,000. Again, from 1857 to 1861, under slave labor, there were produced 18,230,738 bales of cotton; from 1878 to 1882 under free labor, 27,667,367 bales, being a balance in favor of free labor of

9,436,639 bales. There does not appear to be much ground for the charge of laziness to stand up in this handsome showing.

A still more gratifying illustration is furnished in the products of South Carolina. In 1849 and 1859 she raised 654,313 bales of cotton with slave labor; in 1879 and 1882, she raised with free labor 1,153,306 bales, a difference in favor of free labor of 498,993 bales. In 1859 her wheat crop was 1,285,631 bushels, in 1882, 2,973,600 – a difference of 1,687,969 bushels in favor of free labor. In 1859 her oat crop was 936,974 bushels; in 1882, 8,094,600 – a difference in favor of free labor of 7,057,626 bushels. Speaking of these marvellous and satisfactory figures the Boston Herald of a recent date says: "Free labor, protected in its rights, improved transportation, better fertilization and culture, and the subdivision of the lands are at the bottom of this wonderful growth."

I have no doubt that if comparisons were made as to the production of other States like favorable results would be shown. And yet there are men who seriously allege that the negroes are lazy. I am free to admit that a large percentum of the negroes squander much time and money in fishing, hunting and loafing; still the great mass of the people are honest, steady laborers. They must of necessity be, else how account for the steady increase in production in the South?

Compensation of farm laborers in southern states

Now, in view of these facts, it will naturally be asked why the negro population continues poor and ignorant. The answer, in part, is a direct refutation of the statement made to your honorable committee on Thursday last by Mr. John C. Calhoun as to the rate of wages and how it is paid in the South. The average rate of wages of a farm laborer in the South is nearer fifty than seventy-five cents, out of which the laborer must feed and clothe his family. He seldom ever pays rent and he seldom ever sees a cent of currency. He is paid in "orders" on some storekeeper friendly to the planter. He cannot negotiate these precious "orders" at any other than the store indicated. Hence a system of fraud is connived at and practiced, to the utter demoralization and impoverishment of the ignorant, helpless laborer.

I remember an instance which strikingly illustrates the pernicious features of the "orders" system. At a place on the Suwannee River in Florida there is a large saw-mill, owned by a gentleman who also operates a large farm. This man owns the entire village and all the land for miles around, and he will not allow any one to sell on his land. He owns the only store within forty miles of his place. He pays his employees in "orders" on his store, white and black alike, and it is a rare occasion indeed when any one of them gets his hand on a real dollar bill. So expensive is it to live at this place because of the miserly monopoly of everything by the proprietor, that I have known men who had fallen out with the proprietor to walk away, having been unable, from the earnings of many months, to save sufficient to indulge the luxury of a railroad ticket. I once attended a panoramic exhibition in the little church at his place, when the bookkeeper of the firm, a very fine gentleman, stood at the door and "passed in" all his employés who desired to see the sights, noting the name of each in his little book. When they had all passed in he gave the showman an "order" for his money and told him to call at the office the following day and collect, which was done. This sort of thing breeds improvidence, but not thriftlessness, because to be improvident the "orders" must be obtainable, and they are only obtainable when the work has been performed.

Share-labor system on farms

The system of share labor is equally unsatisfactory to the laborer. He is compelled to give a lien on his unplanted or unharvested crop to be able to run his farm, and his account at the store at the end of the year usually brings him in debt. My father once kept an account in the liberal sense; that is to say, he kept an account of the things he "took up" at the store as well as the storekeeper. When the accounts were footed up at the end of the year the thing became serious. The storekeeper had one hundred and fifty dollars more against my father than appeared on the latter's book. Of course there was a wide difference of opinion, but my father settled the account according to his book and told the merchant he was at liberty to sue for the remainder. But the merchant failed to do it, and his books will show a shortage of $150 today if he has not balanced the account to profit and loss. But of course the mass of colored men who farm on shares or labor by the year and keep an account do not, because they cannot, keep a record of every purchase; and it is by this means that they are swindled and kept forever in debt.

I have known honest but ignorant colored men who have lost large farms, magnificently accoutered, by such thievery. The black farmers, and those in other occupations at the South, are robbed year after year by the simplest sort of devices; and the very men who rob them are the loudest in complaint that the negroes are lazy and improvident. For my part, I am surprised that a larger number of them do not go to fishing, hunting, and loafing.

Artisan labor – its compensation

The artisans and laborers in the cities of the South fare better, but the wages they receive would be spurned by the white artisans and day laborers of any Northern or Western city. Masons and carpenters average not $2.50 to $5, as stated by Mr. Calhoun, but $1.50 to $3.25; other laborers receive from 75 cents to $1.25 per diem.

The statement has been made to your honorable committee that a better feeling between the whites and blacks is becoming more and more apparent, but I doubt it. There is an undercurrent of restlessness in the South which the newspapers and reform politicians attempt to smother, but nothing can smother it. The longer the blacks enjoy the state of freedom, the more education and property they acquire, the more restless they become; so that I am free to admit that the starting conclusions arrived at by Professor Gilliam in a recent article in the Popular Science Monthly will, in the main, be largely verified within the time specified by him. The man who thinks the blacks of the South will always patiently endure the wrongs heaped upon them, misapprehends that human nature which is the same in the Spartan helot, the Russian serf, and the Irish peasant.

Penitentiary labor

The penitentiary system of the South, with its infamous chain-gang and convict features, is not equaled in inhumanity, cruelty, and deliberate fraud in any other institution outside of Russian Siberia. Even the Charleston News and Courier and the Savannah morning newspapers, which no man will claim are oversensitive as to how much a negro suffers, have declared the convict system of Alabama, Georgia, and South Carolina a disgrace to civilization. When such papers as these cry out "horror!", it is time for less hidebound papers to look into the matter. The penitentiaries of the South are full of honest men as well as thieves, for the law of the South has been purposely framed to convict the negro, guilty or not guilty. These men are sentenced to long terms of imprisonment upon charges and evidence which would not be entertained for a moment in any court of law north of Mason and Dixon's line, the object being to terrorize the blacks and furnish victims for contractors, who purchase the labor of these wretches from the State for a song. Of course this one-sided administration of justice demoralizes the ignorant blacks, as it is intended to do. The white man who shoots a negro always goes free, while the negro who steals a hog is sent to the chain-gang for ten years. During the past month I noticed three instances of the acquittal of white murderers of colored men.

Rights of colored men

Colored men are, generally speaking, denied the right to serve on jury in the South. Hence they never expect justice, and they always receive the full extent of punishment cunningly devised to reach their case. They hold no offices by appointment under the State governments, and, because of open intimidation and violence and fraud, they hold very few through the suffrage of their fellow citizens. Their educational interests suffer in consequence. Respectable colored men refuse to travel in the South, because corporations sell them $25 worth of accommodation and force them to accept $10 worth when they can. They refuse to be thus outrageously robbed. They cannot receive shelter in hotels and inns, and places of amusement are barred against them. All these wrongs retard the progress of the race, and make the suggestion of amicable relations ridiculous. The condition of affairs in the South is volcanic in the extreme, and is becoming more so year after year, not less because of the apparent calm.

Source: Report of the Committee of the Senate upon the Relations between Labor and Capital, 1885.

Civil Rights

2.1 The Civil Rights Act

March 1, 1875

The Civil Rights Act of 1875 was notable for attempting to guarantee rights of a social character, including access to public places, to the black population.

An act to protect all citizens in their civil and legal rights.

Whereas it is essential to just government we recognize the equality of all men before the law, and hold that it is the duty of government in its dealings with the people to mete out equal and exact justice to all, of whatever nativity, race, color, or persuasion, religious or political; and it being the appropriate object of legislation to enact great fundamental principles into law: Therefore,

Be it enacted, That all persons within the jurisdiction of the United States shall be entitled to the full and equal enjoyment of the accommodations, advantages, facilities, and privileges of inns, public conveyances on land or water, theaters, and other places of public amusement; subject only to the conditions and limitations established by law, and applicable alike to citizens of every race and color, regardless of any previous condition of servitude.

SEC. 2. That any person who shall violate the foregoing section by denying to any citizen, except for reasons by law applicable to citizens of every race and color, and regardless of any previous condition of servitude, the full enjoyment of any of the accommodations, advantages, facilities, or privileges in said section enumerated, or by aiding or inciting such denial, shall, for every such offense, forfeit and pay the sum of five hundred dollars to the person aggrieved thereby, . . . and shall also, for every such offense, be deemed guility of a misdemeanor, and, upon conviction thereof, shall be fined not less than five hundred nor more than one thousand dollars, or shall be imprisoned not less than thirty days nor more than one year . . .

SEC. 3. That the district and circuit courts of the United States shall have exclusively of the courts of the several States, cognizance of all crimes and offenses against, and violations of, the provisions of this act . . .

SEC. 4. That no citizen possessing all other qualifications which are or may be prescribed by law shall be disqualified for service as grand or petit juror in any court of the United States, or of any State, on account of race, color, or previous condition of servitude; and any officer or other person charged with any duty in the selection or summoning of jurors who shall exclude or fail to summon any citizen for the cause aforesaid shall, on conviction thereof, be deemed guilty of a misdemeanor, and be fined not more than five thousand dollars.

SEC. 5. That all cases arising under the provisions of this act ... shall be renewable by the Supreme Court of the United States, without regard to the sum in controversy ...

Source: *US Statutes at Large*, Vol. XVIII, p. 335 ff.

2.2 Civil Rights Cases
1883

Judgement was given in five civil rights cases on appeal to the Supreme Court, involving the validity and interpretation of the Civil Rights Act of 1875. In each case, a black person had been denied some accommodation or privilege on account of colour. The majority decision was that social rights could not be guaranteed by legislation, and that the black population, now freed from slavery, could not indefinitely expect special treatment.

BRADLEY, J. [After holding that the statute derived no support from the Fourteenth Amendment].

. . . But the power of the Congress to adopt direct and primary, as distinguished from corrective legislation, on the subject in hand, is sought in the second place, from the Thirteenth Amendment, which abolishes slavery . . .

It is true that slavery cannot exist without law any more than property in lands and goods can exist without law, and therefore the Thirteenth Amendment may be regarded as nullifying all state laws which establish or uphold slavery. But it has a reflex character also, establishing and decreeing universal civil and political freedom throughout the United States; and it is assumed that the power in Congress to enforce the articles by appropriate legislation, clothes Congress with power to pass all laws necessary and proper for abolishing all badges and incidents of slavery in the United States; and upon this assumption it is claimed that this is sufficient authority for declaring by law that all persons shall have equal accommodations and privileges in all inns, public conveyances, and places of public amusement; the argument being that the denial of such equal accommodations and privileges is in itself a subjection to a species of servitude within the meaning of the amendment. Conceding the major proposition to be true, that Congress has a right to enact all necessary and proper laws for the obliteration and prevention of slavery with all its badges and incidents, is the minor proposition also true, that the denial to any person of admission to the accommodations and privileges of an inn, a public conveyance, or a theatre, does subject that person to any form of servitude, or tend to fasten upon him any badge of slavery? If it does not, then power to pass the law is not found in the Thirteenth Amendment. . . .

But is there any similarity between such servitudes and a denial by the owner of an inn, a public conveyance, or a theatre, of its accommodations and privileges to an individual, even though the denial be founded on the race or color of that individual? Where does any slavery or servitude, or badge of either, arise from such an act of denial? Whether it might not be a denial of a right which, if sanctioned by the state law, would be obnoxious to the prohibitions of the Fourteenth Amendment, is another question. But what has it to do with the question of slavery? . . .

The long existence of African slavery in this country gave us very distinct notions of what it was, and what were its necessary incidents. Compulsory service of the slave for the benefit of the master, restraint of his movements except by the master's will, disability to hold property, to make contracts, to have a standing in court, to be a witness against a white person, and such like burdens and incapacities were the inseparable incidents of the institution. . . . Can the act of a mere individual, the owner of the inn, the public conveyance, or place of amusement, refusing the accommodation, be justly regarded as imposing any badge of slavery or servitude upon the applicant, or only as inflicting an ordinary civil injury, properly cognizable by the laws of the State, and presumably subject to redress by those laws until the contrary appears?

After giving to these questions all the consideration which their importance demands, we are forced to the conclusion that such an act of refusal has nothing to do with slavery or involuntary servitude, and that if it is violative of any right of the party, his redress is to to be sought under the laws of the State; or, if those laws are adverse to his rights and do not protect him, his remedy will be found in the corrective legislation which Congress has adopted, or may adopt, for counteracting the effect of state laws, or state action, prohibited by the Fourteenth Amendment. It would be running the slavery argument into the ground to make it apply to every act of discrimination which a person may see fit to make as to the guests he will entertain, or as to the people he will take into his coach or cab or car, or admit to his concert or theatre, or deal with in other matters of intercourse or business. . . .

When a man has emerged from slavery, and by the aid of beneficent legislation has shaken off the inseparable concomitants of that state, there must be some stage in the progress of his elevation when he takes the rank of a mere citizen, and ceases to be the special favorite of the laws, and when his rights as a citizen, or a man, are to be protected in the ordinary modes by which other men's rights are protected. There were thousands of free colored people in this country before the abolition of slavery, enjoying all the essential rights of life, liberty and property the same as white citizens; yet no one, at that time, thought that it was any invasion of his personal status as a freeman because he was not admitted to all the privileges enjoyed by white citizens, or because he was subjected to discriminations in the enjoyment of accommodations in inns, public conveyances and places of amusement. Mere discriminations on account of race or color were not regarded as badges of slavery. If, since that time, the enjoyment of equal rights in all these respects has become established by constitutional enactment, it is not by force of the Thirteenth Amendment (which merely abolishes slavery), but by force of the Fourteenth and Fifteenth Amendments.

On the whole we are of the opinion that no countenance of authority for the passage of the law in question can be found in either the Thirteenth or Fourteenth Amendment of the Constitution; and no other ground of authority for its passage being suggested, it must necessarily be declared void, at least so far as its operation in the several States is concerned . . .

HARLAN, J., delivered a dissenting opinion.

Source: *Civil Rights Cases 109,* U.S. 3 (1883).

2.3 Frederick Douglass on the Civil Rights Cases Decision, 1883

Frederick Douglass, an ex-slave and leading spokesman since the days of anti-slavery, condemns the decision in the Civil Rights Cases at a Civil Rights Mass Meeting in Washington, D.C.

Friends and fellow-citizens:

I have only a very few words to say to you this evening, and in order that those few words shall be well-chosen, and not liable to be misunderstood, distorted or misrepresented, I have been at the pains of writing them out in full. It may be, after all, that the hour calls more loudly for silence than for speech. Later on in this discussion when we shall have the full text of the recent decision of the Supreme Court before us, and the dissenting opinion of Judge Harlan, who must have weighty reasons for separating from all his associates, and incurring thereby, as he must, an amount of criticism from which even the bravest man might shrink, we may be in better frame of mind, better supplied with facts, and better prepared to speak calmly, correctly, and wisely, than now. The temptation at this time is, of course, to speak more from feeling than reason, more from impulse than reflection. . . .

The cause which has brought us here to-night is neither common nor trivial. Few events in our national history have surpassed it in magnitude, importance and significance. It has swept over the land like a moral cyclone, leaving moral desolation in its track.

We feel it, as we felt the furious attempt, years ago, to force the assursed system of slavery upon the soil of Kansas, the enactment of the Fugitive Slave Bill, the repeal of the Missouri Compromise, the Dred Scott decision. I look upon it as one more shocking development of that moral weakness in high places which has attended the conflict between the spirit of slavery from the beginning, and I venture to predict that it will be so regarded by after-coming generations.

Far down the ages, when men shall wish to inform themselves as to the real state of liberty, law, religion and civilization in the United States at this juncture of our history, they will overhaul the proceedings of the Supreme Court, and read the decision declaring the Civil Rights Bill unconstitutional and void.

From this they will learn more than from many volumes, how far we have advanced, in this year of grace, from barbarism toward civilization.

Fellow-citizens: Among the great evils which now stalk abroad in our land, the one, I think, which most threatens to undermine and destroy the foundations of our free institutions, is the great and apparently increasing want of respect entertained for those to whom are committed the responsibility and the duty of administering our government. On this point, I think all good men must agree, and against this evil I trust you feel, and we all feel, the deepest repugnance, and that we will, neither here nor elsewhere, give it the least breath of sympathy or encouragement. We should never forget, that, whatever may be the incidental mistakes or misconduct of rulers, government is better than anarchy, and patient reform is better than violent revolution.

But while I would increase this feeling, and give it the emphasis of a voice from heaven, it must not be allowed to interfere with free speech, honest expression, and fair criticism. To give up this would be to give up liberty, to give up progress, and to consign the nation to moral stagnation, putrefaction, and death.

In the matter of respect for dignitaries, it should never be forgotten, however, that duties are reciprocal, and while the people should frown down every manifestation of levity and contempt for those in power, it is the duty of the possessors of power so to use it as to deserve and to insure respect and reverence.

To come a little nearer to the case now before us. The Supreme Court of the United States, in the exercise of its high and vast constitutional power, has suddenly and unexpectedly decided that the law intended to secure to colored people the civil rights guaranteed to them by the following provision of the Constitution of the United States, is unconstitutional and void. Here it is:

> "No State," says the 14th Amendment, "shall make or enforce any law which shall abridge the privileges or immunities of citizens of the United States; nor shall any State deprive any person of life, liberty, or property without due process of law; nor deny any person within its jurisdiction the equal protection of the laws." . . .

Inasmuch as the law in question is a law in favor of liberty and justice, it ought to have had the benefit of any doubt which could arise as to its strict constitutionality. This, I believe, will be the view taken of it, not only by laymen like myself, but by eminent lawyers as well . . .

Now let me say here, before I go on a step further in this discussion, if any man has come here to-night with his breast heaving with passion, his heart flooded with acrimony, wishing and expecting to hear violent denunciation of the Supreme Court, on account of this decision, he has mistaken the object of this meeting, and the character of the men by whom it is called. . . .

What will be said here to-night, will be spoken, I trust, more in sorrow than in anger, more in a tone of regret than of bitterness.

We cannot, however, overlook the fact that though not so intended, this decision has inflicted a heavy calamity upon seven millions of the people of this country, and left them naked and defenceless against the action of a malignant, vulgar, and pitiless prejudice.

It presents the United States before the world as a Nation utterly destitute of power to protect the rights of its own citizens upon its own soil.

It can claim service and allegiance, loyalty and life, of them, but it cannot protect them against the most palpable violation of the rights of human nature, rights to secure which, governments are established. It can tax their bread and tax their blood, but has no protecting power for their persons. Its National power extends only to the District of Columbia, and the Territories – where the people have no votes – and where the land has not people. All else is subject to the States. In the name of common sense, I ask, what right have we to call ourselves a Nation, in view of this decision, and this utter destitution of power?

In humiliating the colored people of this country, this decision has humbled the Nation. It gives to a South Carolina, or a Mississippi, Rail-Road Conductor, more power than it gives to the National Government. . . .

The lesson of all the ages on this point is, that a wrong done to one man, is a wrong done to all men. It may not be felt at the moment, and the evil day may be long delayed, but so sure as there is a moral government of the universe, so sure will the harvest of evil come. . . .

To-day, our Republic sits as a Queen among the nations of the earth. Peace is within her walls and plenteousness within her palaces, but he is a bolder and a far more hopeful man than I am, who will affirm that this peace and prosperity will always last. History repeats itself. What has happened once may happen again.

The negro, in the Revolution, fought for us and with us. In the war of 1812 Gen. Jackson, at New Orleans, found it necessary to call upon the colored people to assist in its defence against England. Abraham Lincoln found it necessary to call upon the negro to defend the Union against rebellion, and the negro responded gallantly in all cases.

Our legislators, our Presidents, and our judges should have a care, lest, by forcing these people, outside of law, they destroy that love of country which is needful to the Nation's defence in the day of trouble.

I am not here, in this presence, to discuss the constitutionality or unconstitutionality of this decision of the Supreme Court. The decisions may or may not be constitutional. That is a question for lawyers, and not for laymen, and there are lawyers on this platform as learned, able, and eloquent as any who have appeared in this case before the Supreme Court, or as any in the land. To these I leave the exposition of the Constitution; but I claim the right to remark upon a strange and glaring inconsistency with former decisions, in the action of the court on this Civil Rights Bill. It is a new departure, entirely out of the line of the precedents and decisions of the Supreme Court at other times and in other directions where the rights of colored men were concerned. It has utterly ignored and rejected the force and application of object and intention as a rule of interpretation. It has construed the Constitution in defiant disregard of what was the object and intention of the adoption of the Fourteenth Amendment. It has made no account whatever of the intention and purpose of Congress and the President in putting the Civil Rights Bill upon the Statute Book of the Nation. It has seen fit in this case, affecting a weak and much-persecuted people, to be guided by the narrowest and most restricted rules of legal interpretation. It has viewed both the Constitution and the law with a strict regard to their letter, but without any generous recognition of their broad and liberal spirit. Upon those narrow principles the decision is logical and legal, of course. But what I complain of, and what every lover of liberty in the United States has a right to complain of, is this sudden and causeless reversal of all the great rules of legal interpretation by which this Court was governed in other days, in the construction of the Constitution and of laws respecting colored people. . . .

Fellow-citizens! while slavery was the base line of American society, while it ruled the church and the state, while it was the interpreter of our law and the exponent of our religion, it admitted no quibbling, no narrow rules of legal or scriptural interpretations of Bible or Constitution. It sternly demanded its pound of flesh, no matter how much blood was shed in the taking of it. It was enough for it to be able to show the *intention* to get all it asked in the Courts or out of the Courts. But now slavery is abolished. Its reign was long, dark and bloody. Liberty *now*, is the base line of the Republic. Liberty has supplanted slavery, but I fear it has not supplanted the spirit or power of slavery. Where slavery was strong, liberty is now weak.

O for a Supreme Court of the United States which shall be as true to the claims of humanity, as the Supreme Court formerly was to the demands of slavery! When that day comes, as come it will, a Civil Rights Bill will not be declared unconstitutional and void, in utter and flagrant disregard of the objects and intentions of the National legislature by which it was enacted, and of the rights plainly secured by the Constitution.

This decision of the Supreme Court admits that the Fourteenth Amendment is a prohibition of the States. It admits that a State shall not abridge the privileges or immunities of citizens of the United States, but commits the seeming absurdity of allowing the people of a State to do what it prohibits the State itself from doing.

It used to be thought that the whole was more than a part; that the greater included the less, and that what was unconstitutional for a State to do was equally unconstitutional for an individual member of a State to do. What is a State, in the absence of the people who compose it? Land, air and water. That is all. As individuals, the people of the State of South Carolina may stamp out the rights of the negro wherever they please, so long as they do not do so as a State. All the parts can violate the Constitution, but the whole cannot. It is not the act itself, according to this decision, that is unconstitutional. The unconstitutionality of the case depends wholly upon the party committing the act. If the State commits it, it is wrong, if the citizen of the State commits it, it is right.

O consistency, thou art indeed a jewel! What does it matter to a colored citizen that a State may not insult and outrage him, if a citizen of a State may? The effect upon him is the same, and it was just this effect that the framers of the Fourteenth Amendment plainly intended by that article to prevent.

It was the act, not the instrument, which was prohibited. It meant to protect the newly enfranchised citizen from injustice and wrong, not merely from a State, but from the individual members of a State. It meant to give him the protection to which his citizenship, his loyalty, his allegiance, and his services entitled him; and this meaning, and this purpose, and this intention, is now declared unconstitutional and void, by the Supreme Court of the United States.

I say again, fellow-citizens, O for a Supreme Court which shall be as true, as vigilant, as active, and exacting in maintaining laws enacted for the protection of human rights, as in other days was that Court for the destruction of human rights!

It is said that this decision will make no difference in the treatment of colored people; that the Civil Rights Bill was a dead letter, and could not be enforced. There is some truth in all this, but it is not the whole truth. That bill, like all advance legislation, was a banner on the outer wall of American liberty, a noble moral standard, uplifted for the education of the American people. There are tongues in trees, books, in the running brooks — sermons in stones. This law, though dead, did speak. It expressed the sentiment of justice and fair play, common to every honest heart. Its voice was against popular prejudice and meanness. It appealed to all the noble and patriotic instincts of the American people. It told the American people that they were all equal before the law; that they belonged to a common country and were equal citizens. The Supreme Court has hauled down this flag of liberty in open day, and before all the people, and has thereby given joy to the heart of every man in the land who wishes to deny to others what he claims for himself. It is a concession to race pride, selfishness and meanness, and will be received with joy by every upholder of caste in the land, and for this I deplore and denounce that decision. . . .

Another illustration of this tendency to put opponents in a false position, is seen in the persistent effort to stigmatize the "Civil Rights Bill" as a "Social Rights Bill." Now, nowhere under the whole heavens, outside of the United States, could any such perversion of truth have any chance of success. No man in Europe would ever dream that because he has a right to ride on a railway, or stop at a hotel, he therefore has the right to enter into social relations with anybody. No one has a right to speak to another without the other's permission. Social equality and civil equality rest upon an entirely different basis, and well enough the American people know it; yet to inflame a popular prejudice, respectable papers like the New York Times and the Chicago Tribune, persist in describing the Civil Rights Bill as a Social Rights Bill.

When a colored man is in the same room or in the same carriage with white people, as a servant, there is no talk of social equality, but if he is there as a man and a gentleman, he is an offence. What makes the difference? It is not color, for his color is unchanged. The whole essence of the thing is a studied purpose to degrade and stamp out the liberties of a race. It is the old spirit of slavery, and nothing else. To say that because a man rides in the same car with another, he is therefore socially equal, is one of the wildest absurdities. . . .

If it is a Bill for social equality, so is the Declaration of Independence, which declares that all men have equal rights; so is the Sermon on the Mount, so is the Golden Rule, that commands us to do to others as we would that others should do to us; so is the Apostolic teaching, that of one blood God has made all nations to dwell on all the face of the earth; so is the Constitution of the United States, and so are the laws and customs of every civilized country in the world; for no where, outside of the United States, is any man denied civil rights on account of his color.

Source: Frederick Douglass, Speech to Civil Rights Meeting, Washington, 1883. *Proceedings of the Civil Rights Mass-Meeting Held at Lincoln Hall*, October 22, 1883 (pamphlet, Washington, D.C., 1883), pp. 4-14.

2.4 "Shall Negro Majorities Rule?"

John T. Morgan, a white supremacist, criticises the enfranchisement of the black population.

The population of the United States is made up, mainly, of two races of men, the Caucasian and the African, more than one-seventh being of the latter. In thirteen contiguous States nearly 40 per cent. of the inhabitants are Negroes. In three States the Negroes outnumber the whites. In all political matters the law declares these races to be equal, and secures to men of each all the rights, privileges, and immunities of citizenship that belong to men of the other. In the relations of these races, so different from each other in mental, moral, and physical characteristics, is the "Negro question," which is now receiving, and will hereafter demand in greater degree, the most serious consideration of thinking men of every class and of all sections of the country. . . .

It is a question of race conflict. In whatever connection it is considered, whether in church or social relations, in business, professional, or industrial employments, or in politics, it is a matter of race. Every result that we have reached, or that we can reach, whether it has been worked out by the Negroes in their natural progress, or by the whites in their endeavors to elevate the Negroes, is a consequence of race conflict. Neither race is responsible for the conditions that make this conflict instinctive and irreconcilable, and neither can avoid the issue or its consequences under the circumstances in which both are placed.

These races, brought together here on terms of political equality, are not equal or homogeneous. Their amalgamation is impossible, because it is forbidden by the instincts of both. The whites of the United States have been remarkably firm and persistent in their insistence upon the maintenance of race distinctions in everything that relates to social existence and progress, and the Negroes have as distinctly shown their aversion to any relaxation of race ties and exclusiveness. The aversion is mutual, and, in a general sense, fixed. . . .

Between the African and the white race the bar to union is still more absolute. To remove it, if it could be removed, would be to lower the whites to the level of the intellectual, moral, and social condition of the Negroes. It would be to destroy the white race. One drop of Negro blood known to exist in the veins of a woman in this country draws her down to the social status of the Negro, and impresses upon her whole life the stamp of the fateful Negro caste, though she may rival the Easter lily in the whiteness of her skin. The Negroes, though they may accept almost any form of association with the whites, are never satisfied with any admixture of the blood of the races. It relaxes the hold of their own race upon their affections. Negroes of mixed blood are inferior among the race to which they belong.

It is irrational to attribute these race antipathies and aversions to the laws of this country or to anything in the manner of their administration and enforcement. They rest upon foundations that men have not built, and are supported by ordinances that human power can neither enact nor amend nor repeal. After we have done all that we can to abolish or to neutralize these race distinctions and the feelings that grow out of them — attempting to set aside the eternal laws of nature — we shall find that we have only marked more plainly the differences between the races, and that we have rooted race prejudices more deeply in the hearts of the inferior races and the whites, at least so far as the Chinese and Negroes are concerned. The Negro question is not, therefore, a southern question, but a race question, that appears in every phase of human existence as distinctly in the North, wherever a considerable number of Negroes is found, as in the South.

The personal relations between the Negroes and the white people are more friendly in the South than in the North, because in the South they are based upon the recognition, by both races, of the leadership and superiority of the white race. This recognition of a natural and obvious fact is not offensive to the Negroes, and the relations that accord with it are not constrained or disagreeable to either race.

The southern white man, from long association with the Negroes as a dependent and inferior race, can afford to indulge for them an honest and cordial regard; while the white man in the North feels that, in any exhibition of regard for the Negro, he is sacrificing the dignity of his race and making a personal condescension. He is willing to punish himself with a certain self-abasement to prove to the Negro that he is no more than his equal, while the Negro is compelled to lower his opinion of the white man in order to believe what he says.

If these race instincts and proclivities are wrong, and appeal to humanity for their correction, it by no means follows that the remedy is to be found within the domain of the legislative power, either State or federal. . . . When we come to make laws for the regulation of the political powers accorded to the African race, this important factor – public opinion – cannot be disregarded. Without its support such laws will fail of their purpose, however they may be sustained by force. Public opinion, in any part of the United States, will ultimately neutralize statutes that violate the instincts of the white race. . . .

It is certain that no law can long be enforced among a people as free as ours when their opposition to it is sincere. This is especially true when such laws demand the humiliation of the white race, or the admission of the Negroes to a dangerous participation, as a race, in the affairs of our government. . . .

The laws that give the ballot to one-fifth of the Negro race appeal to the race prejudice which incites them to persistent effort to accomplish the impossible result of race equality. "Equality before the law" is the phrase in which this demand is expressed, but this condition is impossible without equality in the opinion and conscience of the white race. The question is the same in every State, North or South, where any considerable body of Negroes is found, and the decree of public opinion is the same.

The Negroes are no more capable than we are of setting aside the natural influence of race. The honest Negro will vote with his race at every opportunity, just as the honest white man will vote with his. Every sentiment and affection of the human heart is engaged on behalf of the race to which the voter belongs. It is impossible that any man can vote impartially when a question is presented in which his race is believed to be vitally concerned, and it is folly to expect such a vote. The sentiment or public opinion of his race will control him beyond his power of resistance. Education refinement, wealth, and the consciousness of personal merit add a stronger jealousy to the power of race, and continually widen the separation between the white and Negro races. This effect is more decided with the Negro than it is with the white race. It has increased every day since the Negroes were emancipated. They demand, with greater earnestness than ever before, that their representatives shall be Negroes, and not white men. No solidity of political affiliation can resist this borrowing suspicion of the Negro race that a white man is the natural enemy of the Negro power in government.

We have not accomplished any good to either race by conferring upon 1,500,000 Negroes the privilege of voting. Its effect is only to neutralize the same number of white votes that would otherwise be cast with reference to the general welfare and prosperity of the country. It is needless to recall the history of the race contests that have pervaded the ballot-box under this mistaken policy. The facts are present, in every election, to establish the existence of this national misfortune. Unless the voter can sink his race proclivities and aversions in his sense of duty to his country, it is in vain that we endeavor to compel by law the harmonious action of the white and Negro races, either in voting or in conducting the government. This impossible condition is hidden in the core of the Negro question, and neither law-makers, judges, nor executive officers can remove it. . . .

Outside pressure from people who are in no immediate danger and have nothing at stake but their sentiments of justice or philanthropy, cannot change the conduct or modify the opinions of those who have at risk and in charge, as a trust imposed upon them by the blood of kindred, all that is sacred in society and in family. Such pressure must result in permanent harm to the Negro race, while it may also seriously injure the white race temporarily. If the laws of the States in reference to elections, of which no complaint is made, are evaded, or if they are not enforced, it is because public opinion sets too strongly against them. Laws of Congress which can be executed only through the assistance of the people of the States would meet a similar fate. . . .

The southern people are not mistaken as to the dangers of the ballot in the hands of the Negro race. Twenty years of experience, beginning with eight years of the horrors of enforced Negro rule, has demonstrated to them that a relapse into that condition would be the worst form of destruction. They are no more amenable to moral censure for attempting to avoid that desperate fate than are the people who, in all parts of our country, punish with instant death the Indian or Chinaman or Negro who inflicts a worse fate than death upon an innocent woman. Congress can do nothing to prevent such violations of the laws, even in the Territories and against its wards the Indians and Negroes, or its *protégés* the Chinamen. . . .

If this is a race question that the existing amendments of the Constitution could not settle or suppress, and if it must be solved at last by the will of the people as it shall be expressed either in support of or against the safety of entrusting political power, under our system of government, to the inferior Negro race, the question will be whether the public sentiment, or public opinion, or the laws, which shall furnish the ultimate solution of the problem, shall be those of the people of the States respectively which have this trouble to meet, or whether other States must interfere, through the action of Congress, to settle the matter in all its details.

In support of the proposition that the people of the States respectively should be left free, under the Constitution, to deal with this difficult problem without the interference of other States, it is first assumed, with evident reason, that Congress cannot successfully control the suffrage of the people in the States by any means. Military coercion would only increase the difficulties, and that resort may be dismissed as impossible. Whatever is done to secure to the Negroes the full use of the ballot must be done through State laws and through public opinion in the States. If the belief of the white race is that the enforcement of these laws will destroy their civilization, the laws will not be executed, though the refusal to execute them should cost the States their representation in Congress.

It must be remembered that it was an entire race of people that we enfranchised with the ballot, and not the individuals of that race who may have been personally competent to use it with judgment for the general good of the people. Our process of enfranchising the Indians is just the reverse of this. We make citizens of them, man by man, and upon the condition of their proving their capacity for citizenship by dissolving their tribal relations and taking lands in severalty. A plan looking to some personal fitness of the Negro for the high duties and corresponding powers of citizenship would not have shocked the common sense of the people, and would have collected into the body of voters in the States those Negroes who had at least some idea of the uses and value of the ballot. The plan we adopted, of transferring the whole of this inferior race into the body of our citizenship, with the power of government, was a rash experiment, that has not succeeded in accomplishing any good to either race. . . .

Protestations of good will for the Negro race, when made by southern people, are not accepted as being sincere by those who believe that the ex-slaveholder and his posterity are incapable of sympathy or regard for that race of men. The argument, if applied to the ex-slave-catcher and his posterity, would carry with it much more logical strength. If we compare the condition of the Negro, caught in his native land and enslaved, with that of his posterity in the South as it was at the date of the 13th Amendment, simple justice cannot deny to the former slaveholding South the credit of having dealt far more generously with the Negroes than those who caught them in Africa or brought them from the slave ships.

The southern people do not desire to deprive the Negro race of any power or facility that will make freedom a blessing to them. What they seek to avoid is the consolidation of power in the hands of the Negro race that will be used, through the incentives of race aversion, to put them in control of the government of the white race.

Agitation in Congress and in political clubs will keep the prospect of such ascendency ever before the Negroes, and will create opposition to the Negro voter that, otherwise, would be of little effect in any respect, and would never endanger the personal rights of that race. If these questions are permitted to await the solution that experience alone can provide, through the conduct of the people who have befriended this race when they had no other counselors or guides than the slave-hunters, and who have developed this class into a condition that no African Negro ever aspired to, the solution will not, at least, cost us the shame of surrendering Anglo-Saxon civilization to the rule of ignorance and race prejudice. If they are forced into such shape as Negro instincts and the greed for power, common to them and their white leaders, shall compel them to assume, the world cannot censure the southern people if they do not welcome such a solution of the questions as will degrade the race to which we belong from its traditional prestige and wipe out the memory of its former grand achievements. This will not be expected of the South; neither will it be done.

The safe, benevolent, and wise solution of the Negro question can be left to the people of the States respectively, under the Constitution, with far greater security for every right now accorded to the Negroes, and for every blessing that may follow, than it can be to the politicians and agitators in other States.

Source: John T. Morgan, "Shall Negro Majorities Rule?" *Forum*, VI (February 1889), pp. 586-599.

2.5 "Shall White Minorities Rule?"

A response to John T. Morgan by Albion W. Tourgée, once a carpet-bagger, and a supporter of equal rights for black citizens. Tourgée was a lawyer and former judge, and later acted as chief counsel in the test case against enforced segregation which led to the Supreme Court decision in Plessy vs Ferguson.

The "Negro question" is unquestionably the most momentous problem of our civilization. Considered with regard either to its scope or character it is almost unprecedented in importance, difficulty, and the possible peril involved in its solution. It is not a new question. Slavery and the slave trade were only its earlier phases. Rebellion, reconstruction, and ku-kluxism were incidents attending its partial solution. For a hundred years it has almost constantly threatened the life of the republic. . . .

The present phase of the question is a controversy touching the Negro's right to exercise freely, peacefully, and effectually the elective franchise, and to enjoy without hinderance its resulting incidents. It is not fairly presented by the inquiry, "Shall black majorities rule?" The rule of the majority is the fundamental principle of our government. It is one of the incidents of the right to exercise the elective franchise, of which no individual or class can lawfully be deprived while that right remains unrestricted. Some confusion has been produced in the discussion of this question by attempting to treat the elective franchise as a privilege instead of a right. Until duly conferred it is a privilege – a privilege which no individual or class has any legal right to demand. Once granted, however, the exercise and enjoyment of it and of all its natural incidents becomes a right which the sovereign must maintain and enforce, or submit to nullification of the law. The particular point in controversy is not whether the colored man shall be allowed a new privilege, but whether he shall be permitted to exercise a right already guaranteed by law. The proper form of inquiry, therefore, is, "Shall white minorities rule?"

The arguments advanced in support of this monstrous proposition thus far are identical with those adduced in favor of slavery and the slave trade, nullification, secession, rebellion, ku-kluxism — all varying phases, let us not forget, of the same idea. They are urged by the same class of our people, with the same unanimity, the same positiveness, and the same arrogant assumption of infallibility as of old. They not only boastfully admit that for a decade and a half they have nullified the law and defied the national power, but boldly proclaim their determination to continue to do so as long as they may see fit. . . .

In its present phase, the Negro question is not one of sentiment, so far as the colored man is concerned. He asks nothing as a Negro. On the score of "race, color, or previous condition of servitude" he makes no demand, asks no favors. It is as a citizen merely that we are called on to consider what rights and privileges he is entitled to exercise, and how far and in what manner it is just, politic, and safe to permit them to be restricted, abridged, or revoked. Like most political questions, it presents a mixed issue of policy and principle. What is best to be done must depend to a great extent upon what we have the right to do. These elements cannot be separated, and must both be allowed due weight in the final decision.

Even if the claim of inherent superiority of the white race be admitted, it does not follow that it constitutes a sufficient ground for the disfranchisement of the inferior race. The world has moved since it was recognized as a fundamental principle that a divine right to rule inhered in particular classes. The chief function of government at the present time is to protect the weak against the strong. . . .

"Ignorance may struggle up to enlightenment," says Mr. Henry W. Grady, in a recent self-reported speech; "out of corruption may come the incorruptible; but the supremacy of the white race at the South must be maintained forever, simply because it is the white race and is the superior race!" There is no doubt that in this he expresses the conviction of the majority of the white race of the South; and a people who within thirty years punished as a felon the man who uttered the name of liberty in the slave's hearing or taught him to spell it out himself, would not hesitate to destroy the Negro's opportunity for development in order to keep him weak, dependent, and manageable. Not because the Negro is ignorant or incapable do they object to his exercise of the right of suffrage, but because he is a Negro, and as such they will spare no pains to keep him weak.

But even if the inherent superiority of the white race is admitted, and a consequent right to rule not denied, the means by which alone the rule of white minorities can be secured must make the proposition a most serious one. There are but three methods by which it may be accomplished. Two of them would require an appeal at least to the forms of law; the other pre-supposes a steady and persistent defiance of law. The most direct method would be to restore the term "white" as an essential qualification for citizenship in the State constitutions. . . . Another method in which the derived result might be temporarily attained by apparently legal means, is by imposing an educational qualification upon the voter. Such a course would probably command the approval of a majority of the people of the North. They would no doubt be willing to punish the Negro still further for the crime of having been kept in compulsory ignorance by his white Christian brethren for two centuries and a half, in order to conciliate the white people of the South, and get rid, for a time at least, of the unpleasant and annoying Negro question. There is one difficulty in the way of adopting this plan, to wit: forty-five per cent. of the voters of the eight States in which the matter is most pressing are unable to read their ballots. . . .

There remains only the alternative of deterrent violence or neutralizing fraud, which is frankly admitted to have been in operation for a dozen years or more, and which, it is unmistakably intimated by such men as Mr. Watterson, Senator Eustis, Senator Morgan, and Mr. Grady, is to be indefinitely continued as a means of perpetuating the rule of white minorities. This answers all the required conditions. It saves the Negro as a constituent and neutralizes him as a factor in government. This is what southern writers mean when they insist that white minorities at the South shall be left to deal with the Negro question in their own way. . . .

Another difficulty in the way of this indefinite continuance of unlawful usurpation, is the uncertainty that exists as to the course the Negro himself will pursue in regard to the matter. Thus far the Negro has been counted only a silent factor in the problem to which he has given a name. Slavery no more thought of asking him how he enjoyed his condition than the owner does of inquiring whether his horse prefers to go on the road or disport himself in the pasture.

The discussion of the present phase of the problem was started by the grave inquiry of an eminent ecclesiastic, "What shall we do with the Negro?" Is it not about time that we asked ourselves, What will the Negro permit us to do with him? To this inquiry the advocate of the inherent right of white minorities to rule responds with his usual confidence in his own infallibility: "Just let us alone; we will take care of him; we understand the Negro; leave us to manage him." This confidence is very largely based on the docility and submissiveness of the colored race in the past. The man who advocates continued unlawful repression, seems not to realize that a race which has been a perfect type of humility for centuries when in a position of abject servitude, invariably shows altogether different qualities when once it has set its foot upon the lower rung of the ladder of opportunity. . . .

In view of this, it is well to consider briefly who and what the American Negro is. In the first place, he is an American. Since 1802, when the slave trade was abolished, very few African Negroes have entered the United States. In the second place, he is not a heathen. A larger proportion of the colored people of the United States than of any equal body of whites in the country are actual members of a Christian church. It may be well to remember, too, that very few of them are pure Negroes. . . .

There are other qualities which the colored man has displayed that should incline the enthusiastic advocates of the supremacy of white minorities to pause and think very seriously before they decide upon an indefinite perpetuation of this policy of unlawful and defiant despoliation of political rights. Twenty-four years ago the five millions of newly-enfranchised freemen were not worth all together five million cents. They were naked, helpless, inept. They had hands, and a sort of dull, incomprehensible power to endure; that was all. Within a decade they had $12,000,000 in the savings banks alone. They lived on wages and flourished on conditions that would have exterminated the northern white laborer in a generation. Today they claim a valuation in the southern States alone of $100,000,000. In Georgia they own nearly a million acres of land. . . .

We often hear the idea advanced that what is termed the "race question" will disappear from politics just as soon as a proper issue is presented. No race can separate into parties or factions while its rights and liberties are assailed by another on the ground of race alone. Their rights must be freely admitted before they will dare to surrender whatever power there may be in cohesion. To do otherwise would be an act of stupendous and incredible folly. One might as well expect a herd of sheep to separate in the presence of wolves. Their only hope is in union. So, too, we hear it said that when the present generation dies off slavery will be only a dream to the colored man. Such is not the lesson of history. The farther people recede from bondage, the keener is their appreciation of the wrong and the more intense their hate of the oppressor. The horror which the American Negro feels for the institution of slavery will become greater rather than less for several generations at least. When did the Jewish prophets cease to anathematize the Egyptian oppressor? Such antipathies were curable only by continued and undeniable recognition of the right.

"But what can they do?" is the triumphant inquiry which greets the objector who calls attention to these things. "We have the arms, the skill, the experience, the wealth; what can they do?" Truly, the question is not an idle one, yet history clearly teaches that whenever an inferior class, intimately intermingled with a dominant and oppressive caste, becomes both intelligent enough to organize and desperate enough to resist, it is sure to overwhelm the arrogant and better-equipped minority. No man can say when the limit of endurance will be reached if this policy is continued, but that it will be reached in the near future is just as certain as that a boiler will explode if the safety valve is fastened down and the fire kept up. When that day shall come, the advocates of a policy of forcible repression and unlawful subjection will find the battle is not always to the strong.

Should a conflict arise to-morrow, the odds would by no means be entirely with the white race. Their very wealth might constitute a source of weakness. Black eyes and black ears would take note of every white man's movements. In every camp there would be spies; in every household informers. While the Negro has not so heroic a record as the southern white man, it should not be forgotten that there are 50,000 still living who wore the federal blue and fought for the freedom of their race. Besides that, in a strife such as must result if the occasion for it is not carefully and wisely avoided, it is not valor alone that counts, nor excellence of equipment that assures victory. In such a conflict a box of matches is equal to a hundred Winchester rifles!

In the meantime, neither the nation nor the world would sit still and witness the *auto da fé* of a race. Eight millions of people cannot very long be kept in a subordinate position and despoiled of their guaranteed rights by a minority, however superior and arrogant, through the instrumentality of the shot-gun, the cow-hide, the falsified return, or perjured election officials. It is quite probable that the North might not awake to its duty in the prevention of evil until blood had been shed. Thus far it has entirely failed to realize its responsibility. It has left the Negro to his fate, in seeming unconsciousness that the wrongs of the past must be atoned for either by justice or by disaster. The solution of the Negro question is of all the problems of civilization the simplest and yet the most difficult. The trouble is not with the Negro, who has always been content with half a chance in the world's scramble, but with the southern white man, who is not willing that any one should differ with him in opinion or dissent from his in practice; who is the traditional if not inveterate enemy of free thought and free speech, and is so confident of his own infallibility that he would rather appeal to arms or become a cowardly and disguised murderer, than submit to the control of a lawfully-ascertained majority of legal voters. There cannot be any security for our institutions or any guarantee of our domestic peace, so long as the question of depriving a majority of the qualified electors of any State of the rights which they are solemnly guaranteed by law through any unlawful means is coolly discussed as a living issue in the great organs through which popular thought finds expression. The remedy is a simple one – justice and knowledge. These are all the Negro asks. The superior white race should be ashamed to grant him less. It is not a question of sentiment, nor entirely one of right. As a matter of policy, it resolves itself into an inquiry as to what the American people can afford to do or leave undone — whether we can afford even negatively to admit that white minorities have the right not only to rule, but to nullify and subvert the law of the land, boldly, defiantly, and persistently, in order to bar a lawful majority from the exercises of political power, merely because the minority demand it.

Source: Albion W. Tourgée "Shall White Minorities Rule?" *Forum*, VII (April 1889), pp. 143-155.

2.6 Why the Solid South?

A celebration of the end of the rule of Radical Republican governments in the states of the South, and of the restoration of "home rule" by white Democrats.

SUNRISE

PROSPERITY FOLLOWS THE RESTORATION OF GOOD GOVERNMENT.

The days during which the reconstruction governments ruled in the several Southern states were the darkest that ever shrouded any portion of our country.

The slaughter and the sacrifices during our great civil war were terrible indeed, but those dark days were lighted by the shining valor of the patriot soldier; the storm clouds were gilded with glory. . . .

The facts stated in the preceding portions of this book and those shown by these figures present, it is believed, the most startling contrast between the results of good government and bad that can be found in the history of mankind. . . .

The political earthquake that convulsed the Southern States for years, some of them from 1865 to 1876, of course left great fissures, some of which are not yet closed; but the kindly processes of nature are carrying on the work of restoration.

It was and is the misfortune of the Southern people to have to deal with the problems arising out of race prejudices.

The negro had neither the will nor the power to resist the forces which arrayed him against his late master, and the solidification of his vote, by those who were to profit by it, meant, of course, a black man's party; for its majority sentiment determines the complexion of every political party. The domination of the black man's party, officered as it was, meant ruin. To avert ruin white men united; and then came a struggle, the issue of which was in all the States the same. It could not anywhere be doubtful. The race against which the negro had allowed himself to be arrayed has never yet met its master. It could not go down before the African.

No true friend of the colored man would, except in ignorance, precipitate such a conflict.

But victor though the white man was, no one could regret the enforced conflict more than did the people of the South. And they set to work at once to make a kindly use of their victories. Under the laws passed by Southern white men the negroes in every Southern State are far more prosperous than they ever were under the rule of those who claimed to be their especial friends.

There is no large body of men of African descent anywhere in the world superior in morals, equal in industry and intelligence, or as well to do as the negroes in the Southern States of this Union. In everything going to make up a prosperous and happy career their condition is infinitely better than that of their brethren in such countries as Hayti, where the colored man reigns supreme. And yet there are those who seem to think it an especial duty to foment among these colored people a spirit of strife and discontent. There is none of this spirit among the masses of their white fellow-citizens in the South. They understand well enough that the one condition upon which prosperity can be hoped for is peace and not strife between the races. They know full well, too, that the laborer will not be valuable either as a citizen or a worker unless he is contented, and that he will not be content unless he is fairly treated. So in every State in the South the effort is being made, and successfully, too, to better the condition of the negro, to train him in the duties of citizenship. These States are expending many millions per annum for educational purposes. . . .

When the negro was a slave the white men of the South made it unlawful to teach him to read. This was to prevent his learning the lesson of insurrection which certain writers in the abolition press were seeking to instil into his mind. The Southern whites then desired to keep the negro in slavery. Now that he is free these same whites are taxing themselves to fit him for freedom.

Let the reader ponder this fact and then answer to himself the question whether the Congress of the United States can wisely enact any law that would tend to revive the conflict of races in the South. Is not the problem of the hour being worked out by the people most interested in its correct solution? Are they not proceeding in the only possible manner? No such problem can be solved at once. Time, and patience, and tact, and experience, gathered on the spot and applied to legislation by those most interested, all these are necessary to its solution.

Any legislation at Washington, based upon the assumption that the negro is wronged and having for its object the ostensible purpose of righting the assumed wrongs by arraying the negro again in solid phalanx against the white man in a contest for supremacy in governmental affairs may result in a catastrophe more appalling than misgovernment, for it would tend towards a conflict of races in the South.

When the reconstruction laws gave the negro the ballot the party that passed these laws claimed of the colored man his vote and secured it. The negroes went to the polls in solid masses for that party. We have seen the results. Wherever they got power their leaders robbed and plundered. Wherever the negro majorities were greatest the degradation of society was most complete and despoliation the most absolute – as in South Carolina and Louisiana. If Congress shall again take control of suffrage the negro will again claim title to all his ballots, will again urge that he muster all his forces under its banner. The theory upon which these laws are urged undoubtedly must be that this appeal would again succeed; and if it should, then negro majoritieswould again dominate South Carolina, Mississippi and Louisiana, as well as also many of the richest counties in each of the former slave states.

To the people whose lives and fortunes would thus be imperiled, how appalling the prospect! And not only the properties of Southern, but of Northern men also – railroad stocks, state bonds, city bonds, county bonds, mining and manufacturing interests – all would be in peril. Nay, if the program should be carried out, as it is claimed it would be, with the United States army to enforce the law, and negro domination should again be forced at the South, many a princely fortune would vanish into air. It is amazing that capitalists, proverbially sagacious in their forecasts, should be so quiescent and complacent in view of this threatened legislation. The Southern people themselves look on with the profoundest concern. They judge the future by the past. They themselves passed through the scenes that are only faintly pictured in the preceding pages. Experience has demonstrated to them what reason itself would teach, that Federal control over election laws and election methods, interference by the General Government, expressly in favor of the blacks and against the whites, would tend to array one race against the other in bitter hostility, that such hostility in a contest for supremacy in affairs of government would engender race conflicts and that race conflicts would furnish an excuse for military interference.

It will not answer to say that conditions have changed. There will be Northern adventurers and native whites in great plenty to lead the negroes. No mass of voters able to put men in power have ever yet lacked for leaders, and it matters not what prejudices the voters have, they will find men to pander to them, and, how great soever their cupidity may be, their chosen representatives will answer to the demands that may be made upon them. No section of our country can impute to any other the exclusive possession of bad men. The North never showed an adventurer who could over-match Moses or Crews of South Carolina and every other Southern state can point to similar examples.

As to whether the attempt to put the South under the dominion of the negro again would succeed, the history of the past may furnish an instructive lesson. Would the army be used more freely than it was in South Carolina, Mississippi or Louisiana, and would the results now be different?

There was a time, just after the close of our Civil War, when Northern capitalists began to look upon the South as a field for investments, but after the carpet-bag governments had had opportunity fully to demonstrate their capacity for evil not a single dollar for investment went into that region for years. Years had elapsed even after the overthrow of these governments, before confidence was restored. Southern men they were, who, with their own capital, demonstrated to the world the resources of the South. At last the North has ceased to doubt either the stability of state governments or the values of Southern properties; and now Northern capital is flowing southward in a steady stream. It is said that to one town in Alabama – now not more than eighteen months old – investors have come from thirty-two of the states of the Union. The flow has only fairly begun. If not checked by some untoward movement it will steadily increase in volume. There is no finer field for investing the surplus capital of the North. There is no better customer for the Northern merchant than the Southerner. There is no more steady demand for the products of the Northwest than comes from the South; and no one can deny that the continued prosperity of that section is necessary to the prosperity of the North and West.

Source: Extracts from Hilary A. Herbert *et al.*, *Why the Solid South? or Reconstruction and its Results* (Baltimore, Md.: 1890), pp. 430-443.

2.7 The Process of Redemption

A description of tactics formulated to ensure that the Southern white Democrats regained control of the state government of South Carolina in the election of 1876. Both Democrats and Republicans proceeded as if victory was theirs till the withdrawal of the last Federal troops in the South in April 1877 left the "redeeming" Democrats in full control.

(a) Redeemer tactics in 1876

State also & state positively that the majority of the Radicals is only nominal, that it has been obtained by the Negroes repeating & the lukewarmness of the Whites, that at this Election the Whites are determined that the Negro shall have a showing for once, and that after the Election the names of the Democratic Negroes will be made public if desired, (& if we carry the Election the trouble will be to find a Negro who dident vote our ticket).

Under the second head of Preparation action, we must prepare the minds of the Negroes by showing our ability to prevent a thorough organization of their party.

By meeting their Leaders before their faces and hacking them publicly. By swinging their most active Leaders up, if they become offensive. By telling them that their party has gone to pieces – their bell-wether has jumped the fence – and the friends who accomplished their emancipation have turned against them on account of the Rascality of their Representatives, &c. That we are *determined* to see that they vote as they please, but that we don't care a picaune how they vote as so many have left the County that we are now in the majority. That we are not talking to gain their votes but on account of kind feelings &c we are simply telling them how things are &c., assure them of kind treatment after our success if they behave &c.

Tell the Negroes that if they will put up good men who can give good security for faithful performance of duty, we will give them a fair fight at the Ballot Box & beat them too as we have the majority.

Under the 3d head of preparatory action, we must prepare the Democrats, so that they can use to advantage their powers influence & time.

We must be thoroughly organized, so that at short notice we can throw a given body of men in any given position.

We must rouse them if possible to the fullest appreciation of our position.

Every man must know his duty and be willing to do it.

We must have plenty of tickets judiciously distributed, so that we can use them freely.

Those who are to remain at the Boxes must be selected, & those who are to visit (just to see how things are going on) neighboring precincts, must also be selected & have their programs prepared for them.

We must prepare to mass our men at weak boxes, & post our managers so that when a stranger rides up he may vote and ride on.

Our execution Committee must see every White man in their respective Townships & urge him to vote at home if no more & if he is slow to agree come out, he must be looked after, & talked to by his neighbors. We must be prepared to do our level best or die day of election. This exhausts the Preparitory action.

Under the head of Real action only a few General ideas can be laid down, & from these such subplans may be deduced as meet the exegencies of the case and suit the capacity or genius of the Individual.

First every strange Negro must be challenged – & in fact every Negro should be challenged – kill time should be our motto when the Negroes are voting.

It is not yet too late to hack the Leaders if opportunity occurs.

Assure the Mass that they shall have a fair showing but that they must vote according to law.

Vote every white man who is willing to vote.

These suggestion form the basis of a general plan.

Under the Experimental head so much can be said, & so many different plans successfully carried out by enterprising and fearless men that I will only touch on it briefly. We must have some one for clerk who can cook the record make no distinction between white & black voters but put them all down indiscriminately. Have a private clerk to check off the votes of the party & if towards the close of day you find that they have the majority stuff the box. Take away the votes from the Distributors if possible, but so manage it that no box shall be broken. We want every box if they are manipulated correctly. If they are very much in majority make two boy load their pistols with blank cartridges & get up a fight at the box, shoot in good earnest if a Negro is impertinent, but shoot straight & hit a leader & if once hit be sure to finish him &c.

(b) Consolidation of redeemer control, 1878

To return to the history of South Carolina. After the withdrawal of the United States troops the Carpetbaggers were entirely routed and put to flight, and Wade Hampton assumed the undisputed government. He has certainly had much success. His party claim (I believe with justice) that he has done much to restore the finances, promote education, and protect blacks and whites in the exercise of peaceful callings. As regards political matters, his policy amounts, I think, to this; – it is in effect said to the blacks: "If you will accept the present regime, follow us, and vote Democratic; we will receive you, cherish you, and give you a reasonable share of representation, local office, &c.; but there shall be nothing for those who persist in voting Republican." Some of them accept these terms, but to vote Democratic is the one thing which the great majority will not do. They may be on excellent terms with white men with whom they have relations, will follow them and be guided by them in everything else, but they have sufficient independence to hold out on that point of voting, even when they have lost their white leaders and are quite left to themselves. They know that they owe their freedom to the Republicans, and it is to them a sort of religion to vote Republican, I think it was in Georgia (where they have not held out so stoutly) that, talking to a small black farmer, an ex-slave, as to the situation, I asked him about the black vote. "Well," he said, "some vote straight, and some don't; some is 'suaded and some is paid, but I vote according to my principles, and my principles is Republican." In South Carolina that is the view of the great body of the blacks, as the Democrats fully admit. Stories are told of personal dependents of the present Governor who owe everything to him and would do anything else in the world for him, but who will yet openly vote against him. Such, then, was the state of things when the elections of November 1878 came on.

It seemed to be well known beforehand that the Democrats were determined to win everything in the South. It was said to be a necessity finally to emancipate *all* the States from the scandal of black and Carpet-bag rule, and so far one could not but sympathise with the feeling; but so much had been already achieved, and there was not the least risk of a reaction. On the contrary, the power of the native whites was thoroughly re-established. In South Carolina Wade Hampton's re-election was not opposed, and there was no question whatsoever that by moderate means the Democrats could retain a very decided majority in the State Legislature. But they were not content with this; they aimed at an absolute possession of everything, leaving no representation to their opponents at all, and especially at a "solid South," in the United States Congress. "They are determined to win," I was told. "They will get the votes by fair means, if they can; and if not I am sorry to say they will steal 'em." And that is just what was done in South Carolina.

To understand what took place we must look at the election law prevailing in the United States. It seems to me that if the law had been designed to facilitate fraud, make detection difficult, and render the settlement of disputed elections impossible, it could not have been more skilfully devised. There is something to be said for open voting and something for a well-managed ballot, but the pretended ballot of the United States seems to combine all the evils of both systems. It may be just possible for an independent man connected with no party, who manages the thing skilfully, to conceal his vote; but if he consents to make it known, there can be, and in practice there is, no secrecy whatever. There are no official ballotpapers, numbered and checked, so as to be afterwards traced, as with us; every man may deposit in the box any ballot-paper he chooses, written or printed in whatever form he chooses. In practice voters use papers in a particular form supplied by their own party, so that there can be no mistake which way they vote. There being no means of identifying the papers so cast, everything depends on the honesty and fair dealing of those who have the official management of the polls. In all things the executive Government has much greater power in America than with us, and the party which has the executive power has also the control of the ballot-boxes. They appoint returning boards and election managers at each polling-place, who, when party spirit runs high, are in the interest of the dominant majority. This was carried to an excess in South Carolina during the recent elections. The United States officers are entitled to take certain precautions to see that the United States election law is fairly carried out, but they could only be present at the principal places, and sent very subordinate agents to the other polling places, where they were hustled and treated with no respect whatever. Under these conditions the elections were held in South Carolina.

There is a remarkable frankness and openness in speaking of the way in which things were managed, and I believe I violate no confidences, because there was no whispering or confidence about it. There was not a very great amount of violence or intimidation. Some Republican meetings were violently interfered with before the election, and on the day of the election there was at some places a certain amount of galloping about, firing guns, and such-like demonstration by men in red shirts; but any intimidation used was rather moral than physical. In all districts where the parties in any degree approach equality perhaps there would be no very strong grounds for disputing the victory of the Democrats. It is in the lower districts, where the Republicans are admittedly in an immense majority, that great Democratic majorities were obtained by the simple process of what is called "stuffing the ballot-boxes." For this purpose the Democrats used ballot-papers of the thinnest possible tissue-paper, such that a number of them can be packed inside of one larger paper and shaken out as they are dropped into the box. These papers were freely handed about; they were shown to me, and I brought away specimens of them. I never heard a suggestion that these extraordinary little gossamer-web things were designed for any other purpose than that of fraud. Of course the result of such a system was that there were many more ballot-papers in the box than voters. At one place in the Charleston district, where not above one thousand persons voted, there were found, I believe, three thousand five hundred papers in the box. In such case the practice (whether justified by law or not, I know not) is that the election managers blindfold a man, who draws out and destroys the number of papers in excess of the voters. Of course he takes care to draw out the thick papers of the opposite party, and to leave in the thin papers of his own party; so when the process is completed the Democrats are found to be in a great majority, and the return is so made by the returning board. There are some other grounds of complaint. In some of the black districts the number of polling-places has been so reduced that it is impossible for all who wish to poll to do so in the time allowed. At one or two places the ballot-boxes were stolen and carried off. At one place of which I have personal knowledge the appointed election managers simply kept out of the way, and had no poll at all. Hundreds of blacks who came to vote were told they must go elsewhere when it was too late to do so. In short, I have no hesitation in saying, as matter within my own knowledge, that, if these elections had taken place in England, there were irregularities which must have vitiated them before an election judge a hundred times over.

The result of these elections was that, except in the single county of Beaufort, not one Republican or Independent was returned to the State Legislature nor, I believe, was a single office-bearer of those persuasions elected. The dominant party took everything, and the Republican members of Congress were all ejected. South Carolina returns a solid Democratic representation to the next Congress.

I have throughout, on the spot, as I do now, expressed the opinion that there is no excuse whatever for the lengths to which the triumph of the Democrats has been pushed. Granting that they were fairly justified in vigorous measures to give them the control of the Government and Legislature, and that they were in a position thus to obtain a good working majority, there could be no reason for unfairly depriving their opponents of a certain representation. It was bad policy, too, for the things that have been done have roused the indignation of the North, and it is believed that the somewhat unexpected Republican successes in the North were in great degree due to the feeling excited by unfair attempts to make a solid South. Perhaps, for the time, it may not be a matter of the very first importance whether the Democrats have only a good majority in the Southern State Legislatures, or almost the whole representation; but in the present state of parties in Congress two or three seats, or say, including Louisiana and Florida, half a dozen seats, won by extreme and palpable irregularities and fraud, make a great difference; and the question of these elections raises very large and difficult issues. Not only are nearly-balanced parties very much affected, but, in the case of a struggle over the next Presidential election, these votes might just turn the scale; and the question whether there is any remedy practically available to redress wrongs which are, I may almost say, admitted, puts in issue the wider question whether the 15th Amendment of the United States Constitution, securing equal electoral rights to the blacks, is really to be enforced, or whether it may be set aside in practice by the action of individual States. Is, in fact, the settlement at the end of the war to be maintained or surrendered? The excuse made by the Southern whites for their proceedings is, that throughout the United States elections are not pure and free from fraud; that there has been as much of it in New York as in the South; that the laws admitting of such things were made by their enemies to crush them; that the Presidency was "stolen" from them by fraud; and that they are justified in reprisals. I have no doubt that it is an absolute necessity that the election laws should be improved. But besides this there is need of a final laying of the issue between North and South, depending on a due execution of the war settlement.

Sources: (a) Martin W. Gary Papers, University of South Carolina
(b) Sir George Campbell, '*White and Black: The Outcome of a Visit to the United States* (New York (1879), pp. 180-187.

2.8 Disfranchisement of Black Voters

Once in control of the state governments of the South by the 1880s, the conservative Democrats set about trying to capture the black vote, appealing to past associations and understanding, – i.e., as masters and slaves. This was unacceptable to the emergent reforming wing in the Democratic party, which preferred to see blacks removed as far as possible from the political process, as explained by "Pitchfork Ben" Tillman, the "one-eyed plowboy" of South Carolina and later state Governor. Disfranchisement of black voters was largely achieved, state by state, through variants of the Mississippi Plan.

South Carolina Constitutional Convention, 1895

Now, I have alluded to the fact of this villainy, anarchy, misrule and robbery, and I cannot, in any words I possess, paint it. There is no man on this floor living in the country who dared during that dark period* to leave his fireside without dread that when he returned he would find some harm to his family; and he dared not go forth without being armed, fearful of robbery. The sky was lit almost every night by the glare of burning dwellings and ginhouses. Our Courts of Justice were filled with bribe-takers, and the Judges themselves were not free from bribery. How did it come about, and who must bear the blame? We are told the negroes didn't do it. "Oh, we didn't do it," they say. [Addressing the negro delegates.]† You blindly followed and obeyed the orders of the Freedmen's Bureau and the Union League and ignored the appeals of your former masters, who treated you with kindness and furnished you with your daily bread. I myself can testify that appeal after appeal was made by me, and by almost every white man in this State, with the negroes with whom he came in contact on his plantation: "Stop! come back! help us free ourselves from this burden!" But every one of you, almost up to 1876, blindly followed wherever these white thieves ordered. Was it negro government? The negroes furnished the ballots, and that is what we are dealing with. The negroes put the little pieces of paper in the box that

* Reconstruction.

† Six Negro Republican delegates were present at the convention.

gave the commission to these white scoundrels who were their leaders and the men who debauched them; and this must be our justification, our vindication and our excuse to the world that we are met in Convention openly, boldly, without any pretense of secrecy, to annouce that it is our purpose, as far as we may, without coming in conflict with the United States Constitution, to put such safeguards around this ballot in future, to so restrict the suffrage and circumscribe it, that this infamy can never come about again.

The negroes were the tools of designing white men, I acknowledge – participators and willing tools. The poor, ignorant cotton field hand, who never reaped any advantage, nor saw anything except a pistol, blindly followed like sheep wherever their black and white leaders told them to go, voted unanimously every time for the Republican ticket during the dark period, and these results were achieved solely and wholly by reason of the ballot being in the hands of such cattle. Is the danger gone? No. How did we recover our liberty? By fraud and violence. We tried to overcome the thirty thousand majority by honest methods, which was a mathematical impossibility.

How did we bring it about? Every white man sunk his personal feelings and ambitions. The white people of the State, illustrating our glorious motto, "Ready with their lives and fortunes," came together as one. By fraud and violence, if you please, we threw it off. In 1878 we had to resort to more fraud and violence, and so again in 1880. Then the Registration Law and eight-box system was evolved from the superior intelligence of the white man to check and control this surging, muddy stream of ignorance and to tell it back, and since then we have carried our elections without resort to any illegal methods, simply because the whites were united.‡ If we were to remain united it would still be desirable that we should guard against the possibility of this flood, which is now dammed up, breaking loose; or, like the viper that is asleep, only to be warmed into life again and sting us whenever some more white rascals, native or foreign, come here and mobilize the ignorant blacks. Therefore, the only thing we can do as patriots and as statesmen is to take from them every ballot that we can under the laws of our national government.

I read a moment ago from the report of the Committee that good government can only rest on intelligence and good morals. I will go further and say that good government and the very life of republics rest on virtue, patriotism and intelligence. The chief amongst the three is intelligence. It has been said, and it must be apparent to any one who thinks, even if we restrict the suffrage as we propose, that with 40,000 Conservatives and 40,000 Reformers, divided and striving for mastery, and 15,000 illiterate white men disfranchised, that the negroes are still here in sufficient numbers to control us. Are we so besotted, so forgetful and oblivious of the record which I have just read to you? Have our memories grown so callous that we as a white race – kinsmen, brothers, common inheritors of the glorious past and of the freedom transmitted to us by our forefathers – have we got to the point where we cannot unite

‡ The Registration Law of 1882 limited the time when eligible voters could register, increased the discretionary powers of electoral officials, and penalized Negro sharecroppers who migrated from one precinct to another. The eight-box system placed a sign on each ballot box directing the voter to a specific one. White illiterates were helped to find the right box, Negroes were not.

as brothers, throwing aside the petty bickerings and animosities that have been engendered in the last five years, and, without regard to personal ambition or partisan advantage to anybody, can we not provide so that we will not have to appeal to these people as arbiters of our fate? Can we not rise to the necessities of the occasion and put into this Constitution such an Article in reference to suffrage as will guarantee, as far as the law can guarantee, to future generations that they shall have the blessings of Anglo-Saxon civilization and liberty in this State? How pitiable, how puerile, how ineffably, unutterably contemptible appear the personal ambitions and petty spites of men alongside of this grand and glorious purpose!

Alabama Constitutional Convention, 1901

And what is it that we do want to do? Why, it is, within the limits imposed by the Federal Constitution, to establish white supremacy in this State.

This is our problem, and we should be permitted to deal with it, unobstructed by outside influences, with a sense of our responsibilities as citizens, and our duty to posterity.

. . . If we would have white supremacy, we must establish it by law – not by force or fraud. If you teach your boy it is right to buy a vote, it is an easy step for him to learn to use money to bribe or corrupt officials or trustees of any class. If you teach your boy that it is right to steal votes, it is an easy step for him to believe that it is right to steal whatever he may need or greatly desire. The results of such an influence will enter every branch of society; it will reach your bank cashiers, and affect positions of trust in every department; it will ultimately enter your courts, and affect the administration of justice.

I submit it to the intelligent judgment of this Convention that there is no higher duty resting upon us, as citizens and as delegates, than that which requires us to embody in the fundamental law such provisions as will enable us to protect the sanctity of the ballot in every portion of the State.

The justification for whatever manipulation of the ballot that has occurred in this State has been the menace of negro domination. After the war, by force of Federal bayonets, the negro was placed in control of every branch of our government. Inspired and aided by unscrupulous white men, he wasted money, created debts, increased taxes until it threatened to amount to confiscation of our property. While in power, and within a few years, he increased our State debt from a nominal figure to nearly thirty millions of dollars. The right of revolution is always left to every people. Being prostrated by the effects of the war, and unable to take up arms in their own defense, in some portions of this State, white men, greatly in the minority, it is said, resorted to stratagem – used their great intellect to overcome the greater numbers of their black opponents. If so, such a course might be warranted when considered as the right of revolution, and as an act of necessity for self-preservation. But a people cannot always live in a state of revolution. The time comes when, if they would be a free, happy and contented people they must return to a constitutional form of government, where law and order prevail, and where every citizen stands ready to stake his life and his honor to maintain it.

Upon the threshold of our deliberations, I will not undertake to indicate to you how you should solve this new and difficult question of Constitutional reform. At the outset of this movement, I venture to suggest that delegates should be cautious in undertaking to define just what provisions would be or should be embodied in the Constitution; that the new Constitution, when made and placed before the people for ratification, would be and ought to be the result of the united action of the Convention; that if one came here with his mind made up his Constitution in his pocket, he would hardly be in a fit condition to confer with his fellow-delegates on this important subject. I still hold this view. I fail to appreciate the idea of those who seem to think it the duty of delegates to this Convention to write out and publish their views before the Convention meets. Under this plan, we would be liable to have as many Constitutions as delegates. What the people want, in my judgment, is an earnest consideration of and consultation upon these important questions, so that the finished work will represent the united wisdom and experience of the Convention.

Mississippi is the pioneer State in this movement. In addition to the payment of a poll tax, there it is provided that only those can vote who have been duly registered, and only those can register who can read, or understand when read to them, any clause in the Constitution. The decision as to who are sufficiently intelligent to meet the requirements of the understanding clause is exclusively in the hands of the registrars.

But to this plan, the objection has been urged with force that it perpetuates the very form of abuse from which we are seeking to escape; that elections by managers or registrars is not what we want. Our aim should be for a correction of all evils which threaten the purity of the ballot and the morals of the people.

The provision adopted in South Carolina requires the payment of the poll tax, assessed against him for the previous year, six months before any election, and that the voter shall be duly registered. To be qualified for registration up to January 1st, 1898, voters must have been able to read a clause in the Constitution, or understand or explain it when read by the registration officer; and all who register subsequent to that time must be able both to read and write any section of the Constitution, or else show ownership of property assessed at three hundred dollars or more, and the payment of all taxes assessed against him and collectable during the previous year.

In Louisiana and North Carolina, the methods of relief adopted are substantially the same, and require in addition to the poll tax clause, that the voter shall register in accordance with the provisions of the Constitution, and only those are authorized to register who are able to read and write any section of the Constitution in the English language, with the further proviso that no male person who was, on January 1st, 1867, or at any time prior thereto, entitled to vote under the laws of any State in the United States wherein he then resided, and no lineal descendant of any such person shall be denied the right to register and vote at any election by reason of his failure to possess the educational qualifications prescribed, provided he registers within the time limited by the terms of the Constitution, which in Louisiana is about six months, in North Carolina about eight years.

It is contended in defense of this provision, that while in effect, it will exclude the great mass of ignorant negro voters, it does not, in terms, exclude them, and applies generally to all classes of voters, without reference to their race, color or previous condition of servitude; that all negroes who were voters prior to January, 1867, – of whom it was claimed, there were quite a number–could vote, and the descendants – whether slaves or not – of these free negroes, were entitled to vote, and that these were quite numerous. And, on the other hand, that white people born in other countries – emigrants – who cannot read and write, could not vote, nor could white people who were unable to vote in the State in which they lived prior to 1867, unless they were able to read and write. If it be said that this exception permits many more white people to vote than negroes, the answer was that this would be equally true of any proper property qualification which might be proposed. It would be true of an educational qualification, and it would be true of a property qualification, the validity of which has never been questioned.

These provisions are justified in law and in morals, because it is said that the negro is not discriminated against on account of his race, but on account of his intellectual and moral condition. There is a difference it is claimed with great force, between the uneducated white man and the ignorant negro. There is in the white man an inherited capacity for government which is wholly wanting in the negro. Before the art of reading and writing was known, the ancestors of the Anglo-Saxon had established an orderly system of government, the basis, in fact, of the one under which we now live. That the negro, on the other hand, is descended from a race lowest in intelligence and moral perception of all the races of men.

Sources: Speech of Ben Tillman from the *Journal of the Constitutional Convention of the State of South Carolina, 1895* (Columbia, S.C., 1895), pp. 462-464.
Extracts from the *Journal of the Proceedings of the Constitutional Convention of the State of Alabama, 1901* (Montgomery, 1901), pp. 8-15.

2.9 Afro-Americans and the People's Party

One reason for poor white hostility towards black voters was the failure of black and white farmers to make common electoral cause in the South in the Populist Party of the early 1890s, thereby prompting the white reformers to operate within the Democratic Party against the "Bourbons".

At the convention of the Farmers' Alliance, or Peoples party, in Texas, there were a few Afro-American delegates. Upon the attitude that the Alliance should bear to the Afro-American in that State, there was considerable discussion, and greater freedom of speech was permitted to the delegates than they have had in any political convention outside of the Republican party, and as a result two of them were put on the committee representing the State at large, but whose special work should be among Afro-Americans.

The Plaindealer has always welcomed these side issues in the South, since for a time it sets faction against faction among the bourbons, and opens a wedge for free speech and greater political liberty, and enables the race to make a step forward. Some impression, too, is made by these issues, toward dividing the whites on political subjects, impels all to enlist the support of the Afro-American, causing them also to divide on issues, unrestrained by a unity of purpose growing out of their condition.

Free speech in Texas in the ordinary assembly, unless used in glorifying the lost cause and eulogizing its dead and living leaders, and abusing Washington and Lincoln, has not been tolerated, and they who used it otherwise than according to Texas thought, did so at their peril, hence it is that the position assumed by Afro-American delegates seems all the more encouraging from the sturdy independence manifested. *The Plaindealer* gives a part of the debate to show its nature.

The speaker having referred to the claims of the colored man, the following colloquy followed.

> Melvin Ward, colored, – I would like to know what you mean by considering the colored man's claims in contradistinction to the claims of any other citizen of the United States?

The chair disclaimed drawing distinctions. He had been asked who were entitled to work in the organization. The committee would proclaim the answer to the world.

> Captain Evans – Every colored citizen in these United States has the same privileges that any white citizen has, and that is what is meant.
>
> Melvin Ward – When it comes down to practice, such is not the fact. If we are equal why does not the Sheriff summon Negroes on juries? And why hang up the sign "Negro" in passenger cars? I want to tell my people what the People's party is going to do. I want to tell them that it is going to work a black and a white horse in the same field.
>
> The Chair – That is what I mean in bringing it before the committee, so that they should know our action.

Dr. Harris suggested that there be white and colored clubs, and let them confer together.

Mr. Johnson – Resolved that each Congressional district, through its chairman, appoint one colored man to co-operate with those already appointed in the organization of the People's party.

A delegate – This will not do. The colored people are a part of the people and they must be recognized as such.

Colored Delegate Hayes – If you cannot take us and elect us in this convention we will not thank you. We do not propose to be appointed by chairman. You must appoint us by the convention and make us feel that we are men. You will lose in spite of the devil and high water if you do not treat the Negro squarely.

Captain Evans – We have no disposition to ostracize the colored people, but they are poorly represented here. The only thing we can do in the absence of their representation is to elect a representative for the State at large, and I recommend that Mr. Hayes be elected, and let him organize the colored people in harmony with the People's party.

Source: *The Plaindealer*, 1890.

2.10 Plessy v. Ferguson

1896

By creating the legal doctrine of "separate but equal", the Supreme Court effectively ended the attempt to establish common civil rights for black American citizens, and legally underwrote racial segregation. The decision remained law for almost 60 years.

BROWN, J. This case turns upon the constitutionality of an act of the general assembly of the state of Louisiana, passed in 1890, providing for separate railway carriages for the white and colored races. . . .

The constitutionality of this act is attacked upon the ground that it conflicts both with the 13th Amendment of the Constitution, abolishing slavery, and the 14th Amendment, which prohibits certain restrictive legislation on the part of the states.

1. That it does not conflict with the 13th Amendment, which abolished slavery and involuntary servitude, except as a punishment for crime, is too clear for argument. . . .

A statute which implies merely a legal distinction between the white and colored races – a distinction which is founded in the color of the two races, and which must always exist so long as white men are distinguished from the other race by color – has no tendency to destroy the legal equality of the two races, or re-establish a state of involuntary servitude. Indeed, we do not understand that the 13th Amendment is strenuously relied upon by the plaintiff in error of this connection. . . .

The object of the amendment was undoubtedly to enforce the absolute equality of the two races before the law, but in the nature of things it could not have been intended to abolish distinctions based upon color, or to enforce social, as distinguished from political, equality, or a commingling of two races upon terms unsatisfactory to either. Laws permitting, and even requiring their separation in places where they are liable to be brought into contact do not necessarily imply the inferiority of either race to the other, and have been generally, if not universally, recognized as within the competency of the state legislatures in the exercise of their police power. The most common instance of this is connected with the establishment of separate schools for white and colored children, which have been held to be a valid exercise of the legislative power even by courts of states where the political rights of the colored race have been longest and most earnestly enforced. . . .

It is claimed by the plaintiff in error that, in any mixed community, the reputation of belonging to the dominant race, in this instance the white race is *property*, in the same sense that a right of action, or of inheritance, is property. Conceding this to be so, for the purposes of this case, we are unable to see how this statute deprives him of, or in any way affects his right to, such property. If he be a white man and assigned to a colored coach, he may have his action for damages against the company for being deprived of his so-called property. Upon the other hand, if he be a colored man and be so assigned, he has been deprived of no property, since he is not lawfully entitled to the reputation of being a white man. . . .

So far, then, as a conflict with the 14th Amendment is concerned, the case reduces itself to the question whether the statute of Louisiana is a reasonable regulation, and with respect to this there must necessarily be a large discretion on the part of the legislature. In determining the question of reasonableness it is at liberty to act with reference to the established usages, customs, and traditions of the people, and with a view to the promotion of their comfort, and the preservation of the public peace and good order. Gauged by this standard, we cannot say that a law which authorizes or even requires the separation of the two races in public conveyances is unreasonable or more obnoxious to the 14th Amendment than the acts of Congress requiring separate schools for colored children in the District of Columbia, the constitutionality of which does not seem to have been questioned, or the corresponding acts of state legislatures.

We consider the underlying fallacy of the plaintiff's argument to consist in the assumption that the enforced separation of the two races stamps the colored race with a badge of inferiority. If this be so, it is not by reason of anything found in the act, but solely because the colored race chooses to put that construction upon it. The argument necessarily assumes that if, as has been more than once the case, and is not unlikely to be so again, the colored race should become the dominant power in the state legislature, and should enact a law in precisely similar terms, it would thereby relegate the white race to an inferior position. We imagine that the white race, at least, would not acquiesce in this assumption. The argument also assumes that social prejudice may be overcome by legislation, and that equal rights cannot be secured to the Negro except by an enforced commingling of the two races. We cannot accept this proposition. If the two races are to meet on terms of social equality, it must be the result of natural affinities, a mutual appreciation of each other's merits and a voluntary consent of individuals. . . . Legislation is powerless to eradicate racial instincts or to abolish distinctions based upon physical differences, and the attempt to do so can only result in accentuating the difficulties of the present situation. If the civil and political right of both races be equal, one cannot be inferior to the other civilly or politically. If one race be inferior to the other socially, the Constitution of the United States cannot put them upon the same plane.

JUSTICE HARLAN, dissenting. . . . In respect of civil rights, common to all citizens, the Constitution of the United States does not, I think, permit any public authority to know the race of those entitled to be protected in the enjoyment of such rights. Every true man has pride of race, and under appropriate circumstances, when the rights of others, his equals before the law, are not to be affected, it is his privilege to express such pride and to take such action based upon it as to him seems proper. But I deny that any legislative body or judicial tribunal may have regard to the race of citizens when the civil rights of those citizens are involved. Indeed such legislation as that here in question is inconsistent, not only with that equality of rights which pertains to citizenship, national and state, but with the personal liberty enjoyed by every one within the United States. . . .

In my opinion, the judgment this day rendered will, in time, prove to be quite as pernicious as the decision made by this tribunal in the Dred Scott Case. It was adjudged in that case that the descendants of Africans who were imported into this country and sold as slaves were not included nor intended to be included under the word "citizens" in the Constitution, and could not claim any of the rights and privileges which that instrument provided for and secured to citizens of the United States; that at the time of the adoption of the Constitution they were "considered as a subordinate and inferior class of beings, who had been subjugated by the dominant race, and, whether emancipated or not, yet remained subject to their authority, and had no rights or privileges but such as those who held the power and the government might choose to grant them." The recent amendments of the Constitution, it was supposed, had eradicated these principles from our institutions. But it seems that we have yet, in some of the states, a dominant race, a superior class of citizens, which assumes to regulate the enjoyment of civil rights, common to all citizens, upon the basis of race. The present decision, it may well be apprehended, will not only stimulate aggression, more or less brutal and irritating, upon the admitted rights of colored citizens, but will encourage the belief that it is possible, by means of state enactments, to defeat the beneficent purposes which the people of the United States had in view when they adopted the recent amendments of the Constitution, by one of which the blacks of this country were made citizens of the United States and of the states in which they respectively reside and whose privileges and immunities, as citizens, the states are forbidden to abridge. Sixty millions of whites are in no danger from the presence here of eight millions of blacks. The destinies of the two races in this country are indissolubly linked together, and the interests of both require that the common government of all shall not permit the seeds of race hate to be planted under the sanction of law. What can more certainly arouse race hate, what more certainly create and perpetuate a feeling of distrust between these races, than state enactments which in fact proceed on the ground that colored citizens are so inferior and degraded that they cannot be allowed to sit in public coaches occupied by white citizens? That, as all will admit, is the real meaning of such legislation as was enacted in Louisiana. . . .

If evils will result from the commingling of the two races upon public highways established for the benefit of all, they will be infinitely less than those that will surely come from state legislation regulating the enjoyment of civil rights upon the basis of race. We boast of the freedom enjoyed by our people above all other peoples. But it is difficult to reconcile that boast with a state of the law which, practically, puts the brand of servitude and degradation upon a large class of our fellow citizens, our equals before the law. The thin disguise of "equal" accommodations for passengers in railroad coaches will not mislead anyone, or atone for the wrong this day done. . . .

I am of opinion that the statute of Louisiana is inconsistent with the personal liberty of citizens, white and black, in that state, and hostile to both the spirit and letter of the Constitution of the United States. If laws of like character should be enacted in the several states of the Union, the effect would be in the highest degree mischievous. Slavery as an institution tolerated by law would, it is true, have disappeared from our country, but there would remain a power in the states, by sinister legislation, to interfere with the full enjoyment of the blessings of freedom; to regulate civil rights, common to all citizens, upon the basis of race; and to place in a condition of legal inferiority a large body of American citizens, now constituting a part of the political community, called the people of the United States, for whom and by whom, through representatives, our government is administered. Such a system is inconsistent with the guarantee given by the Constitution to each state of a republican form of government, and may be stricken down by Congressional action, or by the courts in the discharge of their solemn duty to maintain the supreme law of the land, anything in the Constitution or laws of any state to the contrary notwithstanding.

For the reason stated, I am constrained to withhold my assent from the opinion and judgment of the majority.

Source: *Plessy vs Ferguson* 163 US 537, 1896.

Black Workers and the Unions

3.1 The Knights of Labor

The Knights attempted to establish a national union encompassing skilled and unskilled labour, male and female, and workers of different races. The ideals of the central leadership were not always reflected locally, where worker competition and strike situations could lead to group fragmentation and even racial conflict in the South.

Labor upheavals

All the world, as far as this country is concerned, appears to have gone mad, after the Knights of Labor. The newspapers, and the politicians appear to be as much on the fence as they were forty years ago on the slavery question, doubting which side to take in the conflict impending. The Knights of Labor have sprung into power like a young giant. Only a few years ago and the wailings of the toilers of the land were poohpoohed by the press and unheeded by the politicians, while the lords of capital smiled in their sleeves at complaints and demands which seemed so utterly absurd as to warrant no serious reflection. In the last Presidential election the vote of the Labor party was such a very small thing as actually to have been lost in the great stack of votes polled by the two national parties. How will it be in the future? The power of the leaders of the labor unions as demonstrated during the past six months, puts an entirely new phase on this aspect of the matter. Labor has heretofore been powerless simply because it was a disorganised, leaderless mass. Now it is organized; now it has masterful leadership. At the nod of an authorized person thousands of men in every line of industry desert their posts of duty and simply paralyze the productive and carrying agencies of the country. Before this organized power capital, even the great body of the people, is as powerful as labor once was.

Political economists have for years snarled at the proposition that labor was the productive and capital the non-productive force in our sociology, and that when labor ceased to produce capital would wither into the elements out of which it was delved. But the events of the past few months have gone very far towards vindicating the tenability of the proposition. The political economist of the future will have largely to reconstruct this glaring heresy before he has a correct premise upon which to predicate his deductions and conclusions.

To become an invincible power the Knights of Labor have wisely concluded to enlist the support of all grades of labor, barring out no nationality except that of the Chinese. Hence colored men all over the Union, are rapidly becoming affiliated with the organization. For instance the colored waiters of New York have formed a strong assembly of the Knights of Labor, and meet Thursday every week at Garnet Hall, and some of the ablest speakers of the Central organization are present to instruct them in the requirements of the parent Union. In most other branches of labor colored men are affiliated with white organizations, not being strong enough to form a separate assembly. We predicted this result a year ago in the book we published under the title of "Black and White", but we did not expect so speedy a consummation of the prediction then made."

We do not hesitate to say we fear the conflict which must result from organized capital on the one hand and organized labor on the other. The gravity of such conflict is correctly estimated by those more directly interested pro and con. We believe in that absolute justice which it is so very difficult to secure in either the social or political relations of men. Tyranny, some one of its multiform variations, seems far more natural in the practice than equity. It therefore almost reduces itself to a choice between the tyrants we shall have, and of which of them is the safer. For centuries we have had the tyranny of capital, and an odious and unjust tyranny it has been, and if we are to have the tyranny of labor we shall after awhile be in position to judge which of them is the more odious, which the more conducive to the happiness of the greatest number and to the general progress of the race.

After all it is a matter of how far forth the masses shall share with the capitalistic oligarchs and sharks the interest of the fruits and labor – whether the fellow who develops the gold mine shall sleep on a board and eat pone cake and hog, while the fellow who claims to own the mine, but does not work it, shall sleep in a palace and fill his stomach with caramels and ice cream.

The revolution is upon us, and since we are largely of the laboring population it is very natural that we should take sides with the labor forces in their flight, for a juster distribution of the results of labor.

New York *Freeman*, c. 1880

John R. Lynch on the color line in ranks of labor

Mr. J. S. Woods, president of the Hod Carrier's Union, told me that I was misinformed about the hod carriers taking part in the parade of May 1. Said he: "There were only four of our members in the procession out of 275, and they are the only four of our Union who belong to the Knights of Labor. The Knights of Labor sent a committee to wait upon our Union asking us to adopt their charter as our own. We inquired if they would concede the right of apprenticeship to our children and admit those of us who are mechanics to full membership in all of their different lodges, allow us to work upon the same scaffold together as their brother?"

Said he: "What reply do you think that committee gave us? The chairman of that committee told our Union that these questions would be an after consideration. Isn't that proof that the Knights of Labor intend to use the colored man as a tool? Suppose our Union had accepted the proposition, without asking them for equal rights? We would have been duped into a second slavery. Further than that the Negroes are barred out of the machine shops, the factories, off of railroad engine and all other mechanical doors are closed against him controlled by the Knights of Labor."

I asked Mr. Woods if the Hod Carriers' Union was a secret organization? "No , sir," was his answer, "but the Knights of Labor and trades unions are, I have no objections to any secret orders that do justice to all nationalities alike."

He asked me if I had ever heard of a colored society being boisterous in the strikes of 1877 and 1878. The few colored men who took part were hunted down, arrested, tried, punished in the courts and kept out of employment by the same white working men who inaugurated the strikes. There were several colored unions that did turn out May 1. Among them the Teamster's Union, which number 200 and over; the Coachman's Union, 160 strong; Hotel Waiters, Butlers and a number of others that would have added a thousand more to the procession.

The Trades Unions or the Knights of Labor cannot succeed as long as the color line exists. Mr. Wood said: "We are well aware of that and there is an agreement among all the colored Unions of this city to stand aloof from all white labor organizations that refuse to recognize us as their brother. These white organizations must concede all rights to the colored man themselves. When they do this then the Hod Carriers' Union will unite with them." . . . The colored laborers should not allow themselves to be placed in an antagonistic position towards the laboring classes of other races, unless the hostility and opposition of those classes make such a course on their part, a necessity.

We all know it to be a fact that labor organizations, in many parts of the country, among the whites, do not recognize the meritorious claims of colored people. Why? That race prejudice has something to do with it cannot be truthfully denied, but this, in my opinion, is not the principle reason. Less than a quarter of a century ago the colored people of this country had no political, social or industrial status. The laboring people of that race represented, at the time, contrary to their own wishes, it is true, opposition to free, intelligent and remunerative labor. This was one of the principal causes of the late civil war – the war between free and slave labor. The colored laborers were justly looked upon, at that time, and consequently unjustly looked upon in many localities now, as a degraded and servile class. It is the present duty of the coloured people to do whatever is necessary to eradicate this erroneous impression. Let them impress the white laborers with the fact that while they are not disposed to antagonize their interests, and are determined not to do so, unless it becomes a necessity, yet they insist upon justice themselves – a right to an equal participation in the enjoyment of the fruits of honest and well paid labor.

I do not wish to be understood as endorsing all the means that are employed by some labor organizations to secure a recognition of the justice of their claims. Lawlessness should never be countenanced or encouraged. The laboring people of the country can, in my opinion, through organization and cooperation, secure for themselves the just rewards of labor without resorting to any methods that cannot be sanctioned by the most law abiding people of the community . . . Colored men should not identify themselves with any organization that seeks the accomplishment of its purposes through a resort of lawlessness and violence. They should maintain their reputation of being a law-abiding and law-observing people, except so far as may be necessary for the protection of themselves and their families. They should discountenance, discourage and condemn lawlessness, violence, communism, socialism and anarchy. . . .

The laboring people in this country can secure all the rights to which they are justly entitled without violating law, and there is no better way to bring about this result than through organization. The legitimate object and purpose of labor organizations should be to call public attention to the condition and wants of the laboring people with a view to creating a sentiment that will enforce a recognition of their just and reasonable demands – to unite their efforts and labors in an intelligent direction for their mutual aid, protection and advancement. Such organizations, created and organized for such purposes, are entitled to and should receive the assistance and support of laboring colored people. It is understood, of course, that I refer to such organizations as do not discriminate on account of race or color in the admission of persons to membership. I hope it is not necessary to advise the laboring colored people to strongly oppose and antagonize every organization that will exclude persons of color from the organization without regard to merit . . . It is the duty of the colored people of the present generation to give their sons and daughters an industrial education and have them contend for recognition by, and admission into, reputable and intelligent labor organizations, and take their chances in the race of life upon terms of equality with the whites.

The A.M.E. Church Review, III (October 1886); 165-67

A General Strike

ABOUT FACE OR 2,000 LABORERS QUIT WORK IN GALVESTON – THE KNIGHTS OF LABOR MAKE AN ISSUE WITH THE MALLORY STEAMSHIP COMPANY, AND ORDER A GENERAL STRIKE OF THEIR OWN – A SUSPENSION OF WORK.

The recent strike of white laborers on the New York wharf, and their substitution by colored laborers, is of too recent occurrence to require any recapitulation here, and is merely referred to as the cause which has resulted in one of the most general labor upheavings ever known in the history of Galveston. The Knights of Labor on Sunday held in this city an important meeting of their executive committee. This meeting was followed up by another held on Monday night, and rumors were then afloat that the result would be a general strike ordered by the association of Knights of Labor. These were merely rumors, but they culminated yesterday in a very serious reality when, at 1 p.m., a general strike was ordered throughout the city by which some 1,500 or 2,000 men employed in various capacities throughout the city quit work, creating a general excitement, as the facts in the case became known. The strike permeated every department of work where Knights of Labor are employed, including the men at the cotton presses, on railroads, along the docks, screwmen and longshoremen, printing offices and even the barber shops. A general stagnation of business was the result, but matters were in such a confused state during the afternoon, and the actual situation so little known, that it was difficult to ascertain accurately the extent of the movement. About 500 men employed in the four compresses quit work almost to a man, excepting probably the clerical force, all employed in the yards and at the freight depot of the Gulf, Colorado and Santa Fe Railway company, while the work along the docks was almost completely suspended.

The cause of the movement

The cause of the present movement is briefly stated by the following correspondence between the Knights of Labor and Captain Sawyer, representing the Mallory Line in this city:

GALVESTON, Tex., November 1, 1885. – J. N. Sawyer, Esq., Agent Mallory Line Steamships, – Dear Sir: At a meeting of the executive board of Knights of Labor of the state of Texas, held in this city on this day, the following resolution was adopted:

Whereas it has been made known to the executive board of the Knights of Labor of the state of Texas at the Mallory Line of steamships and its agents are discriminating against this order by discharging and refusing to allow them to work upon the Mallory or New York wharf, therefore be it

Resolved that we, as the executive board of the Knights of Labor do hereby request that you reinstate said men and also allow the Knights of Labor of the city of Galveston an equal representation upon said wharf. This board will be very much gratified to receive an answer from you by Tuesday, the 3rd day of November, A.D. 1885, at 12 o'clock m. Very respectfully,

P.H. Golden

D.M.W.D.A. No. 18, of the State of Texas, and Chairman of the Executive Board.

This communication was submitted yesterday morning, the committee stating that they would return at noon for an answer. Promptly at noon the executive committee returned and were handed the following reply:

GALVESTON, Tex. – Dear Sir: Your favor of the 1st ultimo, covering preamble and resolutions as adopted by your board on that date, as follows:

"Whereas it has been made known to the executive board of the Knights of Labor of the state of Texas that the Mallory line of steamships and the agents are discriminating against this order by discharging and refusing to allow them to work upon the Mallory or New York wharf; therefore be it

"Resolved that we, as the executive board of the Knights of Labor, do hereby request that you reinstate said men, and also allow the Knights of Labor of the city of Galveston an equal representation upon said wharf," is received, and replying thereto we desire to say that the charges presented in the preamble of your resolution is without foundation, inasmuch as we have not, to our knowledge, discharged any member of your order, or any other well behaved laborer.

In a conference held in this office October 18, 1885, we were informed by Mr. Patrick Nugent, a representative of your order, acting in an advisory capacity, that the men who had been employed at discharging and loading the Mallory steamers were not members of the order of Knights of Labor.

These men were not discharged, but (excepting nine white men who did not leave, and who are now working on the wharf) they of their own volition abandoned their positions as laborers for the Mallory line. Compliance with your request would compel us to enact the injustice of which you unwarrantably complain, of discharging laborers who are performing their duties faithfully to employ others in their stead. So, conforming to our reply to the joint committee of October 27, 1885, we decline to disturb the present status of labor on the Mallory line wharf, and are, sir, yours very truly,

J. N. Sawyer & Co., Agents.

The committee, after considering the above, asked Captain Sawyer if this was his final answer, and he replied in the affirmative; when they informed him that they would be at their meeting-room until 1 p.m., where he could communicate with them if he had anything further to say upon the subject. No further conference took place, and at 1 p.m. sharp the strike was ordered.

Matters were thrown into such confusion for the time being, that no very intelligent opinions could be expressed, and but few seemed to know the cause or the extent of the movement. The corner of Market and Twenty-second streets in the Alvey building, where the Knights of Labor have their meeting-room, seemed to be the general rendezvous, and being the headquarters of the executive committee, it was here that large numbers of the striking laborers congregated causing quite an animated scene. The Knights of Labor generally were reticent as to the details of the movement and a reporter of THE NEWS, with a view of ascertaining the extent of the strike, called upon Captain Sawyer and the management of the different road and compresses to ascertain to what extent they were affected. Captain Sawyer kindly furnished the above correspondence, which is unquestionably the basis of the strike. In recapitulating the recent trouble out of which the present one has grown he referred to his letter as published above defining his position in the matter. He referred to the recent tacit agreement between the white and colored laborers as to a division of the work, but the Mallory company was under moral obligations to continue the colored laborers so long as they gave satisfaction. He had been further advised subsequent to the recent strike that the Knights of Labor would take no definite steps in the matter, merely acting in an advisory capacity to secure, if possible, an amicable adjustment of the difficulties. He could not say at the time what effect the strike would have on the Mallory business. The colored laborers were still at work there, and while work had been stopped at the presses, the cotton already compressed there was being hauled to the wharf. At the four compresses work was at a standstill, and none of them were running in the afternoon, in all about 500 laborers had quit work here. Along the docks members of the Screwmen's and Longshoremen's associations who are members of the Knights of Labor had quit work, disabling the crews to that extent that work was virtually suspended. All the men in the yards and at the shops and freight depot of the Gulf, Colorado and Santa Fe quit work, and until the matter is settled it is a matter of doubt whether any freights will be permitted to move. The forces of the Missouri Pacific railway had not quit, at least up to a later hour, the cause assigned for this being that these laborers are under a different jurisdiction, and were awaiting orders from their assembly. In all, it is estimated that about 1500 or 2000 laborers of this city have obeyed the mandate of the Knights of Labor. It applies to every interest where members of their order are employed, and the printing offices generally were deserted during the afternoon, and in one instance even a hand in a barber shop knocked off work. This instance is cited merely to show how general is the present movement.

The issues involved

While the employment of the colored labor on the New York wharf is the main issue upon which the strike is based, some of the strikers claim that it is a movement of organized labor against unorganized labor and a protection of white labor as against a substitution of colored labor in this city. Besides citing the condition of affairs on the

New York wharf, it was very generally rumored yesterday that two carloads of colored laborers had been brought in the night previous from Brasoria, and that a boat had brought in some forty or fifty more during the day from the mouth of the Brasoe. These rumors could not be verified, and in conversation with N. W. Cubey, last night, he informed a reporter of THE NEWS that such was not the case, and that there was no foundation for the statement very generally made that there was a movement on foot to substitute colored for white labor in the cotton presses and other positions now occupied by white labor, and in connection with which his name was mentioned. He says that if such an importation of colored labor had been made he would surely have known of it, and his denial of the charge was quite positive and emphatic.

Mr. Golden, the master workman of the Knights of Labor, and as such the leader of the present movement, stated to a reporter during the afternoon that it was a matter of self-preservation. A means of adjustment of the late strike on the New York wharf had been submitted to the Mallory company, but they had not accepted it and the white laborers at Galveston who had their families to support; and whose interests are here, could not afford to and their subsistence thus taken from them. The Knights of Labor had done all in their power to settle the differences today and without a resort to extreme measures they had notified Captain Sawyer, of the Mallory line; Captain Fowler, of the Morgan line; President Sealy, of the Santa Fe, and several prominent ship brokers that men of their order, who were not in the strike, were being discriminated against and would not be allowed to work. He had hoped that the present trouble might be averted, but unless the matter were settled the strike would be made general.

Galveston (Texas) *Daily News*, November 4, 1885

A sample of national reactions to the Knights position on social equality

The workingmen of this country know no color line. They stand together shoulder to shoulder, and the black man to them is as good as any if he is a true citizen and performs his allotted task faithfully and well. The color line is fading away like the relic of the confederacy.

Harrisburg *Telegraph,* October 5, 1886.

Let those people who can see no good in the work of the Knights of Labor now come forward like men and allow that their action upon the color question in their Richmond convention is magnanimous, consistent, and far ahead of the age.

Lynn (Mass.) *Bee,* October 6, 1886.

It is well that our people should be warned in time of the new and vile use to which the Knights of Labor organization is to be put – that is to say, if the Southern Knights will consent thus to be used. Will they? We don't believe it.

Raleigh News and Observer, October 7, 1886.

It is reported that the liberal views of the Northern delegates touching the colored members has disgusted the aristocratic workingmen of Richmond. The latter threaten to withdraw from the order. If that is their view of the cause of labor, they had better withdraw and stay out until they learn that honest labor ennobles every doer on the face of the green earth.

Philadelphia *North American,* October 7, 1886.

The Knights who marched to the Richmond theater with the colored delegate at their head said by their action that they had no respect for the sentiments of the people of Richmond, or of the local white Knights, so far as the social equality question is concerned. They took it upon themselves to show the Richmond Knights and the Southern delegates their contempt for Southern opposition to social recognition of colored people, and they did it in a very aggressive, not to say offensive, way. It may be well for Southern Knights to inquire whether it is the purpose of the Knights of Labor to settle social as well as labor questions.

Savannah News, October 8, 1886.

Laboring men struggling to better their condition have a common cause which binds them together in a common brotherhood. There can be no color line. They must stand or fail together, and as this becomes more generally recognized the labor question in the South will assume a new and more promising phase.

Philadephia *Press,* October 8, 1886.

The decision of the assembly from New York to lodge in tents because one of their number was refused admission to the hostel was right. It would have been a curious commentary on the doctrine of brotherly love for the white men to accept accommodations from which their colored brother was debarred, and if they had chosen to stay away from the theaters because Ferrell could not be admitted with them that would have been an eminently right and proper protest, and would have had considerable weight with the managerial pocket-book. But the forcing of Ferrell into the lower part of the theater among people who did not want him was quite another matter and a move that could do no good to anybody. Race prejudices fade out slowly; they do not die of single blows in the head. These Knights do not live in Richmond; they can not follow up their effort, and when they depart they will have intensified the race prejudices of the city. The matter is, luckily, not big enough to have any lasting effect, but what influence it had works to the prejudice of the weaker race.

Springfield (Mass.) *Republican,* October 8, 1886, reprinted in "Knights of Labor and the Color Line," *Public Opinion,* October 16, 1886.

If the Knights of Labor intend to make the social equality of the races part of their creed they will gain little strength in the South. The white working man has as little taste for that as anybody and understands very clearly that social intermixture is the first and longest step toward miscegenation, which means mongrelization.

August News (Ga.), October 9, 1886.

The moment Farrell, the colored man, made his appearance in the ranks of "District 49" the Knights were face to face with a very practical and hard-headed problem. It was certainly very loyal in the "Forty-niners" to refuse good quarters which their colored comrade could not share. Everybody appreciates that, and against this fidelity to conviction the hospitable people of Richmond has nothing to say. There was a lesson in the incident, however, which the Knights received very graciously – namely, that not even ardour in a great cause can override old prejudices or fixed customs. They must take the world as it is and not become disheartened because they can not change it in the twinkling of any eye. Therein lies the difference between a true knight and a mere anarchist. The knight, when he finds the wind dead ahead, tacks ship, going where he does not want to go, both the south and the north, but making progress eastward all the time. The anarchist, on the other hand, insists on sailing straight in the eye of the wind, and when he finds he can not do it he brings out his dynamite and wants to blow up the ship and the ocean and everything else.

New York *Herald,* October 12, 1886.

Whatever may be said in criticism or denunciation of the Knights of Labor, the fact remains that they are doing more to blot out color prejudice and recognize the equality of manhood in all the races than any organization in existence.

Salisbury (N.C.) *Star of Zion.*

If the K. of L. will exterminate class prejudice and color-line, not in form, but in reality, we say colored men this is your chance, but if not it would be leaping from the frying-pan into the fire. We must be made to feel comfortable, as if we had friends at our backs and sides.

Staunton (Va.) *Critic.*

The Knights of Labor justifies the confidence placed in it by the Afro-American people, and its course in Richmond justifies the *Plaindealer* in exhorting the people to combine with it to secure the elevation of the masses and in proclaiming it to be the most potent factor ever yet entered into our American life to secure full justice to the Afro-American.

Detroit (Mich.) *Plaindealer.*

The Knights of Labor have shown themselves to be true to their colored brother, and henceforth colored men will feel that labor begets a fraternity that will in time usurp the power of political and sectional prejudice. The action of the Knights of Labor in Richmond show that they are prepared to sacrifice much for principle, and that they do not intend to build up an aristocracy of caste among those who earn their bread by honest labor.

Chicago *Observer.*

The last and most heartless difficulty to be dealt with and destroyed in this free land is race caste. Its citadel is in the late slave States. Thus far the poor colored man has been left to combat it almost alone. Reason and religion both show its flagrant inconsistency – in fact, it is at war with every principle of truth and right. God is surely raising allies for its effectual resistance and final overthrow. If the Knights are destined to help us in this contest, then may God bless the Knights and prosper them.

Philadelphia *Christian Recorder.*

This certainly is a boom for the order among the colored people, because when white men risk so much and deprive themselves of comforts, in order to break down a mean and hellborn prejudice maintained solely on the ground of color, be it assured that the thinking of the race all over the country, no matter what may have been their dispositions towards the Knights of Labor formerly, will surely be convinced of the sincerity of purpose of the order in making no distinctions and protecting the rights and privileges of all its citizens.

Petersburg (Va.) *Lancet.*

The convention of the Knights of Labor of Richmond, Va., afforded but another evidence of the advancement in education and morals that is growing steadily in reference to the position of the Negro of this country. There is further shown a lively appreciation of the relations that bind man to man, Richmond, the former seat of the confederacy and now the home of race prejudice in its most objectionable form, is having a lesson taught it that while it may not eradicate many of the evils, will still have its influence in demonstrating the futility of withstanding the ordinary customs of civilized communities.

Philadephia *Sentinel.*

Will the order of the Knights of Labor insist that its component unions accept the Negro to membership? Though the leading spirits of the organization are full of home and activity, and though they are inspired by the most proper sense of justice, it is doubtful that the rank and file of the order are ready to preach and practice industrial equality. Mr Powderly and District Assembly 49 have immortalized themselves, so far as the Negro is concerned. We have expressed our doubts about the rank and file of the order being ready to accept the Negro as a man. We hope our doubts are unfounded. For should the whites reach this point, the Knights of Labor will undoubtedly hold the future government of the United States in the hollow of its hand. If the Negro has one predominant characteristic it is his gratitude.

New York Freeman, October 16, 1886.

The Knights of Labor show the white feather

The following, taken from Friday of last week's proceedings of the Convention of Knights of Labor, in Session at Richmond, Va., is of general interest to the race at large:

Before they took its noon recess Wm. H. Barrett of District Assembly 70, on behalf of the Southern delegates, offered the following, which was adopted without debate:

Whereas, Reports have been circulated and impressions have been created by the press of the country regarding of position of the Knights of Labor on the question of social equality; and

Whereas, We believe the welfare of the order South requires that this General Assembly take such action as will dispel wrong impressions; therefore

Resolved, That the organization of the Knights of Labor recognizes the civil and political equality of all men, and in the broad field of labor recognizes no distinction on account of colour; but it has no purpose to interfere with or disrupt the social relations which exist between the different races in the various parts of the country.

The Labor Convention was compelled to do in this matter as the white knight of the South dictated.

Northern sentiment however just has always crawled before and fawned upon the domineering sentiment of the South, however unjust and insolent. The wild goose chase the South led the North on the slavery question is illustrative of the point.

In cold-blooded persistence in the maintenance of an infamous position, – in the subjection of all other matters to the vindication of such position, – the North has never proved itself a match for the South. When the issue is joined the Southern dog always wags his Northern tail.

We are not surprised that the Knights of Labor backed down at the command of the Southern delegates. The whole North knuckled to it in 1856 as voiced by Mr. Justice Taney; every Christian denomination has bowed to it since the war; the Republican party bowed to it in 1876.

The black man constitutes the labor element of the South.

The black man does not ask for social equality – there is no such thing; but he demands and he will have that access to places of amusement and accommodation upon which the Richmond "incident" is based, in the course of time, whatever the Southern high-flyers may say or do to the contrary.

New York *Freeman,* October 23, 1886.

The sugar strike

The negroes of the south found themselves at the close of the war emancipated from chattel slavery only to enter into a condition of competitive wage slavery, a little more disguised but even more miserable than their former position. It has often been openly declared by their masters that they (the masters) prefer the present state of affairs to the old, for now the negro must keep himself as he can; they are not responsible for his support when they do not want him.

The sugar-planters of Louisiana have been loud in their demands for protective tariffs – in the interest of their workmen. But as is always the case, "protection" has enriched the proprietor but has failed in every way to protect the toilers.

The inevitable result is now being accomplished. A miserable, half-starved mob of black wretches have undertaken to right the balances by strikes. They have met force by force and death by death. Their leaders have been taken to prison, and without a semblance of law from the prison to the nearest tree. How long will the people be blind?

Labor Enquirer (Chicago), November 26, 1887.

Outrages in Louisiana

The killing of twelve colored men at Thibodaux last week, also the murder of the two Cox brothers, who were arrested as agitators charged with making incendiary speeches, and taken from the jail by the whites and shot to death, are reported as growing out of the Louisiana sugar strikes. The Coxes were leaders in the strike and prominent in the labor organizations. Even if the Coxes were leaders in the strike, by what right were they taken from the custody of the law and riddled with bullets? The whites who participated in the shooting of the Cox brothers were a more pronounced gang of law-breakers than were these brothers. They dyed their hands in innocent blood and stamped upon themselves the brand of cowardice, because they, a party of supposed law-abiding citizens, overstepped the bounds of law by taking unarmed men out of the hands of the constituted authorities, and giving vent to their pent up anger by filling their bodies with bullets. Such a cowardly act could only be performed by bands of sneaking cutthroats, which permeate nearly every one of the Southern States. The law holds every one charged with crime innocent until proven guilty; therefore the Cox brothers were innocent until they had been accorded a fair and impartial trial and adjudged guilty by a jury of their peers. No body of citizens has any right to constitute themselves into a tribunal of justice, and especially such a body as this Louisiana rabble proved itself to be.

The most notable feature about this shooting affair is that, as is usually the case, the majority of the slain, if not all of them, were colored. This is another example of Mr. Grady's "New South". The usages which oppression have been inflicted upon the inoffensive colored people from the dawn of their freedom still follow close and fast upon their heels; and the question may be asked in all seriousness how much longer is this going to last? Do the whites of the South suppose that colored people are going to continue to submit without a practical protest against their inhuman treatment? If they do, they are basing their supposition upon a frail foundation. They may as well make up their minds at once that the colored people will not in the future continue to be led as lambs to the slaughter. Education is enabling them to know and appreciate their rights as American citizens, and in the future they will not be backward in claiming these rights and insisting upon a fair and impartial interpretation of the laws which govern this country.

Power is a dangerous weapon, especially when it is possessed by unscrupulous men. The oppressed always sooner or later arise and shake off the galling chains of oppression, and they do this even if they cause rivers of blood to follow in their wake. Unscrupulous men who possess power which has been obtained by usurpation and fraud should be careful how they exercise it. The whites of the South should take warning in time, or they may have to repent when repentance will avail them naught.

New York Age, December 3, 1887.

The sugar riots

The attitude of the Knights of Labor of Louisiana regarding the riots at Thibodaux, substantiates the reports of the kindly feeling existing between the white and the colored members of the Order. The Knights are very powerful in New Orleans, and they are using their influence to protect the rights as well as the lives of the colored brethren. They denounce in strong terms the killing of the negroes at Pattersonville, and will lay the whole matter before Congress at its coming session. The District Assembly will also appeal to the Order everywhere to ask for the repeal of duties on sugar which will have the effect of bringing the planters to a sense of justice as well as benefiting the people of the country. This resolution has caused great excitement among the planters and every effort has been made to induce the Knights to withdraw it, but they steadily refuse to do so. It is a significant fact that the publication of this manifesto by the sugar planters in St. Mary, in which parish the town of Pattersonville is situated, have generally granted the increase of wages asked by the negroes, the refusal of which led to the strike and the killing of the colored Knights. If with so powerful an organization at their back the colored people are unable to protect their rights, what must be their condition unorganized and alone to meet the opposition of powerful syndicates and combinations? Let those workingmen who think they can get along without organization, simply because they have at the present time no trouble to command good wages, ask themselves what they would do to protect themselves in case that happy time should cease. It is then organization proves its worth.

Journal of United Labor, December 3, 1887

Sources: Various journals as listed above, 1880s.

3.2 The American Federation of Labor

The A F of L was an umbrella organisation for craft unions but its participant bodies invariably resisted the admission of black workers to skilled occupations and consequently union membership.

For sometime past we have received a large number of inquiries relative to the attitude of the American Federation of Labor toward the negro worker, and the subject has been widely discussed by philanthropists, some negro workers themselves, and particularly by some colored men who have advanced to position of prominence in the realm of thought. We have endeavored upon all occasions to give all possible information upon this as well as other matters of interest to the workers; and while we have no desire to impugn the motives of any one by a charge of suppression, yet for some reason or other, the information we have furnished on this topic has not been given that same wide publicity as have the charges of insincerity or antagonism. We believe, therefore, that a few plain statements of facts here will serve to correct erroneous impressions, and will receive wider and better attention.

For years the American Federation of Labor has declared in favor of, and the necessity for, the organization of all workers, without regard to creed, color, sex, nationality, or politics. In making the declaration for the complete organization of all workers, it does not necessarily proclaim that the social barriers which exist between the whites and blacks could or should be obliterated; but it realizes that when white and black workers are compelled to work side by side, under the same equally unfair and adverse conditions, it would be an anomaly to refuse to accord the right of organization to workers because of a difference in their color.

We have more than 700 volunteer organizers and a number of organizers under salary, among which are several who are devoting their time exclusively to the organization of the colored workers. This certainly should indicate not only our desire and interest, but also the work which is being accomplished.

It need not be imagined, however, that because we realize the necessity for the organization of the colored workers that for that reason we can grant to them privileges which are denied to white workers. We want them to organize in the unions of their trades and callings, and to take their equal chance with the white workmen – they are entitled to no less, they should ask no more. We say this because there are some colored men who imagine that the organization of the colored workers comes under their especial superior wing of protection; who manifest a suspicion that the colored workers when organized will require the solicitous and fostering care of these colored "superiors" from what they indirectly intimate to be the design of the unions of white workers. We are frequently in receipt of communications from these self-constituted "superiors", who make inquiries as to "privileges" to which the colored workman would be entitled in the event of these "superiors" giving their consent or assistance in organizing the colored workmen.

The American Federation of Labor grants to national and international unions of a trade the right, autonomy and independence to make and enforce rules governing their trade, so long as they do not infringe upon the jurisdiction of other national or international unions and observe the laws, policy and principles of the American Federation of Labor.

The American Federation of Labor seeks to place the organizations of labor upon the highest possible plane of ethical, progressive, civilized and humane considerations, and among these recognizes potentially the identity of the interests of the workers irrespective of creed, sex, politics, color or nationality. Time and again have our organizations in conventions emphatically declared and insisted upon the practice of these principles; and often have white union men deprived themselves of opportunities and advantages in order to protect the rights of colored workmen. It may not be generally known that the great strike of the New Orleans white union workers some years ago was in defense and for the promotion of the interests of colored laborers.

For their protection, as well as for the promotion of their interests, the colored workers should organize and in all cases become affiliated with the organizations of white wage earners or form colored workers' unions in full sympathy and co-operation of the white workers' unions.

At the Louisville Convention of the American Federation of Labor authority was granted to organize and grant charters to separate local and central bodies of colored workmen, wherever such two bodies would promote the interests of all the workers.

The American Federation of Labor has a large number of unions affiliated, composed exclusively of colored workers, who feel that their interests are safeguarded by the officers of our movement as justly and wisely as the organizations of any other toilers.

Again, we have unions composed of whites and blacks, and generally these work together without any friction at all.

When a white man desires to become a member of an organization he is proposed for membership and is required to submit to rules which experience has demonstrated to be necessary. Certainly, no greater privilege can be conferred upon a negro simply because of the color of his skin. We repeat that he ought to ask and be accorded equal rights and privileges; certainly, no more.

We do not claim perfection for our movement. In a movement composed of such immense numbers as ours, a mistake may be made, and this, too, toward a white man. When this is done, a corrective effort is made; when, however, it occurs with a colored man it is magnified and exaggerated by the "superiors" to whom we have already referred; and an effort is made to convey the notion that is the rule, not the exception, and that the labor movement does not grant the right of the negro to organize.

The real difficulty in the matter is that the colored workers have allowed themselves to be used with too frequent telling effect by their employers as to injure the cause and interests of themselves as well as of the white workers. They have too often allowed themselves to be regarded as "cheap men", and all realize that "cheap men" are not only an impediment to the attainment of the workers' just rights, and the progress of civilization, but will tie themselves to the slough of despond and despair.

The antipathy that we know some union workers have against the colored man is not because of his color, but because of the fact that generally he is a "cheap man". It is the constant aim of our movement to relieve all workers, white and black, from such an unenviable and unprofitable condition.

In a recent article by a distinguished colored writer, he falls into the common error which others of his race make. Booker T. Washington, to whom we refer, intimated that it would be to the advantage of the colored workers if they would be so situated in their home lives that their employers could control them as well as the lives of their families. Certainly, if this policy is pursued, it implies that the economic, social, and moral progress and advancement of the negro is dependent upon the philanthropic and humane consideration of their employers. How much can be expected from this source is well known to any observer of economic and industrial development. Besides this, if workers are to rely upon the "good will and control" of the employers, it presupposes that there is either no need or no inclination for organization. In other words and in truth, it places the position of the colored worker exactly as a cheap man; and it is this feature of the problem which arouses much of the antagonism and feeling among the organized, and more intensely by the unorganized workmen, whose very bitterest antipathies are aroused against the colored workmen because they couple them with an instrument of their employers to force down and keep down wages to the deterioration of the Caucasian race.

If the colored workmen desire to accept the honest invitation of our movement to organize; if those who have influence over the minds of the colored workmen will encourage the earnest, honest effort put forth by our fellow-unionists, we will find larger success attending their efforts, economic bitterness and antagonism between the races reduced, minimized, and obliterated; but, if the colored workers are taught to depend entirely upon the "good will and control" of their employers; that they can be brought from place to place at any time to thwart the struggle of the white workers for material, moral and social improvement; that hostility will increase, and thus countered the very best efforts of those who are earnestly engaged in the endeavor for the unification of labor, the attainment of social improvement of all the people, and their entire disenthrallment from every vestige of tyranny, wrong, and injustice.

American Federationist (April, 1901): 118.

Effects of the strike

Negroes are tacitly but none the less completely excluded from railroad positions on most Northern lines. No Negro is ever seen in a position on a railroad which is in the line of railroad promotion. This industrial exclusion is a most serious injustice and, with other like exclusions, lies at the bottom of much of the industrial deficiencies of the Negro. The Chicago strike has led the Rock Island to place a number of Negroes in its yards and switch towers. As in most great strikes the practical result of this upheaval is to give a chance to men who had no chance or small chance before, and the power of the Government, can be in no better business than opening a path to work for men to whom it was before closed.

The Christian Recorder, July 12, 1894.

The race question: the cause. White employes will not affiliate with colored men

TERRE HAUTE, Ind., Oct. 6 – Grand Master Sargent of the Brotherhood of Locomotive Firemen, who is President of the Supreme Council of the Federation of Railway Employes, today issued a call for the meeting of the council at Houston, Texas, Thursday next, to consider the threatened strike on the Houston and Texas Central Railway. This trouble is the first instance in which the race question has entered into the consideration of a grievance brought before the federation. Mr. Debs said that not one of all the railway organizations accepted colored men as members. The white railway men refuse to take the colored men as members. The white railway refuse to take the colored laborers into their orders. There are many colored firemen, brakemen, and switchmen in the South, but the colored man is not made an engineer or conductor. Wages paid to such employes are not equal to the rates on Northern roads.

The white employes are endeavoring to raise wages in the South, but colored labor can be procured cheaper. The colored railroad men have organizations throughout the South, but they are not permitted to affiliate with the white organizations. Owing to peculiar conditions existing in the South, the questions to be considered by the Executive Council will be grave ones. Mr. Sargent left tonight for St. Louis, where he will spend tomorrow with a grievance committee of the Missouri Pacific, and will proceed to Houston tomorrow night.

New York Times, October 7, 1890.

Appeal to negro workers

When we were organizing the American Railway Union in 1893, I stood on the floor of that Convention all through its deliberations appealing to the delegates to open the door to admit the colored as well as the white man upon equal terms. They refused, and then came a strike and they expected the colored porters and waiters to stand by them. If they had only admitted these porters and waiters to membership in the American Railway Union there would have been a different story of that strike, for it would certainly have had a different result.

I remember one occasion down in Louisville, Kentucky, where we were organizing and they refused to admit colored workers to the union. A strike followed – a strike order exclusively by the white workers. After having ignored the colored workers and refused them admission, the strike came and the colored workers walked out with the white ones. Notwithstanding they had been excluded and insulted, they went out, and the strike had not lasted long until the white men went back to work and broke the strike, leaving the colored men out in the cold in spite of their loyalty to white workers.

Eugene V. Debs, "Appeal to Negro Workers," at Commonwealth Casino in New York City, October 30, 1923.

The race question

The race question in the South seems to be coming forward with more prominence of late than it has for years. It may be that with the acquisition of more territory people with mixed races, by this Government, is the cause of this fresh agitation; the people realizing that with the assumption of more of the "White Man's Burden" by this country, some method of controlling that burden must be established, that will prove more satisfactory than the one now in force.

It appears to thousands of Americans today that the fifteenth amendment, giving the negro the right of franchise, has not been the educator and uplifter of the race that it was designed and expected to be. The placing in office of negroes so illiterate and ignorant as to be unable to understand the first principles of law and justice has had a demoralizing influence on the race and has tended to bring them into greater disrepute, not alone with the people of the Southern States, but of the whole country. The result has been that in South Carolina, Mississippi and Louisiana laws have been passed, amendatory to the State constitutions, prohibiting illiterates from voting, and so worded as to practically disfranchise the negro voters of those States, *and no others*. A similar law is soon to be voted on in North Carolina, and no doubt will be adopted there. The whole tendency is to disfranchise the negro – to literally annul the fifteenth amendment. It is the logical conclusion of the relations that have existed between the white and black races for hundreds of generations, and will continue for hundreds more.

The immoral, shiftless, indolent nature of the negro, an inherent viciousness that leads to the committal of brutal and revolting crimes, their utter lack of ambition and desire to advance, are the things that are bringing about a reaction in public sentiment. Of course there are exceptions, but to the negro as a class it will apply.

It may be charged by some as a result of the conditions brought about by slavery, but while some of it may be traceable to that, and while the introduction of slavery into the United States, with its attendant evils, must always be deplored, yet the ignorant, licentious characteristics of the negro have existed through centuries in countries where he has predominated, as well as in those where he has been in the minority.

It may be classed as a step backward to disfranchise the negro, but the time is not far distant, in the light of present events, when it will be one of the leading questions of the hour. The freedom which has been permitted in the right of franchise in this country has led to much of the political corruption from which we now suffer, and has tended to degrade the right of the ballot. The ballot should be so restricted to foreigners coming to this country that when they did become eligible to the franchise they would esteem it as a privilege to be sought for and desired, and not as a matter of universal license, free to all, as it is today, to the disgrace and detriment of the American people.

While liberty and equality are the boasts of Americanism, liberty is degenerating into license in many ways, and absolute equality, even before the law, let alone socially or morally, have never existed even here. The law never handles the rich, though criminal, Mr. L. as it does the poor thief, Mr. P. It deals with the drunken debauchee, Mr. Z., vastly differently than it does with intoxicated "Weary Willie" who falls into its clutches. Socially, legally, physically or morally there has never been and never will be, equality between the members of the white races. Then why talk of an equality between the white and black races, which has not, and never will have, any existence except in the minds of theorists. It is a condition hoped for, but which will never be realized.

In the Hawaiian Islands, where the franchise was permitted the black race, it was but meagerly taken advantage of, and then not in a manner to be encouraging for its perpetuation. Of course, the consent of the governed is talked of as something that can not be overlooked, and among a people where the capability of self-government exists it should be permitted full sway, but that the negro of the South, or anywhere else, for that matter, has arisen, as a race, to the opportunity offered him, cannot be demonstrated. There is no use trying to avoid the race issue that is being constantly thrust before the people, more and more frequently as the months roll on. Existing conditions in the South have not proven satisfactory to the people, and while allowance must be made for race prejudice, there is no doubt much cause for complaint and room for reformation in the present existing relations between the two races.

* * *

It would appear from the testimony of employes in the Bureau of Immigration before the Industrial Commission that our laws relative to the restriction of immigration are not properly planned and are not doing what they are intended to do. Mr Dobbler, chief of the Board of Immigration Inspectors, testified that it was plain that immigrants were coached so as to give answers to questions asked, in such a manner as to evade our laws. Dr. Lorenzo Ullo, legal adviser of the immigration bureau, testified that the laws were so contradictory that it was difficult to enforce the intent of the law. For instance, a criminal, according to the law, shall be returned to the port from which he came, and to the country to which he belongs. So a German criminal sailing from Paris or a Chinaman from Rome, or other like cases, would be free from the operation of this law.

There is no actual law for the deportation of contract labor. It is only by implying that meaning in the law of 1891 that this can be done, and even means are found to evade this law by having someone who works for the corporation hire men to come and work in this country from foreign lands, and as the man who hires them is a hired man of the corporation, the intent of the law is evaded. It appears there is no law prohibiting the landing of girls for immoral purposes. The laws appear on their face to fall far short of what was claimed for them, and stand in need of radical changes.

While many newspapers and men claim the present immigration laws are all that could be desired, it is evident they are not, and people so claiming are either ignorant of the facts or have something to gain by so claiming.

With better times in the United States the flood of immigration has again set in, and with apparently very little to bar its progress. Corporations prefer the cheap foreign labor to the American article. The former is more servile and more tractable, at least for a time. Pennsylvania receives a large per cent of this undesirable element – Slavs, Poles, Italians, etc. – until one can go in some parts of that State and easily imagine himself in a foreign country. Immigration laws must be framed with due respect of treaty rights, but this can be done and the laws so worded that a big per cent, of this cheap labor, the criminals and paupers could be kept out, were it not for the opposition such a law meets from the corporations that desire to retain the club they have wielded so long over the heads of American workingmen.

Between the cheap negro labor and the cheap foreign labor, the intelligent American workingman is threatened in his desire to live and enjoy the benefits of our laws, to educate and raise up to some honorable calling the family about him without becoming virtually a slave himself, or permitting his family to sink into misery and squalor. The only reason that the safety of the rights of these men, who form the groundwork (and bulwark, in time of need) of the United States, is permitted to be threatened is that wealth is running the Government, without any regard to its welfare, but solely in its own interests. Possibly the coming Congress will amend the present laws so as to be more beneficial to the interests of labor, but so far all pressure that could be brought to bear on past Congresses has failed to secure legislation that was satisfactory, or if such laws as were secured appeared as if they would be of benefit to the common people they were vetoed by those higher in authority.

Locomotive Firemen's Magazine (November, 1899): 593-95.

Negro domination

The JOURNAL has always contended that when a labor organization made any distinction when the question of a general betterment of conditions was concerned, in the race, creed or color of the people interested, it made a mistake. The question of negro labor in the South, and of the cheapest labor of foreign countries in the North, is one that demands careful and thoughtful attention. The white laborer of the South does not take kindly to the competition of its colored labor, and the intelligent labor of the North does not take kindly to the competition of the labor forced upon it by indiscriminate immigration, but, in both cases, it would be well for the laborers themselves to note that the natural tendency of wages and conditions of employment is toward the lowest point, and it is to their interest to give to the lowest class of labor and to the poorest paid every assistance to bring it to the higher level of wages and conditions of employment. Where this is not done, unless some exceptional means are used to maintain wages and conditions of employment, they will naturally drop to the lowest point. In the South, negro labor menaces white labor, and, in several instances, white labor has been supplanted by colored labor because it was cheaper, and because the negro was not at all insistent upon the observance of his rights as an employe. In the North we have the same condition in our foreign labor, and the native laborer suffers in consequence. We have before us a case in point in the trouble at the Atlantic Cotton Mills, in which an attempt was made to substitute white with colored labor. The attempt is supposed to have partly failed, although there is every evidence to prove that the owners of the mill are quietly working to "Africanize" the plant. As it is, the conditions in the mill are now worse than those in the penal camps of the state, and the whole result has been caused by the readiness of the negroes to take the place of the whites at less wages. And now, the white laborer is afraid of the attacks of the colored people, who feel that they have been frozen out of employment, and, altogether, the condition is of a "reign of terror order" that does not promise well for the conditions of employment, or the morals of employes in the future. As it is, the negro controls the situation, and it furnishes an object lesson, in this instance at least, to prove that unless the negro is raised, the white man will have to come down.

Railroad Trainmen's Journal (September, 1899): 880.

Serious mistake

Secretary Riley Complains of Treatment of Colored Miners

Jellico, Tenn., Feb. 27, 1892.

I thought I would write these few lines to let the many readers of your valuable paper see and know the way the colored miners are treated in this part of the country.

Before I left here to go to the Columbus convention I was called to Newcomb, Tenn., to see after some trouble there. When I got to Newcomb I found that a colored checkweighman had been elected and the white miners at that mine declared that no negro should weigh their coal. They made several excuses, such as that the man was not competent, the next excuse was that he kicked against the former checkweighman, the third was that he was not legally elected. After hearing their excuses I offered to take the colored man off that had been elected, if they would agree to support a colored man that was competent and had not kicked against the former checkweighman. Then the Master Workman of that place told me in plain words that the body of white miners had agreed to not support a colored man. After he openly told [of] the determination of the whites, the colored miners said that the white miners had promised to divide the checkweighman's office with them, the whites had promised if there was one half colored they should have the place half of the time, if there was one third they should have it one third of the time, etc., but instead of standing to their promise the whites have filled the office for more than five years, and yet they declare that the negro shall not weigh their coal. At Altamont, Laurel Co., Ky., the company put a colored man in the mine acting as assistant bank boss and the whites declare that they won't work under any negro and the drivers won't pull the coal that is dug under a negro boss. And now I would like to know how under heaven do the white miners expect for the colored people to ever feel free and welcome in the order of Knights of Labor or United Mine Workers of America, when their so-called brothers don't want them to get not one step higher than the pick and shovel. And yet, whenever there is anything in the way of trouble expected, or when anything is wanting in the way of finance these very same men will come up to the colored man and say, "Brother J. we must all stick together, for we are all miners, and your interest is mine and mine is yours; we must band together." This talk you see reminds one of the story of the spider and the fly, the majority of the white miners only need a colored brother in time of trouble.

And how can you ever expect the colored people of the South to become an organized body as long as such work is carried on, which is an open violation of the laws of the order. And yet this matter is given little or no attention. When this subject was brought up by me in the convention at Columbus, that the officers should see that this color line law was fully carried out, that any place or places that made any difference in persons because of their color, and that their character should be taken away from them, they tabled the question and left it so. Now, I think something should be done about this matter. The colored people need to be organized in the South. But how can this be done by the people whom they regard as their enemies? I cannot tell. I hope some steps will be taken at once to right these matters.

Wm. R. Riley,
Sec.-Treas., Dist. 19.
United Mine Workers' Journal, March 3, 1892.

The race problem

RENDVILLE, O., Nov. 4 – As I have been an instrument in placing the United Mine Workers' Journal in the hands of several of my race who have never read a labor paper before, I feel it my duty to write a few lines on a subject that is much talked of every day in this part of the state. That subject is, prejudice on account of color. Mr. Editor, prejudice on account of color is not a natural sentiment. There is a natural prejudice among the civilized nations to certain conditions in life incident to a state of barbarism; there is a natural prejudice to those who are given to immorality and the laws of nature; there is a natural prejudice to those who commit murder and arson; to those who lie and steal; but there is not a natural prejudice to a man simply because he is black, brown or yellow. The influence of a man's complexion is not greater than that of his moral and intellectual culture. Virtue is the highest influence that moves the heart of man, and though it may be clothed in ebony or Parian marble it will command love, honor, obedience and respect in every quarter of the civilized world. Prejudice to an individual of the Negro race can thus be easily removed, but the removal of the prejudice attached to the entire race incident to a state of slavery is a labor of centuries. The problem thereby becomes one for every individual to solve for himself, and thus solving it for himself, he solves it for his race. National progress is the same as individual progress.

There are some writers notably Hamilton Smith, Nott and Gliddon, who deprecate the amalgamation of the races from a pathological point of view, claiming that it tends to lower the vitality and intellectual vigor of the offspring. The assertion has been denied by equally as illustrious writers and will hardly be subscribed to by any Negro American who had made a careful observation of the subject.

There should be no desire to keep up race distinction in this country or in the organization of labor when all have a common interest in it. No benefit can come to the Afro-American by withholding himself apart from white people, a distinctive negro community, a distinctive negro civilization, and social orders, such as churches, beneficial associations, schools, colleges and business enterprises. These are not only not desirable, but indeed are reprehensible, for they create class distinction and foster the race prejudice of which we desire to free ourselves.

This principle is recognized by all other people emigrating to this country. The Frenchman with his high sense of pride soon loses his identity and is absorbed in American homogenity; likewise the German, the Irishman and the Italian; even the Jew, with all his religious instincts, is relaxing his hitherto inflexible exclusiveness and embracing the Americanisms. The Anglo-Saxon civilization, notwithstanding the one black spot on its escutcheon, which has impressed itself upon the heart of the negro as a hot burning brand, must, by its grandeur and its majesty, command our highest admiration. We desire to live, act and move with such a civilization and to say to its people, as Ruth said unto Naomi, "entreat me not to leave thee, or return from following after thee, for whither thou goest I will go, and where thou lodgest, I will lodge. Thy people shall be my people, and they God my God. Where thou diest will I die and there will I be buried. The Lord do so to me and more also if aught, but death part thee and me."

Success to the UNITED MINE WORKERS' JOURNAL

W.E. Clark

United Mine Workers' Journal, November 9, 1893.

3.3 Strike-breaking

Northern workers opposed the recruitment by employers of Southern black labour for purposes of strike-breaking, and also as calculated to reduce prevailing wages rates.

The Southern negro

As a part of the policy adopted by capitalists to depress their wage expense, and thereby increase their profits, negro slaves were first imported. Since the emancipation of the vast army of negro slaves, these slaves have become a part of what Hume called "mixed labor". These millions of negroes, taken with the millions of laborers from Europe and Asia – and the millions of Coolies, Spaniards, Hawaiians, Filipinos, Tagalos, Malays, and numerous other tribes recently annexed, provide a harvest of "mixed labor" for American capitalists. We will write of each in their turn, but now of the Southern negro.

It is probable that the census of 1900 will show nearly eight million negroes in the Southern States. There is no quarrel between the white workingman and his horde of ignorant servile labor. The negro is there not by his own choosing. He is there to stay; a curse visited upon the white workingmen of the South and the North, by the sins of their fathers.

Northern capitalists, within recent years, have begun to realize the profits that can be reaped from Southern negro labor. The Civil War left but few Southern capitalists, and because of the sectional and political prejudices which came as an aftermath of the war, but few Northern capitalists ventured into the negro country. But conditions have changed; sectional prejudice is fast disappearing, and Northern capitalists are rapidly availing themselves of what is said to be the most profitable labor in the world, the Southern negro labor.

It is said that we have the Southern negro with us and we must make the best of it. Too true! But how shall we make the best of it? The ex-slaves of the South and their progeny, are of the same disposition, the same ambitions and hopes, and the same blood as that of their forefathers. While in cities more or less enlightenment has broken in upon their intellects, the vast majority are practically what they were at the time of their emancipation. This is no fault of theirs; there is no war to be made upon them; they are not responsible for their presence in this country, but the white workingman will learn to curse the day, and the men connected with their coming!

One of the leading commercial publications, in America, is *The Tradesman,* of Chattanooga, Tenn., and one of the most interesting numbers of that journal ever published, is the January, 1900, issue. The book is largely devoted to a symposium on the South and its future. Articles are contributed by the representative men south of the Ohio and east of the Mississippi. Ex-Governor Northern, of Georgia, says of the relation between colored labor and capital:

By those who do not know, it is urged that the presence of the negro in the South will greatly hinder industrial development. This result does not necessarily follow. On the contrary, the negro is one of the South's best undeveloped resources. He is, by far, better adapted to outdoor conditions at the South than any labor now accessible to us. Properly trained, as is now the policy of the wisest of his leaders, the negro will be well fitted, technically, for all the demands necessary to meet industrial development along the lines upon which his services may be required.

The average negro is loyal and tractable. He will grow to be easily managed, as the years advance; and he will be found to endure hard labor at the South much more satisfactorily than the foreign element generally used in this way. His furnishings are very much less expensive, and his hire, therefore, requires that much less outlay. Under the system of training now commended and generally pursued for the betterment of the negro, he will grow in a degree commensurate with the South's development, and he will become, more and more, a factor for the South's successful progress. We must handle him as the negro of the future, and not as the negro of reconstruction antipathies and antagonisms.

Whilst the negro is not beyond criticism in some particulars, we cannot afford to displace him, with nothing better in sight than the prospects for supply now open.

The constantly disturbed social conditions of the North and West are unknown at the South. Because of the character of our labor, the South is practically, and in some sections absolutely, a stranger to riots, strikes and ugly uprisings among the people, in the arraignment of classes or conditions. Such business prosperity will be easily maintained if we adhere to our present relations.

In a few years, in my candid judgment, the negro will not only be worth far more, because of his better adaptation, on our farms, but he will be found working intelligently along all lines of industrial development and growth among our people. If we care for the negro properly and train him intelligently for his own profit and our usefulness, he will become a developed resource and a valuable factor in the betterment that awaits us in the future.

The Secretary of the Chamber of Commerce of Huntsville, Ala., contributes an article entitled "The South; Its Opportunities and Necessities," in which he says:

There is one prime and all-important movement needed at this time to put the South in the place where Dame Nature so clearly intended she could occupy, and that is, the creation of a stronger and more general public sentiment in this section favorable to industrial interests and industrial progress. That sentiment should establish as its first work, through proper legislation, the correct relation between labor and capital, and not leave it to the possibility of disturbance at the hands of labor agitators on the one side or political demagogues on the other.

In view of the evils that have afflicted industrial centers in the North from these sources, the South should now take this matter in hand while she can, and make it a crime to inaugurate a strike that in any way affected the general public. It is about time in the career of our common country when the rights of the public should be considered at all times, rather than see them ruthlessly trodden under foot at the behest of labor unions, as is the case in every strike of a general nature. It is the worse stain on the pages of our boasted civilization that public rights can be ignored to make way for the supposed rights of labor, under the command of disgruntled individuals. The South was whipped into giving freedom to the negro, now let her set an example to the world of not only maintaining that freedom, by giving the negro the right to work for whom he pleases and for what he pleases; not only this, but guarantee the same right to every white person within her borders.

Labor outlook for colored men

Seldom does an ill wind blow upon this nation without conveying some good to the Negro. The industrial agitations and upheavals that have not quite subsided seem to forcibly illustrate this fact in point of tendency and indications, to say the least. What the outcome may disclose is not quite so certain, but at present, Negro labor which has hitherto been at a discount, if not generally ignored as an industrial factor, has clothed itself with a prestige and promise which none but the unobservant need gainsay or deny.

At the centre of the great Western strike we have already shown to what extent the colored workman has been invited to enter new industrial avenues. Positions which he has never been able to reach in the line of promotion or competency, has been thrown open to him by considerate railroad companies. In the State of Illinois, mining corporations have agreed to employ him as never before. So encouraging is the premium placed upon his industrial worth and trustworthiness even as a skilled laborer, that numbers of his race are now being trained by a railroad enterprise in Texas, to whom permanent employment has been guaranteed in the event of dissaffection or uprising on the part of the white labor forces now mastering that situation.

The duty of the colored workman under the circumstances and in the light of the logic of the situation is sufficiently clear and incumbent. He must acquire competency as a workman and skillfulness as a laborer. As a skilled laborer he will sooner be in greater demand than ever before. As a reliable factor attention will be taken from foreigners and turned to him. He must become the subject of systematic management. He must become organized, not to control labor but to control himself. Self-protection and self-direction can never be his, as long as he remains outside of methodic and organized government. As he operates so successfully as a religious power in virtue of self-governing institutions, he will serve himself best as an industrial force by standing together with his kind in a judicious manner.

Let the leaders of the race enjoin upon their followers the duty of biding their time with patience and fitness. Let them be shown the folly and danger of co-operating with labor malcontents in their fight against capital. As the balance wheel of industrial power in this country there is an encouraging future for the colored man, if he be cautious and politic in his approach thereto.

The Christian Recorder, July 19, 1894.

The Spring Valley Riot

The Philadelphia *Telegraph* says:

The rioting, the attacks on person and property at Spring Valley, Ill., should not be considered too seriously by anyone who believes that our immigration laws are so nearly perfect as to need no revision, radical or otherwise. The outrages inflicted upon the negro miners of Spring Valley are some of the natural outgrowths of these laws, which the Congress of the United States finds so nearly perfect as to render any material alteration of them undesirable. The colored American citizens were formally notified by the non-English-speaking mob that if they, their women and children, did not leave Spring Valley within the limits of a single day "they would be shot down in their tracks," all of them, without discrimination as to age or sex. Prior to the holding of this meeting, at which it was resolved by 2,000 Italians to issue the notice of expulsion, a number of the negro miners had been shot or clubbed down in their tracks by these non-English-speaking foreigners. Of course they did as they were warned to do, and when later 500 American miners adopted a resolution that they should return and be permitted to work unmolested by others, the Italians again declared that they should not be allowed so to do.

The outrages perpetrated upon the colored workingmen, their women and children, the practical confiscation of their property, the denial of every one of their rights of citizenship, and the terrorism exerted to banish them, were not the acts of the American white miners; they were the acts of the Italian miners, of those ignorant, vicious, morally degraded immigrants from Italy to whom this country has thrown open its generous doors in welcome, and after a brief period, before they can speak the language of the country, to the highest privileges of citizenship – namely, the suffrage. Not only these scum of Italy are voters at Spring Valley, but one of their number is Mayor of the city, and he has been again and again, by the most reliable authorities charged with sympathizing with his murderous countrymen in their assaults upon the persons and property of the colored miners. This affair would serve as a convincing object-lesson to any body of men who cared to learn the truth, but from the manner Congress has so long faltered with the demand for a revision of the Immigration laws, it is obvious that body does not want to learn anything on the subject.

The Detroit *Tribune* says:

It is not a labor strike, but a race riot. These Italians, who are still so un-American that they require to have the mayor's address interpreted to them, have taken it upon themselves to say that no colored man, born upon the soil, shall work or even live in that community. We are told in the dispatches that "The foreign element, which dominates the situation, declares that no man, black or white, shall return to work until the coal company agrees to discharge every colored man in its employ, and also to hire no new men of either race; that all idle men" – whom they approve – "in Spring Valley shall be given employment." This is their modest demand. What country is this, anyway? Can this be America, "the land of the free and the home of the brave?" Is it possible that there is law in Illinois, and peace officers, and a militia, and a governor? Aye! there's the rub! Illinois has a governor, but someway the impression has gone out, since he pardoned the Haymarket anarchists, that his sympathies are not strong for law and order.

The Memphis *Commercial Appeal* says:

So they are learning something of the nature of the negro up in Illinois now. It is well. When they become thoroughly acquainted with him they will know that it is his disposition not to stay in his place, but to take an inch if allowed an ell. They will also come to the conclusion that he knows how to misrepresent the situation – an accomplishment he has probably learned from overzealous coon-bussers north of Mason and Dixon's line. He is putting up the plea of persecution now in the Spring Valley affair, when his side was really the aggressor.

The Chicago *Dispatch* says:

Nothing in the Spring Valley situation warrants the assumption that war is being waged against the negro race. The negro miners at that point belong to the "tough" classes, and they unfortunately have become embroiled with equally "tough" aliens in a riotous outbreak. A handful of lawless negroes are quarreling with a handful of lawless Italians. But there is no discrimination against the colored man and brother here.

The Jacksonville *Times-Union* says:

This is the most disgraceful piece of business that ever soiled the records of a State. It is not a mere case of mob violence. It is the indorsement of mob violence and the protection of mobs by the authorities of the town, county, and State.

Public Opinion (Chicago), August 15, 1895.

Another stab

The following is what John Mitchell, president of the United Mine Workers of America, says concerning the employment of colored labor in the mine:

> "Colored labor has been and is being used for the purpose of reducing wages of workingmen. They are imported from the South to the northern states and frequently are kept working under guards. To prevent this, laws should be enacted, making it a criminal offense for employers to induce laborers to leave their homes under misapprehensions. Colored laborers are used to work in the mines of Illinois more than in any other industry there."

Coming from such a source, these statements and recommendations are no doubt designed and certainly calculated to arouse opposition to colored labor in the mines of the North. It is another instance of the employment of specious forms to mislead the people and grossly misrepresent the colored laborer. There is no truth whatever in the statement that the underlying motive on the part of the mine owners is to reduce wages. The reduction may follow as a result of the law of supply and demand, as where the supply of colored labor is greatly in excess of the demand and where organization has not been effected by which the fluctuation of wages may be prevented or regulated. But that this is the controlling motive of the employer is not true. The fact is that colored labor in the mines is becoming more desirable on account of the absence of colored labor agitators, walking delegates, mischievous demagogues and manplots, whose pleasure and pride it seems to be, to foment discord, encourage idleness, develop insubordination and array labor against capital. The colored miner is satisfied to take what he actually earns, because it is more than he can get in the South where colored labor is poorly paid and because it is but fair. Moreover he is no intruder, he does not seek to dislodge other classes of miners. He accepts the opportunities of labor at fair wages only after they have been ignored or lost by the whites who insist upon unreasonable demands. On more than one occasion his timely assistance in the mines has prevented a coal famine and thus insured moderate prices and home comfort to the masses. Nor are the wages the colored miner receive much less if any, than were received by the whites. The difference is so inconsiderable as not only to justify them in accepting the wages, but constitutes no reason for strikes. When a mine owner has colored labor, whether paid scheduled wages or somewhat less, he is satisfied that the output will be fair and the demands reasonable. The opposition to enact a law to prevent colored people from seeking or accepting labor wheresoever they see fit, is another indication of the spirit of ostracism and injustice on the part of white labor organizations. These labor organizations while professing to be advocating the cause of labor and ameliorating conditions, are seeking to restrict the labor rights of the colored people by a prostitution of the legislative power to the worst forms of prejudice, tyranny and injustice. They would have the law deny to the colored people the right of free locomotion and circumscribe his opportunities for self support. The proposition in itself is enough to show that labor organizations are more grinding and unreasonable than the power of monopoly which they are constantly opposing. It is needless to state that the Congress will be too just to pass so unjust and unconstitutional a measure; but the attempt to secure it indicates the unfriendly spirit of labor organizations toward colored people. Between the policy of refusing to employ colored labor in North Carolina and the proposed legislation to force it to remain there is to place the colored laborer between the upper and nether millstones. Even if it is desirable to displace the colored laborer, it is ungenerous and criminal to seek to do so through the law-making power. The colored people are denied labor by white organizations and he is justified in obtaining it under the best terms possible.

Washington Bee, April 22, 1899

Pittsburg, Kan. June 18. – The striking union coal miners appear to have temporarily stopped the importation of southern negroes by the mine operators. The hearing of the injunction cases brought by strikers to prevent the importation of miners from other States has been postponed until June 26. The miners set up that the negroes are criminals and affected with contagious disease and that their coming would be a menace to the health of the community and the good order of the public.

Booker Washington is right when he says that the negro has a better chance in the South than in any section of the Union. The South does not coddle him or deceive him like the sentimentalists of the North. It lets him work, give him employment, pays him for it, and supports public schools for his children. It says plainly and bluntly that he shall not govern, but does not prate hypocritically of his "rights and privileges" and refuse him admission to places where there is work on the ground that they "are criminals and affected with contagious diseases and that their coming would be a menace to the health of the community and the good order of the public."

Washington Bee, July 8, 1899.

Sources: Various newspapers and journals as indicated, 1890s.

3.4 Opportunities for Black Skilled Labour

In the cities of both the South and the North, the black worker was denied the opportunity of training for skilled work, and, if already skilled, acceptance as a fellow worker by the white work-force. It was claimed that black workers in the South were not only becoming de-skilled, but were also losing out to white labour in their traditional occupations in plantation agriculture.

Skilled labor

Mr Editor:-

Dear Sir:- In your last weeks issue you were kind enough to publish an article relative to the importance of skilled labor among the colored people of our city and state; and the advisability of establishing mechanics institutes in our several communities for the benefit of the colored youth. I see no reason why we should not begin at once a movement, looking forward to the establishment of such an institution in the city of Richmond. Talking about what should be done is vain, unless we act. Now is the time for action.

Can the colored people of this city erect a building suitable for the purposes aforesaid and, meet the expense necessary to the support and maintenance thereof? No man who has a growing family could reasonably object to contributing, at least, one dollar per annum to such a human cause, and all important object. By a little effort we have succeeded in building very many respectable – if not costly and splendid temples of worship. Is it not reasonable to conclude that with determination, and effort commensurate with the importance of the cause, we can succeed in achieving the desired object?

Now we must show ourselves men by sacrificing something for the future welfare of our people, or accept that inevitable alternative resulting from the law of the survival of the fittest in the race of life. Unless we take steps looking forward to the education of our people in the mechanic arts, the future will be a gloomy day for the Negro.

There is every reason to believe that the Southern whites prefer Negro skilled labor to the foreign born mechanic. The Negro is, by nature, peaceable, thoroughly American, and opposed to all revolutionary and dangerous methods in any endeavor to obtain redress for wrongs; and he is satisfied with fair wages.

The opposition to the Negro in the mechanic shops come mainly from the employers, who are, for the most part, foreign born, and, who knowing that the Southern whites have a preference for Negro labor, when efficient, see that it is to their interest to keep up a constant warfare against Negro mechanics. We will never be able to make a successful fight against such prejudice, until we have enough mechanics to take possession of a shop. I am for action along the line indicated.

W. H. Smith
May 7th, 1891, Richmond, Va.
Richmond Planet, May 30, 1891

The negro as a worker

The efficiency of the Negro as a skilled worker, as a factory operative, and as a free laborer generally, is a question of general interest, especially interesting to southern states. *The Tradesman* recently sent out to extensive employers in the south, a circular asking the following question among others;

4. "What degree of efficiency do you find in common and [sic] skilled Negro labor as compared to white labor in like work?
5. Do you intend to continue the employment of Negro labor?
6. Are your Negro laborers improving in efficiency?
7. What effect has such education as the younger generation has acquired on them as laborers?
8. Does it add or detract from a Negro's efficiency as a laborer, in your opinion, to educate him?"

The replies received indicate that the wages now paid the Negroes in the south equal, if not exceed, the average wages of white factory operatives, as shown by the census of 1880.

The Negroes, moreover, are as yet generally exempt from the curse of child labor in mine and factories. The summary of answers received by *The Tradesman* are thus given:

> "Replies were received from 106 persons residing in all the southern states, and employing 7,835 colored workers, of whom 978 are reported to be skilled laborers. The highest wages reported as paid to skilled laborers is $3 per day, the lowest $1.10, and the average wages of skilled laborers $1.75 per day. The highest wages received by unskilled laborers, as shown by these replies, are $1.50 per day, the lowest .60 cents per day, and the average $1.10 per day.
>
> The replies to the fourth question . . . are not so general as the answer to some of the others. Briefly stated, 27 employers of 1,879 colored workers see no difference as to their capacity as compared to white labor; 35 employers of 1,491 colored men prefer white labor, and 49 employers of 5,214 Negroes prefer them to white laborers in the same capacity.
>
> To the inquiry: Does it add to the Negro's efficiency to educate him? the answers are very interesting. To questions 7 and 8, concerning this topic, there were received 139 answers, most of which were quite brief. Employers, 30 in number, having 2,800 colored employees say that the amount of education which the younger Negroes have received has been of benefit to them, and that it adds to the efficiency of a Negro to educate him."

From the answers received there is left no doubt that the Negro is becoming capable of doing better work, and that where the opportunity is given him to do skilled labor, as it is in the south, he is capable of developing so as to improve it. There has been some fear on the part of a few that the Negro was not holding his own, or gaining ground in the industrial or mechanical line. However, in spite of his many drawbacks, he is steadily going forward and to one who has made his progress a study, in this line his advancement is truly marvelous. *The Tradesman's* inquiries were directed to employers in the Southern States only. In the north the wages run considerably higher. For instance, I have been investigating the wages received by Negroes in the North and their acceptance as employees and find that the highest wages paid to skilled Negro laborers in the North is $4.50, $1.50 in excess of what is paid to skilled Negro laborers in the south. The lowest wages paid to skilled colored laborers in the north, $1.75; the average $2.50 per day. For unskilled Negro labor in the north, the average wages per day $1.35; .25 cents in excess of that in the south. I also find that the skilled Negro laborer, when given a chance, is as preferable, if not more, as the whites, and that there is no difference between the efficiency of a skilled Negro laborer and a skilled white laborer.

Larph

Cincinnati Gazette, September 12, 1891

Trade exiles

A City Swarming With Idle Negro Mechanics

Birmingham, Ala., Special

Birmingham is the metropolis of Alabama and the Negroe's paradise. It is to the South what Pittsburgh is to the North, a great mining and manufacturing center, made up of a heterogeneous population. Branded as the "Magic City," its growth within the past eight years has been wonderful. It is a town of machinery, mills, furnaces and a network of railroads and electric cars. The majority of the laboring class is colored, filling such places as the proud Caucasians refuse. Like most other undertakings, the whites have a union which leaves the Negro out when it comes to building. There is little demand for skilled colored labor here. It is safe to say not less than five thousand idle men and hungry women and children wander around the streets in fruitless search for something to do. White supremacy and corrupted Democracy, the prevailing powers, often force the Negro to act the part he otherwise would not. The overplus of broken down farmers and bankrupt merchants from the rural districts, who come daily hoping to find something better, only make it worse for the inhabitants. The twenty-eight furnaces in the Birmingham district, besides rolling mills, factories and hundreds of shops. The city furnishes more attractions than work for these labor seekers. Notwithstanding the bitter opposition to "negro domination," (the interpretation the Bourbon gives to the fact that the Negro is trying to rise), some have arisen above the common level. Birmingham has five colored mail carriers, one jeweler, one undertaking establishment, one inventor, one author, one photographer, one silk grower, the only one in the State, one bank, five editors, three lawyers, two M.D.'s, one S.D., one L.L.D. and D.D.'s by the score.

The Freeman (Indianapolis), October 22, 1892.

Colored women not wanted

The front page picture of *The Freeman* last week was accompanied with an argument deploring the American disposition to close the doors of commercial and industrial employment against the youth of the race. This week we are called upon to record as shameful a story of Democratic disposition to militate against some score of worth qualified women of the race as can be found within the annals of political meanness. Since Chief Johnson of the government Bureau of Engraving and Printing at Washington, took charge of that office in July '93, not two years, there have been eighty women removed. Of this number eighteen were white and seventy colored; leaving only ten colored women remaining in the service. Of the whole number dismissed, eighteen white and seventy colored, twelve of the white women have been reinstated and but one colored woman. Another fact, all these women received their appointment through competitive civil service examination. But let the Civil Service Commission that has recently given publicity to the correspondence with the secretary of the treasury upon this matter, finish this story of small beer politics ergo Democratic narrowness and wrong, and after, kick yourself for not voting that ticket last fall if you can. Said the Commission, writing secretary Carlisle under date of Dec. 15, '94:

> "This nearly clean sweep of colored women extended also to appointments from the certifications of the Civil Service Commission from the regular eligibles. In the year ended June 30, 1894, forty-five women were passed over upon certification without selection, of whom at least ten were colored. Under Mr. Johnson's predecessor, Mr. Meredith, appointments were made in the order of grade, practically none being passed over. Under Mr. Meredith there were only eighteen dismissals out of about 158 women employed between 1888 and 1893, as compared with 88 dismissals to 543 employed in a year and a half under Mr. Johnson. At present there are only eight colored women remaining. Of the women dismissed by Mr. Johnson twelve white were reinstated and one colored."

> "The fact of this large number of discharges of colored women and of passing them over on a certification has greatly reduced the number of colored women applying for examination. During Mr. Meredith's term under President Harrison's administration, there was only one colored woman removed. No allegations have been made to the commission that the colored women were removed for any misconduct."

In stating these facts to the Secretary of the Treasury, the commission said:

> "From these facts it would appear that under the administration of the present chief of the Bureau of Engraving and Printing there has been very marked discriminating on grounds of color merely, not only in the making of appointments from the eligible register, but the dismissal of persons already in the service."

The Freeman (Indianapolis), February 23, 1895.

Spontaneous protest

In 1897 a strike against the employment of Negroes occurred in Atlanta, at the Fulton Bag and Cotton Mill. The strike was a spontaneous protest against the employment of twenty Negro women spinners who were to work along with white women. Fourteen hundred workers quit, and formed a union that afternoon. The strike lasted only a day. The employers agreed to discharge the Negroes, and the employees agreed to work overtime when necessary. When the workers returned, however, they presented an agreement to Mr. Elsas, the manager, which called for the discharge of all Negroes employed by the company except janitors and scrubbers. Mr Elsas refused to sign the agreement, stating that it involved more persons than he had verbally agreed to discharge, and adding that he did not see any reason for the discharge of the additional Negroes. Thereupon the workers went on another strike. This strike lasted only one day also, for Mr Elsas agreed to discharge all Negro employees and to discriminate against none of the strikers. He refused, however, to sign any written agreement. The strike was called off and the workers returned to their places.

Atlanta Constitution, August 5-8, 1897.

Critical position of the negro

Is the Race Losing Ground?

DARK VIEW OF THE PRESENT INDUSTRIAL STATUS OF THE NEGRO OF THE SOUTH – OPINION EXPRESSED THAT THE RACE HAS GONE BACKWARD IN CIVILIZATION AND EFFICIENCY SINCE SLAVERY – A VERY STRIKING TESTIMONY BY A SOUTHERN MAN.

To the Editor of *The Republican*:–

In an editorial article in *The Republican* of November 20 in criticising the study of "The Negro in Africa and America," by James Alexander Tillinghast, you accuse him of "inherited bias against the free blacks," and ask the question:-

"Taking southern agriculture as a whole how was it possible for its farm values to increase in greater percentage in the top decades mentioned (1880-1900) than the farm values of the whole country, if the negro labor, upon which southern agriculture largely depends, was all that time degenerating in quality? Obviously, there is a conflict between Mr Tillinghast's conclusion and the broad fact of the southern uplift in agricultural wealth."

There is no conflict between Mr Tillinghast's contentions and the fact of Southern prosperity and development. These are due to the white man, not to the negro, to the immigration of white men from the West and to the uplifting of the poor white of the South, whose progress during these two decades has been as rapid as the decay of the negro as a laborer and a producer. These statements of Mr. Tillinghast are substantiated by the census and every other statistical report published which lets in any light on the subject, and they cannot be brushed away by the general and vague statement of a North Carolina banker as you suggest.

You very properly take agriculture as the industrial field in which the negro makes the best showing, for he has been an agriculturist for generations. The cotton industry is based on negro (slave) labor. The negro was believed to be the best cotton laborer in days of slavery, and the planters even pretended to find that his hand was better made to pick cotton than that of any other race. Originally the entire cotton crop was raised by negro labor; and, at the depth of slavery, certainly nine-tenths of it was raised and picked by the negroes. If, however, you return to the census of 1900, statistics of agriculture, volume II, you will find that the two counties producing the largest amount of cotton in the South, over 80,000 bales each, are Ellis and Williamson counties in Texas. The negro constitutes only one-tenth of their population, and produces less than one-tenth of their cotton. Of the 19 southern counties producing over 50,000 bales of cotton each, 17 are overwhelmingly white, nearly all the cotton in them being raised by white labor, and only two are black – Washington county, Miss., and Orangeburg county, S.C. A comparison with former censuses will show that the cotton production is drifting away from the black belt to the white counties in nearly every southern state. Thus, in North Carolina the big cotton counties are white. Louisiana, the center of cotton production has shifted from the rich alluvial lands of the Tensas Basin where the cotton is raised by negro labor, to the central district, where the population is mainly white . . . .

Such is the negro in the field of agriculture, where he appears to the greatest advantage. In manufactures no one claims anything for him; in the mechanical trades he is losing ground steadily. In spite of the optimism that you and others feel, the industrial horizon of the negro is growing steadily narrower, and is now actually more limited than in the days of slavery. To those who look only at the surface it seems different, for they see new industrial schools established for negroes, and the old ones enlarged and better endowed. The New Orleans school board has established the higher grades in the negro public schools and will use the money for industrial education of the negro youth, which is proclaimed the panacea for all negro ills.

But when we study the trades, a very different condition of affairs is found. The negro's field of labor is each day more circumscribed. Slavery, as is well known, is not conducive to manufactures, and it was inimical to mechanical work by the whites. "Mechanic" became a word of reproach to a white man in the South of old; in addition to which he found himself placed at a great disadvantage in competing with negro and perhaps with slave labor. As a consequence, nearly all the mechanical work in the Southwest in antebellum days was done by negroes. The gas company imported white mechanics from Philadelphia, but discharged them and replaced them with negro slaves, finding that the raising of pickaninnies paid 20 per cent on the investment in addition to getting the work done cheaper. Most of the mechanical work, however, was done by the free men and women of color. They were the mechanics, the carpenters, blacksmiths, painters, tailors, dressmakers, etc., and originally the policemen and firemen of New Orleans. Their descendants have been crowded more and more out of the trades, until now, their main source of income is shop work for the clothing factories. They have retrograded immensely during the last 40 years in health, education, labor and social standing, and have drifted back almost to the condition of the plantation darkey. Those who believe that the negro is advancing have but to wander through the rear of the 2d district of New Orleans, where probably 25,000 mulattoes and quadroons, "Creole negroes," descendants of the free people of color of antebellum days, live today. He will see at once a retrogression to the African type, for these negroes, having ceased all intercourse with the whites, and marrying among the purer blacks, are growing darker. Some of them were wealthy in old days, nearly all had independent means. Scarcely any of them have anything worth mentioning today.

During this period, as compared with even the days of slavery, the negroes have lost ground industrially. They have ceased to be carpenters, painters, engineers, tailors, cigar-makers, shoemakers, except a few who work mainly among their own people. Their labor has become more and more the roughest manual work, and even in the fields they occupy they are each year more circumscribed. In only one trade have they maintained their former standing – a bricklayer's. Those who are not bricklayers and outside of domestic service are teamsters and loaders, longshoremen who unload and load vessels, or section hands on the railroads. The closing of city contract work to negroes and the division of the ship-loading business between the races has had the effect of crowding a number of negro men out of New Orleans. As a consequence there are more than three negro women to each man, the former supporting themselves by washing and domestic labor. The census figures will probably show fewer negro men at work in New Orleans than 10 years ago, although the colored population of the city has increased.

The statistics read at negro meetings of the property accumulated by negroes in the South are utterly misleading. The negroes own less property in Louisiana than they did in slavery time; the slight increase reported by the auditor is due wholly to improvements in value from greater general prosperity, and it does not keep pace with the general growth of the community or the percentage of increase among the negroes themselves. The proportion of taxpayers among the negroes is growing smaller, and so is the per capita wealth; and if the assessors' tables be examined, it will be found that the bulk of the property with which the negroes are credited is in the hands of a few of the race, who, although called negroes, are nearly white in color, and altogether white in their duties, character and aspirations. One-fourth of all the assessed wealth marked "belonging to negroes" in New Orleans, belongs to a half a dozen persons, who would pass for white in any part of the world save the South, who secured much of this wealth through inheritance and have added to it by their energy and diligence. And yet these millions have figured before every negro convention, and in speeches of white sympathizers, as evidence of the progress the negro has made since slavery.

Mr. Tillinghast declares that slavery civilized the negro and that since the withdrawal of slavery the race has gone backward. This view is sharply substantiated in Louisiana where the deterioration of the negro is mainly due to the separation of the races, which is so marked a feature of the South today. Intermarriage between the races is prohibited in Louisiana; even miscegenation was made a crime by the last Legislature, and that influx of white blood which was at least improving the negro mentally has ceased. The separation is growing more marked every day. The law separates the races in the hotels, theaters, restaurants, on the cars, street railways and boats, even in the penitentiary and insane asylum. The trend of affairs has separated them in other respects. The negroes now occupy distinct quarters of the town. In politics, religion and social affairs they are separate. Visitors to New Orleans are always surprised at the small number of negroes they see on the streets, the reason therefore being that the negroes do not visit the white suburbs or patronize white stores. With this separation, the white control and discipline of the negro race has been lost, the negro is thrown more and more on his own resources and the civilizing work of slavery is being undone. The segregation of the negroes is better for the white man, but it has proved a most unfortunate setback for the negro.

But I do not want to wander off into discussion of the negro problem, but merely to call your attention to the fact that there is a flaw in the line of argument you pursued in criticising Mr. Tillinghast, and that because the South is improving today it does not follow that the negro is improving. If you look over the census more carefully and see in what sections of the South there has been prosperity you will see a disproval of your statement. If you do not I shall be glad to furnish it.

Norman Walker,
New Orleans, Louisiana.

The Springfield Republican, December 1, 1902.

3.5 Black Union Membership at the Turn of the 20th Century

An assessment by W. E. B. DuBois

The Knights of Labor, after a brilliant career, having probably at one time over a half a million members, began to decline owing to internal dissensions and today have perhaps 50,000 – 100,000 members. Coincident with the decline of the Knights of Labor came a larger and more successful movement – the American Federation of Labor which has now nearly a million members. This organisation was started in 1881 at a meeting of disaffected members of the Knights of Labor and others. From the beginning this movement represented the particularistic trade union idea as against the all inclusive centralizing tendencies of the Knights. And although the central administration has grown in power and influence in recent years, it is still primarily a federation of mutually independent and autonomous trade unions, among which it strives to foster co-operation and mutual peace. The declared policy of such a body on the race question is of less importance than in the case of the Knights of Labor, since it is more in the nature of advice than law to the different unions. The attitude of the Federation has summed up as follows:

> "It has always been regarded as one of the cardinal principles of the Federation that 'the working people must unite and organize, irrespective of creed, color, sex, nationality or politics.' The Federation formerly refused to admit any union which, in its written constitution excluded Negroes from membership. It was this that kept out the International Association of Machinists for several years, till it eliminated the word 'white' from its qualifications for membership. It was said at one time that the color line was the chief obstacle in an affiliation of the Brotherhood of Locomotive Firemen with the Federation. The Federation seems, however, to have modified the strictness of the rule. The Railroad Telegraphers and Trackmen have both been welcomed and both restrict their membership to whites.

"In a considerable degree the color line has been actually wiped out in the affiliated organizations. Great Unions controlled by Northern men have insisted in Southern cities on absolute social equality for their colored members. Many local unions receive whites and blacks on equal terms. Where the number of Negroes is large, however, national unions usually organize their white and their colored members into separate locals. In 1898 the Atlanta Federation of Trades declined to enter the peace jubilee parade because colored delegates were excluded.

"The convention of 1897 adopted a resolution condemning a reported statement of Booker T. Washington that the trades unions were placing obstacles in the way of the material advancement of the Negro, and reaffirming the declaration of the Federation that it welcomes to its ranks all labor without regard to creed, color, sex, race or nationality. One delegate from the South declared, however, that the white people of the South would not submit to the employment of the Negro in the mills, and that the federal labor union of which he was a member did not admit Negroes. President Gompers said that a union affiliated with the Federation had no right to debar the Negro from membership.

"With increasing experience in the effort to organize the wage earners of the South, the leaders have become convinced that for local purposes separate organizations of the colored people must be permitted. President Gompers said in his report to the convention of 1900, that here and there a local had refused to accept membership on account of color. In such cases where there were enough colored workers in one calling, an effort had been made to form a separate colored union, and a trades council composed of representatives of the colored and the white. This had generally been acquiesced in. In some parts of the South, however, a more serious difficulty had arisen. Central bodies chartered by the Federation had refused to receive delegates from local unions of Negroes. The Federation had not been able to insist that they be received, because such insistence would have meant the disruption of the central bodies. President Gompers suggested that separate central bodies composed of Negroes be established where it might seem practicable and necessary. The convention accordingly amended the constitution to permit the executive council to charter central labor unions as well as local trade and federal unions, composed exclusively of colored members."

The attitude of the American Federation of Labor may be summed up as having passed through the following stages:

1. *The working people must unite and organize irrespective of creed, color, sex, nationality or politics.*

   This was an early declaration but was not embodied in the constitution. It was reaffirmed in 1897, after opposition. Bodies confining membership to whites were barred from affiliation.

2. *Separate charters may be issued to Central Labor Unions, Local Unions or Federal Labor Unions composed exclusively of colored members.*

   This was adopted by the convention of 1902 and recognizes the legality of excluding Negroes from local unions, city central labor bodies, &c.

3. *A National Union which excludes Negroes expressly by constitutional provision may affiliate with the A.F.L.*

   No official announcement of this change of policy has been made, but the fact is well known in the case of the Railway Trackmen, Telegraphers, and others.

4. *A National Union already affiliated with the A.F.L. may amend its laws so as to exclude Negroes.*

This was done by the Stationary Engineers at their Boston convention in 1902, and an (unsuccessful?) attempt in the same line was made by the Molders at their convention the same year. The A.F.L. has taken no public action in these cases.

This is a record of struggle to maintain high and just ideals and of retrogression; the broader minded labor leaders, like Samuel Gompers, have had to contend with narrow prejudice and selfish greed; it is a struggle parallel with that of the Negro for political and civil rights, and just as black Americans in the struggle upward have met temporary defeat in their aspirations for civil and political rights so, too, they have met rebuff in their search for economic freedom. At the same time there are today probably a larger number of effective Negro members in the trade unions than ever before, there is evidence of renewed inspiration toward mechanical trades and a better comprehension of the labor movement. On the other hand the industrial trial upbuilding of the South has brought to the front a number of white mechanics, who from birth have regarded Negroes as inferiors and can with the greatest difficulty be brought to regard them as brothers in this battle for better conditions of labor. Such are the forces now arrayed in silent conflict.

If we carefully examine the various trade unions now in existence, we may roughly divide them as follows:

1. Those with a considerable Negro membership.
2. Those with few Negro members.
3. Those with no Negro members.

The first two of these classes may be divided into those who receive Negroes freely, those to whom Negroes never apply, and those who receive Negro workmen only after pressure.

Unions with a Considerable Negro Membership. These Unions are as follows:

Trade Unions	Negro Membership 1890	Negro Membership 1900	Total Membership 1901
Journeymen Barbers' International Union	200	800	8,672
International Brick, Tile and Terracotta Workers' Alliance	50	200	1,500
International Broom-makers Union			380
United Brotherhood of Carpenters and Joiners Carriage and Wagon Workers' International Union	240	500	2,025
Cigar-makers' International Union			33,954
Coopers' International Union		200	4,481
International Brotherhood of Stationary Firemen	0	2,700	3,600
International Longshoremen's Assoc.	1,500	6,000	20,000
United Mine Workers of America		20,000	224,000
Brotherhood of Painters, Decorators and Paper-hangers of America	33	169	28,000
International Seaman's Union			8,161
Tobacco Workers' International Union	1,500	1,000	6,170
Brotherhood of Operative Plasterers			7,000
Bricklayers' and Masons' Union			39,000

These unions represent the trades in which the Negro on emerging from slavery possessed the most skill, i.e., the building trades, work in tobacco, and work requiring muscle and endurance. Most of these unions deny any color-discrimination, although the secretary of the carpenters merely says, "None that I know of;" the carriage and wagon workers: "None that has been reported;" the coopers: "If any, it was many years ago;" and the painters' secretary: "I do not know." The carpenters and coopers both admit that local unions could refuse to receive Negroes, and the carpenters and plasterers are not certain that the traveling card of a Negro union man would be recognized by all local unions.

The Knights of Labor claim 6,000 Negro members at present, and 8,000 in 1890, a decrease of 25 per cent. This report came too late for insertion in the table.

To sum up we may make the following list in the order of increasing hostility toward the Negro:

Miners – Welcome Negroes in nearly all cases.
Longshoremen – Welcome Negroes in nearly all cases.
Cigar-makers – Admit practically all applicants.
Barbers – Admit many, but restrain Negroes when possible.
Seamen – Admit many, but prefer whites.
Firemen – Admit many, but prefer whites.
Toacco Workers – Admit many, but prefer whites.
Carriage and Wagon Workers – Admit some, but do not seek Negroes.
Brickmakers – Admit some, but do not seek Negroes.
Coopers – Admit some, but do not seek Negroes.
Broom-makers – Admit some, but do not seek Negroes.

Plasterers – Admit freely in South and a few in North.
Carpenters – Admit many in South, almost none in North.
Masons – Admit many in South, almost none in North.
Painters – Admit a few in South, almost none in North.

Unions with Few Negro Members: The following national unions report a few Negro members:

Trade Unions	Negro Membership	Total Membership†
Journeymen Bakers and Confectioners' International Union	"Several."	6,271
International Brotherhood of Blacksmiths	"Very few."	4,700
National Assn. of Blast Furnace Workers and Smelters of America	100 or more.	
Boot and Shoe Workers' Union	A few.	8,037
Nat'l. Union of United Brewery Workers	12.	25,000
Amalgamated Society of Carpenters and Joiners‡	A few.	2,500
Nat'l. Soc. of Coal Hoisting Engrs	4.	950
Amalgamated Society of Engineers	"Several."	1,779
Intern 'l. Union of Steam Engineers	A few – 1 local.	4,409
United Garment Workers of America	10.	15,000
Granite Cutters National Union	5.	6,500
United Hatters of America	Very few.	7,500
Int'l. Un. of Horse Shoers of U.S. and Canada	?	2,100
Hotel & Rest. Employees' Int'l. Alliance & Bartenders' Int'l League of Amer.	100.	10,962
Amal. Assn. of Iron, Steel & Tin Wkrs.	"Practically none."	8,000
Shirt, Waist & Laundry Wkrs. Int. Un	2 locals	3,066
Tube Workers' Int'l Union	"Some."	
Amal. Meat Cut. & Butcher Workmen of North America	A few.	4,500
Int'l Assn. of Allied Metal Mech	?	2,400
American Federation of Musicians	A few – 1 local	8,100
Journeymen Tailors' Union of America	10.	9,000
National All. of Theatrical Stage Emp.	10.	3,000
International Typographical Union	A few.	38,991
Watch-case Eng. Int'l Association	1.	285
Wood, Wire & Metal Lathers' Int'l Un.	25-50?	
Amal. Woodworkers' Int. Un. of America	?	14,500
Amalgamated Assn. of Street Rlwy. Emp.	10.	4,000

*Possibly the hod-carriers ought to be mentioned under this division as semi-skilled laborers. They have a predominating Negro membership in all parts of the country, but have no national association. The local bodies are usually associated with the various city central labor bodies. The teamsters have a national body and many Negro members.
†Based mainly on actual paid membership tax. Cf. Report Industrial Commission: Vol. 17.
‡Not the same as the Brotherhood of Carpenters and Joiners, but a smaller independent body allied with English unions as well as with the A.F.L.

Source: W. E. B. DuBois (ed), *The Negro Artisan*, 1902.

Booker T. Washington and Accommodation

4.1 Speech at the Atlanta Exposition, 1895

Booker T. Washington had been born into slavery in c.1858 but emerged to gain an education, notably at the Hampton Institute in Virginia to which he later returned to teach. He worked to expand the opportunities for basic education and training in craft skills for blacks in the South, gaining support from white industrialists, particularly for his new foundation at Tuskegee, Alabama in 1881. He also encouraged black entrepreneurialism through the Negro Business League. By the end of the 1890s, Washington had emerged as a significant representative of the black community with whom whites at the highest level were happy to deal.

In his address at the Atlanta Exposition of 1895, he laid out his agenda for the future progress and acceptance of blacks in white America, speaking equally to a black and a white audience in the South. Washington's emphasis on accommodation and rights to be earned by the black community reflected the reality of the ultimate failure of Reconstruction, and of the hostility and harassment to which blacks were subjected in the South. In his subsequent career and utterances, he remained an easy target for the principled and self-righteous among black spokesmen.

MR. PRESIDENT AND GENTLEMEN OF THE BOARD OF DIRECTORS AND CITIZENS

One-third of the population of the South is of the Negro race. No enterprise seeking the material, civil, or moral welfare of this section can disregard this element of our population and reach the highest success. I but convey to you, Mr. President and Directors, the sentiment of the masses of my race when I say that in no way have the value and manhood of the American Negro been more fittingly and generously recognized than by the managers of this magnificent Exposition at every stage of its progress. It is a recognition that will do more to cement the friendship of the two races than any occurrence since the dawn of our freedom.

Not only this, but the opportunity here afforded will awaken among us a new era of industrial progress. Ignorant and inexperienced, it is not strange that in the first years of our new life we began at the top instead of at the bottom; that a seat in Congress or the state legislature was more sought than real estate or industrial skill; that the political convention or stump speaking had more attractions than starting a dairy farm or truck garden.

A ship lost at sea for many days suddenly sighted a friendly vessel. From the mast of the unfortunate vessel was seen a signal, "Water, water; we die of thirst!" The answer from the friendly vessel at once came back, "Cast down your bucket where you are." A second time the signal, "Water, water; send us water!" ran up from the distressed vessel, and was answered, "Cast down your bucket where you are." And a third and fourth signal for water was answered, "Cast down your bucket where you are." The captain of the distressed vessel, at last heeding the injunction, cast down his bucket, and it came up full of fresh, sparkling water from the mouth of the Amazon River. To those of my race who depend on bettering their condition in a foreign land or who underestimate the importance of cultivating friendly relations with the Southern white man, who is their next-door neighbour, I would say: "Cast down your bucket where you are" – cast it down in making friends in every manly way of the people of all races by whom we are surrounded.

Cast it down in agriculture, mechanics, in commerce, in domestic service, and in the professions. And in this connection it is well to bear in mind that whatever other sins the South may be called to bear, when it comes to business, pure and simple, it is in the South that the Negro is given a man's chance in the commercial world, and in nothing is this Exposition more eloquent than in emphasizing this chance. Our greatest danger is that in the great leap from slavery to freedom we may overlook the fact that the masses of us are to live by the productions of our hands, and fail to keep in mind that we shall prosper in proportion as we learn to dignify and glorify common labour and put brains and skill into the common occupations of life; shall prosper in proportion as we learn to draw the line between the superficial and the substantial, the ornamental gewgaws of life and the useful. No race can prosper till it learns that there is as much dignity in tilling a field as in writing a poem. It is at the bottom of life we must begin, and not at the top. Nor should we permit our grievances to overshadow our opportunities.

To those of the white race who look to the incoming of those of foreign birth and strange tongue and habits for the prosperity of the South, were I permitted I would repeat what I say to my own race, "Cast down your bucket where you are." Cast it down among the eight millions of Negroes who habits you know, whose fidelity and love you have tested in days when to have proved treacherous meant the ruins of your firesides. Cast down your bucket among these people who have, without strikes and labour wars, tilled your fields, cleared your forests, builded your railroads and cities, and brought forth treasures from the bowels of the earth, and helped make possible this magnificent representation of the progress of the South. Casting down your bucket among my people, helping and encouraging them as you are doing on these grounds, and to education of head, hand, and heart, you will find that they will buy your surplus land, make blossom the waste places in your fields, and run your factories. While doing this, you can be sure in the future, as in the past, that you and your families will be surrounded by the most patient, faithful, law-abiding, and unresentful people that the world has seen. As we have proved our loyalty to you in the past, in nursing your children, watching by the sick-bed of your mothers and fathers, and often following them with tear-dimmed eyes to their graves, so in the future, in our humble way, we shall stand by you with a devotion that no foreigner can approach, ready to lay down our lives, if need be, in defence of yours, interlacing our industrial, commercial, civil, and religious life with yours in a way that shall make the interests of both races one. In all things that are purely social we can be as separate as the fingers, yet one as the hand in all things essential to mutual progress.

There is no defence or security for any of us except in the highest intelligence and development of all. If anywhere there are efforts tending to curtail the fullest growth of the Negro, let these efforts to be turned into stimulating, encouraging, and making him the most useful and intelligent citizen. Effort or means so invested will pay a thousand per cent interest. These efforts will be twice blessed – "blessing him that gives and him that takes." . . .

Nearly sixteen millions of hands will aid you in pulling the load upward, or they will pull against you the load downward. We shall constitute one-third and more of the ignorance and crime of the South, or one-third its intelligence and progress; we shall contribute one-third to the business and industrial prosperity of the South or we shall prove a veritable body of death, stagnating, depressing, retarding every effort to advance the body politic.

Gentlemen of the Exposition, as we present to you our humble effort at an exhibition of our progress, you must not expect overmuch. Starting thirty years ago with ownership here and there in a few quilts and pumpkins and chickens (gathered from miscellaneous sources), remember the path that has led from these to the inventions and production of agricultural implements, buggies, steam-engines, newspapers, books, statuary, carving, paintings, the management of drug-stores and banks, has not been trodden without contact with thorns and thistles. While we take pride in what we exhibit as a result of our independent efforts, we do not for a moment forget that our part in this exhibition would fall far short of your expectations but for the constant help that has come to our educational life, not only from the Southern states, but especially from Northern philanthropists, who have made their gifts a constant stream of blessing and encouragement.

The wisest among my race understand that the agitation of questions of social equality is the extremist folly, and that progress in the enjoyment of all the privileges that will come to us must be the result of severe and constant struggle rather than of artificial forcing. No race that has anything to contribute to the markets of the world is long in any degree ostracized. It is important and right that all privileges of the law be ours, but it is vastly more important that we be prepared for the exercises of these privileges. The opportunity to earn a dollar in a factory just now is worth infinitely more than the opportunity to spend a dollar in an opera-house.

In conclusion, may I repeat that nothing in thirty years has given us more hope and encouragement, and drawn us so near to you of the white race, as this opportunity offered by the Exposition; and here bending, as it were, over the altar that represents the results of the struggles of your race and mine, both starting practically empty-handed three decades ago, I pledge that in your effort to work out the great and intricate problem which God has laid at the doors of the South, you shall have at all times the patient, sympathetic help of my race; only let this be constantly in mind, that, while from representations in these buildings of the product of field, of forest, of mine, of factory, letters, and art, much good will come, yet far above and beyond material benefits will be that higher good, that, let us pray, will come, in a blotting out of sectional differences and racial animosities and suspicions, a determination to administer absolute justice, in a willing obedience among all classes to the mandates of law. This, this, coupled with our material prosperity, will bring into our beloved South a new heaven and a new earth.

Source: Booker T. Washington, *Up from Slavery*, 1901.

4.2 Citizenship for the Black Population

Washington enlarges on, and provides a rationale for, his programme for black Americans.

Some have advised that the Negro leave the South and take up his residence in the Northern States. I question whether this would leave him any better off than he is in the South, when all things are considered. It has been my privilege to study the condition of our people in nearly every part of America; and I say, without hesitation, that, with some exceptional cases, the Negro is at his best in the Southern States. While he enjoys certain privileges in the North that he does not have in the South, when it comes to the matter of securing property, enjoying business opportunities and employment, the South presents a far better opportunity than the North. Few coloured men from the South are as yet able to stand up against the severe and increasing competition that exists in the North, to say nothing of the unfriendly influence of labour organisations, which in some way prevents black men in the North, as a rule, from securing employment in skilled labour occupations. . . .

. . . As a race, they do not want to leave the South, and the Southern white people do not want them to leave. We must therefore find some basis of settlement that will be constitutional, just, manly, that will be fair to both races in the South and to the whole country. This cannot be done in a day, a year, or any short period of time. We can, it seems to me, with the present light, decide upon a reasonably safe method of solving the problem, and turn our strength and effort in that direction. In doing this, I would not have the Negro deprived of any privilege guaranteed to him by the Constitution of the United States. It is not best for the Negro that he relinquish any of his constitutional rights. It is not best for the Southern white man that he should.

In order that we may, without loss of time or effort, concentrate our forces in a wise direction, I suggest what seems to me and many others the wisest policy to be pursued. . . . But I wish first to mention some elements of danger in the present situation, which all who desire the permanent welfare of both races in the South should carefully consider.

First. – There is danger that a certain class of impatient extremists among the Negroes, who have little knowledge of the actual conditions in the South, may do the entire race injury by attempting to advise their brethren in the South to resort to armed resistance or the use of the torch, in order to secure justice. All intelligent and well-considered discussion of any important question or condemnation of any wrong, both in the North and the South, from the public platform and through the press, is to be commended and encouraged; but ill-considered, incendiary utterances from black men in the North will tend to add to the burdens of our people in the South rather than relieve them.

Second. – Another danger in the South, which should be guarded against, is that the whole white South, including the wise, conservative, law-abiding element, may find itself represented before the bar of public opinion by the mob, or lawless element, which gives expression to its feelings and tendency in a manner that advertises the South throughout the world. Too often those who have no sympathy with such disregard of law are either silent or fail to speak in a sufficiently emphatic manner to offset, in any large degree, the unfortunate reputation which the lawless have too often made for many portions of the South.

Third. – No race or people ever got upon its feet without severe and constant struggle, often in the face of the greatest discouragement. While passing through the present trying period of its history, there is danger that a large and valuable element of the Negro race may become discouraged in the effort to better its condition. Every possible influence should be exerted to prevent this.

Fourth. – There is a possibility that harm may be done to the South and to the Negro by exaggerated newspaper articles which are written near the scene or in the midst of specially aggravating occurrences. Often these reports are written by newspaper men, who give the impression that there is a race conflict throughout the South, and that all Southern white people are opposed to the Negro's progress, overlooking the fact that, while in some sections there is trouble, in most parts of the South there is, nevertheless, a very large measure of peace, good will, and mutual helpfulness. . . .

Fifth. – Under the next head I would mention that, owing to the lack of school opportunities for the Negro in the rural districts of the South, there is danger that ignorance and idleness may increase to the extent of giving the Negro race a reputation for crime, so as to retard its progress for many years. In judging the Negro in this regard, we must not be too harsh. We must remember that it has only been within the last thirty-four years that the black father and mother have had the responsibility, and consequently the experience, of training their own children. That they have not reached perfection in one generation, with the obstacles that the parents have been compelled to overcome, is not to be wondered at.

Sixth. – As a final source of danger to be guarded against, I would mention my fear that some of the white people of the South may be led to feel that the way to settle the race problem is to repress the aspirations of the Negro by legislation of a kind that confers certain legal or political privileges upon an ignorant and poor white man and withholds the same privileges from a black man in the same condition. Such legislation injures and retards the progress of both races. It is an injustice to the poor white man, because it takes from him incentive to secure education and property as prerequisites for voting. He feels that, because he is a white man, regardless of his possessions, a way will be found for him to vote. I would label all such measures, "Laws to keep the poor white man in ignorance and poverty." . . .

Such laws as have been made – as an example, in Mississippi – with the "understanding" clause hold out a temptation for the election officer to perjure and degrade himself by too often deciding that the ignorant white man does understand the Constitution when it is read to him and that the ignorant black man does not. By such a law the State not only commits a wrong against its black citizens; it injures the morals of its white citizens by conferring such a power upon any white man who may happen to be a judge of elections.

Such laws are hurtful, again, because they keep alive in the heart of the black man the feeling that the white man means to oppress him. The only safe way out is to set a high standard as a test of citizenship, and require blacks and whites alike to come up to it. When this is done, both will have a higher respect for the election laws and those who make them. I do not believe that, with his centuries of advantage over the Negro in the opportunity to acquire property and education as prerequisites for voting, the average white man in the South desires that any special law be passed to give him advantage over the Negro, who has had only a little more than thirty years in which to prepare himself for citizenship. In this relation another point of danger is that the Negro has been made to feel that it is his duty to oppose continually the Southern white man in politics, even in matters where no principle is involved, and that he is only loyal to his own race and acting in a manly way when he is opposing him. Such a policy has proved most hurtful to both races. Where it is a matter of principle, where a question of right or wrong is involved, I would advise the Negro to stand by principle at all hazards. A Southern white man has no respect for or confidence in a Negro who acts merely for policy's sake; but there are many cases – and the number is growing – where the Negro has nothing to gain and much to lose by opposing the Southern white man in many matters that relate to government. . . .

In the future, more than in the past, we want to impress upon the Negro the importance of identifying himself more closely with the interests of the South – the importance of making himself part of the South and at home in it. Heretofore, for reasons which were natural and for which no one is especially to blame, the coloured people have been too much like a foreign nation residing in the midst of another nation. . . . The bed-rock upon which every individual rests his chances of success in life is securing the friendship, the confidence, the respect, of his nextdoor neighbour of the little community in which he lives. Almost the whole problem of the Negro in the South rests itself upon the fact as to whether the Negro can make himself of such indispensable service to his neighbour and the community that no one can fill his place better in the body politic. There is at present no other safe course for the black man to pursue. If the Negro in the South has a friend in his white neighbour and a still larger number of friends in his community, he has a protection and a guarantee of his rights that will be more potent and more lasting than any our Federal Congress or any outside power can confer.

We must admit the stern fact that at present the Negro, through no choice of his own, is living among another race which is far ahead of him in education, property, experience, and favourable condition; further, that the Negro's present condition makes him dependent upon the white people for most of the things necessary to sustain life, as well as for his common school education. In all history, those who have possessed the property and intelligence have exercised the greatest control in government, regardless of colour, race or geographical location. This being the case, how can the black man in the South improve his present condition? And does the Southern white man want him to improve it?

The Negro in the South has it within his power, if he properly utilises the forces at hand, to make of himself such a valuable factor in the life of the South that he will not have to seek privileges, they will be freely conferred upon him. To bring this about, the Negro must begin at the bottom and lay a sure foundation, and not be lured by any temptation into trying to rise on a false foundation. While the Negro is laying the foundation he will need help, sympathy, and simple justice. Progress by any other method will be but temporary and superficial, and the latter end of it will be worse than the beginning. American slavery was a great curse to both races, and I would be the last to apologise for it; but, in the presence of God, I believe that slavery laid the foundation for the solution of the problem that is now before us in the South. During slavery the Negro was taught every trade, every industry, that constitutes the foundation for making a living. Now, if on this foundation – laid in rather a crude way, it is true, but a foundation, nevertheless – we can gradually build and improve, the future for us is bright. Let me be more specific. Agriculture is, or has been, the basic industry of nearly every race or nation that has succeeded. The Negro got a knowledge of this during slavery. Hence, in a large measure, he is in possession of this industry in the South to-day. The Negro can buy land in the South, as a rule, wherever the white man can buy it, and at very low prices. Now, since the bulk of our people already have a foundation in agriculture, they are at their best when living in the country, engaged in agricultural pursuits. Plainly, then, the best thing, the logical thing, is to turn the larger part of our strength in a direction that will make the Negro among the most skilled agricultural people in the world. The man who has learned to do something better than anyone else, has learned to do a common thing in an uncommon manner, is the man who has a power and influence that no adverse circumstances can take from him. The Negro who can make himself so conspicuous as a successful farmer, a large tax-payer, a wise helper of his fellow-men, as to be placed in a position of trust and honour, whether the position be political or otherwise, by natural selection, is a hundred-fold more secure in that position than one placed there by mere outside force or pressure. . . .

Let us help the Negro by every means possible to acquire such an education in farming, dairying, stock-raising, horticulture, etc., as will enable him to become a model in these respects and place him near the top in these industries, and the race problem would in a large part be settled, or at least stripped of many of its most perplexing elements. This policy would also tend to keep the Negro in the country and smaller towns, where he succeeds best, and stop the influx into the large cities, where he does not succeed so well. The race, like the individual, that produces something of superior worth that has a common human interest, makes a permanent place for itself, and is bound to be recognised.

At a county fair in the South not long ago I saw a Negro awarded the first prize by a jury of white men, over white competitors, for the production of the best specimen of Indian corn. Every white man at this fair seemed to be pleased and proud of the achievement of this Negro, because it was apparent that he had done something that would add to the wealth and comfort of the people of both races in that county. . . . While race prejudice is strongly exhibited in many directions, in the matter of business, of commercial and industrial development, there is very little obstacle in the Negro's way. A Negro who produces or has for sale something that the community wants finds customers among white people as well as black people. A Negro can borrow money at the bank with equal security as readily as a white man can. A bank in Birmingham, Alabama, that has now existed ten years, is officered and controlled wholly by Negroes. This bank has white borrowers and white depositors. A graduate of the Tuskegee Institute keeps a well-appointed grocery store in Tuskegee, and he tells me that he sells about as many goods to the one race as to the other. What I have said of the opening that awaits the Negro in the direction of agriculture is almost equally true of mechanics, manufacturing, and all the domestic arts. . . .

But it is asked, Would you confine the Negro to agriculture, mechanics, and domestic arts, etc.? Not at all, but along the lines that I have mentioned is where the stress should be laid just now and for many years to come. We will need and must have many teachers and ministers, some doctors and lawyers and statesmen; but these professional men will have a constituency or a foundation from which to draw support just in proportion as the race prospers along the economic lines that I have mentioned. During the first fifty or one hundred years of the life of any people are not the economic occupations always given the greater attention? This is not only the historic, but, I think, the common-sense view. If this generation will lay the material foundation, it will be the quickest and surest way for the succeeding generation to succeed in the cultivation of the fine arts, and to surround itself even with some of the luxuries of life, if desired. What the race now most needs, in my opinion, is a whole army of men and women well trained to lead and at the same time infuse themselves into agriculture, mechanics, domestic employment, and business. As to the mental training that these educated leaders should be equipped with, I should say, Give them all the mental training and culture that the circumstances of individuals will allow, – the more, the better. No race can permanently succeed until its mind is awakened and strengthened by the ripest thought. But I would constantly have it kept in the thoughts of those who are educated in books that a large proportion of those who are educated should be so trained in hand that they can bring this mental strength and knowledge to bear upon the physical conditions in the South which I have tried to emphasise. . . .

To state in detail just what place the black man will occupy in the South as a citizen, when he was developed in the direction named, is beyond the wisdom of any one. Much will depend upon the sense of justice which can be kept alive in the breast of the American people. Almost as much will depend upon the good sense of the Negro himself. That question, I confess, does not give me the most concern just now. The important and pressing question is, Will the Negro with his own help and that of his friends take advantage of the opportunities that now surround him? When he has done this, I believe that, speaking of his future in general terms, he will be treated with justice, will be given the protection of the law, and will be given the recognition in a large measure which his usefulness and ability warrant. If, fifty years ago, any one had predicted that the Negro would have received the recognition and honour which individuals have already received, he would have been laughed at as an idle dreamer. Time, patience, and constant achievement are great factors in the rise of a race.

I do not believe that the world ever takes a race seriously, in its desire to enter into the control of the government of a nation in any large degree, until a large number of individuals, members of that race, have demonstrated, beyond question, their ability to control and develop individual business enterprises. When a number of Negroes rise to the point where they own and operate the most successful farms, are among the largest tax-payers in their county, are moral and intelligent, I do not believe that in many portions of the South such men need long be denied the right of saying by their votes how they prefer their property to be taxed and in choosing those who are to make and administer the laws. . . . But a short time ago I read letters from nearly ever prominent white man in Birmingham, Alabama, asking that the Rev. W. R. Pettiford, a Negro, be appointed to a certain important federal office. What is the explanation of this? Mr. Pettiford for nine years has been the president of the Negro bank in Birmingham to which I have alluded. During these nine years these white citizens have had the opportunity of seeing that Mr. Pettiford could manage successfully a private business, and that he had proven himself a conservative, thoughtful citizen; and they were willing to trust him in a public office. Such individual examples will have to be multiplied until they become the rule rather than the exception. While we are multiplying these examples, the Negro must keep a strong and courageous heart. He cannot improve his condition by any short cut course or by artificial methods. Above all, he must not be deluded into the temptation of believing that his condition can be permanently improved by a mere battledore and shuttlecock of words or by any process of mere mental gymnastics or oratory alone. What is desired, along with a logical defence of his cause, are deeds, results, – multiplied results, – in the direction of building himself up, so as to leave no doubt in the minds of any one of his ability to succeed. . . .

My own feeling is that the South will gradually reach the point where it will see the wisdom and the justice of enacting an educational or property qualification, or both, for voting, that shall be made to apply honestly to both races. The industrial development of the Negro in connection with education and Christian character will help to hasten this end. When this is done, we shall have a foundation, in my opinion, upon which to build a government that is honest and that will be in a high degree satisfactory to both races. . . .

The problem is a large and serious one, and will require the patient help, sympathy, and advice of our most patriotic citizens, North and South, for years to come. But I believe that, if the principles which I have tried to indicate are followed, a solution of the question will come. So long as the Negro is permitted to get education, acquire property, and secure employment, and is treated with respect in the business or commercial world, – as is now true in the greater part of the South, – I shall have the greatest faith of his working out his own destiny in our Southern States. . . .

Source: Booker T. Washington, *The Future of the American Negro* (Boston: Small, Maynard & Co., 1899), pp. 201-244.

4.3 Industrial Education is the Solution

Washington's own description of his college and training centre for craft skills ("industrial education"), the Tuskegee Institute, which was intended to be a model for such institutions to educate black workers to compete on equal terms with white skilled labour in the South.

At Tuskegee, Alabama, starting fifteen years ago in a little shanty with one teacher and thirty students, with no property, there has grown up an industrial and educational village where the ideas that I have referred to are put into the heads, hearts, and hands of an army of colored men and women, with the purpose of having them become centers of light and civilization in every part of the South. One visiting the Tuskegee Normal and Industrial Institute today will find eight hundred and fifty students gathered from twenty-four States, with eighty-eight teachers and officers training these students in literary, religious, and industrial work.

Counting the students and the families of the instructors, the visitor will find a black village of about twelve hundred people. Instead of the old, worn-out plantation that was there fifteen years ago, there is a modern farm of seven hundred acres cultivated by student labor. There are Jersey and Holstein cows and Berkshire pigs, and the butter used is made by the most modern process.

Aside from the dozens of neat, comfortable cottages owned by individual teachers and other persons, who have settled in this village for the purpose of educating their children, he will find thirty-six buildings of various kinds and sizes, owned and built by the school, property valued at three hundred thousand dollars. Perhaps the most interesting thing in connection with these buildings is that, with the exception of three, they have been built by student labor. The friends of the school have furnished money to pay the teachers and for material.

When a building is to be erected, the teacher in charge of the mechanical and architectural drawing department gives to the class in drawing a general description of the building desired, and then there is a competition to see whose plan will be accepted. These same students in most cases help do the practical work of putting up the building – some at the sawmill, the brickyard, or in the carpentry, brickmaking, plastering, painting, and tinsmithing departments. At the same time care is taken to see not only that the building goes up properly, but that the students, who are under intelligent instructors in their special branch, are taught at the same time the principles as well as the practical part of the trade.

The school has the building in the end, and the students have the knowledge of the trade. This same principle applies, whether in the laundry, where the washing for seven or eight hundred people is done, or in the sewing-room, where a large part of the clothing for this colony is made and repaired, or in the wheelwright and blacksmith departments, where all the wagons and buggies used by the school, besides a large number for the outside public, are manufactured, or in the printing-office, where a large part of the printing for the white and colored people in this region is done. Twenty-six different industries are here in constant operation.

When the student is through with his course of training he goes out feeling that it is just as honorable to labor with the hand as with the head, and instead of his having to look for a place, the place usually seeks him, because he has to give that which the South wants. One other thing should not be overlooked in our efforts to develop the black man. As bad as slavery was, almost every large plantation in the South during that time was, in a measure, an industrial school. It had its farming department, its blacksmith, wheelwright, brickmaking, carpentry, and sewing departments. Thus at the close of the war our people were in possession of all the common and skilled labor in the South. For nearly twenty years after the war we overlooked the value of the antebellum training, and no one was trained to replace these skilled men and women who were soon to pass away; and now, as skilled laborers from foreign countries, with not only educated hands but trained brains, begin to come into the South and take these positions once held by us, we are gradually waking up to the fact that we must compete with the white man in the industrial world if we would hold our own.

Source: Booker T. Washington, *Industrial Education is the Solution*, 1896.

4.4 The Treatment of Negroes in the United States

In his later years, Washington wrote extensively on his assessment of black living conditions and treatment in the United States. He was in no doubt that blacks had more opportunities there than elsewhere, but he condemned unequivocally the unequal treatment of black citizens wherever he perceived it.

IS THE NEGRO HAVING A FAIR CHANCE?

If I were asked the simple, direct question, "Does the Negro in America have a fair chance?" it would be easy to answer simply, "No," and then refer to instances with which every one is familiar to justify this reply. Such a statement would, however, be misleading to any one who was not intimately acquainted with the actual situation. For that reason I have chosen to make my answer not less candid and direct, I hope, but a little more circumstantial.

The Negro treated better in America than elsewhere

Although I have never visited either Africa or the West Indies to see for myself the condition of the people in these countries, I have had opportunities from time to time, outside of the knowledge I have gained from books, to get some insight into actual conditions there. But I do not intend to assert or even suggest that the condition of the American Negro is satisfactory, nor that he has in all things a fair chance. Nevertheless, from all that I can learn I believe I am safe in saying that nowhere are there ten millions of black people who have greater opportunities or are making greater progress than the Negroes in America.

I know that few native Africans will agree with me in this statement. For example, we had at Tuskegee a student from the Gold Coast who came to America to study in our Bible Training School and incidentally to learn something of our methods of study and work. He did not approve at all of our course of study. There was not enough theology, and too much work to suit him. As far as he was concerned, he could not see any value in learning to work and he thought it was a pretty poor sort of country in which the people had to devote so much time to labor. "In my country," he said, "everything grows of itself. We do not have to work. We can devote all our time to the larger life."

Little immigration of Negroes

In the last ten years the official records show that 37,000 Negroes have left other countries to take residence in the United States. I can find no evidence to show that any considerable number of black people have given up residence in America.

The striking fact is, that Negroes from other countries are constantly coming into the United States, and few are going out. This seems in part to answer the question as to whether the Negro is having a fair chance in America as compared with any other country in which Negroes live in any large numbers.

By far the largest number of Negro immigrants come from the West Indies. Even Haiti, a free Negro republic, furnishes a considerable number of immigrants every year. In all my experience and observation, however, I cannot recall a single instance in which a Negro has left the United States to become a citizen of the Haitian Republic. On the other hand, not a few leaders of thought and action among the Negroes in the United States are those who have given up citizenship in the little Black Republic in order to live under the Stars and Stripes. The majority of the colored people who come from the West Indies do so because of the economic opportunities which the United States offers them. Another large group, however, comes to get education. Here at the Tuskegee Institute in Alabama we usually have not far from one hundred students from South America and the various West Indian Islands. In the matter of opportunity to secure the old-fashioned, abstract book education several of the West Indian Islands give Negroes a better chance than is afforded them in most of our Southern States, but for industrial and technical education they are compelled to come to the United States.

In the matter of political and civil rights; including protection of life and property and even-handed justice in the courts, Negroes in the West Indies have the advantage of Negroes in the United States. In the island of Jamaica, for example, there are about 15,000 white people and 600,000 black people, but of the "race problem," in regard to which there is much agitation in this country, one hears almost nothing there. Jamaica has neither mobs, race riots, lynchings, nor burnings, such as disgrace our civilization. In that country there is likewise no bitterness between white man and black man. One reason for this is that the laws are conceived and executed with exact and absolute justice, without regard to race or color.

Unequal laws the cause of racial trouble in America

Reduced to its lowest terms, the fact is that a large part of our racial troubles in the United States grow out of some attempt to pass and execute a law that will make and keep one man superior to another, whether he is intrinsically superior or not. No greater harm can be done to any group of people than to let them feel that a statutory enactment can keep them superior to anybody else. No greater injury can be done to any youth than to let him feel that because he belongs to this or that race, or because of his color, he will be advanced in life regardless of his own merits or efforts.

In what I have said I do not mean to suggest that in the West Indian Islands there is any more social intermingling between whites and blacks than there is in the United States. The trouble in most parts of the United States is that mere civil and legal privileges are confused with social intermingling. The fact that two men ride in the same railway coach does not mean in any country in the world that they are socially equal.

The facts seem to show, however, that after the West Indian Negro has carefully weighted his civil and political privileges against the economic and other advantages to be found in the United States, he decides that, all things considered, he has a better chance in the United States than at home. The Negro in Haiti votes, but votes have not made that country happy; or have not even made it free, in any true sense of the word. There is one other fact I might add to this comparison: nearly all the Negro church organizations in the United States have mission churches in the islands, as they have also in Africa.

Does the Negro in our country have a fair chance as compared with the native black man in Africa, the home of the Negro? In the midst of the preparation of this article, I met Bishop Isaiah B. Scott of the Methodist Episcopal Church, one of the strongest and most intelligent colored men that I know. Bishop Scott has spent the greater part of his life in the Southern States, but during the last seven years he has lived in Liberia and traveled extensively on the west coast of Africa, where he has come into contact with all classes of European white people. In answer to my question, Bishop Scott dictated the following sentence, which he authorized me to use:

> The fairest white man that I have met in dealing with the colored man is the American white man. He understands the colored man better because of his contact with him, and he has more respect for the colored man who has accomplished something.

Basing my conclusions largely on conversations which I have had with native Africans, with Negro missionaries, and with Negro diplomatic officials who have lived in Africa, especially on the west coast and in South Africa, I am led to the conclusion that, all things considered, the Negro in the United States has a better chance than he has in Africa.

The Negro as a dependent race

In certain directions the Negro has had greater opportunities in the States in which he served as a slave than he has had in the States in which he has been for a century or more a free man. This statement is borne out by the fact that in the South the

Negro rarely has to seek labor, but, on the other hand, labor seeks him. In all my experience in the Southern States, I have rarely seen a Negro man or woman seeking labor who did not find it. In the South the Negro has business opportunities that he does not have elsewhere. While in social matters the lines are strictly drawn, the Negro is less handicapped in business in the South than any other part of the country. He is sought after as a depositor in banks. If he wishes to borrow money, he gets it from the local bank just as quickly as the white man with the same business standing. If the Negro is in the grocery business or in the dry-goods trade, or if he operates a drug store, he gets his goods from the wholesale dealer just as readily and on as good terms as his white competitor. If the Southern white man has a dwelling-house, a storehouse, factory, school, or court-house to erect, it is natural for him to employ a colored man as builder or contractor to perform that work. What is said to be the finest school building in the city of New Orleans was erected by a colored contractor. In the North a colored man who ran a large grocery store would be looked upon as a curiosity. The Southern white man frequently buys his groceries from a Negro merchant.

Fortunately, the greater part of the colored people in the South have remained as farmers on the soil. The late census shows that eighty per cent of Southern Negroes live on the land.

There are few cases where a black man cannot buy and own a farm in the South. It is as a farmer in the Southern States that the masses of my race have economically and industrially the largest opportunity. No one stops to ask before purchasing a bale of cotton or a bushel of corn if it has been produced by a white hand or a black hand.

The Negro now owns, as near as I can estimate, 15,000 grocery and dry-goods stores, 300 drug stores, and 63 banks. Negroes pay taxes on between $600,000,000 and $700,000,000 of property of various kinds in the United States. Unless he had had a reasonably fair chance in the South, the Negro could not have gained and held this large amount of property, and would not have been able to enter in the commerce of this country to the extent that he has.

Skilled Negro labor better treated in the South than in the North

As a skilled laborer, the Negro has a better opportunity in the South than in the North. I think it will be found generally true in the South as elsewhere that wherever the Negro is strong in numbers and in skill he gets on well with the trades-unions. In these cases the unions seek to get him in, or they leave him alone, and in the latter case do not seek to control him. In the Southern States, where the race enters in large numbers in the trades, the trades-unions have not had any appreciable effect in hindering the progress of the Negro as a skilled laborer or as a worker in special industries, such as coal-mining, etc. In border cities, like St. Louis, Washington, and Baltimore, however, the Negro rarely finds work in such industries as brick-laying and carpentry. One of the saddest examples of this fact that I ever witnessed was in the City of Washington, where on the campus of Howard University, a Negro institution, a large brick building was in process of erection. Every man laying brick on this building was white, every man carrying a hod was a Negro. The white man, in this instance, was willing to erect a building in which Negroes could study Latin, but was not willing to give Negroes a chance to lay the bricks in its walls.

Let us consider for a moment the Negro in the professions in the Southern States. Aside from school teaching and preaching, into which the racial question enters in only a slight degree, there remain law and medicine. All told, there are not more than 700 colored lawyers in the Southern States, while there are perhaps more than 3000 doctors, dentists and pharmacists. With few exceptions, colored lawyers feel, as they tell me, that they do not have a fair chance before a white jury when a white lawyer is on the other side of the case. Even in communities where Negro lawyers are not discriminated against by juries, their clients feel that there is danger in intrusting cases to a colored lawyer. Mainly for these two reasons, colored lawyers are not numerous in the South; yet, in cases where lawyers combine legal practice with trading and real estate, they have in several instances been highly successful.

The difficulty of obtaining uniform treatment

Here again, however, it is difficult to generalize. People speak of the "race question" in the South, overlooking the fact that each one of the 1300 counties in the Southern States is a law unto itself. The result is that there are almost as many race problems as there are counties. The Negro may have a fair chance in one county, and have no chance at all in the adjoining county. The Hon. Josiah T. Settles, for example, has practised both criminal and civil law for thirty years in Memphis. He tells me that he meets with no discrimination on account of his color either from judges, lawyers, or juries. There are other communities, like New Orleans and Little Rock, where Negro lawyers are accorded the same fair treatment, and, I ought to add, that, almost without exception, Negro lawyers tell me they are treated fairly by white judges and white lawyers.

The professional man who is making the greatest success in the South is the Negro doctor, and I should include the pharmacists and dentists with the physicians and surgeons. Except in a few cities, white doctors are always willing to consult with Negro doctors.

The young Negro physician in the South soon finds himself with a large and paying practice, and, as a rule, he makes use of this opportunity to improve the health conditions of his race in the community. Some of the most prosperous men of my race in the South are Negro doctors. Again, the very fact that a Negro cannot buy soda-water in a white drug store makes an opportunity for the colored drug store, which often becomes a sort of social center for the colored population.

From an economic point of view, the Negro in the North, when compared with the white man, does not have a fair chance. This is the feeling not only of the colored people themselves, but of almost every one who has examined into the conditions under which colored men work. But here also one is likely to form a wrong opinion. There is, to begin with, this general difference between the North and the South, that whereas in the South there is, as I have already suggested, a job looking for every idle man, in the North, on the contrary, there are frequently two or three idle men looking for every job. In some of the large cities of the North there are organizations to secure employment for colored people. For a number of years I have kept in pretty close touch with those at the head of these organizations, and they tell me that in many cases they have been led to believe that the Negro has a harder time in finding employment than is actually true. The reason is that those who are out of employment seek these organizations. Those who have steady work, in positions which they have held for years, do not seek them.

As a matter of fact, I have been surprised to find how large a number of colored people there are in Boston, New York, Philadelphia, and Chicago who hold responsible positions in factories, stores, banks, and other places. In regard to those people one hears very little. There is a colored man, for example, in Cleveland who has been for years private secretary to a railway president. In St. Paul there is a colored man who holds a similar position; in Baltimore there is still another colored private secretary to a railway president.

The shifting of occupations

In recent years there has been a great shifting of employment between the races. A few years ago all the rough work in the mines, on the railway, and elsewhere was performed by Irish immigrants. Now this work is done by Poles, Hungarians, and Italians. In cities like New York, Chicago, and Pittsburgh one finds to-day fewer colored people employed as hotel waiters, barbers, and porters than twenty years ago. In New York, however, many colored men are employed in the streets and in the subways. In Pittsburgh thousands of colored men are employed in the iron mills. In Chicago Negroes are employed very largely in the packing-houses. Twenty years ago in these cities there were almost no colored people in these industries. In addition to the changes I have mentioned, many colored people have gone into businesses of various kinds on their own account. It should be remembered, also, that, while in some trades and in some places discrimination is made against the Negro, in other trades and in other places this discrimination works in his favor. The case in point is the Pullman-car service. I question whether any white man, however efficient, could secure a job as a Pullman-car porter.

Better opportunity for education in the North

In the North, as a rule, the Negro has the same opportunities for education as his white neighbor. When it comes to making use of this education, however, he is frequently driven to a choice between becoming an agitator, who makes his living out of the troubles of his race, or emigrating to the Southern States, where the opportunities for educated colored men are large. One of the greatest sources of bitterness and despondency among colored people in the North grows out of their inability to find a use for their education after they have obtained it. Again, they are seldom sure of just what they may or may not do. If one is a stranger in a city, he does not know in what hotel he will be permitted to stay; he is not certain what seat he may occupy in the theater, or whether he will be able to obtain a meal in a restaurant.

The uncertainty of treatment of the race in the North

The uncertainty, the constant fear and expectation of rebuff which the colored man experiences in the North, is often more humiliating and more wearing than the frank and impersonal discrimination which he meets in the South. This is all the more true because the colored youth in most of the Northern States, educated as they are in the same schools with white youths, taught by the same teachers, and inspired by the same ideals of American citizenship, are not prepared for the discrimination that meets them when they leave school.

Despite all this, it cannot be denied that the Negro has advantages in the North which are denied him in the South. They are the opportunity to vote and to take part, to some extent, in making and administering the laws by which he is governed, the opportunity to obtain an education, and, what is of still greater importance, fair and unbiased treatment in the courts, the protection of the law.

I have touched upon conditions North and South, which, whether they affect the Negro favorably or adversely, are for the most part so firmly entrenched in custom, prejudice, and human nature that they must perhaps be left to the slow changes of time. There are certain conditions in the South, however, in regard to which colored people feel perhaps more keenly because they believe if they were generally understood they would be remedied. Very frequently the Negro people suffer injury and wrong in the South because they have or believe they have no way of making their grievances known. Not only are they not represented in the legislatures, but it is sometimes hard to get a hearing even in the press. On one of my educational campaigns in the South I was accompanied by a colored newspaper man. He was an enterprising sort of chap and at every public meeting we held he would manage in some way to address the audience on the subject of his paper. On one occasion, after appealing to the colored people for some time, he turned to the white portion of the audience.

"You white folks," he said, "ought to read our colored papers to find out what colored people are doing. You ought to find out what they are doing and what they are thinking. You don't know anything about us," he added. "Don't you know a colored man can't get his name in a white paper unless he commits a crime?"

I do not know whether the colored newspaper man succeeded in getting any subscriptions by this speech or not, but there was much truth in his statement.

The greatest source of dissatisfaction to the Negro in the South

One thing that many Negroes feel keenly, although they do not say much about it to either black or white people, is the conditions of railway travel in the South.

Now and then the Negro is compelled to travel. With few exceptions, the railroads are almost the only great business concerns in the South that pursue the policy of taking just as much money from the black traveler as from the white traveler without feeling that they ought, as a matter of justice and fair play, not as a matter of social equality, to give one man for his money just as much as another man. The failure of most of the roads to do justice to the Negro when he travels is the source of more bitterness than any one other matter of which I have any knowledge.

It is strange that the wide-awake men who control the railroads in the Southern States do not see that, as a matter of dollars and cents, to say nothing of any higher consideration, they ought to encourage, not discourage, the patronage of nine millions of the black race in the South. This is a traveling population that is larger than the whole population of Canada, and yet, with here and there an exception, railway managers do not seem to see that there is any business advantage to them in giving this large portion of the population fair treatment.

What embitters the colored people in regard to railroad travel, I repeat, is not the separation, but the inadequacy of the accommodations. The colored people are given half of a baggage-car or half of a smoking-car. In most cases, the Negro portion of the car is poorly ventilated, poorly lighted, and, above all, rarely kept clean; and then, to add to the colored man's discomfort, no matter how many colored women may be in the colored end of the car, nor how clean or how well educated these colored women may be, this car is made the headquarters for the newsboy. He spreads out his papers, his magazines, his candy, and his cigars over two or three seats. White men are constantly coming into the car and almost invariably light cigars while in the colored coach, so that these women are required to ride in what is virtually a smoking-car.

On some of the roads colored men and colored women are forced to use the same toilet-room. This is not true of every Southern railway. There are some railways in the South, notably the Western Railway of Alabama, which make a special effort to see that the colored people are given every facility in the day coaches that the white people have, and the colored people show in many ways that they appreciate this consideration.

Here is an experience of R. S. Lovinggood, a colored man of Austin, Texas. I know Mr. Lovinggood well. He is neither a bitter nor a foolish man. I will venture to say that there is not a single white man in Austin, Texas, where he lives, who will say that Professor Lovinggood is anything but a conservative, sensible man.

"At one time," he said to me, in speaking of some of his traveling experiences, "I got off at a station almost starved. I begged the keeper of the restaurant to sell me a lunch in a paper and hand it out of the window. He refused, and I had to ride a hundred miles farther before I could get a sandwich.

"At another time I went to a station to purchase my ticket. I was there thirty minutes before the ticket-office was opened. When it did finally open I at once appeared at the window. While the ticket-agent served the white people at one window, I remained there beating the other until the train pulled out. I was compelled to jump aboard the train without my ticket and wire back to get my trunk expressed. Considering the temper of the people, the separate coach law may be the wisest plan for the South, but the statement that the two races have equal accommodations is all bosh. I pay the same money, but I cannot have a chair or a lavatory and rarely a through car. I must crawl out at all times of night, and in all kinds of weather, in order to catch another dirty 'Jim Crow' coach to make my connections. I do not ask for a ride with white people. I do ask for equal accommodations for the same money."

Lack of a "square deal" in education in the South

In the matter of education, the Negro in the South has not had what Colonel Roosevelt calls a "square deal." In the North, not only the Jew, the Slav, the Italian, many of whom are such recent arrivals that they have not yet become citizens and voters, even under the easy terms granted them by the naturalization laws of the Northern States, have all the advantages of education that are granted to every other portion of the population, but in several States an effort is now being made to give immigrant peoples special opportunities for education over and above those given to the average citizens. In some instances, night schools are started for their special benefit. Frequently schools which run nine months in the winter are continued throughout the summer, whenever a sufficient number of people can be induced to attend them. Sometimes, as for example, in New York State, where large numbers of men are employed in digging the Erie Canal and in excavating the Croton Aqueduct, camp schools are started where the men employed on these public works in the day may have an opportunity to learn the English language at night. In some cases a special kind of text-book, written in two or three different languages, has been prepared for use in these immigrant schools, and frequently teachers are specially employed who can teach in the native languages if necessary.

While in the North all this effort is being made to provide education for these foreign peoples, many of whom are merely sojourners in this country, and will return in a few months to their homes in Europe, it is only natural that the Negro in the South should feel that he is unfairly treated when he has, as is often true in the country districts, either no school at all, or one with a term of no more than four or five months, taught in the wreck of a log-cabin and by a teacher who is paid about half the price of a first-class convict.

This is no mere rhetorical statement. If a Negro steals or commits a murderous assault of some kind, he will be tried and imprisoned, and then if he is classed as a first-class convict, he will be rented out at the rate of $46 per month for twelve months in the year. The Negro who does not commit a crime, but prepares himself to serve the State as a first-grade teacher, will receive from the State for that service perhaps $30 per month for a period of not more than six months.

Taking the Southern States as a whole, about $10.23 per capita is spent in educating the average white boy or girl, and the sum of $2.82 per capita in educating the average black child.

Let me take as an illustration one of our Southern farming communities, where the colored population largely outnumbers the white. In Wilcox County, Alabama, there are nearly 11,000 black children and 2,000 white children of school age. Last year $3569 of the public school fund went for the education of the black children in that county, and $30,294 for the education of the white children, this notwithstanding that there are five times as many Negro children as white. In other words, there was expended for the education of each Negro child in Wilcox County thirty-three cents, and for each white child $15. In the six counties surrounding and touching Wilcox County there are 55,000 Negro children of school age. There was appropriated for their education last year from the public school fund $40,000, while for the 19,622 white children in the same counties there was appropriated from the public fund $199,000.

There are few, if any intelligent white people in the South or anywhere else who will claim that the Negro is receiving justice in these counties in the matter of the public school fund. Especially will this seem true when it is borne in mind that the Negro is the main dependence for producing the farm products which constitute the chief wealth of that part of Alabama. I say this because I know there are thousands of fair-minded and liberal white men in the South who do not know what is actually going on in their own States.

In the State of Georgia, Negroes represent forty-two per cent. of the farmers of the State, and are largely employed as farm laborers on the plantations. Notwithstanding this fact, Georgia has two agricultural colleges and eleven district agricultural high schools for whites, supported at an annual cost to the State of $140,000, while there is only one school where Negroes have a chance to study agriculture, and to the support of this the State contributes only $8000 a year. When one hears it said that the Negro farmer of Georgia is incompetent and inefficient as compared with the white farmer of Minnesota or Wisconsin, can any one say that this is fair to the Negro?

Not a few Southern white men see what is needed and are not afraid to say so. A A. Gunby of Louisiana recently said: "Every one competent to speak and honest enough to be candid knows that education benefits and improves the Negro. It makes him a better neighbor and workman, no matter what you put him at."

Every one agrees that a public library in a city tends to make better citizens, keeping people usefully employed instead of spending their time in idleness or in committing crime. It is fair, as is true of most of the large cities of the South, to take the Negro's money in the form of taxes to support a public library, and then to make no provision for the Negro using any library? I am glad to say that some of the cities, for instance, Louisville, Kentucky, and Jacksonville, Florida, have already provided library facilities for their black citizens or are preparing to do so.

One excuse that is frequently made in the South for not giving the Negro a fair share of the moneys expended for education is that the Negro is poor and does not contribute by his taxes sufficient to support the schools that now exist. True, the Negro is poor; but in the North that would be a reason for giving him more opportunities for education, not fewer, because it is recognized that one of the greatest hindrances to progress is ignorance. As far as I know, only two men have ever given thorough consideration to the question as to the amount the Negro contributes directly or indirectly toward his own education. Both of these are Southern white men. One of them is W. N. Sheats, former Superintendent of Education for the State of Florida. The other is Charles L. Coon, Superintendent of Schools at Wilson, North Carolina, and formerly connected with the Department of Education for that State.

The Negro pays more than his share to education in the South

In his annual report for 1900, Mr. Sheats made a thorough analysis of the sources of the school fund in Florida, and of the way in which it is distributed between the white and Negro schools. In referring to the figures which he obtained, he said:

> A glance at the foregoing statistics indicates that the section of the State designated as "Middle Florida" is considerably behind all the rest in all stages of educational progress. The usual plea is that this is due to the intolerable burden of Negro education, and a general discouragement and inactivity is ascribed to this cause. The following figures are given to show that the education of the Negroes of Middle Florida does not cost the white people of that section one cent. Without discussing the American principle that it is the duty of all property to educate every citizen as a means of protection to the State, and with no reference to what taxes that citizen

> may pay, it is the purpose of this paragraph to show that the backwardness of education of the white people is in no degree due to the presence of the Negro, but that the presence of the Negro has been actually contributing to the sustenance of white schools.

Mr. Sheats shows that the amount paid for Negro schools from Negro taxes or from a division of other funds to which Negroes contribute indirectly with the whites, amounted to $23,984. The actual cost of Negro schools, including their pro rata for administration expenses, was $19,476.

"If this is a fair calculation," Mr. Sheats concludes, "the schools for Negroes are not only no burden on the white citizens, but $4525 for Negro schools contributed from other sources was in some way diverted to the white schools. A further loss to the Negro schools is due to the fact that so few polls are collected from Negroes by county officials."

Mr. Coon, in an address on "Public Taxation and Negro Schools" before the 1909 Conference for Education in the South, at Atlanta, Georgia, said:

> The South is spending $32,068,851 on her public schools, both white and black, but what part of this sum is devoted to Negro public schools, which must serve at least forty per cent. of her school population? It is not possible to answer this question with absolute accuracy, but it is possible from the several State reports to find out the whole amount spent for teachers, and in all the States, except Arkansas, what was spent for white and Negro teachers separately. The aggregate amount now being spent for public teachers of both races in these eleven States is $23,856,914, or 74.4 per cent. of the whole amount expended. Of this sum not more than $3,818,705 was paid to Negro teachers, or twelve per cent. of the total expenditures.

He also brought out the fact that in Virginia, if, in addition to the direct taxes paid by Negroes, they had received their proportion of the taxes on corporate property and other special taxes, such as fertilizers, liquor, etc., there would have been expended on the Negro schools $18,077 more than was expended; that is, they would have received $507,305 instead of $489,228. In North Carolina there would have been expended $26,539 more than was expended, the Negroes receiving $429,197 instead of $402,658. In Georgia there would have been expended on the Negro schools $141,682 more than was expended.

In other words, Superintendent Coon seems to prove that Negro schools in the States referred to are not only no burden to the white taxpayers, but that the colored people do not get back all the money for their schools that they themselves pay in taxes. In each case there is a considerable amount taken from the Negroes' taxes and spent somewhere else or for other purposes.

Convict labor a great evil in the South

It would help mightily toward the higher civilization for both races if more white people would apply their religion to the Negro in their community, and ask themselves how they would like to be treated if they were in the Negro's place. For example, no white man in America would feel that he was being treated with justice if every time he had a case in court, whether civil or criminal, every member of the jury was of some other race. Yet this is true of the Negro in nearly all of the Southern States. There are few white lawyers or judges who will not admit privately that it is almost impossible for a Negro to get justice when he has a case against a white man and all the members of the jury are white. In these circumstances, when a Negro fails to receive justice, the injury to him is temporary, but the injury to the character of the white man on the jury is permanent.

In Alabama eighty-five per cent. of the convicts are Negroes. The official records show that last year Alabama had turned into its treasury $1,085,854 from the labor of its convicts. At least $900,000 of this came from Negro convicts, who were for the most part rented to the coal-mining companies in the northern part of the State. The result of this policy has been to get as many able-bodied convicts as possible into the mines, so that contractors might increase their profits. Alabama, of course, is not the only State that has yielded to the temptation to make money out of human misery. The point is, however, that while $900,000 is turned into the State treasury from Negro-convict labor, to say nothing of Negro taxes, there came out of the State treasury, to pay Negro teachers, only $357,585.

I speak of this matter as much in the interest of the white man as of the black. Whenever and wherever the white man, acting as a court officer, feels that he cannot render absolute justice because of public sentiment, that white man is not free. Injustice in the courts makes slaves of two races in the South, the white and the black.

The ballot to the intelligent Negro

No influence could ever make me desire to go back to the conditions of Reconstruction days to secure the ballot for the Negro. That was an order of things that was bad for the Negro and bad for the white man. In most Southern States it is absolutely necessary that some restriction be placed upon the use of the ballot. The actual methods by which this restriction was brought about have been widely advertised, and there is no necessity for me discussing them here. At the time these measures were passed I urged that, whatever law went upon the statute-book in regard to the use of the ballot, it should apply with absolute impartiality to both races. This policy I advocate again in justice to both white man and Negro.

Let me illustrate what I mean. In a certain county of Virginia, where the county board had charge of registering those who were to be voters, a colored man, a graduate of Harvard University, who had long been a resident of the county, a quiet, unassuming man, went before the board to register. He was refused on the ground that he was not intelligent enough to vote. Before this colored man left the room a white man came in who was so intoxicated that he could scarcely tell where he lived. This white man was registered, and by a board of intelligent white men who had taken an oath to deal justly in administering the law.

Will any one say that there is wisdom or statesmanship in such a policy as that? In my opinion it is a fatal mistake to teach the young black man and the young white man that the dominance of the white race in the South rests upon any other basis than absolute justice to the weaker man. It is a mistake to cultivate in the mind of any individual or group of individuals the feeling and belief that their happiness rests upon the misery of some one else, or that their intelligence is measured by the ignorance of some one else; or their wealth by the poverty of some one else. I do not advocate that the Negro make politics or the holding of office an important thing in his life. I do urge, in the interest of fair play for everybody, that a Negro who prepares himself in property, in intelligence, and in character to cast a ballot, and desires to do so, should have the opportunity.

In these pages I have spoken plainly regarding the South because I love the South as I love no other part of our country, and I want to see her white people equal to any white people on the globe in material wealth, in education, and in intelligence. I am certain, however, that none of these things can be secured and permanently maintained except [where] they are founded on justice.

The crime of lynching

In most parts of the United States the colored people feel that they suffer more than others as the result of the lynching habit. When he was Governor of Alabama, I heard Governor Jelks say in a public speech that he knew of five cases during his administration of innocent colored people having been lynched. If that many innocent people were known to the governor to have been lynched, it is safe to say that there were other innocent persons lynched whom the governor did not know about. What is true of Alabama in this respect is true of other States. In short, it is safe to say that a large proportion of the colored people lynched are innocent.

A lynching-bee usually has its origin in a report that some crime has been committed. The story flies from mouth to mouth. Excitement spreads. Few take the time to get the facts. A mob forms and fills itself with bad whisky. Some one is captured. In case rape is charged, the culprit is frequently taken before the person said to have been assaulted. In the excitement of the moment, it is natural that the victim should say that the first person brought before her is guilty. Then comes more excitement and more whisky. The comes the hanging, the shooting, or burning of the body.

Not a few cases have occurred where white people have blackened their faces and committed a crime, knowing that some Negro would be suspected and mobbed for it. In other cases it is known that where Negroes have committed crimes, innocent men have been lynched and the guilty ones have escaped and gone on committing more crimes.

Within the last twelve months there have been seventy-one cases of lynching, nearly all of colored people. Only seventeen were charged with the crime of rape. Perhaps they are wrong to do so, but colored people in the South do not feel that innocence offers them security against lynching. They do feel, however, that the lynching habit tends to give greater security to the criminal, white or black. When ten millions of people feel that they are not sure of being fairly tried in a court of justice, when charged with crime, is it not natural that they should feel that they have not had a fair chance?

I am aware of the fact that in what I have said in regard to the hardships of the Negro in this country I throw myself open to the criticism of doing what I have all my life condemned and everywhere sought to avoid; namely, laying over-emphasis on matters in which the Negro race in America has been badly treated, and thereby overlooking those matters in which the Negro has been better treated in America than anywhere else in the world.

Despite all any one has said or can say in regard to the injustice and unfair treatment of the people of my race at the hands of the white men in this country, I venture to say that there is no example in history of the people of one race who have had the assistance, the direction, and the sympathy of another race in all its efforts to rise to such an extent as the Negro in the United States.

Notwithstanding all the defects in our system of dealing with him, the Negro in this country owns more property, lives in better houses, is in a larger measure encouraged in business, wears better clothes, eats better food, has more school-houses and churches, more teachers and ministers, than any similar group of Negroes anywhere else in the world.

What has been accomplished in the past years, however, is merely an indication of what can be done in the future.

As white and black learn day by day to adjust, in a spirit of justice and fair play, those interests which are individual and racial, and to see and feel the importance of those fundamental interests which are common, so will both races grow and prosper. In the long run no individual and no race can succeed which sets itself at war against the common good.

November, 1912.

MY VIEW OF SEGREGATION LAWS

In all of my experience I have never yet found a case where the masses of the people of any given city were interested in the matter of the segregation of white and colored people; that is, there has been no spontaneous demand for segregation ordinances. In certain cities politicians have taken the leadership in introducing such segregation ordinances into city councils, and after making an appeal to racial prejudices have succeeded in securing a backing for ordinances which would segregate the Negro people from their white fellow citizens. After such ordinances have been introduced it is always difficult, in the present state of public opinion in the South, to have any considerable body of white people oppose them, because their attitude is likely to be misrepresented as favoring Negroes against white people. They are, in the main, afraid of the stigma, "Negro-lover."

It is probably useless to discuss the legality of segregation; that is a matter which the courts will finally pass upon. It is reasonably certain, however, that the courts in no section of the country would uphold a case where Negroes sought to segregate white citizens. This is the most convincing argument that segregation is regarded as illegal, when viewed on its merits by the whole body of our white citizens.

Personally I have little faith in the doctrine that it is necessary to segregate the whites from the blacks to prevent race mixture. The whites are the dominant race in the South, they control the courts, the industries and the government in all of the cities, counties and states except in those few communities where the Negroes, seeking some form of self-government, have established a number of experimental towns or communities.

I have never viewed except with amusement the sentiment that white people who live next to Negro populations suffer physically, mentally and morally because of their proximity to colored people. Southern white people who have been brought up in this proximity are not inferior to other white people. The President of the United States was born and reared in the South in close contact with black people. Five members of the present Cabinet were born in the South; and many of them, I am sure, had black "mammies." The Speaker of the House of Representatives is a Southern man, the chairman of leading committees in both the United States Senate and the Lower House of Congress are Southern men. Throughout the country to-day, people occupying the highest positions not only in the government but in education, industry and science, are persons born in the South in close contact with the Negro.

Attempts at legal segregation are unnecessary for the reason that the matter of residence is one which naturally settles itself. Both colored and whites are likely to select a section of the city where they will be surrounded by congenial neighbors. It is unusual to hear of a colored man attempting to live where he is surrounded by white people or where he is not welcome. Where attempts are being made to segregate the races legally, it should be noted that in the matter of business no attempt is made to keep the white man from placing his grocery store, his dry goods store, or other enterprise right in the heart of a Negro district. This is another searching test which challenges the good faith of segregationists.

It is true that the Negro opposes these attempts to restrain him from residing in certain sections of a city or community. He does this not because he wants to mix with the white man socially, but because he feels that such laws are unnecessary. The Negro objects to being segregated because it usually means that he will receive inferior accommodations in return for the taxes he pays. If the Negro is segregated, it will probably mean that the sewerage in his part of the city will be inferior; that the streets and sidewalks will be neglected, that the street lighting will be poor; that his section of the city will not be kept in order by the police and other authorities, and that the "undesirables" of other races will be placed near him, thereby making it difficult for him to rear his family in decency. It should always be kept in mind that whilst the Negro may not be directly a large taxpayer, he does pay large taxes indirectly. In the last analysis, all will agree that the man who pays house rent pays large taxes, for the price paid for the rent includes payment of the taxes on the property.

Right here in Alabama nobody is thinking or talking about land and home segregation. It is rather remarkable that in the very heart of the Black Belt where the black man is most ignorant the white people should not find him so repulsive as to set him away off to himself. If living side by side is such a menace as some people think, it does seem as if the people who have had the bulk of the race question to handle during the past fifty years would have discovered the danger and adjusted it long ago.

A segregated Negro community is a terrible temptation to many white people. Such a community invariably provides certain types of white men with hiding-places – hiding-places from the law, from decent people of their own race, from their churches and their wives and daughters. In a Negro district in a certain city in the South a house of ill-repute for white men was next door to a Negro denominational school. In another town a similar kind of house is just across the street from the Negro grammar school. In New Orleans the legalized vice section is set in the midst of the Negro section, and near the spot where stood a Negro school and a Negro church, and near the place where the Negro orphanage now operates. Now when a Negro seeks to buy a house in a reputable street he does it not only to get police protection, lights and accommodations, but to remove his children to a locality in which vice is not paraded.

In New Orleans, Atlanta, Birmingham, Memphis – indeed in nearly every large city in the South – I have been in the homes of Negroes who live in white neighborhoods, and I have yet to find any race friction; the Negro goes about his business, the white man about his. Neither the wives nor the children have the slightest trouble.

White people who argue for the segregation of the masses of black people forget the tremendous power of objective teaching. To hedge any set of people off in a corner and sally among them now and then with a lecture or a sermon is merely to add misery to degradation. But put the black man where day by day he sees how the white man keeps his lawns, his windows; how he treats his wife and children, and you will do more real helpful teaching than a whole library of lectures and sermons. Moreover, this will help the white man. If he knows that his life is to be taken as a model, that his hours, dress, manners, are all to be patterns for someone less fortunate, he will deport himself better than he would otherwise. Practically all the real moral uplift the black people have got from the whites – and this has been great indeed – has come from this observation of the white man's conduct. The South to-day is still full of the type of Negro with gentle manners. Where did he get them? From some master or mistress of the same type.

Summarizing the matter in the large, segregation is ill-advised because

1. It is unjust.
2. It invites other unjust measures.
3. It will not be productive of good, because practically every thoughtful Negro resents its injustice and doubts its sincerity. Any race adjustment based on injustice finally defeats itself. The Civil War is the best illustration of what results where it is attempted to make wrong right or seem to be right.
4. It is unnecessary.
5. It is inconsistent. The Negro is segregated from his white neighbor, but white business men are not prevented from doing business in Negro neighborhoods.
6. There has been no case of segregation of Negroes in the United States that has not widened the breach between the two races. Wherever a form of segregation exists it will be found that it has been administered in such a way as to embitter the Negro and harm more or less the moral fibre of the white man. That the Negro does not express this constant sense of wrong is no proof that he does not feel it.

It seems to me that the reasons given above, if carefully considered, should serve to prevent further passage of such segregation ordinances as have been adopted in Norfolk, Richmond, Louisville, Baltimore, and one or two cities in South Carolina.

Finally, as I have said in another place, as white and black learn daily to adjust, in a spirit of justice and fair play, those interests which are individual and racial, and to see and feel the importance of those fundamental interests which are common, so will both races grow and prosper. In the long run no individual and no race can succeed which sets itself at war against the common good; for "in the gain or loss of one race, all the rest have equal claim".

December 4, 1915.

Source: Booker T. Washington, 'Is the Negro having a Fair Chance?' *The Century Magazine*, November 1912.
Booker T. Washington, 'My View of Segregation Laws', *The New Republic*, December 1915.

W. E. B. DuBois and the NAACP

5.1 Critique of Washington's Policy

W. E. B. DuBois was a Harvard-educated historian who subsequently became Professor of Sociology at Atlanta University. He led the intellectual opposition to Washington's accommodationism and "bottom-up" model for advancing the education of the black community, offering instead an élitist "top down" model. Till the 1930s, DuBois championed the cause of black civil rights in a fully integrated United States. Growing disillusion with the prospects of white acceptance of black political and social equality led him to turn to segregation as the only way forward.

Easily the most striking thing in the history of the American Negro since 1876 is the ascendancy of Mr Booker T. Washington. It began at the time when war memories and ideals were rapidly passing; a day of astonishing commercial development was dawning; a sense of doubt and hesitation overtook the freedmen's sons, – then it was that his leading began. Mr Washington came, with a simple definite programme, at the psychological moment when the nation was a little ashamed of having bestowed so much sentiment on Negroes, and was concentrating its energies on Dollars. His programme of industrial education, conciliation of the South, and submission and silence as to civil and political rights, was not wholly original; the Free Negroes from 1830 up to war-time had striven to build industrial schools, and the American Missionary Association had from the first taught various trades; and Price[1] and others had sought a way of honorable alliance with the best of the Southerners. But Mr. Washington first indissolubly linked these things; he put enthusiasm, unlimited energy, and perfect faith into this programme, and changed it from a by-path into a veritable Way of Life. And the tale of the methods by which he did this is a fascinating study of human life.

It startled the nation to hear a Negro advocating such a programme after many decades of bitter complaint; it startled and won the applause of the South, it interested and won the admiration of the North; and after a confused murmur of protest, it silenced if it did not convert the Negroes themselves.

To gain the sympathy and cooperation of the various elements comprising the white South was Mr. Washington's first task; and this, at the time Tuskegee was founded, seemed, for a black man, well-nigh impossible. And yet ten years later it was done in the word spoken at Atlanta: "In all things purely social we can be as separate as five fingers, and yet one as the hand in all things essential to mutual progress." This "Atlanta Compromise" is by all odds the most notable thing in Mr. Washington's career. The South interpreted it in different ways: the radicals received it as a complete surrender of the demand for civil and political equality; the conservatives, as a generously conceived working basis for mutual understanding. So both approved it, and to-day its author is certainly the most distinguished Southerner since Jefferson Davis, and the one with the largest personal following.

Next to this achievement comes Mr. Washington's work in gaining place and consideration in the North. Others less shrewd and tactful had formerly essayed to sit on these two stools and had fallen between them; but as Mr. Washington knew the heart of the South from birth and training, so by singular insight he intuitively grasped the spirit of the age which was dominating the North. And so thoroughly did he learn the speech and thought of triumphant commercialism, and the ideals of material prosperity, that the picture of a lone black boy poring over a French grammar amid the weeds and dirt of a neglected home soon seemed to him the acme of absurdities. One wonders what Socrates and St. Francis of Assisi would say to this.

And yet this very singleness of vision and thorough oneness with his age is a mark of the successful man. It is as though Nature must needs make men narrow in order to give them force. So Mr. Washington's cult has gained unquestioning followers, his work has wonderfully proposed, his friends are legion and his enemies are confounded. To-day he stands as the one recognized spokesman of his ten million fellows, and one of the most notable figures in a nation of seventy millions. One hesitates, therefore, to criticise a life which, beginning with so little, has done so much. And yet the time is come when one may speak in all sincerity and utter courtesy of the mistakes and shortcomings of Mr Washington's career, as well as of his triumphs, without being thought captious or envious, and without forgetting that it is easier to do ill than well in the world.

The criticism that has hitherto met Mr. Washington has not always been of this broad character. In the south especially has he had to walk warily to avoid the harshest judgments – and naturally so, for he is dealing with the one subject of deepest sensitiveness to that section. Twice – once when at the Chicago celebration of the Spanish-American War he alluded to the color-prejudice that is "eating away the vitals of the South," and once when he dined with President Roosevelt – has the resulting Southern criticism been violent enough to threaten seriously his popularity. In the North the feeling has several times forced itself into words, that Mr. Washington's counsels of submission overlooked certain elements of true manhood, and that his educational programme was unnecessarily narrow. Usually, however, such criticism has not found open expression, although, too, the spiritual sons of the Abolitionists have not been prepared to acknowledge that the schools founded before Tuskegee, by men of broad ideals and self-sacrificing spirit, were wholly failures or worthy of ridicule. While, then, criticism has not failed to follow Mr. Washington, yet the prevailing public opinion of the land has been but too willing to deliver the solution of a wearisome problem into his hands, and say, "If that is all you and your race ask, take it."

Among his own people, however, Mr. Washington has encountered the strongest and most lasting opposition, amounting at times to bitterness, and even to-day continuing strong and insistent even though largely silenced in outward expression by the public opinion of the nation. Some of this opposition is, of course, mere envy; the disappointment of displaced demagogues and the spite of narrow minds. But aside from this, there is among educated and thoughtful colored men in all parts of the land a feeling of deep regret, sorrow, and apprehension at the wide currency and ascendancy which some of Mr. Washington's theories have gained. These same men admire his sincerity of purpose, and are willing to forgive much to honest endeavor which is doing something worth the doing. They cooperate with Mr. Washington as far as they conscientiously can; and, indeed, it is no ordinary tribute to this man's tact and power that, steering as he must between so many diverse interests and opinions, he so largely retains the respect of all.

But the hushing of the criticism of honest opponents is a dangerous thing. It leads some of the best of the critics to unfortunate silence and paralysis of effort, and others to burst into speech so passionately and intemperately as to lose listeners. Honest and earnest criticism from those whose interests are most nearly touched – criticism of writers by readers, of government by those governed, of leaders by those led, – this is the soul of democracy and the safeguard of modern society. If the best of the American Negroes receive by outer pressure a leader whom they had not recognized before, manifestly there is here a certain palpable gain. Yet there is also irreparable loss, – a loss of that peculiarly valuable education which a group receives when by search and criticism it finds and commissions its own leaders. The way in which this is done is at once the most elementary and the nicest problem of social growth. History is but the record of such group-leadership; and yet how infinitely changeful is its type and character! And of all types and kinds, what can be more instructive than the leadership of a group within a group? – that curious double movement where real progress may be negative and actual advance be relative retrogression. All this is the social student's inspiration and despair. . . .

Then came the Revolution of 1876, the suppression of the Negro votes, the changing and shifting of ideals, and the seeking of new lights in the great night. Douglass[2], in his old age, still bravely stood for the ideals of his early manhood, – ultimate assimilation *through* self-assertion, and on no other terms. For a time Price arose as a new leader, destined, it seemed, not to give up, but to re-state the old ideals in a form less repugnant to the white South. But he passed away in his prime. Then came the new leader. Nearly all the former ones had become leaders by the silent suffrage of their fellows, had sought to lead their own people alone, and were usually, save Douglass, little known outside their race. But Booker T. Washington arose as essentially the leader not of one race but of two, – a compromiser between the South, the North, and the Negro. Naturally the Negroes resented, at first bitterly, signs of compromise which surrendered their civil and political rights, even though this was to be exchanged for larger chances of economic development. The rich and dominating North, however, was not only weary of the race problem, but was investing largely in Southern enterprises, and welcomed any method of peaceful cooperation. Thus, by national opinion, the Negroes began to recognize Mr. Washington's leadership; and the voice of criticism was hushed.

Mr Washington represents in Negro thought the old attitude of adjustment and submission; but adjustment at such a peculiar time as to make his programme unique. This is an age of unusual economic development, and Mr. Washington's programme naturally takes an economic cast, becoming a gospel of Work and Money to such an extent as apparently almost completely to overshadow the higher aims of life. Moreover, this is an age when the more advanced races are coming in closer contact with the less developed races, and the race-feeling is therefore intensified; and Mr. Washington's programme practically accepts the alleged inferiority of the Negro races. Again, in our own land, the reaction from the sentiment of war time has given impetus to race-prejudice against Negroes, and Mr. Washington withdraws many of the high demands of Negroes as men and American citizens. In other periods of intensified prejudice all the Negro's tendency to self-assertion has been called forth; at this period a policy of submission is advocated. In the history of nearly all other races and peoples the doctrine preached at such crises has been that manly self-respect is worth more than lands and houses, and that a people who voluntarily surrender such respect, or cease striving for it, are not worth civilizing.

In answer to this, it has been claimed that the Negro can survive only through submission. Mr Washington distinctly asks that black people give up, at least for the present, three things, –

First, political power,
Second, insistence on civil rights,
Third, higher education of Negro youth, –

and concentrate all their energies on industrial education, the accumulation of wealth, and the conciliation of the South. This policy has been courageously and insistently advocated for over fifteen years, and has been triumphant for perhaps ten years. As a result of this tender of the palm-branch, what has been the return? In these years there have occurred:

1. The disfranchisement of the Negro.
2. The legal creation of a distinct status of civil inferiority for the Negro.
3. The steady withdrawal of aid from institutions for the higher training of the Negro.

These movements are not, to be sure, direct results of Mr. Washington's teachings; but his propaganda has, without a shadow of doubt, helped their speedier accomplishment. The question them comes: It is possible, and probable, that nine millions of men can make effective progress in economic lines if they are deprived of political rights, made a servile caste, and allowed only the most meagre chance for developing their exceptional men? If history and reason give any distinct answer to these questions, it is an emphatic *No*. And Mr Washington thus faces the triple paradox of his career:

1. He is striving nobly to make Negro artisans business men and property-owners; but it is utterly impossible, under modern competitive methods, for workingmen and property-owners to defend their rights and exist without the right of suffrage.
2. He insists on thrift and self-respect, but at the same time counsels a silent submission to civic inferiority such as is bound to sap the manhood of any race in the long run.
3. He advocates common-school and industrial training, and deprecates institutions of higher learning; but neither the Negro common-schools, nor Tuskegee itself, could remain open a day were it not for teachers trained in Negro colleges, or trained by their graduates.

This triple paradox in Mr. Washington's position is the object of criticism by two classes of colored Americans. One class is spiritually descended from Toussaint the

Saviour, through Gabriel, Vesey, and Turner,[3] and they represent the attitude of revolt and revenge; they hate the white South blindly and distrust the white race generally, and so far as they agree on definite action, think that the Negro's only hope lies in emigration beyond the borders of the United States. And yet, by the irony of fate, nothing has more effectively made this programme seem hopeless than the recent course of the United States toward weaker and darker peoples in the West Indies, Hawaii, and the Philippines, – for where in the world may we go and be safe from lying and brute force?

The other class of Negroes who cannot agree with Mr. Washington has hitherto said little aloud. They deprecate the sight of scattered counsels, of internal disagreement; and especially they dislike making their just criticism of a useful and earnest man an excuse for a general discharge of venom from small-minded opponents. Nevertheless, the questions involved are so fundamental and serious that it is difficult to see how men like the Grimkes, Kelly Miller, J. W. E. Bowen,[4] and other representatives of this group, can much longer be silent. Such men feel in conscience bound to ask of this nation three things:

1. The right to vote.
2. Civic equality.
3. The education of youth according to ability.

They acknowledge Mr. Washington's invaluable service in counselling patience and courtesy in such demands; they do not ask that ignorant black men vote when ignorant whites are debarred, or that any reasonable restrictions in the suffrage should not be applied; they know that the low social level of the mass of the race is responsible for much discrimination against it, but they also know, and the nation knows, that relentless color-prejudice is more often a cause than a result of the Negro's degradation; they seek the abatement of this relic of barbarism, and not its systematic encouragement and pampering by all agencies of social power from the Associated Press to the Church of Christ. They advocate, with Mr. Washington, a broad system of Negro common schools supplemented by thorough industrial training; but they are surprised that a man of Mr. Washington's insight cannot see that no educational system ever has rested or can rest on any other basis than that of the well-equipped college and university, and they insist that there is a demand for a few such institutions throughout the South to train the best of the Negro youth as teachers, professional men, and leaders.

This group of men honor Mr. Washington for his attitude of conciliation toward the white South; they accept the "Atlanta Compromise" in its broadest interpretation; they recognize, with him, many signs of promise, many men of high purpose and fair judgment, in this section; they know that no easy task has been laid upon a region already tottering under heavy burdens. But, nevertheless, they insist that the way to truth and right lies in straightforward honesty, not in indiscriminate flattery; in praising those of the South who do well and criticising uncompromisingly those who do ill; in taking advantage of the opportunities at hand and urging their fellows to do the same, but at the same time in remembering that only a firm adherence to their higher ideals and aspirations will ever keep those ideals within the realm of possibility.

They do not expect that the free right to vote, to enjoy civic rights, and to be educated, will come in a moment; they do not expect to see the bias and prejudices of years disappear at the blast of a trumpet; but they are absolutely certain that the way for a people to gain their reasonable rights is not by voluntarily throwing them away and insisting that they do not want them; that the way for a people to gain respect is not by continually belittling and ridiculing themselves; that, on the contrary, Negroes must insist continually, in season and out of season, that voting is necessary to modern manhood, that color discrimination is barbarism, and that black boys need education as well as white boys. . . .

It would be unjust to Mr. Washington not to acknowledge that in several instances he has opposed movements in the South which were unjust to the Negro; he sent memorials (opposing disfranchisement of Negroes only; and proposing instead the application of identical literacy and property qualifications to whites and Negroes alike) to the Louisiana and Alabama constitutional conventions, he has spoken against lynching, and in other ways has openly or silently set his influence against sinister schemes and unfortunate happenings. Notwithstanding this, it is equally true to assert that on the whole the distinct impression left by Mr. Washington's propaganda is, first, that the South is justified in its present attitude toward the Negro because of the Negro's degradation; secondly, that the prime cause of the Negro's failure to rise more quickly is his wrong education in the past; and, thirdly, that his future rise depends primarily on his own efforts. Each of these propositions is a dangerous half-truth. The supplementary truths must never be lost sight of: first, slavery and race prejudice are potent if not sufficient causes of the Negro's position; second, industrial and common-school training were necessarily slow in planting because they had to await the black teachers trained by higher institutions – it being extremely doubtful if any essentially different development was possible, and certainly a Tuskegee was unthinkable before 1880; and, third, while it is a great truth to say that the Negro must strive and strive mightily to help himself, it is equally true that unless his striving be not simply seconded, but rather aroused and encouraged, by the initiative of the richer and wiser environing group, he cannot hope for great success.

In his failure to realize and impress this last point, Mr. Washington is especially to be criticised. His doctrine has tended to make the whites, North and South, shift the burden of the Negro problem to the Negro's shoulders and stand aside as critical and rather pessimistic spectators; when in fact the burden belongs to the nation, and the hands of none of us are clean if we bend not our energies to righting these great wrongs.

The South ought to be led, by candid and honest criticism, to assert her better self and do her full duty to the race she has cruelly wronged and is still wronging. The North – her co-partner in guilt – cannot salve her conscience by plastering it with gold. We cannot settle this problem by diplomacy and suaveness, by "policy" alone. If worse come to worst, can the moral fibre of this country survive the slow throttling and murder of nine millions of men?

The black men of America have a duty to perform, a duty stern and delicate, – a forward movement to oppose a part of the work of their greatest leader. So far as Mr. Washington preaches Thrift, Patience, and Industrial Training for the masses, we must hold up his hands and strive with him, rejoicing in his honors and glorying in the strength of this Joshua called of God and of man to lead the headless host. But so far as Mr. Washington apologizes for injustice, North or South, does not rightly value the privilege and duty of voting, belittles the emasculating effects of caste distinctions, and opposes the higher training and ambition of our brighter minds, – so far as he, the South, or the Nation, does this, – we must unceasingly and firmly oppose them. By every civilized and peaceful method we must strive for the rights which the world accords to men, clinging unwaveringly to those great words which the sons of the Father would fain forget: "We hold these truths to be self-evident: That all men are created equal; that they are endowed by their Creator with certain unalienable rights; that among these are life, liberty, and the pursuit of happiness."

Notes

1. J.C. Price, founder and president of Livingstone College, Salisbury, N.C.; the first president of the Afro-American League, he was a renowned orator and conciliatory leader from about 1890 until his death in 1894 (Ed.).
2. The death of the renowned protest leader Frederick Douglass in 1895, the year of Washington's Atlanta address, has often been described as symbolizing the transition from the philosophy of protest to that of accommodation. But Douglass's leadership and point of view were in fact being eclipsed several years before his death (Ed.).
3. Gabriel Prosser, Denmark Vesey, and Nat Turner, leaders of the three most famous slave revolts in American history (Ed.).
4. Archibald Grimké, Boston lawyer, consul in Santo Domingo, 1894-1898; Francis J. Grimké, minister of the 16th Street Presbyterian Church in Washington, D.C.; Kelly Miller, professor and later dean at the college of liberal arts at Howard University, and a noted essayist on racial affairs; J. W. E. Bowen, professor and later president at Gammon Theological Seminary, Atlanta, Ga. The Grimké brothers later joined the radicals; Bowen remained a conservative; Miller, known as a "straddler," attempted to synthesize both points of view (Ed.).

Source: W. E. B. DuBois, 'Of Mr. Booker T. Washington and Others,' *The Souls of Black Folk* (Chicago: A.C. McClurg & Co., 1903), pp. 41-59.

5.2 A College-educated Elite

DuBois argues for the importance of the education of the "Talented Tenth"

The Negro race, like all races, is going to be saved by its exceptional men. The problem of education, then, among Negroes must first of all deal with the Talented Tenth; it is the problem of developing the Best of this race that they may guide the Mass away from the contamination and death of the Worst, in their own and other races. Now the training of men is a difficult and intricate task. Its technique is a matter for educational experts, but its object is for the vision of seers. If we make money the object of man-training, we shall develop money-makers but not necessarily men; if we make technical skill the object of education, we may possess artisans but not, in nature, men. Men we shall have only as we make manhood the object of the work of the schools – intelligence, broad sympathy, knowledge of the world that was and is, and of the relation of men to it – this is the curriculum of that Higher Education which must underlie true life. On this foundation we may build bread winning, skill of hand and quickness of brain, with never a fear lest the child and man mistake the means of living for the object of life.

* * *

If this be true – and who can deny it – three tasks lay before me; first to show from the past that the Talented Tenth as they have risen among American Negroes have been worthy of leadership; secondly, to show how these men may be educated and developed; and thirdly, to show their relation to the Negro problem.

* * *

From the very first it has been the educated and intelligent of the Negro people that have led and elevated the mass, and the sole obstacles that nullified and retarded their efforts were slavery and race prejudice; . . .

And so we come to the present – a day of cowardice and vacillation, of strident wide-voiced wrong and faint hearted compromise; of double-faced dallying with Truth and Right. Who are to-day guiding the work of the Negro people? The "exceptions" of course. And yet so sure as this Talented Tenth is pointed out, the blind worshippers of the Average cry out in alarm; "These are exceptions, look here at death, disease and crime – these are the happy rule." Of course they are the rule, because a silly nation made them the rule: Because for three long centuries this people lynched Negroes who dared to be brave, raped black women who dared to be virtuous, crushed dark-hued youth who dared to be ambitious, and encouraged and made to flourish servility and lewdness and apathy. But not even this was able to crush all manhood and chastity and aspiration from black folk. A saving remnant continually survives and persists, continually aspires, continually shows itself in thrift and ability and character. Exceptional it is to be sure, but this is its chiefest promise; it shows the capability of Negro blood, the promise of black men. . . . Is it fair, is it decent, is it Christian to ignore these facts of the Negro problem, to belittle such aspiration, to nullify such leadership and seek to crush these people back into the mass out of which by toil and travail, they and their fathers have raised themselves?

Can the masses of the Negro people be in any possible way more quickly raised than by the effort and example of this aristocracy of talent and character? Was there ever a nation on God's fair earth civilized from the bottom upward? Never; it is, ever was and ever will be from the top downward that culture filters. The Talented Tenth rises and pulls all that are worth the saving up to their vantage ground. This is the history of human progress; . . .

How then shall the leaders of a struggling people be trained and the hands of the risen few strengthened? There can be but one answer: The best and most capable of their youth must be schooled in the colleges and universities of the land. . . .

All men cannot go to college but some men must; every isolated group or nation must have its yeast, must have for the talented few centers of training where men are not so mystified and befuddled by the hard and necessary toil of earning a living, as to have no aims higher than their bellies, and no God greater than Gold. This is true training, and thus in the beginning were the favored sons of the freedom trained. Out of the colleges of the North came, after the blood of war, Ware, Cravath, Chase, Andrews, Bumstead and Spence* to build the foundations of knowledge and civilization in the black South. Where ought they to have begun to build? At the bottom, of course, quibbles the mole with his eyes in the earth. Aye! truly at the bottom, at the very bottom; at the bottom of knowledge, down in the very depth of knowledge there where the roots of justice strike into the lowest soil of Truth. And so they did begin; they founded colleges, and up from the colleges shot normal schools, and out from the normal schools went teachers, and around the normal teachers clustered other teachers to teach the public schools; the college trained in Greek and Latin and mathematics, 2,000 men; and these men trained full 50,000 others in morals and manners, and they in turn taught thrift and the alphabet to nine millions of men who to-day hold £300,000,000 of property. If was a miracle – the most wonderful peace-battle of the 19th century, and yet to-day men smile at it, and in fine superiority tell us that it was all a strange mistake; that a proper way to found a system of education is first to gather the children and buy them spelling books and hoes; afterward men may look about for teachers, if haply they may find them; or again they would teach men Work, but as for Life – why, what has Work to do with Life, they ask vacantly. . . .

These figures illustrate vividly the function of the college-bred Negro. He is, as he ought to be, the group leader, the man who sets the ideals of the community where he lives, directs its thoughts and heads its social movements. It need hardly be argued that the Negro people need social leadership more than most groups; that they have no traditions to fall back upon, no long established customs, no strong family ties, no well defined social classes. All these things must be slowly and painfully evolved. The preacher was, even before the war, the group leader of the Negroes, and the church their greatest social institution. Naturally this preacher was ignorant and often immoral, and the problem of replacing the older type by better educated men has been a difficult one. Both by direct work and by direct influence on other preachers, and on congregations, the college-bred preacher has an opportunity for reformatory work and moral inspiration, the value of which cannot be overestimated.

It has, however, been in the furnishing of teachers that the Negro college has found its peculiar function. Few persons realize how vast a work, how mighty a revolution has been thus accomplished. To furnish five millions and more of ignorant people with teachers of their own race and blood, in one generation, was not only a very difficult undertaking, but a very important one, in that it placed before the eyes of almost every Negro child an attainable ideal. It brought the masses of the blacks in contact with modern civilization, made black men the leaders of their communities and trainers of the new generation. In this work college-bred Negroes were first teachers, and then teachers of teachers. And here it is that the broad culture of college work has

* Presidents of Negro colleges established by northern churches (Ed.).

been of peculiar value. Knowledge of life and its wider meaning, has been the point of the Negro's deepest ignorance, and the sending out of teachers whose training has not been simply for bread winning, but also for human culture, has been of inestimable value in the training of these men. . . .

The main question, so far as the Southern Negro is concerned, is: What under the present circumstance, must a system of education do in order to raise the Negro as quickly as possible in the scale of civilization? The answer to this question seems to me clear: It must strengthen the Negro's character, increase his knowledge and teach him to earn a living. Now it goes without saying, that it is hard to do all these things simultaneously or suddenly, and that at the same time it will not do to give all the attention to one and neglect the others; we could give black boys trades, but that alone will not civilize a race of ex-slaves; we might simply increase their knowledge of the world, but this would not necessarily make them wish to use this knowledge honestly; we might seek to strengthen character and purpose, but to what end if this people have nothing to eat or to wear? . . . . If then we start out to train an ignorant and unskilled people with a heritage of bad habits, our system of training must set before itself two great aims – the one dealing with knowledge and character, the other part seeking to give the child the technical knowledge necessary for him to earn a living under the present circumstances. These objects are accomplished in part by the opening of the common schools on the one, and of the industrial schools on the other. But only in part, for there must also be trained those who are to teach these schools – men and women of knowledge and culture and technical skill who understand modern civilization, and have the training and aptitude to impart it to the children under them. There must be teachers, and teachers of teachers, and to attempt to establish any sort of a system of common and industrial school training, without *first* (and I say *first* advisedly) without *first* providing for the higher training of the very best teachers, is simply throwing your money to the winds . . . Nothing, in these latter days, has so dampened the faith of thinking Negroes in recent educational movements, as the fact that such movements have been accompanied by ridicule and denouncement and decrying of those very institutions of higher training which made the Negro public school possible, and make Negro industrial schools thinkable. . . . .

I would not deny, or for a moment seem to deny, the paramount necessity of teaching the Negro to work, and to work steadily and skillfully; or seem to depreciate in the slightest degree the important part industrial schools must play in the accomplishment of these ends, but I *do* say, and insist upon it, that it is industrialism drunk with its vision of success, to imagine that its own work can be accomplished without providing for the training of broadly cultured men and women to teach its own teachers, and to teach the teachers of the public schools.

But I have already said that human education is not simply a matter of schools; it is much more a matter of family and group life – the training of one's home, of one's daily companions, of one's social class. Now the black boy of the South moves in a black world – a world with its own leaders, its own thoughts, its own ideals. In this world he gets by far the larger part of his life training, and through the eyes of this dark world he peers into the veiled world beyond. Who guides and determines the education which he receives in his world? His teachers here are the group-leaders of the Negro people – the physicians and clergymen, the trained fathers and mothers, the influential and forceful men about him of all kinds; here it is, if at all, that all culture of the surrounding world trickles through and is handed on by the graduates of the higher schools. Can such culture training of group leaders be neglected? Can we afford to ignore it? . . . You have no choice; either you must help furnish this race from within its own ranks with thoughtful men of trained leadership, or you must suffer the evil consequences of a headless misguided rabble.

I am an earnest advocate of manual training and trade teaching for black boys, and for white boys, too. I believe that next to the founding of Negro colleges the most valuable addition to Negro education since the war, has been industrial training for black boys. Nevertheless, I insist that the object of all true education is not to make men carpenters, it is to make carpenters men; there are two means of making the carpenter a man, each equally important: the first is to give the group and community in which he works, liberally trained teachers and leaders to teach him and his family what life means; the second is to give him sufficient intelligence and technical skill to make him an efficient workman; the first object demands the Negro college and college-bred men – not a quantity of such colleges, but a few of excellent quality; not too many college-bred men, but enough to leaven the lump, to inspire the masses, to raise the Talented Tenth to leadership; the second object demands a good system of common schools, well-taught, conventionally located and properly equipped . . . .

Further than this, after being provided with group leaders of civilization, and a foundation of intelligence in the public schools, the carpenter, in order to be a man, needs technical skill. This calls for trade schools. . . .

Even at this point, however, the difficulties were not surmounted. In the first place modern industry has taken great strides since the war, and the teaching of trades is no longer a simple matter. Machinery and long processes of work have greatly changed the work of the carpenter, the ironworker and the shoemaker. A really efficient workman must be to-day an intelligent man who has had good technical training in addition to thorough common school, and perhaps even higher training. . . .

Thus, again, in the manning of trade schools and manual training schools we are thrown back upon the higher training as its source and chief support. There was a time when any aged and wornout carpenter could teach in a trade school. But not so to-day. Indeed the demand for college-bred men by a school like Tuskegee, ought to make Mr. Booker T. Washington the firmest friend of higher training. Here he has as helpers the son of a Negro senator, trained in Greek and the humanities, and graduated at Harvard; the son of a Negro congressman and lawyer, trained in Latin and mathematics, and graduated at Oberlin; he has as his wife, a woman who read Virgil and Homer in the same class room with me; he has as college chaplain, a classical graduate of Atlanta University; as teacher of science, a graduate of Fisk; as teacher of history, a graduate of Smith, – indeed some thirty of his chief teachers are college graduates, and instead of studying French grammars in the midst of weeds, or buying pianos for dirty cabins, they are at Mr. Washington's right hand helping him in a noble work. And yet one of the effects of Mr. Washington's propaganda has been to throw doubt upon the expediency of such training for Negroes, as these persons have had.

Men of America, the problem is plain before you. Here is a race transplanted through the criminal foolishness of your fathers. Whether you like it or not the millions are here, and here they will remain. If you do not lift them up, they will pull you down. Education and work are the levers to uplift a people. Work alone will not do it unless inspired by the right ideals and guided by intelligence. Education must not simply teach work – it must teach Life. The Talented Tenth of the Negro race must be made leaders of thought and missionaries of culture among their people. No others can do this and Negro colleges must train men for it. The Negro race, like all other races, is going to be saved by its exceptional men.

Source: W. E. B. DuBois, 'The Talented Tenth,' in Booker T. Washington and others, *The Negro Problem: A Series of Articles by Representative Negroes of To-day* (New York: James Pott & Co., 1903), pp. 33-75, passim.

5.3 The Beginning of the NAACP

During this integrationist period, DuBois operated within the NAACP, editing its journal, The Crisis, *and bringing his own black organisation, the Niagara Movement, within its multi-racial confines.*

The National Association for the Advancement of Colored People is five years old – old enough, it is believed, to have a history; and I, who am perhaps its first member, have been chosen as the person to recite it.

In the summer of 1908, the country was shocked by the account of the race riots at Springfield, Illinois. Here, in the home of Abraham Lincoln, a mob containing many of the town's "best citizens," raged for two days, killed and wounded scores of Negroes, and drove thousands from the city. Articles on the subject appeared in newspapers and magazines. Among them was one in the *Independent* of September 3d, by William English Walling, entitled "Race War in the North." After describing the atrocities committed against the colored people, Mr. Walling declared:

"Either the spirit of the abolitionists, of Lincoln and of Lovejoy must be revived and we must come to treat the Negro on a plane of absolute political and social equality, or Vardaman and Tillman will soon have transferred the race war to the North." And he ended with these words, "Yet who realizes the seriousness of the situation, and what large and powerful body of citizens is ready to come to their aid?"

It so happened that one of Mr. Walling's readers accepted his question and answered it. For four years I had been studying the status of the Negro in New York. I had investigated his housing conditions, his health, his opportunities for work. I had spent many months in the South, and at the time of Mr. Walling's article, I was living in a New York Negro tenement on a Negro street. And my investigations and my surroundings led me to believe with the writer of the article that "the spirit of the abolitionists must be revived."

So I wrote to Mr. Walling, and after some time, for he was in the West, we met in New York in the first week of the year 1909. With us was Dr. Henry Moskowitz, now prominent in the administration of John Purroy Mitchell, Mayor of New York.* It was then that the National Association for the Advancement of Colored People was born.

It was born in a little room of a New York apartment. It is to be regretted that there are no minutes of the first meeting, for they would make interesting if unparliamentary reading. Mr. Walling had spent some years in Russia where his wife, working in the cause of the revolutionists, had suffered imprisonment; and he expressed his belief that the Negro was treated in greater inhumanity in the United States than the Jew was treated in Russia. As Mr. Walling is a Southerner we listened with conviction. I knew something of the Negro's difficulty in securing decent employment in the North and of the insolent treatment awarded him at Northern hotels and restaurants, and I voiced my protest. Dr. Moskowitz, with his broad knowledge of conditions among New York's helpless immigrants, aided us in properly interpreting our facts. And so we talked and talked, voicing our indignation.

Of course, we wanted to do something at once that should move the country. It was January. Why not choose Lincoln's birthday, February 12, to open our campaign? We decided, therefore, that a wise, immediate action would be the issuing on Lincoln's birthday of a call for a national conference on the Negro question. At this conference we might discover the beginnings, at least, of that "large and powerful body of citizens" of which Mr. Walling had written.

And so the meeting adjourned. Something definite was determined upon, and our next step was to call others into our councils. We at once turned to Mr. Oswald Garrison Villard, president of the N.Y. Evening Post Company. He received our suggestions with enthusiasm, and aided us in securing the co-operation of able and representative men and women. It was he who drafted the Lincoln's birthday call and helped to give it wide publicity. I give the Call in its entirety . . . . since it expresses, I think, better than anything else we have published, the spirit of those who are active in the Association's cause.

"The celebration of the Centennial of the birth of Abraham Lincoln, widespread and grateful as it may be, will fail to justify itself if it takes no note of and makes no recognition of the colored men and women for whom the great Emancipator labored to assure freedom. Besides a day of rejoicing, Lincoln's birthday in 1909 should be one of taking stock of the nation's progress since 1865.

"How far has it lived up to the obligations imposed upon it by the Emancipation Proclamation? How far has it gone in assuring to each and every citizen, irrespective of color, the equality of opportunity and equality before the law, which underlie our American institutions and are guaranteed by the Constitution?

"If Mr Lincoln could revisit this country in the flesh, he would be disheartened and discouraged. He would learn that on January 1, 1909, Georgia had rounded out a new

* Moskowitz later became a member of the ethnic coterie that supported the political ambitions of Al Smith.

confederacy by disfranchising the Negro, after the manner of all the other Southern States. He would learn that the Supreme Court of the United States, supposedly a bulwark of American liberties, had refused every opportunity to pass squarely upon this disfranchisement of millions, by laws avowedly discriminatory and openly enforced in such manner that the white men may vote and black men be without a vote in their government; he would discover, therefore, that taxation without representation is the lot of millions of wealth-producing American citizens, in whose hands rests the economic progress and welfare of an entire section of the country.

"He would learn that the Supreme Court, according to the official statement of one of its own judges in the Berea College case, has laid down the principle that if an individual State chooses, it may 'make it a crime for white and colored persons to frequent the same market place at the same time, or appear in an assemblage of citizens convened to consider questions of a public or political nature in which all citizens, without regard to race, are equally interested.'

"In many states Lincoln would find justice enforced, if at all, by judges elected by one element in a community to pass upon the liberties and lives of another. He would see the black men and women, for whose freedom a hundred thousand of soldiers gave their lives, set apart in trains, in which they pay first-class fares for third-class service, and segregated in railway stations and in places of entertainment; he would observe that State after State declines to do its elementary duty in preparing the Negro through education for the best exercise of citizenship.

"Added to this, the spread of lawless attacks upon the Negro, North, South, and West – even in the Springfield made famous by Lincoln – often accompanied by revolting brutalities, sparing neither sex nor age nor youth, could but shock the author of the sentiment that 'government of the people, by the people, for the people; shall not perish from the earth.'

"Silence under these conditions means tacit approval. The indifference of the North is already responsible for more than one assault upon democracy, and every such attack reacts as unfavorably upon whites as upon blacks. Discrimination once permitted cannot be bridled; recent history in the South shows that in forging chains for the Negros the White voters are forging chains for themselves. 'A house divided against itself cannot stand'; this government cannot exist half-slave and half-free any better to-day than it could in 1861.

"Hence we call upon all the believers in democracy to join in a national conference for the discussion of present evils, the voicing of protests, and the renewal of the struggle for civil and political liberty."

It was thus decided that we should hold a conference, and the next two months were busily spent arranging for it. . . . It was agreed that the conference should be by invitation only, with the one open meeting at Cooper Union. Over a thousand people were invited, the Charity Organization Hall was secured, and, on the evening of May 30th, the conference opened with an informal reception at the Henry Street Settlement, given by Miss Lillian D. Wald, one of the Association's first and oldest friends. The next morning our deliberations began.

We have had five conferences since 1909, but I doubt whether any have been so full of a questioning surprise, mounting swiftly to enthusiasm, on the part of the white people in attendance. These men and women, engaged in religious, social and educational work, for the first time met the Negro who demands, not a pittance, but his full rights in the commonwealth. They received a stimulating shock and one which they enjoyed. They did not want to leave the meetings. We conferred all the time, formally and informally, and the Association gained in those days many of the earnest and uncompromising men and women who have since worked unfalteringly in its cause. Mr. William Hayes Ward, senior editor of the *Independent,* opened the conference, and Mr. Charles Edward Russell, always the friend of those who struggle for opportunity, presided at the stormy session at the close.

Out of this conference we formed a committee of forty and secured the services of Miss Frances Blascoer,* as secretary. We were greatly hampered by lack of funds. Important national work would present itself which we were unable to handle. But our secretary was an excellent organizer, and at the end of a year we had held four mass meetings, had distributed thousands of pamphlets, and numbered our membership in the hundreds. In May, 1910, we held our second conference in New York, and again our meetings were attended by earnest, interested people. It was then that we organized a permanent body to be known as the National Association for the Advancement of Colored People.

The securing of a sufficient financial support to warrant our calling Dr. Du Bois from Atlanta University into an executive office in the Association was the most important work of the second conference.

When Dr. Du Bois came to us we were brought closely in touch with an organization of colored people, formed in 1905 at Niagara and known as the Niagara Movement. This organization had held important conferences at Niagara, Harpers Ferry, and Boston, and had attempted a work of legal redress along very much the lines upon which the National Association for the Advancement of Colored People was working.

The Niagara Movement, hampered as it was by lack of funds and by a membership confined to one race only, continued to push slowly on, but when the larger possibilities of this new Association were clear, the members of the Niagara Movement were advised to join, as the platforms were practically identical. Many of the most prominent members of the Niagara Movement thus brought their energy and ability into the service of the Association, and eight are now serving on its Board of Directors.

Our history, after 1910, may be read in our annual reports, and in the numbers of THE CRISIS. We opened two offices in the *Evening Post* building. With Dr. Du Bois came Mr. Frank M. Turner, a Wilberforce graduate, who has shown great efficiency in handling our books. In November of 1910 appeared the first number of THE CRISIS, with Dr. Du Bois as editor, and Mary Dunlop MacLean, whose death has been the greatest loss the Association has known, as managing editor. Our propaganda work was put on a national footing, our legal work was well under way, and we were in

* Miss Blascoer was a social worker and author of *Colored School Children in New York* (New York, 1915).

truth, a National Association, pledged to a nation-wide work for justice to the Negro race.

I remember the afternoon that THE CRISIS received its name. We were sitting around the conventional table that seems a necessary adjunct to every Board, and were having an informal talk regarding the new magazine. We touched the subject of poetry.

"There is a poem of Lowell's," I said, "that means more to me today than any other poem in the world – 'The Present Crisis.'

And if we had a creed to which our members, black and white, our branches North and South and East and West, our college societies, our children's circles, should all subscribe, it should be the lines of Lowell's noble verse, lines that are as true today as when they were written seventy years ago.

Source: Mary White Ovington, *How the National Association for the Advancement of Colored Peoples Began* (New York, 1914).

5.4 The NAACP and Segregation

DuBois argues the inevitability of racial segregation.

There is a good deal of misapprehension as to the historic attitude of the National Association for the Advancement of Colored People and race segregation. As a matter of fact, the Association, while it has from time to time discussed the larger aspects of this matter, has taken no general stand and adopted no general philosophy. Of course its action, and often very effective action, has been in specific cases of segregation where the call for a definite stand was clear and decided. For instance, in the preliminary National Negro Convention which met in New York May 31st and June 1st, 1909, segregation was only mentioned in a protest against Jim-Crow car laws and that because of an amendment by William M. Trotter. In the First Annual Report, January 1, 1911, the Association evolved a statement of its purpose, which said that "it seeks to uplift the colored men and women of this country by securing to them the full enjoyment of their rights as citizens, justice in all courts, and equality of opportunity everywhere." Later, this general statement was epitomized in the well-known declaration: "It conceives its mission to be the completion of the work which the great Emancipator began. It proposes to make a group of ten million Americans free from the lingering shackles of past slavery, physically free from peonage, mentally free from ignorance, politically free from disfranchisement, and socially free from insult." This phrase which I first wrote myself for the Annual Report of 1915 still expresses pregnantly the object of the N.A.A.C.P. and it has my own entire adherence.

It will be noted, however, that here again segregation comes in only by implication. Specifically, it was first spoken of in the Second Report of the Association, January 1, 1912, when the attempt to destroy the property of Negroes in Kansas City because they had moved into a white section was taken up. This began our fight on a specific phase of segregation, namely, the attempt to establish a Negro ghetto by force of law. This phase of segregation we fought vigorously for years and often achieved notable victories in the highest courts of the land.

But it will be noted here that the N.A.A.C.P. expressed no opinion as to whether it might not be a feasible and advisable thing for colored people to establish their own residential sections, or their own towns; and certainly there was nothing expressed or implied that Negroes should not organize for promoting their own interests in industry, literature or art. Manifestly, here was opportunity for considerable difference of opinion, but the matter never was thoroughly threshed out.

The Association moved on to other matters of color discrimination: the "Full Crew" bills which led to dismissal of so many Negro railway employees;* the "Jim-Crow" car laws on railway trains and street cars; the segregation in government departments. In all these matters, the stand of the Association was clear and unequivocal: it held that it was a gross injustice to make special rules which discriminated against the color of employees or patrons.

In the Sixth Annual Report issued in March, 1916, the seven lines of endeavor of the Association included change of unfair laws, better administration of present laws, justice in the courts, stoppage of public slander, the investigation of facts, the encouragement of distinguished work by Negroes, and organizations.

Very soon, however, there came up a more complex question and that was the matter of Negro schools. The Association had avoided from the beginning any thoroughgoing pronouncement on this matter. In the resolutions of 1909, the conference asked: "Equal educational opportunities for all and in all the states, and that public school expenditure be the same for the Negro and white child." This of course did not touch the real problem of separate schools. Very soon, however, definite problems were presented to the Association: the exclusion of colored girls from the Oberlin dormitories in 1919; the discrimination in the School of Education at the University of Pennsylvania; and the Cincinnati fight against establishing a separate school for colored children, brought the matter squarely to the front. Later, further cases came: the Brooklyn Girls' High School, the matter of a colored High School in Indianapolis, and the celebrated Gary case.†

Gradually, in these cases the attitude of the Association crystallized. It declared that further extension of segregated schools for particular races and especially for Negroes was unwise and dangerous, and the Association undertook in all possible cases to oppose such further segregation. It did not, however, for a moment feel called upon to attack the separate schools where most colored children are educated throughout the United States and it refrained from this not because it approved of separate schools, but because it was faced by a fact and not a theory. It saw no sense in tilting against windmills.

* After World War I.

† Gary, Indiana, established separate high schools for Negroes.

The case at Cheyney was a variation; here was an old and separate private school which became in effect though not in law a separate public normal school; and in the city of Philadelphia a partial system of elementary Negro schools was developed with no definite action on the part of the N.A.A.C.P.

It will be seen that in all these cases the Association was attacking specific instances and not attempting to lay down any general rule as to how far the advancement of the colored race in the United States was going to involve separate racial action and segregated organization of Negroes for certain ends.

To be sure, the overwhelming and underlying thought of the N.A.A.C.P. has always been that any discrimination based simply on race is fundamentally wrong, and that consequently purely racial organizations must have strong justification to be admissable. On the other hand, they faced certain unfortunate but undeniable facts. For instance, War came. The Negro was being drafted. No Negro officers were being commissioned. The N.A.A.C.P. asked for the admission of Negroes to the officers' schools. This was denied. There was only one further thing to do and that was to ask for a school for Negro officers. There arose a bitter protest among many Negroes against this movement. Nevertheless, the argument for it was absolutely unanswerable, and Joel E. Spingarn, Chairman of the Board, supported by the students of Howard University, launched a movement which resulted in the commissioning of seven hundred Negro officers in the A.E.F. In all the British Dominions, with their hundreds of millions of colored folk, there was not a single officer of known Negro blood. The American Negro scored a tremendous triumph against the Color Line by their admitted and open policy of segregation. This did not mean that Mr. Springarn or any of the members of the N.A.A.C.P. thought it right that there should be a separate Negro camp, but they thought a separate Negro camp and Negro officers was infinitely better than no camp and no Negro officers and that was the only practical choice that lay before them.

Similarly, in the question of the Negro vote, the N.A.A.C.P. began in 1920 an attempt to organize the Negro vote and cast it in opposition to open enemies of the Negro race who were running for office. This was without doubt a species of segregation. It was appealing to voters on the grounds of race, and it brought for that reason considerable opposition. Nevertheless, it could be defended on the ground that the election of enemies of the Negro race was not only a blow to that race but to the white race and to all civilization. And while our attitude, even in the Parker case,* has been criticized, it has on the whole found abundant justification.

The final problem in segregation presented to us was that of the Harlem Hospital. Here was a hospital in the center of a great Negro population which for years did not have and would not admit a single Negro physician to its staff. Finally, by agitation and by political power, Negroes obtained representation on the staff in considerable numbers and membership on the Board of Control. It was a great triumph. But it was

* The NAACP and the AF of L successfully opposed the appointment of John J. Parker to the Supreme Court in 1930. Parker, in 1920, had praised the exclusion of Negroes from Southern politics.

accompanied by reaction on the part of whites and some Negroes who had opposed this movement, and an attempt to change the status of the hospital so that it would become a segregated Negro hospital, and so that presumably the other hospitals of the city would continue to exclude Negroes from their staffs. With this arose a movement to establish Negro hospitals throughout the United States.

Here was an exceedingly difficult problem. On the one hand, there is no doubt of the need of the Negro population for wider and better hospitalization; and of the demand on the part of Negro physicians for opportunities of hospital practice. This was illustrated by the celebrated Tuskegee hospital where nearly all the Negro veterans are segregated but where an efficient Negro staff has been installed. Perhaps nothing illustrates better than this the contradiction and paradox of the problem of race segregation in the United States, and the problem which the N.A.A.C.P. faced and still faces.

The N.A.A.C.P. opposed the initial establishment of the hospital at Tuskegee although it is doubtful if it would have opposed such a hospital in the North. On the other hand, once established, we fought to defend the Tuskegee hospital and give it widest opportunity.

In other words, the N.A.A.C.P. has never officially opposed separate Negro organizations – such as churches, schools and business and cultural organizations. It has never denied the recurrent necessity of united separate action on the part of Negroes for self-defense and self-development; but it has insistently and continually pointed out that such action is in any case a necessary evil involving often a recognition from within of the very color line which we are fighting without. That race pride and race loyalty, Negro ideals and Negro unity, have a place and function today, the N.A.A.C.P. never has denied and never can deny.

But all this simply touches the whole question of racial organization and initiative. No matter what we may wish or say, the vast majority of the Negroes in the United States are born in colored homes, educated in separate colored schools, attend separate colored churches, marry colored mates, and find their amusement in colored Y.M.C.A.'s and Y.W.C.A.'s. Even in their economic life, they are gradually being forced out of the place in industry which they occupied in the white world and are being compelled to seek their living among themselves. Here is segregation with a vengeance, and its problems must be met and its course guided. It would be idiotic simply to sit on the side lines and yell: "No segregation" in an increasingly segregated world.

On the other hand, the danger of easily and eagerly yielding to suggested racial segregation without reason or pressure stares us ever in the face. We segregate ourselves. We herd together. We do things such as this clipping from the *Atlanta Constitution* indicates:

> A lecture on the raising of Lazarus from the dead will be delivered at the city auditorium on Friday night. The Big Bethel choir will sing and the Graham Jackson band will give additional music. Space has been set aside for white people.

The "Jim Crow" galleries of Southern moving picture houses are filled with some of the best Negro citizens. Separate schools and other institutions have been asked by Negroes in the north when the whites had made no real demand.

Such are the flat and undeniable facts. What are we going to go about them? We can neither yell them down nor make them disappear by resolutions. We must think and act. It is this problem which THE CRISIS desires to discuss during the present year in all its phases and with ample and fair representation to all shades of opinion.

Source: W. E. B. DuBois, *The Crisis*, XLI (February, 1934), pp. 52-53. Reprinted by permission of *The Crisis Magazine*.

5.5 The Need for Racial Pride

DuBois emphasises the lack of recognition by whites of black worth.

Many persons have interpreted my reassertion of our current attitude toward segregation as a counsel of despair. We can't win, therefore, give up and accept the inevitable. Never, and nonsense. Our business in this world is to fight and fight again, and never to yield. But after all, one must fight with his brains, if he has any. He gathers strength to fight. He gathers knowledge, and he raises children who are proud to fight and who know what they are fighting about. And above all, they learn that what they are fighting for is the opportunity and the chance to know and associate with black folk. They are not fighting to escape themselves. They are fighting to say to the world; the opportunity of knowing Negroes is worth so much to us and is so appreciated, that we want you to know them too.

Negroes are not extraordinary human beings. They are just like other human beings, with all their foibles and ignorance and mistakes. But they are human beings, and human nature is always worth knowing, and withal, splendid in its manifestations. Therefore, we are fighting to keep open the avenues of human contact; but in the meantime, we are taking every advantage of what opportunities of contact are already open to us, and among those opportunities which are open, and which are splendid and inspiring, is the opportunity of Negroes to work together in the twentieth century for the uplift and development of the Negro race. It is no counsel for despair to emphasize and hail the opportunity for such work.

The assumptions of the anti-segregation campaign have been all wrong. This is not our fault, but it is our misfortune. When I went to Atlanta University to teach in 1897, and to study the Negro problem, I said, confidently, that the basic problem is our racial ignorance and lack of culture. That once Negroes know civilization, and whites know Negroes, then the problem is solved. This proposition is still true, but the solution is much further away than my youth dreamed. Negroes are still ignorant, but the disconcerting thing is that white people on the whole are just as much opposed to Negroes education and culture, as to any kind, and perhaps more so. Not all whites, to be sure, but the overwhelming majority.

Our main method, then, falls flat. We stop training ability. We lose our manners. We swallow our pride, and beg for things. We agitate and get angry. And with all that, we face the blank fact: Negroes are not wanted; neither as scholars nor as business men; neither as clerks nor as artisans; neither as artists nor as writers. What can we do about it? We cannot use force. We cannot enforce law, even if we get it on the statute books. So long as overwhelming public opinion sanctions and justifies and defends color segregation, we are helpless, and without remedy. We are segregated. We are cast back upon ourselves, to an Island Within; "To your tents, Oh Israel!"

Surely then, in this period of frustration and disappointment, we must turn from negation to affirmation, from the ever-lasting "No" to the ever-lasting "Yes." Instead of sitting, sapped of all initiative and independence; instead of drowning our originality in imitation of mediocre white folks; instead of being afraid of ourselves and cultivating the art of skulking to escape the Color Line; we have got to renounce a program that always involves humiliating self-stultifying scrambling to crawl somewhere where we are not wanted; where we crouch panting like a whipped dog. We have got to stop this and learn that on such a program they cannot build manhood. No, by God, stand erect in a mud-puddle and tell the white world to go to hell, rather than lick boots in a parlor.

Affirm, as you have a right to affirm, that the Negro race is one of the great human races, inferior to none in its accomplishment and in its ability. Different, it is true, and for most of the difference, let us reverently thank God. And this race, with its vantage grounds in modern days, can go forward of its own will, of its own power, and its own initiative. It is led by twelve million American Negroes of average modern intelligence; three or four million American educated African Negroes are their full equals, and several million Negroes in the West Indies and South America. This body of at least twenty-five million modern men are not called upon to commit suicide because somebody doesn't like their complexion or their hair. It is their opportunity and their day to stand up and make themselves heard and felt in the modern world.

Indeed, there is nothing else we can do. If you have passed your resolution, "No segregation, Never and Nowhere," what are you going to do about it? Let me tell you what you are going to do. You are going back to continue to make your living in a Jim-Crow school; you are going to dwell in a segregated section of the city; you are going to pastor a Jim-Crow Church; you are going to occupy political office because of Jim-Crow political organizations that stand back of you and force you into office. All these things and a thousand others you are going to do because you have got to.

If you are going to do this, why not say so? What are you afraid of? Do you believe in the Negro race or do you not? If you do not, naturally, you are justified in keeping still. But if you do believe in the extraordinary accomplishment of the Negro church and the Negro college, the Negro school and the Negro newspaper, then say so and say so plainly, not only for the sake of those who have given their lives to make these things worthwhile, but for those young people whom you are teaching, by that negative attitude, that there is nothing that they can do, nobody that they can emulate, and no field worthwhile working in. Thinking of what Negro art and literature has yet to accomplish if it can only be free and untrammeled by the necessity of pleasing white folks! Think of the splendid moral appeal that you can make to a million children tomorrow, if once you can get them to see the possibilities of the American Negro today and now, whether he is segregated or not, or in spite of all possible segregation.

Source: W. E. B. DuBois, *The Crisis*, XLI (June 1934), p. 182. Reprinted by permission of *The Crisis Magazine*.

5.6 Critique of DuBois and Segregation

James Weldon Johnson of the NAACP – educator, man of letters and journalist – argues against the position of DuBois on segregation.

. . . We have reduced choices of a way out to two. There remain, on the one hand, the continuation of our efforts to achieve integration and, on the other hand, an acknowledgment of our isolation and the determination to accept and make the best of it.

Throughout our entire intellectual history there has been a division of opinion as to which of these two divergent courses the race should follow. From early times there have been sincere thinkers among us who were brought to the conclusion that our only salvation lies in the making of the race into a self-contained economic, social, and cultural unit; in a word, in the building of an *imperium in imperio*.

All along, however, majority opinion has held that the only salvation worth achieving lies in the making of the race into a component part of the nation, with all the common rights and privileges, as well as duties, of citizenship. This attitude has been basic in the general policy of the race – so far as it has had a general policy – for generations, the policy of striving zealously to gain full admission to citizenship and guarding jealously each single advance made.

But this question of direction, of goal, is not a settled one. There is in us all a stronger tendency toward isolation than we may be aware of. There come times when the most persistent integrationist becomes an isolationist, when he curses the White world and consigns it to hell. This tendency toward isolation is strong because it springs from a deep-seated, natural desire – a desire for respite from the unremitting, grueling struggle; for a place in which refuge might be taken. We are again and again confronted by this question. It is ever present, though often dormant. Recently it was emphatically brought forward by the utterances of so authoritative a voice as that of Dr. Du Bois.

The question is not one to be lightly brushed aside. Those who stand for making the race into a self-sufficient unit point out that after years of effort we are still Jim-Crowed, discriminated against, segregated, and lynched; that we are still shut out from industry, barred from the main avenues of business, and cut off from free participation in national life. They point out that in some sections of the country we have not even secured equal protection of life and property under the laws. They declare that entrance of the Negro into full citizenship is as distant as it was seventy years ago. And they ask: What is the Negro to do? Give himself over to wishful thinking? Stand shooting at the stars with a popgun? Is it not rather a duty and a necessity for him to face the facts of his condition and environment, to acknowledge them as facts, and to make the best use of them that he can? These are questions which the thinkers of the race should strive to sift clearly.

To this writer it seems that one of the first results of clear thinking is a realization of the truth that the making of the race into a self-sustaining unit, the creating of an *imperium in imperio,* does not offer an easier or more feasible task than does the task of achieving full citizenship. Such an *imperium* would have to rest upon a bias of separate group economic independence, and the trend of all present-day forces is against the building of any foundation of that sort.

After thoughtful consideration, I cannot see the slightest possibility of our being able to duplicate the economic and social machinery of the country. I do not believe that any other special group could do it. The isolationists declare that because of imposed segregation we have, to a large degree, already done it. But the situation they point to is more apparent than real. Our separate schools and some of our other race institutions, many of our race enterprises, the greater part of our employment, and most of our fundamental activities are contingent upon our interrelationship with the country as a whole.

Clear thinking reveals that the outcome of voluntary isolation would be a permanent secondary status, so acknowledged by the race. Such a status would, it is true, solve some phases of the race question. It would smooth away a good part of the friction and bring about a certain protection and security. The status of slavery carried some advantages of that sort. But I do not believe we shall ever be willing to pay such a price for security and peace.

If Negro Americans could do what reasonably appears to be impossible, and as a separate unit achieve self-sufficiency built upon group economic independence, does anyone suppose that that would abolish prejudice against them and allay opposition, or that the struggle to maintain their self-sufficiency would be in any degree less bitter than the present struggle to become an integral part of the nation? Taking into account human nature as it is, would not the achievement be more likely to arouse envy and bring on even more violent hatreds and persecutions?

Certainly, the isolationists are stating a truth when they contend that we should not, ostrich-like, hide our heads in the sand, making believe that prejudice is non-existent; but in so doing they are apostles of the obvious. Calling upon the race to realize that prejudice is an actuality is a needless effort; it is placing emphasis on what has never been questioned. The danger for us does not lie in a possible failure to acknowledge prejudice as a reality, but in acknowledging it too fully. We cannot ignore the fact that we are segregated, no matter how much we might wish to do so; and the smallest amount of common sense forces us to extract as much good from the situation as there is in it. Any degree of sagacity forces us at the same time to use all our powers to abolish imposed segregation; for it is an evil *per se* and the negation of equality either of opportunity or of awards. We should by all means make our schools and institutions as excellent as we can possibly make them – and by that very act we reduce the certainty that they will forever remain schools and institutions "for Negroes only." We should make our business enterprises and other strictly group undertakings as successful as we can possibly make them. We should gather all the strength and experience we can from imposed segregation. But any good we are able to derive from the system we should consider as a means, not an end. The strength and experience we gain from it should be applied to the objective of *entering into*, not *staying out* of the body politic.

Clear thinking shows, too, that, as bad as conditions are, they are not as bad as they are declared to be by discouraged and pessimistic isolationists. To say that in the past two generations or more Negro Americans have not advanced a single step toward a fuller share in the commonwealth becomes in the light of easily ascertainable facts, an absurdity. Only the shortest view of the situation gives color of truth to such a statement; any reasonably long view proves it to be utterly false.

With our choice narrowed down to these two courses, wisdom and far-sightedness and possibility of achievement demand that we follow the line that leads to equal rights to us, based on the common terms and conditions under which they are accorded and guaranteed to the other groups that go into the making up of our national family. It is not necessary for our advancement that such an outcome should suddenly eradicate all prejudices. It would not, of course, have the effect of suddenly doing away with voluntary grouping in religious and secular organizations or of abolishing group enterprises – for example, Negro newspapers. The accordance of full civil and political rights has not in the case of the greater number of groups in the nation had that effect. Nevertheless, it would be an immeasurable step forward, and would place us where we had a fair start with the other American groups. More than that we do not need to ask.

Source: James Weldon Johnson, *Negro Americans, What Now?* (New York, 1935), pp. 12-18. James Weldon Johnson's material from *Negro Americans, What Now?* by permission of Mrs Ollie Sims Okala.

The Early Twentieth Century

6.1 Progressivism and the Negro

Ray Stannard Baker was a Northern Progressive journalist who investigated race relations in the South at first hand. In his book, Following the Color Line, *and in this article, he concluded that the potential for racism in the North was as great as the actuality in the South.*

The South does not now believe and never has believed in a democracy which applies to every man regardless of race, religion or condition. But neither does the North. Undoubtedly the North possesses more of the democratic spirit than the South; and yet, studying the growth of negro communities in Northern cities, I am convinced that if we had anything like the proportion of negroes that the South struggles with, we should also find ourselves developing a spirit not unlike that of the South. Lynchings, mob-law, discrimination, prejudice, are not unknown today in the North. I found discrimination and separation growing even in Boston, and I could not find that mob law in Springfield, Ohio, was any less ferocious than in Huntsville, Alabama. The same spirit which drives the man with the colored face out of certain counties in Indiana is found burning negro colleges in Texas.

We of the North do not, most of us, believe in any real sense in a democracy which includes black men as well as white men.

If there were enough colored voters in New York to carry the city, or even to exercise a balance of power, and they all voted one ticket as they do in the South, disfranchisement would immediately become an important issue. As it is, we are contented to disfranchise most of our negro voters at every election by bribery. Let us be willing to face the truth, and not cast stones at our Southern neighbors. The plain fact is, most of us in the North do not believe in any real democracy as between white and colored men. Nor do we believe in it among our own white people, for we are divided into warring classes and societies. Nor does the negro on his part believe in it, for no line among white people is more strictly drawn than the line, in some localities, between the mulatto and his black brother. I have known negroes as intolerably aristocratic in their prejudices as any white men I have had the pleasure of meeting.

The point I am making here is that the *spirit* of democracy, which, after all, is the only thing that really counts, is not exhausted with exercise anywhere in this land. We have made a little relative progress toward democracy; we have exprest its shining ideal in some of our institutions, but for the most part the human heart of us is wofully aristocratic, ungenerous, prejudiced, and it expresses its haughtiness not only in the South, where the negro suffers most, but in the North, where we employ swarms of underpaid women and children, and build selfish palaces out of the labor of wretched foreigners. We have no stones to cast at the South. This is our problem, too. I have heard much talk against the passage of the disfranchisement and "Jim Crow" laws, in the South, but I cannot consider them without feeling that whatever else they may express, they also constitute a genuine protest against the lie of the law. The Supreme Court decision in the Berea College case has been attacked in some quarters, but does it not represent the real view of the mass of American citizens? In Chicago, in St. Paul, in Boston, white parents do not often want their children to sit in schools where many negroes attend. This is the plain truth.

But a tremendous endowment of power follows any effort to arrive at the real truth of things. Thus the discussion in the South regarding the limitation of democracy on the statute books has opened the question as to where, having begun to limit, the line shall henceforth be drawn. If you study the political campaigns in the South, if you read the proceedings of the recent legislatures of Southern States, you will discover that, however blindly, the discussions have turned upon these questions:

How many colored men can be cut off from participation in the political rights of the democracy? How many seats at the rear of the car shall the negroes occupy? At what door shall the negro enter the railroad station? Shall negroes be confined in the same prisons with white men, or take the oath with their hands on the same Bible, or be buried in the same cemeteries? How many parts of white blood shall admit a negro to real participation in the democracy? What occupation must negroes pursue in the democracy? Some would compel them all to be servants, others would admit them as small businessmen but not as professional men, others still would let them practise medicine *if* they practise only among their own people.

All these discussions may seem amusingly trivial to the outsider who cannot understand that they are, after all, profoundly and fundamentally educative.

Think what a tremendous experimental laboratory in applied democracy is this South of ours! A whole people trying to draw an elusive line between some men who belong and some who do not! In each legislature, in each campaign, the line wavers, is broken down at some point, is newly drawn. Some awful event like the Atlanta riot comes along and the best white men and the best negroes, who have never come together or known one another, are irresistibly forced into common effort. A white man says: "I did not know there were any such intelligent negroes in the country." Another says: "After all, are we not brothers?"

Or some man arises – a liberator, like Booker T. Washington – who will not be classified, who breaks thru many lines "What shall be done with such a man?" these campaigners and legislators ask themselves. "He serves the South. He is useful to all of us. How can we legislate such a man out of the democracy? But can we let him in and keep out the dark-skinned man who follows close behind?"

So these Southern men are concerning themselves with real questions; they are being driven onward by the tremendous logic of events. They will see sooner, perhaps, than we see the utter absurdity and impossibility of limiting a democracy. It must either be democracy or else a caste system or graded aristocracy, which, if it is forced, will petrify our civilization as it has petrified that of India. Once an attempt is made to draw lines and it is discovered that the whole attention of the people is centered, as it is today in the South, on drawing and redrawing the lines – to let a few more in or to keep a few more out. So we shall discover in time and by painful experience that if the negro does not fit into our present sort of democracy, it is not the negro who is wrong, but the democracy. The final test of any democracy is its humblest citizen.

Science has taught us that every atom is necessary to every other atom in the universe. It is also teaching us that every human being is necessary to every other human being; that there can be no real democracy which leaves any one out. Emerson says . . ."To science there is no poison; to botany no weed; to chemistry no dirt." To this we may add: "To democracy, no negro."

The spirit of true democracy is faint in this country; and it is not surprising that the United States Supreme Court should express what the people feel. What we need is a revival of the spirit of democracy, both South and North. How can this be attained? Again only by old-fashioned remedies: I mean by education and the passionate preaching of the religion of service.

Hearing these commonplace things suggested, some of us grow weary; the way seems so long and so hard. What we really need is new fervor in our work along these lines. It is not enough to believe; there must burn behind that belief the true fire of faith. If I have any message to deliver today it lies in the reinforcement of our conviction that these old remedies are the true remedies.

What we need today is not less democracy, but more democracy. We need the constant re-assertion of the validity of the highest levels of democracy: the sort of democracy which leaves no man out. That must be our religion from now on.

Source: Ray Stannard Baker, 'The Negro in a Democracy', *The Independent*, LXVII, September 2, 1909, pp. 584-588.

6.2 A Delegation to President Wilson against Segregation

An inter-racial delegation, led by William Monroe Trotter, editor of the Boston Guardian, *complained about segregation in the Federal Government offices of the Treasury and the Postmaster General to the President, Woodrow Wilson, who, as a Democratic candidate, had promised fair treatment for blacks.*

Washington, D.C., Nov. 20 – Thursday afternoon of last week President Wilson became indignant when William Monroe Trotter, editor of the Boston *Guardian,* as chairman of a committee of protest from the National Independence Equal Rights League against the segregation of Afro-American employees in the government departments in Washington, plainly told the nation's chief executive about it.

The committee met the president by appointment, after waiting a year for a personal interview with him. Mr. Trotter was the spokesman, and in the fervor of his plea for equal rights for his people he forgot the servile manner and speech once characteristic of the Afro-American and he talked to the president as man to man, addressing the head of the government as any American citizen should, especially when discussing a serious matter. But the president did not like Mr. Trotter's attitude and told the committee that if it called on him again it would have to get a new chairman. The president added he had not been addressed in such a manner since he entered the White House.

The delegation charged that Secretary McAdoo and Comptroller Williams in the treasury and Postmaster General Burleson had enforced segregation rules in their offices. The president replied that he had investigated the question and had been assured there had been no discrimination in the comforts and surroundings given to the Afro-American workers. He added he had been informed by officials that the segregation had been started to avoid friction between the races and not with the object of injuring the Afro-American employees.

The president said he was deeply interested in the race and greatly admired its progress. He declared the thing to be sought by the Afro-American people was complete independence of white people, and that he felt the white race was willing to do everything possible to assist them.

Mr. Trotter and other members at once took issue with the president, declaring the Afro-American people did not seek charity or assistance, but that they took the position that they had equal rights with whites and that those rights should be respected. They denied there had been any friction between the two races before segregation was begun.

The president listened to what they had to say, and then told the delegation that Mr. Trotter was losing control of his temper, and that he (the president) would not discuss the matter further with him.

The president said he thought his colleagues in the government departments were not trying to put the employees at a disadvantage, but simply to make arrangements which would prevent friction. He added that the question involved was not a question of intrinsic qualities, because all had human souls and were equal in that respect, but that for the present it was a question of economic policy whether the Afro-American race could do the same things that the white race could do with equal efficiency. He said he thought the Afro-American people were proving that they could, and that everyone wished to help them and that their conditions of labor would be bettered. The entire matter, however, should be treated with a recognition of its difficulties. The president said he was anxious to do what was just, and asked for more memoranda from the committee as to instances of segregation about which they complained.

Mr. Trotter said in his address that his committee did not come "as wards looking for charity, but as full-fledged American citizens, vouchsafed equality of citizenship by the federal constitution."

"Two years ago," said Mr Trotter, "You were thought to be a second Abraham Lincoln." The president tried to interrupt, asking that personalities be left out of the discussion. Mr. Trotter continued to speak and the president finally told him that if the organization he represented wished to approach him again it must choose another spokesman.

The spokesman continued to argue that he was merely trying to show how the Afro-American people felt, and asserted that he and others were now being branded as traitors to the race because they advised the people "to support the ticket."

This mention of votes caused the president to say politics must be left out, because it was a form of blackmail. He said he would resent it as quickly from one set of men as from another, and that his auditors could vote as they pleased, it mattered little to him.

Source: *Chicago Defender*, November 21, 1914.

6.3 The Chicago Race Riot, 1919

The Chicago race riot of 1919 was one of several in the United States following the end of the First World War, when blacks, including those who had enjoyed new employment opportunities, or had seen service overseas, had to adjust once more to the reality of their restricted position in the country.

Thirty-eight persons killed, 537 injured, and about 1,000 rendered homeless and destitute was the casualty list of the race riot which broke out in Chicago on July 27, 1919, and swept uncontrolled through parts of the city for four days. By August 2 it had yielded to the forces of law and order, and on August 8 the state militia withdrew.

A clash between whites and Negroes on the shore of Lake Michigan at Twenty-ninth Street, which involved much stone-throwing and resulted in the drowning of a Negro boy, was the beginning of the riot. A policeman's refusal to arrest a white man accused by Negroes of stoning the Negro boy was an important factor in starting mob action. Within two hours the riot was in full sway, had scored its second fatality, and was spreading throughout the south and southwest parts of the city. Before the end came it reached out to a section of the West Side and even invaded the "Loop," the heart of Chicago's downtown business district. Of the thirty-eight killed, fifteen were whites and twenty-three Negroes; of 537 injured, 178 were whites, 342 were Negroes, and the race of seventeen was not recorded.

In contrast with many other outbreaks of violence over racial friction the Chicago riot was not preceded by excitement over reports of attacks on women or of any other crimes alleged to have been committed by Negroes. It is interesting to note that not one of the thirty-eight deaths was of a woman or girl, and that only ten of the 537 persons injured were women or girls. In further contrast with other outbreaks of racial violence, the Chicago riot was marked by no hangings or burnings.

The rioting was characterized by much activity on the part of gangs of hoodlums, and the clashes developed from sudden and spontaneous assaults into organized raids against life and property.

In handling the emergency and restoring order, the police were effectively reinforced by the state militia. Help was also rendered by deputy sheriffs, and by ex-soldiers who volunteered.

In nine of the thirty-eight cases of death, indictments for murder were voted by the grand jury, and in the ensuing trials there were four convictions. In fifteen other cases the coroner's jury recommended that unknown members of mobs be apprehended, but none of these was ever found.

The Commission's inquiry concerning the facts of the riot included a critical analysis of the 5,584 pages of the testimony taken by the coroner's jury; a study of the records of the office of the state's attorney; studies of the records of the Police Department, hospitals, and other institutions with reference to injuries, and of the records of the Fire Department with reference to incendiary fires; and interviews with many public officials and citizens having special knowledge of various phases of the riot. Much information was also gained by the Commission in a series of four conferences to which it invited the foreman of the riot grand jury, the chief and other commanding officers of the Police Department, the state's attorney and some of his assistants, and officers in command of the state militia during the riot.

Background of the riot

The Chicago riot was not the only serious outbreak of interracial violence in the year following the war. The same summer witnessed the riot in Washington, about a week earlier; the riot in Omaha, about a month later; and then the week of armed conflict in a rural district of Arkansas due to exploitation of Negro cotton producers.

Nor was the Chicago riot the first violent manifestation of race antagonism in Illinois. In 1908 Springfield had been the scene of an outbreak that brought shame to the community which boasted of having been Lincoln's home. In 1917 East St. Louis was torn by a bitter and destructive riot which raged for nearly a week, and was the subject of a Congressional investigation that disclosed appalling underlying conditions.

Chicago was one of the northern cities most largely affected by the migration of Negroes from the South during the war. The Negro population increased from 44,103 in 1910 to 109,594 in 1920, an increase of 148 percent. Most of this increase came in the years 1916-19. It was principally caused by the widening of industrial opportunities due to the entrance of northern workers into the army and to the demand for war workers at much higher wages than Negroes had been able to earn in the South. An added factor was the feeling, which spread like a contagion through the South, that the great opportunity had come to escape from what they felt to be a land of discrimination and subserviency to places where they could expect fair treatment and equal rights. Chicago became to the southern Negro the "top of the world."

It is necessary to point out . . . . that friction in industry was less than might have been expected. There had been a few strikes which had given the Negro the name of "strike breaker." But the demand for labor was such that there were plenty of jobs to absorb all the white and Negro workers available. This condition continued even after the end of the war and demobilization.

In housing, however, there was a different story. Practically no new building had been done in the city during the war, and it was a physical impossibility for a doubled Negro population to live in the space occupied in 1915. Negroes spread out of what had been known as the "Black Belt" into neighborhoods near-by which had been exclusively white. This movement . . . developed friction, so much so that in the "invaded" neighborhoods bombs were thrown at the houses of Negroes who had moved in, and of real estate men, white and Negro, who sold or rented property to the newcomers. From July 1, 1917, to July 27, 1919, the day the riot began, twenty-four such bombs had been thrown. The police had been entirely unsuccessful in finding those guilty, and were accused of making little effort to do so.

A third phase of the situation was the increased political strength gained by Mayor Thompson's faction in the Republican party. Negro politicians affiliated with this faction had been able to sway to its support a large proportion of the voters in the ward most largely inhabited by Negroes. Negro aldermen elected from this ward were prominent in the activities of this faction. The part played by the Negro vote in the hard-fought partisan struggle is indicated by the fact that in the Republican primary election on February 25, 1919, Mayor Thompson received in this ward 12,143 votes, while his two opponents, Olson and Merrian, received only 1,492 and 319 respectively. Mayor Thompson was re-elected on April 1, 1919, by a plurality of 21,622 in a total vote in the city of 698,920; his vote in this ward was 15,569, to his nearest opponent's 3,323, and was therefore large enough to control the election. The bitterness of this factional struggle aroused resentment against the race that had so conspicuously allied itself with the Thompson side.

As part of the background of the Chicago riot, the activities of gangs of hoodlums should be cited. There had been friction for years, especially along the western boundary of the area in which the Negroes mainly live, and attacks upon Negroes by gangs of young toughs had been particularly frequent in the spring just preceding the riot. They reached a climax on the night of June 21, 1919, five weeks before the riot, when two Negroes were murdered. Each was alone at the time and was the victim of unprovoked and particularly brutal attack. Molestation of Negroes by hoodlums had been prevalent in the vicinity of parks and playgrounds and at bathing-beaches.

On two occasions shortly before the riot the forewarnings of serious racial trouble had been so pronounced that the chief of police sent several hundred extra policemen into the territory where trouble seemed imminent. But serious violence did not break out until Sunday afternoon, July 27, when the clash on the lake shore at Twenty-ninth Street resulted in the drowning of a Negro boy.

Events followed so fast in the train of the drowning that this tragedy may be considered as marking the beginning of the riot.

It was four o'clock Sunday afternoon, July 27, when Eugene Williams, a seventeen-year-old Negro boy, was swimming offshore at the foot of Twenty-ninth Street. This beach was not one of those publicly maintained and supervised for bathing, but it was much used. Although it flanks an area thickly inhabited by Negroes, it was used by both races, access being had by crossing the railway tracks which skirt the lake shore. The part near Twenty-seventh Street had by tacit understanding come to be considered as reserved for Negroes, while the whites used the part near Twenty-ninth Street. Walking is not easy along the shore, and each race had kept pretty much to its own part, observing, moreover, an imaginary boundary extending into the water.

Williams, who had entered the water at the part used by Negroes, swam and drifted south into the part used by the whites. Immediately before his appearance there, white men, women, and children had been bathing in the vicinity and were on the beach in considerable numbers. Four Negroes walked through the group and into the water. White men summarily ordered them off. The Negroes left, and the white people resumed their sport. But it was not long before the Negroes were back, coming from the north with others of their race. Then began a series of attacks and retreats, counterattacks, and stone-throwing. Women and children who could not escape hid behind debris and rocks. The stone-throwing continued, first one side gaining the advantage, then the other.

Williams, who had remained in the water during the fracas, found a railroad tie and clung to it, stones meanwhile frequently striking the water near him. A white boy of about the same age swam toward him. As the white boy neared, Williams let go of the tie, took a few strokes, and went down. The coroner's jury rendered a verdict that he had drowned because fear of stone-throwing kept him from shore. His body showed no stone bruises, but rumor had it that he had actually been hit by one of the stones and drowned as a result.

On shore guilt was immediately placed upon a certain white man by several Negro witnesses who demanded that he be arrested by a white policeman who was on the spot. No arrest was made.

The tragedy was sensed by the battling crowd and, awed by it, they gathered on the beach. For an hour both whites and Negroes dived for the boy without results. Awe gave way to excited whispers. "They" said he was stoned to death. The report circulated through the crowd that the police officer had refused to arrest the murderer. The Negroes in the crowd began to mass dangerously. At this crucial point the accused policeman arrested a Negro on a white man's complaint. Negroes mobbed the white officer, and the riot was under way.

Source: Chicago Commission on Race Relations, *The Negro in Chicago: a Study of Race Relations and a Race Riot*, (Chicago, 1922), pp. 1-4.

6.4 Marcus Garvey and the Universal Negro Improvement Association

Marcus Garvey came from Jamaica to the United States in 1916 with a background of journalism and union activism, and proceeded to build up an organisation with mass support from the black urban poor – the result of heavy migration from the South to the cities of the North. Garvey set up a variety of black businesses, encouraging economic self-sufficiency and racial pride in the black community. His professed aim was to create the option for all people of African descent ultimately to return to Africa. His ideas and style attracted the hostility of other black leaders and also of the government, which regarded him as an agitator. In 1923, he was convicted of fraudulent use of the mails in supporting his ventures, imprisoned in 1925, and deported in 1927.

(a) "The true solution of the Negro problem"

As far as Negroes are concerned, in America we have the problem of lynching, peonage and dis-franchisement.

In the West Indies, South and Central America we have the problem of peonage, serfdom, industrial and political governmental inequality.

In Africa we have, not only peonage and serfdom, but outright slavery, racial exploitation and alien political monopoly.

We cannot allow a continuation of these crimes against our race. As four hundred million men, women and children, worthy of the existence given us by the Divine Creator, we are determined to solve our own problem, by redeeming our Motherland Africa from the hands of alien exploiters and found there a government, a nation of our own, strong enough to lend protection to the members of our race scattered all over the world, and to compel the respect of the nations and races of the earth.

Do they lynch Englishmen, Frenchmen, Germans or Japanese? No. And Why? Because these people are represented by great governments, mighty nations and empires, strongly organized. Yes, and ever ready to shed the last drop of blood and spend the last penny in the national treasury to protect the honor and integrity of a citizen outraged anywhere.

Until the Negro reaches this point of national independence, all he does as a race will count for naught, because the prejudice that will stand out against him even with his ballot in his hand, with his industrial progress to show, will be of such an overwhelming nature as to perpetuate mob violence and mob rule, from which he will suffer and which he will not be able to stop with his industrial wealth and with his ballot.

You may argue that he can use his industrial wealth and his ballot to force the government to recognize him, but he must understand that the government is the people. That the majority of the people dictate the policy of governments, and if the majority are against a measure, a thing, or a race, then the government is impotent to protect that measure, thing or race.

If the Negro were to live in this Western Hemisphere for another five hundred years he would still be outnumbered by other races who are prejudiced against him. He cannot resort to the government for protection for government will be in the hands of the majority of the people who are prejudiced against him, hence for the Negro to depend on the ballot and his industrial progress alone, will be hopeless as it does not help him when he is lynched, burned, jim-crowed and segregated. The future of the Negro therefore, outside of Africa, spells ruin and disaster.

(b) The aims of the Universal Negro Improvement Association

Generally the public is kept misinformed of the truth surrounding new movements of reform. Very seldom, if ever, reformers get the truth told about them and their movements. Because of this natural attitude, the Universal Negro Improvement Association has been greatly handicapped in its work, causing thereby one of the most liberal and helpful human movements of the twentieth century to be held up to ridicule by those who take pride in poking fun at anything not already successfully established.

The white man of America has become the natural leader of the world. He, because of his exalted position, is called upon to help in all human efforts. From nations to individuals the appeal is made to him for aid in all things affecting humanity, so, naturally, there can be no great mass movement or change without first acquainting the leader on whose sympathy and advice the world moves.

It is because of this, and more so because of a desire to be Christian friends with the white race, why I explain the aims and objects of the Universal Negro Improvement Association.

The Universal Negro Improvement Association is an organization among Negroes that is seeking to improve the condition of the race, with the view of establishing a nation in Africa where Negroes will be given the opportunity to develop by themselves, without creating the hatred and animosity that now exist in countries of the white race through Negroes rivaling them for the highest and best positions in government, politics, society and industry. The organization believes in the rights of all men, yellow, white and black. To us, the white race has a right to the peaceful possession and occupation of countries of its own and in like manner the yellow and black races have their rights. It is only by an honest and liberal consideration of such rights can the world be blessed with the peace that is sought by Christian teachers and leaders.

The spiritual brotherhood of man

The following preamble to the constitution of the organization speaks for itself:

> "The Universal Negro Improvement Association and African Communities' League is a social, friendly, humanitarian, charitable, educational, institutional, constructive, and expansive society, and is founded by persons, desiring to the utmost to work for the general uplift of the Negro peoples of the world. And the members pledge themselves to do all in their power to conserve the rights of their noble race and to

respect the rights of all mankind, believing always in the Brotherhood of Man and the Fatherhood of God. The motto of the organization is: One God! One Aim! One Destiny! Therefore, let justice be done to all mankind, realizing that if the strong oppresses the weak confusion and discontent will ever mark the path of man, but with love, faith and charity toward all the reign of peace and plenty will be heralded into the world and the generation of men shall be called Blessed."

The declared objects of the association are:

> "To establish a Universal Confraternity among the race; to promote the spirit of pride and love; to reclaim the fallen; to administer to and assist the needy; to assist in civilizing the backward tribes of Africa; to assist in the development of Independent Negro Nations and Communities; to establish a central nation for the race; to establish Commissaries or Agencies in the principal countries and cities of the world for the representation of all Negroes; to promote a conscientious Spiritual worship among the native tribes of Africa; to establish Universities, Colleges, Academies and Schools for the racial education and culture of the people; to work for better conditions among Negroes everywhere."

Supplying a long-felt want

The organization of the Universal Negro Improvement Association has supplied among Negroes a long-felt want. Hitherto the other Negro movements in America, with the exception of the Tuskegee effort of Booker T. Washington, sought to teach the Negro to aspire to social equality with the whites, meaning thereby the right to intermarry and fraternize in every social way. This has been the source of much trouble and still some Negro organizations continue to preach this dangerous "race destroying doctrine" added to a program of political agitation and aggression. The Universal Negro Improvement Association on the other hand believes in and teaches the pride and purity of race. We believe that the white race should uphold its racial pride and perpetuate itself, and that the black race should do likewise. We believe that there is room enough in the world for the various race groups to grow and develop by themselves without seeking to destroy the Creator's plan by the constant introduction of mongrel types.

The unfortunate condition of slavery as imposed upon the Negro, and which caused the mongrelization of the race, should not be legalized and continued now to the harm and detriment of both races.

The time has really come to give the Negro a chance to develop himself to a moral-standard-man, and it is for such an opportunity that the Universal Negro Improvement Association seeks in the creation of an African nation for Negroes, where the greatest latitude would be given to work out this racial ideal.

There are hundreds of thousands of colored people in America who desire race amalgamation and miscegenation as a solution of the race problem. These people are, therefore, opposed to the race pride ideas of black and white; but the thoughtful of both races will naturally ignore the ravings of such persons and honestly work for the solution of a problem that has been forced upon us.

Liberal white America and race loving Negroes are bound to think at this time and thus evolve a program or plan by which there can be a fair and amicable settlement of the question.

We cannot put off the consideration of the matter, for time is pressing on our hands. The educated Negro is making rightful constitutional demands. The great white majority will never grant them, and thus we march on to danger if we do not now stop and adjust the matter.

The time is opportune to regulate the relationship between both races. Let the Negro have a country of his own. Help him to return to his original home, Africa, and there give him the opportunity to climb from the lowest to the highest positions in a state of his own. If not, then the nation will have to hearken to the demand of the aggressive, "social equality" organization, known as the National Association for the Advancement of Colored People, of which W. E. Du Bois is leader, which declares vehemently for social and political equality, viz: Negroes and whites in the same hotels, homes, residential districts, public and private places, a Negro as president, members of the Cabinet, Governors of States, Mayors of cities, and leaders of society in the United States. In this agitation, Du Bois is ably supported by the "Chicago Defender", a colored newspaper published in Chicago. This paper advocates Negroes in the Cabinet and Senate. All these, as everybody knows, are the Negroes' constitutional rights, but reason dictates that the masses of the white race will never stand by the ascendency of an opposite minority group to the favored positions in a government, society and industry that exist by the will of the majority, hence the demand of the Du Bois group of colored leaders will only lead, ultimately, to further disturbances in riots, lynching and mob rule. The only logical solution therefore, is to supply the Negro with opportunities and environments of his own, and there [by] point him to the fullness of his ambition.

Negroes who seek social equality

The Negro who seeks the White House in America could find ample play for his ambition in Africa. The Negro who seeks the office of Secretary of State in America would have a fair chance of demonstrating his diplomacy in Africa. The Negro who seeks a seat in the Senate or of being governor of a State of America, would be provided with a glorious chance for statesmanship in Africa.

The Negro has a claim on American white sympathy that cannot be denied. The Negro has labored for 300 years in contributing to America's greatness. White America will not be unmindful, therefore, of this consideration, but will treat him kindly. Yet it is realized that all human beings have a limit to their humanity. The humanity of white America, we realize, will seek self-protection and self-preservation, and that is why the thoughtful and reasonable Negro sees no hope in America for satisfying the aggressive program of the National Association for the Advancement of Colored People, but advances the reasonable plan of the Universal Negro Improvement Association, that of creating in Africa a nation and government for the Negro race.

This plan when properly undertaken and prosecuted will solve the race problem in America in fifty years. Africa affords a wonderful opportunity at the present time for colonization by the Negroes of the Western world. There is Liberia, already established as an independent Negro government. Let white America assist Afro-Americans to go there and help develop the country. Then, there are the late German colonies; let white sentiment force England and France to turn them over to the American and West Indian Negroes who fought for the Allies in the World's War. Then, France, England and Belgium owe America billions of dollars which they claim they cannot afford to repay immediately. Let them compromise by turning over Sierra Leone and the Ivory Coast on the West Coast of Africa and add them to Liberia and help make Liberia a state worthy of her history.

The Negroes of Africa and America are one in blood. They have sprung from the same common stock. They can work and live together and thus make their own racial contribution to the world.

Will deep thinking and liberal white America help? It is a considerate duty.

It is true that a large number of self-seeking colored agitators and so-called political leaders, who hanker after social equality and fight for the impossible in politics and governments, will rave, but remember that the slave-holder raved, but the North said, "Let the slaves go free"; the British Parliament raved when the Colonists said, "We want a free and American nation,"; the Monarchists of France raved when the people declared for a more liberal form of government.

The masses of Negroes think differently from the self-appointed leaders of the race. The majority of Negro leaders are selfish, self-appointed and not elected by the people. The people desire freedom in a land of their own, while the colored politician desires office and social equality for himself in America, and that is why we are asking white America to help the masses to realize their objective. . . .

Help the Negro to return home

Surely the time has come for the Negro to look homeward. He has won civilization and Christianity at the price of slavery. The Negro who is thoughtful and serviceable, feels that God intended him to give to his brothers still in darkness, the light of his civilization. The very light element of Negroes do not want to go back to Africa. They believe that in time, through miscegenation, the American race will be of their type. This is a fallacy and in that respect the agitation of the mulatto leader, Dr. W. E. B. Du Bois and the National Association for the Advancement of Colored People is dangerous to both races.

The off-colored people, being children of the Negro race, should combine to re-establish the purity of their own race, rather than seek to perpetuate the abuse of both races. That is to say, all elements of the Negro race should be encouraged to get together and form themselves into a healthy whole, rather than seeking to lose their identities through miscegenation and social intercourse with the white race. These statements are made because we desire an honest solution of the problem and no flattery or deception will bring that about.

Let the white and Negro people settle down in all seriousness and in true sympathy and solve the problem. When that is done, a new day of peace and good will will be ushered in.

The natural opponents among Negroes to a program of this kind are that lazy element who believe always in following the line of least resistance, being of themselves void of initiative and the pioneering spirit to do for themselves. The professional Negro leader and the class who are agitating for social equality feel that it is too much work for them to settle down and build up a civilization of their own. They feel it is easier to seize on to the civilization of the white man and under the guise of constitutional rights fight for those things that the white man has created. Natural reason suggests that the white man will not yield them, hence such leaders are but fools for their pains. Teach the Negro to do for himself, help him the best way possible in that direction; but to encourage him into the belief that he is going to possess himself of the things that others have fought and died for, is to build up in his mind false hopes never to be realized. As for instance, Dr. W. E. B. Du Bois, who has been educated by white charity, is a brilliant scholar, but he is not a hard worker. He prefers to use his higher intellectual abilities to fight for a place among white men in society, industry and in politics, rather than use that ability to work and create for his own race that which the race could be able to take credit for. He would not think of repeating for his race the work of the Pilgrim Fathers or the Colonists who laid the foundation of America, but he prefers to fight and agitate for the privilege of dancing with a white lady at a ball at the Biltmore or at the Astoria hotels in New York. That kind of leadership will destroy the Negro in America and against which the Universal Negro Improvement Association is fighting.

The Universal Negro Improvement Association is composed of all shades of Negroes – blacks, mulattoes and yellows, who are all working honestly for the purification of their race, and for a sympathetic adjustment of the race problem.

Source: Marcus Garvey, 'The True Solution of the Negro Problem' (1922) and 'Aims and Objects of Movement for Solution of Negro Problem' (1923?) from *Philosophy and Opinions of Marcus Garvey*, ed. Amy Jacques - Garvey, (New York: Universal Publishing House, 1923 and 1925), pp. 52-53 and 37-43 respectively.

6.5 The Communist Party and the "Negro Question"

The Communist Party in the United States was active in promoting racial equality, particularly in unions and among workers, in pursuit of the larger aim of working class solidarity against capitalist oppression and imperialism.

1. The industrialization of the South, the concentration of a new Negro working class population in the big cities of the East and North and the entrance of the Negroes into the basic industries on a mass scale, create the possibility for the Negro workers, under the leadership of the Communist Party, to assume the hegemony of all Negro liberation movements, and to increase their importance and role in the revolutionary struggle of the American proletariat.

The Negro working class has reached a stage of development which enables it, if properly organized and well led, to fulfill successfully its double historical mission:

(a) To play a considerable role in the class struggle against American imperialism as an important part of the American working class; and

(b) To lead the movement of the opposed masses of the Negro population.

2. The bulk of the Negro population (86 percent) live in the southern states: of this number 74 per cent live in the rural districts and are dependent almost exclusively upon agriculture for a livelihood. Approximately one-half of these rural dwellers live in the so-called "Black Belt," in which area they constitute more than 50 per cent of the entire population. The great mass of the Negro agrarian population are subject to the most ruthless exploitation and persecution of a semi-slave character. In addition to the ordinary forms of capitalist exploitation, American imperialism utilized every possible form of slave exploitation (peonage, share-cropping, landlord supervision of crops and marketing, etc.) for the purpose of extracting super-profits. On the basis of these slave remnants, there has grown up a super-structure of social and political inequality that expresses itself in lynching, segregation, Jim Crowism, etc.

Necessary condition for national revolutionary movement

3. The various forms of oppression of the Negro masses, who are concentrated mainly in the so-called "Black Belt," provide the necessary conditions for a national revolutionary movement among the Negroes. The Negro agricultural laborers and the tenant farmers feel the pressure of the white persecution and exploitation. Thus, the agrarian problem lies at the root of the Negro national movement. The great majority of Negroes in the rural districts of the South are not "reserves of capitalist reaction," but potential allies of the revolutionary proletariat. Their objective position facilitates their transformation into a revolutionary force, which, under the leadership of the proletariat, will be able to participate in the joint struggle with all other workers against capitalist exploitation.

4. It is the duty of the Negro workers to organize through the mobilization of the broad masses of the Negro population the struggle of the agricultural laborers and tenant farmers against all forms of semi-feudal oppression. On the other hand, it is the duty of the Communist Party of the U.S.A. to mobilize and rally the broad masses of the white workers for active participation in this struggle. For that reason the Party must consider the beginning of systematic work in the south as one of its main tasks, having regard for the fact that the bringing together of the workers and toiling masses of all nationalities for a joint struggle against the land-owners and the bourgeoisie is one of the most important aims of the Communist International, as laid down in the resolutions on the national and colonial question of the Second and Sixth Congresses of the Comintern.

For complete emancipation of oppressed Negro race

5. To accomplish this task, the Communist Party must come out as the champion of the right of the oppressed Negro race for full emancipation. While continuing and intensifying the struggle under the slogan of full social and political equality for the Negroes, which must remain the central slogan of our Party for work among the masses, the Party must come out openly and unreservedly for the right of Negroes to national self-determination in the southern states, where the Negroes form a majority of the population. The struggle for equal rights and the propaganda for the slogan of self-determination must be linked up with the economic demands of the Negro masses, especially those directed against the slave remnants and all forms of national and racial oppression. Special stress must be laid upon organizing active resistance against lynching. Jim Crowism, segregation and all other forms of oppression of the Negro population.

6. All work among the Negroes, as well as the struggle for the Negro cause among the whites, must be used, based upon the changes which have taken place in the relationship of classes among the Negro population. The existence of a Negro industrial proletariat of almost two million workers makes it imperative that the main emphasis should be placed on these new proletarian forces. The Negro workers must be organized under the leadership of the Communist Party, and thrown into joint struggle together with the white workers. The Party must learn to combine all demands of the Negroes with the economic and political struggle of the workers and the poor farmers.

American Negro question part of world problem

7. The Negro question in the United States must be treated in its relation to the Negro questions and struggles in other parts of the world. The Negro race everywhere is an oppressed race. Whether it is a minority (U.S.A., etc.) majority (South Africa) or inhabits a so-called independent state (Liberia, etc.) the Negroes are oppressed by imperialism. Thus, a common tie of interest is established for the revolutionary struggle of race and national liberation from imperialist domination of the Negroes in various parts of the world. A strong Negro revolutionary movement in the U.S.A. will be able to influence and direct the revolutionary movement in all those parts of the world where the Negroes are oppressed by imperialism.

8. The proletarianization of the Negro masses makes the trade unions the principal form of mass organization. It is the primary task of the Party to play an active part and lead in the work of organizing the Negro workers and agricultural laborers in trade unions. Owing to the refusal of the majority of the white unions in the U.S.A., led by the reactionary leaders, to admit Negroes to membership, steps must be immediately taken to set up special unions for those Negro workers who are not allowed to join the white unions. At the same time, however, the struggles for the inclusion of Negro workers in the existing unions must be intensified and concentrated upon, special attention must be given to those unions in which the statutes and rules set up special limitations against

the admission of Negro workers. The primary duty of the Communist Party in this connection is to wage a merciless struggle against the A. F. of L. bureaucracy, which prevents the Negro workers from joining the white workers' unions. The organization of special trade unions for the Negro masses must be carried out as part and parcel of the struggle against the restrictions imposed upon the Negro workers and for their admission to the white workers' unions. The creation of separate Negro unions should in no way weaken the struggle in the old unions for the admission of Negroes on equal terms. Every effort must be made to see that all the new unions organized by the left wing and by the Communist Party should embrace the workers of all nationalities and of all races. The principle of one union for all workers in each industry, white and black, should cease to be a mere slogan of propaganda, and must become a slogan of action.

Party trade union work among Negroes

9. While organizing the Negroes into unions and conducting an aggressive struggle against the anti-Negro trade union policy of the A. F. of L., the Party must pay more attention than it has hitherto done to the work in the Negro workers' organizations, such as the Brotherhood of Sleeping Car Porters, Chicago Asphalt Workers Union, and so on. The existence of two million Negro workers and the further industrialization of the Negroes demand a radical change in the work of the Party among the Negroes. The creation of working class organizations and the extension of our influence in the existing working class Negro organizations, are of much greater importance than the work in bourgeois and petty-bourgeois organizations, such as the National Association for the Advancement of Colored People, the Pan-African Congress, etc.

10. The American Negro Labor Congress* continues to exist only nominally. Every effort should be made to strengthen this organization as a medium through which we can extend the work of the Party among the Negro masses and mobilize the Negro workers under our leadership. After careful preparatory work, which must be started at once, another convention of the American Negro Labor Congress should be held. A concrete plan must also be presented to the Congress for an intensified struggle for the economic, social, political and national demands of the Negro masses. The program of the American Negro Labor Congress must deal specially with the agrarian demands for the Negro farmers and tenants in the South.

11. The importance of trade union work imposes special tasks upon the Trade Union Unity League. The T.U.U.L. has completely neglected the work among the Negro workers, notwithstanding the fact that these workers are objectively in a position to play a very great part in carrying through the program of organizing the unorganized. The closest contact must be established between the T.U.U.L. and the Negro masses. The T.U.U.L. must become the champion in the struggle for the rights of the Negroes in the old unions, and in the

* Founded in 1925.

organizing of new unions for both Negroes and whites, as well as separate Negro unions.

White chauvinism evidenced in the American Party

(12.) The C.E.C.† of the American Communist Party itself stated in its resolution of April 30, 1928, that "the Party as a whole has not sufficiently realized the significance of work among the Negroes." Such an attitude toward the Party work among the Negroes is, however, not satisfactory. The time is ripe to begin within the Party a courageous campaign of self-criticism concerning the work among the Negroes. Penetrating self-criticism is the necessary preliminary condition for directing the Negro work along new lines.

13. The Party must bear in mind that white chauvinism, which is the expression of the ideological influence of American imperialism among the workers, not only prevails among different strata of the white workers in the U.S.A., but is even reflected in various forms in the Party itself. White chauvinism has manifested itself even in open antagonism of some comrades to the Negro comrades. In some instances where Communists were called upon to champion and to lead in the most vigorous manner the fight against white chauvinism, they instead, yielded to it. In Gary, white members of the Workers Party protested against Negroes eating in the restaurant controlled by the Party. In Detroit, Party members, yielding to pressure, drove out Negro comrades from a social given in aid of the miners' strike.

While the Party has taken certain measures against these manifestations of white chauvinism, nevertheless those manifestations must be regarded as indications of race prejudice even in the ranks of the Party which must be fought with the utmost energy.

14. An aggressive fight against all forms of white chauvinism must be accompanied by a widespread and thorough educational campaign in the spirit of internationalism within the Party, utilizing for this purpose to the fullest possible extent the Party schools, the Party press and the public platform, to stamp out all forms of antagonism, or even indifference among our white comrades toward the Negro work. This educational work should be conducted simultaneously with a campaign to draw the white workers and the poor farmers into the struggle for the support of the demands of the Negro workers.

Tasks of Party in relation to Negro work

15. The Communist Party of the U.S.A., in its treatment of the Negro question must all the time bear in mind this twofold task:

(a) To fight for the full rights of the oppressed Negroes and for their right to self-determination and against all forms of chauvinism, especially among the workers of the oppressing nationality.

† Central Executive Committee.

(b) The propaganda and the day-to-day practice of international class solidarity must be considered as one of the basic tasks of the American Communist Party. The fight – by propaganda and by deeds – should be directed first and foremost against the chauvinism of the workers of the oppressing nationality as well as against bourgeois segregation tendencies of the oppressed nationality. The propaganda of international class solidarity is the necessary prerequisite for the unity of the working class in the struggle.

"The center of gravity in educating the workers of the oppressing countries in the principles of internationalism must inevitably consist in the propaganda and defense of these workers of the right of segregation by the oppressed countries. We have the right and duty to treat every socialist of an oppressing nation, who does not conduct such propaganda, as an imperialist and as a scoundrel." (Lenin, selected articles on the national question.)

16. The Party must seriously take up the task of training a cadre of Negro comrades as leaders, bring them into the Party schools in the U.S.A., and abroad, and make every effort to draw Negro proletarians into active and leading work in the Party, not confining the activities of the Negro comrades exclusively to the work among Negroes. Simultaneously, white workers must specially be trained for work among the Negroes.

17. Efforts must be made to transform the "Negro Champion"* into a weekly mass organ of the Negro proletariat and tenant farmers. Every encouragement and inducement must be given to the Negro comrades to utilize the Party press generally.

Negro work part of general work of Party

18. The Party must link up the struggle on behalf of the Negroes with the general campaigns of the Party. The Negro problem must be part and parcel of all and every campaign conducted by the Party. In the election campaigns, trade union work, the campaigns for the organization of the unorganized, anti-imperialist work, labor party campaign, International Labor Defense, etc., the Central Executive Committee must work out plans designed to draw the Negroes into active participation in all these campaigns, and at the same time to bring the white workers into the struggle on behalf of the Negroes' demands. It must be borne in mind that the Negro masses will not be won for the revolutionary struggles until such time as the most conscious section of the white workers show, by action, that they are fighting with the Negroes against all racial discrimination and persecution. Every member of the Party must bear in mind that "the age-long oppression of the colonial and weak nationalities by the imperialist powers, has given rise to a feeling of bitterness among the masses of the enslaved countries as well as a feeling of distrust toward the oppressing nations in general and toward the proletariat of those nations." (See resolution on Colonial and National Question of Second Congress.)

* Communist newspaper founded in the twenties.

19. The Negro women in industry and on the farms constitute a powerful potential force in the struggle for Negro emancipation. By reason of being unorganized to an even greater extent than male Negro workers, they are the most exploited section. The A. F. of L. bureaucracy naturally exercises toward them a double hostility, by reason of both their color and sex. It therefore becomes an important task of the Party to bring the Negro women into the economic and political struggle.

20. Only by an active and strenuous fight on the part of the white workers against all forms of oppression directed against the Negroes, will the Party be able to draw into its ranks the most active and conscious Negro workers – men and women – and to increase its influence in those intermediary organizations which are necessary for the mobilization of the Negro masses in the struggle against segregation, lynching, Jim Crowism, etc.

21. In the present struggle in the mining industry, the Negro workers participate actively and in large numbers. The leading role the Party played in this struggle has helped greatly to increase its prestige. Nevertheless, the special efforts being made by the Party in the work among the Negro strikers cannot be considered as adequate. The Party did not send enough Negro organizers into the coal fields, and it did not sufficiently attempt, in the first stages of the fight, to develop the most able Negro strikers and to place them in leading positions. The Party must be especially criticized for its failure to put Negro workers on the Presidium of the Pittsburgh Miners' Conference,* doing so only after such representation was demanded by the Negroes themselves.

22. In the work among the Negroes, special attention should be paid to the role played by the churches and preachers who are acting on behalf of American imperialism. The party must conduct a continuous and carefully worked out campaign among the Negro masses, sharpened primarily against the preachers and the churchmen, who are the agents of the oppressors of the Negro race.

Party work among Negro proletariat and peasantry

23. The Party must apply united front tactics for specific demands to the existing Negro petty bourgeois organizations. The purpose of these united front tactics should be the mobilizing of the Negro masses under the leadership of the Party, and to expose the treacherous petty bourgeois leadership of those organizations.

24. The Negro Miners Relief Committee and the Harlem Tenants League are examples of joint organizations of action which may serve as a means of drawing the Negro masses into struggle. In every case the utmost effort must be made to combine the struggle of the Negro workers with the struggle of the white workers, and to draw the white workers' organizations into such joint campaigns.

25. In order to reach the bulk of the Negro masses, special attention should be paid to the work among the Negroes in the South. For that purpose, the Party should

* A. T. U. U. L. affiliate.

† Birmingham became the center of party activity in the South.

establish a district organization in the most suitable locality in the South†. Whilst continuing trade union work among the Negro workers and the agricultural laborers, special organizations of tenant farmers must be set up. Special efforts must also be made to secure the support of the share croppers in the creation of such organizations. The Party must undertake the task of working out a definite program of immediate demands, directed against all slave remnants, which will serve as the rallying slogans for the formation of such peasant organizations.

Henceforth the Communist Party must consider the struggle on behalf of the Negro masses, the task of organizing the Negro workers and peasants and the drawing of these oppressed masses into the proletarian revolutionary struggle, as one of its major tasks, remembering, in the words of the Second Congress resolution, that "the victory over capitalism cannot be fully achieved and carried to its ultimate goal unless the proletariat and the toiling masses of all nations of the world rally of their own accord in a concordant and close union."

Source: The Communist International Resolution on the Negro Question in the US, *The Communist*, January 1930.

6.6 Negro Housing in the Urban North

The migration of blacks from the South to the cities of the North resulted in black ghettoes of sub-standard housing characterised by poverty, ill-health and crime. The conditions were publicised by the Committee on Negro Housing of President Hoover's Conference on Home Building and Home Ownership. The National Urban League was active in assisting incoming blacks to find employment and accommodation.

NEGRO HOUSING

Albany, New York

With the exception of a relatively small number of homes built by Negro owners for their own use, not one new structure has been made available for the Negro tenant since 1900. A large portion of the houses occupied by Negroes are very old brick buildings and their death, barring accidental destruction, is so lingering and drawn out over so many years of decline and decay that they are undesirable from external appearances alone. In some cases essential repairs were made and the life of the building prolonged, while in other cases no repairs have been made and the buildings remain occupied. The houses do not represent what the city approves according to its Building Ordinance, but it does represent what Albany tolerates and offers to the increasing Negro population group. The Negro population is widely scattered in Albany, being distributed throughout 17 of the 19 wards of the city.

In general there is a low standard of housing for the Negro population in Albany. The scanty equipment and poor repair of the average Negro dwelling make the rent paid comparatively high.

Chicago, Illinois

A selection was made of 274 Negro families living in all sections of Chicago. . .

For the most part the physical surroundings of the Negro family, as indicated by these family histories, are poor . . .

On the South Side, where most of the Negro population lives, the low quality of housing is widespread, although there are some houses of a better grade which are greatly in demand.

The ordinary conveniences, considered necessities by the average white citizen, are often lacking. Bathrooms are often missing. Gas lighting is common, and electric lighting is a rarity. Heating is commonly done by wood or coal stoves, and furnaces are rather exceptional; when furnaces are present, they are sometimes out of commission . . .

An almost complete cessation in the building of dwellings in Chicago extended over the greater part of the period when Negro migration was heaviest. As the most recent comers into the tenement districts of the city, Negroes and Mexicans have found shelter in the most used, most outworn and derelict housing which the city keeps. The old tenement districts have long been experiencing a steady encroachment by industry and commerce. In whole or in part as residence sections they are destined for extinction. Already deterioration is general in them, both in their houses and in their neighborhood conditions. It is unlikely that anything will be done to make these districts more fit for dwelling places. Although in many cases it seems hardly conceivable, it nevertheless is probable that further decline and deterioration are all that can be predicted with certainty for much of the renting property in them . . .

About 8 per cent of the 770 buildings in which the families included in this study dwelt occupied the rear of the lots and had another building in front of them. Almost six out of every ten buildings (59 per cent) had not more than two floors. Fifty-six per cent had only one or two dwellings in them. Fully half were of frame construction though within the fire limits. These are characteristics of older buildings rather than of recent construction in the thickly populated sections of a large city. As a city grows, the one-family frame houses give way to larger multi-family buildings of brick. Land values increase and the ideal of having a city of one-family homes fades into impracticability. . . .

Columbus, Ohio

It is well known that unsatisfactory housing conditions are associated with poverty, both as a cause and as an effect. The very poor man, especially if he has lived only under rural conditions, does not know how to care for modern equipment when he secures a good house. He justifies the landlord's claim that poor people have poor ways. On the other hand, the lack of sanitary facilities is a real reason for dirt and disorder. The housewife who must carry all water from a distant well or hydrant cannot be held entirely to blame if the house is not immaculate. Under such conditions good habits of housekeeping are likely to suffer degeneration.

Negro migrants are poor. Their poverty and the barriers of race restrict them severely in their selection of a home. To this home they bring their country habits, thus helping to keep housing standards low; especially is this true in a district like Champion Avenue, where many of the lots are almost entirely taken up with cheap structures built primarily to produce income from rentals. . .

Two types of dwellings prevail in this district. There is the old, solidly built house which was originally built for the use of its owner. Some of these houses have been remodeled and modernized by their present owners; others have been divided into tenements; still others remain unchanged – substantial, but not modern. There is also the type of dwelling which had been built more recently and less substantially, not to house its owner, but rather to supply him with an income from rents. Dwellings of this type are usually built at the least possible cost and with the fewest possible conveniences. Costs of repair on such houses would be heavy if repairs were made, but it is seldom found necessary to keep such houses in repair in order to rent them. Several cases can be pointed out in which the landlord has built two four-family flats on one lot with a sixty-foot frontage on the street. One flat is built close to the sidewalk and facing the street, and the other is built on the rear of the lot, facing the alley. The prevailing size of these flats is four rooms. Practically all of them are rental properties, as is shown by the fact that of the 84 households living in four-room apartments, only three were reported as living in their own homes.

These built-up alleys are often dignified by the term "court". A row of sheds built between the two flats, over the sewer-main, contains the fuel supply and the toilets. The latter was generally of the long-hopper type, with a funnel tile connected directly with the sewer-main, but with no flush arrangement to clear the funnel, which in many cases becomes clogged, especially in freezing weather or when used as a garbage receiver. When this happens, such a "toilet" becomes in fact a poor kind of vault privy, in violation of the real intent of the public health laws.

Detroit, Michigan

Housing is one of the most serious problems of the Negro in Detroit. For some years the fluctuating shortage in the number of houses for the population in general has had it greatest effect upon the Negro group. . .

This St. Antoine district (which holds the largest Negro population) may be termed a deteriorating area from the standpoint of family housing. Bordering on the main commercial center of the city, it is no longer a favorable location for residential purposes, as factories, garages and other commercial establishments have been built. The paving is not generally of the best and traffic is heavy. Land values are high since the area is chiefly used for manufacturing or commercial purposes. A preponderance of the houses are old frame dwellings, and as the landlords are interested in them only as a temporary source of income until the property can be sold for other than residential purposes, sanitary conditions are often far from the best. In some blocks the houses are so dilapidated that expenditure on the part of the owner to make them suitable for living purposes would be useless. However, since houses still remain and Negro tenants can be obtained for them at any reasonable rent, most of them are still occupied.

The fact that the whites in Detroit feel that the presence of a Negro in a neighborhood depreciates property values is one of the most important factors in "the race problem."

Elizabeth, New Jersey

In Elizabeth, as in many other northern cities, there are no new houses built for occupancy by Negro tenants. Today a number of the houses occupied by Negroes, particularly in Elizabethport, are unfit for human habitation. The life of such houses is so long and their death, barring accidental destruction, is so lingering and drawn out over so many years of decline and decay that they are undesirable on external appearances alone. In some cases essential repairs have been made, and the buildings have remained occupied. Such conditions do not represent what the City of Elizabeth approves as satisfactory according to its ordinances, but they do represent what Elizabeth tolerates and offers to the ever-increasing Negro population.

Kansas City, Missouri

. . . Few cities in the United States have better housing for the middle classes and for a large part of the working class; yet, in spite of these hopeful conditions, Kansas City has a housing problem of sufficient gravity to call for a vigorous movement to eradicate the evils which now exist. The housing problem as related to the Negro is an especially serious one, since only limited districts are available to him for residence purposes; and, as the population increases, these districts must either be enlarged or become overcrowded. The latter course has usually prevailed, and as a result the conditions have been gradually growing worse. . .

Toilet accommodations are also totally inadequate. The present requirements of the sanitary ordinances of the city provide that not less than one water-closet or privy shall be furnished for every twenty persons, while the new building code provides that there must be one of these for every fifteen persons. Little effort has been made to enforce these provisions, especially in the old buildings where the mass of the Negroes are living . . . .

Only a small percentage of the houses in the congested Negro districts are provided with baths, either tub or shower, though the nature of the daily work done by both the Negro men and the Negro women makes it absolutely necessary for them to keep clean, if they are to retain their health and self-respect; yet the houses in which they are forced to live are not provided with the means. In an investigation made by the Board of Public Welfare near Garrison Square only two bathtubs were found in 827 Negro houses. However, the conditions are not so bad in the other sections of the city. Since baths are not provided by the Negro in his house, there remains no place in the entire city, save the free baths in the Allen Chapel African Methodist Church and a few Negro barber shops, where the Negro can secure a bath.

A SURVEY OF THE EFFECTS OF URBANISATION

Urbanization on a large scale is comparatively new among Negroes. Up to 1900, 77 per cent of Negroes were rural dwellers. Since 1910, they have been making up for lost time . . . In spite of the fact that many of the forces pulling the Negroes to cities during the last two decades have diminished in intensity, the drift has continued. Attempts to arouse interest in the "back-to-the farm movement" have generally fallen on deaf ears. The story is told of a labor agent from the South who went to Chicago some years ago to recruit workers in lumber mills. He was asked, "Mister, where did you say them logs is?" When told "Mississippi," his reply was, "If you'll bring them up here we'll saw them for you." The Negro in the North was predominantly urban before the opening of the present century. In 1920 he was 70 per cent urban in sharp contrast to native whites, who were only 38.6 per cent.

The movement was primarily to the four centers – New York, Chicago, Philadelphia, and Detroit . . . Whatever influence Horace Greeley may have exerted on the Negro question before and during the Civil War, his advice to young men to go west has apparently not been taken seriously by the Negro of the present generation. For in 1930 there were only 130,000 Negroes in the entire western area. In about fifteen years Detroit's Negro population jumped from 6,000 to over 100,000. New York City rose from 150,000 in 1920 to 327,000 in 1930 – an increase of 115 per cent against a 20 per cent increase for its white population.

What has been the effect of this new, unassimilated group on the community life? Everywhere this concentration of Negroes in segregated colonies has been followed by an aggravation of social problems.

According to the White House Conference on Child Health, tuberculosis among Negro children under five years of age is double that of white children; for those between the ages of five and nine, it is four times as great; and from ten to nineteen years of age, it is five times that of whites.

In Chicago, Negro girls and young women have constituted nearly one-third of females confined in the jails. The Department of Correction of New York reported for 1930 that of 59,000 males arraigned in the four courts, 16,391, or about 28 per cent, were Negroes – five times as great as the population should warrant. One would think that Negroes are especially fond of going to jail. According to studies made by the National Urban League, unemployment runs all the way from four to six times that of the city as a whole. In juvenile delinquency, crime, disease, and the other ills that so vitally affect family life, the story is generally the same. Harlem is referred to in a report of the New York Vice Committee as a place where whites go on a moral vacation.

The causes are not far to seek. A study of 4,000 Negro families of Harlem in 1920 revealed that one-half the income of the heads of these families ($102 per month average) was expended for rent. To supplement this income, over 80 per cent of mothers worked away from home; 65 per cent resorted to taking in of lodgers.

Restriction to definite areas and denial of opportunities to work at the more remunerative jobs were the main contributing factors. A study just completed by the New York Building Congress divides Manhattan into four rental zones. Although the majority of the Negro population falls within the lowest-income group, 75 per cent of them live in the fifty to one-hundred-dollar-per-month rental zone – the third highest rental section for the city.

Negroes . . . have usually taken over declining areas, houses abandoned as undesirable in the general forward movement of whites to other sections and supply tenants for houses that would otherwise remain unoccupied. Strange as it may seem, these newcomers have been compelled to pay from 10 to 40 per cent more for these houses than was paid by white tenants who preceded them. In Chicago, Negro tenants paid from $8.00 to $20.00 for the same room for which white tenants formerly paid $4.00 to $5.00. In New York, Negroes were found paying, in some instances, $110.00 per month for the same apartments for which whites had previously paid $55.00. Similar conditions were found in Philadelphia and Buffalo . . .

The mobility of the urbanized Negro within the city is also greater than that of whites. It is estimated that the average Negro tenant in New York moves once every fifteen months, while the average white family moves only once in five years.

A study of census tracts by the President's Research Commission on recent social trends shows a pronounced tendency for immigrants to abandon their colonies, and disperse among the general population. Negro colonies, on the contrary, show a different history. Instead of scattering, they tend to become more compact and racially more homogeneous.

Many students of the race problem in America have looked to urbanization and northern migration as one possible solution. But in deserting the country for the city, the Negro appears to have merely jumped from the frying pan into the fire . . . Urbanization has accentuated the growing conviction that, regardless of efforts, the Negro finds it increasingly difficult to "make it on the level"; that he cannot beat the color line; that the barrier of race has condemned him to the lower level of life.

Sources: President's Conference on Home Building and Home Ownership, Negro Housing, 1931.
James H Hubert, 'Urbanisation and the Negro', *Proceedings of the National Conference of Social Work, 1933* (Chicago, 1933), pp. 420-425.

6.7 Exposition of "Negro"

Much contemporary academic and scientific thinking about Afro-Americans in the United States was encapsulated in an article on the "Negro" which first appeared in the celebrated 11th Edition of the *Enclopaedia Britannica* of 1910/11 and was carried forward unaltered into the 13th Edition of 1926.

It is claimed that negroes apparently occupied "a lower evolutionary plane" than the white and yellow races owing to the less challenging environment in which they had developed. The article repeats the perceptions of the white South about black Americans: their possession of the typical "Sambo" personality – child-like, generally cheerful, but given to violent changes of mood; and their obsessive concern with sexual activity. It is argued that a resolution of the difficulties over race relations in the United States was leading to an accommodation somewhere between the racial controls of the slave system and the freedom of the period of Radical Reconstruction.

It is accepted that black Americans have benefited since emancipation, but unevenly, with the leading 10% having advanced significantly, but the bottom 10% having regressed to a condition arguably worse than they endured under slavery. Nevertheless, the article concludes that their experience as slaves had a beneficial effect in preparing them for incorporation into American life, although doubts are expressed about their capacity to contribute as much as they had in the past to the increasingly complex industrial and commercial life of the South. The imposition of white-imposed segregation in the South is seen as part of the development of a caste system.

This treatment of racial difference may be contrasted with the UNESCO statement on "Race" of 1950 (8.2).

Blacks and the New Deal

7.1 Unequal Wages in New Deal Projects

Under the New Deal, Federal projects continued the common practice of paying blacks less than whites for the same work: the implications and rationale are explored in this article.

No issue affecting Negroes under the recovery program is of more importance than that of wage policy under the NRA. There is no other question arising out of the new deal which has excited more discussion among enlightened Negroes. Like most important controversies, this is a complicated matter. To discuss it intelligently, one must consider the philosophy of the recovery program and the implications of the Negro's position in American life.

There are two observations which are fundamental. In the first place, Southern industrial life is personal and paternalistic. The employers like to keep in touch with the workers. This paternalism is especially present in the relationship between the white employer and his Negro workers. A manufacturer of the deep South explained why he preferred Negro workers saying that he could handle them easier – they felt close to the boss and he felt close to them. On the other hand, the philosophy behind minimum wage provisions (and all social legislation) is that of an impersonal and highly developed industrial life. Thus there is a fundamental conflict between the Southern system and the labor provisions of the NRA.

The very idea of a sub-marginal minimum for Negro workers is an expression of the second important feature of the situation – the tendency to lump all Negroes together and judge them by the least desirable and the least able in the group. This tendency is, of course, the most arbitrary and pernicious feature of race prejudice.

Since the inauguration of the NRA there has been a series of attempts to establish lower minimum rates of wages for Negro workers. First it was said that Negroes have a lower standard of living. Then, lower wages were defended on the basis of the Negro's slower efficiency. Lastly, it was pointed out that lower wages for Negroes were traditional and should be incorporated as a feature of the New Deal. However, the most telling and important argument for a lower minimum wage for Negroes was the fact that they were being displaced from industry as a result of the operation of labor provision of the NRA.

Long before the New Deal was thought of, there was a constant displacement of Negroes by white workers. Certain cities in the South replaced their colored workers with whites; in other places organizations were initiated to foster the substitution of white for black laborers in all positions. The minimum wage regulations of the NRA accelerated this tendency. Indeed, it resulted in wholesale discharges in certain areas. More recently, the tendency has been arrested.

There are many causes for the failure of the program to be carried further. In the first place, there is reason to believe that employers resorted to the discharge of colored workers as a means of forcing the NRA to grant a racial differential. They declared that if a man has to be paid as much as twelve dollars a week, they would pay a white worker that wage. Then, too, there are many instances where it is impossible to discharge a whole working force. Even modern industry with its automatic machinery requires workers of some training, and training is a time and money consuming process. Thus, where Negroes formed a large percentage of the total working force, it was often impracticable to displace them and hire a new all-white labor force.

Nevertheless, there have been many displacements of Negroes. All the available evidence seems to indicate, as one would expect, that perhaps the greater part of this substitution of white for Negro workers has occurred in small enterprises where the Negro is often the marginal worker. In such plants, the separation of Negro workers presented no important question of organizational integrity or of training.

Out of these developments a movement for a racial differential has arisen. The motivating force for such a campaign has come from the Southern employers who have, for the most part, shifted their emphasis from standard of living and tradition to efficiency and displacement. The latter feature – the loss of job opportunities to Negroes – has been made much of in recent months. Appeals have been made to Negro leaders to endorse a lower minimum wage for Negroes on the ground that such action is necessary if Negroes are not to be forced out of industry. The colored leaders have been careful in their championing of this cause. A few have been convinced that it is the only possible way out; some have supported the policy because of local pressure in the South but most have tried to keep out of the discussion. Many are almost convinced that it is the proper choice but fear a loss of prestige among Negroes if they speak in favor of such a measure.

Briefly, the only possible argument for a racial wage differential is one based upon a *de facto* situation. Negroes have lost jobs as a result of the NRA, and a lower wage for them would counteract this tendency. It would assure Negroes of retaining their old jobs and perhaps it would lead to a few additional ones. It may be observed that this reasoning is correct as far as it goes. Certainly, a racial differential would do much to arrest and, perchance, offset the displacement of Negro workers. But there is more involved in this question than the arresting of Negro displacement. In it are the elements which combine to establish the whole industrial position of colored Americans.

The establishment of a lower minimum wage for Negroes would have far reaching effects. It would brand black workers as a less efficient and sub-marginal group. It would increase the ill-will and friction between white and colored workers. It would destroy much of the advance Negroes have made in the industrial North. It would destroy any possibility of ever forming a strong and effective labor movement in the nation. The ultimate effect would be to relegate Negroes into a low wage caste and place the federal stamp of approval upon their being in such a position.

It was pointed out above that the most damnable feature of racial prejudice in America is the tendency to judge all Negroes by the least able colored persons. Obviously, a racial minimum is an expression of such an attitude. Were this not true, why should Negroes be singled out for a special – -and lower–rate of pay? There have been no satisfactory or convincing studies of racial efficiency. (Efforts along this line are even more crude than the measures we have which have been set up to gauge intelligence.) Indeed, it is absurd to talk about racial efficiency since Negroes, like every other group of human beings, vary in their effectiveness. The efficiency of a worker depends upon his native ability, environment and specific training. These factors differ between individuals rather than between races. A racial differential on the other hand would say, in effect, that efficiency is based on race and the individual black worker – because he is a Negro – is less efficient.

Now, there is still another phase of this matter. The very attitude which dictates a racial differential would make such a provision most discriminatory against colored workers. Any minimum wage tends to become a maximum. In the case of Negro workers this tendency would be accentuated. Since all Negroes are usually considered the same regardless of their ability, a lower minimum for black labor would in fact, mean that practically all Negroes would receive wages lower than their white prototypes. Not only would this be manifestly unfair, but in certain areas it would undermine the race's industrial progress of the last twenty years. During the period, Negroes have entered the industries of the North and the West as never before. They came from the South, where they were treated with mercy (as opposed to justice), and faced a situation which was new to them. Standards of efficiency were higher and they had to measure up to these new standards. Some failed but the recent data on Negro participation in Northern industry shows that many succeeded. It has been a difficult process of adaptation. The fruits have been higher wages and less racial discrimination in rates of pay. To establish a differential based on race, would be, in effect, to take away the fruits of this hard-won victory.

Nor would the white worker respond favorably to the notion of a lower minimum for Negro workers. His first response in the South would be favorable because his ego would be flattered. But when the lower minimum destroyed the effectiveness of the higher minimum, the white recipient of the latter would blame the Negro. The black worker, North and South, would be regarded as the force which rendered it impossible for workers to demand a decent wage and find employment. This would occasion no end of misunderstanding and hatred between the white and black worker.

It is clear that the unity of all labor into an organized body would be impossible if there were a racial differential. The essence of collective bargaining is an impersonal and standard wage. Unionism rests upon the cooperation of all workers. A racial wage differential prevents both of these developments. It would, therefore, destroy the possibility of *a real labor movement* in this country.

Source: *The Crisis*, XLI, August 1934, pp. 236, 238. Reprinted by permission of *The Crisis Magazine*.

7.2 The CIO and the National Negro Congress

The Committee for Industrial Organization (CIO) looked to organise workers in industries ignored by the American Federation of Labor, and also across the colour line. Philip Murray, Chairman of the Steel Workers Organizing Committee, seeks black support for the new unions.

Since the founders of the Committee for Industrial Organization met in Atlantic City two years ago to form that Committee, they set out to organize the great mass production industries of this nation upon the firm belief that each international and each national union should admit to membership upon a basis of absolute equality every man and woman eligible to membership, regardless of race, creed, political or religious belief.

Eight international unions, in November, 1935, founded the Committee for Industrial Organization – having a total membership of one million. Now our membership is four million constituting 32 internationals. We have reduced hours of labor, increased wages for the wage earners who are members of the Committee for Industrial Organization by a sum of money approximating one billion dollars. We admit into our international and national unions colored workers upon the same basis of economic equality as white workers. All members of our several unions enjoy the same economic provisions as the others. That is one of the reasons why the CIO is extremely popular with the workers of this nation. This is true because it is the kind of union that the wage earners want.

Let us analyze in a few situations just what this great organization has done to help the poor. Some eighteen months ago, I was assigned by the CIO to assume the chairmanship of the Steel Workers Organizing Committee. For a period of approximately fifty years, the steel industry has been completely non-union. The steel industry represents the greatest and most powerful combination of wealth in American industry – five billion dollars. That five billion dollars has been utilized with all of its influence – to prevent steel workers from getting membership in independent labor unions; to prevent the enactment of social legislation of all kinds and descriptions, not only in our state legislatures, but in the seat of our federal government as well; to corrupt our courts and to corrupt men holding important public office; to depress wages and worsen the condition of employment of steel workers, not only in the steel industry, because the repercussions of what this powerful combination was doing in steel was felt in every industry, small and large, and in every enterprise where people were working. And this is the steel industry with its power, lust and greed.

Eighteen months ago, when we set out to organize the steel workers, there was nothing. Let us look at the picture today. A crusade on the part of the CIO and the Steel Workers Organizing Committee has resulted in the following: We have organized

1052 lodges in the United States and Canada. We have a signed membership of 532,000. We have 785 independent grievance committees which are peacefully adjusting all grievances affecting the men in those plants. We have reduced hours of labor from 48 to 40. We have improved conditions of labor. Last, but not least, our Research Bureau has found, resulting from our efforts, that the wages of the steel workers have increased by a sum of $236,000,000 annually.

Surely, trade unions along industrial lines or any other lines if they fulfill their mission in life, have but one service to render – a better distribution of the world's goods, a greater opportunity to improve your status economically, socially and politically. Unions without this purpose are useless. But a union such as the Steel Workers Organizing Committee rendering such a service has made friends in the steel industry and among the workers of the nation generally.

Let us visualize another union in the CIO – the United Automobile Workers of America. For fifty years the AFL tried to organize steel and couldn't succeed. And when they did set up unions in steel, what did they do? They barred colored workers from their unions and they still exercise the same form of discrimination. Recently they decided, and I speak now of the AFL, to amend their organizing policy in craft unions so that colored workers may be brought into what is known as Class B membership – the other people can be Class A, thereby separating them and establishing unjust wage differentials for colored wage earners.

To return to the auto workers. I met with the United Auto Workers at their national office in Detroit where the President told me that they had 23,000 members. I asked him how long the AFL had been trying to organize. He told me they started to organize in 1933 when the National Recovery Act came about and Section 7A gave the workers the right to organize. They established a few federal labor unions here and then left. The workers regretted the unwillingness of the AFL to take advantage of its opportunities during the NRA to organize this industry. So when the CIO was formed, they immediately affiliated with this Committee for the protection and for the assistance which the CIO promptly gave them.

There is only one large automobile manufacturer in this country who has not executed a written agreement with the union – Henry Ford. But the officers and members of the union will convince Mr. Ford of the need of establishing a different kind of relationship than he has now.*

Another situation – you have in Philadelphia the International Brotherhood of Electrical Workers, a powerful craft organization that undoubtedly has rendered some service to the labor movement. But never in its history has it attempted to organize the electrical manufacturing industry. Nothing was done to organize the large plants of Westinghouse, General Electric, etc., but this small group of men in Philadelphia working in Philco Radio just a year ago determined to affiliate to the CIO and set out on their own a union to organize the electrical industry, and the President of the Electrical Union reported to the CIO conference this week that they now have 135,000 members dues paying with contracts for closed shops.

* The National Negro Congress cooperated with Walker P. Reuther and the UAW in their fight with Ford.

Who ever heard of the AFL attempting to organize the rubber industry? Never, except in Akron where a few men established a federal labor union and divided that union into six separate crafts. That small union, 2,800 in number, rebelled against the autocratic leadership of the A. F. of L.

I could follow industry after industry. There is a striking example in New York. The great transport system in the city of New York operating for years – no organization. Finally just about eighteen months ago a few men formed a small local union. They went to Mr. Green of the A. F. of L. and asked for an industrial charter to organize all the workers on that system. Mr. Green replied that they couldn't do it, and that the only basis on which those workers could be organized is on a basis of eighteen craft unions. Mr. Quill, President of the Transport Workers Union replied that they couldn't be organized that way. These men were, after this, determined to ask the CIO for a charter. That was only six months ago. Now this company is completely organized.

I could continue down the list, giving you the history of the international and national unions that have been formed by the CIO in the past eighteen months. Behind it all lies your opportunity. I speak now particularly with reference to the Negro workers. It is the only labor organization in this country that affords the Negro worker the gain that we are entitled to in this life. I might say to you that since we have started this campaign, we have had small conventions of Negro workers and the representatives of Negro organizations in almost every large city throughout the country. Your distinguished chairman, Mr. Randolph, has participated in these conferences and attended the last conference with your Secretary, Mr. John P. Davis, held in Pittsburgh.

But what has happened in the past eighteen months? We have organized the steel towns. I have often maintained that no nation can be politically free unless it is economically free. The Steel Workers Organizing Committee and the CIO gave to the steel workers of all the steel communities throughout the state their economic freedom, and when the people of those towns realized and appreciated the fact that economic freedom had come, they then set in motion an organism, the mechanism, the instrument that might make possible their political freedom. In recent primaries in the State of Pennsylvania in every steel town or almost every steel town the lodges of steel workers that had been set up nominated their own candidates – nominated them in the primaries and have taken from the steel corporations the political control which they formerly held over the people residing in the towns. Thus, the CIO has given every wage earner also the right to exercise his franchise without danger of interference.

Now I have attempted to describe to you the nature of the work now being done by the CIO. We have come to regard this institution as the most powerful labor movement in America. We regard its leaders as the type of leadership that the wage earners want, its policies as the policies which workers also want. We contend that our efforts have had their effect in great non-union industries and enterprises, that many men and women who were not and are not affiliated with unions have enjoyed some of the benefits given to members of the CIO. And I am going to ask your Congress, representing the great Negro population of the United States to take action in the labor division of the Congress; to return to your homes and communities and render every assistance you can to this crusade.

There is no other labor organization in this country that affords the Negro worker the same opportunity as do the great international and national unions affiliated with the CIO. I can conceive your situation – 90 to 95% of our entire colored population poor. Thousands of them are undernourished and underprivileged. They have the same ideals and aspirations and the same hopes beating within their breasts that beat within the breast of a white man. Their wives and children have the same feelings and emotions and they are entitled by all the laws of nature itself to the same opportunity in the game of life as any white man.

We tell you your economic and political salvation lies in assisting the CIO in the course of its activities. I speak to you today as an officer of the CIO without prejudices, without passions. I do have a deep-rooted feeling that you can do much in your communities and towns and in your organizations, societies, churches – in all your activities–to assist the CIO in the furtherance of its campaign to help you.

So, my friends, I am happy to have had this opportunity of being with you this afternoon. I want to encourage you. I want you to believe that the CIO is ready to lend every effort to help you in your efforts. And I beseech your support and the support of your officers (many of whom I know personally and whom I have collaborated with in the development of institutions such as you are interested in) in this great undertaking which the CIO has now begun.

Source: Second National Negro Congress, *Official Proceedings, 1937*, (Washington, D.C., 1937).

7.3 The March on Washington Movement

A. Philip Randolph had successfully organised the strongest black labour union, the Brotherhood of Sleeping Car Porters in 1925. In 1941, he and other black leaders combined to prepare for a march on Washington to persuade President F. D. Roosevelt to end discrimination in employment in the defence industries. In order to forestall the march, FDR issued Executive Order 8802.

July 1, 1941

We call upon you to fight for jobs in National Defense.

We call upon you to struggle for the integration of Negroes in the armed forces, such as the Air Corps, Navy, Army and Marine Corps of the Nation.

We call upon you to demonstrate for the abolition of Jim-Crowism in all Government departments and defense employment.

This is an hour of crisis. It is a crisis of democracy. It is a crisis of minority groups. It is a crisis of Negro Americans.

What is this crisis?

To American Negroes, it is the denial of jobs in Government defense projects. It is racial discrimination in Government departments. It is widespread Jim-Crowism in the armed forces of the Nation.

While billions of the taxpayers' money are being spent for war weapons, Negro workers are being turned away from the gates of factories, mines and mills – being flatly told, "NOTHING DOING." Some employers refuse to give Negroes jobs when they are without "union cards," and some unions refuse Negro workers union cards when they are "without jobs."

What shall we do?

What a dilemma!

What a runaround!

What a disgrace!

What a blow below the belt!

'Though dark, doubtful and discouraging, all is not lost, all is not hopeless. 'Though battered and bruised, we are not beaten, broken or bewildered.

Verily, the Negroes' deepest disappointments and direst defeats, their tragic trials and outrageous oppressions in these dreadful days of destruction and disaster to democracy and freedom, and the rights of minority peoples, and the dignity and independence of the human spirit, is the Negroes' greatest opportunity to rise to the highest heights of struggle for freedom and justice in Government, in industry, in labor unions, education, social service, religion and culture.

With faith and confidence of the Negro people in their own power for self-liberation, Negroes can break down the barriers of discrimination against employment in National Defense. Negroes can kill the deadly serpent of race hatred in the Army, Navy, Air and Marine Corps, and smash through and blast the Government, business and labor-union red tape to win the right to equal opportunity in vocational training and re-training in defense employment.

Most important and vital to all, Negroes, by the mobilization and coordination of their mass power, can cause PRESIDENT ROOSEVELT TO ISSUE AN EXECUTIVE ORDER ABOLISHING DISCRIMINATIONS IN ALL GOVERNMENT DEPARTMENTS, ARMY, NAVY, AIR CORPS AND NATIONAL DEFENSE JOBS.

Of course, the task is not easy. In very truth, it is big, tremendous and difficult.

It will cost money.

It will require sacrifice.

It will tax the Negroes' courage, determination and will to struggle. But we can, must and will triumph.

The Negroes' stake in national defense is big. It consists of jobs, thousands of jobs. It may represent millions, yes, hundreds of millions of dollars in wages. It consists of new industrial opportunities and hope. This is worth fighting for.

But to win our stakes, it will require an "all-out," bold and total effort and demonstration of colossal proportions.

Negroes can build a mammoth machine of mass action with a terrific and tremendous driving and striking power that can shatter and crush the evil fortress of race prejudice and hate, if they will only resolve to do so and never stop, until victory comes.

Dear fellow Negro Americans, be not dismayed in these terrible times. You possess power, great power. Our problem is to harness and hitch it up for action on the broadest, daring and most gigantic scale.

In this period of power politics, nothing counts but pressure, more pressure, and still more pressure, through the tactic and strategy of broad, organized, aggressive mass action behind the vital and important issues of the Negro. To this end, we propose that ten thousand Negroes MARCH ON WASHINGTON FOR JOBS IN NATIONAL DEFENSE AND EQUAL INTEGRATION IN THE FIGHTING FORCES OF THE UNITED STATES.

An "all-out" thundering march on Washington, ending in a monster and huge demonstration at Lincoln's Monument will shake up white America.

It will shake up official Washington.

It will give encouragement to our white friends to fight all the harder by our side, with us, for our righteous cause.

It will gain respect for the Negro people.

It will create a new sense of self-respect among Negroes.

But what of national unity?

We believe in national unity which recognizes equal opportunity of black and white citizens to jobs in national defense and the armed forces, and in all other institutions and endeavors in America. We condemn all dictatorships, Fascist, Nazi and Communist. We are loyal, patriotic Americans, all.

But, if American democracy will not defend its defenders; if American democracy will not protect its protectors; if American democracy will not give jobs to its toilers because of race or color; if American democracy will not insure equality of opportunity, freedom and justice to its citizens, black and white, it is a hollow mockery and belies the principles for which it is supposed to stand.

To the hard, difficult and trying problem of securing equal participation in national defense, we summon all Negro Americans to march on Washington. We summon Negro Americans to form committees in various cities to recruit and register marchers and raise funds through the sale of buttons and other legitimate means for the expenses of marchers to Washington by buses, train, private automobiles, trucks, and on foot.

We summon Negro Americans to stage marches on their City Halls and Councils in their respective cities and urge them to memorialize the President to issue an executive order to abolish discrimination in the Government and national defense.

However, we sternly counsel against violence and ill-considered and intemperate action and the abuse of power. Mass power, like physical power, when misdirected is more harmful than helpful.

We summon you to mass action that is orderly and lawful, but aggressive and militant, for justice, equality and freedom.

Crispus Attucks marched and died as a martyr for American independence. Nat Turner, Denmark Vesey, Gabriel Prosser, Harriet Tubman and Frederick Douglass fought, bled and died for the emancipation of Negro slaves and the preservation of American democracy.

Abraham Lincoln, in times of the grave emergency of the Civil War, issued the Proclamation of Emancipation for the freedom of Negro slaves and the preservation of American democracy.

Today, we call upon President Roosevelt, a great humanitarian and idealist, to follow in the footsteps of his noble and illustrious predecessor and take the second decisive step in this world and national emergency and free American Negro citizens of the stigma, humiliation and insult of discrimination and Jim-Crowism in Government departments and national defense.

The Federal Government cannot with clear conscience call upon private industry and labor unions to abolish discrimination based upon race and color as long as it practices discrimination itself against Negro Americans.

Executive Order 8802: Franklin D. Roosevelt

REAFFIRMING POLICY OF FULL PARTICIPATION IN THE DEFENSE PROGRAM BY ALL PERSONS, REGARDLESS OF RACE, CREED, COLOR, OR NATIONAL ORIGIN, AND DIRECTING CERTAIN ACTION IN FURTHERANCE OF SAID POLICY

WHEREAS it is the policy of the United States to encourage full participation in the national defense program by all citizens of the United States, regardless of race, creed, color, or national origin, in the firm belief that the democratic way of life within the Nation can be defended successfully only with the help and support of all groups within its borders; and

WHEREAS there is evidence that available and needed workers have been barred from employment in industries engaged in defense production solely because of considerations of race, creed, color, or national origin, to the detriment of workers' morale and of national unity:

NOW, THEREFORE, by virtue of the authority vested in me by the Constitution and the statutes, and as a prerequisite to the successful conduct of our national defense production effort, I do hereby reaffirm the policy of the United States that there shall be no discrimination in the employment of workers in defense industries or government because of race, creed, color, or national origin, and I do hereby declare that it is the duty of employers and of labor organizations, in furtherance of said policy and of this order, to provide for the full and equitable participation of all workers in defense industries, without discrimination because of race, creed, color, or national origin;

And it is hereby ordered as follows:

1. All departments and agencies of the Government of the United States concerned with vocational and training programs for defense production shall take special measures appropriate to assure that such programs are administered without discrimination because of race, creed, color, or national origin;

2. All contracting agencies of the Government of the United States shall include in all defense contracts hereafter negotiated by them a provision obligating the contractor not to discriminate against any worker because of race, creed, color, or national origin;

3. There is established in the Office of Production Management a Committee on Fair Employment Practice, which shall consist of a chairman and four other members* to be appointed by the President. The Chairman and members of the Committee shall serve as such without compensation but shall be entitled to actual and necessary transportation, subsistence and other expenses incidental to performance of their duties. The Committee shall receive and investigate complaints of discrimination in violation of the provisions of this order and shall take appropriate steps to redress grievances which it finds to be valid. The Committee shall also recommend to the several departments and agencies of the Government of the United States and to the President all measures which may be deemed by it necessary or proper to effectuate the provsions of this order.

Franklin D. Roosevelt
The White House,
June 25, 1941.

* The Committee was increased in size to six members on July 18, 1941.

Sources: *The Black Worker*, July 1941.
Federal Register, July 1941

7.4 The Roosevelt Record

Prior to the Presidential election of 1940, an assessment of FDR's stance on civil rights in the course of his Presidency, particularly in relation to the New Deal programs.

On the subject of the Negro, the Roosevelt record is spotty, as might be expected in an administration where so much power is in the hands of the southern wing of the Democratic party. And yet Mr. Roosevelt, hobbled as he has been by the Dixie diehards, has managed to include Negro citizens in practically every phase of the administration program. In this respect, no matter how far behind the ideal he may be, he is far ahead of any other Democratic president, and of recent Republican ones.

The best proof that Mr. Roosevelt has not catered always to the South and has insisted on carrying the Negro along with his program is to be found in the smearing, race-hating propaganda used against him in the 1936 campaign by southern white groups. Both he and Mrs. Roosevelt were targets of filthy mud-slinging simply because they did not see eye to eye with the South on the Negro.

This does not mean that the Roosevelt administration has done all that it could have done for the race. Its policies in many instances have done Negroes great injustice and have helped to build more secure walls of segregation.

On the anti-lynching bill Mr. Roosevelt has said not a mumbling word. His failure to endorse this legislation, to bring pressure to break the filibuster, is a black mark against him. It does no good to say that the White House could not pass down some word on this bill. The White House spoke on many bills. Mr. Roosevelt might have pressed the anti-lynching bill to a vote, especially during January and February, 1938, when there was tremendous public opinion supporting the bill. His failure to act, or even speak, on the anti-lynching bill was the more glaring because, while mobs in America were visiting inhumanities upon Negroes, Mr. Roosevelt periodically was rebuking some foreign government for inhumanity, and enunciating high sentiments of liberty, tolerance, justice, etc.

To declare that the Roosevelt administration has tried to include the Negro in nearly every phase of its program for the people of the nation is not to ignore the instances where government policies have harmed the race.

At Boulder dam, for example, the administration continued the shameful policy begun by Hoover of forbidding Negroes to live in Boulder City, the government-built town. And in its own pet project, the TVA, the administration forbade Negroes to live in Norris, another government-built town at Norris dam.

Full credit must go to the administration for its program of low-cost housing, so sorely needed by low-income families. No one pretends that the American housing program is more than a beginning, but Negroes have shared in it in the most equitable manner. However, there were, outside the slum-clearance program, some damaging practices. The FHA, which insures mortgages for home buyers, has enforced a regulation which puts the power and approval of the government on ghetto life. No Negro family which sought a home outside the so-called "Negro" neighborhood could get a FHA-insured loan.

The vast program for youth, the CCC and the NYA, has included our young people, but in the CCC a justifiable complaint has been that Negro instructors, advisers, and reserve army officers were not appointed in any but the tiniest proportion.

There is little need to mention relief and the WPA. Mr. Roosevelt's critics concede what his administration has done in these two branches of his program by concentrating their attack upon the relief that the New Deal has given Negroes. In relief the government set the tone. That tone was so much higher than the city, county and state standards for Negroes in certain areas that, even though differentials existed, the net result was more than it would have been without government supervision. Collective bargaining and the Wages and Hours act have aided Negro workers in private industry.

The farm program has not been ideally administered, but colored people have shared in the benefits. More than 50,000 families have been assisted by the Farm Security administration.

Mr. Roosevelt had the courage to appoint a Negro to a federal judgeship, the first in the history of the country. His nominee was confirmed by a Democratic senate without a murmur. Complaint has been made that in naming about a score of colored administrative assistants and advisers, Mr. Roosevelt has kept Negroes out of any real posts in the government. If it be true that Mr. Roosevelt has created Negro appendages to various bureaus, it cannot be denied that colored people know more about their government and have penetrated nearer to policy-making desks than ever before.

Heavily on the debit side is Mr. Roosevelt's approval of the War department's notorious jim crow in the armed services.

Most important contribution of the Roosevelt administration to the age-old color line problem in America has been its doctrine that Negroes are a part of the country and must be considered in any program for the country as a whole. The inevitable discriminations notwithstanding, this thought has been driven home in thousands of communities by a thousand specific acts. For the first time in their lives, government has taken on meaning and substance for the Negro masses.

* * *

Negro voters are posed a question on November 5: Do they believe that in spite of admitted mistakes and failures (both as to them and to government generally) the Roosevelt administration is tending toward the kind of government that is best for the majority of the people; or has the Roosevelt record on the Negro specifically and on the government generally been such that a new administration should be voted into power?

Source: *The Crisis*, XLVII, November 1940, 343. Reprinted by permission of *The Crisis Magazine*.

Civil Rights after the Second World War

8.1 Colonialism and Racism in the Post-War World

Walter White, executive secretary to NAACP, went to Europe at the end of the Second World War on reports of tensions between black and white American troops. His resultant book, A Rising Wind, *focused instead on the likely realities of the post-war world in which colonialism and racism could no longer be justified.*

World War II has given to the Negro a sense of kinship with other colored – and also oppressed – peoples of the world. Where he has not thought through or informed himself on the racial angles of colonial policy and master-race theories, he senses that the struggle of the Negro in the United States is part and parcel of the struggle against imperialism and exploitation in India, China, Burma, Africa, the Philippines, Malaya, the West Indies, and South America. The Negro soldier is convinced that as time proceeds that identification of interests will spread even among some brown and yellow peoples who today refuse to see the connection between their exploitation by white nations and discrimination against the Negro in the United States.

The evil effect of misbehavior by a majority and the timorousness of the American Government in meeting such misbehavior will cost America and other white nations dearly so far as colored peoples, constituting two thirds of the earth's population, are concerned. Winston Churchill's recent statement that, as the war nears its end, ideology is being forgotten increasingly means to colored peoples that idealism is being conveniently shelved. Colored peoples, particularly in the Pacific, believed, whether correctly or not, that in its later stages the war was being fought to restore empire to Great Britain, France, Holland, and Portugal. The immediate resumption of control of Hollandia and other sections of Dutch New Guinea by the Dutch, and similar action by the British in Guadalcanal and Tarawa as soon as the Japanese had been driven out, the preparations being made by France to take over again control of Indo-China the minute the Nipponese are ejected, created increasing skepticism of the Allies throughout the Pacific.

Any person of normal intelligence could have foreseen this. With considerable effectiveness, the Japanese by radio and other means have industriously spread in the Pacific stories of lynchings, of segregation and discrimination against the Negro in the American Army, and of race riots in Detroit, Philadelphia, and other American cities. To each of these recitals has been appended the statement that such treatment of a colored minority in the United States is certain to be that given to brown and yellow peoples in the Pacific if the Allies, instead of the Japanese, win the war. No one can accurately estimate at this time the effectiveness of such propaganda. But it is certain that it has had wide circulation and has been believed by many. Particularly damaging has been the circulation of reports of clashes between white and Negro soldiers in the European and other theaters of operation.

Indissolubly tied in with the carrying overseas of prejudice against the Negro is the racial and imperialist question in the Pacific of Great Britain's and our intentions toward India and China. Publication of Ambassador William Phillips' blunt warning to President Roosevelt in May 1944 that India is a problem of the United States as well as of England despite British opposition to American intervention is of the highest significance. It reaffirmed warnings the Western world by Wendell Willkie, Sumner Welles, Pearl Buck, and Henry Wallace, among others, that grave peril which might bring disaster to the entire world was involved in continued refusal to recognize the just claims for justice and equality by the colored people, particularly in the Orient. These people are not as powerless as some naive Americans believe them to be. In the first place they have the strength of numbers, unified by resentment against the condescension and exploitation by white nations which Pearl Buck calls "the suppression of human rights to a degree which has not been matched in its ruthlessness outside of facist-owned Europe," which can and possibly will grow into open revolt. The trend of such awakening and revolution is clearly to be seen in the demand which was made for China at the Dumbarton Oaks Conference of August 1944 that the Allied nations unequivocally declare themselves for complete racial equality. It is to be seen in Ambassador Phillips' warning that though there are four million Indians under arms they are wholly a mercenary army whose allegiance to the Allies will last only as long as they are paid; and in his further revelation that all of these as well as African troops must be used to police other Indians instead of fighting Japan.

Permit me to cite a few solemn warnings of the inevitability of world-wide racial conflict unless the white nations of the earth do an about-face on the issue of race. "Moreover, during the years between 1920 and 1940 a period in the history of the Asiatic and Pacific peoples was in any event drawing to its close," says Sumner Welles, former Undersecretary of State, in his epochal book, *The Time For Decision.*

> The startling development of Japan as a world power, and the slower but nevertheless steady emergence of China as a full member of the family of nations, together with the growth of popular institutions among many other peoples of Asia, notably India, all combined to erase very swiftly indeed the fetish of white supremacy cultivated by the big colonial powers during the nineteenth century. The thesis of white supremacy could only exist so long as the white race actually proved to be supreme. The nature of the defeats suffered by the Western nations in 1942 dealt the final blow to any concept of white supremacy which still remained.

While there are British and Dutch colonial administrators who show a "spirit of devotion, of decency and of self-abnegation," Mr. Welles remarks, there also are "yet only too many British representatives in the Far East [who] have demonstrated that type of thinking which is so well exemplified in the words of a high British official in India at the outset of the present century when he expressed a conviction which he asserted 'was shared by every Englishman in India, from the highest to the lowest . . . the conviction in every man that he belongs to a race whom God has destined to govern and subdue.' "

The distinguished former Undersecretary might well have gone on to point out that had not the Russians and Chinese performed miracles of military offense and defense in World War II, or had not the black Governor-General of French Equatorial Africa, Félix Eboué, retained faith in the democratic process when white Frenchmen lost theirs, the so-called Anglo-Saxon nations and peoples would surely have lost this war. And Mr. Welles could have reminded his readers that brown and yellow peoples in Asia and the Pacific and black peoples in Africa and the West Indies and the United States are not ignorant of the truth that the war was won by men and women – white, yellow, black, and brown. Resumption of white arrogance and domination in the face of such facts may be disastrous to the peace of the world.

The distinguished novelist, Pearl Buck, hits hard on the same issue in her *American Unity and Asia* in the chapter ominously captioned, "Tinder for Tomorrow."

> The Japanese weapon of racial propaganda in Asia is beginning to show signs of effectiveness [she declares]. This is not because of peculiar skill in the way it is being used, but because it is being presented to persons who have had unfortunate experiences with English and American people .... It will be better for us if we acknowledge the danger in this Japanese propaganda. The truth is that the white man in the Far East has too often behaved without wisdom or justice to his fellow man. It is worse than folly – it is dangerous today – not to recognize the truth, for in it lies the tinder for tomorrow. Who of us can doubt it who has seen a white policeman beat a Chinese coolie in Shanghai, a white sailor kick a Japanese in Kobe, an English captain lash out with his whip at an Indian vendor – who of us, having seen such oriental sights or heard the common contemptuous talk of the white man in any colored country, can forget the fearful bitter hatred in the colored face and the blaze in the dark eyes?

Miss Buck tells how such stupid cruelty is put to use by the Japanese among the one billion colored people of the Pacific.

> Race prejudice continues unabated among white people today, the Japanese are saying. Tokyo radio programs daily send their broadcasts over Asia in their campaign to drive out the white man. They dwell upon white exploitation of colored troops and cite mistreatment of Filipinos by the American military and similar treatment of Indian troops by the English . . . "The colored peoples," Japanese propaganda says over and over again in a thousand forms, "have no hope of justice and equality from the white peoples because of their unalterable race prejudice against us." . . . The effect therefore of this Japanese propaganda cannot be lightly dismissed. It lies uneasy in the minds and memories of many at this moment who are loyally allied with Britain and the United States, in the minds and memories of colored peoples of Asia. Yes, and it lies uneasy, too, in the minds and memories of many colored citizens of the United States, who cannot deny the charge and must remain loyal in spite of it. For such minds realize that, though Nazism may give them nothing but death, yet the United States and Britain have given them too little for life in the past

> and not even promises for the future. Our colored allies proceed to war against the Axis not deceived or in ignorance. They know that it may not be the end of the war for them even when Hitler has gone down and Nazism is crushed and Japan returned to her isles again. The colored peoples know that for them the war for freedom may have to go on against the very white men at whose side they are now fighting.

These are grim words not pleasant to the ears of white America and Britain, who believe that the last shot fired in this war will mean the complete restoration of the way of life which preceded it. But the consequences of denying or ignoring them are solemnly voiced by an Englishman, Harold J. Laski, who bluntly warns that "Englishmen who put imperial power before social justice, Americans who think the color of a man's skin determines his rights – these are only some of the elements in our midst who might easily pervert the great victory into an epoch barren and ugly."

Will the United States after the war perpetuate its racial-discrimination policies and beliefs at home and abroad as it did during the war? Will it continue to follow blindly the dangerous and vicious philosophy voiced in Kipling's poem, The White Man's Burden, which Paul Hutchinson characterized in *World Revolution and Religion* as "the most significant cultural expression of the nineteenth century: even more significant than Nietzsche's discovery of the "*Übermensch*"? Will decent and intelligent America continue to permit itself to be led by the nose by demagogues and professional race-hate mongers – to have its thinking and action determined on this global and explosive issue by the lowest common denominator of public opinion?

Or will the United States, having found that prejudice is an expensive luxury, slough off the mistakes of the past and chart a new course both at home and in its relations with the rest of the world? Miss Buck supplies one answer:

> This also the Far Eastern Allies are asking. Japan is busily declaring that we cannot. She is declaring in the Philippines, in China, in India, Malaya, and even Russia that there is no basis for hope that colored peoples can expect any justice from the people who rule in the United States, namely, the white people. For specific proof the Japanese point to our treatment of our own colored people, citizens of generations in the United States. Every lynching, every race riot, gives joy to Japan. The discriminations of the American army and navy and air forces against colored soldiers and sailors, the exclusion of colored labor in our defense industries and trade unions, all our social discriminations, are of the greatest aid today to our enemy in Asia, Japan. "Look at America," Japan is saying to millions of listening ears. "Will white Americans give you equality?"
>
> Who can reply with a clear affirmative? The persistent refusal of Americans to see the connection between the colored American and the colored peoples abroad, the continued, and it seems even willful, ignorance which will not investigate the connection, are agony to those loyal and anxious Americans who know all too well the dangerous possibilities.

Is Japan right in what she says to Asia and the Pacific? And whether right or not, what effect is her propaganda – unhappily based largely on truth – having upon hundreds of millions of people in what were once far places but today are but a few hours away from New York or Washington or San Francisco? Upon people whose good will and faith in our integrity are vital to our own national security?

During the middle stages of the war I made a study of Japanese radio and other propaganda among the people of the Orient and of German propaganda, almost invariably identical in language and content to the Japanese, in Latin America and Africa. Every lynching, every race riot like the one in Detroit in 1943 and the one in Philadelphia in 1944 against employment of qualified Negroes on streetcars, every killing or other mistreatment of a Negro soldier in a Southern training camp or city, every anti-Negro diatribe on the floor of Congress, every refusal to abolish racial segregation in the armed services of the United States was played up over and over again. Significantly enough, there was little embellishment of the details, probably because little was needed. In one form or another this moral was driven home: See what the United States does to its own colored people; this is the way you colored people of the world will be treated if the Allied nations win the war! Be smart and cast your lot with another colored people, the Japanese, who will never mistreat fellow colored people!

What will America's answer be? If already planned race riots and lynchings of returning Negro soldiers "to teach them their place" are consummated, if Negro war workers are first fired, if India remains enslaved, if Eboué's people go back to disease and poverty to provide luxury and ease for Parisian boulevardiers, World War III will be in the making before the last gun is fired in World War II. In *One World,* Wendell Willkie reported that "everywhere I found polite but skeptical people, who met my questions about their problems and difficulties with polite but ironic questions about our own. The maladjustments of races in America came up frequently." Such skepticism is but beginning. The question is posed bluntly: Can the United States, Britain, and other "white" nations any longer afford, in enlightened self-interest, racial superiority?

What to do?

The United States, Great Britain, France, and other Allied nations must choose without delay one of two courses – to revolutionize their racial concepts and practices, to abolish imperialism and grant full equality to all of its people, or else prepare for World War III. Another Versailles Treaty providing for "mandates," "protectorates," and other devices for white domination will make such a war inevitable. One of the chief deterrents will be Russia. Distrustful of Anglo-American control of Europe, many and perhaps all of the Balkan states may through choice or necessity ally themselves with Russia. If Anglo-Saxon practices in China and India are not drastically and immediately revised, it is probable and perhaps certain that the people of India, China, Burma, Malaya, and other parts of the Pacific may also move into the Russian orbit as the lesser of two dangers.

As for the United States, the storm signals are unmistakable. She can choose between a policy of appeasement of bigots – which course she gives every indication now of following – and thus court disaster. Or she can live up to her ideals and thereby both save herself and help to avert an early and more disastrous resumption of war.

A wind *is* rising – a wind of determination by the have-nots of the world to share the benefits of freedom and prosperity which the haves of the earth have tried to keep exclusively for themselves. That wind blows all over the world. Whether that wind develops into a hurricane is a decision which we must make now and in the days when we form the peace.

Source: From *A Rising Wind* by Walter White. Copyright 1945 by Walter White. Used by permission of Doubleday, a division of Bantam Doubleday Dell Publishing Group, Inc.

8.2 UNESCO Statement on Race, 1949

The United Nations Educational, Scientific and Cultural Organisation (UNESCO) held a conference of leading international anthropologists, psychologists and sociologists in Paris in December 1949. The Report included the following statement on the scientific meaning of "Race".

1. Scientists have reached general agreement in recognizing that mankind is one: that all men belong to the same species, *Homo sapiens*. It is further generally agreed among scientists that all men are probably derived from the same common stock; and that such differences as exist between different groups of mankind are due to the operation of evolutionary factors or differentiation such as isolation, the drift and random fixation of the material particles which control heredity (the genes), changes in the structure of these particles, hybridization, and natural selection. In these ways groups have arisen of varying stability and degree of differentiation which have been classified in different ways for different purposes.

2. From the biological standpoint, the species *Homo sapiens* is made up of a number of populations, each one of which differs from the others in the frequency of one or more genes. Such genes, responsible for the hereditary differences between men, are always few when compared to the whole genetic constitution of man and to the vast number of genes common to all human beings regardless of the population to which they belong. This means that the likenesses among men are far greater than their differences.

3. A race, from the biological standpoint, may therefore be defined as one of the group of populations constituting the species *Homo sapiens*. These populations are capable of interbreeding with one another but, by virtue of the isolating barriers which in the past kept them more or less separated, exhibit certain physical differences as a result of their somewhat different biological histories. These represent variations, as it were, on a common theme.

4. In short, the term "race" designates a group or population characterized by some concentrations, relative as to frequency and distribution, of hereditary particles

(genes) or physical characters, which appear, fluctuate, and often disappear in the course of time by reason of geographic and/or cultural isolation. The varying manifestations of these traits in different populations are perceived in different ways by each group. What is perceived is largely preconceived, so that each group arbitrarily tends to misinterpret the variability which occurs as a fundamental difference which separates that group from all others.

5. These are the scientific facts. Unfortunately, however, when most people use the term "race" they do not do so in the sense above defined. To most people, a race is any group of people whom they choose to describe as a race. Thus, many national, religious, geographic, linguistic or cultural groups have, in such loose usage, been called "race," when obviously Americans are not a race, nor are Englishmen, nor Frenchmen, nor any other national group. Catholics, Protestants, Moslems and Jews are not races, nor are groups who speak English or any other language thereby definable as a race; people who live in Iceland or England or India are not races; nor are people who are culturally Turkish or Chinese or the like thereby describable as races.

6. National, religious, geographic, linguistic and cultural groups do not necessarily coincide with racial groups; and the cultural traits of such groups have no demonstrated genetic connexion with racial traits. Because serious errors of this kind are habitually committed when the term "race" is used in popular parlance, it would be better when speaking of human races to drop the term "race" altogether and speak of *ethnic groups*.

7. Now what has the scientist to say about the groups of mankind which may be recognized at the present time? Human races can be and have been differently classified by different anthropologists, but at the present time most anthropologists agree on classifying the greater part of present-day mankind into three major divisions, as follows: the Mongoloid Division, the Negroid Division, the Caucasoid Division. The biological processes which the classifier has here embalmed, as it were, are dynamic, not static. These divisions were not the same in the past as they are at present, and there is every very reason to believe that they will change in the future.

8. Many sub-groups or ethnic groups within these divisions have been described. There is no general agreement upon their number, and in any event most ethnic groups have not yet been either studied or described by the physical anthropologists.

9. Whatever classification the anthropologist makes of man, he never includes mental characteristics as part of those classifications. It is now generally recognized that intelligence tests do not in themselves enable us to differentiate safely between what is due to innate capacity and what is the result of environmental influences, training and education. Wherever it has been possible to make allowances for differences in environmental opportunities, the tests have shown essential similarity in mental characters among all human groups. In short, given similar degrees of cultural opportunity to realize their potentialities, the average achievement of the members of each ethnic group is about the same. The scientific investigations of recent years fully support the dictum of Confucius (551-478 B.C.): "Men's natures are alike; it is their habits that carry them far apart."

10. The scientific material available to us at present does not justify the conclusion that inherited genetic differences are a major factor in producing the differences between the cultures and cultural achievements of different peoples or groups. It does indicate, however, that the history of the cultural experience which each group has undergone is the major factor in explaining such differences. The one trait which above all others has been at a premium in the evolution of men's mental characters has been educability, plasticity. This is a trait which all human beings possess. It is indeed, a species character of *Homo sapiens.*

11. So far as temperament is concerned, there is no definite evidence that there exist inborn differences between human groups. There is evidence that whatever group differences of the kind there might be are greatly over-ridden by the individual differences, and by the differences springing from environmental factors.

12. As for personality and character, these may be considered raceless. In every human group a rich variety of personality and character types will be found, and there is no reason for believing that any human group is richer than any other in these respects.

13. With respect to race-mixture, the evidence points unequivocally to the fact that this has been going on from the earliest times. Indeed, one of the chief processes of race-formation and race-extinction or absorption is by means of hybridization between races or ethnic groups. Furthermore, no convincing evidence has been adduced that race-mixture of itself produces biologically bad effects. Statements that human hybrids frequently show undesirable traits, both physically and mentally, physical disharmonies and mental degeneracies, are not supported by the facts. There is, therefore, no "biological" justification for prohibiting intermarriage between persons of different ethnic groups.

14. The biological fact of race and the myth of "race" should be distinguished. For all practical social purposes "race" is not so much a biological phenomenon as a social myth. The myth "race" has created an enormous amount of human and social damage. In recent years it has taken a heavy toll in human lives and caused untold suffering. It still prevents the normal development of millions of human beings and deprives civilization of the effective co-operation of productive minds. The biological differences between ethnic groups should be disregarded from the standpoint of social acceptance and social action. The unity of mankind from both the biological and social viewpoints is the main thing. To recognize this and to act accordingly is the first requirement of modern man. It is but to recognize what a great biologist wrote in 1875: "As man advances in civilization, and small tribes are united into larger communities, the simplest reason would tell each individual that he ought to extend his social instincts and sympathies to all the members of the same nation, though personally unknown to him. This point being once reached, there is only an artificial barrier to prevent his sympathies extending to the men of all nations and races." These are the words of Charles Darwin in *The Descent of Man* (2nd ed., 1875, pp. 187-188). And, indeed, the whole of human history shows that a co-operative spirit is not only natural to men, but more deeply rooted than any self-seeking tendencies. If this were not so we should not see the growth of integration and organization of his communities which the centuries and the millennia plainly exhibit.

15. We now have to consider the bearing of these statements on the problem of human equality. It must be asserted with the utmost emphasis that equality as an ethical principle in no way depends upon the assertion that human beings are in fact equal in endowment. Obviously individuals in all ethnic groups vary greatly among themselves in endowment. Nevertheless, the characteristics in which human groups differ from one another are often exaggerated and used as a basis for questioning the validity of equality in the ethical sense. For this purpose we have thought it worth while to set out in a formal manner what is at present scientifically established concerning individual and group differences.

(a) In matters of race, the only characteristics which anthropologists can effectively use as a basis for classifications are physical and physiological.

(b) According to present knowledge there is no proof that the groups of mankind differ in their innate mental characteristics, whether in respect of intelligence or temperament. The scientific evidence indicates that the range of mental capacities in all ethnic groups is much the same.

(c) Historical and sociological studies support the view that genetic differences are not of importance in determining the social and cultural differences between different groups of *Homo sapiens,* and that the social and cultural *changes* in different groups have, in the main, been independent of *changes* in inborn constitution. Vast social changes have occurred which were not in any way connected with changes in racial type.

(d) There is no evidence that race-mixture as such produces bad results from the biological point of view. The social results of race-mixture whether for good or ill are to be traced to social factors.

(e) All normal human beings are capable of learning to share in a common life, to understand the nature of mutual service and reciprocity, and to respect social obligations and contracts. Such biological differences as exist between members of different ethnic groups have no relevance to problems of social and political organization, moral life and communication between human beings.

Lastly, biological studies lend support to the ethic of universal brotherhood; for man is born with drives toward co-operation, and unless these drives are satisfied, men and nations alike fall ill. Man is born a social being who can reach his fullest development only through interaction with his fellows. The denial at any point of this social bond between man and man brings with it disintegration. In this sense, every man is his brother's keeper. For every man is a piece of the continent, a part of the main, because he is involved in mankind.

The original statement was drafted at Unesco House, Paris by the following experts:

Professor Ernest Beaglehole, New Zealand;
Professor Juan Comas, Mexico;
Professor L. A. Costa Pinto, Brazil;
Professor E. Franklin Frazier, United States of America;
Professor Morris Ginsberg, United Kingdom;

Dr. Humayun Kabir, India;
Professor Claude Levi-Strauss, France;
Professor M. F. Ashley-Montagu, United States of America
(Rapporteur)

The text was revised by Professor Ashley-Montague, after criticisms submitted by Professors Hadley Cantril, E. G. Conklin, Gunnar Dahlberg, Theodosius Dobzhansky, L. C. Dunn, Donald Hager, Julian S. Huxley, Otto Klineberg, Wilbert Moore, H. J. Muller, Gunner Myrdal, Joseph Needham, Curt Stern.

Source: UNESCO, *Race and Science*, (New York, 1961), pp. 496-501. Reproduced by permission of UNESCO.

8.3 Report of the Committee on Civil Rights, 1947

A measure of the growing concern in the post-war United States about the denial of civil rights to black citizens was the establishment of a Committee on Civil Rights by President Truman in December 1946. The Report of the Committee provided recommendations for Truman's civil rights message to Congress in February 1948.

The condition of our rights

The crime of lynching

In 1946 at least six persons in the United States were lynched by mobs. Three of them had not been charged, either by the police or anyone else, with an offense. Of the three that had been charged, one had been accused of stealing a saddle. (The real thieves were discovered after the lynching). Another was said to have broken into a house. A third was charged with stabbing a man. All were Negroes.

* * *

While available statistics show that, decade by decade, lynchings have decreased, this Committee has found that in the year 1947 lynching remains one of the most serious threats to the civil rights of Americans. It is still possible for a mob to abduct and murder a person in some sections of the country with almost certain assurance of escaping punishment for the crime. The decade from 1936 through 1946 saw at least 43 lynchings. No persons received the death penalty, and the majority of the guilty persons were not even prosecuted.

The communities in which lynchings occur tend to condone the crime. Punishment of lynchers is not accepted as the responsibility of state or local governments in these communities. Frequently, state officials participate in the crime, actively or passively. Federal efforts to punish the crime are resisted. Condonation of lynching is indicated by the failure of some local law enforcement officials to make adequate efforts to break up a mob. It is further shown by failure in most cases to make any real effort to apprehend or try those guilty. If the federal government enters a case, local officials sometimes actively resist the federal investigation.

* * *

Police brutality

We have reported the failure of some public officials to fulfill their most elementary duty – the protection of persons against mob violence. We must also report more widespread and varied forms of official misconduct. These include violent physical attacks by police officers on members of minority groups, the use of third degree methods to extort confessions, and brutality against prisoners. Civil rights violations of this kind are by no means universal and many law enforcement agencies have gone far in recent years toward stamping out these evils.

* * *

Much of the illegal official action which has been brought to the attention of the Committee is centered in the South. There is evidence of lawless police action against whites and Negroes alike, but the dominant pattern is that of race prejudice. J. Edgar Hoover referred, in his testimony before the Committee, to a particular jail where "it was seldom that a Negro man or women was incarcerated who was not given a severe beating, which started off with a pistol whipping and ended with a rubber hose."

* * *

There are other cases in the files of the Department of Justice of officers who seem to be "trigger-happy" where weak or poor persons are concerned. In a number of instances, Negroes have been shot, supposedly in self-defense, under circumstances indicating, at best, unsatisfactory police work in the handling of criminals, and, at worst, a callous willingness to kill.

* * *

The total picture – adding the connivance of some police officials in lynchings to their record of brutality against Negroes in other situations – is, in the opinion of this Committee, a serious reflection on American justice. We know that Americans everywhere deplore this violence. We recognize further that there are many law enforcement officers in the South and the North who do not commit violent acts against Negroes or other friendless culprits. We are convinced, however, that the incidence of police brutality against Negroes is disturbingly high.

The right to vote

The right of all qualified citizens to vote is today considered axiomatic by most Americans. To achieve universal adult suffrage we have carried on vigorous political crusades since the earliest days of the Republic. In theory the aim has been achieved, but in fact there are many backwaters in our political life where the right to vote is not assured to every qualified citizen. The franchise is barred to some citizens because of race; to others by institutions or procedures which impede free access to the polls. Still other Americans are in substance disfranchised whenever electoral irregularities or corrupt practices dissipate their votes or distort their intended purposes. Some citizens – permanent residents of the District of Columbia – are excluded from political representation and the right to vote as a result of outmoded national traditions. As a result of such restrictions, all of these citizens are limited, in varying degrees, in their opportunities to seek office and to influence the conduct of government on an equal plane with other American citizens.

The denial of the suffrage on account of race is the most serious present interference with the right to vote. Until very recently, American Negro citizens in most southern states found it difficult to vote. Some Negroes have voted in parts of the upper South for the last twenty years. In recent years the situation in the deep South has changed to the point where it can be said that Negroes are beginning to exercise the political rights of free Americans. In the light of history, this represents progress, limited and precarious, but nevertheless progress.

* * *

Discriminatory hiring practices

Discrimination is most acutely felt by minority group members in their inability to get a job suited to their qualifications. Exclusions of Negroes, Jews, or Mexicans in the process of hiring is effected in various ways – by newspaper advertisements requesting only whites or gentiles to apply, by registration or application blanks on which a space is reserved for "race" or "religion," by discriminatory job orders placed with employment agencies, or by the arbitrary policy of a company official in charge of hiring.

A survey conducted by the United States Employment Service and contained in the Final Report of the Fair Employment Practice Committee reveals that of the total job orders received by USES offices in 11 selected areas during the period of February 1-15, 1946, 24 percent of the orders were discriminatory. Of 38,195 orders received, 9,171 included specifications with regard to race, citizenship, religion, or some combination of these factors.

* * *

On-the-job discrimination

If he can get himself hired, the minority worker often finds that he is being paid less than other workers. This wage discrimination is sharply evident in studies made of individual cities and is especially exaggerated in the South. A survey, conducted by the Research and Information Department of the American Federation of Labor, shows that the average weekly income of white veterans ranges from 30 to 78 percent above the average income of Negro veterans in 26 communities, 25 of them in the South. In Houston, for example, 36,000 white veterans had a weekly income of $49 and 4,000 Negro veterans had average income of $30 – a difference of 63 percent. These difficulties are not caused solely by the relegation of the Negroes to lower types of work, but reflect wage discriminations between whites and Negroes for the same type of work. The Final Report of the FEPC states that the hourly wage rates for Negro common laborers averaged 47.4 cents in July, 1942, as compared with 65.3 cents for white laborers.

* * *

In presenting this evidence, the Committee is not ignoring the fact that an individual Negro worker may be less efficient than an individual white worker or vice versa. Nor does it suggest that wage differences which reflect actual differences in the competence of workers are unjustifiable. What is indefensible is a wage discrimination based, not on the worker's ability, but on his race.

While private business provided almost 70 percent of all cases docketed by the FEPC for the fiscal year 1943-44, about a fourth of the complaints were against the federal government itself. This at once calls to question the effectiveness of the Civil Service Commission rules against such discrimination, and the various departments' directives and executive orders that have restated this policy on non-discrimination from time to time.

* * *

Finally, labor unions are guilty of discriminatory labor practices. Six percent of the complaints received by the FEPC were made against unions, and the FEPC states that when challenged, private industry eliminated discrimination much more readily than did unions. On the other hand, it should be noted that great strides have been made in the admission of minorities to unions. Both the American Federation of Labor and the Congress of Industrial Organizations have repeatedly condemned discriminatory union practices. But the national organizations have not yet fully attained their goals. Some railway unions have "Jim Crow" auxiliaries into which Negroes, Mexicans, or Orientals are shunted, with little or no voice in union affairs. Furthermore, there is a rapid upper limit on the type of job on which these members can be employed.

Government responsibility: securing the rights

The national government should assume leadership in our American civil rights program because there is much in the field of civil rights that it is squarely responsible for in its own direct dealings with millions of persons. It is the largest single employer of labor in the country. More than two million persons are on its payroll. The freedom of opinion and expression enjoyed by these people is in many ways dependent upon the attitudes and practices of the government. By not restricting this freedom beyond a point necessary to insure the efficiency and loyalty of its workers, the government, itself, can make a very large contribution to the effort to achieve true freedom of thought in America. By scrulpulously following fair employment practices, it not only sets a model for other employers to follow, but also directly protects the rights of more than two million workers to fair employment.

* * *

Leadership by the federal government in safeguarding civil rights does not mean exclusive action by that government. There is much that the states and local communities can do in this field, and much that they alone can do. The Committee believes that Justice Holmes' view of the states as 48 laboratories for social and economic experimentation is still valid. The very complexity of the civil rights problem calls for much experimental, remedial action which may be better undertaken by the states than by the national government. Parallel state and local action supporting the national program is highly desirable. It is obvious that even though the federal government should take steps to stamp out the crime of lynching, the states cannot escape the responsibility to employ all of the powers and resources available to them for the same end. Or again, the enactment of a federal fair employment practice act will not render similar state legislation unnecessary.

In certain areas the states must do far more than parallel federal action. Either for constitutional or administrative reasons, they must remain the primary protectors of civil rights. This is true of governmental efforts to control or outlaw racial or religious discrimination practiced by privately supported public-service institutions such as schools and hospitals, and of places of public accommodation such as hotels, restaurants, theaters, and stores.

Furthermore, government action alone, whether federal, state, local, or all combined, cannot provide complete protection of civil rights. Everything that government does stems from and is conditioned by the state of public opinion. Civil rights in this country will never be adequately protected until the intelligent will of the American people approves and demands that protection. Great responsibility, therefore, will always rest upon private organizations and private individuals who are in a position to educate and shape public opinion. The argument is sometimes made that because prejudice and intolerance cannot be eliminated through legislation and government control we should abandon that action in favor of the long, slow, evolutionary effects of education and voluntary private efforts. We believe that this argument misses the point and that the choice it poses between legislation and education as to the means of improving civil rights is an unnecessary one. In our opinion, both approaches to the goal are valid, and are, moreover, essential to each other.

Source: *Secure These Rights: The Report of the President's Committee on Civil Rights*, (New York, 1947) IX, X-XI, 20-103.

8.4 Equality in the Armed Services

President Truman issued Executive Orders in July 1948 dealing with equality of treatment and opportunity in government employment and in the armed services. The degree of discrimination which had to be addressed in the armed services may be gauged from the Report of the President's Committee on Equality of Treatment and Opportunity in the Armed Services.

The course of the inquiry

The scope of the executive order required that there be equality of treatment and opportunity for all persons in the armed services without regard to race, color, religion, or national origin. Members of various minority groups have asserted the existence of discrimination on these grounds, but no evidence was presented to the Committee and no specific facts were found indicating formally defined service policies denying equality of treatment and opportunity except with respect to Negroes. In their case practices resulting in inequality of treatment and opportunity had the sanction of official policy and were embodied in regulations.

The Committee felt, therefore, that its examination should leave room for gathering facts and developing conclusions affecting all minorities, but that it should proceed with the material on hand concerning the specific status of Negroes in the services. Once this racial factor should be satisfactorily disposed of, the Committee believed a formula would be evolved applicable to all minorities. For this reason specific mention is limited throughout the report to recommendations and changes affecting Negroes.

There follows a summary account of the extent to which the President's executive order presently is being implemented, with an indication of the policy changes that have been put into effect by the services since the order was issued in July 1948.

The Navy

All jobs and ratings in the naval general service now are open to all enlisted men without regard to race or color. Negroes are currently serving in every job classification in general service.

All courses in Navy technical schools are open to qualified personnel without regard to race or color and without racial quotas. Negroes are attending the most advanced technical schools and are serving in their ratings both in the fleet and at shore installations.

Negroes in general service are completely integrated with whites in basic training, technical schools, on the job, in messes and sleeping quarters, ashore and afloat.

Chief, first-, second-, and third-class stewards now have the rate of chief, first-, second-, and third-class petty officers. (Policy change adopted June 7, 1949).

Stewards who qualify for general ratings now can transfer to general service.

The Marine Corps, which as a part of the Navy is subject to Navy policy, has abolished its segregated Negro training units. (Policy change adopted June 7, 1949). Marine Corps training is now integrated, although some Negro marines are still assigned to separate units after basic training. In this respect the effectuation of Navy policy in the Marine Corps is yet to be completed.

The Air Force

The Air Force announced its new racial policy on May 11, 1949. As a result of this policy, the all-Negro 332d Fighter Wing at Lockbourne Field, Ohio, has been broken up, and its personnel either sent to school for further training, transferred to white units in other commands, or separated under current regulations.

A majority of other Negro units has also been abolished. As of January 31, 1950, only 59 Negro units remained, and, 1,301 units were racially integrated, as compared with 106 Negro units and only 167 mixed units on June 1, 1949, when the Air Force policy went into effect.

Approximately 74 percent of the 25,000 Negroes in the Air Force on January 31, 1950, were serving in integrated units; and 26 percent still were serving in Negro units. This integration process is continuing.

All Air Force jobs and schools are open to qualified personnel without racial restriction or quotas. Six percent of the total personnel attending technical training schools in January 1950 were Negro.

Negroes serving in mixed units and attending service schools are integrated with whites in living conditions.,

The Army

All Army jobs now are open to Negroes, (Policy change adopted September 30, 1949).

All Army school courses are open to Negroes without restriction or quota. (Policy change adopted September 30, 1949).

For the first time Negroes no longer are limited in assignment to Negro and overhead (housekeeping) units, but are to be assigned according to their qualifications to any unit, including formerly white units. (Policy change adopted January 16, 1950).

Negroes serving in mixed units will be integrated on the job, in barracks and messes. (Policy change adopted January 16, 1950).

The 10 percent limitation on Negro strength in the Army has been abolished, and there no longer are Negro quotas for enlistment. (Policy change adopted March 27, 1950.)

Source: Freedom to Serve: a Report of the President's Committee on Equality of Treatment and Opportunity in the Armed Services, 1950.

8.5 Brown *vs* Board of Education of Topeka, Kansas, 1954

The decision in Plessy vs Ferguson *had given legal sanction to segregated public facilities in the states of the South since 1896. The Supreme Court overturned this decision in giving judgement in* Brown vs Board of Education of Topeka, Kansas *in 1954, responding to challenges in respect of school facilities. The following year, the Court laid down the basis for a transition to integrated public education, albeit "with all deliberate speed".*

Brown *v.* Board of Education of Topeka (Kansas)

The plaintiffs contend that segregated public schools are not "equal" and cannot be made "equal," and that hence they are deprived of the equal protection of the laws. Because of the obvious importance of the question presented, the Court took jurisdiction. Argument was heard in the 1952 Term, and reargument was heard this Term on certain questions propounded by the Court.

Reargument was largely devoted to the circumstances surrounding the adoption of the Fourteenth Amendment in 1868. It covered exhaustively consideration of the

Amendment in Congress, ratification by the states, then existing practices in racial segregation, and the views of proponents and opponents of the Amendment. This discussion and our own investigation convince us that, although these sources cast some light, it is not enough to resolve the problem with which we are faced. At best, they are inconclusive. The most avid proponents of the post-War Amendments undoubtedly intended them to remove all legal distinctions among "all persons born or naturalized in the United States." Their opponents, just as certainly, were antagonistic to both the letter and the spirit of the Amendments and wished them to have the most limited effect. What others in Congress and the state legislatures had in mind cannot be determined with any degree of certainty.

An additional reason for the inconclusive nature of the Amendment's history, with respect to segregated schools, is the status of public education at that time. In the South, the movement toward free common schools, supported by general taxation, had not yet taken hold. Education of white children was largely in the hands of private groups. Education of Negroes was almost nonexistent, and practically all of the race were illiterate. In fact, any education of Negroes was forbidden by law in some states. Today, in contrast, many Negroes have achieved outstanding success in the arts and sciences as well as in the business and professional world. It is true that public school education at the time of the Amendment had advanced further in the North, but the effect of the Amendment on Northern States was generally ignored in the congressional debates. Even in the North, the conditions of public education did not approximate those existing today. The curriculum was usually rudimentary; ungraded schools were common in rural areas; the school term was but three months a year in many states; and compulsory school attendance was virtually unknown. As a consequence, it is not surprising that there should be so little in the history of the Fourteenth Amendment relating to its intended effect on public education.

In the first cases in this Court construing the Fourteenth Amendment, decided shortly after its adoption, the Court interpreted it as proscribing all state-imposed discriminations against the Negro race. The doctrine of "separate but equal" did not make its appearance in this Court until 1896 in the case of *Plessy v. Ferguson* involving not education but transportation. American courts have since labored with the doctrine for over half a century. In this Court, there have been six cases involving the "separate but equal" doctrine in the field of public education. In more recent cases, all on the graduate school level, inequality was found in that specific benefits enjoyed by white students were denied to Negro students of the same educational qualifications. In none of these cases was it necessary to re-examine the doctrine to grant relief to the Negro plaintiff.

* * *

In approaching this problem, we cannot turn the clock back to 1868 when the Amendment was adopted, or even to 1896 when *Plessy v. Ferguson* was written. We must consider public education in the light of its full development and its present place in American life throughout the Nation. Only in this way can it be determined if segregation in public schools deprives these plaintiffs of the equal protection of the laws.

Today, education is perhaps the most important function of state and local governments. Compulsory school attendance laws and the great expenditures for education both demonstrate our recognition of the importance of education to our democratic society. It is required in the performance of our most basic public responsibilities, even service in the armed forces. It is the very foundation of good citizenship. Today it is a principal instrument in awakening the child to cultural values, in preparing him for later professional training, and in helping him to adjust normally to his environment. In these days, it is doubtful that any child may reasonably be expected to succeed in life if he is denied the opportunity of an education. Such an opportunity, where the state has undertaken to provide it, is a right which might be made available to all on equal terms.

We come then to the question presented: Does segregation of children in public schools solely on the basis of race, even though the physical facilities and other "tangible" factors may be equal, deprive the children of the minority group of equal educational opportunities? We believe that it does.

In *Sweatt v. Painter* in finding that a segregated law school for Negroes could not provide them equal educational opportunities, this Court relied in large part on "those qualities which are incapable of objective measurement but which make for greatness in a law school." In *McLaurin v. Oklahoma State Regents* the Court, in requiring that a Negro admitted to a white graduate school be treated like all other students, again resorted to intangible considerations: ". . . his ability to study, to engage in discussions and exchange views with other students, and, in general, to learn his profession." Such considerations apply with added force to children in grade and high schools. To separate them from others of similar age and qualifications solely because of their race generates a feeling of inferiority as to their status in the community that may affect their hearts and minds in a way unlikely ever to be undone. The effect of this separation on their educational opportunities was well stated by a finding in the Kansas case by a court which nevertheless felt compelled to rule against the Negro plaintiffs:

> "Segregation of white and colored children in public schools has a detrimental effect upon the colored children. The impact is greater when it has the sanction of the law; for the policy of separating the races is usually interpreted as denoting the inferiority of the negro group. A sense of inferiority affects the motivation of a child to learn. Segregation with the sanction of law, therefore, has a tendency to [retard] the educational and mental development of negro children and to deprive them of some of the benefits they would receive in a racial(ly) integrated school system."

What ever may have been the extent of psychological knowledge at the time of *Plessy v. Ferguson,* this finding is amply supported by modern authority. Any language in *Plessy v. Ferguson* contrary to this finding is rejected.

We conclude that in the field of public education the doctrine of "separate but equal" has no place. Separate educational facilities are inherently unequal. Therefore, we hold that the plaintiffs and others similarly situated for whom the actions have been brought are, by reason of the segregation complained of, deprived of the equal protection of the laws guaranteed by the Fourteenth Amendment.

***Source*: *Brown vs Board of Education of Topeka, [Kansas],* 347, US., 483, 1954.**

8.6 Southern Declaration on Integration

March 12, 1956

A justification for Southern resistance to the integration of educational facilities is put forward in this statement by 96 Southern Congressmen in March 1956.

We regard the decision of the Supreme Court in the school cases as clear abuse of judicial power. It climaxes a trend in the Federal judiciary undertaking to legislate, in derogation of the authority of Congress, and to encroach upon the reserved rights of the states and the people.

The original Constitution does not mention education. Neither does the Fourteenth Amendment nor any other amendment. The debates preceding the submission of the Fourteenth Amendment clearly show that there was no intent that it should affect the systems of education maintained by the states.

The very Congress which proposed the amendment subsequently provided for segregated schools in the District of Columbia.

When the amendment was adopted in 1868, there were thirty-seven states of the Union. Every one of the twenty-six states that had any substantial racial differences among its people either approved the operation of segregated schools already in existence or subsequently established such schools by action of the same law-making body which considered the Fourteenth Amendment.

As admitted by the Supreme Court in the public school case (Brown v. Board of Education), the doctrine of separate but equal schools "apparently originated in Roberts v. City of Boston (1849), upholding school segregation against attack as being violative of a state constitutional guarantee of equality." This constitutional doctrine began in the North, not in the South – and it was followed not only in Massachusetts but in Connecticut, New York, Illinois, Indiana, Michigan, Minnesota, New Jersey, Ohio, Pennsylvania and other northern states until they, exercising their rights as states through the constitutional processes of local self-government, changed their school systems.

In the case of Plessy v. Ferguson in 1896 the Supreme Court expressly declared that under the Fourteenth Amendment no person was denied any of his rights if the states provided separate but equal public facilities. This decision has been followed in many other cases. It is notable that the Supreme Court, speaking through Chief Justice Taft, a former President of the United States, unanimously declared in 1927 in Lum v. Rice that the "separate but equal" principle is ". . . within the discretion of the state in regulating its public schools and does not conflict with the Fourteenth Amendment."

This interpretation, restated time and again, became a part of the life of the people of many of the states and confirmed their habits, customs, traditions and way of life. It is founded on elemental humanity and common sense, for parents should not be deprived by Government of the right to direct the lives and education of their own children.

Though there has been no constitutional amendment or act of Congress changing this established legal principle almost a century old, the Supreme Court of the United States, with no legal basis for such action, undertook to exercise their naked judicial power and substituted their personal political and social idea for the established law of the land.

This unwarranted exercise of power by the court, contrary to the Constitution, is creating chaos and confusion in the states principally affected. It is destroying the amicable relations between the white and Negro races that have been created through ninety years of patient effort by the good people of both races. It has planted hatred and suspicion where there has been heretofore friendship and understanding.

Without regard to the consent of the governed, outside agitators are threatening immediate and revolutionary changes in our public school systems. If done, this is certain to destroy the system of public education in some of the states.

With the gravest concern for the explosive and dangerous condition created by this decision and inflamed by outside meddlers:

We reaffirm our reliance on the Constitution as the fundamental law of the land.

We decry the Supreme Court's encroachments on rights reserved to the states and to the people, contrary to established law and to the Constitution.

We commend the motives of those states which have declared the intention to resist forced integration by any lawful means.

We appeal to the states and people who are not directly affected by these decisions to consider the constitutional principles involved against the time when they too, on issues vital to them, may be the victims of judicial encroachment.

Even though we constitute a minority in the present Congress, we have full faith that a majority of the American people believe in the dual system of government which has enabled us to achieve our greatness and will in time demand that the reserved rights of the states and of the people be made secure against judicial usurpation.

We pledge ourselves to use all lawful means to bring about a reversal of this decision which is contrary to the Constitution and to prevent the use of force in its implementation.

In this trying period, as we all seek to right this wrong, we appeal to our people not to be provoked by the agitators and troublemakers invading our states and to scrupulously refrain from disorder and lawless acts.

Source: *The New York Times*, 12 March 1956.

8.7 CORE and Non-Violent Direct Action

The Chicago Committee of Racial Equality was the forerunner of the Congress of Racial Equality (CORE), which adopted its approach to non-violent, direct action demonstrations.

(a) CORE statement of purpose

CORE has one purpose – to eliminate racial discrimination.

CORE has one method – inter-racial, non-violent, direct action.

CORE asks its members to commit themselves to work as an integrated, disciplined group:

> by abiding by all democratic group decisions and accepting CORE discipline for all projects in which the individual participates:
>
> by renouncing overt violence in opposing racial discrimination and using the method of non-violent direct action:
>
> which refuses the cooperate with racial injustice;
>
> which seeks to change existing practices by using such techniques as negotiation, mediation, demonstration, and picketing;
>
> which develops a spirit of understanding rather than antagonism.

CORE members find a unique field of action:

> in working against discrimination in public places such as schools, restaurants, churches, etc.
>
> in attempting to attack the more basic social, economic, and political problems of discrimination as they are manifested in such forms as the restrictive covenant system.

CORE relates itself to other organizations and individuals on a basis of friendly cooperation with the possibility of mutual action on particular occasions. CORE welcomes the participation of individual members of other groups in specific projects, providing they accept the group discipline.

(b) CORE action discipline

CORE and non-violence

The Congress of Racial Equality is a national federation of local interracial groups committed to the goal of erasing the color-line through methods of direct non-violent action. All groups affiliated with national CORE agree to follow to the best of their ability the non-violent procedure in all action which they sponsor. The discipline which is set forth here, and which has been approved by the national convention, is simply meant to make explicit what seems to be implicit in the non-violent method.

This method consists of relatively undeveloped techniques for solving social conflicts, but it has great possibilities for good. It makes two assumptions. First of all, it assumes that social conflicts are not ultimately solved by the use of violence; that violence perpetuates itself, and serves to aggravate rather than resolve conflict. Moreover, it assumes that it is suicidal for a minority group to use violence since to use it would simply result in complete control and subjugation by the majority group. Secondly, the non-violent method assumes the possibility of creating a world in which non-violence will be used to a maximum degree. In working for this type of world, it confronts injustice without fear, without compromise, and without hate. The type of power which it uses in overcoming injustice is fourfold: (1) the power of active goodwill; (2) the power of public opinion against a wrong-door; (3) the power of refusing to cooperate with injustice, such non-cooperation being illustrated by the boycott and the strike; and (4) the power of accepting punishment if necessary without striking back, by placing one's body in the way of injustice.

Below are listed some of the implications for action of the non-violent method.

Guarantees of the individual to the group

1. A CORE member will investigate the facts carefully before determining whether or not racial injustice exists in a given situation.
2. A CORE member will seek at all times to understand the social situation which engendered the prejudiced attitude of the perpetrator of racial injustice.
3. A CORE member will seek to understand, without compromising his principles, the attitude of the person responsible for a policy of racial discrimination by discussing the problem through with him.
4. A CORE member will habor no malice or hate toward any individual or group of individuals.
5. A CORE member will maintain an attitude of humility, and will be willing to admit his own inadequencies.
6. He will suffer the anger of any individual or group in the spirit of good-will and creative reconciliation.
7. In suffering such anger, he will submit to assault and never retaliate in kind, either by act or word. He will not submit out of personal fear of embarassment or punishment.
8. If a CORE member faces arrest, he will submit willingly to such arrest by a legally constituted official. He will not, however, voluntarily retreat before the threats of legal or non-legal personages. At the same time, he will never violate his pledge of non-violence.
9. The CORE member will never use malicious slogans or labels or discredit any opponent.
10. If in the course of non-violent action any person is violently assaulted, the CORE member will non-violently defend such person even at the risk of his own life.

11. A member will never patronize knowingly an institution which practices discrimination, where there is a choice of places to patronize, except in the event of learning facts, or of participating in action toward elimination of discrimination.

12. A member will never engage in any action in the name of the group except when authorized by the group or one of its action units.

13. When in an action project a CORE member will cheerfully obey the orders issued by the authorized leader or spokesman of the project, whether these orders please him or not. If he does not approve of such orders, he shall later refer the criticism back to the group or back to the committee which was the source of the project plan.

14. No member, after once accepting the discipline of the group for a particular action project, shall have the right of withdrawing from that discipline.

15. No person who is not a recognized member of the group or an accepted participant in a particular project shall be allowed to act as a participant in an action project.

16. No personal, family, or other consideration shall divert a member from his group discipline if he once agrees to a particular project.

Guarantees from the group to the individual

17. Each member has the right to dissent from any group decision, and if dissenting, shall not participate in the specific action planned. A person who dissents, however, shall continue to have a voice in the discussion of the project.

18. Each member shall understand that all decisions on general policy shall be arrived at only through democratic group discussion.

19. If a member gets in trouble carrying out the work of CORE, he shall receive the uncompromising support of CORE, financially and otherwise, as he faces the difficulty.

Source: Chicago Committee of Racial Equality, *Statement of Purpose*, 1942.
CORE Action Discipline: Version adapted by the National Convention of the Congress of Racial Equality, June 1945. CORE Archives, State Historical Society of Wisconsin.

8.8 Martin Luther King, Jr., and the Montgomery Bus Boycott

With the support of local church and union leaders, Martin Luther King, Jr., recently arrived to be the Pastor of Dexter Avenue Baptist Church in Montgomery, Alabama, emerged in 1955 as the leader of the civil rights movement in Montgomery. King shows how the bus and consumer boycott by local blacks which was built on the stand taken by Mrs Rosa Parks took effect, and outlines the rationale for non-violent protest.

A. "We Negroes have replaced self-pity with self-respect and . . . with dignity"

The segregation of Negroes, with its inevitable discrimination, has thrived on elements of inferiority present in the masses of both white and Negro people. Through forced separation from our African culture, through slavery, poverty, and deprivation, many black men lost self-respect.

In their relations with Negroes, white people discovered that they had rejected the very center of their own ethical professions. They could not face the triumph of their lesser instincts and simultaneously have peace within. And so, to gain it, they rationalized – insisting that the unfortunate Negro, being less than human, deserved and even enjoyed second class status.

They argued that his inferior social, economic and political position was good for him. He was incapable of advancing beyond a fixed position and would therefore be happier if encouraged not to attempt the impossible. He is subjugated by a superior people with an advanced way of life. The "master race" will be able to civilize him to a limited degree, if only he will be true to his inferior nature and stay in his place.

White men soon came to forget that the Southern social culture and all its institutions had been organized to perpetuate this rationalization. They observed a caste system and quickly were conditioned to believe that its social results, which they had created, actually reflected the Negro's innate and true nature.

In time many Negroes lost faith in themselves and came to believe that perhaps they really were what they had been told they were – something less than men. So long as they were prepared to except this role, racial peace could be maintained. It was an uneasy peace in which the Negro was forced to accept patiently injustice, insult, injury and exploitation.

Gradually the Negro masses in the South began to re-evaluate themselves – a process that was to change the nature of the Negro community and doom the social patterns of the South. We discovered that we had never really smothered our self-respect and that we could not be at one with ourselves without asserting it. From this point on, the South's terrible peace was rapidly undermined by the Negro's new and courageous thinking and his ever-increasing readiness to organize and to act. Conflict and violence was coming to the surface as the white South desperately clung to its old patterns. The extreme tension in race relations in the South today is explained in part by the revolutionary change in the Negro's evaluation of himself and of his destiny and by his determination to struggle for justice. *We Negroes have replaced self-pity with self-respect and self-depreciation with dignity.*

When Mrs. Rosa Parks, the quiet seamstress whose arrest precipitated the non-violent protest in Montgomery, was asked why she had refused to move to the rear of a bus, she said: "It was a matter of dignity; I could not have faced myself and my people if I had moved."

Many of the Negroes who joined the protest did not expect it to succeed. When asked why, they usually gave one of three answers: "I didn't expect Negroes to stick to it," or "I never thought we Negroes had the nerve," or "I thought the pressure from the white folks would kill it before it got started."

In other words, our non-violent protest in Montgomery is important because it is demonstrating to the Negro, North and South, that many of the stereotypes he has held about himself and other Negroes are not valid. Montgomery has broken the spell and is ushering in concrete manifestations of the thinking and action of the new Negro.

We now know that:

We can stick together. In Montgomery, 42,000 of us have refused to ride the city's segregated buses since December 5. Some walk as many as fourteen miles a day.

Our leaders do not have to sell out. Many of us have been indicted, arrested, and "mugged". Every Monday and Thursday night we stand before the Negro population at the prayer meetings and repeat: "It is an honor to face jail for a just cause."

Threats and violence do not necessarily intimidate those who are sufficiently aroused and non-violent. The bombing of two of our homes has made us more resolute. When a handbill was circulated at a White Citizens Council meeting stating that Negroes should be "abolished" by "guns, bows and arrows, sling shots and knives," we responded with even greater determination.

Our church is becoming militant. Twenty-four ministers were arrested in Montgomery. Each has said publicly that he stands prepared to be arrested again. Even upper-class Negroes who reject the "come to Jesus" gospel are now convinced that the church has no alternative but to provide the non-violent dynamics for social change in the midst of conflict. The $30,000 used for the car pool, which transports over 20,000 Negro workers, school children and housewives, has been raised in the churches. The churches have become the dispatch centers where the people gather to wait for rides.

We believe in ourselves. In Montgomery we walk in a new way. We hold our heads in a new way. Even the Negro reporters who converged on Montgomery have a new attitude. One tired reporter, asked at a luncheon in Birmingham to say a few words about Montgomery, stood up, thought for a moment, and uttered one sentence: "Montgomery has made me proud to be a Negro."

Economics is part of our struggle. We are aware that Montgomery's white businessmen have tried to "talk sense" to the bus company and the city commissioners. We have observed that small Negro shops are thriving as Negroes find it inconvenient to walk downtown to the white stores. We have been getting more polite treatment in the white shops since the protest began. We have a new respect for the proper use of our dollar.

We have discovered a new and powerful weapon – non-violent resistance. Although law is an important factor in bringing about social change, there are certain conditions in which the very effort to adhere to new legal decisions creates tension and provokes violence. We had hoped to see demonstrated a method that would enable us to continue our struggle while coping with the violence it aroused. Now we see the answer: face violence if necessary, but refuse to return violence. If we respect those who oppose us, they may achieve a new understanding of the human relations involved.

We now know that the Southern Negro has become of age, politically and morally. Montgomery has demonstrated that we will not run from the struggle, and will support the battle for equality. The attitude of many young Negroes a few years ago was reflected in the common expression, "I'd rather be a lamp post in Harlem than Governor of Alabama." Now the idea expressed in our churches, schools, pool rooms, restaurants and homes is: "Brother, stay here and fight non-violently. 'Cause if you don't let them make you mad, you can win." The official slogan of the Montgomery Improvement Association is "Justice without Violence."

Modest demands rejected

The leaders of the old order in Montgomery are not prepared to negotiate a settlement. This is not because of the conditions we have set for returning to the buses. The basic question of segregation in intra-state travel is already before the courts. Meanwhile we ask only for what in Atlanta, Mobile, Charleston and most other cities of the South is considered the Southern pattern. We seek the right, under segregation, to seat ourselves from the rear forward on a first come, first served basis. In addition, we ask for courtesy and the hiring of some Negro bus drivers on predominantly Negro routes.

A prominent judge of Tuscaloosa was asked if he felt there was any connection between Autherine Lucy's effort to enter the University of Alabama and the Montgomery non-violent protest. He replied, "Autherine is just an unfortunate girl who doesn't know what she is doing, but in Montgomery it looks like all the niggers have gone crazy."

Later the judge is reported to have explained that "of course the good niggers had undoubtedly been riled up by outsiders, Communists and agitators." It is apparent that at this historic moment most of the elements of the white South are not prepared to believe that "our Negroes could of themselves act like this."

Because the mayor and city authorities cannot admit to themselves that we have changed, every move they have made has inadvertently increased the protest and united the Negro community.

Dec. 1 – They arrested Mrs. Parks, one of the most respected Negro women in Montgomery.

Dec. 3 – They attempted to intimidate the Negro population by publishing a report in the daily paper that certain Negroes were calling for a boycott of the buses. They thereby informed the 30,000 Negro readers of the planned protest.

Dec. 5 – They found Mrs. Parks guilty and fined her $14. This action increased the number of those who joined the boycott.

Dec. 5 – They arrested a Negro college student for "intimidating passengers." Actually, he was helping an elderly women cross the street. This mistake solidified the college students' support of the protest.

Two policemen on motorcycles followed each bus on its rounds through the Negro community. This attempt at psychological coercion further increased the number of Negroes who joined the protest.

In a news telecast at 6:00 p.m. a mass meeting planned for that evening was announced. Although we had expected only 500 people at the meeting over 5,000 attended.

Dec. 6 – They began to intimidate Negro taxi drivers. This led to the setting up of a car pool and a resolution to extend indefinitely our protest, which had originally been called for one day only.

Dec 7 – They began to harass Negro motorists. This encouraged the Negro middle class to join the struggle.

Dec 8 – The lawyer for the bus company said, "We have no intention of hiring Negro drivers now or in the foreseeable future." To us this meant never. The slogan then became, "Stay off the buses until we win."

Dec. 9 – The mayor invited Negro leaders to a conference presumably for negotiations. When we arrived, we discovered that some of the men in the room were white supremacists and members of the White Citizens Council. The mayor's attitude was made clear when he said, "Comes the first rainy day and the Negroes will be back in the buses." The next day it did rain, but the Negroes did not ride the buses.

At this point over 42,000 Montgomery Negroes had joined the protest. After a period of uneasy quiet, elements in the white community turned to further police intimidation and to violence.

Jan 26 – I was arrested for travelling 30 miles per hour in a 25-mile zone. This arrest occurred just 2 hours before a mass meeting. So, we had to hold seven mass meetings to accommodate the people.

Jan 30 – My home was bombed.

Feb. 1 – The home of E. D. Nixon, one of the protest leaders and former state president of the NAACP, was bombed. This brought moral and financial support from all over the state.

Feb. 22 – Eighty-nine persons, including the 24 ministers, were arrested for participating in the non-violent protest.

The method of non-violence

Every attempt to end the protest by intimidation, by encouraging Negroes to inform, by force and violence, further cemented the Negro community and brought sympathy for our cause from men of good will all over the world. The great appeal for the world appears to lie in the fact that we in Montgomery have adopted the method of non-violence. In a world in which most men attempt to defend their highest values by the accumulation of weapons of destruction, it is morally refreshing to hear 5,000 Negroes in Montgomery shout "Amen" and "Halleluh" when they are exhorted to "pray for those who oppose you," or pray "Oh Lord, give us strength of body to keep walking for freedom," and conclude each mass meeting with: "Let us pray that God shall give us strength to remain non-violent though we may face death."

And death there may be. Many white men in the South see themselves as a fearful minority in an ocean of black men. They honestly believe with one side of their minds that Negroes are depraved and disease-ridden. They look upon any effort at equality as leading to "mongrelization." They are convinced that racial equality is a Communist idea and that those who ask for it are subversive. They believe that their caste system is the highest form of social organization.

The enlightened white Southerner, who for years has preached gradualism, now sees that even the slow approach finally has revolutionary implications. Placing straws on a camel's back, no matter how slowly, is dangerous. This realization has immobilized the liberals and most of the white church leaders. They have no answer for dealing with or absorbing violence. They end in begging for retreat, lest "things get out of hand and lead to violence."

Writing in *Life,* William Faulkner, Nobel prize-winning author from Mississippi, recently urged the NAACP to "stop now for a moment." That is to say, he encouraged Negroes to accept injustice, exploitation and indignity for a while longer. It is hardly a moral act to encourage others patiently to accept injustice which he himself does not endure.

In urging delay, which in this dynamic period is tantamount to retreat, Faulkner suggests that those of us who press for change now may not know that violence could break out. He says we are "dealing with a fact: the fact of emotional conditions of such fierce unanimity as to scorn the fact that it is a minority and which will go to any length and against any odds at the moment to justify and, if necessary, defend that condition and its right to it."

The answer to Faulkner

We Southern Negroes believe that it is essential to defend the right of equality now. From this position we will not and cannot retreat. Fortunately, we are increasingly aware that we must not try to defend our position by methods that contradict the aim of brotherhood. We in Montgomery believe that the only way to press on is by adopting the philosophy and practice of non-violent resistance.

This method permits a struggle to go on with dignity and without the need to retreat. It is a method that can absorb the violence that is inevitable in social change whenever deep-seated prejudices are challenged.

If, in pressing for justice and equality in Montgomery, we discover that those who reject equality are prepared to use violence, we must not despair, retreat, or fear. Before they make this crucial decision, they must remember: whatever they do, we will not use violence in return. We hope we can act in the struggle in such a way that they will see the error of their approach and will come to respect us. Then we can all live together in peace and equality.

The basic conflict is not really over the buses. Yet we believe that, if the method we use in dealing with equality in the buses can eliminate injustice within ourselves, we shall at the same time be attacking the basis of injustice – man's hostility to man. This can only be done when we challenge the white community to re-examine its assumptions as we are now prepared to re-examine ours.

We do not wish to triumph over the white community. That would only result in transferring those now on the bottom to the top. But, if we can live up to non-violence in thought and deed, there will emerge an interracial society based on freedom for all.

B. ". . . a nonviolent protest against injustice"

The present protest here in Montgomery on the part of the Negro citizens, grows out of many experiences – experiences that have often been humiliating and have led to deep resentment. The Negro citizens of Montgomery compose about 75% of the bus riders. In riding buses, they have confronted conditions which have made for a great deal of embarrassment, such as having to stand over empty seats, having to pay fares at the front door and going out to the back to get on, and then the very humiliating experience of being arrested for refusing to get up and give a seat to a person of another race.

These conditions and those experiences have now reached the point that the Negro citizens are tired, and this tiredness was expressed on December 5, when more than 99 percent of the Negro bus riders decided not to ride the buses, in a protest against these unjust conditions. This protest has lasted now for many, many weeks and is still in process.

From the beginning, we have insisted on nonviolence. This is a protest – a *nonviolent* protest against injustice. We are depending on moral and spiritual forces. To put it another way, this is a movement of passive resistance, and the great instrument is the instrument of love. We feel that this is our chief weapon, and that no matter how long we are involved in the protest, no matter how tragic the experiences are, no matter what sacrifices we have to make, we will not let anybody drag us so low as to hate them.

Love *must* be at the forefront of our movement if it is to be a successful movement. And when we speak of love, we speak of understanding, good will toward *all* men. We speak of a creative, a redemptive sort of love, so that as we look at the problem, we see that the real tension is not between the Negro citizens and the white citizens of

Montgomery, but it is a conflict between justice and injustice, between the forces of light and the forces of darkness, and if there is a victory – and there *will* be a victory – the victory will not be merely for the Negro citizens and a defeat for the white citizens, but it will be a victory for justice and a defeat of injustice. It will be a victory for goodness in its long struggle with the forces of evil.

Violence is immoral

This is a spiritual movement, and we intend to keep these things in the forefront. We know that violence will defeat our purpose. We know that in our struggle in America and in our specific struggle here in Montgomery, violence will not only be impractical but immoral. We are outnumbered; we do not have access to the instruments of violence. Even more than that, not only is violence impractical, but it is *immoral;* for it is my firm conviction that to seek to retaliate with violence does nothing but intensify the existence of evil and hate in the universe.

Along the way of life, someone must have *sense* enough and morality enough to cut off the chain of hate and evil. The greatest way to do that is through love. I believe firmly that love is a transforming power that can lift a whole community to new horizons of fair play, good will and justice.

Love vs. bombs

Love is our great instrument and our great weapon, and that alone. On January my home was bombed. My wife and baby were there; I was attending a meeting. I first heard of the bombing at the meeting, when someone came to me and mentioned it, and I tried to accept it in a very calm manner. I first inquired about my wife and daughter; then after I found out that they were all right, I stopped in the midst of the meeting and spoke to the group, and urged them not to be panicky and not to do anything about it because that was not the way.

I immediately came home and, on entering the front of the house, I noticed there were some 500-1000 persons. I came in the house and looked it over and went back to see my wife and to see if the baby was all right, but as I stood in the back of the house, hundreds and hundreds of people were still gathering, and I saw there that violence was a possibility.

It was at that time that I went to the porch and tried to say to the people that we could not allow ourselves to be panicky. We could not allow ourselves to retaliate with any type of violence, but that we were still to confront the problem with *love*.

One statement that I made – and I believe it very firmly – was: "He who lives by the sword will perish by the sword." I urged the people to continue to manifest love, and to continue to carry on the struggle with the same dignity and with the same discipline that we had started out with. I think at that time the people did decide to go home, things did get quiet, and it ended up with a great deal of calmness and a great deal of discipline, which I think our community should be proud of and which I was very proud to see because our people were determined not to retaliate with violence.

"Stand up to the finish"

Some twenty-six of the ministers and almost one hundred of the citizens of the city were indicted in this boycott. But we realized in the beginning that we would confront experiences that make for great sacrifices, experiences that are not altogether pleasant. We decided among ourselves that we would stand up to the finish, and this is what we are determined to do. In the midst of the indictments, we still hold to this nonviolent attitude, and this primacy of love.

Pray for justice

Even though convicted, we will not retaliate with hate, but will still stand with love in our hearts, and stand resisting injustice, with the same determination with which we started out. We need a great deal of encouragement in this movement. Of course one thing that we are depending on, from not only other communities but from our own community, is prayer. We ask people everywhere to pray that God will guide us, pray that justice will be done and that righteousness will stand. And I think through these prayers we will be strengthened; it will make us feel the unity of the nation and the presence of Almighty God. For as we said all along, this is a spiritual movement.

8.9 Southern Christian Leadership Conference

The Southern Christian Leadership Conference (SCLC) was founded by Martin Luther King, Jr., in 1957 to co-ordinate local protest movements in the South.

Aims and purposes of SCLC

The Southern Christian Leadership Conference has the basic aim of achieving full citizenship rights, equality, and the integration of the Negro in all aspects of American life. SCLC is a service agency to facilitate coordinated action of local community groups within the frame of their indigenous organizations and natural leadership. SCLC activity revolves around two main focal points: the use of nonviolent philosophy as a means of creative protest; and securing the right of the ballot for every citizen.

Philosophy of SCLC

The basic tenets of Hebraic-Christian tradition coupled with the Gandhian concept of *satyagraha* – truth force – is at the heart of SCLC's philosophy. Christian nonviolence actively resists evil in any form. It never seeks to humiliate the opponent, only to win him. Suffering is accepted without retaliation. Internal violence of the spirit is as much to be rejected as external physical violence. At the center of nonviolence is redemptive love. Creatively used, the philosophy of nonviolence can restore the broken community in America. SCLC is convinced that nonviolence is the most potent force available to an oppressed people in their struggle for freedom and dignity.

SCLC and nonviolent mass direct action

SCLC believes that the American dilemma in race relations can best and most quickly be resolved through the action of thousands of people, committed to the philosophy of nonviolence, who will physically identify themselves in a just and moral struggle. It is not enough to be intellectually dissatisfied with an evil system. The true nonviolent resister presents his physical body as an instrument to defeat the system. Through nonviolent mass direct action, the evil system is creatively dramatized in order that the conscience of the community may grapple with the rightness or wrongness of the issue at hand . . . .

SCLC and voter-registration

The right of the ballot is basic to the exercise of full citizenship rights. All across the South, subtle and flagrant obstacles confront the Negro when he seeks to register and vote. Poll taxes, long form questionnaires, harassment, economic reprisal, and sometimes death, meet those who dare to seek this exercise of the ballot. In areas where there is little or no attempt to block the voting attempts of the Negro, apathy generally is deeply etched upon the habits of the community. SCLC, with its specialized staff, works on both fronts; aiding local communities through every means available to secure the right to vote (e.g. filing complaints with the Civil Rights Commission) and arousing interest through voter-registration workshops to point up the importance of the ballot. Periodically, SCLC, upon invitation, conducts a voter-registration drive to enhance a community's opportunity to free itself from economic and political servitude. SCLC believes that the most important step the Negro can take is that short walk to the voting booth.

SCLC and civil disobedience

SCLC sees civil disobedience as a natural consequence of nonviolence when the register is confronted by unjust and immoral laws. This does not imply that SCLC advocates either anarchy or lawlessness. The Conference firmly believes that all people have a moral responsibility to obey laws that are just. It recognizes, however, that there also are unjust laws. From a purely moral point of view, an unjust law is one that is out of harmony with the moral law of the universe, or, as the religionist would say, out of harmony with the Law of God. More concretely, an unjust law is one in which the minority is compelled to observe a code which is not binding on the majority. An unjust law is one in which people are required to obey a code that they had no part in making because they were denied the right to vote. In the face of such obvious inequality, where difference is made legal, the nonviolent resister has no alternative but to disobey the unjust law. In disobeying such a law, he does so peacefully, openly and nonviolently. Most important, he *willingly* accepts the penalty for breaking the law. This distinguishes SCLC's position on civil disobedience from the "uncivil disobedience" of the racist opposition in the South. In the face of laws they consider unjust, they seek to defy, evade, and circumvent the law, BUT they are *un-*

willing to accept the penalty for breaking the law. The end result of their defiance is anarchy and disrespect for the law. SCLC, on the other hand, believes that civil disobedience involves the highest respect for the law. He who openly disobeys a law that conscience tells him is unjust and willingly accepts the penalty is giving evidence that he so respects the law that he belongs in jail until it is changed. . .

SCLC and segregation

SCLC is firmly opposed to segregation in any form that it takes and pledges itself to work unrelentingly to rid every vestige of its scars from our nation through nonviolent means. Segregation is an evil and its presence in our nation has blighted our larger destiny as a leader in world affairs. Segregation does as much harm to the *segregator* as it does to the *segregated.* The *segregated* develops a false sense of inferiority and the *segregator* develops a false sense of superiority, both contrary to the American ideal of democracy. America must rid herself of segregation not alone because it is politically expedient, but because it is morally right!

SCLC and constructive program

SCLC's basic program fosters nonviolent resistance to all forms of racial injustice, including state and local laws and practices, even when this means going to jail; and imaginative, bold constructive action to end the demoralization caused by the legacy of slavery and segregation – inferior schools, slums, and second-class citizenship. Thus, the Conference works on two fronts. On the one hand, it resists continuously the system of segregation which is the basic cause of lagging standards; on the other hand, it works constructively to improve the standards themselves. There MUST be a balance between attacking the causes and healing the effects the segregation.

SCLC and the beloved community

The ultimate aim of SCLC is to foster and create the "beloved community" in America where brotherhood is a reality. It rejects any doctrine of black supremacy for this merely substitutes one kind of tyranny for another.

8.10 Civil Rights Act, 1964

President John F. Kennedy's Civil Rights Bill was inherited by President Lyndon B. Johnson, who successfully steered it through Congress. Since the Act provided insufficient protection against infringements of black voting rights, a Voting Rights Act was passed in 1965 and this finally brought to an end Southern practices aimed at disfranchising black voters.

Title 1 – voting

Prohibits registrars from applying different standards to white and Negro voting applicants and from disqualifying applicants because of inconsequential errors on their forms. Requires that literacy tests be in writing, except under special arrangements for blind persons, and that any applicant desiring one be given a copy of the questions and his answers. Make a sixth-grade education a rebuttable presumption of literacy. Allows the Attorney General or defendant state officials in any voting suit to request trial by a three-judge Federal Court.

Title II – public accommodations

Prohibits discrimination or refusal of service on account of race in hotels, motels, restaurants, gasoline stations and places of amusement if their operations affect interstate commerce or if their discrimination "is supported by state action". Permits the Attorney General to enforce the title by suit in the Federal courts if he believes that any person or group is engaging in a "pattern or practice of resistance" to the rights declared by the title. The latter language was added in the Senate, which also authorized three-judge courts for suits under this title.

Title III – public facilities

Requires that Negroes have equal access to, and treatment in, publicly owned or operated facilities such as parks, stadiums and swimming pools. Authorizes the Attorney General to sue for enforcement of these rights if private citizens are unable to sue effectively.

Title IV – public schools

Empowers the Attorney General to bring school desegregation suits under the same conditions as in Title III. Authorizes technical and financial aid to school districts to assist in desegregation. The Senate strengthened a provision in the House bill saying that the title does not cover busing of pupils or other steps to end "racial imbalance."

Title V – Civil Rights Commission

Extends the life of the Civil Rights Commission until Jan 31, 1968.

Title VI – federal aid

Provides that no person shall be subjected to racial discrimination in any program receiving Federal aid. Direct Federal agencies to take steps against discrimination, including – as a last resort, and after hearings – withholding of Federal funds from state or local agencies that discriminate.

Title VII – employment

Bans discrimination by employers or unions with 100 or more employees or members the first year the act is effective, reducing over four years to 25 or more. Establishes a commission to investigate alleged discrimination and use persuasion to end it. Authorizes the Attorney General to sue if he believes any person or group is engaged in a "pattern or practice" of resistance to the title, and to ask for trial by a three-judge court. The Senate added the "pattern-or-practice" condition and shifted the power to sue from the commission to the Attorney General.

Title VIII – statistics

Directs the Census Bureau to compile statistics of registration and voting by race in areas of the country designated by the Civil Rights Commission. This might be used to enforce the long-forgotten provision of the 14th Amendment that states that [to] discriminate in voting shall lose seats in the House of Representatives.

Title IX – courts

Permits appellate review of decisions by Federal District judges to send back to the state courts criminal defendants who have attempted to remove their cases on the ground that their civil rights would be denied in state trials. Permits the Attorney General to intervene in suits filed by private persons complaining that they have been denied the equal protection of the laws.

Title X – conciliation

Establishes a Community Relations Service in the Commerce Department to help conciliate racial disputes. The Senate removed a House ceiling of seven employees.

Trial XI – miscellaneous

Guarantees jury trials for criminal contempt under any part of the act but Title I – a provision added in the Senate. Provides that the statue shall not invalidate state laws with consistent purposes, and that it shall not impair any existing powers of Federal officials.

The Voting Rights Act of 1965

A Digest of the Act

On January 4, 1965, President Johnson proposed in his State of the Union Message that ". . . we eliminate every remaining obstacle to the right and the opportunity to vote."

In March, a week after Negro civil rights marchers had been attacked by Alabama law enforcement officers as they attempted to walk from Selma to Montgomery to dramatize their appeal for full voting rights, the President appeared before a special session of Congress to urge speedy enactment of voting legislation and told Congress that ". . . the harsh fact is that in many places in this country men and women are kept from voting simply because they are Negroes." He added, "No law we now have on the books . . . can ensure the right to vote when local officials are determined to deny it."

The Administration's proposal to eliminate barriers to the right to vote was introduced in the House of Representatives on March 17 and in the Senate the following day. The Administration bill contained two central features, similar to proposals previously made by the Commission on Civil Rights, which were designed to attack the problem of systematic discrimination by local voting officials.

It provided that all literacy tests and other devices used to deny Negroes their voting rights would be suspended in States where less than 50 percent of the population had been registered or had voted in the 1964 Presidential election.

The proposal also provided for the appointment of Federal examiners who would list voters in designated areas covered by the legislation. It gave the Attorney General of the United States broad discretionary power to designate the counties in which the U.S. Civil Service Commission would appoint examiners.

In determining the political subdivisions to which examiners would be assigned, the Attorney General could assign examiners to any political subdivision from which he had received 20 meritorious complaints alleging voter discrimination or upon a determination that in his judgement examiners were needed to prevent denial of the right to vote in a subdivision.

Although the Administration bill was modified during the more than four months it was considered by Congress, its two central features – elimination of literacy tests and assignment of Federal examiners – remained in the final version.

The bill contained a provision dealing with poll taxes – a device which has been used to effect both racial and economic discrimination. The original measure modified State poll tax procedures by allowing new voters to vote if they tendered poll tax payment for the current year within 45 days before an election. The House bill abolished all poll taxes. The Senate-approved measure, however, provided for accelerated court challenge by the Attorney General of State poll tax requirements rather than outright abolition. As finally approved, the bill contained the Senate's proposal for challenging the poll tax and retained the Administration's provision for its payment.

The Attorney General's discretionary power to assign examiners was clarified by a provision that in exercising his discretion he could consider such factors as differences in registration level for whites and nonwhites and affirmative indications of compliance with the law.

The Administration bill required a would-be voter to allege to a Federal examiner that he had been refused registration or found not qualified to register by State officials sometime during a 90-day period before he appeared before the examiner. Some Congressmen argued that in counties where disfranchisement was most acute, registration would continue to be limited by reluctance of Negroes to confront hostile State officials. The Act, as passed, did not contain this requirement.

To assure the proper conduct of an election, Congress added a provision giving the Civil Service Commission authority to appoint, at the request of the Attorney General, poll watchers to be stationed at polling places in examiner counties to observe whether any persons were denied the opportunity to vote and to observe the tabulation of ballots.

The Senate added to the Administration bill a provision dealing with language literacy. It allows a prospective voter to qualify, without taking a literacy test, by demonstrating that he has completed at least six grades in a school under the American flag conducted in a language other than English. This provision will result in enfranchising persons educated in Puerto Rico who now reside on the mainland of the United States

The Senate began debating the Administration measure on April 13 and approved its version on May 26. The bill was called up in the House on July 6 and passed after three days of debate. The Senate-House Conference Committee reported out its version on August 2. The House approved the Voting Rights Act of 1965 with a 328-74 vote on August 3 and the Senate added its approval by a vote of 79-18 on August 4.

The Final Bill

The Voting Rights Act of 1965, signed by the President on August 6, suspends all literacy tests and other devices as qualifications for voting in any Federal, State, local, general, or primary election. It applies to the States of Alabama, Alaska, Georgia, Louisiana, Mississippi, South Carolina, Virginia, at least 26 counties in North Carolina, and one county in Arizona. The Act also covers election to political party office.

Sources: The digest of the Civil Rights Act's provisions is from *The New York Times*, June 20, 1964. United States Commission on Civil Rights, *The Voting Rights Act: The First Months* (Washington, D.C., 1965), pp. 10-13.

Separatism and Black Power

9.1 Malcolm X and the Black Muslims

Between 1952 and 1963, Malcolm X was a leading spokesman for the Nation of Islam (Black Muslims), arguing for cultural nationalism and segregation for the black community. His appeal was to the constituency of Marcus Garvey in the 1920s: the black population of (predominantly) the cities of the North, for whom the message and objectives of Martin Luther King, Jr., in the 1950s had little meaning.

Malcolm X

In the name of Allah, the Beneficent, the Merciful, to whom all praise is due whom we forever thank for giving America's 20 million so-called Negroes, the most honorable Elijah Muhammad as our leader and our teacher and our guide.

I would point out at the beginning that I wasn't born Malcolm Little. Little is the name of the slave master who owned one of my grandparents during slavery, a white man, and the name Little was handed down to my grandfather, to my father and on to me. But after hearing the teachings of the Honorable Elijah Muhammad and realizing that Little is an English name, and I'm not an Englishman, I gave the Englishman back his name; and since my own had been stripped from me, hidden from me, and I don't know it, I use X; and someday, as we are taught by the Honorable Elijah Muhammad, every black man, woman and child in America will get back the same name, the same language, and the same culture that he had before he was kidnapped and brought to this country and stripped of these things.

I would like to point out in a recent column by James Reston on the editorial page of the *New York Times*, December 15, 1961, writing from London, Mr. Reston, after interviewing several leading European statesmen, pointed out that the people of Europe, or the statesmen in Europe, don't feel that America or Europe have anything to worry about in Russia; that the people in Europe foresee the time when Russia, Europe, and America will have to unite together to ward off the threat of China and the non-white world. And if this same statement was made by a Muslim, or by the honorable Elijah Muhammad, it would be classified as racist; but Reston who is one of the leading correspondents in this country and writing for one of the most respected newspapers, points out that the holocaust that the West is facing is not something from Russia, but threats of the combined forces of the dark world against the white world.

Why do I mention this? Primarily because the most crucial problem facing the white world today is the race problem. And the most crucial problem facing white America today is the race problem. Mr. Farmer pointed out beautifully and quoted one writer actually as saying that the holocaust that America is facing is primarily still based upon race. This doesn't mean that when people point these things out that they are racist; this means that they are facing the facts of life that we are confronted with today. And one need only to look at the world troubles in its international context, national context, or local context, and one will always see the race problem right there, a problem that is almost impossible to duck around.

It so happens that you and I were born at a time of great change, when changes are taking place. And if we can't react intelligently to these changes, then we are going to be destroyed. When you look into the United Nations set-up, the way it is, we see that there is a change of power taking place, a change of position, a change of influence, a change of control. Wherein, in the past, white people used to exercise unlimited control and authority over dark mankind, today they are losing their ability to dictate unilateral terms to dark mankind. Whereas, yesterday dark nations had no voice in their own affairs, today the voice that they exercise in their own affairs is increasing, which means in essence that the voice of the white man or the white world is becoming more quiet every day, and the voice of the non-white world is becoming more loud every day. These are the facts of life and these are the changes that you and I, this generation, have to face up to on an international level, a national level, or a local level before we can get a solution to the problems that confront not only the white man, but problems that confront also the black man, or the non-white man.

When we look at the United Nations and see how these dark nations get their independence – they can out-vote the western block or what is known as the white world – and to the point where up until last year the U.N. was controlled by the white powers, or Western powers, mainly Christian powers, and the secretaryship used to be in the hands of a white European Christian; but now when we look at the general structure of the United Nations we see a man from Asia, from Burma, who is occupying the position of Secretary, who is a Buddhist, by the way, and we find the man who is occupying the seat of President is a Moslem from Africa, namely Tunisia. Just in recent times all of these changes are taking place, and the white man has got to be able to face up to them, and the black man has to be able to face up to them, before we can get our problem solved, on an international level, a national level, as well as on the local level.

In terms of black and white, what this means is that the unlimited power and prestige of the white world is decreasing, while the power and prestige of the non-white world is increasing. And just as our African and Asian brothers wanted to have their own land, wanted to have their own country, wanted to exercise control over themselves – they didn't want to be governed by whites or Europeans or outsiders, they wanted control over something among the black masses here in America. I think it would be mighty naive on the part of the white man to see dark mankind all over the world stretching out to get a country of his own, a land of his own, an industry of his own, a society of his own, even a flag of his own, it would be mighty naive on the part of the white man to think that same feeling that is sweeping through the dark world is not going to leap 9000 miles across the ocean and come into the black people here in this country, who have been begging you for 400 years for something that they have yet to get.

In the areas of Asia and Africa where the whites gave freedom to the non-whites a transition took place, of friendliness and hospitality. In the areas where the non-whites had to exercise violence, today there is hostility between them and the white man. In this, we learn that the only way to solve a problem that is unjust, if you are wrong, is to take immediate action to correct it. But when the people against whom these actions have been directed have to take matters in their own hands, this creates hostility, and lack of friendliness and good relations between the two.

I emphasize these things to point up the fact that we are living in an era of great change; when dark mankind wants freedom, justice, and equality. It is not a case of wanting integration or separation, it is a case of wanting freedom, justice, and equality.

Now if certain groups think that through integration they are going to get freedom, justice, equality and human dignity, then well and good, we will go along with the integrationists. But if integration is not going to return human dignity to dark mankind, then integration is not the solution to the problem. And oft times we make the mistake of confusing the objective with the means by which the objective is to be obtained. It is not integration that Negroes in America want, it is human dignity. They want to be recognized as human beings. And if integration is going to bring us recognition as human beings, then we will integrate. But if integration is not going to bring us recognition as human beings, then integration "out the window," and we have to find another means or method and try that to get out objectives reached.

The same hand that has been writing on the wall in Africa and Asia is also writing on the wall right here in America. The same rebellion, the same impatience, the same anger that exists in the hearts of the dark people in Africa and Asia is existing in the hearts and minds of 20 million black people in this country who have been just as thoroughly colonized as the people in Africa and Asia. Only the black man in America has been colonized mentally, his mind has been destroyed. And today, even though he goes to college, he comes out and still doesn't even know he is a black man; he is ashamed of what he is, because his culture has been destroyed, his identity has been destroyed; he has been made to hate his black skin, he has been made to hate the texture of his hair, he has been made to hate the features that God gave him. Because the honorable Elijah Muhammad is coming along today and teaching us the truth about black people to make us love ourselves instead of realizing that it is you who taught us to hate ourselves and our own kind, you accuse the honorable Elijah Muhammad of being a hate teacher and accuse him of being a racist. He is only trying to undo the white supremacy that you have indoctrinated the entire world with.

I might point out that it makes America look ridiculous to stand up in the world conferences and refer to herself as the leader of the free world. Here is a country, Uncle Sam, standing up and pointing a finger at the Portuguese, and at the French, and at other colonizers, and there are 20 million black people in this country who are still confined to second-class citizenship, 20 million black people in this country who are still segregated and Jim-Crowed, as my friend, Dr. Farmer has already pointed out. And despite the fact that 20 million black people here yet don't have freedom, justice and equality, Adlai Stevenson has the nerve enough to stand up in the United Nations and point the finger at South Africa, and at Portugal and at some of these other countries. All we say is that South Africa preaches what it practices and practices what it preaches; America preaches one thing and practices another. And we don't want to integrate with hypocrites who preach one thing and practice another.

The good point in all of this is that there is an awakening going on among whites in America today, and this awakening is manifested in this way: two years ago you didn't know that there were black people in this country who didn't want to integrate with you; two years ago the white public had been brainwashed into thinking that every black man in this country wanted to force his way into your community, force his way into your schools, or force his way into your factories; two years ago you thought that all you would have to do is give us a little token integration and the race problem would be solved. Why? Because the people in the black community who didn't want integration were never given a voice, were never given a platform, were never given an opportunity to shout out the fact that integration would never solve the problem. And it has only been during the past year that the white public has begun to realize that the problem will never be solved unless a solution is devised acceptable to the black masses, as well as the black bourgeoisie – the upper class or middle class Negro. And when the whites began to realize that these integration-minded Negroes were in the minority, rather than in the majority, they began to offer an open forum and give those who want separation an opportunity to speak their mind to.

We who are black in the black belt, or black community, or black neighborhood can easily see that our people who settle for integration are usually the middle-class so-called Negroes, who are in the minority. Why? Because they have confidence in the white man; they have absolute confidence that you will change. They believe that they can change you, they believe that there is still hope in the American dream. But what to them is an American dream to us is an American nightmare, and we don't think that it is possible for the American white man in sincerity to take the action necessary to correct the unjust conditions that 20 million black people here are made to suffer morning, noon, and night. And because we don't have any hope or confidence or faith in the American white man's ability to bring about a change in the injustices that exist, instead of asking or seeking to integrate into the American society we want to face the facts of the problem the way they are, and separate ourselves. And in separating ourselves this doesn't mean that we are anti-white or anti-America, or anti-anything. We feel, that if integration all these years hasn't solved the problem yet, then we want to try something new, something different and something that is in accord with the conditions as they actually exist.

The honorable Elijah Muhammad teaches as that there are over 725 million Moslems or Muslims on this earth. I use both words interchangeably. I use the word Moslem for those who can't undergo the change, and I use the word Muslim for those who can. He teaches us that the world of Islam stretches from the China Seas to the shores of West Africa and that the 20 million black people in this country are the lost-found members of the nation of Islam. He teaches us that before we were kidnapped by your grandfathers and brought to this country and put in chains, our religion was Islam, our culture was Islamic, we came from the Muslim world, we were kidnapped and brought here out of the Muslim world. And after being brought here we were stripped of our language, stripped of our ability to speak our mother tongue, and it's a crime today to have to admit that there are 20 million black people in this country who not only can't speak their mother tongue, but don't even know they ever had one. This points up the crime of how thoroughly and completely the black man in America has been robbed by the white man of his culture, of his identity, of his soul, of his self. And because he has been robbed of his self, he is trying to accept yourself. Because he doesn't know who he is, now he wants to be who you are. Because he doesn't know what belongs to him, he is trying to lay claim to what belongs to you. You have brainwashed him and made him a monster. He is black on the outside, but you have made him white on the inside. Now he has a white heart and white brain, and he's breathing down your throat and down your neck because he thinks he's a white man the same as you are. He thinks that he should have your house, that he should have your factory, he thinks that he should even have your school, and most of them even think that they should have your woman, and most of them are after your woman.

The honorable Elijah Muhammad teaches us that the black people in America, the so-called Negroes, are the people who are referred to in the Bible as the lost sheep, who are to be returned to their own in the last days. He says that we are also referred to in the Bible, symbolically, as the lost tribe. He teaches us in our religion, that we are those people whom the Bible refers to who would be lost until the end of time. Lost in a house that is not theirs, lost in a land that is not theirs; lost in a country that is not theirs, and who will be found in the last days by the Messiah who will awaken them and enlighten them, and teach them that which they had been stripped of, and then this would give them the desire to come together among their own kind and go back among their own kind.

And this, basically, is why we who are followers of the honorable Elijah Muhammad don't accept integration: we feel that we are living at the end of time, by this, we feel that we are living at the end of the world. Not the end of the earth, but the end of the world. He teaches us that there are many worlds. The planet is an earth, and there is only one earth, but there are many worlds on this earth, the Eastern World and the Western World. There is a dark world and a white world. There is the world of Christianity, and the world of Islam. All of these are worlds and he teaches us that when the book speaks of the end of time, it doesn't mean the end of the earth, but it means the end of time for certain segments of people, or a certain world that is on this earth. Today, we who are here in America who have awakened to the knowledge of ourselves; we believe that there is no God but Allah, and we believe that the religion of Islam is Allah's religion, and we believe that it is Allah's intention to spread his religion throughout the entire earth. We believe that the earth will become all Muslim, all Islam, and because we are in a Christian country we believe that this Christian country will have to accept Allah as God, accept the religion of Islam as God's religion, or otherwise God will come in and wipe it out. And we don't want to be wiped out with the American white man, we don't want to integrate with him, we want to separate from him.

The method by which the honorable Elijah Muhammad is straightening out our problem is not teaching us to force ourselves into your society, or force ourselves even into your political, economic or any phase of your society, but he teaches us that the best way to solve this problem is for complete separation. He says that since the black man here in America is actually the property that was stolen from the East by the American white man, since you have awakened today and realized that this is what we are, we should be separated from you, and your government should ship us back from where we came from, not at our expense, because we didn't pay to come here. We were brought here in chains. So the honorable Elijah Muhammad and the Muslims who follow him, we want to go back to our own people. We want to be returned to our own people.

But in teaching this among our people and the masses of black people in this country, we discover that the American government is the foremost agency in opposing any move by any large number of black people to leave here and go back among our own kind. The honorable Elijah Muhammad's words and work is harassed daily by the F.B.I. and every other government agency which use various tactics to make the so-called Negroes in every community think that we are all about to be rounded up, and they will be rounded up too if they will listen to Mr. Muhammad; but what the American government has failed to realize, the best way to open up a black man's head today and make him listen to another black man is to speak against that black man. But when you begin to pat a black man on the back, no black man in his right mind will trust that black man any longer. And it is because of this hostility on the part of the government toward our leaving here that the honorable Elijah Muhammad says then, if the American white man or the American government doesn't want us to leave, and the government has proven its inability to bring about integration or give us freedom, justice and equality on a basis, equally mixed up with white people, then what are we going to do? If the government doesn't want us to go back among our own people, or to our own people, and at the same time the government has proven its inability to give us justice, the honorable Elijah Muhammad says if you don't want us to go and we can't stay here and live in peace together, then the best solution is separation. And this is what he means when he says that some of the territory here should be set aside, and let our people go off to ourselves and try and solve our own problem.

Some of you may say, Well, why should you give us part of this country? The honorable Elijah Muhammad says that for 400 years we contributed our slave labor to make the country what it is. If you were to take the individual salary or allowances of each person in this audience it would amount to nothing individually, but when you take it collectively all in one pot you have a heavy load. Just the weekly wage. And if you realize that from anybody who could collect all of the wages from the persons in this audience right here for one month, why they would be so wealthy they couldn't walk. And if you see that, then you can imagine the result of millions of black people working for nothing for 310 years. And that is the contribution that we made to America. Not Jackie Robinson, not Marian Anderson, not George Washington Carver, that's not our contribution; our contribution to American society is 310 years of free slave labor for which we have not been paid one dime. We who are Muslims, followers of the honorable Elijah Muhammad, don't think that an integrated cup of coffee is sufficient payment for 310 years of slave labor.

Source: Malcolm X (and James Farmer), 'Separation or Integration: a Debate', *Dialogue Magazine*, May 1962.

9.2 A Case for Separation

A reasoned case for the partition of the United States into white and black geographical regions and nations.

There is a growing ambivalence in the Negro community which is creating a great deal of confusion both within the black community itself, and within those segments of the white community that are attempting to relate to the blacks. It arises from the question of whether the American Negro is a cultural group, significantly distinct from the majority culture in ways that are ethnically rather than socio-economically based.

If one believes the answer to this is yes, then one is likely to favor emphasizing the cultural distinctiveness and to be vigorously opposed to any efforts to minimize or to submerge the differences. If, on the other hand, one believes that there are no cultural differences between the blacks and the whites or that the differences are minimal and transitory, then one is likely to resist the placing of great emphasis on the differences and to favor accentuating the similarities.

These two currents in the black community are symbolized, and perhaps over-simplified, by the factional labels of separatists and integrationists.

The separatist would argue that the Negro's foremost grievance is not solvable by giving him access to more gadgets, although this is certainly part of the solution, but that his greatest thirst is in the realm of the spirit – that he must be provided an opportunity to reclaim his own group individuality and to have that individuality recognized as having equal validity with the other major cultural groups of the world.

The integrationist would argue that what the Negro wants, principally, is exactly what the whites want – that is, that the Negro wants "in" American society, and that operationally this means providing the Negro with employment, income, housing, and education comparable to that of the whites. This having been achieved, the other aspects of the Negro's problem of inferiority will disappear.

The origins of this ideological dichotomy are easily identified. The physical characteristics that distinguish blacks from whites are obvious enough; and the long history of slavery, supplemented by the post-emancipation pattern of exclusion of the blacks from so many facets of American society, are equally undeniable. Whether observable behavioral differences between the mass of the blacks and the white majority are more properly attributable to this special history of the black man in America or are better viewed as expressions of racial differences in life style is an arguable proposition.

What is not arguable, however, is the fact that at the time of the slave trade the blacks arrived in America with a cultural background and a life style that was quite distinct from that of the whites. Although there was perhaps as much diversity amongst those Africans from widely scattered portions of the continent as there was amongst the European settlers, the differences between the two racial groups was unquestionably far greater, as attested by the different roles which they were to play in the society.

Integrationist and separatist viewpoints

Over this history there seems to be little disagreement. The dispute arises from how one views what happened during the subsequent 350 years.

The integrationist would focus on the transformation of the blacks into imitators of the European civilization. European clothing was imposed on the slaves; eventually their languages were forgotten; the African homeland receded ever further into the background. Certainly after 1808, when the slave trade was officially terminated, thus cutting off the supply of fresh injections of African culture, the Europeanization of the blacks proceeded apace. With emancipation, the national constitution recognized the legal manhood of the blacks, United States citizenship was unilaterally conferred upon the ex-slave, and the Negro began his arduous struggle for social, economic, and political acceptance into the American mainstream.

The separatist, however, takes the position that the cultural transformation of the black man was not complete. Whereas the integrationist is more or less content to accept the destruction of the original culture of the African slaves as a *fait accompli,* irrespective of whether he feels it to have been morally reprehensible or not, the separatist is likely to harbor a vague sense of resentment toward the whites for having perpetrated this cultural genocide and he is concerned to nurture whatever vestiges may have survived the North American experience and to encourage a renaissance of these lost characteristics. In effect, he is sensitive to an identity crisis which presumably does not exist in the mind of the integrationist.

To many observers, the separatist appears to be romantic and even reactionary. On the other hand, his viewpoint strikes an harmonious chord with mankind's most fundamental instinct – the instinct for survival. With so powerful a stimulus and with the oppressive tendencies congenitally present in the larger white society, one almost could have predicted the emergence of the burgeoning movement toward black separatism. Millions of black parents have been confronted with the poignant agony of raising black, kinky-haired children in a society where the standard of beauty is a milk-white skin and long, straight hair. To convince a black child that she is beautiful when every channel of value formation in the society is telling her the opposite is a heart-rending and well-nigh impossible task. It is a challenge that confronts all Negroes, irrespective of their social and economic class, but the difficulty of dealing with it is likely to vary directly with the degree to which the family leads an integrated existence. A black child in a predominantly black school may realize that she doesn't look like the pictures in the books, magazines, and TV advertisements, but at least she looks like her schoolmates and neighbors. The black child in a predominantly white school and neighborhood lacks even this basis for identification.

The problem of identity

This identity problem is not peculiar to the Negro, of course, nor is it limited to questions of physical appearance. Minorities of all sorts encounter it in one form or another – the immigrant who speaks with an accent; the Jewish child who doesn't celebrate Christmas; the vegetarian who shuns meat. But for the Negro the problem has a special dimension, for in the American ethos a black man is not only "different," he is classed as ugly and inferior.

This is not an easy situation to deal with, and the manner in which a Negro chooses to handle it will be both determined by and a determinant of his larger political outlook. He can deal with it as an integrationist, accepting his child as being ugly by prevailing standards and urging him to excel in other ways to prove his worth; or he can deal with it as a black nationalist, telling the child that he is not a freak but rather part of a larger international community of black-skinned, kinky-haired people who have a beauty of their own, a glorious history, and a great future. In short, he can replace shame with pride, inferiority with dignity, by imbuing the child with what is coming to be known as black nationalism. The growing popularity of this latter viewpoint is evidenced by the appearance of "natural" hair styles among Negro youth and by the surge of interest in African and Negro culture and history.

Black Power, black consciousness and American society

Black Power may not be the ideal slogan to describe this new self-image that the black American is developing, for to guilt-ridden whites the slogan conjures up violence, anarchy, and revenge. To frustrated blacks, however, it symbolizes unity and a newly found pride in the blackness with which the Creator endowed us and which we realize must always be our mark of identification. Heretofore this blackness has been a stigma, a curse with which we were born. Black Power means that henceforth this curse will be a badge of pride rather than of scorn. It marks the end of an era in which black men devoted themselves to pathetic attempts to be white men and inaugurates an era in which black people will set their own standards of beauty, conduct, and accomplishment.

Is this new black consciousness in irreconcilable conflict with the larger American society?

In a sense, the heart of the American cultural problem always has been the need to harmonize the inherent contradiction between racial (or national) identity and integration into the melting pot which was America. In the century since the Civil War, the society has made little effort to find a measure to afford the black minority a sense of racial pride and independence while at the same time accepting it as a full participant in the larger society.

Now that the implications of that failure are becoming apparent, the black community seems to be saying "Forget it! We'll solve our own problems." Integration, which never had a high priority among the black masses, now is being written off by them as not only unattainable but as actually harmful – driving a wedge between those black masses and the so-called Negro elite.

To these developments has been added the momentous realization by many of the "integrated" Negroes that, in the United States, full integration can only mean full assimilation – a loss of racial identity. This sobering prospect has caused many a black integrationist to pause and reflect, even as have his similarly challenged Jewish counterparts.

Integration – a painless genocide?

Thus, within the black community there are two separate challenges to the traditional integration policy which long has constituted the major objective of established Negro leadership. There is the general skepticism that the Negro, even after having transformed himself into a white black-man, will enjoy full acceptance into American society; and there is the longer-range doubt that even should complete integration somehow be achieved, it would prove to be really desirable, for its price may be the total absorption and disappearance of the race – a sort of painless genocide.

Understandably, it is the black masses who have most vociferously articulated these dangers of assimilation, for they have watched with alarm as the more fortunate among their ranks have gradually risen to the top only to be promptly "integrated" off into the white community – absorbed into another culture, often with undisguised contempt for all that had previously constituted their racial and cultural heritage. Also, it was the black masses who first perceived that integration actually increases the white community's control over the black one by destroying black institutions, and by absorbing black leadership and coinciding its interests with those of the white community.

The international "brain drain" has its counterpart in the black community, which is constantly being denuded of its best trained people and many of its natural leaders. Black institutions of all sorts – colleges, newspapers, banks, even community organizations – are experiencing the loss of their better people to the newly available openings in white establishments, thereby lowering the quality of the Negro organizations and in some cases causing their demise or increasing their dependence on whites for survival. Such injurious, if unintended, side effects of integration have been felt in almost every layer of the black community.

Negro distrust of white America

If the foregoing analysis of the integrationist *vs.* separatist conflict exhausted the case, we might conclude that all the problems have been dealt with before, by other immigrant groups in America. (It would be an erroneous conclusion, for while other groups may have encountered similar problems, their solutions do not work for us, alas.) But there remains yet another factor which is cooling the Negro's enthusiasm for the integration path: he is becoming distrustful of his fellow Americans.

The American culture is one of the youngest in the world. Futhermore, as has been pointed out repeatedly in recent years, it is essentially a culture that approves of violence, indeed enjoys it. Military expenditures absorb roughly half the national budget. Violence predominates on the TV screen and the toys of violence are best-selling items during the annual rites for the much praised but little imitated Prince of Peace. In Vietnam, the zeal with which America has pursued its effort to destroy a poor and illiterate peasantry has astonished civilized people around the globe.

In such an atmosphere the Negro is understandably restive about the fate his white compatriots may have in store for him. The veiled threat by President Johnson at the time of the 1966 riots, suggesting that riots might beget pogroms and pointing out that Negroes are only 10 percent of the population was not lost on most blacks. It enraged them, but it was a sobering thought. The manner in which Germany herded the Jews into concentration camps and ultimately into ovens was a solemn warning to minority peoples everywhere. The casualness with which America exterminated the

Indians and later interned the Japanese suggests that there is no cause for the Negro to feel complacent about his security in the United States. He finds little consolation in the assurance that if it does become necessary to place him in concentration camps it will only be as a means of protecting him from uncontrollable whites. "Protective incarceration" to use governmental jargonese.

The very fact that such alternatives are becoming serious topics of discussion has exposed the Negro's already raw and sensitive psyche to yet another heretofore unfelt vulnerability – the insecurity he suffers as a result of having no homeland which he can honestly feel is his own. Among the major ethnocultural groups in the world he is unique in this respect.

Need for nationhood

As the Jewish drama during and following World War II painfully demonstrated, a national homeland is a primordial and urgent need for a people, even though its benefits do not always lend themselves to ready measurement. For some, the homeland constitutes a vital place of refuge from the strains of a life led too long within a foreign environment. For others, the need to reside in the homeland is considerably less intense than the need merely for knowing that such a homeland exists. The benefit to the expatriate is psychological, a sense of security in knowing that he belongs to a culturally and politically identifiable community. No doubt this phenomenon largely accounts for the fact that both the West Indian Negro and the Puerto Rican exhibit considerably more self-assurance than does the American Negro, for both of the former groups have ties to an identifiable homeland which honors and preserves their cultural heritage.

It has been marvelled that we American Negroes, almost alone among the cultural groups of the world, exhibit no sense of nationhood. Perhaps it is true that we do lack this sense, but there seems to be little doubt that the absense of a homeland exacts a severe if unconscious price from our psyche. Theoretically, our homeland is the U.S.A. We pledge allegiance to the stars and stripes and sing the national anthem. But from the age when we first begin to sense that we are somehow "different", that we are victimized, these rituals begin to mean less to us than to our white compatriots. For many of us they become a cruel and bitter mockery of our dignity and good sense; for relatively few of us do they retain a significance in any way comparable to their hold on our white brethren.

The recent coming into independence of many African states stimulated some interest among Negroes that independent Africa might become the homeland which they so desperately needed. A few made the journey and experienced a newly-found sense of community and racial dignity. For many who went, however, the gratifying racial fraternity which they experienced was insufficient to compensate for the cultural estrangement that accompanied it. They had been away from Africa for too long and the differences in language, food, and custom barred them from experiencing that "at home" sensation they were eagerly seeking. Symbolically, independent Africa could serve them as a homeland: practically, it could not. Their search continues – a search for a place where they can experience the security that comes from being a part of the majority culture, free at last from the inhibiting effects of cultural repression and induced cultural timidity and shame.

"This land is our rightful home"

If we have been separated from Africa for so long that we are no longer quite at ease there, then we are left with only one place to make our home, and that is in this land to which we were brought in chains. Justice would indicate such a solution in any case, for it is North America, not Africa, into which our toil and effort have been poured. This land is our rightful home and we are well within our rights in demanding an opportunity to enjoy it on the same terms as the other immigrants who have helped to develop it.

Since few whites will deny the justice of this claim, it is paradoxical that we are offered the option of exercising this birthright only on the condition that we abandon our culture, deny our race, and integrate ourselves into the white community. The "accepted" Negro, the "integrated" Negro, are mere euphemisms, hiding a cruel and relentless cultural destruction which is sometimes agonizing to the middle class Negro but which is becoming intolerable to the black masses. A Negro who refuses to yield his identity and to ape the white model finds he can survive in dignity only by rejecting the entire white society, which ultimately must mean challenging the law and the law enforcement mechanisms. On the other hand, if he abandons his cultural heritage and succumbs to the lure of integration he risks certain rejection and humiliation along the way, with absolutely no guarantee of ever achieving complete acceptance.

That such unsatisfactory options are leading to almost continuous disruption and dislocation of our society should hardly be cause for surprise.

Partition as a solution

A formal partitioning of the United States into two totally separate and independent nations, one white and one black, offers one way out of this tragic situation. Many will condemn it as a defeatist solution, but what they see as defeatism may better be described as a frank facing up to the realities of American society. A society is stable only to the extent that there exists a basic core of value judgments that are unthinkingly accepted by the great bulk of its members. Increasingly, Negroes are demonstrating that they do not accept the common core of values that underlies America – whether because they had little to do with drafting it or because they feel it is weighted against their interests.

The alleged disproportionately large number of Negro law violators, of unwed mothers, of illegitimate children, of non-working adults *may* be indicators that there is no community of values such as has been supposed, although I am not unaware of racial socio-economic reasons for these statistics also. But whatever the reasons for observed behavioral differences, there clearly is no reason *why* the Negro should not have his own ideas about what the societal organization should be. The Anglo-Saxon system of organizing human relationships certainly has not proved itself to be superior to all other systems and the Negro is likely to be more acutely aware of this fact than are most Americans.

This unprecedented challenging of the "conventional wisdom" on the racial question is causing considerable consternation within the white community, especially the white liberal community, which has long felt itself to be the sponsor and guardian of the blacks. The situation is further confused because the challenges to the orthodox integrationist views are being projected by persons whose roots are authentically within the black community – whereas the integrationist spokesmen of the past often have been persons whose credentials were partly white-bestowed. This situation is further aggravated by the classical inter-generational problem – with black youth seizing the lead and speaking out for nationalism and separatism whereas their elders look on askance, a development which has at least a partial parallel within the contemporary white community, where youth is increasingly strident in its demands for thoroughgoing revision of our social institutions.

The black nationalists

If one were to inquire as to who the principal spokesmen for the new black nationalism or for separatism are, one would discover that the movement is essentially locally based rather than nationally organized. In the San Francisco Bay area, the Black Panther party is well known as a leader in the tactics of winning recognition for the black community. Their tactic is *via* a separate political party for black people, a format which I suspect we will hear a great deal more of in the future. The work of the Black Muslims is well known, and perhaps more national in scope than that of any other black nationalist group. Out of Detroit there is the Malcolm X Society, led by attorney Milton Henry, whose members reject their United States citizenship and are claiming five southern states for the creation of a new Black Republic. Another major leader in Detroit is the Rev. Albert Cleage, who is developing a considerable following for his preachings of black dignity and who has also experimented with a black political party, thus far without success.

The black students at white colleges are one highly articulate group seeking for some national organizational form. A growing number of black educators are also groping toward some sort of nationally coordinated body to lend strength to their local efforts for developing educational systems better tailored to the needs of the black child. Under the name of Association of Afro-American Educators, they recently held a national conference in Chicago which was attended by several hundred public school teachers and college and community workers.

This is not to say that every black teacher or parent-teacher group that favors community control of schools is necessarily sympathetic to black separatism. Nevertheless, the general thrust of the move toward decentralized control over public schools, at least in the larger urban areas, derives from an abandoning of the idea of integration in the schools and a decision to bring to the ghetto the best and most suitable education that can be obtained.

Ghetto improvement efforts

Similarly, a growing number of community-based organizations are being formed for the purpose of facilitating the economic development of the ghetto, for replacement of absentee business proprietors and landlords by black entrepreneurs and resident owners. Again, these efforts are not totally separatist in that they operate within the framework of the present national society, but they build on the separatism that already exists in the society rather than attempting to eliminate it. To a black who sees salvation for the black man only in a complete divorce of the two races, these efforts at ghetto improvement appear futile – perhaps even harmful. To others, convinced that co-existence with white America is possible within the national framework if only the white will permit the Negro to develop as he wishes and by his own hand rather than in accordance with a white-conceived and white-administered pattern, such physically and economically upgraded black enclaves will be viewed as desirable steps forward.

Source: Robert S Browne, 'A Case for Separatism', in *Separatism or Integration: Which Way for America?, – A Dialogue* (New York: A. Philip Randolph Educational Funds, 1968), pp. 7-15.

9.3 SNCC Urges Revolutionary Action

The Student National Co-ordinating Committee (SNCC) had provided many activists for the campaigns of Martin Luther King, Jr., and SCLC in the South in pursuit of civil rights. By the 1960s, the left-wing leadership of SNCC had developed a revolutionary agenda in the context of poverty and riots in the black ghettoes of Northern cities. Particular targets for their wrath were white exploitation and the accommodationism of the black middle class.

Black men of America are a captive people

The black man in America is in a perpetual state of slavery no matter what the white man's propaganda tells us.

The black man in America is exploited and oppressed the same as his black brothers are all over the face of the earth by the same white man. We will never be free until we are all free and that means all black oppressed people all over the earth.

We are not alone in this fight, we are a part of the struggle for self-determination of all black men everywhere. We here in America must unite ourselves to be ready to help our brothers elsewhere.

We must first gain BLACK POWER here in America. Living inside the camp of the leaders of the enemy forces, it is our duty to our Brothers to revolt against the system and create our own system so that we can live as MEN.

We must take over the political and economic systems where we are in the majority in the heart of every major city in this country as well as in the rural areas. We must create our own black culture to erase the lies the white man has fed our minds from the day we were born.

The black man in the ghetto will lead the Black Power Movement

The black Brother in the ghetto will lead the Black Power Movement and make the changes that are necessary for its success.

The black man in the ghetto has one big advantage that the bourgeois Negro does not have despite his 'superior' education. He is already living outside the value system white society imposes on all black Americans.

He has to look at things from another direction in order to survive. He is ready. He received his training in the streets, in the jails, from the ADC check his mother did not receive in time and the head-beatings he got from the cop on the corner.

Once he makes that first important discovery about the great pride you feel inside as a BLACK MAN and the great heritage of the mother country, Africa, there is no stopping him from dedicating himself to fight the white man's system.

This is why the Black Power Movement is a true revolutionary movement with the power to change men's minds and unmask the tricks the white man has used to keep black men enslaved in modern society.

The bourgeois Negro cannot be a part of the Black Power Movement

The burgeois Negro has been force-fed the white man's propaganda and has lived too long in the half-world between white and phony black bourgeois society. He cannot think for himself because he is a shell of a man full of contradictions he cannot resolve. He is not to be trusted under any circumstances until he has proved himself to be 'cured.' There are a minute handful of these 'cured' bourgeois Negroes in the Black Power Movement and they are most valuable but they must not be allowed to take control. They are aware intellectually but under stress will react emotionally to the pressures of white society in the same way a white 'liberal' will expose an unconscious prejudice that he did not even realize he possessed.

What Brother Malcolm X taught us about ourselves

Malcolm X was the first black man from the ghetto in America to make a real attempt to get the white man's fist off the black man. He recognized the true dignity of man – without the white society prejudices about status, education and background that we all must purge from our minds.

Even today, in the Black Power Movement itself we find Brothers who look down on another Brother because of the conditions that life has imposed upon him. The most beautiful thing that Malcolm X taught us is that once a black man discovers for himself a pride of his blackness, he can throw off the shackles of mental slavery and become a MAN in the truest sense of the word. We must move on from the point our Great Black Prince had reached.

We must become leaders for ourselves

We must not get hung-up in the bag of having one great leader who we depend upon to make decisions. This makes the Movement too vulnerable to those forces the white man uses to keep us enslaved, such as the draft, murder, prison or character assassination.

We have to all learn to become leaders for ourselves and remove all white values from our minds. When we see a Brother using a white value through error it is our duty to the Movement to point it out to him. We must thank our Brothers who show us our own errors. We must discipline ourselves so that if necessary we can leave family and friends at a moment's notice, maybe forever, and know our Brothers have pledged themselves to protect the family we have left behind.

As a part of our education, we must travel to other cities and make contracts with the Brothers in all the ghettos in America so that when the time is right we can unite as one under the banner of BLACK POWER.

Learning to think Black and remove white things from our minds

We have got to begin to say and understand with complete assuredness what black is. Black is an inner pride that the white man's language hampers us from expressing. Black is being a complete fanatic, who white society considers insane.

We have to learn that black is so much better than belonging to the white race with the blood of millions dripping from their hands that it goes far beyond any prejudice or resentment. We must fill ourselves with hate for all white things. This is not vengeance or trying to take the white oppressors' place to become new black oppressors but is a oneness with a worldwide black brotherhood.

We must regain respect for the lost religion of our fathers, the spirits of the black earth of Africa. The white man has so poisoned our minds that if a Brother told you he practiced Voodoo you would roll around on the floor laughing at how stupid and superstitious he was.

We have to learn to roll around on the floor laughing at the black man who says he worships the white Jesus. He is truly sick.

We must create our own language for these things that the white man will not understand because a Black Culture exists and it is not the wood-carvings or native dancing it is the black strength inside of true men.

Ideas on planning for the future of Black Power

We must infiltrate all government agencies. This will not be hard because black clerks work in all agencies in poor paying jobs and have a natural resentment of the white men who run these jobs.

People must be assigned to seek out these dissatisfied black men and women and put pressure on them to give us the information we need. Any man in overalls, carrying a tool box, can enter a building if he looks like he knows what he is doing.

Modern America depends on many complex systems such as electricity, water, gas, sewerage and transportation and all are vulnerable. Much of the government is run by computers that must operate in air conditioning. Cut off the air conditioning and they cannot function.

We must begin to investigate and learn all of these things so that we can use them if it becomes necessary. We cannot train an army in the local park but we can be ready for the final confrontation with the white man's system.

Remember your Brothers in South Africa and do not delude yourselves that it could not happen here. We must copy the white man's biggest trick, diversion, (Hitler taught them that) and infiltrate all civil rights groups, keep them in confusion so they will be neutralized and cannot be used as a tool of the white power structure.

The civil rights, integrationist movement says to the white man, "If you please, Sir, let us, the 10 percent minority of America have our rights. See how nice and nonviolent we are?"

This is why SNCC calls itself a Human Rights Organization. We believe that we belong to the 90 percent majority of the people on earth that the white man oppresses and that we should not beg the white man for anything. We want what belongs to us as human beings and we intend to get it through BLACK POWER.

How to deal with black traitors

Uncle Tom is too kind of a word. What we have are black traitors, quisslings, collaborators, sell-outs, white Negroes.

We have to expose these people for once and for all for what they are and place them on the side of the oppressor where they belong. Their black skin is a lie and their guilt the shame of all black men. We must ostracize them and if necessary exterminate them.

We must stop fighting a "fair game." We have to hate and disrupt and destroy and blackmail and lie and steal and become blood-brothers like the Mau-Mau.

We must eliminate or render ineffective all traitors. We must make them fear to stand up like puppets for the white men, and we must make the world understand that these so-called men do not represent us or even belong to the same black race because they sold out their birthright for a mess of white society pottage. Let them choke on it.

Pitfalls to avoid on the path to Black Power

We must learn how close America and Russia are politically. The biggest lie in the world is the cold-war. Money runs the world and it is controlled completely by the white man.

Russia and America run the two biggest money systems in the world and they intend to keep it under their control under any circumstances. Thus, we cannot except any help from Communism or any other "ism."

We must seek out poor peoples movements in South America Africa and Asia and make our alliances with them. We must not be fooled into thinking that there is a ready-made doctrine that will solve all our problems.

There are only white man's doctrines and they will never work for us. We have to work out our own systems and doctrines and culture.

Why propaganda is our most important tool

The one thing that the white man's system cannot stand is the TRUTH because his system is all based on lies.

There is no such thing as "justice" for a black man in America. The white man controls everything that is said in every book, newspaper, magazine, TV and radio broadcast.

Even the textbooks used in the schools and the bible that is read in the churches are designed to maintain the system for the white man. Each and every one of us is forced to listen to the white man's propaganda every day of our lives.

The political system, economic system, military system, educational system, religious system and anything else you name is used to preserve the status quo of white America getting fatter and fatter while the black man gets more and more hungry.

We must spend our time telling our Brothers the truth.

We must tell them that any black woman who wears a diamond on her finger is wearing the blood of her Brothers and Sisters in slavery in South Africa where one out of every three black babies die before the age of one, from starvation, to make the white man rich.

We must stop wearing the symbols of slavery on our fingers.

We must stop going to other countries to exterminate our Brothers and Sisters for the white man's greed.

We must ask our Brothers which side they are on.

Once you know the truth for yourself it is your duty to dedicate your life to recruiting your Brothers and to counteract the white man's propaganda.

We must disrupt the white man's system to create our own. We must publish newspapers and get radio stations. Black Unity is strength – let's use it now to get BLACK POWER.

Source: Chicago Office of SNCC, *We Want Black Power*, leaflet (Chicago: Chicago Office of SNCC, 1967).

9.4 The Black Panther Party

The Black Panthers emerged in California in 1966 with a program of revolutionary nationalism and self-defence for the black community against hostile white authorities. By the end of the 1960s, local law enforcement had killed or imprisoned many of the leaders.

(a) The Black Panther program

BLACK PANTHER

PARTY

FOR SELF DEFENSE

WHAT WE WANT WHAT WE BELIEVE

What we want now!:

1. We want freedom. We want power to determine the destiny of our black community.
2. We want full employment for our people.
3. We want an end to the robbery by the white man of our black community.
4. We want decent housing fit for shelter of human beings.
5. We want education for our people that exposes the true nature of this decadent American society. We want education that teaches us our true history and our role in the present day society.
6. We want all black men to be exempt from military service.
7. We want an immediate end to *police brutality* and *murder* of black people.
8. We want freedom for all black men and women held in federal, state, county, and city prisons and jails.
9. We want all black people when brought to trial, to be tried in court by a jury of their peer group or people from their black communities, as defined by the Constitution of the United States.
10. We want land, bread, housing, education, clothing, justice and peace.

What we believe:

1. We believe that black people will not be free until we are able to determine our destiny.
2. We believe that the federal government is responsible and obligated to give every man employment or a guaranteed income.

   We believe that if the white American business men will not give full employment, then the means of production should be taken from the business men and placed in the community so that the people of the community can organize and employ all of its people and give a high standard of living.
3. We believe that this racist government has robbed us and now we are demanding the overdue debt of forty acres and two mules. Forty acres and two mules was promised 100 years ago as retribution for slave labor and mass murder of black people. We will accept the payment in currency which will be distributed to our many communities. The Germans are now aiding the Jews in Israel for the genocide of the Jewish people. The Germans murdered 6,000,000 million Jews. The American racist has taken part in the slaughter of over 50,000,000 million black people; therefore, we feel that this is a modest demand that we make.
4. We believe that if the white landlords will not give decent housing to our black community then the housing and the land should be made into cooperatives so that our community, with government aide, can build and make decent housing for its people.

5. We believe in an educational system that will give to our people a knowledge of self. If a man does not have knowledge of himself and his position in society and the world, then he has little chance to relate to anything else.

6. We believe that black people should not be forced to fight in the military service to defend a racist government that does not protect us. We will not fight and kill other people of color in the world who, like black people, are being victimized by the white racist government of America. We will protect ourselves from the force and violence of the racist police and the racist military, by whatever means necessary.

7. We believe we can end police brutality in our black community by organizing black *self defense* groups that are dedicated to defending our black community from racist police oppression and brutality. The Second Amendment of the Constitution of the United States gives us a right to bear arms. We therefore believe that all black people should arm themselves for *self defense.*

8. We believe that all black people should be released from the many jails and prisons because they have not received a fair and impartial trial.

9. We believe that the courts should follow the United States Constitution so that black people will receive fair trials. The 14th Amendment of the U.S. Constitution gives a man a right to be tried by his peer group. A peer is a person from a similar economical, social, religious, geographical, environmental, historical and racial background. To do this the court will be forced to select a jury from the black community from which the black defendant came. We have been, and are being tried by all white juries that have no understanding of the "average reasoning man" of the black community.

10. When in the course of human events, it becomes necessary for one people to dissolve the political bonds which have connected them with another, and to assume among the powers of the earth, the separate and equal station to which the laws of nature and nature's God entitle them, a decent respect to the opinions of mankind requires that they should declare the causes which impel them to the separation.

We hold these truths to be self-evident, that all men are created equal, that they are endowed by their Creator with certain unalienable rights, that among these are life, liberty and the pursuit of happiness. That to secure these rights, governments are instituted among men, deriving their just powers from the consent of the governed, – *that whenever any form of government becomes destructive of these ends, it is the right of people to alter or to abolish it, and to institute new government, laying its foundation on such principles and organizing its powers in such form, as to them shall seem most likely to effect their safety and happiness.*

Prudence, indeed, will dictate that governments long established should not be changed for light and transient causes; and accordingly all experience hath shewn, that mankind are more disposed to suffer, while evils are sufferable, than to right themselves by abolishing the forms to which they are accustomed. *But when a long train of abuses and usurpations, pursuing invariably the same object, evinces a design to reduce them under absolute despotism, it is their right, it is their duty, to throw off such government, and to provide new guards for their future security.*

B. Interview with Huey Newton

THE MOVEMENT: The question of nationalism is a vital one in the black movement today. Some have made a distinction between cultural nationalism and revolutionary nationalism. Would you comment on the differences and give us your views?

HUEY P. NEWTON: There are two kinds of nationalism, revolutionary nationalism and reactionary nationalism. Revolutionary nationalism is first dependent upon a people's revolution with the end goal being the people in power. Therefore to be a revolutionary nationalist you would by necessity have to be a socialist. If you are a reactionary nationalist you are not a socialist and your end goal is the oppression of the people.

Cultural nationalism, or pork chop nationalism, as I sometimes call it, is basically a problem of having the wrong political perspective. It seems to be a reaction instead of responding to political oppression. The cultural nationalists are concerned with returning to the old African culture and thereby regaining their identity and freedom. In other words, they feel that the African culture will automatically bring political freedom. Many times cultural nationalists fall into line as reactionary nationalists.

Source: Black Panther Party Program, *Key List Mailing: Selected Documents of Current and Lasting Interest in the Civil Rights Movement* (San Francisco Office of SNCC, March 19, 1967).

The View from the Centre

10.1 The Negro Family

In Beyond the Melting Pot, *Nathan Glaser and Daniel P. Moynihan contrasted the failure of blacks in general to make social and economic progress equally with other (immigrant) groups. Moynihan's report for the United States Department of Labor,* The Negro Family, *particularly linked economic deprivation with unstable family structure among the black population.*

At the heart of the deterioration of the fabric of Negro society is the deterioration of the Negro family.

It is the fundamental source of the weakness of the Negro community at the present time.

There is probably no single fact of Negro American life so little understood by whites. The Negro situation is commonly perceived by whites in terms of the visible manifestations of discrimination and poverty, in part because Negro protest is directed against such obstacles, and in part, no doubt, because these are facts which involve the actions and attitudes of the white community as well. It is more difficult, however, for whites to perceive the effect that three centuries of exploitation have had on the fabric of Negro society itself. Here the consequences of the historic injustices done to Negro Americans are silent and hidden from view. But here is where the true injury has occurred: unless this damage is repaired, all the effort to end discrimination and poverty and injustice will come to little.

The role of the family in shaping character and ability is so pervasive as to be easily overlooked. The family is the basic social unit of American life; it is the basic socializing unit. By and large, adult conduct in society is learned as a child.

A fundamental insight of psychoanalytic theory, for example, is that the child learns a way of looking at life in his early years through which all later experience is viewed and which profoundly shapes his adult conduct.

It may be hazarded that the reason family structure does not loom larger in public discussion of social issues is that people tend to assume that the nature of family life is about the same throughout American society. The mass media and the development of suburbia have created an image of the American family as a highly standardized phenomenon. It is therefore easy to assume that whatever it is that makes for differences among individuals or groups of individuals, it is not a different family structure.

There is much truth to this; as with any other nation, Americans are producing a recognizable family system. But that process is not completed by any means. There are still, for example, important differences in family patterns surviving from the age of the great European migration to the United States, and these variations account for notable differences in the progress and assimilation of various ethnic and religious groups. A number of immigrant groups were characterized by unusually strong family bonds; these groups have characteristically progressed more rapidly than others.

But there is one truly great discontinuity in family structure in the United States at the present time: that between the white world in general and that of the Negro American.

The white family has achieved a high degree of stability and is maintaining that stability.

By contrast, the family structure of lower class Negroes is highly unstable, and in many urban centers is approaching complete breakdown.

N.b. There is considerable evidence that the Negro community is in fact dividing between a stable middle-class group that is steadily growing stronger and more successful, and an increasingly disorganized and disadvantaged lower-class group. There are indications, for example, that the middle-class Negro family puts a higher premium on family stability and the conserving of family resources than does the white middle-class family. The discussion of this paper is not, obviously, directed to the first group excepting as it is affected by the experiences of the second – an important exception. . . .

There are two points to be noted in this context.

First, the emergence and increasing visibility of a Negro middle-class may beguile the nation into supposing that the circumstances of the remainder of the Negro community are equally prosperous, whereas just the opposite is true at present, and is likely to continue so.

Second, the lumping of all Negroes together in one statistical measurement very probably conceals the extent of the disorganization among the lower-class group. If conditions are improving for one and deteriorating for the other, the resultant statistical averages might show no change. Further, the statistics on the Negro family and most other subjects treated in this paper refer only to a specific point in time. They are a vertical measure of the situation at a given moment. They do not measure the experience of individuals over time. Thus the average monthly unemployment rate for Negro males for 1964 is recorded as 9 percent. But *during* 1964, some 29 percent of Negro males were unemployed at one time or another. Similarly, for example, if 36 percent of Negro children are living in broken homes *at any specific moment,* it is likely that a far higher proportion of Negro children find themselves in that situation *at one time or another* in their lives.

Nearly a quarter of urban Negro marriages are dissolved

Nearly a quarter of Negro women in cities who have ever married are divorced, separated, or are living apart from their husbands.

The rates are highest in the urban Northeast where 26 percent of Negro women ever married are either divorced, separated, or have their husbands absent.

On the urban frontier, the proportion of husbands absent is even higher. In New York City in 1960, it was 30.2 percent, *not* including divorces.

Among ever-married nonwhite women in the nation, the proportion with husbands present *declined* in *every* age group over the decade 1950-60, as follows:

Age	**Percent with husbands present**	
	1950	1960
15-19 years	77.8	72.5
20-24 years	76.7	74.2
25-29 years	76.1	73.4
30-34 years	74.9	72.0
35-39 years	73.1	70.7
40-44 years	68.9	68.2

Although similar declines occurred among white females, the proportion of white husbands present never dropped below 90 percent except for the first and last age group.

Nearly one-quarter of Negro births are now illegitimate

Both white and Negro illegitimacy rates have been increasing, although from dramatically different bases. The white rate was 2 percent in 1940; it was 3.07 percent in 1963. In that period, the Negro rate went from 16.8 percent to 23.6 percent.

The number of illegitimate children per 1,000 live births increased by 11 among whites in the period 1940-63, but by 68 among nonwhites. There are, of course, limits to the dependability of these statistics. There are almost certainly a considerable number of Negro children who, although technically illegitimate, are in fact the offspring of stable unions. On the other hand, it may be assumed that many births that are in fact illegitimate are recorded otherwise. Probably the two opposite effects cancel each other out.

On the urban frontier, the nonwhite illegitimacy rates are usually higher than the national average, and the increase of late has been drastic.

In the District of Columbia, the illegitimacy rate for nonwhites grew from 21.8 percent in 1950, to 29.5 percent in 1964.

A similar picture of disintegrating Negro marriages emerges from the divorce statistics. Divorces have increased of late for both whites and nonwhites, but at a much greater rate for the latter. In 1940 both groups had a divorce rate of 2.2 percent. By 1964 the white rate had risen to 3.6 percent, but the nonwhite rate had reached 5.1 percent – 40 percent greater than the formerly equal white rate.

Almost one-fourth of Negro families are headed by females

As a direct result of this high rate of divorce, separation, and desertion, a very large percent of Negro families are headed by females. While the percentage of such families among whites has been dropping since 1940, it has been rising among Negroes.

The percent of nonwhite families headed by a female is more than double the percent for whites. Fatherless nonwhite families increased by a sixth between 1950 and 1960, but held constant for white families.

It has been estimated that only a minority of Negro children reach the age of 18 having lived all their lives with both their parents.

Once again, this measure of family disorganization is found to be diminishing among white families and increasing among Negro families.

The breakdown of the Negro family has led to a startling increase in welfare dependency

The majority of Negro children receive public assistance under the AFDC program at one point or another in their childhood.

At present, 14 percent of Negro children are receiving AFDC assistance, as against 2 percent of white children. Eight percent of white children receive such assistance at some time, as against 56 percent of nonwhites, according to an extrapolation based on HEW data. (Let it be noted, however, that out of a total of 1.8 million nonwhite illegitimate children in the nation in 1961, 1.3 million were *not* receiving aid under the AFDC program, although a substantial number have, or will, receive aid at some time in their lives.)

Again, the situation may be said to be worsening. The AFDC program, deriving from the long established Mothers' Aid programs, was established in 1935 principally to care for widows and orphans, although the legislation covered all children in homes deprived of parental support because one or both of their parents are absent or incapacitated.

In the beginning, the number of AFDC families in which the father was absent because of desertion was less than a third of the total. Today it is two-thirds. HEW estimates "that between two-thirds and three-fourths of the 50 percent increase from 1948 to 1955 in the number of absent-father families receiving ADC may be explained by an increase in broken homes in the population."

A 1960 study of Aid to Dependent Children in Cook County, Ill. stated:

> The "typical" ADC mother in Cook County was married and had children by her husband, who deserted; his whereabouts are unknown, and he does not contribute to the support of his children. She is not free to remarry and has had an illegitimate child since her husband left. (Almost 90 percent of the ADC families are Negro.)

The steady expansion of this welfare program, as of public assistance programs in general, can be taken as a measure of the steady disintegration of the Negro family structure over the past generation in the United States.

Source: Daniel P. Moynihan, 'A Study of the Negro Family' from The Moyniham Report: United States Department of Labor, *The Negro Family: The Case for National Action* (Washington, D.C., 1965), pp. 5-14.

10.2 Report of the Kerner Commission

Following widespread unrest in Northern cities in the 1960s, President Lyndon B. Johnson established a Commission under Governor Otto B. Kerner of Illinois to investigate the causes and context. The Report, which appeared in 1968, presented an impressive array of data and the same attention to detailed analysis which had typified Gunnar Myrdal's study a quarter of a century earlier. Unequivocal blame for the plight of inner city blacks was placed on a history of white racism and on the indifference of local (white) authorities. The remedies proposed for the urban unrest included: improved communications between ghetto residents and a more responsive and accountable local government; greater opportunities for black communities to particpate in the making of policy and decisions which would be likely to affect them; and the provision of central government and private finance to support community programmes and initiatives.

THE FORMATION OF THE RACIAL GHETTOS

Major trends in Negro population

Throughout the 20th century, and particularly in the last three decades, the Negro population of the United States has been steadily moving – from rural areas to urban, from South to North and West.

In 1910, 2.7 million Negroes lived in American cities – 28 percent of the nation's Negro population of 9.8 million. Today, about 15 million Negro Americans live in metropolitan areas, or 69 percent of the Negro population of 21.5 million. In 1910, 885,000 Negroes – 9 percent – lived outside the South. Now, almost 10 million, about 45 percent, live in the North or West.

These shifts in population have resulted from three basic trends:

A rapid increase in the size of the Negro population.

A continuous flow of Negroes from Southern rural areas, partly to large cities in the South, but primarily to large cities in the North and West.

An increasing concentration of Negroes in large metropolitan areas within racially segregated neighborhoods.

Taken together, these trends have produced large and constantly growing concentrations of Negro population within big cities in all parts of the nation. Because most major civil disorders of recent years occurred in predominantly Negro neighborhoods, we have examined the causes of this concentration.

The growth rate of the Negro population

During the first half of this century, the white population of the United States grew at a slightly faster rate than the Negro population. Because fertility rates among Negro women were more than offset by death rates among Negroes and large-scale immigration of whites from Europe, the proportion of Negroes in the country declined from 12 percent in 1900 to 10 percent in 1940.

By the end of World War II – and increasingly since then – major advances in medicine and medical care, together with the increasing youth of the Negro population resulting from higher fertility rates, caused death rates among Negroes to fall much faster than among whites. This is shown in Table 1.

Table 1 Death rate/1,000 population

Year	Whites	Nonwhites	Ratio of nonwhite rate to white rate
1900	17.0	25.0	1.47
1940	10.4	13.8	1.33
1965	9.4	9.6	1.02

In addition, white immigration from outside the United States dropped dramatically after stringent restrictions were adopted in the 1920's. [See Table 2.]

Table 2

20-year period	Total immigration (millions)
1901-20	14.5
1921-40	4.6
1941-60	3.6

Thus, by mid-century, both factors which had previously offset higher fertility rates among Negro women no longer were in effect.

While Negro fertility rates, after rising rapidly to 1957, have declined sharply in the past decade, white fertility rates have dropped even more, leaving Negro rates much higher in comparison. [See Table 3.]

The result is that Negro population is now growing significantly faster than white population. From 1940 to 1960, the white population rose 34.0 percent, but the Negro population rose 46.6 percent. From 1960 to 1966, the white population grew 7.6 percent, whereas Negro population rose 14.4 percent, almost twice as much.

Table 3 Live births per 1,000 women aged 15-44

Year	White	Nonwhite	Ratio of nonwhite to white
1940	77.1	102.4	1.33
1957	117.4	163.4	1.39
1965	91.4	133.9	1.46

Consequently, the proportion of Negroes in the total population has risen from 10.0 percent in 1950 to 10.5 percent in 1960, and 11.1 percent in 1966.

In 1950, at least one of every ten Americans was Negro; in 1966, one of nine. If this trend continues, one of every eight Americans will be Negro by 1972.

Another consequence of higher birth rates among Negroes is that the Negro population is considerably younger than the white population. In 1966, the median age among whites was 29.1 years, as compared to 21.1 among Negroes. About 35 percent of the white population was under 18 years of age, compared with 45 percent for Negroes. About one of every six children under five and one of every six new babies are Negro.

Negro-white fertility rates bear an interesting relationship to educational experience. Negro women with low levels of education have more children than white women with similar schooling, while Negro women with four years or more of college education have fewer children than white women similarly educated. Table 4 illustrates this.

Table 4

	Number of children ever born to all women (married or unmarried) 35-39 years old, by level of education (based on 1960 census)	
Education level attained	Nonwhite	White
Completed elementary school	3.0	2.8
Four years of high school	2.3	2.3
Four years of college	1.7	2.2
Five years or more of college	1.2	1.6

This suggests that the difference between Negro and white fertility rates may decline in the future if Negro educational attainment compares more closely with that of whites, and if a rising proportion of members of both groups complete college.

The migration of Negroes from the South

The magnitude of this migration

In 1910, 91 percent of the Nation's 9.8 million Negroes lived in the South. Twenty-seven percent of American Negroes lived in cities of 2,500 persons or more, as compared to 49 percent of the Nation's white population.

By 1966, the Negro population had increased to 21.5 million, and two significant geographic shifts had taken place. The proportion of Negroes living in the South had dropped to 55 percent, and about 69 percent of all Negroes lived in metropolitan areas compared to 64 percent for whites. While the total Negro population more then doubled from 1910 to 1966, the number living in cities rose over fivefold (from 2.7 million to 14.8 million) and the number outside the South rose elevenfold (from 885,000 to 9.7 million).

Negro migration from the South began after the Civil War. By the turn of the century, sizable Negro populations lived in many large Northern cities – Philadelphia, for example, had 63,400 Negro residents in 1900. The movement of Negroes out of the rural South accelerated during World War I, when floods and boll weevils hurt farming in the South and the industrial demands of the war created thousands of new jobs for unskilled workers in the North. After the war, the shift to mechanized farming spurred the continuing movement of Negroes from rural Southern areas.

The Depression slowed this migratory flow, but World War II set it in motion again. More recently, continuing mechanization of agriculture and the expansion of industrial employment in Northern and Western cities have served to sustain the movement of Negroes out of the South, although at a slightly lower rate. [See Table 5].

From 1960 to 1963, annual Negro out-migration actually dropped to 78,000 but then rose to over 125,000 from 1963 to 1966.

Table 5

Period	Net Negro out-migration from the South	Annual average rate
1910-20	454,000	45,400
1920-30	749,000	74,900
1930-40	348,000	34,800
1940-50	1,597,000	159,700
1950-60	1,457,000	145,700
1960-66	613,000	102,500

Important characteristics of this migration

It is useful to recall that even the latest scale of Negro migration is relatively small when compared to the earlier waves of European immigrants. A total of 8.8 million immigrants entered the United States between 1901 and 1911, and another 5.7 million arrived during the following decade. Even during the years from 1960 through 1966, the 1.8 million immigrants from abroad were almost three times the 613,000 Negroes who departed the South. In these same 6 years, California alone gained over 1.5 million new residents from internal shifts of American population.

Three major routes of Negro migration from the South have developed. One runs north along the Atlantic Seaboard toward Boston, another north from Mississippi toward Chicago, and the third west from Texas and Louisiana toward California. Between 1955 and 1960, 50 percent of the nonwhite migrants to the New York metropolitan area came from North Carolina, South Carolina, Virginia, Georgia, and Alabama; North Carolina alone supplied 20 percent of all New York's nonwhite immigrants. During the same period, almost 60 percent of the nonwhite migrants to Chicago came from Mississippi, Tennessee, Arkansas, Alabama and Louisiana; Mississippi accounted for almost one-third. During these years, three-fourths of the nonwhite migrants to Los Angeles came from Texas, Louisiana, Mississippi, Arkansas, and Alabama.

The flow of Negroes from the South has caused the Negro population to grow more rapidly in the North and West, as indicated [in Table 6].

Table 6

Period	Total Negro population gains (millions)		Percent of gain in North & West
	North & West	South	
1940-50	1.859	0.321	85.2
1950-60	2.741	1.086	71.6
1960-66	2.119	0.517	80.4

As a result, although a much higher proportion of Negroes still reside in the South, the distribution of Negroes throughout the United States is beginning to approximate that of whites, as Tables 7 and 8 show.

Table 7 Percent distribution of the population by region – 1950, 1960, and 1966

	Negro			White		
	1950	1960	1966	1950	1960[1]	1966
United States	100	100	100	100	100	100
South	68	60	55	27	27	28
North	28	34	37	59	56	55
Northeast	13	16	17	28	26	26
North Central	15	18	20	31	30	29
West	4	6	8	14	16	17

[1] Rounds to 99.

Table 8 Negroes as a percentage of the total population in the United States and each region 1950, 1960, and 1966

	1950	1960	1966
United States	10	11	11
South	22	21	20
North	5	7	8
West	3	4	5

Negroes in the North and West are now so numerous that natural increase rather than migration provides the greater part of Negro population gains there. And even though Negro migration has continued at a high level, it comprises a constantly declining proportion of Negro growth in these regions. [See Table 9.]

Table 9

Period	Percentage of total North and West Negro gain from Southern in-migration
1940-50	85.9
1950-60	53.1
1960-66	28.9

In other words, we have reached the point where the Negro populations of the North and West will continue to expand significantly even if migration from the South drops substantially.

Future migration

Despite accelerating Negro migration from the South, the Negro population there has continued to rise. [See Table 10.]

Nor is it likely to halt. Negro birth rates in the South, as elsewhere, have fallen sharply since 1957, but so far this decline has been offset by the rising Negro population base remaining in the South. From 1950 to 1960, Southern Negro births generated an average net increase of 254,000 per year and, from 1960 to 1966, an average of 188,000 per year. Even if Negro birth rates continue to fall they are likely to remain high enough to support significant migration to other regions for some time to come.

Table 10

Date	Negro population in the South (millions)	Change from preceding date	
		Total	Annual average
1940	9.9	–	–
1950	10.2	321,000	32,100
1960	11.3	1,086,000	108,600
1966	11.8	517,000	86,200

The Negro population in the South is becoming increasingly urbanized. In 1950, there were 5.4 million Southern rural Negroes; by 1960, 4.8 million. But the decline has been more than offset by increases in the urban population. A rising proportion of interregional migration now consists of persons moving from one city to another. From 1960 to 1966, rural Negro population in the South was far below its peak, but the annual average migration of Negroes from the South was still substantial.

These facts demonstrate that Negro migration from the South, which has maintained a high rate for the past 60 years, will continue unless economic conditions change dramatically in either the South or the North and West. This conclusion is reinforced by the fact that most Southern states in recent decades have also experienced outflows of white population. From 1950 to 1960, 11 of the 17 Southern states (including the District of Columbia) "exported" white population – as compared to 13 which "exported" Negro population. Excluding Florida's net gain by migration of 1.5 million, the other 16 Southern states together had a net loss by migration of 1.46 million whites.

The concentration of Negro population in large cities

Where Negro urbanization has occurred

Statistically, the Negro population in America has become more urbanized, and more metropolitan, than the white population. According to Census Bureau estimates, almost 70 percent of all Negroes in 1966 lived in metropolitan areas, compared to 64 percent of all whites. In the South, more than half the Negro population now lives in cities. Rural Negroes outnumber urban Negroes in only four states: Arkansas, Mississippi, North Carolina, and South Carolina.

Basic data concerning Negro urbanization trends, presented in tables at the conclusion of this chapter, indicate that:

> Almost all Negro population growth is occurring within metropolitan areas, primarily within central cities. From 1950 to 1966, the U.S. Negro population rose 6.5 million. Over 98 percent of that increase took place in metropolitan areas – 86 percent within central cities, 12 percent in the urban fringe.
>
> The vast majority of white population growth is occurring in suburban portions of metropolitan areas. From 1950 to 1966, 77.8 percent of the white population increase of 35.6 million took place in the suburbs. Central cities received only 2.5 percent of this total white increase. Since 1960, white central-city population has actually declined by 1.3 million.
>
> As a result, central cities are steadily becoming more heavily Negro, while the urban fringes around them remain almost entirely white. The proportion of Negroes in all central cities rose steadily from 12 percent in 1950, to 17 percent in 1960, to 20 percent in 1966. Meanwhile, metropolitan areas outside of central cities remained 95 percent white from 1956 to 1960 and became 96 percent white by 1966.
>
> The Negro population is growing faster, both absolutely and relatively, in the larger metropolitan areas than in the smaller ones. From 1950 to 1966, the proportion of nonwhites in the central cities of metropolitan areas with 1 million or more persons doubled, reaching 26 percent, as compared with 20 percent in the central cities of metropolitan areas containing from 250,000 to 1 million persons and 12 percent in the central cities of metropolitan areas containing under 250,000 persons.
>
> The 12 largest central cities – New York, Chicago, Los Angeles, Philadelphia, Detroit, Baltimore, Houston, Cleveland, Washington, D.C., St. Louis, Milwaukee, and San Francisco – now contain over two-thirds of the Negro population outside the South and almost one-third of the total in the United States. All these cities have experienced rapid increases in Negro population since 1950. In six – Chicago, Detroit, Cleveland, St. Louis, Milwaukee, and San Francisco – the proportion of Negroes at least doubled. In two others – New York and Los Angeles – it probably doubled. In 1968 seven of these cities are over 30 percent Negro, and one, Washington, D.C., is two-thirds Negro.

Factors causing residential segregation in metropolitan areas

The early pattern of Negro settlement within each metropolitan area followed that of immigrant groups. Migrants converged on the older sections of the central city because the lowest cost housing was located there, friends and relatives were likely to be living there, and the older neighborhoods then often had good public transportation.

But the later phases of Negro settlement and expansion in metropolitan areas diverge sharply from those typical of white immigrants. As the whites were absorbed by the larger society, many left their predominantly ethnic neighborhoods and moved to outlying areas to obtain newer housing and better schools. Some scattered randomly over the suburban area. Others established new ethnic clusters in the suburbs, but even these rarely contained solely members of a single ethnic group. As a result, most middle-class neighborhoods – both in the suburbs and within central cities – have no distinctive ethnic character, except that they are white.

Nowhere has the expansion of America's urban Negro population followed this pattern of dispersal. Thousands of Negro families have attained incomes, living standards, and cultural levels matching or surpassing those of whites who have "upgraded" themselves from distinctly ethnic neighborhoods. Yet most Negro families have remained within predominantly Negro neighborhoods, primarily because they have been effectively excluded from white residential areas.

Their exclusion has been accomplished through various discriminatory practices, some obvious and overt, others subtle and hidden. Deliberate efforts are sometimes made to discourage Negro families from purchasing or renting homes in all-white neighborhoods. Intimidation and threats of violence have ranged from throwing garbage on lawns and making threatening phone calls to burning crosses in yards and even dynamiting property. More often, real estate agents simply refuse to show homes to Negro buyers.

Many middle-class Negro families, therefore, cease looking for homes beyond all-Negro areas or nearby "changing" neighborhoods. For them, trying to move into all-white neighborhoods is not worth the psychological efforts and costs required.

Another form of discrimination just as significant is white withdrawal from, or refusal to enter, neighborhoods where large numbers of Negroes are moving or already residing. Normal population turnover causes about 20 percent of the residents of average U.S. neighborhoods to move out every year because of income changes, job transfers, shifts in life-cycle position or deaths. This normal turnover rate is even higher in apartment areas. The refusal of whites to move into changing areas when vacancies occur there from normal turnover means that most of these vacancies are eventually occupied by Negroes. An inexorable shift toward heavy Negro occupancy results.

Once this happens, the remaining whites seek to leave, thus confirming the existing belief among whites that complete transformation of a neighborhood is inevitable once Negroes begin to enter. Since the belief itself is one of the major causes of the transformation, it becomes a self-fulfilling prophecy which inhibits the development of racially integrated neighborhoods.

As a result, Negro settlements expand almost entirely through "massive racial transition" at the edges of existing all-Negro neighborhoods, rather than by a gradual dispersion of population throughout the metropolitan area.

Two points are particularly important:

> "Massive transition" requires no panic or flight by the original white residents of a neighborhood into which Negroes begin moving. All it

requires is the failure or refusal of other whites to fill the vacancies resulting from normal turnover.

Thus, efforts to stop massive transition by persuading present white residents to remain will ultimately fail unless whites outside the neighborhood can be persuaded to move in.

It is obviously true that some residential separation of whites and Negroes would occur even without discriminatory practices by whites. This would result from the desires of some Negroes to live in predominantly Negro neighborhoods and from differences in meaningful social variables, such as income and educational levels. But these factors alone would not lead to the almost complete segregation of whites and Negroes which has developed in our metropolitan areas.

The exodus of whites from central cities

The process of racial transition in central-city neighborhoods has been only one factor among many others causing millions of whites to move out of central cities as the Negro populations there expanded. More basic perhaps have been the rising mobility and affluence of middle-class families and the more attractive living conditions – particularly better schools – in the suburbs.

Whatever the reason, the result is clear. In 1950, 45.5 million whites lived in central cities. If this population had grown from 1950 to 1960 at the same rate as the Nation's white population as a whole, it would have increased by 8 million. It actually rose only 2.2 million, indicating an outflow of 5.8 million.

From 1960 to 1966, the white outflow appears to have been even more rapid. White population of central cities declined 1.3 million instead of rising 3.6 million – as it would if it had grown at the same rate as the entire white population. In theory, therefore, 4.9 million whites left central cities during these 6 years.

Statistics for all central cities as a group understate the relationship between Negro population growth and white outflow in individual central cities. The fact is, many cities with relatively few Negroes experienced rapid white-population growth, thereby obscuring the size of white outmigration that took place in cities having large increases in Negro population. For example, from 1950 to 1960, the 10 largest cities in the United States had a total Negro population increase of 1.6 million, or 55 percent, while the white population there declined 1.4 million. If the two cities where the white population (Los Angeles and Houston) are excluded, the nonwhite population in the remaining eight rose 1.4 million, whereas their white population declined 2.1 million. If the white population in these cities had increased at only half the rate of the white population in the United States as a whole from 1950 to 1960, it would have risen by 1.4 million. Thus, these eight cities actually experienced a white outmigration of at least 3.5 million, while gaining 1.4 million nonwhites.

The extent of residential segregation

The rapid expansion of all-Negro residential areas and large-scale white withdrawal have continued a pattern of residential segregation that has existed in American cities for decades. A recent study reveals that this pattern is present to a high degree in every large city in America. The authors devised an index to measure the degree of residential segregation. The index indicates for each city the percentage of Negroes who would have to move from the blocks where they now live to other blocks in order to provide a perfectly proportional, unsegregated distribution of population.

According to their findings, the average segregation index for 207 of the largest U.S. cities was 86.2 in 1960. This means that an average of over 86 percent of all Negroes would have had to change blocks to create an unsegregated population distribution. Southern cities had a higher average index (90.9) than cities in the Northeast (79.2), the North Central (87.7), or the West (79.3). Only eight cities had index values below 70, whereas over 50 had values above 91.7.

The degree of residential segregation for all 20 cities has been relatively stable, averaging 85.2 in 1940, 87.3 in 1950, and 86.2 in 1960. Variations within individual regions were only slightly larger. However, a recent Census Bureau study shows that in most of the 12 large cities where special censuses were taken in the mid-1960's, the proportions of Negroes living in neighborhoods of greatest Negro concentration had increased since 1960.

Residential segregation is generally more prevalent with respect to Negroes than for any other minority group, including Puerto Ricans, Orientals, and Mexican-Americans. Moreover, it varies little between central city and suburb. This nearly universal pattern cannot be explained in terms of economic discrimination against all low-income groups. Analysis of 15 representative cities indicates that white upper and middle income households are far more segregated from Negro upper and middle-income households than from white lower income households.

In summary, the concentration of Negroes in central cities results from a combination of forces. Some of these forces, such as migration and initial settlement patterns in older neighborhoods, are similar to those which affected previous ethnic minorities. Others – particularly discrimination in employment and segregation in housing and schools – are a result of white attitudes based on race and color. These forces continue to shape the future of the central city. [See Tables 11 through 15.]

Table 11 Proportion of Negroes in each of the 30 largest cities, 1950, 1960, and estimated 1965

	1950	1960	Estimate[1] 1965
New York, N.Y.	10	14	18
Chicago, Ill.	14	23	28
Los Angeles, Calif.	9	14	17
Philadelphia, Pa.	18	26	31
Detroit, Mich.	16	29	34
Baltimore, Md.	24	35	38
Houston, Tex.	21	23	23
Cleveland, Ohio	16	29	34
Washington, D.C.	35	54	66
St. Louis, Mo.	18	29	36
Milwaukee, Wis.	3	8	11

(Cont)	1950	1960	Estimate[1] 1965
San Francisco, Calif.	6	10	12
Boston, Mass.	5	9	13
Dallas, Tex.	13	19	21
New Orleans, La.	32	37	41
Pittsburgh, Pa.	12	17	20
San Antonio, Tex.	7	7	8
San Diego, Calif.	5	6	7
Seattle, Wash.	3	5	7
Buffalo, N.Y.	6	13	17
Cincinnati, Ohio	16	22	24
Memphis, Tenn.	37	37	40
Denver, Colo.	4	6	9
Atlanta, Ga.	37	38	44
Minneapolis, Minn.	1	2	4
Indianapolis, Ind.	15	21	23
Kansas City, Mo.	12	18	22
Columbus, Ohio	12	16	18
Phoenix, Ariz.	5	5	5
Newark, N.J.	17	34	47

[1] Except for Cleveland, Buffalo, Memphis, and Phoenix, for which a special census has been made in recent years, these are very rough estimations computed on the basis of the change in relative proportions of Negro births and deaths since 1960.

Source: U.S. Department of Commerce, Bureau of the Census, BLS Report No. 332, p. 11.

UNEMPLOYMENT, FAMILY STRUCTURE AND SOCIAL DISORGANISATION

Recent economic trends

The Negro population in our country is as diverse in income, occupation, family composition, and other variables as the white community. Nevertheless, for purposes of analysis, three major Negro economic groups can be identified.

The first and smallest group consists of middle and upper income individuals and households whose educational, occupational, and cultural characteristics are similar to those of middle and upper income white groups.

The second and largest group contains Negroes whose incomes are above the "poverty level" but who have not attained the educational, occupational, or income status typical of middle-class Americans.

The third group has very low educational, occupational, and income attainments and lives below the "poverty level."

A recent compilation of data on American Negroes by the Departments of Labor and Commerce shows that although incomes of both Negroes and whites have been rising rapidly,

Negro incomes still remain far below those of whites. Negro median family income was only 58 percent of the white median in 1966.

Negro family income is not keeping pace with white family income growth. In constant 1965 dollars, median nonwhite income in 1947 was $2,174 lower than median white income. By 1966, the gap had grown to $3,036.

The Negro upper income group is expanding rapidly and achieving sizeable income gains. In 1966, 28 percent of all Negro families received incomes of $7,000 or more, compared with 55 percent of white families. This was 1.6 times the proportion of Negroes receiving comparable incomes in 1960, and four times greater than the proportion receiving such incomes in 1947. Moreover, the proportion of Negroes employed in high-skill, high-status, and well-paying jobs rose faster than comparable proportions among whites from 1960 to 1966.

As Negro incomes have risen, the size of the lowest income group has grown smaller, and the middle and upper groups have grown larger – both relatively and absolutely. [See Table 1.]

About two-thirds of the lowest income group – or 20 percent of all Negro families–are making no significant economic gains despite continued general prosperity. Half of these hard-core disadvantaged – more than 2 million persons – live in central-city neighborhoods. Recent special censuses in Los Angeles and Cleveland indicate that the incomes of persons living in the worst slum areas have not risen at all during this period, unemployment rates have declined only slightly, the proportion of families with female heads has increased, and housing conditions have worsened even though rents have risen.

Table 1

	Percentage of Negro families			**Percentage of white families**
Group	1947	1960	1966	1966
$7,000 and over	7	17	28	55
$3,000 to $6,999	29	40	41	33
Under $3,000	65	44	32	13

Thus, between 2.0 and 2.5 million poor Negroes are living in disadvantaged neighborhoods of central cities in the United States. These persons comprise only slightly more than 1 percent of the Nation's total population, but they make up about 16 to 20 percent of the total Negro population of all central cities, and a much higher proportion in certain cities.

Unemployment and underemployment

The critical significance of employment

The capacity to obtain and hold a "good job" is the traditional test of participation in American society. Steady employment with adequate compensation provides both purchasing power and social status. It develops the capabilities, confidence, and self-esteem an individual needs to be a responsible citizen, and provides a basis for a stable family life. As Daniel P. Moynihan has written:

> The principal measure of progress toward equality will be that of employment. It is the primary source of individual or group identity. In America what you do is what you are: to do nothing is to be nothing; to do little is to be little. The equations are implicable and blunt, and ruthlessly public.
>
> For the Negro American it is already, and will continue to be, the master problem. It is the measure of white bona fides. It is the measure of Negro competence, and also of the competence of American society. Most importantly, the linkage between problems of employment and the range of social pathology that afflicts the Negro community is unmistakable. Employment not only controls the present for the Negro American but, in a most profound way, it is creating the future as well.

For residents of disadvantaged Negro neighborhoods, obtaining good jobs is vastly more difficult than for most workers in society. For decades, social, economic, and psychological disadvantages surrounding the urban Negro poor have impaired their work capacities and opportunities. The result is a cycle of failure – the employment disabilities of one generation breed those of the next.

Negro unemployment

Unemployment rates among Negroes have declined from a post-Korean War high of 12.6 percent in 1958 to 8.2 percent in 1967. Among married Negro men, the employment rate for 1967 was down to 3.2 percent.

Notwithstanding this decline, unemployment rates for Negroes are still double those for whites in every category, including married men, as they have been throughout the postwar period. Moreover, since 1954, even during the current unprecedented period of sustained economic growth, unemployment among Negroes has been continuously above the 6 percent "recession" level widely regarded as a sign of serious economic weakness when prevalent for the entire work force.

While the Negro unemployment rate remains high in relation to the white rate, the number of additional jobs needed to lower this to the level of white unemployment is surprisingly small. In 1967, approximately 3 million persons were unemployed during an average week, of whom about 638,000, or 21 percent, were nonwhites. When corrected for undercounting, total nonwhite unemployment was approximately 712,000 or 8 percent of the nonwhite labor force. To reduce the unemployment rate to 3.4 percent, the rate prevalent among whites, jobs must be found for 57.5 percent of these unemployed persons. This amounts to nearly 409,000 jobs, or about 27 percent of the net number of new jobs added to the economy in the year 1967 alone and only slightly more than one-half of 1 percent of all jobs in the United States in 1967.

The low-status and low-paying nature of many Negro jobs

Even more important perhaps than unemployment is the related problem of the undesirable nature of many jobs open to Negroes. Negro workers are concentrated in the lowest skilled and lowest paying occupations. These jobs often involve substandard wages, great instability and uncertainty of tenure, extremely low status in the eyes of both employer and employee, little or no chance for meaningful advancement, and unpleasant or exhausting duties. Negro men in particular are more than three times as likely as whites to be in unskilled or service jobs which pay far less than most. [See Table 2.]

Table 2

Type of occupation	**Percentage of male workers in each type of occupation, 1966** White	Nonwhite	**Median earnings of all male civilians in each occupation, 1965**
Professional, technical, and managerial	27	9	$7,603[1]
Clerical and sales	14	9	5,532[1]
Craftsmen and foremen	20	12	6,270
Operatives	20	27	5,046
Service workers	6	16	3,436
Nonfarm laborers	6	20	2,410
Farmers and farm workers	7	8	1,669[1]

[1]Average of two categories from normal Census Bureau categories as combined in data presented in *The Social and Economic Conditions of Negroes in the United States* (BLS No. 332).

This concentration in the least desirable jobs can be viewed another way by calculating the changes which would occur if Negro men were employed in various occupations in the same proportions as the male labor force as a whole (not solely the white labor force). [See Table 3.]

Table 3

	Number of male nonwhite workers, 1966			
			Difference	
Type of occupation	As actually distributed[1]	If distributed the same as all male workers	*Number*	*Percent*
Professional, technical, and managerial	415,000	1,173,000	+758,000	+183
Clerical and sales	415,000	628,000	+213,000	+51
Craftsmen and foremen	553,000	894,000	+341,000	+62
Operatives	1,244,000	964,000	–280,000	–23
Service workers	737,000	326,000	–411,000	–56
Nonfarm laborers	922,000	340,000	–582,000	–63
Farmers and farm workers	369,000	330,000	–39,000	–11

[1]Estimates based upon percentages set forth in BLS No. 332, p. 41.

Thus, upgrading the employment of Negro men to make their occupational distribution identical with that of the labor force as a whole would have an immense impact upon the nature of their occupations. About 1.3 million nonwhite men – or 28 percent of those employed in 1966 – would move up the employment ladder into one of the higher status and higher paying categories. The effect of such a shift upon the incomes of Negro men would be very great. Using the 1966 job distribution, the shift indicated above would produce about $4.8 billion more earned income for nonwhite men alone if they received the 1965 median income in each occupation. This would be a rise of approximately 30 percent in the earnings actually received by all nonwhite men in 1965 (not counting any sources of income other than wages and salaries).

Of course, the kind of "instant upgrading" visualized in these calculations does not represent a practical alternative for national policy. The economy cannot drastically reduce the total number of low-status jobs it now contains, or shift large numbers of people upward in occupation in any short period. Therefore, major upgrading in the employment status of Negro men must come through a faster relative expansion of higher level jobs than lower jobs (which has been occurring for several decades), an improvement in the skills of nonwhite workers so they can obtain a high proportion of those added better jobs, and a drastic reduction of discriminatory hiring and promotion practices in all enterprises, both private and public.

Nevertheless, this hypothetical example clearly shows that the concentration of male Negro employment at the lowest end of the occupational scale is greatly depressing the incomes of U.S. Negroes in general. In fact, this is the single most important source of poverty among Negroes. It is even more important than unemployment, as can be shown by a second hypothetical calculation. In 1966, there were about 724,000 unemployed nonwhites in the United States on the average, including adults and teenagers, and allowing for the Census Bureau undercount of Negroes. If every one of these persons had been employed and had received the median amount earned by nonwhite males in 1966 ($3,864), this would have added a total of $2.8 billion to nonwhite income as a whole. If only enough of these persons had been employed at that wage to reduce nonwhite unemployment from 7.3 to 3.3 percent – the rate among whites in 1966 – then the income gain for nonwhites would have totaled about $1.5 billion. But if nonwhite unemployment remained at 7.3 percent, and nonwhite men were upgraded so that they had the same occupational distribution and incomes as all men in the labor force considered together, this would have produced about $4.8 billion in additional income, as noted above (using 1965 earnings for calculation). Thus the potential income gains from upgrading the male nonwhite labor force are much larger than those from reducing nonwhite unemployment.

This conclusion underlines the difficulty of improving the economic status of Negro men. It is far easier to create new jobs than either to create new jobs with relatively high status and earning power, or to upgrade existing employed or partly employed workers into such better quality employment. Yet only such upgrading will eliminate the fundamental basis of poverty and deprivation among Negro families.

Access to good-quality jobs clearly affects the willingness of Negro men actively to seek work. In riot cities surveyed by the Commission with the largest percentage of Negroes in skilled and semiskilled jobs, Negro men participated in the labor force to the same extent as, or greater than, white men. Conversely, where most Negro men were heavily concentrated in menial jobs, they participated less in the labor force than white men.

Even given similar employment, Negro workers with the same education as white workers are paid less. This disparity doubtless results to some extent from inferior training in segregated schools, and also from the fact that large numbers of Negroes are only now entering certain occupations for the first time. However, the differentials are so large and so universal at all educational levels that they clearly reflect the patterns of discrimination which characterize hiring and promotion practices in many segments of the economy. For example, in 1966, among persons who had completed high school, the median income of Negroes was only 73 percent that of whites. Even among persons with an eighth-grade education, Negro median income was only 80 percent of white median income.

At the same time, a higher proportion of Negro women than white women participates in the labor force at nearly all ages except 16 to 19. For instance, in 1966, 55 percent of nonwhite women from 25 to 34 years of age were employed, compared to only 38 percent of white women in the same age group. The fact that almost half of all adult Negro women work reflects the fact that so many Negro males have unsteady and low-paying jobs. Yet even though Negro women are often better able to find work than Negro men, the unemployment rate among adult nonwhite women (20 years old and over) in 1967 was 7.1 percent, compared to the 4.3 percent rate among adult nonwhite men.

Unemployment rates are, of course, much higher among teenagers, both Negro and white, than among adults; in fact about one-third of all unemployed Negroes in 1967 were between 16 and 19 years old. During the first 9 months of 1967, the unemployment rate among nonwhite teenagers was 26.5 percent; for whites, it was 10.6 percent. About 219,300 nonwhite teenagers were unemployed. About 58,300 were still in school but were actively looking for jobs.

Subemployment in disadvantaged Negro neighborhoods

In disadvantaged areas, unemployment conditions for Negroes are in a chronic state of crisis. Surveys in low-income neighborhoods of nine large cities made by the Department of Labor late in 1966 revealed that the rate of unemployment there was 9.3 percent, compared to 7.3 percent for Negroes generally and 3.3 percent for whites. Moreover, a high proportion of the persons living in these areas were "underemployed," that is, they were either part-time workers looking for full-time employment, or full-time workers earning less than $3000 per year, or had dropped out of the labor force. The Department of Labor estimated that this underemployment is 2½ times greater than the number of unemployed in these areas. Therefore, the "subemployment rate," including both the unemployed and the under-employed, was about 32.7 percent in the nine areas surveyed, or 8.8 times greater than the overall unemployment rate for all U.S. workers. Since underemployment also exists outside disadvantaged neighborhoods, comparing the full subemployment rate in these areas with the unemployment rate for the Nation as a whole is not entirely valid. However, it provides some measure of the enormous disparity between employment conditions in most of the Nation and those prevalent in disadvantaged Negro areas in our large cities.

Table 4

Group	Nonwhite subemployment in disadvantaged areas of all central cities, 1967		
	Unemployment	Underemployment	Total subemployment
Adult men	102,000	230,000	332,000
Adult women	118,000	266,000	384,000
Teenagers	98,000	220,000	318,000
Total	318,000	716,000	1,034,000

The critical problem is to determine the actual number of those unemployed and underemployed in central-city Negro ghettos. This involves a process of calculation which is detailed in the note at the end of this chapter. The outcome of this process is summarized in Table 4.

Therefore, in order to bring subemployment in these areas down to a level equal to unemployment alone among whites, enough steady, reasonably paying jobs (and the training and motivation to perform them) must be provided to eliminate all underemployment and reduce unemployment by 65 percent. For all three age groups combined, this deficit amounted to 923,000 jobs in 1967.

The magnitude of poverty in disadvantaged neighborhoods

The chronic unemployment problems in the central city, aggravated by the constant arrival of new unemployed migrants, is the fundamental cause of the persistent poverty in disadvantaged Negro areas.

"Poverty" in the affluent society is more than absolute deprivation. Many of the poor in the United States would be well off in other societies. Relative deprivation – inequality – is a more useful concept of poverty with respect to the Negro in America because it encompasses social and political exclusions as well as economic inequality. Because of the lack of data of this type, we have had to focus our analysis on a measure of poverty which is both economic and absolute – the Social Security Administration "poverty level" concept. It is clear, however, that broader measures of poverty would substantiate the conclusions that follow.

In 1966, there were 29.7 million persons in the United States – 15.3 percent of the Nation's population – with incomes below the "poverty level," as defined by the Social Security Administration. Of these, 20.3 million were white (68.3 percent), and 9.3 million nonwhite (31.7 percent). Thus, about 11.9 percent of the Nation's whites and 40.6 percent of its nonwhites were poor under the Social Security definition.

The location of the Nation's poor is best shown from 1964 data as indicated by Table 5.

Table 5

Group	Percentage of those in poverty in each group living in metropolitan areas		Other areas	Total
	In central cities	Outside central cities		
Whites	23.8	21.8	54.4	100
Nonwhites	41.7	10.8	47.5	100
Total	29.4	18.4	52.2	100

Source: Social Security Administration.

The following facts concerning poverty are relevant to an understanding of the problems faced by people living in disadvantaged neighborhoods.

In central cities 30.7 percent of nonwhite families of two or more persons lived in poverty compared to only 8.8 percent of whites.

Of the 10.1 million poor persons in central cities in 1964, about 4.4 million of these (43.6 percent) were nonwhites, and 5.7 million (56.4 percent) were whites. The poor whites were much older on the average than the poor nonwhites. The proportion of poor persons 65 years old or older was 23.2 percent among whites, but only 6.8 percent among nonwhites.

Poverty was more than twice as prevalent among nonwhite families with female heads than among those with male heads, 57 percent compared to 21 percent. In central cities, 26 percent of all nonwhite families of two or more persons had female heads, as compared to 12 percent of white families.

Among nonwhite families headed by a female, and having children under 6, the incidence of poverty was 81 percent. Moreover, there were 243,000 such families living in poverty in central cities – or over 9 percent of all nonwhite families in those cities.

Among all children living in poverty within central cities, nonwhites outnumbered whites by over 400,000. The number of poor nonwhite children equalled or surpassed the number of white poor children in every age group. [See Table 6.]

Table 6 Number of children living in poverty (millions)

Age group	White	Nonwhite	Percent of total nonwhite
Under 6	0.9	1.0	53
6 to 15	1.0	1.3	57
16-21	0.4	0.4	50
Total	2.3	2.7	54

Two stark facts emerge:

> 54 percent of all poor children in central cities in 1964 were nonwhites.
>
> Of the 4.4 million nonwhites living in poverty within central cities in 1964, 52 percent were children under 16 and 61 percent were under 21.

Since 1964, the number of nonwhite families living in poverty within central cities has remained about the same; hence, these poverty conditions are probably still prevalent in central cities in terms of absolute numbers of persons, although the proportion of persons in poverty may have dropped slightly.

The social impact of employment problems in disadvantaged Negro areas

Unemployment and the family

The high rates of unemployment and underemployment in racial ghettos are evidence, in part, that many men living in these areas are seeking, but cannot obtain, jobs which will support a family. Perhaps equally important, most jobs they can get are at the low end of the occupational scale, and often lack the necessary status to sustain a worker's self-respect, or the respect of his family and friends. These same men are also constantly confronted with the message of discrimination: "You are inferior because of a trait you did not cause and cannot change." This message reinforces feelings of inadequacy arising from repeated failure to obtain and keep decent jobs.

Wives of these men are forced to work and usually produce more money. If the men stay at home without working, their inadequacies constantly confront them and tensions arise between them and their wives and children. Under these pressures, it is not surprising that many of these men flee their responsibilities as husbands and fathers, leaving home, and drifting from city to city, or adopting the style of "street corner men."

Statistical evidence tends to document this. A close correlation exists between the number of nonwhite married women separated from their husbands each year and the unemployment rate among nonwhite males 20 years old and over. Similarly, from 1948 to 1962, the number of new Aid to Families with Dependent Children cases rose and fell with the nonwhite male unemployment rate. Since 1963, however, the number of new cases – most of them Negro children – has steadily increased even though the unemployment rate among nonwhite males has declined. The impact of marital status on employment among Negroes is shown by the fact that in 1967 the proportion of married men either divorced or separated from their wives was more than twice as high among unemployed nonwhite men as among employed nonwhite men. Moreover, among those participating in the labor force, there was a higher proportion of married men with wives present than with wives absent. [See Table 7.]

Table 7 Unemployment rate and particpation in total labor force, 25- to 54-year-old nonwhite men, by marital status, March, 1967

	Unemployment rate, nonwhite	Labor force participation (percent), nonwhite
Married, wife present	3.7	96.7
Other (separated, divorced, widowed)	8.7	77.6

Fatherless families

The abandonment of the home by many Negro males affects a great many children growing up in the racial ghetto. As previously indicated, most American Negro families are headed by men, just like most other American families. Yet the proportion of families with female heads is much greater among Negroes than among whites at all income levels, and has been rising in recent years. [See Table 8].

This disparity between white and nonwhite families is far greater among the lowest income families – those most likely to reside in disadvantaged big-city neighborhoods – than among higher income families. Among families with incomes under $3,000 in 1966, the proportion with female heads was 42 percent for Negroes but only 23 percent for whites.

Table 8 Proportion of families of various types

[In Percent]

	Husband-wife		Female head	
Date	White	Nonwhite	[White]	Nonwhite
1950	88.0	77.7	8.5	17.6
1960	88.7	73.6	8.7	22.4
1966	88.8	72.7	8.9	23.7

In contrast, among families with incomes of $7,000 or more, 8 percent of Negro families had female heads compared to 4 percent of whites.

The problems of "fatherlessness" are aggravated by the tendency of the poor to have large families. The average poor, urban, nonwhite family contains 4.8 persons, as compared with 3.7 for the average poor, urban, white family. This is one of the primary factors in the poverty status of nonwhite households in large cities.

The proportion of fatherless families appears to be increasing in the poorest Negro neighborhoods. In the Hough section of Cleveland, the proportion of families with female heads rose from 23 to 32 percent from 1960 to 1965. In the Watts section of Los Angeles it rose from 36 to 39 percent during the same period.

The handicap imposed on children growing up without fathers, in an atmosphere of poverty and deprivation, is increased because many mothers must work to provide support. Table 9 illustrates the disparity between the proportion of nonwhite women in the child-rearing ages who are in the labor force and the comparable proportion of white women:

Table 9

Age group	**Percentage of women in the labor force**	
	Nonwhite	White
20 to 24	55	51
25 to 34	55	38
35 to 44	61	45

With the father absent and the mother working, many ghetto children spend the bulk of their time on the streets – the streets of a crime-ridden, violence-prone, and poverty-stricken world. The image of success in this world is not that of the "solid citizen," the responsible husband and father, but rather that of the "hustler" who promotes his own interests by exploiting others. The dope sellers and the numbers runners are the "successful" men because their earnings far outstrip those men who try to climb the economic ladder in honest ways.

Young people in the ghetto are acutely conscious of a system which appears to offer rewards to those who illegally exploit others, and failure to those who struggle under traditional responsibilities. Under these circumstances, many adopt exploitation and the "hustle" as a way of life, disclaiming both work and marriage in favor of casual and temporary liaisons. This pattern reinforces itself from one generation to the next, creating a "culture of poverty" and an ingrained cynicism about society and its institutions.

The "Jungle"

The culture of poverty that results from unemployment and family disorganization generates a system of ruthless, exploitative relationships within the ghetto. Prostitution, dope addiction, casual sexual affairs, and crime create an environmental jungle characterized by personal insecurity and tension. The effects of this development are stark:

> The rate of illegitimate births among nonwhite women has risen sharply in the past two decades. In 1940, 16.8 percent of all nonwhite births were illegitimate. By 1950 this proportion was 18 percent; by 1960, 21.6 percent; by 1966, 26.3 percent. In the ghettos of many large cities, illegitimacy rates exceed 50 percent.
>
> The rate of illegitimacy among nonwhite women is closely related to low income and high unemployment. In Washington, D.C., for example, an analysis of 1960 census tracts shows that in tracts with unemployment rates of 12 percent or more among nonwhite men, illegitimacy was over 40 percent. But in tracts with unemployment rates of 2.9 percent and below among nonwhite men, reported illegitimacy was under 20 percent. A similar contrast existed between tracts in which median non-white income was under $4,000 (where illegitimacy was 38 percent) and those in which it was $8,000 and over (where illegitimacy was 12 percent).
>
> Narcotics addiction is also heavily concentrated in low-income Negro neighborhoods, particularly in New York City. Of the 59,720 addicts known

> to the U.S. Bureau of Narcotics at the end of 1966, just over 50 percent were Negroes. Over 52 percent of all known addicts lived within New York State, mostly in Harlem and other Negro neighborhoods. These figures undoubtedly greatly understate the actual number of persons using narcotics regularly – especially those under 21.
>
> Not surprisingly, at every age from 6 through 19, the proportion of children from homes with both parents present who actually attend school is higher than the proportion of children from homes with only one parent or neither present.
>
> Rates of juvenile delinquency, venereal disease, dependency upon AFDC support, and use of public assistance in general are much higher in disadvantaged Negro areas than in other parts of large cities. Data taken from New York City contrasting predominantly Negro neighborhoods with the city as a whole clearly illustrate this fact. [See Table 10.]

In conclusion: in 1965, 1.2 million nonwhite children under 16 lived in central city families headed by a woman under 65. The great majority of these children were growing up in poverty under conditions that make them better candidates for crime and civil disorder than for jobs providing an entry into American society. . . .

CONDITIONS OF LIFE IN THE RACIAL GHETTO

The conditions of life in the racial ghetto are strikingly different from those to which most Americans are accustomed – especially white, middle-class Americans. We believe it is important to describe these conditions and their effect on the lives of people who cannot escape from the ghetto.[1]

Crime and insecurity

Nothing is more fundamental to the quality of life in any area than the sense of personal security of its residents, and nothing affects this more than crime.

In general, crime rates in large cities are much higher than in other areas of our country. Within such cities, crime rates are higher in disadvantaged Negro areas than anywhere else.

The most widely used measure of crime is the number of "index crimes" (homicide, forcible rape, aggravated assault, robbery, burglary, grand larceny, and auto theft) in relation to population. In 1966, 1,754 such crimes were reported to police for every 100,000 Americans. In cities over 250,000 the rate was 3,153, and in cities over 1 million, it was 3,630 – or more than double the national average. In suburban areas alone, including suburban cities, the rate was only 1,300, or just over one-third the rate in the largest cities.

Within larger cities, personal and property insecurity has consistently been highest in the older neighborhoods encircling the downtown business district. In most cities, crime rates for many decades have been higher in these inner areas than anywhere, except in downtown areas themselves, where they are inflated by the small number of residents.

High crime rates have persisted in these inner areas even though the ethnic character of their residents continually changed. Poor immigrants used these areas as "entry ports," then usually moved on to more desirable neighborhoods as soon as they acquired enough resources. Many "entry port" areas have now become racial ghettos.

Table 1 Incidence of index crimes and patrolmen assignments per 100,000 residents in 5 Chicago police districts, 1965

Number	High-income white district	Low middle-income white district	Mixed high- and low-income white district	Very low income Negro district No. 1	Very low income Negro district No. 2
Index crimes against persons	80	440	338	1,615	2,820
Index crimes against property	1,038	1,750	2,080	2,508	2,630
Patrolmen assigned	93	133	115	243	291

The difference between crime rates in these disadvantaged neighborhoods and in other parts of the city is usually startling, as a comparison of crime rates in five police districts in Chicago for 1965 illustrates. These five include one high-income, all-white district at the periphery of the city, two very low-income, virtually all-Negro districts near the city core with numerous public housing projects, and two predominantly white districts, one with mainly lower middle-income families, the other containing a mixture of very high-income and relatively low-income households. The table shows crime rates against persons and against property in these five districts, plus the number of patrolmen assigned to them per 100,000 residents, as [seen in Table 1].

These data indicate that:

> Variations in the crime rate against persons within the city are extremely large. One very low income Negro district had 35 times as many serious crimes against persons per 100,000 residents as did the high-income white district.
>
> Variations in the crime rate against property are much smaller. The highest rate was only 2.5 times larger than the lowest.
>
> The lower the income in an area, the higher the crime rate there. Yet low-income Negro areas have significantly higher crime rates than low-income white areas. This reflects the high degree of social disorganization in Negro areas described in the previous chapter, as well as the fact that poor Negroes as a group have lower incomes than poor whites as a group.
>
> The presence of more police patrolmen per 100,000 residents does not necessarily offset high crime in certain parts of the city. Although the Chicago Police Department had assigned over three times as many patrolmen per 100,000 residents to the highest crime areas shown as to the lowest, crime rates in the highest crime area for offenses against both persons and property combined were 4.9 times as high as in the lowest crime area.

Because most middle-class Americans live in neighborhoods similar to the more crime-free district described above, they have little comprehension of the sense of insecurity that characterizes the ghetto resident. Moreover, official statistics normally greatly understate actual crime rates because the vast majority are not reported to the police. For example, studies conducted for the President's Crime Commission in Washington, D.C., Boston, and Chicago, showed that three to six times as many crimes were actually committed against persons and homes as were reported to the police.

Two facts are crucial to an understanding of the effects of high crime rates in racial ghettos; most of these crimes are committed by a small minority of the residents, and the principal victims are the residents themselves. Throughout the United States, the great majority of crimes committed by Negroes involve other Negroes as victims. A special tabulation made by the Chicago Police Department for the President's Crime Commission indicated that over 85 percent of the crimes committed against persons by Negroes between September, 1965, and March, 1966, involved Negro victims.

As a result, the majority of law-abiding citizens who live in disadvantaged Negro areas face much higher probabilities of being victimized than residents of most higher income areas, including almost all suburbs. For nonwhites, the probability of suffering from any index crime except larceny is 78 percent higher than for whites. The probability of being raped is 3.7 times higher among nonwhite women, and the probability of being robbed is 3.5 times higher for nonwhites in general.

The problems associated with high crime rates generate widespread hostility toward the police in these neighborhoods for reasons described elsewhere in this Report. Thus, crime not only creates an atmosphere of insecurity and fear throughout Negro neighborhoods but also causes continuing attrition of the relationship between Negro residents and police. This bears a direct relationship to civil disorder.

There are reasons to expect the crime situation in these areas to become worse in the future. First, crime rates throughout the United States have been rising rapidly in recent years. The rate of index crimes against persons rose 37 percent from 1960 to 1966, and the rate of index crimes against property rose 50 percent. In the first 9 months of 1967, the number of index crimes was up 16 percent over the same period in 1966, whereas the U.S. population rose about 1 percent. In cities of 250,000 to 1 million, index crime rose by over 20 percent, whereas it increased 4 percent in cities of over 1 million.[2]

Second, the number of police available to combat crime is rising much more slowly than the amount of crime. In 1966, there were about 20 percent more police employees in the United States than in 1960, and per capita expenditures for police rose from $15.29 in 1960 to $20.99 in 1966, a gain of 37 percent. But over the 6-year period, the number of reported index crimes had jumped 62 percent. In spite of significant improvements in police efficiency, it is clear that police will be unable to cope with their expanding workload unless there is a dramatic increase in the resources allocated by society to this task.

Third, in the next decade, the number of young Negroes aged 14 to 24 will increase rapidly, particularly in central cities. This group is responsible for a disproportionately high share of crimes in all parts of the Nation. In 1966, persons under 25 years of age comprised the following proportions of those arrested for various major crimes: murder, 37 percent; forcible rape, 64 percent; robbery, 71 percent; burglary, 81 percent; larceny, about 77 percent; and auto theft, 89 percent. For all index crimes together, the arrest rate for Negroes is about four times higher than that for whites. Yet the number of young Negroes aged 14 to 24 in central cities will rise about 63 percent from 1966 to 1975, as compared to only 32 percent for the total Negro population of central cities.[3]

Health and sanitation conditions

The residents of the racial ghetto are significantly less healthy than most other Americans. They suffer from higher mortality rates, higher incidence of major diseases, and lower availability and utilization of medical services. They also experience higher admission rates to mental hospitals.

These conditions result from a number of factors.

Poverty

From the standpoint of health, poverty means deficient diets, lack of medical care, inadequate shelter and clothing and often lack of awareness of potential health needs. As a result, almost 30 percent of all persons with family incomes less than $2,000 per year suffer from chronic health conditions that adversely affect their employment – as compared with less than 8 percent of the families with incomes of $7,000 or more.

Poor families have the greatest need for financial assistance in meeting medical expenses. Only about 34 percent of families with incomes of less than $2,000 per year use health insurance benefits, as compared to nearly 90 percent of those with incomes of $7,000 or more.[4]

These factors are aggravated for Negroes when compared to whites for the simple reason that the proportion of persons in the United States who are poor is 3.5 times as high among Negroes (41 percent in 1966) as among whites (12 percent in 1966).

Maternal mortality

Mortality rates for nonwhites are four times as high as those for white mothers. There has been a sharp decline in such rates since 1940, when 774 nonwhite and 320 white mothers died for each 100,000 live births. In 1965, only 84 nonwhite and 21 white mothers died per 100,000 live births – but the gap between nonwhites and whites actually increased.

Infant mortality

Mortality rates among nonwhite babies are 58 percent higher than among whites for those under 1 month old and almost three times as high among those from 1 month to 1 year old. This is true in spite of a large drop in infant mortality rates in both groups since 1940. [See Table 2.]

Table 2 Number of infants who died per 1,000 live births

Year	Less than 1 month old		1 month to 1 year old	
	White	Nonwhite	White	Nonwhite
1940	27.2	39.7	16.0	34.1
1950	19.4	27.5	7.4	17.0
1960	17.2	26.9	5.7	16.4
1965	16.1	25.4	5.4	14.9

Life expectancy

To some extent because of infant mortality rates, life expectancy at birth was 6.9 years longer for whites (71.0 years) than for nonwhites (64.1 years) in 1965. Even in the prime working ages, life expectancy is significantly lower among nonwhites than among whites. In 1965, white persons 25 years old could expect to live an average of 48.6 more years, whereas nonwhites 25 years old could expect to live another 43.3 years, or 11 percent less. Similar but smaller discrepancies existed at all ages from 25 through 55; some actually increased slightly between 1960 and 1965.

Lower utilization of health services

A fact that also contributes to poorer health conditions in the ghetto is that Negro families with incomes similar to those of whites spend less on medical services and visit medical specialists less often. [See Table 3].

Since the lowest income group contains a much larger proportion of nonwhite families than white families, the overall discrepancy in medical care spending between those two groups is very significant, as shown by Table 4.

Table 3 Percent of family expenditure spent for medical care, 1960-61

Income group	White	Nonwhite	Ratio, white to nonwhite
Under $3,000	9	5	1.8:1
$3,000 to $7,499	7	5	1.4:1
$7,500 and over	6	4	1.5:1

These data indicate that nonwhite families in the lower income group spent less than half as much per person on medical services as white families with similar incomes. This discrepancy sharply declines but is still significant in the higher income group, where total nonwhite medical expenditures per person equal, on the average, $74.3 percent of white expenditures.

Table 4 Health expenses per person per year for the period from July to December 1962

Income by racial group	Expenses					
	Total medical	Hospital	Doctor	Dental	Medicine	Other
Under $2,000 per family per year:						
White	$130	$33	$41	$11	$32	$13
Nonwhite	63	15	23	5	16	5
$10,000 and more per family per year:						
White	179	34	61	37	31	16
Nonwhite	133	34	50	19	23	8

Negroes spend less on medical care for several reasons. Negro households generally are larger, requiring greater nonmedical expenses for each household and leaving less money for meeting medical expenses. Thus, lower expenditures per person would result even if expenditures per household were the same. Negroes also often pay more for other basic necessities such as food and consumer durables, as discussed in the next part of this chapter. In addition, fewer doctors, dentists, and medical facilities are conveniently available to Negroes than to most whites – a result both of geographic concentration of doctors in higher income areas in large cities and of discrimination against Negroes by doctors and hospitals. A survey in Cleveland indicated that there were 0.45 physicians per 1,000 people in poor neighborhoods, compared to 1.13 per 1,000 in nonpoverty areas. The result nationally is fewer visits to physicians and dentists. [See Table 5.]

Table 5 Percent of population making one or visits to indicated type of medical specialist from July 1963 to June 1964

Type of medical specialist	Family incomes of $2,000-$3,999		Family incomes of $7,000-$9,999	
	White	Nonwhite	White	Nonwhite
Physician	64	56	70	64
Dentist	31	20	52	33

Although widespread use of health insurance has led many hospitals to adopt nondiscriminatory policies, some private hospitals still refuse to admit Negro patients or to accept doctors with Negro patients. And many individual doctors still discriminate against Negro patients. As a result, Negroes are more likely to be treated in hospital clinics than whites and they are less likely to receive personalized service. This conclusion is confirmed by the data [in Table 6].

Table 6 Percent of all visits to physicians from July 1963 to June 1964, made in indicated ways

	Family incomes of $2,000-$3,000		Family incomes of $7,000-$9,999	
Type of visit to physician	White	Nonwhite	White	Nonwhite
In physician's office	68	56	73	66
Hospital clinic	17	35	7	16
Other (mainly telephone)	15	9	20	18
Total	100	100	100	100

Environmental factors

Environmental conditions in disadvantaged Negro neighborhoods create further reasons for poor health conditions there. The level of sanitation is strikingly below that which is prevalent in most higher income areas. One simple reason is that residents often lack proper storage facilities for food – adequate refrigerators, freezers, even garbage cans, which are sometimes stolen as fast as landlords can replace them.

In areas where garbage collection and other sanitation services are grossly inadequate – commonly in the poorer parts of our large cities – rats proliferate. It is estimated that in 1965, there were over 14,000 cases of ratbite in the United States, mostly in such neighborhoods.

The importance of these conditions was outlined for the Commission as follows:[5]

> Sanitation Commissioners of New York City and Chicago both feel this [sanitation] to be an important community problem and report themselves as being under substantial pressure to improve conditions. *It must be concluded that slum sanitation is a serious problem in the minds of the urban poor and well merits, at least on that ground, the attention of the Commission.* A related problem, according to one Sanitation Commissioner, is the fact that residents of areas bordering on slums feel that sanitation and neighborhood cleanliness is a crucial issue, relating to the stability of their blocks and constituting an important psychological index of "how far gone" their area is.
>
> . . . There is no known study comparing sanitation services between slum and non-slum areas. The experts agree, however, that there are more services in the slums on a quantitative basis, although perhaps not on a per capita basis. In New York, for example, garbage pickups are supposedly scheduled for about six times a week in slums, compared to three times a week in other areas of the city; the comparable figures in Chicago are two to three times a week versus once a week.
>
> The point, therefore, is not the relative quantitative level of services but the peculiarly intense needs of ghetto areas for sanitation services. This high demand is the product of numerous factors including: (1) higher population density; (2) lack of well managed buildings and adequate garbage services provided by landlords, number of receptacles, carrying to

curbside, number of electric garbage disposals; (3) high relocation rates of tenants and businesses, producing heavy volume of bulk refuse left on streets and in buildings; (4) different uses of the streets – as outdoor living rooms in summer, recreation areas – producing high visibility and sensitivity to garbage problems; (5) large numbers of abandoned cars; (6) severe rodent and pest problems; (7) traffic congestion blocking garbage collection; and (8) obstructed street cleaning and snow removal on crowded, car-choked streets. Each of these elements adds to the problem and suggests a different possible line of attack.

Exploitation of disadvantaged consumers by retail merchants

Much of the violence in recent civil disorders has been directed at stores and other commercial establishments in disadvantaged Negro areas. In some cases, rioters focused on stores operated by white merchants who, they apparently believed, had been charging exorbitant prices or selling inferior goods. Not all the violence against these stores can be attributed to "revenge" for such practices. Yet it is clear that many residents of disadvantaged Negro neighborhoods believe they suffer constant abuses by local merchants.

Significant grievances concerning unfair commercial practices affecting Negro consumers were found in 11 of the 20 cities studied by the Commission. The fact that most of the merchants who operate stores in Negro areas are white undoubtedly contributes to the conclusion among Negroes that they are exploited by white society.

It is difficult to assess the precise degree and extent of exploitation. No systematic and reliable survey comparing consumer pricing and credit practices in all-Negro and other neighborhoods has ever been conducted on a nationwide basis. Differences in prices and credit practices between white middle-income areas and Negro low-income areas to some extent reflect differences in the real costs of serving these two markets (such as differential losses from pilferage in supermarkets), but the exact extent of these cost differences has never been estimated accurately. Finally, an examination of exploitative consumer practices must consider the particular structure and functions of the low-income consumer durables market.

Installment buying

This complex situation can best be understood by first considering certain basic facts:

Various cultural factors generate constant pressure on low-income families to buy many relatively expensive durable goods and display them in their homes. This pressure comes in part from continuous exposure to commercial advertising, especially on television. In January, 1967, over 88 percent of all Negro households had TV sets. A 1961 study of 464 low-income families in New York City showed that 95 percent of these relatively poor families had TV sets.

Many poor families have extremely low incomes, bad previous credit records, unstable sources of income or other attributes which make it virtually impossible for them to buy merchandise from established large national or local retail firms. These families lack enough savings to pay cash, and they cannot meet the standard credit requirements of established general merchants because they are too likely to fall behind in their payments.

Poor families in urban areas are far less mobile than others. A 1967 Chicago study of low-income Negro households indicated their low automobile ownership compelled them to patronize neighborhood merchants. These merchants typically provided smaller selection, poorer services and higher prices than big national outlets. The 1961 New York study also indicated that families who shopped outside their own neighborhoods were far less likely to pay exorbitant prices.

Most low-income families are uneducated concerning the nature of credit purchase contracts, the legal rights and obligations of both buyers and sellers, sources of advice for consumers who are having difficulties with merchants and the operation of the courts concerned with these matters. In contrast, merchants engaged in selling goods to them are very well informed.

In most states, the laws governing relations between consumers and merchants in effect offer protection only to informed, sophisticated parties with understanding of each other's rights and obligations. Consequently, these laws are little suited to protect the rights of most low-income consumers.

In this situation, exploitative practices flourish. Ghetto residents who want to buy relatively expensive goods cannot do so from standard retail outlets and are thus restricted to local stores. Forced to use credit, they have little understanding of the pitfalls of credit buying. But because they have unstable incomes and frequently fail to make payments, the cost to the merchants of serving them is significantly above that of serving middle-income consumers. Consequently, a special kind of merchant appears to sell them goods on terms designed to cover the high cost of doing business in ghetto neighborhoods.

Whether they actually gain higher profits, these merchants charge higher prices than those in other parts of the city to cover the greater credit risks and other higher operating costs inherent in neighborhood outlets. A recent study conducted by the Federal Trade Commission in Washington, D.C., illustrates this conclusion dramatically. The FTC identified a number of stores specializing in selling furniture and appliances to low-income households. About 92 percent of the sales of these stores were credit sales involving installment purchases, as compared to 27 percent of the sales in general retail outlets handling the same merchandise.

The median income annually of a sample of 486 customers of these stores was about $4,200, but one-third had annual incomes below $3,600, and about 6 percent were receiving welfare payments, and another 76 percent were employed in the lowest paying occupations (service workers, operatives, laborers and domestics), as compared to 36 percent of the total labor force in Washington in those occupations.

Definitely catering to a low-income group, these stores charged significantly higher prices than general merchandise outlets in the Washington area. According to testimony by Paul Rand Dixon, Chairman of the FTC, an item selling wholesale at $100 would retail on the average for $165 in a general merchandise store and for $250 in a low-income specialty store. Thus, the customers of these outlets were paying an average price premium of about 52 percent.

White higher prices are not necessarily exploitative in themselves, many merchants in ghetto neighborhoods take advantage of their superior knowledge of credit buying by engaging in various exploitative tactics – high-pressure salesmanship, "bait advertising," misrepresentation of prices, substitution of used goods for promised new ones, failure to notify consumers of legal actions against them, refusal to repair or replace substandard goods, exorbitant prices or credit charges, and use of shoddy merchandise. Such tactics affect a great many low-income consumers. In the New York study, 60 percent of all households had suffered from consumer problems (some of which were purely their own fault). About 23 percent had experienced serious exploitation. Another 20 percent, many of whom were also exploited, had experienced repossession, garnishment, or threat of garnishment.

Garnishment

Garnishment practices in many states allow creditors to deprive individuals of their wages through court action, without hearing or trial. In about 20 states, the wages of an employee can be diverted to a creditor merely upon the latter's deposition, with no advance hearing where the employee can defend himself. He often receives no prior notice of such action and is usually unaware of the law's operation and too poor to hire legal defense. Moreover, consumers may find themselves still owing money on a sales contract even after the creditor has repossessed the goods. The New York study cited earlier in this chapter indicated that 20 percent of a sample of low-income families had been subjected to legal action regarding consumer purchases. And the Federal Trade Commission study in Washington, D.C., showed that, on the average, retailers specializing in credit sales of furniture and appliances to low-income consumers resorted to court action once for every $2,200 of sales. Since their average sale was for $207, this amounted to using the courts to collect from one of every 11 customers. In contrast, department stores in the same area used court action against approximately one of every 14,500 customers.[6]

Variations in food prices

Residents of low-income Negro neighborhoods frequently claim that they pay higher prices for food in local markets than wealthier white suburbanites and receive inferior quality meat and produce. Statistically reliable information comparing prices and quality in these two kinds of areas is generally unavailable. The U.S. Bureau of Labor Statistics, studying food prices in six cities in 1966, compared prices of a standard list of 18 items in low-income areas and higher income areas in each city. In a total of 180 stores, including independent and chain stores, and for items of the same type sold in the same types of stores, there were no significant differences in prices between low-income and high-income areas. However, stores in low-income areas were more likely to be small independents (which had somewhat higher prices), to sell low-quality produce and meat at any given price, and to be patronized by people who typically bought smaller sized packages which are more expensive per unit of measure. In other words, many low-income consumers in fact pay higher prices, although the situation varies greatly from place to place.

Although these findings must be considered inconclusive, there are significant reasons to believe that poor households generally pay higher prices for the food they buy and receive lower quality food. Low-income consumers buy more food at local groceries because they are less mobile. Prices in these small stores are significantly higher than in major supermarkets because they cannot achieve economies of scale and because real operating costs are higher in low-income Negro areas than in outlying suburbs. For instance, inventory "shrinkage" from pilfering and other causes is normally under 2 percent of sales but can run twice as much in high-crime areas. Managers seek to make up for these added costs by charging higher prices for food or by substituting lower grades.

These practices do not necessarily involve exploitation, but they are often perceived as exploitative and unfair by those who are aware of the price and quality differences involved but unaware of operating costs. In addition, it is probable that genuinely exploitative pricing practices exist in some areas. In either case, differential food prices constitute another factor convincing urban Negroes in low-income neighborhoods that whites discriminate against them.

Notes

1. We have not attempted here to describe conditions relating to the fundamental problems of housing, education, and welfare, which are treated in detail in later chapters.
2. The problem of interpreting and evaluating "rising" crime rates is complicated by the changing age distribution of the population, improvements in reporting methods, and the increasing willingness of victims to report crimes. Despite these complications, there is general agreement on the serious increase in the incidence of crime in the United States.
3. Assuming those cities will experience the same proportion of total United States Negro population growth that they did from 1960 to 1966. The calculations are derived from population projections in Bureau of the Census, Population Estimates, Current Population Reports, Series P-25, No. 381, Dec. 1967, p. 63.
4. Public programs of various kinds have been providing significant financial assistance for medical care in recent years. In 1964, over $1.1 billion was paid out by various governments for such aid. About 52 percent of medical vendor payments came from Federal Government agencies, 33 percent from states, and 12 percent from local governments. The biggest contributions were made by the Old Age Assistance Program and the Medical Assistance for the Aged Program. The enactment of Medicare in 1965 has significantly added to this flow of public assistance for medical aid. However, it is too early to evaluate the results upon health conditions among the poor.
5. Memorandum to the Commission dated Nov. 16, 1967, from Robert Patricelli, minority counsel, Subcommittee on Employment, Manpower and Poverty, U.S. Senate.
6. Assuming their sales also averaged $207 per customer.

COMPARING THE IMMIGRANT AND NEGRO EXPERIENCE

In the preceding chapters we have surveyed the historical background of racial discrimination and traced its effects on Negro employment, on the social structure of the ghetto community and on the conditions of life that surround the urban Negro poor. Here we address a fundamental question that many white Americans are asking today: Why has the Negro been unable to escape from poverty and the ghetto like the European immigrants?

The maturing economy

The changing nature of the American economy is one major reason. When the European immigrants were arriving in large numbers, America was becoming an urban-industrial society. To build its major cities and industries, America needed great pools of unskilled labor. The immigrants provided the labor, gained an economic foothold and thereby enabled their children and grandchildren to move up to skilled, white-collar and professional employment.

Since World War II especially, America's urban-industrial society has matured; unskilled labor is far less essential than before, and blue-collar jobs of all kinds are decreasing in number and importance as a source of new employment. The Negroes who migrated to the great urban centers lacked the skills essential to the new economy, and the schools of the ghetto have been unable to provide the education that can qualify them for decent jobs. The Negro migrant, unlike the immigrant, found little opportunity in the city; he had arrived too late, and the unskilled labor he had to offer was no longer needed.

The disability of race

Racial discrimination is undoubtedly the second major reason why the Negro has been unable to escape from poverty. The structure of discrimination has persistently narrowed his opportunities and restricted his prospects. Well before the high tide of immigration from overseas, Negroes were already relegated to the poorly paid, low status occupations. Had it not been for racial discrimination, the North might well have recruited southern Negroes after the Civil War to provide the labor for building the burgeoning urban-industrial economy. Instead, northern employers looked to Europe for their sources of unskilled labor. Upon the arrival of the immigrants, the Negroes were dislodged from the few urban occupations they had dominated. Not until World War II were Negroes generally hired for industrial jobs, and by that time the decline in the need for unskilled labor had already begun. European immigrants, too, suffered from discrimination, but never was it so pervasive. The prejudice against color in America has formed a bar to advancement unlike any other.

Entry into the political system

Political opportunities also played an important role in enabling the European immigrants to escape from poverty. The immigrants settled for the most part in rapidly growing cities that had powerful and expanding political machines which gave them economic advantages in exchange for political support. The political machines were decentralized, and ward-level grievance machinery as well as personal representation enabled the immigrant to make his voice heard and his power felt. Since the local political organizations exercised considerable influence over public building in the cities, they provided employment in construction jobs for their immigrant voters. Ethnic groups often dominated one or more of the municipal services – police and fire protection, sanitation and even public education.

By the time the Negroes arrived, the situation had altered dramatically. The great wave of public building had virtually come to an end; reform groups were beginning to attack the political machines; the machines were no longer so powerful or so well equipped to provide jobs and other favors.

Although the political machines retained their hold over the areas settled by Negroes, the scarcity of patronage jobs made them unwilling to share with Negroes the political positions they had created in these neighborhoods. For example, Harlem was dominated by white politicians for many years after it had become a Negro ghetto; even today, New York's Lower East Side, which is now predominantly Puerto Rican, is strongly influenced by politicians of the older immigrant groups.

This pattern exists in many other American cities. Negroes are still underrepresented in city councils in most city agencies.

Segregation played a role here too. The immigrants and their descendants, who felt threatened by the arrival of the Negro, prevented a Negro-immigrant coalition that might have saved the old political machines. Reform groups, nominally more liberal on the race issue, were often dominated by businessmen and middle-class city residents who usually opposed coalition with any low-income group, white or black.

Cultural factors

Cultural factors also made it easier for the immigrants to escape from poverty. They came to America from much poorer societies, with a low standard of living, and they came at a time when job aspirations were low. When most jobs in the American economy were unskilled, they sensed little deprivation in being forced to take the dirty and poorly paid jobs. Moreover, their families were large, and many breadwinners, some of whom never married, contributed to the total family income. As a result, family units managed to live even from the lowest paid jobs and still put some money aside for savings or investment, for example, to purchase a house or tenement or to open a store or factory. Since the immigrants spoke little English and had their own ethnic culture, they needed stores to supply them with ethnic foods and other services. Since their family structures were patriarchal, men found satisfactions in family life that helped compensate for the bad jobs they had to take and the hard work they had to endure.

Negroes came to the city under quite different circumstances. Generally relegated to jobs that others would not take, they were paid too little to be able to put money in savings for new enterprises. In addition, Negroes lacked the extended family characteristic of certain European groups; each household usually had only one or two breadwinners. Moreover, Negro men had fewer cultural incentives to work in a dirty job for the sake of the family. As a result of slavery and of long periods of male unemployment afterwards, the Negro family structure had become matriarchal; the man played a secondary and marginal role in his family. For many Negro men, then, there were few of the cultural and psychological rewards of family life; they often abandoned their homes because they felt themselves useless to their families.

Although Negro men worked as hard as the immigrants to support their families, their rewards were less. The jobs did not pay enough to enable them to support their families, for prices and living standards had risen since the immigrants had come, and the entrepreneurial opportunities that had allowed some immigrants to become independent, even rich, had vanished. Above all, Negroes suffered from segregation, which denied them access to the good jobs and the right unions and which deprived them of the opportunity to buy real estate or obtain business loans or move out of the ghetto and bring up their children in middle-class neighborhoods. Immigrants were able to leave their ghettos as soon as they had the money; segregation has denied Negroes the opportunity to live elsewhere.

The vital element of time

Finally, nostalgia makes it easy to exaggerate the ease of escape of the white immigrants from the ghettos. When the immigrants were immersed in poverty, they, too, lived in slums, and these neighborhoods exhibited fearfully high rates of alcoholism, desertion, illegitimacy and the other pathologies associated with poverty. Just as some Negro men desert their families when they are unemployed and their wives can get jobs, so did the men of other ethnic groups, even though time and affluence has clouded white memories of the past.

Today, whites tend to contrast their experience with poverty-stricken Negroes. The fact is, among the southern and eastern Europeans who came to America in the last great wave of immigration, those who came already urbanized were the first to escape from poverty. The others who came to America from rural background, as Negroes did, are only now, after three generations, in the final stages of escaping from poverty. Until the last 10 years or so, most of these were employed in blue-collar jobs, and only a small proportion of their children were able or willing to attend college. In other words, only the third, and in many cases only the fourth, generation has been able to achieve the kind of middle-class income and status that allows it to send its children to college. Because of favorable economic and political conditions, these ethnic groups were able to escape from lower class status to working class and lower middle-class status, but it has taken them three generations.

Negroes have been concentrated in the city for only two generations, and they have been there under much less favorable conditions. Moreover, their escape from poverty has been blocked in part by the resistance of the European ethnic groups; they have been unable to enter some unions and to move into some neighborhoods outside the ghetto because descendants of the European immigrants who control these unions and neighborhoods have not yet abandoned them for middle-class occupations and areas.

Even so, some Negroes have escaped poverty, and they have done so in only two generations; their success is less visible than that of the immigrants in many cases, for residential segregation has forced them to remain in the ghetto. Still, the proportion of nonwhites employed in white-collar, technical and professional jobs has risen from

10.2 percent in 1950 to 20.8 percent in 1966 and the proportion attending college has risen an equal amount. Indeed, the development of a small but steadily increasing Negro middle class while a great part of the Negro population is stagnating economically is creating a growing gap between Negro haves and have-nots.

The awareness of this gap by those left behind undoubtedly adds to the feelings of desperation and anger which breed civil disorders. Low-income Negroes realize that segregation and lack of job opportunities have made it possible for only a small proportion of all Negroes to escape poverty, and the summer disorders are at least in part a protest against being left behind and left out.

The immigrant who labored long hours at hard and often menial work had the hope of a better future, if not for himself then for this children. This was the promise of the "American dream" – the society offered to all a future that was open-ended; with hard work and perseverance, a man and his family could in time achieve not only material well-being but "position" and status.

For the Negro family in the urban ghetto, there is a different vision – the future seems to lead only to a dead end.

What the American economy of the late 19th and early 20th century was able to do to help the European immigrants escape from poverty is now largely impossible. New methods of escape must be found for the majority of today's poor.

THE COMMUNITY RESPONSE

Introduction

The racial disorders of last summer in part reflect the failure of all levels of government – Federal and state as well as local – to come to grips with the problems of our cities. The ghetto symbolizes the dilemma: a widening gap between human needs and public resources and a growing cynicism regarding the commitment of community institutions and leadership to meet these needs.

The problem has many dimensions – financial, political and institutional. Almost all cities – and particularly the central cities of the largest metropolitan regions – are simply unable to meet the growing need for public services and facilities with traditional sources of municipal revenue. Many cities are structured politically so that great numbers of citizens – particularly minority groups – have little or no representation in the processes of government. Finally, some cities lack either the will or the capacity to use effectively the resources that are available to them.

Instrumentalities of Federal and state government often compound the problems. National policy expressed through a very large number of grant programs and institutions rarely exhibits a coherent and consistent perspective when viewed at the local level. State efforts, traditionally focused on rural areas, often fail to tie in effectively with either local or Federal programs in urban areas.

Meanwhile, the decay of the central city continues – its revenue base eroded by the retreat of industry and white middle-class families to the suburbs, its budget and tax rate inflated by rising costs and increasing numbers of dependent citizens and its public plant – schools, hospitals, and correctional institutions deteriorated by age and long-deferred maintenance.

Yet to most citizens, the decay remains largely invisible. Only their tax bills and the headlines about crime or "riots" suggest that something may be seriously wrong in the city.

There are, however, two groups of people that live constantly with the problem of the city: the public officials and the poor, particularly the residents of the racial ghetto. Their relationship is a key factor in the development of conditions underlying civil disorders.

Our investigations of the 1967 riot cities establish that:

> Virtually every major episode of urban violence in the summer of 1967 was foreshadowed by an accumulation of unresolved grievances by ghetto residents against local authorities (often, but not always, the police). So high was the resulting underlying tension that routine and random events, tolerated or ignored under most circumstances (such as the raid on the "blind pig" in Detroit and the arrest of the cab driver in Newark), became the triggers of sudden violence.
>
> Coinciding with this high level of dissatisfaction, confidence in the willingness and ability of local government to respond to Negro grievances was low. Evidence presented to this Commission in hearings, field reports and research analyses of the 1967 riot cities establishes that a substantial number of Negroes were disturbed and angry about local governments' failures to solve their problems.

Several developments have converged to produce this volatile situation.

First, there is a widening gulf in communications between local government and the residents of the erupting ghettos of the city. As a result, many Negro citizens develop a profound sense of isolation and alienation from the processes and programs of government. This lack of communication exists for all residents in our larger cities; it is, however, far more difficult to overcome for low-income, less educated citizens who are disproportionately supported by and dependent upon programs administered by agencies of local government. Consequently, they are more often subject to real or imagined official misconduct ranging from abrasive contacts with public officials to arbitrary administrative actions.

Further, as a result of the long history of racial discrimination, grievances experienced by Negroes often take on personal and symbolic significance transcending the immediate consequences of the event. For example, inadequate sanitation services are viewed by many ghetto residents not merely as instances of poor public service but as manifestations of racial discrimination. This perception reinforces existing feelings of alienation and contributes to a heightened level of frustration and dissatisfaction, not only with the administrators of the sanitation department but with all the representatives of local government. This is particularly true with respect to the police, who are the only public agents on duty in the ghetto 24 hours a day and who bear this burden of hostility for the less visible elements of the system.

The lack of communication and the absence of regular contacts with ghetto residents prevent city leaders from learning about problems and grievances as they develop. As a result, tensions, which could have been dissipated if responded to promptly, mount unnecessarily, and the potential for explosion grows inevitably. Once disorder erupts, public officials are frequently unable to fashion an effective response; they lack adequate information about the nature of the trouble and its causes, and they lack rapport with local leaders who might be able to influence the community.

Second, many city governments are poorly organized to respond effectively to the needs of ghetto residents, even when those needs are made known to appropriate public officials. Most middle-class city dwellers have limited contacts with local government. When contacts do occur, they tend to concern relatively narrow and specific problems. Furthermore, middle-class citizens, although subject to many of the same frustrations and resentments as ghetto residents in dealing with the public bureaucracy, find it relatively easy to locate the appropriate agency for help and redress. If they fail to get satisfaction, they can call on a variety of remedies – assistance of elected representatives, friends in government, a lawyer. In short, the middle-class city dweller has relatively fewer needs for public services and is reasonably well positioned to move the system to his benefit.

On the other hand, the typical ghetto resident has interrelated social and economic problems which require the services of several government and private agencies. At the same time, he may be unable to identify his problems to fit the complicated structure of government. Moreover, he may be unaware of his rights and opportunities under public programs and unable to obtain the necessary guidance from either public or private sources.

Current trends in municipal administration have had the effect of reducing the capacity of local government to respond effectively to these needs. The pressures for administrative efficiency and cost cutting have brought about the withdrawal of many operations of city government from direct contact with neighborhood and citizen. Red tape and administrative complexity have filled the vacuum by the centralization of local government. The introduction of a merit system and a professionalized civil service has made management of the cities more businesslike, but it has also tended to depersonalize and isolate government. The rigid patterns of segregation prevalent within the central city have widened the distance between Negro citizens and city hall.

In most of the riot cities surveyed by the Commission, we found little or no meaningful coordination among city agencies, either in responding to the needs of ghetto residents on an ongoing basis or in planning to head off disturbances. The consequences of this lack of coordination were particularly severe for the police. Despite the fact that they were being called upon increasingly to deal with tensions and citizen complaints often having little, if anything, to do with police services, the police departments of many large cities were isolated from other city agencies, sometimes including the mayor and his staff. In these cities, the police were compelled to deal with ghetto residents angered over dirty streets, dilapidated housing, unfair commercial practices or inferior schools – grievances which they had neither the responsibility for creating nor the authority to redress.

Third, ghetto residents increasingly believe that they are excluded from the decision-making process which affects their lives and community. This feeling of exclusion, intensified by the bitter legacy of racial discrimination, has engendered a deep seated hostility toward the institutions of government. It has severely compromised the effectiveness of programs intended to provide improved services to ghetto residents.

In part, this is the lesson of Detroit and New Haven where well intentioned programs designed to respond to the needs of ghetto residents were not worked out and implemented sufficiently in cooperation with the intended beneficiaries. A report prepared for the Senate Subcommittee on Employment, Manpower and Poverty, presented just prior to the riot in Detroit, found that:

> Area residents . . . complain almost continually that . . . their demands for program changes are not heeded, that they have little voice in what goes on. . . . As much as the area residents are involved, listened to, and even heeded, . . . it becomes fairly clear that the relationship is still one of superordinate-subordinate, rather than one of equals. . . . The procedures by which HRD (the Mayor's Committee for Human Resources Development, the Detroit Community Action Agency) operates by and large admit the contributions of area residents only after programs have been written, after policies have already operated for a time or already been formulated and to a large degree, only in formal and infrequent meetings rather than in day-to-day operations. . . . The meaningfulness of resident involvement is reduced by its after-the-fact nature and by relatively limited resources they have at their disposal.

Mayor Alfonso J. Cervantes of St. Louis was even more explicit. In testimony before this Commission, he stated:

> We have found that ghetto neighborhoods cannot be operated on from outside alone. The people within them should have a voice, and our experience has shown that it is often a voice that speaks with good sense, since the practical aspects of the needs of the ghetto people are so much clearer to the people there than they are to anyone else.

The political system, traditionally an important vehicle of minorities to participate effectively in decisions affecting the distribution of public resources, has not worked for the Negro as it has for other groups. The reasons are fairly obvious.

We have found that the number of Negro officials in elected and appointed positions in the riot cities is minimal in proportion to the Negro population. The alienation of the Negro from the political process has been exacerbated by his racial and economic isolation.

Specifically, the needs of ghetto residents for social welfare and other public services have swelled dramatically at a time when increased affluence has diminished the need for such services by the rest of the urban population. By reducing disproportionately the economic disability of other portions of the population, particularly other ethnic urban minorities, this affluence has left the urban Negro few potential local allies with whom to make common cause for shared objectives. The development of political alliances, essential to effective participation of minority groups in the political process, has been further impaired by the polarization of the races, which on both sides has transformed economic considerations into racial issues.

Finally, these developments have coincided with the demise of the historic urban political machines and the growth of the city manager concept of government. While this tendency has produced major benefits in terms of honest and efficient administration, it has eliminated an important political link between city government and low-income residents.

These conditions have produced a vast and threatening disparity in perceptions of the intensity and validity of Negro dissatisfaction. Viewed for the perspective of the ghetto resident, city government appears distant and unconcerned, the possibility of effective change remote. As a result, tension rises perceptibly; the explosion comes as the climax to a progression of tension-generating incidents. To the city administration, unaware of this growing tension or unable to respond effectively to it, the outbreak of disorder comes as a shock.

No democratic society can long endure the existence within its major urban centers of a substantial number of citizens who feel deeply aggrieved as a group, yet lack confidence in the government to rectify perceived injustice and in their ability to bring about needed change.

We are aware that reforms in existing instruments of local government and their relationship to the ghetto population will mean little unless joined with sincere and comprehensive response to the severe social and economic needs of ghetto residents. Elsewhere in this report, we make specific recommendations with respect to employment, education, welfare, and housing which we hope will meet some of these needs.

We believe, however, that there are measures which can and should be taken now; that they can be put to work without great cost and without delay; that they can be built upon in the future and that they will effectively reduce the level of grievance and tension as well as improve the responsiveness of local government to the needs of ghetto residents.

Source: *Report of the National Advisory Commission on Civil Disorders, 1968,* Part II, pp. 115-121; 123-131;133-141; 143-145; 147-150.

10.3 Institutional Racism in America

The United States Commission on Civil Rights produced this Report in 1970 on the nature of white racism in the country.

White racism exhibits itself in hundreds of ways in American society, and acts in hundreds of other ways that are not recognized by most citizens. Yet all of these can be usefully grouped into two basic categories: *overt racism,* and *indirect institutional subordination because of color.* (For convenience, the second category will be referred to as just *institutional subordination.)*

Overt racism is the use of color *per se* (or other visible characteristics related to color) as a subordinating factor. *Institutional subordination* is placing or keeping persons in a position or status of inferiority by means of attitudes, actions, or institutional structures which do not use color itself as the subordinating mechanism, but instead use other mechanisms indirectly related to color. . . .

Racism is one of those words that many people use, and feel strongly about, but cannot define very clearly. Those who suffer from racism usually interpret the word one way while others interpret it quite differently. This ambiguity is possible in part because the word refers to ideas that are very complicated and hard to pin down. Yet, before we can fully understand how racism works or how to combat its harmful effects we must first try to define it clearly even though such an attempt may be regarded as wrong by many.

Perhaps the best definition of *racism* is an operational one. This means that it must be based upon the way people actually behave, rather than upon logical consistency or purely scientific ideas. Therefore, racism may be viewed as *any attitude, action, or institutional structure which subordinates a person or group because of his or their color.* Even though "race" and "color" refer to two different kinds of human characteristics, in America it is the visibility of skin color – and of other physical traits associated with particular colors or groups – that marks individuals as "targets" for subordination by members of the white majority. This is true of Negroes, Puerto Ricans, Mexican Americans, Japanese Americans, Chinese Americans, and American Indians. Specifically, white racism subordinates members of all these other groups primarily because they are not white in color, even though some are technically considered to be members of the "white race" and even view themselves as "whites."

As a matter of further explanation, racism is not just a matter of attitudes: actions and institutional structures, especially, can also be forms of racism. An "institutional structure" is any well-established, habitual, or widely accepted pattern of action or organizational arrangement, whether formal or informal. For example, the residential segregation of almost all Negroes in large cities is an "institutional structure." So is the widely used practice of denying employment to applicants with any nontraffic police record because this tends to discriminate unfairly against residents of low-income areas where police normally arrest young men for minor incidents that are routinely overlooked in wealthy suburbs.

Just being aware of someone's color or race, or even taking it into account when making decisions or in other behavior, is not necessarily racist. Racism occurs only when these reactions involve some kind of subordination. Thus, pride in one's black heritage, or Irish ancestry, is not necessarily racist.

Racism can occur even if the people causing it have no intention of subordinating others because of color, or are totally unaware of doing so. Admittedly, this implication is sure to be extremely controversial. Most Americans believe racism is bad. But how can anyone be "guilty" of doing something bad when he does not realize he is doing it? Racism can be a matter of *result* rather than *intention* because many institutional structures in America that most whites do not recognize as subordinating others because of color actually injure minority group members far more than deliberate racism.

The separation of races is not racism unless it leads to or involves subordination of one group by another (including subordination of whites by Negroes). Therefore, favoring the voluntary separation of races is not necessarily a form of racism. However, it would become racism if members of one group who wanted to cluster together tried to restrict the locational choices of members of some other group in order to achieve such clustering; for example, if whites tried to discourage Mexican Americans from moving into all-white neighborhoods or if a group of black students forced other black students to live in a specific dormitory. Furthermore, separation of groups is one of the oldest and most widespread devices for subordination in all societies. It is particularly effective in modern urbanized societies because it is extremely difficult, if not impossible, to provide different but truly equal opportunities and conditions for separated groups within an economically integrated society. . . .

For more than 300 years, overt racism was a central part of American life, particularly in the South. During these centuries, thousands of overtly racist laws, social institutions, behavior patterns, living conditions, distributions of political power, figures and forms of speech, cultural viewpoints and habits, and even thought patterns continually forced colored Americans[1] into positions of inferiority and subordination. It took the bloodiest of all American wars to abolish the most terrible form of legal subordination – slavery – just 100 years ago. . . .

In the past two decades, there has been important progress in striking down legal support for most of the forms of overt racism. The actual effects of many such forms of racism have been greatly reduced, too. Moreover, this type of conscious and deliberate subordination by color is now considered wrong by most Americans. As a result, many whites *believe* that overt racism – which is the only form they recognize–is disappearing from America.

Yet hundreds of forms of overt racism remain throughout most of the Nation. Examples are the deliberate exclusion of Negroes, Mexican Americans, and other colored persons from labor unions, law firms, school districts, all-white residential neighborhoods, college fraternities, and private social clubs.

. . . taken as a whole, Americans of color are still severely handicapped by the residual efforts of past overt racism – plus the many forms of overt racism that still exist.

The deeply embedded effects of overt white racism will not instantly disappear if the white majority suddenly reduces or even eliminates the use of color as an explicit factor in making decisions or influencing its actions. Many whites now say: "All right, we recognize the injustice of overt racism. So we will stop using color as a factor in making decisions. Instead we will use other factors which are clearly and reasonably related to the activities and privileges concerned." Examples of these other factors used in making decisions are skill levels in relation to jobs, place of residence in relation to school attendance, ability to score well on entrance examinations in relation to higher education, self-confidence and leadership of whites in relation to job promotions, and savings plus present income in relation to buying homes.

Usually, the use of such factors is free from overt racism. Hence, it constitutes great progress in relation to most of American history. . . .

Nevertheless, even "merit employment" programs can conceal many forms of indirect institutional subordination by color. In fact, we can use the example of such programs to illustrate how present elimination of overtly racist action does *not* destroy or even significantly weaken the continuing racist effects of *past* overtly racist behavior. This can occur because many of those effects are embedded in institutional structures that no longer appear related to race or color.

Consider an employer who needs workers to fill certain jobs that demand advanced carpentry skills. Naturally, he requires that applicants have such skills in order to be hired. But what if the local carpenters' union excludes all Negroes and Mexican Americans as members? Then this very reasonable behavior of the employer has racist effects because of overt racism of another organization upon which he relies to carry out his own activities. Or what if unions accept minority group apprentices specially trained in local high schools, but the only high schools providing such training are in all-white neighborhoods, either too far from minority group neighborhoods for convenient attendance, or far enough to be placed in different school districts because all school boundaries are based upon the "neighborhood proximity" principle? In this case, no decision-makers are using overtly racist principles. Yet the result clearly continues systematic subordination of minority groups by excluding them from important economic opportunities. Returning to the example, assume that the employer saves money by never advertising available job openings. Instead, he relies solely upon word-of-mouth communications from his present employees to their friends to find applicants – but all his present employees are white. This is an extremely widespread practice, since most workers find their jobs by hearing of openings from friends. Yet it has the effect of excluding nearly all minority group members from consideration for available jobs. Because of past overt racism, most whites have mainly white friends, particularly since they live in all-white neighborhoods.

Again, the employer is taking actions which are not overtly racist in either nature or intent – but which nevertheless have racist effects – that is, they subordinate people because of their color. In this case, these effects occur because the seemingly reasonable and "unbiased" behavior of the employer takes place in an institutional context that still contains profoundly racist elements remaining from three centuries of overt racism. . . .

This "invisibility" of institutional subordination is even more striking concerning those forms which result from *geographic exclusion* of minority group members from all-white areas, or *perceptual distortion* in the way people see reality. Overt racism – both past and present – is the main cause of the spatial separation of where most whites live from where most nonwhite minorities live. The major form of such racism is deliberate discouragement of Negro and other nonwhite families from buying or renting homes in all-white neighborhoods. Such discouragement is systematically practiced by white realtors, renting agents, landlords, and homeowners. This clearly racist behavior has become so well entrenched that many minority group members no longer even try to find homes in all-white areas because they fear they will "get the run-around" or receive hostile treatment from at least some neighbors. So the pattern of exclusion is continued – in spite of recent laws and court decisions to the contrary.

Yet dozens of other forms of institutional subordination are indirectly caused by the absence of nonwhites from white residential areas. For example, most new jobs are being created in suburban shopping centers, industrial parks, new office buildings, and schools or universities. But American suburban areas are overwhelmingly white in population (about 95 percent in 1966). So the suburban sources of new employment are usually far from where nonwhites live. . . . Even if they do get jobs in the suburbs, they have great difficulty in finding housing near their work. This difficulty does not result only from overt racism: it is also caused by zoning laws which deliberately discourage any housing serving relatively lower-income groups, or local actions which prevent use of Federal subsidies for such housing. Such laws are usually defended on grounds of "maintaining high community standards" of housing and open space, or protecting the existing residents from tax increases that would be caused by building more schools to serve new low-income residents.

All these conditions discourage minority group members from even trying to get suburban jobs. This perpetuates their exclusion from all-white suburban areas. Yet many of the best quality schools, housing developments, recreational facilities, and general residential environments are found in the suburbs. So most minority group members find themselves cut off not only from the fastest growing sources of new jobs, but also from many of the best amenities in American society. This is clearly racism or "institutional subordination."

. . . invisibility of institutional subordination occurs in part because minority group members themselves are "invisible" in the normal lives of most white Americans – especially white children. Most white children are brought up in neighborhoods where Negroes, Mexican Americans, and other nonwhite persons are totally absent, or constitute an extremely small minority – usually engaged in menial jobs. These children form an unconscious but deeply rooted mental image of "normal" society as consisting only of white people, and of all colored persons as "strange" and "different" from "normal people." This image is further reinforced by the world they see on television. . . .

. . . this perception of whites as the only "normal Americans" was further reinforced for more than 100 years by the elementary and other textbooks used in almost all American schools. The exclusion of minority group members from such texts is one more way in which millions of Americans were – and still are – made both "invisible" and "strange" in the minds of the white majority.

Note

1. The terms colored and nonwhite refer to Negroes, Puerto Ricans, Mexican Americans, Japanese Americans, Chinese Americans, and American Indians because this is how most whites really view and identify them.

Source: The U.S. Commission on Civil Rights, *Racism in America and How to Combat It*, Clearing House Publication, Urban Series No. 1 (Washington: Government Printing Office, January 1970), pp. 6-11 *passim*. The report was prepared by Dr. Anthony Downs.

Theoretical Perspectives

11.1 Robert Ezra Park on Race Relations

Robert Ezra Park wrote extensively about the nature and origins of racial and other group relations, emphasising the effects of competition for scarce resources. Both these excerpts from his writings were published on the eve of major conflicts between European nations, and show a consciousness of the competitive activities of European groups both within and outside their continent. The second excerpt is particularly concerned with the effects of the ending of slavery on subsequent black progress in the United States.

(a) The nature of race relations (1939)

The races of mankind seem to have had their own origin at a time when man, like all other living creatures, lived in immediate dependence upon the natural resources of his habitat. Under pressure of the food quest, man, like the other animals, was constantly urged to roam farther afield in search of (1) a more abundant food supply and (2) of some niche or coign of vantage where life was relatively secure. This was the period of what one may describe as "the great dispersion."

The first movements of mankind seem, therefore, to have been like the migrations of plants and animals, centrifugal. It was as if they were engaged in a general recognizance and exploration in order to spy out the land and discover the places where the different species might safely settle. It was, presumably, in the security of these widely dispersed niches that man developed, by natural selection and inbreeding, those special physical and cultural traits that characterize the different racial stocks.

The process of dispersion still continues, and no permanent biotic equilibrium is yet in sight. As a matter of fact, the dispersion of living organisms, including human beings, is taking place today as a result of the multiplication of new means of transportation, more rapidly than ever before. However, the consequences, so far as they concern human beings at least, are profoundly different now from what they were at earlier stages in the historical process. As populations have increased and man – having learned to subjugate and domesticate not merely other animals but other men – has become the dominant species, his dependence upon cultural, as distinguished from natural, resources has vastly increased. One consequence of this is that human migrations have taken a different direction. The movements of peoples that had been centrifugal, away from the centers of population, have long since begun to take the opposite direction, and have become, particularly in recent times, centripetal, i.e., toward the cities. Settled villages have taken the place of nomadic tribes, and villages have become more and more dependent upon, or superseded by, urban and metropolitan communities. The result of this is that man is no longer so immediately dependent, as he once was, upon the natural resources of his habitat but has become increasingly dependent upon society. For the same reason the condition of isolation in which the different races slowly accumulated and funded, so to speak, their different racial and cultural traits, no longer exists, certainly not to the extent that it once did.

Evidence of this is the increasing in hybridization of peoples which seems everywhere to be the inevitable consequence of racial contact.

"The degree of ethnical purity of a human race," says Pittard, "is first and foremost a function of its geographical isolation. An unmixed stock is assured to a human group by the very difficulty it experiences in leaving its natural environment or, and this comes to the same thing, the difficulty any other group experiences in approaching it." [4]

On the other hand, he continues, "primitive races became mixed from the time that the wanderings of humanity over the continents became intensive," In fact, the mingling of races has increased progressively from that time to the present day so that it is impossible, as far as Europe is concerned, to speak of pure races. "In Europe the Lapps and the Samoyeds," says Pittard, "are better protected by their geographical position from admixture, than others. However, the Lapps have very largely mixed with the Scandinavians and the Samoyeds with Russians." [5]

If it is true that the different races, like the different species, came into existence under conditions imposed by their dispersion, it is likewise true that civilization, if not society, is a product of the city. In the city peoples of diverse races and cultures come together not to participate in and perpetuate a common life as is the case of a family, kinship group, or a religious sect, but as individuals who have discovered that they are useful to one another. Society and the moral order indubitably have had their origin in the family, but civilization has grown up around the market place and has expanded with the expansion of the market.

Sumner suggests that we should conceive primitive society as composed of little ethnic and ethnocentric groups scattered over a territory – a territory with no very clearly defined limits. Within this territory every ethnic or tribal unit lives with every other in a state of potential, if not actual, warfare. Under these conditions one may expect to find peace, order, and security within the family or tribe, or as Sumner describes it, the "in-group". On the other hand, the permanence of this peace, security, and solidarity within is more or less determined by the degree or imminence of conflict without. The "in-group" and the "out-group" are to be conceived, therefore, as in a relation like that of compensating or countervailing forces. The sentiments with which these groups regard one another reflect the moral isolation in which they live, and they define, in so far as races rather than mere tribal units are involved, the racial situation.

Ethnocentrism, as Sumner explains, "is the technical name for this view of things in which one's own group is the center of everything, and all others are scaled and rated with reference to it." [6] Under such circumstances the members of every little society or ethnic group tend to regard the members of every other as somewhat less human than themselves. People living in tribal isolation think of themselves as "men" or "human beings." All others they are likely to regard, as they do the trees in the forest, or the animals who inhabit it, as part of the flora and fauna. As such they may appear interesting or quaint, but such interest is always qualified by the fact that one cannot tell what those "foreign devils," to use a term with which the Chinese have made us familiar, will do next.

This does not mean, of course, that in primitive society the stranger and the alien may be welcomed if they come endowed with a certain amount of prestige. When Captain Cook made his first visit to the Hawaiian Islands he was received by the natives with divine honors. But that did not prevent his being killed and, it is suspected, ceremonially eaten, when the natives discovered later that he was not wholly immune to attack by the weapons of ordinary mortals.

All this indicates that primitive peoples have lived, and to an extent which it is difficult for most of us to comprehend, still do live in an isolation which I have described as "moral." By moral in this sense I mean a relation which exists only when, and in so far as, one individual recognizes another as human like himself. Physical distances which separate races and peoples are important socially only as they serve to maintain social distances. Social distance is measured by the degree of intimacy and understanding which individuals or social groups have anywhere achieved.

Primitive society, so far as it is organized on the basis of the kinship group, survives only to the extent to which it is able to maintain and transmit a tradition of solidarity and interdependence which has grown up in the intimate association of primary groups and is maintained by custom and tradition. In a civic society, in which kinship has been replaced by citizenship, relations are more formal and not so binding.[7]

* * *

Preliterate peoples do not, however, live in complete isolation, and the routine of their tribal life has not infrequently – until Europe imposed its peace upon them – been interrupted by the alarms of tribal wars as well as the milder excitements of intertribal trade. With the increase of commerce and communication, however, a form of association eventually came into existence of a sort very different from anything primitive man had hitherto known. The new and more inclusive social unit which emerged included all the peoples within a territory of which the market place was the center. For this reason and for others it tended to assume, with the growth of permanent settlement, the character of a territorial, as distinguished from the familial, organization, such as its characteristic of primitive and particularly nomadic peoples. Such a society, held together in unstable equilibrium by a process of competitive co-operation, is obviously of a very different sort from the little genetic and ethnocentric societies of which it is composed. It is a type of association that is fundamentally economic in the sense in which plant and animal ecologists use that term.[8]

The thing that most definitely characterizes it is, perhaps, the absence of that mystic sense of solidarity which, at certain times and seasons, unites the members of a family, a clan, or religious sect into a consensus so intimate that it can be felt but hardly analyzed. I mention the religious sect in this connection because of all forms of a society, not genetic in origin, it seems to be one that more nearly conforms to the organization of the clan and tribe. It is an interesting fact in this connection that, in the breakup of primitive societies under the impact of European civilization, a mission station of some religious society, with its little community of converts – or if not the mission then some newly organized sect – has frequently performed functions that had formerly been performed by the class or tribe. In a religious community, it seems, the detribalized native feels himself at home once more – perhaps more than ever before – in a world in which he had been otherwise quite lost.[9]

The conditions under which men buy and sell, have undoubtedly had a profound influence on human relations and upon human nature. Not all that is characteristically human is the product, as Cooley seems to say, of man's relations in the primary group.[10] Men go to market and women too, not as they go to church, namely, to revive a sense of their social solidarity and of their participation in common destiny. One meets at the market place, not friends merely, but strangers, possibly enemies. They have all, each motivated by interests presumably personal to himself, come together because they need one another and because, by an exchange of goods and services, they hope not only to satisfy their own needs but also profit by the needs of others. Besides, the market place, aside from the mere social excitement of being a member of the crowd, offers the prospect of hearing the latest news, and that is always an interest that is as intriguing to primitive as to more sophisticated peoples. There is, also, the consideration that in the market one may have, among strangers, a better chance to drive a bargain since it is always difficult to bargain with friends and relatives. On the other hand, it is notoriously easy and interesting to trade with strangers. It is even possible, under certain circumstances, to carry on a rather brisk trade with the enemy.

The familiar rule of the market place, *caveat emptor,* "Let the purchaser beware," is an indication of what was, and still is, the normal relation between buyer and seller. The situation in which men bargain and chaffer is psychologically complex and tricky, and for that reason, perhaps the capacity to trade is one of the last of the fundamental human traits that mankind has acquired. Among the many definitions of man that seek to identify him with, but at the same time distinguish him from, the other animals is that which describes him as a trading animal. Man is the only animal that has learned to dicker and trade.[11] But trade is necessarily a complex affair since it requires that one know, at the same instant, both his own mind and that of the other party. Each must understand the need of the other in order that each may make for himself the best bargain. This is inevitably the case because in this unique form of co-operation one man's necessity is another man's opportunity. But at the same time one does not wish to know the other party and his necessity too well either. One must, if possible, remain objective. It is for this reason, among others, that trade has so frequently gotten into the hands of foreigners.[12] It is easier to be objective if one maintain the normal distances. Detachment is the secret of the academic attitude.

It was around the market place that cities originally grew up. When city states first came into existence in Egypt and Asia Minor, later in Greece, they seem to have been at first and in many instances little more than market places with walls around them. The market, with the industries that grew up about it, may have been there first and the place later fortified, or a market may have grown up under the protection of a citadel.[13]

City states came into existence, not always perhaps, but often, when some nomadic chieftain with his tribal followers invaded and conquered a settled and sedentary population. In that case he made the market place the seat of a totalitarian government. Every city as it became a center of political power acquired its local deity, just as among more primitive peoples every clan had its totem. It was at once the emblem of its authority and the symbol of its solidarity.

"The war-like character of the nomads," says Friedrich Ratzel, "is a great factor in the creation of states. It finds expression in the immense nations of Asia controlled by nomad dynasties and nomad armies, such as Persia, ruled by the Turks; China, conquered and governed by the Mongols and Manchus; and in the Mongol and Radjaputa states of India, as well as in the states on the border of the Soudan. . . Their importance lies in the capacity of the nomads to hold together the sedentary races who otherwise would easily fall apart. This, however, does not exclude their learning much from their subjects. . . . Yet all these industrious and clever folk did not have and could not have the will and the power to rule, the military spirit, and the sense for the order and subordination that befits a state. For this reason, the desert-born lords of the Soudan rule over their Negro folk just as the Manchus rule their Chinese subjects."[14]

The rise of the city state gave a new direction to the historical process which profoundly affected and presently transformed tribal and racial relations. The first consequence was to change a relationship between ethnic groups, which had been territorial – modified and mitigated to be sure by commerce and politics, that is to say, intertribal war and peace – into a relationship of dominance and subjection, a relationship which eventually assumed the hierarchical form of caste and class organization. The second consequence was to hasten the process of ethnic amalgamation which, up to that point, had taken place mainly, but not wholly, by the incorporation of the women and children of the conquered tribes into the tribal organizations of the conquerors.

It was inevitable, perhaps, that a state based on conquest should seek to extend its boundaries so as to include more territory and more peoples. But there were always limits to territorial expansion, and as the city state approached these limits, the possibility and the necessity for amalgamation disappeared with the necessity for conquest. With peace, society tended to crystallize, and the form which it invariably took, particularly in a society based on conquest rather than trade, was that of a caste and class system. As a matter of course, there was, particularly at first, a certain amount of miscegenation between the different castes, but caste distinctions were still based on ethnic differences. In short, the contrast and conflict of ethnic groups were still the basis of the new social and political, as they were earlier of the tribal, society. But race consciousness and race conflict were in process of supersession by class consciousness and class conflict.

The existence of a permanent caste system in India seems to have had its origin in the obvious diversity of racial types in the Indian population. It was a well-organized fact that visibility is an important factor in maintaining social distances and incidentally making class distinction hereditary. It is notable in this connection that while domestic slavery has always, apparently, existed in China where racial differences in the population are slight, there has never been anything that could be described as caste among Chinese people, although the relation between the Hakka and Punti peoples in South China tends to assume that character. In China, also, where feudalism disappeared relatively early, social classes were not closed and social status was not based on inheritance. In Japan, on the other hand, where society is notoriously more regimental than elsewhere in the Orient, there still exists, in spite of efforts to ameliorate their condition, an outcaste group called the Eta, which in origin seems to have been foreign although it has been recruited from all classes, even from the Samurai at times when these knightly warriors sought oblivion, because for some reason, perhaps as a consequence of defeat in battle, they had lost caste.

* * *

In the modern world, and particularly outside of Europe, wherever race relations – or what, in view of the steadily increasing race mixture, we have called race relations – have assumed a character that could be described as problematic, such problems have invariably arisen in response to the expansion of European peoples and European civilization.

In the period of four hundred years and more since Vasco da Gama rounded the Cape of Good Hope and Columbus landed at San Salvador, European discoveries and European enterprise have penetrated to the most remote regions of the earth. There is nowhere now, it seems – either in the jungles of the Malayan peninsula or the remote islands of New Guinea – a primitive people that has not, directly or indirectly, come under the influence of European peoples and European culture.[22]

The growth of European population is, among other evidences of European expansion, the one that is perhaps least obvious. However, the growth and decline of populations are basic to every other form of social or cultural change.

Between 1800 and 1930 the population of Europe increased from 180,000,000 to 480,000,000, and the number of individuals of European origin overseas amounts at the present to 160,000,000. During this period, and indirectly as a result of this emigration of European peoples, a corresponding movement of African and Asiatic peoples has been in progress. The number of people of African origin in the New World, that is, in North America, the West Indies, and South America, is at the present time, as near as can be estimated 37,000,000. Of this number, something over 12,000,000 are in the United States and Canada; 8,148,000 are in Bermuda, Central America, and the West Indies; 14,200,000, including, according to the best estimates, 8,800,000 mulattoes, are in Brazil. The remainder, 2,400,000, are in South America.

Meanwhile oriental peoples, mainly Chinese and East Indians, in response to the demands for crude labor to do the rough work on Europe's advancing frontier, have been imported into almost every part of the world outside of Europe. There are settlements of both Hindus and Chinese in the West Indies, in Australia, South and East Africa, and the islands of the Pacific, particularly the Dutch East Indies, the Philippines, and the Hawaiian Islands. They are employed mainly, but not wholly, in plantation agriculture. They are imported to work in the gold mines. There are Chinese in Cuba, in Jamaica, and British Guiana. They were imported in the first instance to replace Negroes on the sugar plantations after emancipation. There are Japanese in Brazil as in the United States. They were brought to Brazil to work in the coffee plantations in São Paulo and to the United States to work in the fruit and vegetable gardens of the Pacific coast.

The number of Chinese, Indians, and Japanese who have gone abroad and are now living outside of their native states has been estimated at 16,084,371. There is in South Africa a Chinese community in the Transvaal and an Indian community in

Natal. The Chinese were imported as laborers to work in the Rand gold mines; the Indians, to work on sugar plantations in Natal. In the West Indies, Indians and Chinese took the places, after emancipation in 1834, of Negroes on the plantations. Japanese, who are more recent emigrants, have gone mainly to Hawaii and Brazil.

There are, at the present time, between 16,000,000 and 17,000,000 people of Asiatic origin living in the diaspora, if I may use that term to designate not merely the condition but the place of dispersion of peoples.[23]

Of the Orientals in this diaspora, 10,000,000, it is estimated, are Chinese, 2,125,000 are Indians, and 1,973,960 are Japanese. There are 1,900,000 Chinese in Siam; 1,800,00 in Malaya; 1,240,000 in the Dutch East Indies; 700,000 in Indo-China; 150,000 in Burma; 74,954 in the United States; 45,000 in Canada; and 4,090,046 in other parts of the world.

Of the 4,125,000 Indians abroad, 1,300,000 are in Burma; 628,000 in Malaya; 1,133,000 in Ceylon; 281,000 in the island of Mauritius; 278,00 are in South and East Africa; 133,277 are in the British island of Trinidad; 181,600 in British and Dutch Guiana; 76,000 are in the Fiji Islands; 6,101 in the United States and Canada; and 100,225 in other countries.

Of the 1,969,371 Japanese living outside Insular Japan; 1,351,383 are in Korea, the Island of Sakhalin, Manchuria, Formosa, or other parts of the world including China, which have become, or are in a process of incorporation in, the Japanese Empire. Of the remaining 617,988 Japanese abroad, 162,537 are in Brazil, and 297,651 are in the United States and Canada. Of the number of Japanese in the United States, 139,634 are in Hawaii.[24]

The Hawaiian Islands are occupied by what, from the point of race and cultural differences, is probably the most thoroughly scrambled community in the world. The census for the Hawaiian Islands, where, different from continental America, the population is classified by racial origin, recognizes twelve different racial categories, two of them hyphenated. They are: Hawaiian, Caucasian-Hawaiian, Asiatic-Hawaiian, Other Caucasian, Portuguese, Chinese, Japanese, Korean, Porto Rican, and Filipino. Among the laborers that have at various times been imported to perform the work on the plantations a considerable number were from Europe, among them Scandinavians, Germans, Galicians, Russians, Poles, Portuguese, and Spaniards.

Of the total population of 347,799 in Hawaii in 1930, 236,673, were Orientals, 562 were Negroes and 46,311 were hybrids. Of this 46,311 or 47,560 according to another and different calculation, 5,040 were persons who counted their ancestry in more than two races.[25] Commenting on the situation, one of these products of miscegenation, a very charming young lady, incidentally, remarked: “Mixed? Yes; I am a kind of league of nations in myself.”

I have conceived the emigration of European peoples and the emigration of extra-European peoples – since most, if not all, of these movements have taken place in direct and indirect response to conditions in Europe – as integral parts of a single mass migration. So considered, this is, undoubtedly, the most extensive and momentous movement of populations in history. Its consequences, likewise, have been in proportion to its numbers. Everywhere that European peoples – including their commerce and culture – have penetrated they have invariably disturbed the existing population balance; undermined the local economic organization; imposed upon native societies, sometimes a direct form of control, more often political and judicial processes which are strange to them, but processes which have, at any rate, more or less completely superseded those of the native and local authorities. The invaders have frequently, but not always, inoculated the native peoples with new and devastating diseases. They have invariably infected them with the contagious ferment of new and subversive ideas.

All this disorganization and demoralization seems to have come about, however, in the modern world as it did in the ancient, as an incident of ineluctable historical and cultural processes; the processes by which the integration of peoples and cultures have always and everywhere taken place, though not always and everywhere at a pace so rapid or on so grand a scale.

It is obvious that race relations and all that they imply are generally, and on the whole, the products of migration and conquest. This was true of the ancient world and it is equally true of the modern. The interracial adjustments that follow such migration and conquest are more complex than is ordinarily understood. They involve racial competition, conflict, accommodation, and eventually assimilation, but of a new social and cultural organism to achieve a new biotic and social equilibrium.

The fact that these adjustments involve different processes, each operating in relative independence of one another, suggests that one may conceive race relations as existing and assuming different forms at different levels of association. Thus the invasion by one race or one people of the territories occupied and settled by another involves first of all a struggle for mere existence, that is to say, a struggle to maintain a place on the land and in the habitat which has been invaded. This has often resulted in a catastrophic decline in the numbers and sometimes, as in the case of the Tasmanians, in the extinction of the native population, who seem to have been hunted like wild animals by the European immigrant as were, at one time, the Indians in the United States.[26] But disease is often more deadly to primitive people than war. The native population of Hawaii declined in the period from 1778 to 1875 from 300,000 or more to 55,347. Since that time the total population of the islands has increased, largely by the importation of Orientals to work on the plantations, until in 1930 it was 368,336, inclusive of military personnel.[27]

In other parts of the Pacific the native population has multiplied under European domination. The population of Java has increased in the centenary 1830 to 1930 from about 5,000,000 to 36,745,537.

The effects of infections and contagious diseases introduced by foreigners are the more devastating in the first years of the intercourse. Eventually some sort of biotic equilibrium is achieved, but racial competition on the biotic or ecological level continues, although its consequences are not so obvious. "Throughout human history," says S. J. Holmes, "stocks have continually been replaced, peacefully or otherwise, by their successful rivals. Even relatively stable populations represent but a temporary retardation in the general course of racial change. What is of greater importance than military prowess in the biological fortunes of peoples is the more obscure factors which affect the balance of births and deaths."[28] But any change in the conditions of life which affects the biotic or population balance is inevitably reflected at every other level on which race relations may be said to exist. This is particularly well illustrated in a recent analysis by S. J. Holmes of the vital statistics of the Negro in the United States. He has described his investigation as "A Study in Human Ecology." However, his estimate of the Negro's chances of survival in the American environment is, as he himself admits, necessarily inconclusive. It is inconclusive because there are factors to be reckoned with for which we have as yet no adequate statistical data.

"There are," he says, "four ways in which the racial struggle may conceivably work out:

1. We may all become black;
2. We may all become white;
3. Whites and blacks may fuse into a hybrid stock; or
4. We may become permanently biracial, either mingled together, or occupying different local areas.[29]

But this list does not include all the factors that one needs to take account of in making such a forecast as is here proposed. The Negro population, for example – and this is characteristic of almost every other population element in America – is sometimes slowly, sometimes rapidly, but continuously in motion, moving out of its original location and settlement into some other part of the country. There has been a very considerable concentration of Negro population in recent years in Northern cities. Nevertheless, the population is with every decade more widely dispersed. Associated with this dispersal is a tendency for Negroes, as for all other races, living in communities where they are a small or negligible minority, to intermarry and interbreed and so lose their racial identity. On the other hand, in the Black Belt where the Negro is, or has constituted, 50 per cent or more of the population, the Negro's complexion has not noticeably changed.

The migration and dispersion of Negroes involves new social contacts and new race relations. Negroes in every part of the country, even on the plantations in the Southern states, are now, as they were not formerly, in a competition with whites for jobs and places of relative security in the occupational organization of the community in which they live.

In one of its aspects this competition is not merely a struggle of the individual to find a place in the local economy, it is at the same time a struggle of a racial unit to discover a niche in which Negroes will enjoy relative security from competition with white competitors. This is the way in which the caste interest and caste organization, where it exists, cuts across the class interest and class organization. When, and to the extent that the Negro finds the niche into which he fits, or into which he has succeeded in accommodating himself, then the degree of this economic security will be registered in the balance of births and deaths.

Moving North, the Negro has become a factor in politics to an extent that was not permitted him in the South. The Northern migration and dispersion have given him opportunities for education which he did not have in the South. But the effect of education, and conspicuously the education of Negro women, has had a devastating effect upon the Negro birth rate. There is apparently no way in which a people can so effectively commit race suicide as by educating its women. At the present time colored women have more opportunities for education, and for higher education, than colored men.

The effect of education, especially higher education, in so far as it has increased the number of occupations, particularly in the professions to which Negroes have access, has brought into existence a Negro middle class, which fact has also had effects that will eventually be registered in the balance of Negro births and deaths. In proportion to the numbers of Negroes in the population, I might add, the number in the professions is much smaller than is normal for the population as a whole.[30]

The effects of education and dispersion in so far as they tend to increase the number of Negro occupations tend likewise to undermine the caste system. The consequence of this is, on the one hand, to diminish the distances between the races at the different class levels and, on the other, to transform the status of the Negro in the United States from that of a caste to that of a racial minority.[31]

It seems, then, that one may think of race relations as existing not only on different levels, that is (1) ecological, (2) economic (3) political, (4) personal and cultural, but one may think of these different levels as constituting a hierarchy of relations of such a nature that change upon any one level will invariably have repercussions, not immediately, but finally, upon every other.

* * *

There are, it seems, two distinct and opposite points of view from which it is possible to survey an historical movement, such as that referred to by historians as "The Expansion of Europe." From one point of view this movement appears as a progressive extension of European culture and domination in the world, accompanied by an increasing integration of, and intimacy with, the races and peoples within this imperium. The movement may, however, be viewed in a temporal perspective in which it presents itself as a succession of changes which have come about in connection with, and incidental to, the expansion and integration of a vast and new social organism, if it is permissible to apply that term to any or all of the typical forms of interdependence – ecological, economic, political, and cultural – which the European social and cultural complex has assumed in the course of its expansion. At any rate, the changes which have come about with the expansion of European dominance seem to have come about everywhere, though not everywhere at the same pace.

The earliest cultural and racial contacts seem to have arisen out of the necessities of trade and barter. At the outset this trade was likely to proceed very cautiously as in the case of the so-called "silent trade".[32]

There is always, it appears, something uncanny about people who are complete strangers, particularly when they arrive in great ships, or, as has recently happened in the New Guinea archipelago, in flying boats. However, as trade relations progress, everything foreign tends to acquire a certain prestige, partly because it is unfamiliar and exotic. Presently barter is superseded by something like commercial exploitation. Articles of foreign manufacture replace the native products because, being machine made, they are cheaper.

Trade relations are invariably succeeded, eventually if not immediately, by some form of political domination. This is made necessary in order to protect not merely trade but the trader. Political domination may, in the natural course, take forms as different as that represented, on the one hand, by "spheres of influence." At this point in the race relations cycle the foreign missionary is likely to make his appearance.

We ordinarily think of missionary societies, so far as their secular activities are concerned, as agencies for salving the wounds and mitigating the grievances which an unregulated commerce inevitably provokes. This conception is justified when one considers to what extent colonial or "missionary peoples," if I may use that term in a general and generic sense, have benefited by the schools, hospitals, and other welfare agencies which European missionary societies have established in every part of the world in which Europeans are now or have been dominant. But missions, in planting the seeds of a new and competing culture, in countries like India and China – that is, in countries which are now, or will be presently, involved in a struggle to emancipate themselves from European domination and tutelage – have sometimes intensified the confusion and raised new points of conflict. But that, too, is an inescapable incident of the historical process. As a matter of fact, the formal education begun in the missionary schools is carried on and completed by the informal education which native peoples inevitably receive on the plantations, in the factories, and the commercial establishments where they work within the limits of a European economic and social system, and under the direct supervision of European agents.

Thus every plantation in Java, the Philippines, or Hawaii, every factory, commercial organization or bank in Hong Kong, Calcutta, or Bombay, is a means of completing the education begun by the missionary schools, and incidentally of hastening the time when the native peoples will be able to dispense with the luxury of foreign tutors and foreign tutelage.

The final stage in European expansion is reached when Europe begins to export not goods but capital, capital first of all to finance mining operations, the tin mines of Billiton, in the Dutch East Indies, for example, or the rubber plantations in Sumatra and the Malay peninsula, and finally, to build factories to employ native laborers in the manufacture of commodities which are then sold not only in the colonies, but, as in the case of Japan, in Europe and in competition with European products.

This imposes upon European expansion the limit to which it has been steadily trending. The cycle is now complete. Communication, to be sure, is still expanding and acculturation continues, but the great migration is, apparently, ended. In a recent volume, entitled *An Island Community,* Andrew Lind describes this movement as it is reflected in the history of economic and race relations in the Hawaiian Islands.

Here we may see, as in a microcosm, within the compass of a territory smaller than Massachusetts and within a period of 160 years, the operation of processes which Oswald Spengler has described in cosmic proportions and in the grand style of a philosopher of history, in his *Decline of the West (Untergang des Abendlandes).*[33]

From a somewhat similar point of view Hermann Schneider has written a *History of World Civilization*. In this unique history – unique because it attempts to make history systematic – the civilization of Egypt, Babylon, Crete, Persia, Greece, and Rome, and the Jews are treated as individual organic units, each repeating with individual variations the same life cycle. It is Schneider's thesis that every civilization begins with migration, invasion, and conquest. There follows a period of miscegenation, in the course of which a new race is formed by the fusion of the invaders with the natives. After a period of internal conflict a class organization finally crystallizes, and then, in due course, a new culture arises which finds expression in a characteristic literature, philosophy, and technology. This process is repeated with the rise of each succeeding civilization, except that, in so far as each later civilization is able to appropriate and assimilate the inheritance transmitted to it from its predecessors, the latter represents an advance over the earlier. In this way progress is achieved. The transmission of a cultural heritage from an earlier to a later civilization is always problematic, never complete, and its advance, when achieved at all, is not a continuous and consistent as the popular conception of progress assumes.

One of the consequences of the European expansion that is not ordinarily taken into the reckoning is the appearance, in the wake of every European invasion, of a mixed blood population due in part to the intermarriage and interbreeding of Europeans with the native populations and in part to the mixture of races outside of Europe imported into the colonies to do the rough work on the plantations for which natives are not fitted.[34]

Hybrid peoples, particularly if they are the product of the interbreeding of stocks so physically divergent that the resulting hybrid can be readily distinguished from both parents, will ordinarily occupy a status somewhat below that of the colonizing European but above that of the native or pure blood. In this situation the half-caste tends to conform to the personality of the so-called "marginal man," that is to say, a man who is predestined to live in two cultures and two worlds. It is characteristic of marginal types that they are able to look with a certain degree of critical detachment upon the diverse worlds of their parents. At the same time they are likely to feel themselves not quite at home in either.[35] This is especially the case when, as has happened in Hawaii, the parents speak habitually each a different language, Chinese and Hawaiian for example. In that case the offspring will probably speak English. They will have, in short, no mother tongue.

Living, so to speak, on the margin of two races, the half-caste ordinarily functions either as a mediator or a buffer between the European and the Asiatic or African. In some cases, as for example in the West Indies, the man of mixed blood may, indirectly and quite unintentionally, assist in keeping the African of pure blood in subordination and by so doing make the position of the dominant European more secure. This happens when the man of mixed blood, representing a rising middle class, interposes himself between the European at the top and the man of pure blood at the bottom in such fashion that no man of pure blood can rise except in so far as he is accepted by the mulatto middle class or caste. This is, in a general way, the situation in India though the racial situation is complicated by the existence of a caste system – and a caste system maintained by religious as well as social sanctions. The caste system of the Hindu necessarily affects the status of every other ethnic or religious unit in India. The Anglo-Indians, being Christians, actually occupy a position in the Indian Empire comparable with that of the Parsis in Bombay. They are described in the report on which the new Indian constitution is based as a "community," although as employees of the state they are dispersed throughout the Empire.

In Brazil, where *métis,* or mixed bloods, are neither a class nor a caste but merely the advance guard of a population of African origin in process of assimilation, the mulatto seems to have no special social function. The situation in the United States, on the other hand, is profoundly different. Here, where every man with a tincture of the African in him is classed as Negro, and racial distinctions within the race have been pretty thoroughly abolished, the Negroes of mixed blood have made themselves protagonists of the American Negro minority. They have been likewise the most aggressive leaders of the race.[36]

* * *

One of the incidental consequences of European expansion that inevitably impresses the world traveler is the sudden rise along great ocean thoroughfares through which the currents of world commerce flow, of a succession of great metropolitan cities. Most of them are new cities and if they are not wholly European in character they all sport a European façade. The most outstanding of these cities, which circle the world like a girdle, are: San Francisco, Yokohama, Shanghai, Hong Kong, Colombo, Bombay, Marseilles, London, and New York. And then there is Johannesburg, one of the world's most interesting metropolitan cities, which has apparently strayed inland, but which, as the primary market for most of the world's gold, performs a distinctly metropolitan function. Aside, also, from the fact that Johannesburg is much like San Francisco in the early years of the Gold Rush, it is interesting from the point of view of race relations because in its gold mines some two hundred thousand tribal natives are getting their first lessons in European civilization.

The function of the great port cities in the new world economy is to facilitate the movement of raw materials and commodities from their sources in the interior through continental gateways, into the world market. Almost all the great and growing cities of the world are now located on this main street of the world.

Spengler has described these cities as the centers "in which the whole life of broad regions is collecting while the rest dries up." These are the places where "the type-true people, born of and grown on the soil," are being superseeded by "a new sort of nomad, cohering unstably in fluid masses, the parasitical city dweller, traditionless, utterly matter-of-fact, religionless, clever, unfruitful, deeply contemptuous of the countryman and especially that highest form of countryman, the country gentleman."[37]

If it is true that in the cosmopolitan life all that was characteristic of earlier and more provincial cultures is obviously losing its local characteristics and disappearing in a welter and mishmash of local cultures and that we are now living, most of us, in a world which, in comparison with the life-forms of a more mature and stable social order, is almost without form and wholly without distinction, it is nevertheless equally true that in these cities a new civilization, new peoples, the modern world, with new local varieties of culture, is visibly coming into existence.

One of the evidences of this is the sudden and widespread interest in nationalism and in local nationalities. The struggle of minor racial and language groups for some sort of independent and individual expression of their traditional and national lives, which began in Europe in the early part of the last century, has now spread, as if it was contagious, to every part of the world; every part of the world, at any rate, which has felt or still feels itself oppressed in its local, provincial autonomous life, or for any another reason, inferior in its international status.

It is interesting that this ambition of minority nationalities, if I may so describe them, to control and direct their own destinies, in accordance with their own tradition and sense of values, has not in the least diminished their interest in, or determination to possess and use, in their own interest, all the technical knowledge and all the technical devices upon which the dominance of Europe in the modern world seems to have been based.[38]

The present nationalist movement, associated as it is by the practical cessation of migration and the so-called "devolution" of missions, is evidence that we are at the end of one epoch in human and racial relations and at the beginning of another.

What then, finally, is the precise nature of race relations that distinguish them, in all the variety of conditions in which they arise, from other fundamental forms of human relations? It is the essence of race relations that they are the relations of strangers; of peoples who are associated primarily for secular and practical purposes; for the exchange of goods and services. They are otherwise the relations of people of diverse races and cultures who have been thrown together by the fortunes of war, and who, for any reason, have not been sufficiently knit together by intermarriage and interbreeding to constitute a single ethnic community, with all that it implies.

Obviously that does not imply as much in the modern world as it did in the ancient; it does not imply as much in the Occident as it does in the Orient, where society is still organized on the familial pattern. It possibly implies less in America, or parts of America where divorce is easy and people are not generally interested in genealogies, as it does in Europe.

Although people in America and the modern world are no longer bound and united as people once were by familial and tribal ties, we are, nevertheless, profoundly affected by sentiments of nationality, particularly where they have an ethnic and a cultural basis. Furthermore, national and cultural differences are often re-enforced by divergence of physical and racial traits. But racial differences would not maintain social distances to the extent they actually do if they were not symptoms of differences in custom, tradition, and religion, and of sentiments appropriate to them. Differences of race and custom mutually re-enforce one another, particularly when they are not broken up by intermarriage.[39]

Traditions and customs are ordinarily transmitted through the family and can be most effectively maintained by intermarrying, i.e., endogamous groups. Evidence of this is the fact that every religious society tends to assume the character of a caste or endogamous group in so far at least as it prohibits or discourages marriage outside of the church or the sect. The Catholic clergy are profoundly opposed to marriage outside of the church, and the Jews who are, perhaps, the most mixed of peoples, have only been able to preserve their tribal religion for three thousand years and more because by endogamy they converted a religious society into a racial minority.

It has become commonplace among students of anthropology that most of the traits which we attribute to the different historic races are, like language and a high-school education, acquired by each succeeding generation for itself, sometimes by painful experience and always by a more or less extended formal education. Nevertheless, it is likewise becoming more obvious to students of human nature and society that the things that one learns in the intimate association of the family are likely to be the more permanent and more profound in their effects upon one's character in determining the individual's conception of himself, his outlook on life, his relations to other people.

It is obvious that society, so far as it is founded on a familial or genetic basis is concerned – as a secular society based on commercial and political interest is not – with maintaining not merely a definite life program, but a manner, moral order, and style of life consistent with that conception.

All this implies that the family and religion, the home and the church, in spite of public schools and social welfare institutions of every sort, still have the major responsibility for directing the career of youth and transmitting that intimate personal and moral order in accordance with which individuals freely govern themselves. Where custom breaks down, order may still be maintained, not by custom but by the police.

The consequence of this is that where there are racial and cultural minorities, whether Jews, Negroes, Catholics or religious sects that do not intermarry, the conflicts ordinarily described as racial but which are mainly cultural, do everywhere tend to arise. They arise even in an equalitarian society, like our own where "all men are," in principle if not in fact, "born equal," and they arise perhaps more readily here than they do in a society based on caste, because in theory they should not arise.

The obvious source and origin of most, if not all of the cultural and racial conflicts which constitute our race problems, are, therefore, conflicts of the "we groups" and the "other groups," as Sumner calls them, groups which are, however, integral parts of a great cosmopolitan and a free society. They are the ineluctable conflicts between the "little world" of the family in its struggle to preserve its sacred heritage against the disintegrating consequences of contact with an impersonal "great world" of business and politics.

They are, in fact, individual instances of an irrepressible conflict between a society founded on kinship and a society founded on the market place; the conflict between the folk culture of the provinces and the civilization of the metropolis.

Looking at race relations in the long historical perspective, this modern world which seems destined to bring presently all the diverse and distant peoples of the earth together within the limits of a common culture and a common social order, strikes one as something not merely unique but milennial! Nevertheless, this new civilization is the product of essentially the same historical processes as those that preceded it. The same forces which brought about the diversity of races will inevitably bring about, in the long run, a diversity in the peoples in the modern world corresponding to that which we have seen in the old. It is likely, however, that these diversities will be based in the future less on inheritance and race and rather more on culture and occupation. That means that race conflicts in the modern world, which is already or presently will be a single great society, will be more and more in the future confused with, and eventually superseded by, the conflicts of classes.

Notes

4. Eugène Pittard, *Race and History: An Ethnological Introduction to History* (New York: Alfred A. Knopf, 1926), p.17

5. The conditions under which racial purity is maintained have been briefly summarized in a paragraph by Pittard: "The isolation of high valleys, great poverty (bad economic conditions have never attracted strangers from without), religious fanaticism and extreme conservatism in the matter of ancestral customs, all conduce to a fierce hostility to anything new; still other reasons may explain the comparative lack of mixed blood in certain districts. In such conditions of ethnical preservation we have the chance of finding a considerable percentage of individuals of the same type. Many European countries can still show smaller or larger groups of this kind today, relatively well preserved. We can count on a similar percentage in still another set of circumstances, as when the primitive 'human kingdom' finds itself situated far from the beaten tract – Scandinavia, for example – and when, in addition, the conditions of existence offered by this 'kingdom' are very poor. Consequently its more favored neighbours did not seek to fall upon it. If a high birthrate increased its population unduly, portions of it would swarm from the hive and settle elsewhere; the groups that remained behind, being almost undisturbed by foreign elements, were able, like an untroubled spring, to maintain their primitive purity. The anthropological map of Scandinavia is of almost uniform tint. Furthermore, all the other reasons for preservation already indicated – or some of them – can add their quota to this geographical cause for homogeneity." Pittard, *op. cit.*, p. 18.

6. William Graham Sumner, *Folkways* (Boston: Ginn and Co., 1906) p. 13.

7. So-called primitive societies resemble the most perfect animal societies in the rigidity of their organization. Quoting a recent writer, an author adds, "The individual from the moment of his birth is the prisoner of the group to which he belongs, which imposes upon him its customs, its beliefs, its manner of life, which obliges him to take a wife from a specific circle. The solidarity of members of this group extends to every domain." It involves, he continues, the responsibility of all for the faults of one of their number, the responsibility of descendants for the faults of their ancestors. Property has a social character. The rites, in which all collaborate, aim at ensuring the prosperity of the group. The social bond is indurated, and life, as it were, mechanized within the narrow sheath of institutions. Not only the activity of individuals, but their very thought is subject to social constraint – no less than to the burden of heredity. Henri Berr in the Forward to *From Tribe to Empire: Social Organization among Primitives and in the Ancient East*, by A. Moret and G. Davy (New York: Alfred A. Knopf, 1926,) pp. xiii-xiv.

8. "In every habitat we find that there is a sort of community or society of organisms not only preying upon but depending upon each other, and that certain balance, though often a

violently swaying balance, is maintained between the various species so that the community *keeps* on . . . The particular name given to this subject of vital balances and interchanges is called Ecology. Ecology is a term coined by Haeckel, the celebrated German biologist, in 1878; its root is the Greek olkos, a house, which is also the root of the kindred older word economics. Economics is used only for human affairs; ecology is really an extension of economics to the whole world of life" (H. G. Wells, Julian S. Huxley, and G. P. Wells, *The Science of Life*, New York, 1931, III, 961).

9. The government of South Africa a few years ago registered the names of no less than 206 native separatist churches. All of them were organized by detribalized natives. See J. Merle Davis, *Modern Industry and the African* (London, 1933), Appendix E.

10. Charles H. Cooley, *Human Nature and the Social Order* (New York, 1902)

11. See Edward Westermarck, *History of Human Marriage* (3d ed., London, 1901), p.400.

12. See Gustave Glotz, *Ancient Greece at Work* (New York: Alfred A. Knopf, 1926), pp.170-177.

13. "The agora, the town market, was originally a neutral, sacred ground where the members of different gene met for peaceful transactions such as exchange and arbitration. When the sovereignty of the city was extended over a larger territory there were 'border agoras', protected against violence by religious laws" (*ibid.*, p.113).

14. Friedrich Ratzel, *Völkerkunde* (2d ed., Leipzig and Wien, 1894-95), p. 370. Quoted by Franz Oppenheimer, *The State*, trans. John M. Gitterman (Indianapolis, 1914), pp. 54-55.

22. The situation seems to have brought about something approaching an anthropological crisis. Since there are now, or soon will be, no living examples of primitive peoples to investigate, anthropologists seem to have arrived at a crossroads with the following result: One school of thought is directing its attention more exclusively to antiquarian and prehistorical investigation, seeking to extend the limits of our knowledge of historical facts; another school is more particularly interested in the historical processes they observe going on about them in contemporary life – the processes of history in the making. But the processes of history, so far as they reveal the manner in which new societies and new civilizations have arisen on the ruins of their predecessors, are the processes by which new and more sophisticated types of personality have succeeded earlier and simpler types. Anthropology thus merges into sociology.

23. Diaspora is a Greek term for a nation or part of a nation separate from its own state or territory and dispersed among other nations but preserving its national culture. In a sense Magna Graecia constituted a Greek diaspora in the ancient Roman Empire, and a typical case of diaspora is presented by the Armenians, many of whom have voluntarily lived outside their small national territory for centuries. Generally, however, the term is used with reference to those parts of the Jewish people residing outside Palestine. It was used at first to describe the sections of Jewry scattered in the ancient Greco-Roman world and later to designate Jewish dispersion throughout the world in the twenty-five hundred years since the Babylonian captivity. Diaspora has its equivalents in the Hebrew words *galuth* (exile) and *golah* (the exiled), which, since the Babylonian captivity, have been used to describe the dispersion of Jewry, *Encyclopedia of the Social Sciences*, V, 126-127.

24. Radhakamal Mukerjee, Migrant Asia (Roma, 1936), Appendix A. The figures for the Japanese in the United States and Brazil have been corrected in accordance with more recent figures.

25. Romanzo Adams, *Interracial Marriage in Hawaii* (New York, 1937), pp. 12-20. See also Appendix C, pp, 334-345, for data relating to interracial marriages.

26. During the Indian wars in the United States bounties were frequently offered for Indian scalps to encourage settlers and frontier men to kill Indians as they would be encouraged to kill wolves and other pests. In a note in the volume, *Alien Americans* (New York: The Viking Press, Inc., 1936), p.5, B. Schrieke states: "This method was introduced in 1641 by Wilhelmus Kieft, Dutch director-general of New Netherlands – presumably imitating a similar practice in the East Indies – and later on was adopted by the Puritans. It was, in a way, a money-saving expedient. If the frontier farmers could be encouraged to make offensive war against the Indians on a commission basis, fewer regular soldiers – paid and maintained by the government during long periods of inactivity – would be needed. The last American scalp bounty was offered by the Territory of Indiana in 1814 as an 'encouragement to the enterprise and bravery of our fellow citizens.'"

27. Adams, *op. cit.*, pp. 1-12. Also George H. Pitt-Rivers, *The Clash of Cultures and the Contact of Races in the Pacific* (London, 1927).

28. S. J. Holmes, *The Negro's Struggle for Survival: A Study in Human Ecology* (Berkeley: University of California Press, 1937), p.2.

29. *Ibid.*, p.2.

30. Charles S. Johnson, *The Negro College Graduate* (Chapel Hill, 1938).

31. Bertram W. Doyle, *The Etiquette of Race Relations in the South* (Chicago, 1937), Introduction, p. xxii.

32. This area (the Congo forest) "is famous for the development of 'silent trading' between the pygmies and the Negroes. Many pygmy groups are tacitly attached to a Negro village and have an understanding for the barter of game for agricultural crops. After a successful hunt the negritoes enter the banana groves of the villagers, gather fruit, and hang suitable meat in its place; the villagers when needing game will also lay out agricultural produce in an accustomed place for the hunters, who will in due course bring to that place a portion of their bag." C. Daryll Forde, *Habitat, Economy and Society* (2d ed., New York: Harcourt, Brace and Co., 1937), p.23. See also Sir P. J. H. Grierson, *The Silent Trade* (Edinburgh, 1903).

33. From Spengler's point of view there is no such thing as civilization; there are only civilizations, each an organism unique and individual, limited in its possibilities, and expressing itself in a characteristic rhythm, form, and duration. "I see," he says, "in place of that empty figment of *one* linear history which can only be kept up by shutting one's eyes to the overwhelming multitude of the facts, the drama of a *number* of mighty Cultures, each springing with primitive strength from the soil of a mother-region to which it remains firmly bound throughout its whole life-cycle; each stamping its material, its mankind, in *its own* image; each having *its own* idea, *its own* passions, *its own* life, will and feeling, *its own* depth," Oswald Spengler, *The Decline of the West* (New York: Alfred A. Knopf, 1926), I, 21.

34. No attempt has been made to estimate the number of persons in the world who are today reckoned as "mixed bloods". As a matter of fact, unless the races which interbreed are sufficiently different in respect to those traits by which we ordinarily distinguish races, no mixed or half-caste arises. Thus if a Jew marries a Christian, their offspring become either Jews or Gentiles. The individual may, to be sure, be reckoned as a part-Jew and part-Gentile, but there is no part-Jew-part-Gentile class or caste. The opposite is the case with an African or an Asiatic who is born of mixed parentage.

    However the number of persons who are of recognized racial origin, but are not sufficiently amalgamated to constitute them as distinct racial varieties, is considerable.

There were in the United States 1,660,554 persons reckoned as mulattoes in 1920. The Cape Coloured, mainly mixed Hottentots and Dutch, numbered 545,548 in 1930. The Eurasians of India, or Anglo-Indians, as they prefer to call themselves, numbered in 1921, 113,090. In Brazil "persons of color", that is, persons recognized as of mixed Negro-white origin, numbered 8,800,000. Forty-three per cent of the population is of mixed Indian and European origin. In Java the Indo-Europeans, or Eurasians, numbered 290,408.

If we add to the numbers of those who are recognized as of mixed racial origin those who have been or could properly be classed as "racial and cultural minorities", that is, those who, because of racial or language differences, have not been wholly assimilated or regard themselves in any sense as alien in the country in which they live, we should know how extensive the diaspora – that is to say, the region in which peoples live more or less as strangers, the region in which race relations may be said to exist – actually is.

35. Everett V. Stonequist, *The Marginal Man* (New York, 1937).

36. Alfred Holt Stone, *Studies in the American Race Problem* (New York, 1908), chap, ix, "The Mulatto Factor in the Race Problem," pp. 425-439. See also Robert E. Park, "Mentality of Racial Hybrids," *American Journal of Sociology*, XXXVI, 534-551 (Jan., 1931)

37. Spengler, *op. cit.*, I, 32.

38. The only instance of an outstanding personality in the modern world who has opposed this tendency to appropriate European technology is Mr. Gandhi, of India, who in other respects seems to be the most modern of moderns. He advised the Indian people to go back to the spinning wheel rather than forward to the factory. See René Fulop-Miller, *Lenin and Gandhi* (London, 1927), p. 289.

39. See Romanzo Adams, *op. cit.*

(b) Racial assimilation in secondary groups (1913)

Assimilation, as the word is here used, brings with it a certain borrowed significance which it carried out from physiology where it is employed to describe the process of nutrition. By a process of nutrition, somewhat similar to the physiological one, we may conceive alien peoples to be incorporated with, and made part of, the community or state. Ordinarily assimilation goes on silently and unconsciously, and only forces itself into popular conscience when there is some interruption or disturbance of the process.

At the outset it may be said, then, that assimilation rarely becomes a problem except in secondary groups. Admission to the primary group, that is to say, the group in which relationships are direct and personal, as, for example, in the family and in the tribe, makes assimilation comparatively easy, and almost inevitable.

The most striking illustration of this is the fact of domestic slavery. Slavery has been, historically, the usual method by which peoples have been incorporated into alien groups. When a member of an alien race is adopted into the family as a servant, or as a slave, and particularly when that status is made hereditary, as it was in the case of the Negro after his importation to America, assimilation followed rapidly and as a matter of course.

It is difficult to conceive two races farther removed from each other in temperament and tradition than the Anglo-Saxon and the Negro, and yet the Negro in the southern states, particularly where he was adopted into the household as a family servant, learned in a comparatively short time the manners and customs of his master's family. He very soon possessed himself of so much of the language, religion, and the technique of the civilization of his master as, in his station, he was fitted or permitted to acquire. Eventually, also, Negro slaves transferred their allegiance to the state, of which they were only indirectly members, or at least to their masters' families, with whom they felt themselves in most things one in sentiment and interest.

The assimilation of the Negro field hand, where the contact of the slave with his master and his master's family was less intimate, was naturally less complete. On the large plantations, where an overseer stood between the master and the majority of his slaves, and especially on the Sea Island plantations off the coast of South Carolina, where the master and his family were likely to be merely winter visitors, this distance between master and slave was greatly increased. The consequence is that the Negroes in these regions are less touched today by the white man's influence and civilization than elsewhere in the southern states. The size of the plantation, the density of the slave population, and the extent and character of the isolation in which the master and his slave lived are factors to be reckoned with in estimating the influence which the plantation exerted on the Negro. In Virginia the average slave population on the plantation has been estimated at about ten. On the Sea Islands and farther south it was thirty; and in Jamaica it was two hundred.[5]

As might be expected there were class distinctions among the slaves as among the whites, and these class distinctions were more rigidly enforced on the large plantations than on the smaller ones. In Jamaica, for example, it was customary to employ the mulattoes in the lighter and the more desirable occupations about the master's house. The mulattoes in that part of the country, more definitely than was true in the United States, constituted a separate caste midway between the white man and black. Under these conditions the assimilation of the masses of the Negro people took place more slowly and less completely in Jamaica than in the United States.

In Virginia and the border states, and in what was known as the Back Country, where the plantations were smaller and the relation of the races more intimate, slaves gained relatively more of the white man's civilization. The kindly relations of master and slave in Virginia are indicated by the number of free Negroes in that state. In 1860 one Negro in every eight was free and in one county in the Tidewater Region, the county of Nansemond, there were 2,473 Negroes and only 581 slaves. The differences in the Negro population which existed before the Civil War are still clearly marked today. They are so clearly marked, in fact, that an outline of the areas in which the different types of plantation existed before the War would furnish the basis for a map showing distinct cultural levels in the Negro population in the South today.

The first Negroes were imported into the United States in 1619. At the beginning of the nineteenth century there were 900,000 slaves in the United States. By 1860 that number had increased to nearly 4,000,000. At that time, it is safe to say, the great mass of the Negroes were no longer, in any true sense, an alien people. They were, of course, not citizens. They lived in the smaller world of the particular plantation to which they belonged. It might, perhaps, be more correct to say that they were less assimilated than domesticated.

In this respect, however, the situation of the Negro was not different from that of the Russian peasant, at least as late as 1860. The Russian noble and the Russian peasant were likely to be of the same ethnic stock, but mentally they were probably not much more alike than the Negro slave and his master. The noble and the peasant did not intermarry. The peasant lived in the little world of the *mir* or commune. He had his own customs and traditions. His life and thought moved in a smaller orbit and he knew nothing about the larger world which belonged exclusively to the noble. The relations between the serf and the proprietor of the estate to which he was attached were, perhaps, less familiar and less frank than those which existed between the Negro slave and his master. The attitude of the serf in the presence of the noble was more abject. Still, one could hardly say that the Russian peasant had not been assimilated, at least in the sense in which it has been decided to use that term in this paper.

A right understanding of conditions in the South before the War will make clear that the southern plantation was founded in the different temperaments, habits, and sentiments of the white man and the black. The discipline of the plantation puts its own impress upon, and largely formed the character of, both races. In the life of the plantation white and black were different but complementary, the one bred to the role of a slave and the other to that of master. This, of course, takes no account of the poor white man who was also formed by slavery, but rather as a by-product.

Where the conditions of slavery brought the two races, as it frequently did, into close and intimate contact, there grew up a mutual sympathy and understanding which frequently withstood not only the shock of the Civil War, but the political agitation and chicane which followed it in the southern states.

Speaking of the difference between the North and the South in its attitude toward the Negro, Booker T. Washington says: "It is the individual touch which holds the races together in the South, and it is this individual touch which is lacking to a large degree in the North."

No doubt kindly relations between individual members of the two races do exist in the South to an extent not known in the North. As a rule, it will be found that these kindly relations had their origin in slavery. The men who have given the tone to political discussion in southern states in recent years are men who did not own slaves. The men from the mountain districts of the South, whose sentiments found expression in a great antislavery document, like Hinton Helper's *Impending Crisis,* hated slavery with an intensity that was only equaled by their hatred for the Negro. It is the raucous note of the Hill Billy and the Red Neck that one hears in the public utterances of men like Senator Vardaman, of Mississippi, and Govenor Blease, of South Carolina.

* * *

The Civil War weakened but did not fully destroy the *modus vivendi* which slavery had established between the slave and his master. With emancipation the authority which had formerly been exercised by the master was transferred to the state, and Washington, D.C., began to assume in the mind of the freedman the position that formerly had been occupied by the "big house" on the plantation. The masses of the Negro people still maintained their habit of dependence, however, and after the first confusion of the change had passed, life went on, for most of them, much as it had before the War. As one old farmer explained, the only difference he could see was that in slavery he "was working for old Marster and now he was working for himself."

There was one difference between slavery and freedom, nevertheless, which was very real to the freedman. And this was the liberty to move. To move from one plantation to another in case he was discontented was one of the ways in which a freedman was able to realize his freedom and to make sure that he possessed it. This liberty to move meant a good deal more to the plantation Negro than one not acquainted with the situation in the South is likely to understand.

If there had been an abundance of labor in the South; if the situation had been such that the Negro laborer was seeking the opportunity to work, or such that the Negro tenant farmers were competing for the opportunity to get a place on the land, as is so frequently the case in Europe, the situation would have been fundamentally different from what it actually was. But the South was, and is today, what Nieboer called a country of "open," in contradistinction to a country of "closed" resources. In other words there is more land in the South than there is labor to till it. Land owners are driven to competing for laborers and tenants to work their plantations.

Owing to his ignorance of business matters and to a long-established habit of submission the Negro after emancipation was placed at a great disadvantage in his dealings with the white man. His right to move from one plantation to another became, therefore, the Negro tenants's method of enforcing consideration from the planter. He might not dispute the planter's accounts, because he was not capable of doing so, and it was unprofitable to attempt it, but if he felt aggrieved he could move.

This was the significance of the exodus in some of the southern states which took place about 1879, when 40,000 people left the plantations in the Black Belts of Louisiana and Mississippi and went to Kansas. The masses of the colored people were dissatisfied with the treatment they were receiving from the planters and made up their minds to move to "a free country", as they described it. At the same time it was the attempt of the planter to bound the Negro tenant who was in debt to him, to his place on the plantation, that gave rise to the system of peonage that still exists in a mitigated form in the South today.

When the Negro moved off the plantation upon which he was reared he severed the personal relations which bound him to his master's people. It was just at this point that the two races began to lose touch with each other. From this time on the relations of the black man and the white, which in slavery had been direct and personal, became every year, as the old associations were broken, more and more indirect and secondary. There lingers still the disposition on the part of the white man to treat every Negro familiarly, and the disposition on the part of every Negro to treat every white man respectfully. But these are habits which are gradually disappearing. The breaking down of the instincts and habits of servitude, and the acquisition, by the masses of the Negro people, of the instincts and habits of freedom have proceeded slowly but steadily. The reason the change seems to have gone on more rapidly in some cases than others is explained by the fact that at the time of emancipation 10 per cent of the Negroes in the United States were already free, and others, those who had worked in trades, many of whom had hired their own time from their masters, had become more or less adapted to the competitive conditions of free society.

One of the effects of the mobilization of the Negro has been to bring him into closer and more intimate contact with his own people. Common interests have drawn the blacks together, and caste sentiment has kept the black and white apart. The segregation of the races, which began as a spontaneous movement on the part of both, has been fostered by the policy of the dominant race. The agitation of the Reconstruction Period made the division between the races in politics absolute. Segregation and separation in other matters have gone on steadily ever since. The Negro at the present time has separate churches, schools, libraries, hospitals, Y.M.C.A. associations, and even separate towns. There are, perhaps, a half-dozen communities in the United States, every inhabitant of which is a Negro. Most of these so-called Negro towns are suburban villages; two of them, at any rate, are the centers of a considerable Negro farming population. In general it may be said that where the Negro schools, churches, and Y.M.C.A. associations are not separate they do not exist.

It is hard to estimate the ultimate effect of this isolation of the black man. One of the most important effects has been to establish a common interest among all the different colors and classes of the race. This sense of solidarity has grown up gradually with the organization of the Negro people. It is stronger in the South, where segregation is more complete, than it is in the North where, twenty years ago, it would have been safe to say it did not exist. Gradually, imperceptibly, within the larger world of the white man, a smaller world, the world of the black man, is silently taking form and shape.

Every advance in education and intelligence puts the Negro in possession of the technique of communication and organization of the white man, and so contributes to the extension and consolidation of the Negro world within the white.

The motive for this increasing solidarity is furnished by the increasing pressure, or perhaps I should say, by the increasing sensibility of Negroes to the pressure and the prejudice without. The sentiment of racial loyalty, which is a comparatively recent manifestation of the growing self-consciousness of the race, must be regarded as a response and "accommodation" to changing internal and external relations of the race. The sentiment which Negroes are beginning to call "race pride" does not exist to the same extent in the North as in the South, but an increasing disposition to enforce racial distinctions in the North, as in the South, is bringing it into existence.

One or two incidents in this connection are significant. A few years ago a man who is the head of the largest Negro publishing business in this country sent to Germany and had a number of Negro dolls manufactured according to specifications of his own. At the time this company was started Negro children were in the habit of playing with white dolls. There were already Negro dolls on the market, but they were for white children and represented the white man's conception of the Negro and not the Negro's ideal of himself. The new Negro doll was a mulatto with regular features slightly modified in favor of the conventional Negro type. It was a neat, prim, well-dressed, well-behaved, self-respecting doll. Later on, as I understand, there were other dolls, equally tidy and respectable in appearance, but in darker shades with Negro features a little more pronounced. The man who designed these dolls was perfectly clear in regard to the significance of the substitution that he was making. He said that he thought it was a good thing to let Negro girls become accustomed to dolls of their own color. He thought it important, as long as the races were to be segregated, that the dolls, which like other forms of art, are patterns and represent ideals, should be segregated also.

This substitution of the Negro model for the white is a very interesting and a very significant fact. It means that the Negro has begun to fashion his own ideals and in his own image rather than in that of the white man. It is also interesting to know that the Negro doll company has been a success and that these dolls are now widely sold in every part of the United States. Nothing exhibits more clearly the extent to which the Negro has become assimilated in slavery or the extent to which he has broken with the past in recent years than this episode of the Negro doll.

The incident is typical. It is an indication of the nature of tendencies and of forces that are stirring in the background of the Negro's mind, although they have not succeeded in forcing themselves, except in special instances, into clear consciousness.

In this same category must be reckoned the poetry of Paul Lawrence Dunbar, in whom, as William Dean Howells has said, the Negro "attained civilization." Before Paul Lawrence Dunbar, Negro literature had been either apologetic or self-assertive, but Dunbar "studied the Negro objectively." He represented him as he found him, not only without apology, but with an affectionate understanding and sympathy which one can have only for what is one's own. In Dunbar, Negro literature attained an ethnocentric point of view. Through the medium of his verses the ordinary shapes and forms of the Negro's life have taken on the color of his affections and sentiments and we see the black man, not as he looks, but as he feels and is.

It is a significant fact that a certain number of educated – or rather the so-called educated – Negroes were not at first disposed to accept at their full value either Dunbar's dialect verse or the familiar pictures of Negro life which are the symbols in which his poetry usually found expression. The explanation sometimes offered for the dialect poems was that "they were made to please white folk." The assumption seems to have been that if they have been written for Negroes it would have been impossible in his poetry to distinguish black people from white. This was a sentiment which was never shared by the masses of the people, who, upon the occasions when Dunbar recited to them, were fairly bowled over with amusement and delight because of the authenticity of the portraits he offered them. At the present time Dunbar is so far accepted as to have hundreds of imitators.

Literature and art have played a similar and perhaps more important role in the racial struggles of Europe than of America. One reason seems to be that racial conflicts, as they occur in secondary groups, are primarily sentimental and secondarily economic. Literature and art, when they are employed to give expression to racial sentiment and form to racial ideals, serve, along with other agencies, to mobilize the group and put the masses *en rapport* with their leaders and with each other. In such case art and literature are like silent drummers which summon into action the latent instincts and energies of the race.

These struggles, I might add, in which a submerged people seek to rise and make for themselves a place in a world occupied by superior and privileged races, are not less vital or less important because they are bloodless. They serve to stimulate ambitions and inspire ideals which years, perhaps, of subjection and subordination have suppressed. In fact, it seems as if it were through conflicts of this kind, rather than through war, that the minor peoples were destined to gain the moral concentration and discipline that fit them to share, on anything like equal terms, in the conscious life of the civilized world.

* * *

The progress of race adjustment in the southern states since the emancipation has, on the whole, run parallel with the nationalist movement in Europe. The so-called "nationalities" are, for the most part, Slavic peoples, fragments of the great Slavic race, that have attained national self-consciousness as a result of their struggle for freedom and air against their German conquerors. It is a significant face that the nationalist movement, as well as the "nationalities" that it has brought into existence, had its rise in that twilight zone, upon the eastern border of Germany and the western border of Russia, and is part of the century-long conflict, partly racial, partly cultural, of which this meeting-place of the East and West has been the scene.

Until the beginning of the last century the European peasant, like the Negro slave, bound as he was to the soil, lived in the little world of direct and personal relations, under what we may call a domestic régime. It was military necessity that first turned the attention of statesmen like Frederick the Great of Prussia to the welfare of the peasant. It was the overthrow of Prussia by Napoleon in 1807 that brought about his final emancipation in that country. In recent years it has been the international struggle for economic efficiency which has contributed most to mobilize the peasant and laboring classes in Europe.

As the peasant slowly emerged from serfdom he found himself a member of a depressed class, without education, political privileges, or capital. It was the struggle of this class for wider opportunity and better conditions of life that made most of the history of the previous century. Among the peoples in the racial borderland the effect of this struggle has been, on the whole, to substitute for a horizontal organization of society – in which the upper stratum, that is to say the wealthy or privileged class, was mainly of one race and the poorer and subject class was mainly of another – a vertical organization in which all classes of each racial group were united under the title of their respective nationalities. Thus organized, the nationalities represent, on the one hand, intractable minorities engaged in a ruthless partisan struggle for political privilege or economic advantage and, on the other, they represent cultural groups, each struggling to maintain a sentiment of loyalty to the distinctive traditions, language, and institutions of the race they represent.

This sketch of the racial situation in Europe is, of course, the barest abstraction and should not be accepted realistically. It is intended merely as an indication of similarities, in the broader outlines, of the motives that have produced nationalities in Europe and are making the Negro in America, as Booker Washington says, "a nation within a nation."

It may be said that there is one profound difference between the Negro and the European nationalities, namely, that the Negro has had his separateness and consequent race consciousness thrust upon him, because of his exclusion and forcible isolation from white society. The Slavic nationalities, on the contrary, have segregated themselves in order to escape assimilation and escape racial extinction in the larger cosmopolitan states.

The difference is, however, not so great as it seems. With the exception of the Poles, nationalistic sentiment may be said hardly to have existed fifty years ago. Forty years ago when German was the language of the educated classes, educated Bohemians were a little ashamed to speak their own language in public. Now nationalist sentiment is so strong that, where the Czech nationality has gained control, it has sought to wipe out every vestige of the German language. It has changed the names of streets, buildings, and public places. In the city of Prag, for example, all that formerly held German associations now fairly reeks with the sentiment of Bohemian nationality.

On the other hand, the masses of the Polish people cherished very little nationalist sentiment until after the Franco-Prussian War. The fact is that nationalist sentiment among the Slavs, like racial sentiment among the Negroes, has sprung up as the result of a struggle against privilege and discrimination based upon racial distinctions. The movement is not so far advanced among Negroes; sentiment is not so intense, and for several reasons probably never will be. One reason is that Negroes, in their struggle for equal opportunities, have the democratic sentiment of the country on their side.

From what has been said it seems fair to draw one conclusion, namely: under conditions of secondary contact, that is to say, conditions of individual liberty and individual competition, characteristic of modern civilization, depressed racial groups tend to assume the form of nationalities. A nationality, in this narrower sense, may be defined as the racial group which has attained self-consciousness, no matter whether it has at the same time gained political independence or not.

In societies organized along horizontal lines the disposition of individuals in the lower strata is to seek their models in the strata above them. Loyalty attaches to individuals, particularly to the upper classes, who furnish, in their persons and in their lives, the models for the masses of the people below them. Long after the nobility has lost every other social function connected with its vocation the ideals of the nobility have survived in our conception of the gentlemen, genteel manners and bearing – gentility.

The sentiment of the Negro slave was, in a certain sense, not merely loyalty to his master, but to the white race. Negroes of the older generations speak very frequently, with a sense of proprietorship, of "our white folk." This sentiment was not always confined to the ignorant masses. An educated colored man once explained to me "that we colored people always want our white folks to be superior." He was shocked when I showed no particular enthusiasm for that form of sentiment.

The fundamental significance of the nationalist movement must be sought in the effort of subject races, sometimes consciously, sometimes unconsciously, to substitute, for those supplied them by aliens, models based on their own racial individuality and embodying sentiments and ideals which spring naturally out of their own lives.

Note

5. Documentary History of American and Industrial Society, Vol. I, "Plantation and Frontier": Introduction, pp. 80-81.

Source: Robert Ezra Park, "The Nature of Race Relations", pp. 84-91 and 100-116; "Racial Assimilation in Secondary Groups", pp. 209-219. Reprinted with permission of The Free Press, a Division of Simon & Schuster from *Race and Culture. Essays in the Sociology of Contemporary Man*, by Robert Ezra Park and Everett C. Hughes.

11.2 John H. Dollard on Race Relations in the American South

John Dollard was identified with the "caste school of race relations" led by W. Lloyd Warner among others. He spent five months in the American South ("Southerntown"), experiencing and enquiring into the nature of race relations there, and produced a classic work of social psychology.

Caste has replaced slavery as a means of maintaining the essence of the old status order in the South.[2] By means of it racial animosity is held at a minimum.[3] Caste is often seen as a barrier to social contact or, at least, to some forms of social contact. It defines a superior and inferior group and regulates the behavior of the members of each group. In essence the caste idea seems to be a barrier to legitimate descent. A union of members of the two castes may not have a legitimate child. All such children are members of the lower caste and cannot be legitimated into the upper caste by the fact that they have an upper-caste father or mother. Caste in Southerntown is also a categorical barrier to sexual congress between upper-caste women and lower-caste men, within or without the married state. It does not result in such a barrier between upper-caste men and lower-caste women. In this it seems to be modeled on the patriarchal family with its possessive prerogatives of the male; it has a double standard of the same type. Nothing else seems absolute about the caste barrier. It does not totally exclude social contact and seems to have no other mark so distinctive as the marriage and sexual prohibition.

It is necessary to remind ourselves that American democratic mores are set in quite another current. They do not recognize barriers to legitimate descent or preferential rights to sex relationships. Democratic society guarantees equal opportunity to enjoy whatever goods and services society has to offer; there are no arbitrary limitations based on race or color. This is the sense in which northerners seem theoretical to southerners when the Negro is discussed. Northerners look at the Negro through the constitutional window; southerners look at him through the caste window. In the train of the barriers to legitimate descent and sexual contact come other limitations. The caste line works out also as an automatic block to social advancement for the Negro and this means that the highest prestige prizes are not accessible to him. For example, we bring millions of boys into the world who are in training as future presidents of the United States; no one expects, however, that Negro boys are really included. Their caste membership silently excludes them from such high hopes.

American caste is pinned not to cultural but to biological features – to color, features, hair form, and the like. This badge is categorical regardless of the social value of the individual. It is in this sense that caste is "undemocratic" since it accepts an arbitrary token as a means of barring Negroes from equal opportunity and equal recognition of social merit.[4] Negroid body form was at one time a mark of a Negro culture and is still to some degree a mark of an inferior assimilation of white culture; but both of these differentiating marks of Negroes are rapidly diminishing and in the course of time the physical stigmata may be left isolated as the only warrant of caste difference. The cultural stigmata of the past seem likely to disappear altogether.

Inferior caste results in a degree of social isolation for the individuals concerned. It tends to limit the personal development of members so that it is more difficult for them to compete for the highest social rewards and position. American policy is somewhat contradictory on this score, since we really do not keep the caste barrier fixed by the most effective methods. Slavery in this sense is much superior as a method of holding a population as a subject group. The upper caste would be more secure if the inferior caste were to have a separate language, or at least if its acquisition of our speech were limited. It would be safer also if lower-caste members were not able to read, if there were no social or religious sharing, and if the group were geographically immobile and extremely limited in social participation. The leaven of our dominant democratic mores has, however, made such a firm adjustment impossible; war broke up the southern approximation of it and we have a system of subjugation which is, for all its seeming firmness, shaky and contradictory.

Caste members tend to develop a distinctive psychology. This is no less true of the white caste than of the Negro, and we must never forget that we have two castes in the South and not just one. Southern white solidarity is caste solidarity. Nor should we overlook the fact that most of us, in the North as well as South, are members of the white caste, that we do, in practice, define the Negro as something categorically inferior and demand special privileges for ourselves and fellow whites. Our sympathy also tends to run along caste lines, even if it is not so acute in the North by virtue of the absence of the problem in a crucial form; northern Negroes are not numerous enough to be designated as out-groups in most northern communities.

The slogans of the white caste are among the most common expressions in Southerntown: "Niggers are all right in their place." "Would you want your sister to marry a nigger?" "Whenever whites have come in contact with blacks the world over, they have always been the dominant race," etc. Here is certainly a situation in which prediction is possible in the social sciences because these beliefs may be elicited at will from high and low in the southern white caste. Their repetition can in fact become tedious, and one is surprised at the sense of originality which those who repeat them often seem to feel. These expressions are always heavily supported from the emotional side and are impressive in the actual situation. White-caste members exhibit an appropriate pride in the achievements of their caste and like to stress its superiority in management and social responsibility.[5] In the Negro caste also a distinctive emotional set tends to develop, a psychology which is an accurate response to the caste position of the Negro.

The solidarity of the white caste on sexual and social issues has been widely noticed. When southern white people tell a northerner that after a few years in the South he will feel about Negroes just as southerners do, they are making the point that he joins the white caste. The solicitation is extremely active, though informal, and one must stand by one's caste to survive. Negroes, of course, know the power of white solidarity better than any one else. A Negro put it this way: Although white men often appear to be good friends to Negroes, if a Negro commits a crime against a white man, the white friend will invariably turn against him; whereas if a white man has any little trouble, all his white friends flock to him and defend him. He says it is different with Negro friends: they stick by you better. Raper has cited the case of a white infantryman who actually used a bayonet in defending a Negro charged with rape. This white man was never able to keep a position in his town thereafter; his white fellow workers forced him to leave for one reason or another.

A feature of white solidarity, as has been noted, is the harsh term that brands the caste traitor – "nigger-lover." Such a man enjoys the benefits of white solidarity, but does not stand by his caste. In the epithet there is an implication of inferiority and perhaps a threat of being classed with the scorned Negro.

To the Negro, of course, the caste barrier is an ever-present solid fact. His education is incomplete until he has learned to make some adjustment to it, usually the one preferred by the white caste. Since our democratic society is built on equal opportunity to achieve the highest social distinction, highest class position, and highest financial rewards, the caste barrier is obviously in contradiction with it. The Negro must haul down his social expectations and resign himself to a relative immobility in contrast to the dominant spirit of our society. This dominant spirit is well expressed by the notion of "beginning at the bottom and working to the top." Moton has pointed out that the Negro may begin at the bottom but, on the average, he may expect to stay there, or pretty close to it.

Notes

2. W. A. Dunning, 'The Undoing of Reconstruction,' *Atlantic Monthly* (1901), Vol. 88, p 449; also W. E. B. Du Bois, *The Negro* (New York, 1915), p. 149.
3. James E. Cutler, *Lynch-law* (New York, 1905), p. 218.
4. Donald Young, *American Minority Peoples* (New York, 1932), pp. 580-581.
5. A. H. Stone, *Studies in the American Race Problem* (New York, 1908), p. 87.

Source: John Dollard, *Caste and Class in a Southern Town*, pp. 62-65, c. 1937, 1949, 1957, 1964.

11.3 Gunnar Myrdal on American Race Relations

The Swedish economist, Gunnar Myrdal, was invited by the Carnegie Foundation to undertake a detailed study of the black population in the United States towards the end of the 1930s. His investigation of historical, sociological and economic aspects of the black experience was comprehensive, and the insights which were offered by his analysis of the data were profound. He remained optimistic about the future of race relations in the United States, with a European's confidence in American democratic ideals. His book influenced liberal opinion in the United States, although the concentration on the difficulties of the situation in the South made its acceptance there problematic. Black experience has moved on since Myrdal wrote in the early 1940s, but this was a landmark study which summarised a multi-faceted historical situation when it appeared.

FACETS OF THE NEGRO PROBLEM

The white man's theory of color caste

We have attempted to present in compressed and abstract formulation the white supremacy doctrine as applied to amalgamation, sex relations and marriage. The difficulty inherent in this task is great. As no scientifically controlled nation-wide investigations have been made, the author has here, as in other sections, had to rely on his own observations.[1]

Every widening of the writer's experience of white Americans has only driven home to him more strongly that the opinion that the Negro is unassimilable, or, rather, that his amalgamation into the American nation is undesirable, is held more commonly, absolutely, and intensely than would be assumed from a general knowledge of American thoughtways. Except for a handful of rational intellectual liberals – who also, in many cases, add to their acceptance in principle of amalgamation an admission that they personally feel an irrational emotional inhibition against it – it is a rare case to meet a white American who will confess that, if it were not for public opinion and social sanctions not removable by private choice, he would have no strong objection to intermarriage.

The intensity of the attitude seems to be markedly stronger in the South than in the North. Its strength seems generally to be inversely related to the economic and social status of the informant and his educational level. It is usually strong even in most of the non-colored minority groups, if they are above the lowest plane of indifference. To the poor and socially insecure, but struggling, white individual, a fixed opinion on this point seems an important matter of prestige and distinction.

But even a liberal-minded Northerner of cosmopolitan culture and with a minimum of conventional blinds will, in nine cases out of ten, express a definite feeling against amalgamation. He will not be willing usually to hinder intermarriage by law. Individual liberty is to him a higher principle and, what is more important, he actually invokes it. But he will regret the exceptional cases that occur. He may sometimes hold a philosophical view that in centuries to come amalgamation is bound to happen and might become the solution. But he will be inclined to look on it as an inevitable deterioration.[1]

This attitude of refusing to consider amalgamation – felt and expressed in the entire country – constitutes the center in the complex of attitudes which can be described as the "common denominator" in the problem. It defines the Negro group in contradistinction to all the non-colored minority groups in America and all other lower class groups. The boundary between Negro and white is not simply a class line which can be successfully crossed by education, integration into the national culture, and individual economic advancement. The boundary is fixed. It is not a temporary expediency during an apprenticeship in the national culture. It is a bar erected with the intention of permanency. It is directed against the whole group. Actually, however, "passing" as a white person is possible when a Negro is white enough to conceal his Negro heritage. But the difference between "passing" and ordinary social climbing reveals the distinction between a class line, in the ordinary sense, and a caste line.

This brings us to the point where we shall attempt to sketch, only in an abstract and preliminary form, the social mechanism by which the anti-amalgamation maxim determines race relations. This mechanism is perceived by nearly everybody in America, but most clearly in the South. Almost unanimously white Americans have communicated to the author the following logic of the caste situation which we shall call the "*white man's theory of color caste.*"

(1) The concern for "race purity" is basic in the whole issue; the primary and essential command is to prevent amalgamation; the whites are determined to utilize every means to this end.

(2) Rejection of "social equality" is to be understood as a precaution to hinder miscegenation and particularly intermarriage.

(3) The danger of miscegenation is so tremendous that the segregation and discrimination inherent in the refusal of "social equality" must be extended to nearly all spheres of life. There must be segregation and discrimination in recreation, in religious service, in education, before the law, in politics, in housing, in stores and in breadwinning.

This popular theory of the American caste mechanism is, of course, open to criticism. It can be criticized from a valuational point of view by maintaining that hindering miscegenation is not a worthwhile end, or that as an end it is not sufficiently worthwhile to counterbalance the sufferings inflicted upon the suppressed caste and the general depression of productive efficiency, standards of living and human culture in the American society at large – costs appreciated by all parties concerned. This criticism does not, however, endanger the theory which assumes that white people actually are following another valuation of means and ends and are prepared to pay the costs for attaining the ends. A second criticism would point out that, assuming the desirability of the end, this end could be reached without the complicated and, in all respects, socially expensive caste apparatus now employed. This criticism, however adequate though it be on the practical or political plane of discussion, does not disprove that people believe otherwise, and that the popular theory is a true representation of their beliefs and actions.

To undermine the popular theory of the caste mechanism, as based on the anti-amalgamation maxim, it would, of course, be necessary to prove that people really are influenced by other motives than the ones pronounced. Much material has, as we shall find, been brought together indicating that, among other things, competitive economic interests, which do not figure at all in the popular rationalization referred to, play a decisive role. The announced concern about racial purity is, when this economic motive is taken into account, no longer awarded the exclusive role as the *basic* cause in the psychology of the race problem.

Though the popular theory of color caste turns out to be a rationalization, this does not destroy it. For among the forces in the minds of the white people are certainly not only economic interests (if these were the only ones, the popular theory would be utterly demolished), but also sexual urges, inhibitions, and jealousies, and social fears and cravings for prestige and security. When they come under the scrutiny of scientific research, both the sexual and the social complexes take on unexpected designs. We shall then also get a clue to understanding the remarkable tendency of this presumably biological doctrine, that it refers only to legal marriage and to relations between Negro men and white women, but not to extra-marital sex relations between white man and Negro women.

However these sexual and social complexes might turn out when analyzed, they will reveal the psychological nature of the anti-amalgamation doctrine and show its "meaning". They will also explain the compressed emotion attached to the Negro problem. It is inherent in our type of modern Western civilization that sex and social status are for most individuals the danger points, the directions whence he fears the sinister onslaughts on his personal security. These two factors are more likely than anything else to push a life problem deep down into the subconscious and load it with emotions. There is some probability that in America both complexes are particularly laden with emotions. The American puritan tradition gives everything connected with sex a higher emotional charge. The roads for social climbing have been kept more open in America than perhaps anywhere else in the world, but in this upward struggle the competition for social status has also become more absorbing. In a manner and to a degree most uncomfortable for the Negro people in America, both the sexual and the social complexes have become related to the Negro problem.

These complexes are most of the time kept concealed. In occasional groups of persons and situations they break into the open. Even when not consciously perceived or expressed, they ordinarily determine interracial behavior on the white side.

The "rank order of discriminations"

The anti-amalgamation doctrine represents a strategic constellation of forces in race relations. Their charting will allow us a first general overview of the discrimination patterns and will have the advantage that white Americans themselves will recognise their own paths on the map we draw. When white Southerners are asked to rank, in order of importance, various types of discrimination[2], they consistently present a list in which these types of discrimination are ranked according to the degree of closeness of their relation to the anti-amalgamation doctrine. This rank order – which will be referred to as "the white mans" rank order of discriminations" – will serve as an organizing principle in this book. It appears, actually, only as an elaboration of the popular theory of color caste sketched above. Like that theory, it is most clearly and distinctly perceived in the South; in the North ideas are more vague but, on the whole, not greatly divergent. Neither the popular theory of caste nor the rank order of discriminations has been noted much in scientific literature on the Negro problem.

The rank order held nearly unanimously is the following:

Rank 1. Highest in this order stands the bar against intermarriage and sexual intercourse involving white women.

Rank 2. Next come the several etiquettes and discriminations, which specifically concern behavior in personal relations. (These are the barriers against dancing, bathing, eating, drinking together, and social intercourse generally; peculiar rules as to handshaking, hat lifting, use of titles, house entrance to be used, social forms when meeting on streets and in work, and so forth. These patterns are sometimes referred to as the denial of "social equality" in the narrow meaning of the term.)

Rank 3. Thereafter follow the segregations and discriminations in use of public facilities such as schools, churches and means of conveyance.

Rank 4. Next comes politicial disfranchisement.

Rank 5. Thereafter come discriminations in law courts, by the police, and by other public servants.

Rank 6. Finally come the discriminations in securing land, credit, jobs, or other means of earning a living, and discriminations in public relief and other social welfare activities.

It is unfortunate that this cornerstone in our edifice of basic hypotheses, like many of our other generalizations, has to be constructed upon the author's observations. It is desirable that scientifically controlled, quantitative knowledge be substituted for impressionistic judgments as soon as possible. It should be noted that the rank order is very apparently determined by the factors of sex and social status, so that the closer the association of a type of interracial behavior is to sexual and social intercourse on an equalitarian basis, the higher it ranks among the forbidden things.

Next in importance to the fact of the white man's rank order of discriminations is the fact that *the Negro's own rank order is just about parallel, but inverse, to that of the white man*. The Negro resists least the discrimination on the ranks placed highest in the white man's evaluation and resents most any discrimination on the lowest level. This is in accord with the Negro's immediate interests. Negroes are in desperate need of jobs and bread, even more so than of justice in the courts, and of the vote. These latter needs are, in their turn, more urgent even than better schools and playgrounds, or, rather, they are primary means of reaching equality in the use of community facilities. Such facilities are, in turn, more important than civil courtesies. The marriage matter, finally, is of rather distant and doubtful interest.

Such reflections are obvious; and most Negroes have them in their minds. It is another matter, however, whether the white man is prepared to stick honestly to the rank order which he is so explicit and emphatic in announcing. The question is whether he is really prepared to give the Negro a good job, or even the vote, rather than to allow him entrance to his front door or to ride beside him in the street car.

Upon the assumption that this question is given an affirmative answer, that the white man is actually prepared to carry out in practice the implications of his theories, this inverse relationship between the Negro's and the white man's rank orders becomes of strategical importance in the practical and political sphere of the Negro problem. Although not formulated in this way, such a relationship, or such a minimum moral demand on the ordinary white man, has always been the basis of all attempts to compromise and come to a better understanding between leaders of the two groups. It has been the basis for all interracial policy and also for most of the practical work actually carried out by Negro betterment organizations. Followed to its logical end, it should fundamentally change the race situation in America.

It has thus always been a primary requirement upon every Negro leader – who aspires to get any hearing at all from the white majority group, and who does not want to appear dangerously radical to the Negro group and at the same time hurt the "race pride" it has built up as a defense – that he shall explicitly condone the anti-amalgamation maxim, which is the keystone in the white man's structure of race prejudice, and forbear to express any desire on the part of the Negro people to aspire to intermarriage with the whites. The request for intermarriage is easy for the Negro leader to give up. Intermarriage cannot possibly be a practical object of Negro public policy. Independent of the Negroes' wishes, the opportunity for intermarriage is not favorable as long as the great majority of the white population dislikes the very idea. As a defense reaction a strong attitude against intermarriage has developed in the Negro people itself. And the Negro people have no interest in defending the exploitative illicit relations between white men and Negro women. This race mingling is, on the contrary, commonly felt among Negroes to be disgraceful. And it often arouses the jealousy of Negro men.

The required soothing gesture toward the anti-amalgamation doctrine is, therefore, readily delivered. It is iterated at every convenient opportunity and belongs to the established routine of Negro leadership. For example, Robert R. Moton writes:

> As for amalgamation, very few expect it; still fewer want it; no one advocates it; and only a constantly diminishing minority practise it, and that surreptitiously. It is generally accepted on both sides of the colour line that it is best for the two races to remain ethnologically distinct.

There seems thus to be unanimity among Negro leaders on the point deemed crucial by white Americans. If we attend carefully, we shall, however, detect some important differences in formulation. The Negro spokesman will never, to begin with, accept the common white premise of racial inferiority of the Negro stock. To quote Moton again:

> . . . even in the matter of the mingling of racial strains, however undesirable it might seem to be from a social point of view, he (the Negro) would never admit that his blood carries any taint of physiological, mental, or spiritual inferiority.

A doctrine of equal natural endowments – a doctrine contrary to the white man's assumption of Negro inferiority, which is at the basis of the anti-amalgamation theory – has been consistently upheld. If a Negro leader publicly even hinted at the possibility of inherent racial inferiority, he would immediately lose his following. The entire Negro press watches the Negro leaders on this point.

Even Booker T. Washington, the supreme diplomat of the Negro people through a generation filled with severe trials, who was able by studied unobtrusiveness to wring so many favors from the white majority, never dared to allude to such a possibility, though he sometimes critized most severely his own people for lack of thrift, skill, perseverance and general culture. In fact, there is no reason to think that he did not firmly believe in the fundamental equality of inherent capacities. Privately, local Negro leaders might find it advisable to admit Negro inferiority and, particularly earlier, many individual Negroes might have shared the white man's view. But it will not be expressed by national leaders and, in fact, never when they are under public scrutiny. An emphatic assertion of equal endowments is article number one in the growing Negro "race pride."

Another deviation of the Negro faith in the anti-amalgamation doctrine is the stress that they, for natural reasons, lay on condemning exploitative illicit amalgamation. They turn the tables and accuse white men of debasing Negro womanhood, and the entire white culture for not rising up against this practice as their expressed antagonism against miscegenation should demand. Here they have a strong point, and they know how to press it.

A third qualification in the Negro's acceptance of the anti-amalgamation doctrine, expressed not only by the more "radical" and outspoken Negro leaders, is the assertion that intermarriage should not be barred by law. The respect for individual liberty is invoked as an argument. But, in addition, it is pointed out that this barrier, by releasing the white man from the consequences of intimacy with a Negro woman, actually has the effect of inducing such intimacy and thus tends to increase miscegenation. Moton makes this point:

> The Negro woman suffers not only from the handicap of economic and social discriminations imposed upon the race as a whole, but is in addition the victim of unfavourable legislation incorporated in the marriage laws of twenty-nine states, which forbid the intermarriage of black and white. The disadvantage of these statutes lies, not as is generally represented, in the legal obstacle they present to social equality, but rather in the fact that

> such laws specifically deny to the Negro woman and her offspring that safeguard from abuse and exploitation with which the women of the white race are abundantly surrounded. On the other side, the effect of such legislation leaves the white man, who is so inclined, free of any responsibility attending his amatory excursions across the colour line and leaves the coloured woman without redress for any of the consequences of her defencelessness; whereas white women have every protection, from fine and imprisonment under the law to enforced marriage and lynching outside the law.

But even with all these qualifications, the anti-amalgamation doctrine, the necessity of assenting to which is understood by nearly everybody, obviously encounters some difficulties in the minds of intellectual Negroes. They can hardly be expected to accept it as a just rule of conduct. They tend to accept it merely as a temporary expedient necessitated by human weakness. Kelly Miller thus wrote:

> . . . you would hardly expect the Negro, in derogation of his common human qualities, to proclaim that he is so diverse from God's other human creatures as to making the blending of the races contrary to the law of nature. The Negro refuses to become excited or share in your frenzy on this subject. The amalgamation of the races is an ultimate possibility, though not an immediate probability. But what have you and I to do with ultimate questions, anyway?

And a few years later, he said:

> It must be taken for granted in the final outcome of things that the color line will be wholly obliterated. While blood may be thicker than water, it does not possess the spissitude or inherency of everlasting principle. The brotherhood of man is more fundamental than the fellowship of race. A physical and spiritual identity of all peoples occupying common territory is a logical necessity of thought. The clear seeing mind refuses to yield or give its assent to any other ultimate conclusion. This consummation, however, is far too removed from the sphere of present probability to have decisive influence upon pratical procedure.

This problem is, of course, tied up with the freedom of the individual. "Theoretically Negroes would all subscribe to the right of freedom of choice in marriage even between the two races," wrote Moton. And Du Bois formulates it in stronger terms:

> . . . a woman may say, I do not want to marry this black man, or this red man, or this white man . . . But the impudent and vicious demand that all colored folk shall write themselves down as brutes by a general assertion of their unfitness to marry other decent folk is a nightmare.

Negroes have always pointed out that the white man must not be very certain of his woman's lack of interest when he rises to such frenzy on behalf of the danger to her and feels compelled to build up such formidable fences to prevent her from marrying a Negro.

With these reservations both Negro leadership and the Negro masses acquiesce in the white anti-amalgamation doctrine. This attitude is noted with satisfaction in the white camp. The writer has observed, however, that the average white man, particularly in the South, does not feel quite convinced of the Negro's acquiescence. In several conversations, the same white person, in the same breath, has assured me, on the one hand, that the Negroes are perfectly satisfied in their position and would not like to be treated as equals, and on the other hand, that the only thing these Negroes long for is to be like white people and to marry their daughters.

Whereas the Negro spokesman finds it possible to assent to the first rank of discrimination, namely, that involving miscegenation, it is more difficult for him to give his approval to the second rank of discrimination, namely, that involving "etiquette" and consisting in the white man's refusal to extend the ordinary courtesies to Negroes in daily life and his expectation of receiving certain symbolic signs of submissiveness from the Negro. The Negro leader could not do so without serious risk of censorship by his own people and rebuke by the Negro press. In all articulate groups of Negroes there is a demand to have white men call them by their titles of Mr., Mrs., and Miss; to have white men take off their hats on entering a Negro's house; to be able to enter a white man's house through the front door rather than the back door, and so on. But on the whole, and in spite of the rule that they stand up for "social equality" in this sense, most Negroes in the South obey the white man's rules.

Booker T. Washington went a long way, it is true, in his Atlanta speech in 1895 where he explained that: "In all things that are purely social we [the two races] can be as separate as the fingers, yet one as the hand in all things essential to mutual progress." Here there seemed to condone not only these rules of "etiquette" but also the denial of "social equality" in a broader sense, including some of the further categories in the white man's rank order of discrimination. He himself was always most eager to observe the rules. But Washington was bitterly rebuked for this capitulation, particularly by Negroes in the North. And a long time has passed since then; the whole spirit in the Negro world has changed considerably in three decades.

The modern Negro leader will try to solve this dilemma by iterating that no Negroes want to intrude upon white people's private lives. But this is not what Southern white opinion asks for. It is not satisfied with the natural rules of polite conduct that no individual, of whatever race, shall push his presence on a society where he is not wanted. It asks for a general order according to which *all* Negroes are placed under *all* white people and excluded from not only the white man's society but also from the ordinary symbols of respect. No Negro shall ever aspire to them, and no white shall be allowed to offer them.

Thus, on this second rank of discrimination there is a wide gap between the ideologies of the two groups. As we then continue downward in our rank order and arrive at the ordinary Jim Crow practices, the segregation in schools, the disfranchisement, and the discrimination in employment, we find, on the one hand, that increasingly larger groups of white people are prepared to take a stand against these discriminations. Many a liberal white professor in the South who, for his own welfare, would not dare to entertain a Negro in his home and perhaps not even speak to him in a friendly manner on the street, will be found prepared publicly to condemn disfranchisement, lynching, and the forcing of the Negro out of employment. Also, on the other hand, Negro spokesmen are becoming increasingly firm in their opposition to discrimination on these lower levels. It is principally on these lower levels of the white man's rank order of discriminations that the race struggle goes on. The struggle will widen to embrace all the thousand problems of education, politics, economic standards, and so forth, and the frontier will shift from day to day according to varying events.

Even a superficial view of discrimination in America will reveal to the observer: first, that there are great differences, not only between larger regions, but between neighboring communities; and, second, that even in the same community, changes occur from one time to another. There is also, contrary to the rule that all Negroes are to be treated alike, a certain amount of discretion depending upon the class and social status of the Negro in question. A white person, especially if he has high status in the community, is, furthermore, supposed to be free, within limits, to overstep the rules. The rules are primarily to govern the Negro's behavior.

Some of these differences and changes can be explained. But the need for their interpretation is perhaps less than has sometimes been assumed. The variations in discrimination between local communities or from one time to another are often not of primary consequence. All of these thousand and one precepts, etiquettes, taboos, and disabilities inflicted upon the Negro have a common purpose: to express the subordinate status of the Negro people and the exalted position of the whites. They have their meaning and chief function as symbols. As symbols they are, however, interchangeable to an extent: one can serve in place of another without causing material difference in the essential social relations in the community.

The differences in patterns of discrimination between the larger regions of the country and the temporal changes of patterns within one region, which reveal a definite trend, have, on the contrary, more material import. These differences and changes imply, in fact, a considerable margin of variation within the very notion of American caste, which is not true of all the other minor differences between the changes in localities within a single region – hence the reason for a clear distinction. For exemplification it may suffice here to refer only to the differentials in space. As one moves from the Deep South through the Upper South and the Border states to the North, the manifestations of discrimination decrease in extent and intensity; at the same time the rules become more uncertain and capricious. The "color line" becomes a broad ribbon of arbitrariness. The old New England states stand, on the whole, as the antipode to the Deep South. This generalization requires important qualifications, and the relations are in process of change.

The decreasing discrimination as we go from South to North in the United States is apparently related to a weaker basic prejudice. In the North the Negroes have fair justice and are not disfranchised; they are not Jim-Crowed in public means of conveyance; educational institutions are less segregated. The interesting thing is that the decrease of discrimination does *not* regularly follow the white man's rank order. Thus intermarriage, placed on the top of the rank order, is legally permitted in all but one of the Northern states east of the Mississippi. The racial etiquette, being the most conspicuous element in the second rank, is, practically speaking, absent from the North. On the other hand, employment discriminations, placed at the bottom of the rank order, at times are equally severe, or more so, in some Northern communities than in the South, even if it is true that Negroes have been able to press themselves into many more new avenues of employment during the last generation in the North than in the South.

There is plenty of discrimination in the North. But it is – or rather its rationalization is – kept hidden. We can, in the North, witness the legislators' obedience to the American Creed when they solemnly pass laws and regulations to condemn and punish such acts of discrimination which, as a matter of routine, are committed daily by the great majority of the white citizens and by the legislators themselves. In the North, as indeed often in the South, public speakers frequently pronounce principles of human and civic equality. We see here revealed in relief the Negro problem as an American Dilemma.

Relationships between lower class groups

It was important to compare the Negro problem with American minority problems in general because both the similarities and the dissimilarities are instructive. Comparisons give leads, and they furnish perspective.

The same reason permits us to point out that the consideration of the Negro problem as one minority problem among others is far too narrow. The Negro has usually the same disadvantages and some extra ones in addition. To these other disadvantaged groups in America belong not only the groups recognized as minorities, but all economically weak classes in the nation, the bulk of the Southern people, women[3], and others. This country is a "white man's country," but, in addition, it is a country belonging primarily to the elderly, male, upper class, Protestant Northerner. Viewed in this setting the Negro problem in America is but one local and temporary facet of that eternal problem of world dimension – how to regulate the conflicting interests of groups in the best interest of justice and fairness. The latter ideals are vague and conflicting, and their meaning is changing in the course of the struggle.

There seems to be a general structure of social relations between groups on different levels of power and advantage. From a consideration of our exaggeratedly "typical" case – the Negro – we may hope to reach some suggestions toward a more satisfactory general theory about this social power structure in general. Our hypothesis is that in a society where there are broad social classes and, in addition, more minute distinctions and splits in the lower strata, *the lower class groups will, to a great extent, take care of keeping each other subdued,* thus relieving, to that extent, the higher classes of this otherwise painful task necessary to the monopolization of the power and the advantages.

It will be observed that this hypothesis is contrary to the Marxian theory of class society, which in the period between the two World Wars has been so powerful, directly and indirectly, consciously and unconsciously, in American social science thinking generally. The Marxian scheme assumes that there is an actual solidarity between the several lower class groups against the higher classes, or, in any case, a potential solidarity which as a matter of natural development is bound to emerge. The inevitable result is a "class struggle" where all poor and disadvantaged groups are united behind the barricades.

Such a construction has had a considerable vogue in all discussions on the American Negro problem since the First World War. We are not here taking issue with the political desirability of a common front between the poorer classes of whites and the Negro people who, for the most part, belong to the proletariat. In fact, we can well see that such a practical judgment is motivated as a conclusion from certain value premises in line with the American Creed. But the thesis has also been given a theoretical content as describing actual trends in reality and not only political *desiderata.* A solidarity between poor whites and Negroes has been said to be "natural' and the conflicts to be due to "illusions." This thesis, which will be discussed in some detail in [Chapter 38], has been a leading one in the field and much has been made of even the faintest demonstration of such solidarity.

In partial anticipation of what is to follow later in this volume, we might be permitted to make a few general, and perhaps rather dogmatic, remarks is criticism of this theory. Everything we know about human frustation and aggression, and the displacement of aggression, speaks against it. For an individual to feel interest solidarity with a group assumes his psychological identification with the group. This identification must be of considerable strength, as the very meaning of solidarity is that he is prepared to set aside and even sacrifice his own short-range private interests for the long-range interests of his group. Every vertical split within the lower class aggregate will stand as an obstacle to the feeling of solidarity. Even within the white working class itself, as within the entire American nation, the feeling of solidarity and loyalty is relatively low[4]. Despite the considerable mobility, especially in the North, the Negroes are held apart from the whites by caste, which furnishes a formidable bar to mutual identification and solidarity.

It has often occurred to me, when reflecting upon the responses I get from white laboring people on this strategic question, that my friends among the younger Negro intellectuals, whose judgment I otherwise have learned to admire greatly, have perhaps, and for natural reasons, not had enough occasion to find out for themselves what a bitter, spiteful, and relentless feeling often prevails against the Negroes among lower class white people in America. Again relying upon my own observations, I have become convinced that the laboring Negroes do not resent whites in any degree comparable with the resentment shown in the opposite direction by the laboring whites. The competitive situation is, and is likely to remain, highly unstable.

It must be admitted that, in the midst of harsh caste resentment, signs of newborn working class solidarity are not entirely lacking; we shall have to discuss these recent tendencies in some detail in order to evaluate the resultant trend and the prospects for the future[5]. On this point there seems, however, to be a danger of wishful thinking present in most writings on the subject. The Marxian solidarity between the toilers of all the earth will, indeed, have a long way to go as far as concerns solidarity of the poor white Americans with the toiling Negro. This is particularly true of the South but true also of the communities in the North where the Negroes are numerous and competing with the whites for employment.

Our hypothesis is similar to the view taken by an older group of Negro writers and by most white writers who have touched this crucial question: that the Negro's friend – or the one who is least unfriendly – is still rather the upper class of white people, the people with economic and social security who are truly a "noncompeting group". There are many things in the economic, political, and social history of the Negro which are simply inexplicable by the Marxian theory of class solidarity but which fit into our hypothesis of the predominance of internal lower class struggle. Du Bois, in *Black Reconstruction,* argues that it would have been desirable if after the Civil War the landless Negroes and the poor whites had joined hands to retain political power and carry out a land reform and a progressive government in the Southern states; one sometimes feels that he thinks it would have been a possibility. From our point of view such a possibility did not exist at all, and the negative outcome was neither an accident nor a result of simple deception or delusion. These two groups, illiterate and insecure in an impoverished South, placed in an intensified competition with each other, lacking every trace of primary solidarity, and marked off from each other by color and tradition, could not possibly be expected to clasp hands.

THE NEGRO CLASS STRUCTURE

The Negro class order in the American caste system[6]

The caste principle, as insisted upon and enforced by white society would undoubtedly be best satisfied by a classless Negro community wherein all Negroes in all respects – educationally, occupationally, and economically – were in the lowest bracket and placed under the lowest class of whites. That "all Negroes are alike" and should be treated in the same way is still insisted upon by many whites, especially in the lower classes, who actually feel, or fear, competition from the Negroes and who are inclined to sense a challenge to their status in the fact that some Negroes rise from the bottom even if they professionally and socially keep entirely within the Negro community.[1] The popular theories rationalizing and justifying the caste order to the whites have been framed to fit this principle of a homogeneous lower caste. None of the Jim Crow legislation distinguishes between classes of Negroes.

This absolutistic principle has, however, never been fully realized even in the South. Already in slavery society there came to be a social stratification within the slave community, as house servants and skilled mechanics acquired a level of living and culture and enjoyed a social prestige different from that of the field slaves. The blood ties of the former group of slaves with the white upper class widened this difference. There may also have been some difference in status between the slaves owned by the aristocracy and the slaves owned by the small farmers. Contemporary sources give us the impression that the hatred between Negro slaves and "poor white trash" was largely due to this social stratification in the Negro group. It was mainly the superior slave who could be a challenge and danger to the poor whites, and it was he who, on his side, would have the social basis for the contemptuous attitude toward them. The early emergence of a class of free Negroes, which at the time of Emancipation had grown to one-half million individuals, strengthened this trend toward a social stratification of the Negro population in America. All sorts of restrictive laws were enacted and also partly enforced to keep the free Negroes down. But in spite of this, their condition of life and social status was different from that of the masses of slaves.

After Emancipation this development continued. The measures to keep the Negroes disfranchised and deprived of full civil rights and the whole structure of social and economic discrimination are to be viewed as attempts to enforce the caste principle against the constitutional prescripts and against the tendency of some Negroes to rise out of complete dependence. The Constitution – and the partial hold of the American Creed even on the Southern whites' own minds – prevented effective caste legislation. All laws, even in the South, had to be written upon the pretense of equality. Education for Negroes was kept backward, but it was given in some measure and gradually improved. Some Negroes become landowners, often under the protection of individual white patronage. And, most important of all, social segregation itself – which has always been maintained as the last absolute barrier – afforded protection for a rising number of Negro professionals and businessmen. Negroes had to be ministered to, their educational institutions had to be manned, their corpses had to be washed and buried, and, as white people did not wish to take on these tasks and as Negroes gradually found out their own needs and chances, a Negro middle and upper class developed to perform these functions, and thus drew its vitality from the very fact of American caste. The dividing line between the two castes did not crack, however. Thus, this dual system of social class developed, *one class system on each side of the caste line.*

Robert E. Park has schematized this development as follows:

> Originally race relatons in the South could be rather accurately represented by a horizontal line, with all the white folk above, and all the Negro folk below. But at present these relations are assuming new forms, and in consequence changing in character and meaning. With the development of industrial and professional classes within the Negro race, the distinction between the races tends to assume the form of a vertical line. On one side of this line the Negro is represented in most of the occupational and professional classes; on the other side of the line the white man is similarly represented. The situation *was* this:
>
> All white
> ———————
> All colored
>
> It is now this:

White		*Colored*
Professional occupation	:	Professional occupation
Business occupation	:	Business occupation
Labor	:	Labor

The result is to develop in every occupational class professional and industrial bi-racial organizations. Bi-racial organizations preserve race distinction, but change their content. The distances which separate the races are maintained, but the attitudes involved are different. *The races no longer look up and down: they look across.*

Warner's Diagram[1]

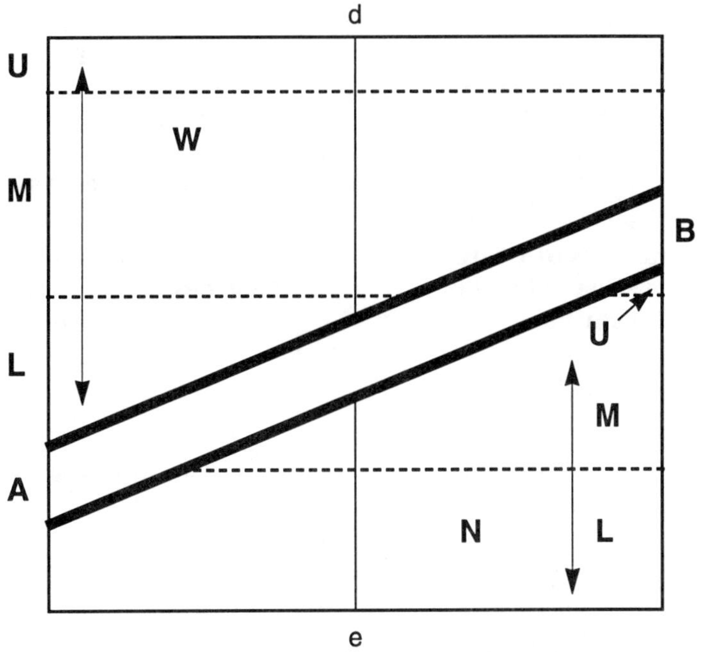

[1] W. Lloyd Warner, Introduction to *Deep South*, by Allison Davis, B. B. Gardner and M. R. Gardner (1941), p. 10.
Legend: W –White. N – Negro. U – Upper Class. M – Middle Class. L – Lower Class. AB – Caste Line. de – Ultimate Position of caste Line.

This description contains – as the author is probably well aware – several overstatements. The caste line is not vertical but rather "diagonal" (that is, a sloped line). The line has moved, and is moving, from horizontal, but it is still far away from the vertical position, as Warner has shown. But Warner is not correct either, since he thinks of the caste line as a straight one, implying that the Negro group gets proportionately smaller as one goes up the social status scale. Actually, the Negro middle and upper class are *more than proportionately* smaller than their lower class. Du Bois brings this out clearly.

> It goes without saying that while Negroes are thus manifestly of low average culture, in no place nor at any time do they form a homogeneous group. Even in the country districts of the lower South, Allison Davis likens the group to a steeple with wide base tapering to a high pinnacle. This means that while the poor, ignorant, sick and anti-social form a vast foundation, that upward from that base stretch classes whose highest members, although few in number, reach above the average not only of the Negroes but of the whites, and may justly be compared to the better-class white culture. The class structure of the whites, on the other hand, resembles a tower bulging near the center with the lowest classes small in number as compared with the middle and lower middle classes; and the highest classes far more numerous in proportion than those among blacks.

We can diagram the caste-class situation in two ways: one, in terms of absolute numbers after the manner of the ordinary population pyramid – as in Du Bois' description; two, in terms of percentages at each social level – after the pattern of a box diagram. The latter diagram brings out the line, in temporal changes in which Warner and others have been interested. The pyramid and the line are drawn hypothetically – it would take an enormous amount of work to draw them with an approximation of empirical quantitative accuracy. But as to their genral shape there can be little doubt: the pyramid is heavier at the bottom of the Negro side than on the white side, and the line is a *diagonal curve,* not a straight line diagonal.

Absolute numbers of whites and Negroes at each level of social status

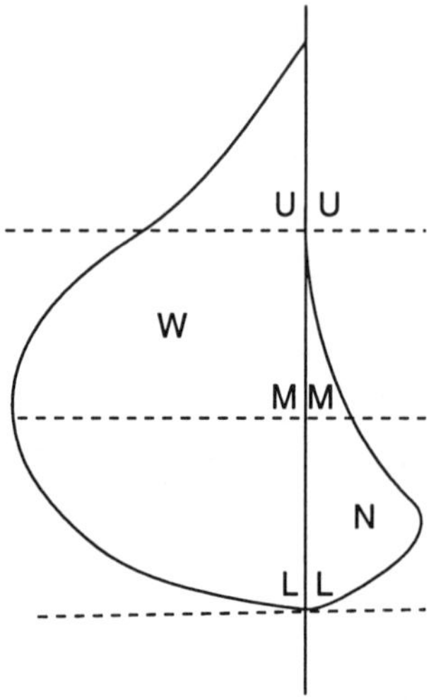

Percentage of white and Negroes at each level of social status

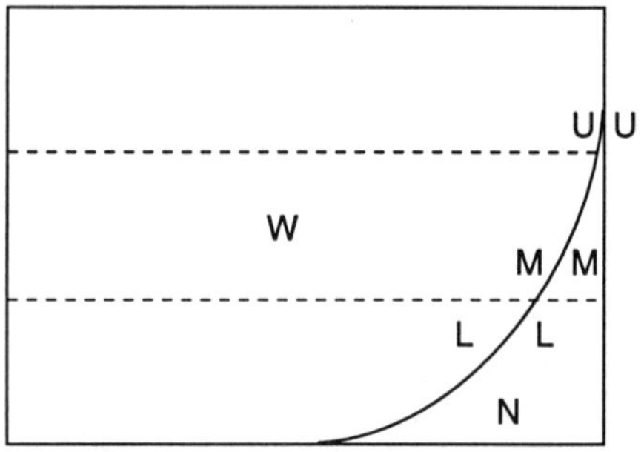

Legend: W – White. N – Negro. U – Upper Class. M – Middle Class. L – Lower Class.

There is at least one weakness of all diagrams of this sort: they assume that the class structures of the two castes are exactly comparable, which they are not. On the same class level – that is, assuming white and Negro individuals with the same education, occupation, income, and so on – the white does *not* "look across" the caste line upon the Negro, but he definitely *looks down* upon him.[7] And this fundamental fact of caste is materialized in a great number of political, judicial, and social disabilities imposed upon Negroes somewhat independent of their class, and in the rigid rule that the Negro is not allowed to pass legitimately from the one side to the other.

The diagonal and curved character of the caste line and this fact that whites can look down on Negroes of the same income, educational, or other level, form one of what Dollard calls the major "gains" of the caste order to the whites. The difference between the South and the North and, in a degree, between rural and urban communities is, from this point of view, that the caste line tends to be somewhat more vertical in the latter than in the former regions and localities. The caste status of the Negro in the North and in cities generally has fewer rigid restrictions of free competition. In this direction the class system has been continually moving in the South and – except for the transitional extraordinary pressure of recent mass immigration – also in the North.

We have seen that Southern whites, especially in the lower brackets, often refuse to recognize class differences in the Negro community and insist upon distinguishing only between "bad niggers," "good niggers," and "uppity niggers," and that they, until recently, have succeeded in retaining a legal and political system which corresponds most closely to this view. But this uncompromising attitude is disappearing under the pressure of the facts of Negro social differentiation. Thus the actual import of caste is gradually changing as the Negro class structure develops – except in the fundamental restriction that no Negro is allowed to ascend into the white caste.

Caste determines class

While the Negro class structure has developed contrary to the caste principle and actually implies a considerable modification of caste relations, fundamentally, this class structure is a function of the caste order. We have repeatedly had to refer to this important fact that, while the caste order has held the Negro worker down, it has at the same time created petty monopolies for a tiny Negro middle and upper class. Negroes understand this, although they seldom discuss is openly.[8]

The lower caste monopolies are strongest in some of the professions and in the service occupations near the professions (funeral work, beauty work, retail trade, and so on); some monopolistic leeway is also afforded small-scale Negro banking, insurance and real estate. For the rest of the occupations, the caste barriers block the way for Negroes.[9] It is thus understandable that, next to the small size of the middle and upper class, the Negro class system has its most characteristic feature in the fact that, on the whole, capitalist business and wealth mean so relatively little, and that general education and professional training mean so relatively much, as criteria for attaining upper class status.[10] This is evidently not due to a lower valuation of wealth among Negroes than among whites. Rather independent of the respectability of the source, wealth is as sure – and perhaps even a little more sure – to give upper class status among American Negroes as it does among whites. But there is so little of it in the Negro community. And education is such a high value to this group, which has to struggle for it, that it is understandable why education is more important, relatively, for Negro status than for white status. Among the consequences of the relative prestige of education among Negroes is that practically all Negro college teachers are upper class, and that most of the national Negro leaders are academic men. In both these respects, the American Negro world is strikingly different from the American white world.

One of the consequences of the small range of wealth and occupation in the Negro community, and of the importance of education, is that there is probably less social distance between bottom and top among Negroes than there is among whites. It is not uncommon for a Negro boy – especially in the North – to rise from the lowest to the highest social status in one generation. While a white boy could rise the same absolute social distance in the white caste during his lifetime – that is, he could attain the same increase in education, wealth, and manners – this distance would not appear so great because he would still be far from the top. This fact has tended to keep the various Negro classes in better contact with each other, except for the declining mulatto aristocracies, than is the case with the white classes. Other factors – such as caste pressure, the northward migration, and the existence of national organizations fighting for the whole caste – have had a similar effect.

Another characteristic of the Negro class structure – which would superficially seem contradictory to the previously mentioned trait, but is not on closer examination – is the smaller amount of pride in individual climbing among upper class Negroes. It is my impression that, in a sense, the typical Negro upper class person attaches more importance to family background than the typical Yankee. At least he is less likely to brag about his lowly origin. In this, as in many other respects, the American Negro seems more similar to the Southern white man, who also places a lower estimation on the self-made man. I should imagine that this is not only a cultural pattern borrowed from Southern white society but also, and more fundamentally, a trait connected with the fact that both Negroes and Southern whites are, though in different degrees, disadvantaged groups and do not feel the security of the Yankee, who can afford to brag about having started as newsboy or shoeshiner.[11]

Also important for the spirit of the Negro class structure is the fact that such a relatively large portion of the Negro middle class groups in all regions of America have positions in personal service of whites. In Southern cities some of the upper class Negroes still engage in some of the service occupations, as they did even in the Northern cities a generation ago. A great number of their sons and daughters have proceeded into the upper class professions. I have also been struck by the relatively high proportion of upper class professionals who during their college years, for lack of other employment opportunities open to Negroes, have done service work for whites. It appears plausible that both the refined and worldly-wise manners, especially in the older generation of upper class Negroes, and their often conservative social and economic views are not unconnected with such earlier experiences in personal service of well-to-do whites.

An individual's relation to white society is of utmost importance for his social status in the Negro community. This aspect of the Negro class structure will be considered in the next part on Negro leadership and concerted action.

Color and class

The American order of color caste has even more directly stamped the Negro class system by including relative whiteness as one of the main factors determining status within the Negro community. This has a history as old as class stratification itself among Negroes. Mixed bloods have always been preferred by the whites in practically all respects. They made a better appearance to the whites and were assumed to be mentally more capable. They had a higher sales value on the slave market. The select classes of trained mechanics and house servants who early came in closer contact with the dominant culture of the whites seem largely to have been drawn from the group of mixed bloods, and their superior training further raised their status.

A sexual selection added its influence to this occupational differentiation. The fair-skinned house girls were more frequently used as mistresses by men of the planter class than were the plantation hands. They became the mothers of successive generations of even whiter children. Many white fathers freed their illegitimate mulatto offspring and often also the children's mothers, or gave them the opportunity to work out their freedom on easy terms. Some were helped to education and sent to the free states in the North. Some were given a start in business or helped to acquire land.

For this reason the free Negro population everywhere contained a greater proportion of mixed bloods than did the slave population. The mulattoes followed the white people's valuation and associated their privileges with their lighter color. They considered themselves superior to the black slave people and attributed their superiority to the fact of their mixed blood. The black slaves, too, came to hold this same valuation. The white people, however, excluded even the fairest of the mulatto group from their own caste – in so far as they did not succeed in passing – and the mulattoes, in their turn, held themselves more and more aloof from the black slaves and the humbler blacks among the free Negroes; thus the mulattoes tended early to form a separate intermediary caste of their own. Although they were constantly augmented by mulatto ex-slaves, they seldom married down into the slave group. In such cities as New Orleans, Charleston, Mobile, Natchez, and later Washington, highly exclusive mulatto societies were formed which still exist, to a certain extent, today. Color thus became a badge of status and social distinction among the Negro people.

Emancipation destroyed any possibility there might have been for the mulatto group to form an intermediary caste of their own in America as a substitute for their not being able to get into the white group.[12] Even their upper class position lost in relative exclusiveness as their monopoly of freedom was extinguished and white philanthropy began to aid the recently emancipated slave masses. The new definition of the Negro problem in the South and the increased antagonism on the white side toward all Negroes who were "out of their place" made the whites less inclined to draw a distinction between light and dark Negroes.

But at the same time Emancipation broadened the basis for a Negro upper class and increased the possibilities for this class relatively even more than for the Negro masses themselves. What there was in the Negro people of "family background," tradition of freedom, education and property ownership was mostly in the hands of mulattoes. They became the political leaders of the freedmen during Reconstruction, as well as their teachers, professionals and business people. Compared with the newly freed slave population they had a tremendous head-start. In the social stratification of the Negro community their social distance toward the Negro masses perpetuated itself. Darker Negroes who rose from the masses to distinction in the Negro community by getting an education or by conducting successful business enterprises showed an almost universal desire to marry light-skinned women and so to become adopted members of the light-colored aristocracy and to give their children a heritage of lighter color. Blackness of skin remained undesirable and even took on an association of badness.

Without any doubt a Negro with light skin and other European features has in the North an advantage with white people when competing for jobs available for Negroes. It is less true in the South, particularly in the humbler occupations. The whites continue to associate the nearness to their own physical type with superior endowments and cultural advancement, and the preponderance of fair-skinned Negroes in the upper strata seems to give this prejudice a basis in fact. Perhaps of even greater importance is the fact that the Negro community itself has accepted this color preference. In conversation Negroes often try to deny or to minimize this fact. But there are a number of indications which an observer cannot help recording. For one thing, many individual Negroes will be found, when speaking about themselves, to rate their own color lighter than it actually is, but practically none to rate it darker. The desire on the part of Negro women of all shades and in all social classes to bleach their skin and straighten their hair – observed decades ago by Ray Stannard Baker and William Archer – has been the basis for some of the most important Negro businesses and some of the largest fortunes. Cosmetics for such purposes are most prominently advertised in the Negro press. The pictures of the social lions displayed on the social pages of the Negro newspapers give evidence in the same direction, as does listening to the undertones of conversation in Negro society even when an outsider is present.

Cliques, clubs, and social life in general seem to be permeated by this color preference. The color problem enters into the Negro home, where children show differences in shades, and into the schools. In marriage selection, as we have had occasion to mention previously, it becomes a dominant factor. It is impossible not to observe that in the higher classes the wives regularly tend to be of a lighter shade of color than the husbands. For a dark Negro woman, especially in the middle or upper classes, the chances of getting a husband are fewer than for a dark Negro man: men achieve more on the basis of merit and also take the initiative in marriage selection. A fair Negro woman, on the other hand, has such superior marriage chances that this fact is generally recognized as the major explanation of why passable women do not seem to pass out of the Negro caste as often as do passable men.

Fair-skinned Negroes have not been allowed by the white caste to establish an intermediary caste of their own. Their superior status has not been recognized. With great consistency they have been relegated to the Negro caste. In the Negro community their exclusiveness has been broken up by social mobility, aided by the growth of the Negro upper classes. Darker Negroes *can* rise to the top among Negroes in social status, and intermarriage with lighter Negroes *is* possible and actually not infrequent. But the marriage selection referred to and the greater opportunities generally for economic and cultural advance of fair-skinned Negroes have preserved an inherited situation where the darker individuals tend to form the lower classes while the fairer individuals tend to belong to the upper strata. The actual quantitative correlation between class and color is not known. It would seem, however, as if it were higher in urban districts than in rural ones. It is also probable that, in spite of the selection factors still working in favor of the fair-skinned individuals, the relative proportion of dark-skined individuals in the upper classes is increasing as these classes are growing. The "blue-veined" societies are breaking up.

As the Negro community is becoming increasingly "race conscious" it is no longer proper to display color preferences publicly. The light-skinned Negroes have to pledge allegiance to the Negro race. There is and has always been much envy on the part of darker Negroes toward lighter ones. There is even some tendency to regard a light skin as a badge of undesirable illegitimacy, especially when the light-skinned individual has a dark-skinned mother or siblings. There is also a slight tendency to attribute bad biological effects to miscegenation. The Garvey Back-to-Africa movement appealed systematically to the darker Negroes and tried to impute superiority to an unmixed African heritage.[13] Other more recent movements have made similar appeals.[14] This reaction has, however, never outweighed the primary tendency, which has always been to regard physical and cultural similarity to white people with esteem and deference. And the reaction itself is in many cases a psychological defense against a dominant belief in the desirability of light skin and "good" features. If has often been remarked that this tendency is not entirely unique among Negroes. It will appear in every disadvantaged group, for instance, among Jews in America. But Negro features also so distinct that only in the Negro problem does this factor become of great social importance.

Their color valuation is only one instance, among many, of the much more general tendency for the Negro people, to the degree that they are becoming acculturated, to take over the valuations of the superior white caste.[15] In other spheres this process can, on the whole, be regarded as a wholesome and advantageous adjustment of the Negroes to American life. In this particular respect, however, a conflict emerges which is unsolvable, as the average Negro cannot effectively change his color and other physical features. If the dark Negro accepts the white man's valuation of skin color, he must stamp himself as inferior. If the light Negro accepts this valuation, he places himself above the darker Negroes but below the whites, and he reduces his loyalty to his caste. The conflict produces a personality problem for practically every single Negro. And few Negroes accomplish an entirely successful adjustment.

There is a considerable literature on the personality problem of the light-skined Negro. He has been characterized as a "marginal man" – "one whom fate has condemned to live in two societies and in two, not merely different but antogonistic cultures" – and he has been assumed to show restlessness, instability, and all sorts of deviations from a harmonious and well-balanced personality type. This literature, which is largely of a speculative character, probably reflects – like the great amount of fiction devoted to the mulatto – more the imaginative expectations of white people as they think of themselves with their white skin, if placed under the caste yoke, than the actual life situation of mulattoes in the Negro caste. It is forgotten that the Negro upper strata enjoy considerable protection behind the wall of segregation and that a light skin in all social strata of the Negro community has definite advantages, two factors which must tend to make mulattoes rather more satisfied to be Negroes than are the darker Negroes.[16] It should not be denied, of course, that there are fair-skinned Negroes in America who develop the personality traits traditionally ascribed to them.[17] But, as Wirth and Goldhamer point out, "It is important to recognize . . . that in a sense *every* Negro, whether light or dark, is a marginal man in American society." And skin color is only one factor among many creating personality problems for Negroes.

The classes in the Negro community[18]

The static or cross-sectional configuration of the Negro class system, particularly as it is observable in the South, has recently been delineated in a number of community studies, and we know much more on this topic today than we did ten years ago. In all these studies the conventional division of a population into three classes – "lower class," "middle class," "upper class" – has been applied to the Negro community. Some of these studies, further, subdivide each of the three classes into two. It is quite convenient for the investigator to describe two extremes – the lower and upper classes – and then handle the great amount of variation by describing a middle class between them. We shall follow this pattern for the convenience of both ourselves and the reader. It should be understood that the description is in terms of the average, the general and the typical. Actually each class has a considerable amount of variation and there are often individuals who are complete exceptions. The actual situation, it must be remembered, is one of a continuum of social status, with an imperfect correlation between the factors making up social status and between social status and the other traits which are to be ascribed to the various classes. There are also differences between regions and communities, and the class structure is constantly changing.

The Negro *lower class,* as it is usually described, contains the large majority of Negroes everywhere. Any reasonable criteria used to describe the white lower class would , when applied to Negroes, put the majority of the latter in the lower class. They are the unskilled or semi-skilled laborers and domestic workers of the cities in the South and the North; and the agricultural wage laborers, tenants and household servants in Southern rural districts. During the 'thirties a large portion of this group has, permanently or temporarily, been on relief. Incomes are low and uncertain; levels of living do not include most of what is considered cultural necessities according to the "American standard."[19] They generally have little education. The older generation is often illiterate or practically illiterate. Books, periodicals, and newspapers, social movements and ideas, play an almost insignificant role in their lives.

This class is Southern in origin and character. Even in the Northern cities the lower class of Negroes is largely made up of recent migrants from the South and of their children. Both economically and culturally the Southern origin projects into present time the attitude and behavior patterns from slavery to a great extent. Lower class Negroes have kept more of the mental servility and dependence of the slave population and developed less resourcefulness, self-reliance and sense of individual dignity. Their situation is not favorable for developing strong incentives to personal accomplishment and improvement. Standards of industry and honesty are generally low. Judged by American standards, their family life is disorganized and their morals are lax.[20] Aggression and violence are neither rare nor censored much by community disapproval.[21] They are the group most subject to lack of legal protection in the South, and they probably have least respect for law and justice as it is applied in that region.[22]

Before the Civil War, ignorance and isolation probably kept most of the slaves accommodated to their inferior caste status. The bulk of this group remained in the lower class after the War. As the intimate servant-master relations have been progressively broken up, Negroes became increasingly resentful, in a sullen and concealed way, and behind their caste mask often manifested bitter resignation and suspicion against the whites. Some of them have been looked upon by the whites as the "good old darkies," but others are turning into "bad niggers," likely to fight back. Their strangeness is increasingly felt. This process has gone much further in the North than in the South and, in the South, further in urban districts than in rural ones.

This Negro lower class is, to reiterate, not homogeneous. In respect to security of employment and level of income, but more fundamentally to variations in family circumstances and individual endowments and propensities, some are falling below the average class norm and some are managing to keep above. To a section of the lower class belong the chronic relief cases, the habitual criminals, prostitutes, gamblers and vagabonds. It is a matter of definition and, partly, a matter of unemployment cycles, where the dividing line is to be drawn. In some cases, a gambler will have the prestige and wealth of a person in the middle or upper class, and during the depression of the 'thirties, the majority of the Negro population became either actual or potential relief clients. For the rural districts, Charles S. Johnson emphasizes rightly that a distinction should be made between the "folk Negro" and the rest of the lower class. The "folk Negro" has a low degree of assimilation to modern American standards but has, nevertheless, some measure of family organization and internal group cohesion. In the upper levels of the lower class, there are many persons who have definite ambitions to better their own, or at least their children's, status. These people will take care not to let their insurance lapse; they will have more permanent affiliation with churches and lodges; they will try to keep their children in school. It is again a matter of definition as to how large a portion of the Negro lower class should be included in this sub-group.

At the other end of the social status scale is the small Negro *upper class*. In rural districts the ownership and successful management of a sizable farm may be said to give a person upper class status. All over the country the training for a profession or the carrying on of a substantial business, particularly in the field of banking or insurance, but also in contracting, real estate, and personal service, is the regular basis for an upper class position. In smaller communities even today, and previously also in big cities, every steady employment where some training or skill was required, and the income was substantially above the average among Negroes, conferred upper class status. Employment by public agencies, particularly federal agencies like the United States postal service, has always carried high social esteem in the Negro community, and if coupled with some home ownership and some education, usually put the person in the upper class. Generally, in the absence of wealth, higher education is becoming practically an essential to an upper class position.

Often family background is stressed in this class. The family is organized upon the paternalistic principle, legal marriage in an accepted form, and illegitimacy and desertion are not condoned. Children are shielded as far as possible both from influences of the lower class Negroes and from humiliating experiences of the caste system. They are ordinarily given a higher education and assisted to acquire professional training. As Negroes are commonly believed to be loud, ignorant, dirty, boisterous, and lax in sexual and all other morals, good manners and respectability become nearly an obsession in the Negro upper class. If the community offers a choice, they will tend to belong to Episcopal, Congregational, or Presbyterian churches, or, in any case, to those churches where there is less "shouting" and where the preacher also has some education and refinement. In Southern cities the Negro upper class will often adhere more closely to strict puritanical standards of conduct than the white upper or middle class. In the larger cities, however, the younger generation in the upper class shows allegiance to the modern American fashion of being "smart" and "sporting." Conspicuous consumption in automobiles, dresses, and parties – carried on with "good taste" – is becoming of increasing importance and may even supplant respectability as the major characteristic of upper class status.

The Negro upper class is most thoroughly assimilated into the national culture, but it is also most isolated from the whites.[23] They are the most race conscious. They provide the leadership and often almost the entire membership of the nationally established Negro defense organizations, such as the local branches of the N.A.A.C.P. But they sometimes feel great difficulty in identifying themselves with the Negro masses whose spokesmen they are, although, perhaps, no more than the white upper class with the white lower class. *The Negro upper class is characterized by many of the traits which are in complete contrast to those of the masses of Negroes in the lower class.* Their social ambition is to keep up this distinction. In private they are often the severest critics of the Negro masses. Their resentment against the "lazy, promiscuous, uneducated, good-for-nothing" lower class Negro is apparent to every observer. W. E. B. Du Bois talks about the "inner problems of contact with their own lower classes with which they have few or no social institutions capable of dealing."

But their small numbers in rural districts and small cities of the South and the segregation everywhere enforce physical proximity to the lower class Negroes and make isolation difficult. The Negro masses, further, usually form the basis of their economic position and their income: usually they cannot afford too much exclusiveness. Moreover, they think of themselves, and are thought of by all other Negroes and by the whites, as the "Negro élite," membership in which confers the presumption of local leadership. This ties them spiritually to the protective Negro community. "Though the upper class is relatively small in numbers, . . . it provides the standards and values, and symbolizes the aspirations of the Negro community; being the most articulate element in the community, its outlook and interests are often regarded as those of the community at large." Not only as a basis for its economic livelihood but also as a sounding board for its role of leadership, the Negro upper class needs contact with the Negro masses. They have their social status and, indeed, their existence as an upper class only *by virtue of their relationship to the lower classes of Negroes.*

The conflict in their attitudes toward the lower class creates a tension and confusion in the political convictions of the upper class. Their wealth and security tend to make them conservative; their extreme dependence on the lower class forces them to sympathize with reforms which would aid the lower class – and, therefore, themselves indirectly. Negro doctors, for example, have reasons to be against socialized medicine, as do many white doctors, since they might lose some of their clients. But they stand to profit enormously if the government should use Negro doctors to treat Negro patients under a socialized set-up.[24]

The Negro *middle* class is usually assumed to be larger than the upper class but smaller than the lower class.[25] There would be a good deal of difference of opinion among experts as to what occupations were associated with middle class status. They have usually achieved a small but, in comparison with the lower class, less insecure occupational position, but are characterized even more by a striving toward a better economic position. Usually they have had primary or secondary education, but few have been to college except the school teachers. Education has a high ranking in their scale of social values, and they want to give their children this means of fuller cultural emancipation. They also look down on the lower class Negroes and attempt to appear respectable. Thrift, independence, honesty and industriousness are included in their standards. In the middle class, it becomes a proud boast never to have been in trouble with the law. Their family life is rather stabilized. Even if many of them are married under common law,[26] these marriages tend to be relatively stable. Extra-marital relations are not uncommon, at least for the men, but it is expected that affairs shall be carried on in decent secrecy. They are ordinarily energetic and loyal members of lodges and of churches – usually of the Baptist or Methodist variety.

In the bigger cities where prostitution, gamblng, and other types of "protected" businesses reach considerable importance, there is, parallel to the ordinary "respectable" class structure, a less respectable, or "shady", class structure. Its upper class consists of the successful racketeers. The middle class may be said to consist of their lieutenants and the less successful independents. The lower class would then consist of hangers-on and petty criminals. Wealth and power is the main criterion of status in this society. Education, family background, and respectability have no significance. The upper and middle classes of this shady society have a certain prestige with the lower classes of the general Negro society in the cities. For this reason, vice and crime can appear as a desirable career to almost any lower class urban youth. This shady Negro society has a parallel in the white world, but the shady white society probably has less general prestige.[27]

The foregoing picture of the Negro class structure is, like most other descriptions, static. Actually, however, the Negro class structure is dynamic: not only is there movement between the classes and changes within each of the classes, but also the entire class system is moving upward.

* * *

AMERICAN IDEALS AND THE AMERICAN CONSCIENCE

Unity of ideals and diversity of culture

It is a commonplace to point out the heterogeneity of the American nation and the swift succession of all sorts of changes in all its component parts and, as it often seems, in every conceivable direction. America is truly a shock to the stranger. The bewildering impression it gives of dissimilarity throughout and of chaotic unrest is indicated by the fact that few outside observers – and indeed, few native Americans –

have been able to avoid the intellectual escape of speaking about America as "paradoxical."

Still there is evidently a strong unity in this nation and a basic homogeneity and stability in its valuations. Americans of all national origins, classes, regions, creeds, and colors, have something in common: a social *ethos,* a political creed. It is difficult to avoid the judgment that this "American Creed" is the cement in the structure of this great and disparate nation.

When the American Creed is once detected, the cacophony becomes a melody. The further observation then becomes apparent: that America, compared to every other country in Western civilization, large or small, has the *most explicitly expressed* system of general ideals in reference to human interrelations. This body of ideals is more widely understood and appreciated than similar ideals are anywhere else. The American Creed is not merely – as in some other countries – the implicit background of the nation's political and judicial order as it functions. To be sure, the political creed of America is not very satisfactorily effectuated in actual social life. But as principles which *ought* to rule, the Creed has been made conscious to everyone in American society.

Sometimes one even gets the impression that there is a relation between the intense apprehension of high and uncompromising ideals and the spotty reality. One feels that it is, perhaps, the difficulty of giving reality to the *ethos* in this young and still somewhat unorganized nation – that it is the prevalence of "wrongs" in America, "wrongs" judged by the high standards of the national Creed – which helps make the ideals stand out so clearly. America is continously struggling for its soul. These principles of social ethics have been hammered into easily remembered formulas. All means of intellectual communication are utilized to stamp them into everybody's mind. The schools teach them, the churches preach them. The courts pronounce their judicial decisions in their terms. They permeate editorials with a pattern of idealism so ingrained that the writers could scarcely free themselves from it even if they tried. They have fixed a custom of indulging in high-sounding generalities in all written or spoken addresses to the American public, otherwise so splendidly gifted for the matter-of-fact approach to things and problems. Even the stranger, when he has to appear before an American audience, feels this, if he is sensitive at all, and finds himself espousing the national Creed, as this is the only means by which a speaker can obtain human response from the people to whom he talks.

The Negro people in America are no exception to the national pattern. "It was a revelation to me to hear Negroes sometimes indulge in a glorification of American democracy in the same uncritical way as unsophisticated whites often do," relates the Dutch observer, Bertram Schrieke. A Negro political scientist, Ralph Bunche, observes:

> Every man in the street, white, black, red or yellow, knows that this is "the land of the free," the "land of opportunity," the "cradle of liberty," the "home of democracy," that the American flag symbolizes the "equality of all men" and guarantees to us all "the protection of life, liberty and property," freedom of speech, freedom of religion and racial tolerance.

The present writer has made the same observation. The American Negroes know that they are a subordinated group experiencing, more than anybody else in the nation, the consequences of the fact that the Creed is not lived up to in America. Yet their faith in the Creed is not simply a means of pleading their unfulfilled rights. They, like the whites, are under the spell of the great national suggestion. With one part of themselves they actually believe, as do the whites, that the Creed is ruling America.

These ideals of the essential dignity of the individual human being, of the fundamental equality of all men, and of certain inalienable rights to freedom, justice, and a fair opportunity represent to the American people the essential meaning of the nation's early struggle for independence. In the clarity and intellectual boldness of the Enlightenment period these tenets were written into the Declaration of Independence, the Preamble of the Constitution, the Bill of Rights and into the constitutions of the several states. The ideals of the American Creed have thus become the highest law of the land. The Supreme Court pays its reverence to these general principles when it declares what is constitutional and what is not. They have been elaborated upon by all national leaders, thinkers and statesmen. America has had, throughout its history, a continuous discussion of the principles and implications of democracy, a discussion which, in every epoch, measured by any standard, remained high, not only quantitatively but also qualitatively. The flow of learned treatises and popular tracts on the subject has not ebbed, nor is it likely to do so. In all wars, including the present one, the American Creed has been the ideological foundation of national morale.

American nationalism

The American Creed is identified with America's peculiar brand of nationalism, and it gives the common American his feeling of the historical mission of America in the world – a fact which just now becomes of global importance but which is also of highest significance for the particular problem studied in this book. The great national historian of the middle ninteenth century, George Bancroft, expressed this national feeling of pride and responsibility:

> In the fulness of time a republic rose in the wilderness of America. Thousands of years had passed away before this child of the ages could be born. From whatever there was of good in the systems of the former centuries she drew her nourishment; the wrecks of the past were her warnings. . . The fame of this only daughter of freedom went out into all the lands of the earth; from her the human race drew hope.

And Frederick J. Turner, who injected the naturalistic explanation into history that American democracy was a native-born product of the Western frontier, early in this century wrote in a similar vein:

> Other nations have been rich and prosperous and powerful. But the United States has believed that it had an original contribution to make to the history of society by the production of a self-determining, self-restrained, intelligent democracy.

Wilson's fourteen points and Roosevelt's four freedoms have more recently expressed to the world the boundless idealistic aspirations of this American Creed. For a century and more before the present epoch, when the oceans gave reality to the Monroe Doctrine, America at least applauded heartily every uprising of the people in any corner of the world. This was a tradition from America's own Revolution. The political revolutionaries of foreign countries were approved even by the conservatives in America. And America wanted generously to share its precious ideals and its happiness in enjoying a society ruled by its own people with all who would come here. James Truslow Adams tells us:

> The American dream that has lured tens of millions of all nations to our shores in the past century has not been a dream of merely material plenty, though that has doubtless counted heavily. It has been much more than that. It has been a dream of being able to grow to fullest development as man and woman, unhampered by the barriers which had slowly been erected in older civilizations, unrepressed by social orders which had developed for the benefit of classes rather than for the simple human being of any and every class. And that dream has been realized more fully in actual life here than anywhere else, though very imperfectly even among ourselves.

This is what the Western frontier country could say to the "East." And even the skeptic cannot help feeling that, perhaps, this youthful exuberant America has the destiny to do for the whole Old World what the frontier did to the old colonies. *American nationalism is permeated by the American Creed,* and therefore becomes international in its essence.

* * *

AMERICA AGAIN AT THE CROSSROADS

America's opportunity

But these consequences of the present course of America's and the world's history should not be recorded only in terms of compelling forces. The bright side is that the conquering of color caste in America is America's own innermost desire. This nation early laid down as the moral basis for its existence the principles of equality and liberty. However much Americans have dodged this conviction, they have refused to adjust their laws to their own license. Today, more than ever, they refuse to discuss systematizing their caste order to mutual advantage, apparently because they most seriously mean that caste is wrong and should not be given recognition. They stand warmheartedly against oppression in all the world. When they are reluctantly forced into war, they are compelled to justify their participation to their own conscience by insisting that they are fighting against aggression and for liberty and equality.

America feels itself to be humanity in miniature. When in this crucial time the international leadership passes to America, the great reason for hope is that this country has a national experience of uniting racial and cultural diversities and a national theory, if not a consistent practice, of freedom and equality for all. What America is constantly reaching for is democracy at home and abroad. The main trend in its history is the gradual realization of the American Creed.

In this sense the Negro problem is not only America's greatest failure but also America's incomparably great opportunity for the future. If America should follow its own deepest convictions, its well-being at home would be increased directly. At the same time America's prestige and power abroad would rise immensely. The century-old dream of American patriots, that America should give to the entire world its own freedoms and its own faith, would come true, America can demonstrate that justice, equality and cooperation are possible between white and colored people.

In the present phase of history this is what the world needs to believe. Mankind is sick of fear and disbelief, of pessimism and cynicism. It needs the youthful moralistic optimism of America. But empty declarations only deepen cynicism. Deeds are called for. If America in actual practice could show the world a progressive trend by which the Negro became finally integrated into modern democracy, all mankind would be given faith again – it would have reason to believe that peace, progress and order are feasible. And America would have a spiritual power many times stronger than all her financial and military resources – the power of the trust and support of all good people on earth. *America is free to choose whether the Negro shall remain her liability or become her opportunity.*

The development of the American Negro problem during the years to come is, therefore, fateful not only for America itself but for all mankind. If America wants to make the second choice, she cannot wait and see. She has to do something big and do it soon. For two generations after the national compromise of the 1870s between the North and the South on the Negro problem, the caste status of the Negro was allowed to remain almost unchanged. It was believed by most well-meaning people that self-healing would work, that the Negro problem would come to solve itself by the lapse of time. George Washington Cable wrote in the 'eighties:

> There is a vague hope, much commoner in the North than in the South, that somehow, if everybody will sit still, *"time"* will bring these changes.

Two decades later, Ray Stannard Baker reported from the South:

> All such relationships will work themselves out gradually, naturally, quietly, in the long course of the years: and the less they are talked about the better.

Most of the literature on the Negro problem continues to this day to be written upon this same static assumption.

We have given the reasons why we believe that the *interregnum,* during which the forces balanced each other fairly well, is now at an end. The equilibrium, contrary to common belief, was unstable and temporary. As American Negroes became educated and culturally assimilated, but still found themselves excluded, they grew bitter. Meanwhile the whites were in the process of losing their caste theory. The international upheavals connected with the two World Wars and the world depression brought these developments to a crisis. American isolation was lost. Technical developments brought all nations to be close neighbors even though they were not trained to live together.

We are now in a deeply unbalanced world situation. Many human relations will be readjusted in the present world revolution, and among them race relations are bound to change considerably. As always in a revolutionary situation when society's moorings are temporarily loosened, there is, on the one hand, an opportunity to direct the changes into oragnized reforms and, on the other hand, a corresponding risk involved in letting the changes remain uncontrolled and lead into disorganization. To do nothing is to accept defeat.

From the point of view of social science, this means, among other things, that social engineering will increasingly be demanded. Many things that for a long period have been predominantly a matter of individual adjustment will become more and more determined by political decision and public regulation. We are entering an era where fact-finding and scientific theories of causal relations will be seen as instrumental in planning controlled social change. The peace will bring nothing but problems, one mounting upon another, and consequently, new urgent tasks for social engineering. The American social scientist, because of the New Deal and the War, is already acquiring familiarity with planning and practical action. He will never again be given the opportunity to build up so "disinterested" a social science.

The social sciences in America are equipped to meet the demands of the post-war world. In social engineering they will retain the old American faith in human beings which is all the time becoming fortified by research as the trend continues toward environmentalism in the search for social causation. In a sense, the social engineering of the coming epoch will be nothing but the drawing of practical conclusions from the teaching of social science that "human nature" is changeable and that human deficiencies and unhappiness are, in large degree, preventable.

In this spirit, so intrinsically in harmony with the great tradition of the Enlightenment and the American Revolution, the author may be allowed to close with a personal note. Studying human beings and their behavior is not discouraging. When the author recalls the long gallery of persons whom, in the course of this inquiry, he has come to know with the impetuous but temporary intimacy of the stranger – sharecroppers and plantation owners, workers and employers, merchants and bankers, intellectuals, preachers, organization leaders, political bosses, gangsters, black and white, men and women, young and old, Southerners and Northerners – and general observation retained is the following: Behind all outward dissimilarities, behind their contradictory valuations, rationalizations, vested interests, group allegiances and animosities, behind fears and defense constructions, behind the role they play in life and the mask they wear, people are all much alike on a fundamental level. And they are all good people. They want to be rational and just. They all plead to their conscience that they meant well even when things went wrong.

Social study is concerned with explaining why all these potentially and intentionally good people so often make life a hell for themselves and each other when they live together, whether in a family, a community, a nation or a world. The fault is certainly not with becoming organized *per se*. In their formal organizations, as we have seen, people invest their highest ideals. These institutions regularly direct the individual toward more cooperation and justice than he would be inclined to observe as an isolated private person. The fault is, rather, that our structures of organizations are too imperfect, each by itself, and badly integrated into a social whole.

Notes

1. The response is likely to be anything but pleasant if one jestingly argues that possibly a small fraction of Negro blood in the American people, if it were blended well with all the other good stock brought over to the new continent, might create a race of unsurpassed excellence: a people with just a little sunburn without extra trouble and even through the winter; with some curl in the hair without the cost of a permanent wave; with, perhaps, a little more emotional warmth in their souls; and a little more religion, music, laughter, and carefreeness in their lives. Amalgamation is, to the ordinary American, not a proper subject for jokes at all, unless it can be pulled down to the level of dirty stories, where, however, it enjoys a favored place. Referred to society as a whole and viewed as a principle, the anti-amalgamation maxim is held holy; it is a consecrated taboo. The maxim might, indeed, be a remnant of something really in the "mores". It is kept unproblematic, which is certainly not the case with all the rest of etiquette and segregation and discrimination patterns, for which this quality is sometimes erroneously claimed.

2. In this introductory sketch the distinction between "segregation" and "discrimination" is entirely disregarded. This distinction, signified by the popular theory and legal construct "separate but equal," is mainly to be regarded as an equalitarian rationalization on the part of the white Americans, indicating the fundamental conflict of valuations involved in the matter. "Segregation" means only separation and does not, in principle, imply "discrimination." In practice it almost always does. (See Chapter 28).

3. The parallel between the status of Negroes and of women, who are neither a minority group nor a low social class, is particularly instructive; see Appendix 5, "A Parallel to the Negro Problem."

4. See Chapter 33 of *An American Dilemma.*

5. See Chapter 18 of *An American Dilemma.*

6. In this chapter we shall confine ourselves to the relation between caste and *Negro* classes. This does not mean that caste has no effect on the white class structure. Attitudes and actions toward Negroes have always differentiated the various white classes in the South. (See Chapter 28, Section 8.) Also there have been concrete effects: for example, when practically all Negroes were below them during slavery, the lower class whites probably felt less social distance from upper class whites in the South than today when they realize that many Negroes have a class status above them.

7. On the other hand, *within the Negro community*, the upper class Negro is placed higher than is the white man of comparable income, education, and so on, in the white community. Du Bois observed this:

   ". . . a white Philadelphian with $1,500 a year can call itself poor and live simply. A Negro with $1,500 a year ranks with the richest of his race and must usually spend more in proportion than his white neighbor in rent, dress and entertainment." (W. E. B. Du Bois, The Philadelphia Negro (1899), p. 178.)

8. The author once attended a meeting in Detroit where one of the national Negro leaders gave a speech. The church where the meeting was held was filled with professionals and business people of the local Negro upper class with a sprinkling of humbler people. After the address, there was some discussion, and the eternal question of Negro strategy was brought up. The speaker is answering began to give the standard arguments for a cautious approach. In the middle of his answer he seemed to sense the futility of the question; he smiled and remarked that perhaps segregation should not be bullied so without qualifications: "How would you

all feel if you awakened tomorrow morning and found yourself in the wild sea of white competition?" He cashed in a big laugh, somewhat nervous and bashful, but relieving.

9. See Chapters 13 and 14 of *An American Dilemma.*

10. Two other characteristics that are rather unique make for upper class status in the Negro world: caste leadership and achievement in the white world. Marcus Garvey, Oscar DePriest, and Father Divine, on the one hand, and Joe Louis, Paul Robeson, and Rochester, on the other hand, have high status and would have had it even if they were neither rich nor educated.

11. A special reason why upper class Negroes often make so much of their family background is that if they had free Negro or upper class white ancestry it puts them above the hated slave background. A few Negroes who have risen very high and who are secure may – like the white man – boast of their lowly origin. Frederick Douglass and Booker T. Washington did this.

12. In South Africa, the mulatto group holds itself as a separate caste, even though the blacks are not slaves. A similar situation exists in many other countries. Our statement refers to conditions in the United States only.

13. See Chapter 35, Section 7 of *An American Dilemma.*

14. See Chapter, 39, Section 2 of *An American Dilemma.*

15. See Chapter 44, Section 1 of *An American Dilemma.*

16. Another problem for dark-skinned Negroes who reach the upper class arises out of the fact that they are newly arrived and so have a tenseness which the light-skinned who, for the most part, are long established in the upper class, do not have.

    The studies for the American Youth Commission (see footnote 9 of Chapter 30) corroborate the author's impression that the personality problems of the dark-skinned Negro are often greater than are those of the light-skinned Negro. This is especially true among the educated groups.

17. I have met two violently anti-Negro mulattoes who identified themselves with the whites. One was a passer. The other was just a little bit too dark to pass safely. The latter proudly emphaisized that he was "the descendant of slave owners," which, of course, is not uncommon in the Negro world, but in his announcment it had a definitely sadistic and hateful import. I have been with many passers; with the exception mentioned, they did not show any extraordinary hatred of Negroes or any abnormal fixation on "white blood." Fair-skinned nonpassing Negroes are generally conscious of their social advantage and are sometimes cautiously critical of the black masses. They do not ordinarily appear particularly off balance, but are rather inclined to belong to the complacent type of well-accommodated *petit bourgeois Negro.*

18. For other dynamic interpretations of Negro classes, see: E Franklin Frazier: *The Negro Family in the United States* (1939), pp. 393-475; and Allison Davis, Burleigh B. Gardner, and Mary R. Gardner, *Deep South* (1941), Chapters 9 and 10.

19. Concerning occupational status, unemployment and relief, incomes and levels of living, see Chapters 15 and 16.

20. See Chapter 43, Section 2 of *An American Dilemma.*

21. See Chapter 44, Section 2 of *An American Dilemma.*

22. See Part VI of *An American Dilemma.*

23. See Chapter 30, Section 2. This fact does not, however, prevent upper class Negroes from occasionally enjoying class solidarity over the caste line with upper class whites. See Davis, Gardner, and Gardner, *op. cit.*, p. 53; John Dollard, *Caste and Class in a Southern Town* (1937), p. 83; and Hortense Powdermaker, *After Freedom* (1939), p. 338.

24. See Chapter 15, Section 4 of *An American Dilemma.*

25. This arbitrary assumption would have an empirial justifiation if, as we assumed, the class pyramid has a tapering point and concave sides. See Section 1 of this chapter.

26. There is a divergence of opinion among those who have studied the matter as to whether the middle class among Negroes tends to have formal marriage or only commonlaw marriage. Those who say that the Negro middle class tends to have legalized marriage probably consider that the middle class contains people occupied in skilled work and business. They are also probably thinking of Negroes in the North. We follow Powder-maker (*op. cit.*, pp. 152-153): "In the middle class, licensed marriages are few." We regard the middle class as consisting of mainly semi-skilled workers and workers in the "higher" service occupations, and we are giving main emphasis to conditions in the South. Practically all experts agree that the Negro middle class family is fairly stable, even where it has common-law marriage (see, for example Dollard, *op. cit.*, p. 87; E. Franklin Frazier, *Negro Youth at the Crossways* (1940), p. 278).

27. See Chapter 14, Section 10 of *An American Dilemma.*

11.4 Oliver Cromwell Cox on Caste, Class and Race

In his book, Caste, Class and Race, *Oliver Cromwell Cox presents an alternative, Marxist analysis of the black situation, rejecting the theories of Park on race relations, W. Lloyd Warner and the caste school, and Myrdal on the role of white racism. Instead, Cox argues for black exploitation and ill-treatment to be laid squarely at the door of capitalistic organisation and policy and its encouragement of class antagonism.*

(a) Park's Theory of Race Relations

Shorn of its censual and descriptive support, Park's theory of race relations is weak, vacillating, and misleading; and, to the extent that it lends "scientific" confirmation to the Southern rationalizations of racial exploitation, it is insidious.[30] His teleological approach has diverted him from an examination of specific causal events in the development of modern race antagonism; it has led him inevitably into a hopeless position about "man's inhumanity to man," a state of mind that must eventually drive the student into the open arms of the mystic.

It may seem puerile and even unfair to criticize Professor Park's ideas and views in this fashion. Puerile because one, knowing of Park's kaleidoscopic intellectual style, has no difficulty in finding inconsistencies and occasional contradictions in his writings; and unfair because the citations have been abstracted from their animated setting. But we have been especially careful not to distort these ideas and to consider only that part of Park's theory upon which he seems to put some continued reliance. In fact, this is apparently the whole substance of Dr. Park's contributions to the theory of race relations.[31] Moreover, it is easy to discover inconsistencies but not so easy to show that these inconsistencies are inevitable.

If we know that one believes that the cultural conflicts which existed in ancient times are in fact race conflicts, that race prejudice is caste prejudice, that "the mores" of the white man determine or even maintain the pattern of race relations, then we approach his work with assurance that there will be inconsistencies. Such theories do not explain the facts, and in order to achieve some semblance of logical exposition one must inevitably become inconsistent and contradictory.

Probably the crucial fallacy in Park's thinking is his belief that the beginnings of modern race prejudice may be traced back to the immemorial periods of human associations. As a matter of fact, however, if it is not recognized the color prejudice developed only recently among Europeans, very little, if any, progress could be made in the study of race relations. We must also recognize the peculiar socio-economic necessity for race prejudice. Indeed, Park himself almost put his finger upon this. Thus he writes:

> There was no such thing as a race problem before the Civil War, and there was at the time very little of what we ordinarily call race prejudice, except in the case of the free Negro. The free Negro was the source and origin of whatever race problems there were. Because he was free, he was at once an anomaly and a source of constant anxiety to the slaveholding population.[32]

Although we do not agree entirely with this statement, it might yet have been observed that in the United States the race prolem developed out of the need of the planter class, the ruling class, to keep the freed Negro exploitable. To do this, the ruling class had to do what every ruling class must do; that is, develop mass support for its policy. Race prejudice was and is the convenient vehicle. Apparently it now becomes possible to give meaning to the phenomenon of race prejudice.

Race prejudice in the United States is the socio-attitudinal matrix supporting a calculated and determined effort of a white ruling class to keep some people or peoples of color and their resources exploitable. In a quite literal sense the white ruling class is the Negro's burden; the saying that the white man will do anything for the Negro except get off his back puts the same idea graphically.[33] It is the economic content of race prejudice which makes it a powerful and fearfully subduing force. The "peonization" of Negroes in the South is an extreme form of exploitation and oppression, but this is not caused by race prejudice. The race prejudice is involved with the economic interest. Indeed, "one does not feel prejudice against a beast of burden; one simply keeps him between the shafts." However, it is the human tendency, under capitalism, to break out of such a place, together with the determined counterpressure of exploiters, which produces essentially the lurid psychological complex called race prejudice. Thus race prejudice may be thought of as having its genesis in the propagandistic and legal contrivances of the white ruling class for securing mass support of its interest. It is an attitude of distance and estrangement mingled with repugnance, which seeks to conceptualize as brutes the human objects of exploitation.[34] The integrity of race prejudice must be protected and maintained by the exploiters, for it is constantly strained even at the very few points where sympathetic contact is permitted between the people.

Race prejudice, then, constitutes an attitudinal justification necessary for an easy exploitation of some race. To put it in still another way, race prejudice is the social-attitudinal concomitant of the racial-exploitative practice of a ruling class in a capitalistic society. The substance of race prejudice is the exploitation of the militarily weaker race. The slogan that the colored man shall never have social equality merely means that the colored man must be forever kept exploitable.

We should not be distracted by the illusion of personal repugnance for a race. Whether, as individuals, we feel like or dislike for the colored person is not the crucial fact. What the ruling class requires of race prejudice is that it should uniformly produce racial antagonism; and its laws and propaganda are fashioned for this purpose. The attitude abhors a personal or sympathetic relationship.[35] The following statement by Kelly Miller seems to be relevant:

> Henry W. Grady, not only the mouthpiece, but also the oracle of the South, declared in one of his deliverances that he believed that natural instinct would hold the races asunder, but, if such instinct did not exist, he would strengthen race prejudice so as to make it hold the stubbornness and strength of instinct.[36]

This point may be illustrated further. As an American one might have a great hatred for the English; one might feel the Englishman decidedly repulsive. But normally such an attitude will be personal; it may even have to be private. There are no social sanctions for it. But if the United States should go to war with England, for what real reason the masses of people may not know, then Americans will be propagandized and made to feel dislike for every Englishman. The attitude thus becomes social, and public expressions of hatred for the English will merit the applause of the group. In this situation, to show friendship for the English is to be defined as a traitor, so that to live easily with one's fellows one should both hate and consequently fear the English. Above all, one should never seem to "fraternize" with them; and this even though one's personal experience contradicts the propaganda. Ordinarily, however, individual experience will tend to be consistent with social definitions and pressures.

Perhaps we can now begin to think constructively about race prejudice. The mystification is probably gone. Evidently race prejudice can never be wholly removed under capitalism, because exploitation of militarily weaker peoples is inherent in capitalism. However, within this system the form of race exploitation may be changed.

Capitalist, bourgeois society is modern Western society, which, as a social system, is categorically different from any other contemporary or previously existing society.

Capitalism developed in Europe exclusively; in the East it is a cultural adoption.

In order that capitalism might exist it must proletarianize the masses of workers; that is to say, it must "commoditize" their capacity to work.

To "commoditize" the capacity of persons to work is to conceptualize, consciously or unconsciously, an inanimate or subhuman, these human vehicles of labor power and to behave toward them according to the laws of the market; that is to say, according to the fundamental rules of capitalist society. The capitalist is constrained to regard his labor power "as an abstract quantity, a purchasable, *impersonal* commodity, an item in the cost of production rather than a great mass of human beings."

Labor thus becomes a factor of production to be bought and sold in a non-sentimental market and to be exploited like capital and land, according to the economic interest of producers, for a profit. In production a cheap labor supply is an immediate and *practical* end.

To the extent to which labor can be manipulated as a commodity void of human sensibilities, to that extent also the entrepreneur is free from hindrance to his sole purpose of maximizing his profits. Therefore, capitalism cannot be primarily concerned with human welfare. Slavery, in a capitalist society, presents an ideal situation for easy manipulation of labor power; but it is against free competition, a powerful desideratum of capitalism. Labor, under slavery, is of the nature of capital. It should be observed, however, that long-continued contact between slave and master may develop personal sympathies which tend to limit good business practice in the exploitation of slave labor.

It becomes, then, the immediate pecuniary interest of the capitalists, the bourgeoisie, not only to develop an ideology and world view which facilitate proletarianization, but also, when necessary, to use force in accomplishing this end.

So far as ideology is concerned, the capitalists proceed in a normal way; that is to say, they develop and exploit ethnocentrism and show by any irrational or logical means available that the working class of their own race or whole peoples of other races, whose labor they are bent upon exploiting, are somethng apart: (a) not human at all, (b) only part human, (c) inferior humans, and so on. The bourgeoisie in Europe were faced both with the problem of wresting the power from the agricultural landlords and at the same time keeping the workers from snatching any part of that power. Among the peoples of color, however, the Europeans had only the problem of converting virtually the whole group to worker status.

So far as force is concerned, we might illustrate. In the unrestrained process of "commoditizing" the labor of the American Indians the early European capitalist adventurers accomplished their complete extermination in the West Indies and decimated them on the continent.

The rationalizations for their doing this were that the Indians were not human; they were heathens; they could not be converted to Christianity; therefore, they were exploited, like the beasts of burden, without compunction for infringements of natural human rights. At that time also the argument for the exploitation of the labor of white women and white children in Europe was that the long hours of labor kept them from the concern of the devil, from idleness, and that their supposed suffering was part of the price all human beings must pay for their sins either here or hereafter.

When the great resource of African black labor became available, Indians in the West were not so much relied upon. They were largely pushed back as far as possible from exploitable natural resources.

Slavery became the means by which African labor was used most profitably; hence Negroes were considered producers' capital.

As the tendency to question such overt capitalist exploitation of human beings increased, principally among some articulate persons ordinarily not immediately engaged in business, the rationalizations about the non-human character of Negroes also increased. Moreover, the priests, on the whole, pointed out that God amply sanctioned the ways of the capitalists. The greater the immediacy of the exploitative need, the more insistent were the arguments supporting the rationalizations.

At this time, the early nineteenth century, many white workers in Europe and in America were being killed, beaten, or jailed for attempting to organize themselves so that they might limit their free exploitation by the entrepreneurs. Their unions were considered conspiracies against "society," and thus against the bourgeois state.

In 1861 the Civil War was commenced partly as a reaction to certain social pressures to break the monopoly on black labor in the South and to open up the natural resources of that region for freer exploitation.

At length, however, the Southern agricultural capitalists initiated a counterrevolution and re-established a high degree of control over their labor supply. To do this they had to marshal every force, including the emotional power of the masses of poor whites, in a fanatical campaign of race hatred, with sexual passion as the emotional core.

In support of this restoration the ruling class enacted black codes in which the principal offenses were attempts to whiten the black labor force by sexual contacts and tampering with the labor supply by union organizers or labor recruiters. All sympathetic contact between the white and black masses was scrupulously ruled out by a studied system of segregation. The whole Negro race was defined as having a "place," that of the freely exploitable worker – a place which it could not possibly keep if intermarriage was permitted.

At this time, also, the last quarter of the nineteenth century, the labor movement in the North was being driven underground. Labor had to organize in secret societies – sometimes terroristic societies. Troops, sometimes Federal troops, were being called out from east to west to put down strikes, and the Knights of Labor became a proletarian movement.

Today the ruling class in the South effectively controls legislation in the national Congress favorable to the continued exploitation of the Negro masses mainly by diplomatic bargaining with the politicians of the Northern capitalist exploiters of white labor. The guardians of the racial system in the South control or spend millions of dollars to maintain segregation devices – the most powerful illusory contrivance for keeping poor whites and Negroes antagonized – and to spread anti-color propaganda all over the nation and the world. For this expenditure they expect a return more or less calculable in dollars and cents.

Today it is of vital consequence that black labor and white labor in the South be kept glaring at each other, for if they were permitted to come together in force and to identify their interests as workers, the difficulty of exploiting them would be increased beyond calculation. Indeed, the persistence of the whole system of worker exploitation in the United States depends pivotally upon the maintenance of an active race hatred between white and black workers in the South.

The rationalizations of the exploitative purpose which we know as race prejudice are always couched in terms of the ideology of the age. At first it was mainly religious, then historico-anthropological, then Darwinian-anthropometrical, and today it is sexual, *laissez faire,* and mystical. The intent of these rationalizations, of course, must always be to elicit a collective feeling of more or less ruthless antagonism against and contempt for the exploited race or class. They could never have the meaning that, since the race or class is supposed to be inferior, superior persons ought to be humane toward it – ought to help it along the rugged road whereby full superior stature might be achieved. On the contrary, they must always have the intent and meaning that, since the race is inferior, superior people have a natural right to suppress and to exploit it. The more "inferior" the race is, the more securely the yoke should be clamped around its neck and the saddle fixed upon its back. The rationalizations are thus a defense; race prejudice is a defensive attitude. The obtrusiveness of certain social ideals developed under capitalism as concessions to the masses makes the rationalizations of racial exploitation necessary.

(b) The modern caste school of race relations

During the last decade a prolific school of writer on race relations in the United States, led mainly by social anthropologists, has relied religiously upon an ingenious, if not original, caste hypothesis. Professor W. Lloyd Warner is the admitted leader of the movement, and his followers include scholars of considerable distinction.[1] We propose here to examine critically the position of this school.

The hypothesis

If we think of a hypothesis as a tentative statement of a theory which some researcher sets out to demonstrate or to prove, then the school has no hypothesis. But we shall quote liberally so that the authors might have an opportunity to speak for themselves about the things which they believe. These we shall call loosely the hypothesis. The school is particularly interested in race relations in the Southern states of the United States, and its members believe that they have struck upon an unusually revealing explanation of the situation. In the South, they maintain, Negroes form one caste and whites another, with an imaginary rotating caste line between them. "The white caste is in a superordinate position and the Negro caste in the subordinate social position." The following definition of caste has been most widely accepted.

> Caste . . . describes a theoretical arrangement of the people of a given group in an order in which the privileges, duties, obligations, opportunities, etc., are unequally distributed between the groups which are considered to be higher and lower. . . . Such a definition also describes

> class. A caste or organization. . . can be further defined as one where marriage between two or more groups is not sanctioned and where there is no opportunity for members of the lower groups to rise into the upper groups or of members of the upper to fall into the lower ones.[2]

A class system and a caste system "are antithetical to each other. . . Nevertheless they have accommodated themselves in the southern community. . . ." The caste line is represented as running asymetrically diagonally between the two class systems of Negroes and whites as in the following diagram.[3]

It is assumed that during slavery the caste line, AB in diagram, was practically horizontal but that since then, with the cultural progress of Negroes, it has rotated upward. It may become perpendicular so as to coincide with the line DE; indeed, though unlikely, it may swing over toward the whites. The point here is that it would be possible for the line to take a vertical position while the caste system remains intact.

It is thought further that the social disparity between Negro classes and white classes is particularly disconcerting to upper-class Negroes.

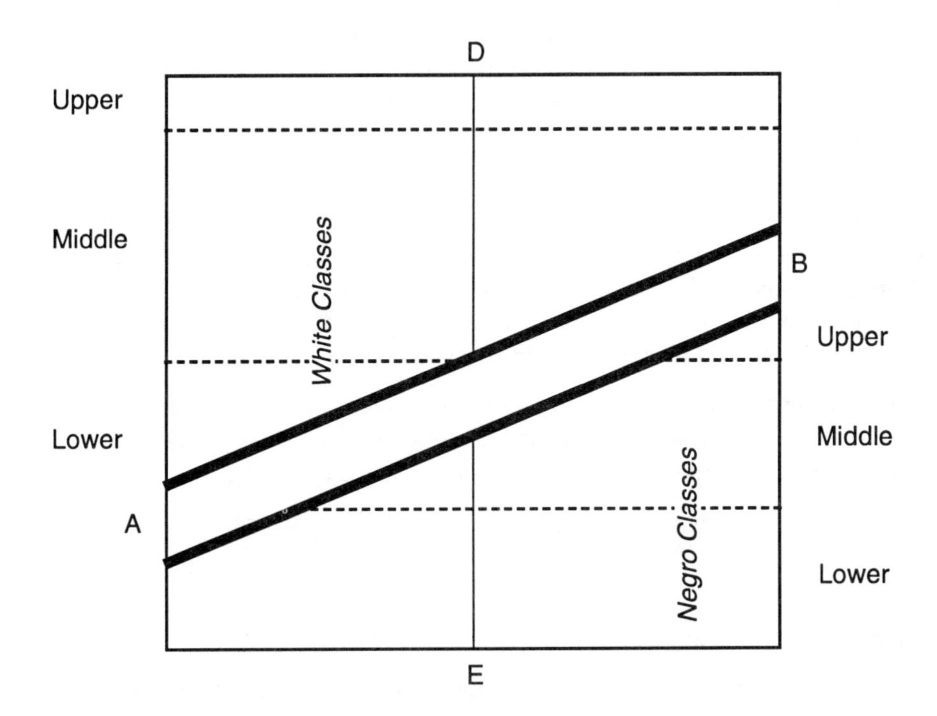

Position of "Caste Line" betweeen White and Negroes in the United States

The "emotional instability of many of the individuals in this group" may be readily explained since:

> In his own personality he feels the conflict of the two opposing structures, and in the thinking and feeling of the members of both groups there is to be found this same conflict about his position . . . Although he is at the top of the Negro class hierarchy, he is constantly butting his head against the caste line.[4]

It is believed that in many countries of the world besides India there are developed caste systems, but the school has never found it convenient to demonstrate this proposition. "Caste," Warner and Davis asset without proof, "is found in most of the major areas of the world; this is particularly true of Africa, Asia, and America. The Indians of the southeastern United States and those of British Columbia have well-developed, if not castes, then caste-like structures. We cannot take time to examine those American systems, but we shall briefly summarize the material on East Indian caste. . . ."[5] Thus the caste system in India has been taken as the criterion; nowhere has the school relied upon any other system.

On the crucial question of marriage among castes Warner and Davis give Emile Senart credit for the belief that castes "isolate themselves to prevent intermarriage"; while they regard hypergamy as an example of "variations from the caste ideal."[6] Kingsley Davis, however, thinks that hypergamy distinguishes two major types of caste systems. In India hypergamy is possible because the Indian caste system is a "non-racial caste system"; in the United States and South Africa, on the other hand, hypergamy is impossible because there are in these situations "racial caste systems."[7] Warner and Davis depend further upon Senart and Bouglé for their significant conclusion that *"no one occupation has but one caste assigned to it."*[8]

Considerable emphasis is put upon the fact that a Negro or a white person, who is born Negro or white, could never hope to become anything other than Negro or white. "Children and grandchildren of Negroes will continue to be born into, live in, and only die out of the Negro 'caste'."[9] Further, this biological fact of inheriting racial marks strikes Kingsley Davis as providing an ideal foundation for a caste system:

> The reason that race serves as an excellent basis of caste is that one gets one's racial traits by birth from parents having those traits, and one cannot change these traits during the rest of one's life.[10]

These, then, are some of the leading postulates of the caste school of race relations. Without continuing to introduce fragmentary statements at this point, we shall attempt an evaluation.[11]

Estimate of basic principles

Although the school has relied completely upon references to the caste system in India for its authority, it has nowhere made anything approaching a careful study of the caste system. Yet, even so, it has been difficult to determine which of their selected "essences" of the caste system will be controlling in given situations; and one is seldom certain about the degree of concentration of these extracts. For example, after their most elaborate discussion of caste in India, the following conclusion is reached:

> There has been no attempt in these last few paragraphs to demonstrate that our caste structure and Indian caste structure are exactly the same, but rather we have attempted to show that they are the same kind of social phenomena.

At this point the question may easily devolve upon the meaning of the expression "same kind". At least the reader might have expected that the authors would now attempt to show that the phenomena are indeed commensurable. But they do not. From this point on they proceed to discuss race relations in the United States, totally oblivious of a theory of caste or of whether caste ever existed in India. Apparently their thin discussion of Indian caste is merely intended to provided subject atmosphere.

We have had considerable difficulty also in finding clear-cut statements of principle. Usually some such phrase as "for our purpose," "as here used," "in so far as," or "generally" limits conclusions that are forthwith given universal applicability. To be sure, one could hardly question such a contrivance, yet it may be likened to the researcher who says: "This animal before us is not a horse, but *for our purpose* it is convenient to call it a horse. If you examine it closely, you will discover that it is a water buffalo. That does not matter, however, for we are not going to use it in the water-buffalo sense. Obviously, you cannot say the animal is not a horse; it is, in so far as it has four legs; and four legs are generally understood to be the essence of all horses and water buffaloes."

At points where clarity is most needed the school invariably becomes obscure, impressionistic, or circuitous. It has been accepted that the form of social organization in Brahmanic India constitutes a caste system. This system has certain distinguishing characteristics; hence we shall consider these the norm.

* * *

Contribution of the School

An astonishing characteristic of this caste school of race relations is its tendency to conceive of itself as being original. It believes not only that it has made a discovery; but also that it has "created" something.[39] It is difficult, however, to determine wherein rests it originality. We do not know who first made the analogy between race relations and the caste system of India, but it is certain that the idea was quite popular during the middle of the last century. One of the most detailed and extended discussions of this hypothesis is that of the Hon. Charles Sumner published in 1869; and in 1904 William I. Thomas brought his full genius into play upon the subject.[40] Since then many textbooks have accepted the idea.[41] Some students, like Sir Herbert Risley, have used the hypothesis as the basis of extensive research.[42] Many writers, such as E. B. Reuter and Charles S. Johnson, have applied the term casually to the racial situation in the United States.[43] Donald Young has discussed the concept rather elaborately.[44] Among these we take somewhat at random from the writings of a journalist who in 1908 published in book form the findings of his study of race relations in the South.

In explaining the "class strata" among Negroes Ray Stannard Baker says:

> I have now described two of the three great classes of Negroes: First, the worthless and idle Negro, often a criminal, comparatively small in

> numbers but perniciously evident. Second, the great middle class of Negroes who do the manual work of the South. Above these, a third class, few in number, but most influential in their race, are the progressive, property owning Negroes, who have wholly severed their old intimate ties with the white people – and who have been getting further and further away from them.[45]

With respect to the color line, called a caste line by the modern school, Baker states:

> When the line began to be drawn, it was drawn not alone against the unworthy Negro, but against the Negro. It was not so much drawn by the highly-intelligent white man as by the white man. And the white man alone has not drawn it, but the Negroes themselves are drawing it – and more and more every day. So we draw the line in this country against the Chinese, the Japanese, and in some measure against the Jews; and they help to draw it.[46]

Baker then proceeds to clinch the full idea of the caste hypothesis:

> More and more they (Negroes) are becoming a people wholly apart – separate in their churches, separate in their schools, separate in cars, conveyances, hotels, restaurants, with separate professional men. In short, we discover tendencies in this country toward the development of a caste system.[47]

It is difficult to see what the modern caste school has added to this, unless it is perhaps publicity and "scientific" prestige.[48] Certainly anyone who has a taste for art might use the information given above to draw a caste line between the white and the black class structures. But Baker, like most other former advocates of the caste hypothesis of race relations in the United States, thinks almost fancifully of the idea and does not stipulate that his work should stand or fall with the belief. He realizes that the consideration of primary significance is not the "caste line" but the way in which that line holds. Thus he concludes:

> This very absence of a clear demarcation is significant of many relationships in the South. The color line is drawn, but neither race knows just where it is. Indeed, it can hardly be definitely drawn in many relationships, because it is constantly changing. This uncertainty is a fertile source of friction and bitterness.[49]

With respect to the scientific precision of the word "caste" the school insists: "By all the physical tests the anthropologists might apply, some social Negroes are *biologically* white," hence the term "race" cannot have meaning when applied to Negroes.[50] We should remember here, however, that the racial situation in the South never depended upon "physical tests of anthropolgists." It developed long before anthropometry became of age. Furthermore, the sociologist is interested not in what the anthropometrists set up as their criteria of race, but in what peoples in interaction come to accept as a race. It is the latter belief which controls their behavior and not what the anthropometrist thinks.

But in reality the term "caste" does not economize thinking on this subject; it is a neology totally unjustified. Before we can know what the Negro caste means it is always necessary first to say what kind of people belong to the Negro caste. Therefore, in the course of defining "Negro caste" we have defined "Negro race," and the final achievement is a substitution of words only. One may test this fact by substituting in the writings of this school the words "Negroes" or "white people" wherever the words "Negro caste" or "white caste" appear and observe that the sense of the statement does not change.

For this reason the burden of the productions of this school is merely old wine in new bottles, and not infrequently the old ideas have suffered from rehandling. In other words, much that has come to us by earlier studies has taken on the glamour of caste, while the school seldom refers to the contributions of out-group students.[51]

One could hardly help recalling as an analogous situation the popularity which William McDougall gave to the instinct hypothesis. Without making any reference to William James, Lloyd Morgan, and others, who had handled the concept with great care, McDougall set out with pioneering zeal to bend all social behavior into his instinct theory. It was not long, however, before reaction came. And so, too, until quite recently, the race-caste idea had a desultory career. This idea has now been made fashionable, yet already students who had once used the term "caste" are beginning to shrink from it.[52] However, we should hasten to add that this school has none of the anti-color complexes of the instinct school; its leadership merely relies a little too much upon sophistry and lacks a sociological tradition.

In the following chapter we shall consider the major contribution of the Carnegie Studies, which also relies upon a "caste hypothesis" but which seems important enough to justify separate discussion.

(c) An American Dilemma[1]: a mystical approach to the study of race relations

If the theoretical structure of our most elaborate study of race relations in America, *An American Dilemma* by Gunnar Myrdal, is correct, then the hypotheses developed in the preceeding [three] chapters cannot be valid, for the two views are antithetical. It thus becomes incumbent upon us to examine carefully Myrdal's approach. In this examination some repetition is unavoidable, and it seems advisable to quote rather than to paraphrase the author. This critical examination, to be sure, is not intended to be a review of *An American Dilemma.* As a source of information and brilliant interpretation of information on race relations in the United States, it is probably unsurpassed.[2] We are interested here only in the validity of the meanings which Dr. Myrdal derives from the broad movements of his data. The data are continually changing and becoming obsolescent; but if we understand their social determinants we can not only predict change but also influence it. In fact, Myrdal himself directs attention to his social logic in saying: "This book is an analysis, not a description. It presents facts only for the sake of their meaning in the interpretation."[3]

In his attempt to explain race relations in the United States the author seems to have been confronted with two principal problems: (a) the problem of avoiding a political-class interpretation, and (b) the problem of finding an acceptable moral or ethical interpretation.[4]

* * *

Rigidity of the caste system

We may reiterate that the caste school of race relations is laboring under the illusion of a simple but vicious truism. One man is white, another is black; the cultural opportunities of these two men may be the same, but since the black man cannot become white, there will always be a white caste and a black caste: "The actual import of caste is gradually changing as the Negro class structure develops – except in the fundamental restrictions that no Negro is allowed to ascend into the white caste."[32] Yet, if this is so, what possible meaning could the following observation have? "We have been brought to view the caste order as fundamentally a system of disabilities forced by the whites upon the Negroes."[33]

Closely related to this amorphous concept of the rigidity of caste is the meaning given to interracial endogamy. Myrdal uses it to identify the races in the United States as castes.

> The scientifically important difference between the terms "caste" and "class" is . . . a relatively large difference in freedom of movement between groups. This difference is foremost in marriage relations. . . . The ban on intermarriage is one expression of the still broader principle . . . that a man born a Negro or a white is not allowed to pass from the one status to the other as he can pass from one class to another.[34]

Now it could hardly be too much emphasized that endogamy of itself is no final criterion of caste. Endogamy is an isolator of social values deemed sacrosanct by social groups, and there are many kinds of social groups besides castes that are endogamous. The final test of caste is an identification of the social values and organization isolated by endogamy. To say that intercaste endogamy in India means the same thing as interracial endogamy in the United States is like saying that a lemon and a potato are the same things because they both have skins.

An illustration of Myrdal's complete disregard of the nature of caste organization is his discussion of "caste struggle". This concept of "caste struggle", to be sure, is totally foreign to our norm, the Indian caste system. Moreover, this must be so because caste in Brahmanic India do not want to be anything other than castes. There is no effort or logical need to homogeneate themselves. A caste is a status entity in an assimilated, self-satisfied society. Regardless of his position in the society, a man's caste is sacred to him; and one caste does not dominate the other. The following description of caste has absolutely no application to caste in India.

The caste distinctions, are actually gulfs which divide the population into antagonistic camps. The caste line . . . is not only an expression of caste differences and caste conflicts, but it has come itself to be a catalyst to widen differences and engender conflicts.[35]

Mysticism

If the scientist has no clear conception of the norm which he is using to interpret social phenomena, the norm itself is likely to become lost in the data. When this happens he will ordinarily have recourse to mystical flights. In our case Myrdal seems to attribute magical powers to caste. Speaking of the cause of the economic position of Negroes in the United States he says: "Their caste position keeps them poor and ill-educated."[36] And, "Caste consigns the overwhelming majority of Negroes to the lower class,"[37] Indeed, the whole meaning of racial exploitation in the United States is laid at the altar of caste. Thus it is observed: "The measures to keep the Negroes disfranchised and deprived of full civil rights and the whole structure of social and economic discrimination are to be viewed as attempts to enforce *the caste principle."*[38]

More immediately, this mysticism is due primarily to a misapprehension of the whole basis of race relations. Caste is vaguely conceived of as something, the preservation of which is valuable *per se*. "The caste system is upheld by its own inertia and by the superior caste's interests in upholding it."[39] It is no wonder, then, that Myrdal falls into the egregious error of thinking that the subordination of Negroes in the South is particularly the business of poor whites. In this light he reasons: "That 'all Negroes are alike' and should be treated in the same way is still insisted upon by many whites, especially in the lower classes, who actually feel, or fear, competition from the Negroes and who are inclined to sense a challenge to their status in the fact that some Negroes rise from the bottom."[40] This, obviously, is a conception of race relations in terms of personal invidiousness. Surely, to say that "Southern whites, *especially in the lower brackets* . . . have succeeded in retaining (the) legal and political system" is to miss the point entirely. We shall return to this question in the following section.

One primary objection to the use of the caste belief in the study of race relations rests not so much upon its scientific untenability as upon its insidious potentialities. It lumps all white people and all Negroes into two antagonistic groups struggling in the interest of a mysterious god called caste. This is very much to the liking of the exploiters of labor, since it tends to confuse them in an emotional matrix with all the people. Observe in illustration how Myrdal directs our view: "All of these thousand and one precepts, etiquettes, taboos, and disabilities inflicted upon the Negro have a common purpose: to express the subordinate status of the Negro people and the exalted position of the whites. They have their meaning and chief function as symbols."[41]

It thus appears that if *white people* were not so wicked, if they would only cease wanting to "exalt" themselves and accept the "American Creed," race prejudice would vanish from America. "Why," asks Myrdal, "is race prejudice . . . not increasing but decreasing?" And he answers sanctimoniously: "This question is . . . only a special variant of the enigma of philosophers for several thousands of years: the problem of Good and Evil in the world."[42] Clearly, this is an escape from the realities of the social system, inexcusable in the modern social scientist.[43] At any rate, the philosophers' enigma apparently leads him directly into a mystical play with imponderables. As he sees it, "white prejudice" is a primary determinant in race relations. "White prejudice and discrimination keep the Negro low in standards of living. . . . This, in turn, gives support to prejudice. White prejudice and Negro standards thus mutually 'cause' each other."[44] Moreover, "the chief hindrance to improving the Negro is *the white man's firm believe in his inferiority*."[45] We shall discuss this controlling idea in a later section.

Poor whites

It should be pointed out again that Myrdal not only closes his eyes to the material interests which support and maintain race prejudice but also labors the point that there is basic antagonism between poor whites and Negroes. Says he: ". . . what a bitter, spiteful, and relentless feeling often prevails against the Negroes among lower class white people in America. . . The Marxian solidarity between the toilers . . . will . . . have a long way to go as far as concerns solidarity of the poor white American with the toiling Negro."[46] In fact, the author goes further to intimate that the poor whites may assume a dominant role in the oppression of Negroes in the South, because the interest of the poor whites is economic, while that of the ruling class is a feeling for superiority:

> Lower class whites in the South have no Negro servants in whose humble demeanors they can reflect their own superiority. Instead, they feel actual economic competition or fear of potential competition from the Negroes. They need the caste demarcations for much more substantial reasons than do the middle and upper classes.[47]
>
> The author hesitates to come to that obvious conclusion so much dreaded by the capitalist ruling class: that the observed overt competitive antagonism is a condition produced and carefully maintained by the exploiters of both the poor whites and the Negroes. Yet he almost says this in so many words: "Plantation owners and employers, who use Negro labor as cheaper and more docile, have at times been observed to tolerate, or co-operate in, the periodic aggression of poor whites against Negroes. It is a plausible thesis that they do so in the interest of upholding the caste system which is so effective in keeping the Negro docile."[48] And even more strikingly he shows by what means white workers are exploited through the perpetuation of racial antagonism. Says he: "If those white workers were paid low wages and held in great dependence, they could at least be offered a consolation of being protected from Negro competition."[49]

At any rate, Myrdal refuses to be consistent. Accordingly, he asserts, attitudes against interracial marriage "seems generally to be inversely related to the economic and social status of the informant and his educational level . . . To the poor and socially insecure, but struggling, white individual, a fixed opinion on this point seems an important matter of prestige and distinction."[50] It would not do, of course, to explain the situation realistically by concluding that if the revised black codes written by the white exploiting class against intermarriage were abrogated an increasing number of marriages between the white and the black proletariat would take place, the consequence of which would be a considerably reduced opportunity for labor exploitation by this class.[51]

The ruling class

Myrdal does not like to talk about the ruling class in the South; the term carries for him an odious "Marxist" connotation. Yet inevitably he describes this class as well as anyone:

> The one-party system in the South . . . and the low political participation of even the white people favor a *de facto* oligarchic regime . . . The oligarchy consists of the big landowners, the industrialists, the bankers, and the merchants. Northern corporate business with big investments in the region has been sharing in the political control by this oligarchy.[52]

And he stresses the ineffectiveness of the exploited masses. "The Southern masses do not generally organize either for advancing their ideals or for protecting their group interests. The immediate reason most often given by Southern liberals is the resistance from the political oligarchy which wants to keep the masses inarticulate."[53] Furthermore, he indicates the desperate pressure endured by Southern workers when he says: "The poorest farmer in the Scandinavian countries or in England . . . would not take benevolent orders so meekly as Negroes and white sharecroppers do in the South."[54]

Sometimes Myrdal shakes off the whole burden of obfuscation spun about caste, creeds,[55] and poor-white control to show, perhaps without intending to do so, the real interest of the ruling class and how it sets race against race to accomplish its exploitative purpose:

> The conservative opponents of reform proposals (that is to say the ruling class in the South) can usually discredit them by pointing out that they will improve the status of the Negroes, and that they prepare for "social equality." This argument has been raised in the South against labor unions, child labor legislation and practically every other proposal for reform.
>
> It has been argued to the white workers that the Wages and Hours Law was an attempt to legislate equality between the races by raising the wage level of Negro workers to that of whites. The South has never been seriously interested in instituting tenancy legislation to protect the tenants' rights . . . and the argument has again been that the Negro sharecropper should not be helped against the white man.[56]

It seems clear that in developing a theory of race relations in the South one must look to the economic policies of the ruling class and not to mere abstract depravity among poor whites. Opposition to social equality has no meaning unless we can see its function in the service of the exploitative purpose of this class. "When the Negro rises socially," says Myrdal, "and is no longer a servant, he becomes a stranger to the white upper class. His ambition is suspected and he is disliked."[57] Again: "The ordinary white upper class people will 'have no use' for such Negroes. They need cheap labor – faithful, obedient, unambitious Labor."[58] And the author observes further: "In most Southern communities the ruling classes of whites want to keep Negroes from joining labor unions. Some are quite frank in wanting to keep Negroes from reading the Constitution or studying social subjects."[59]

In the South the ruling class stands effectively between the Negroes and the white proletariat. Every segregation barrier is a barrier put up between white and black people by the exploiters. Myrdal puts it in this way: "On the local scene the accommodation motive by itself does not usually encourage Negro leaders to such adventures as trying to reach behind the white leaders to the white people."[60] Moreover, it is not the poor whites but the ruling class which uses its intelligence and its money to guard against any movement among Negroes to throw off their yoke of exploitation. "In many communities leading white citizens make no secret of the fact that they are carefully following . . . all signs of 'subversive propaganda' and unrest among the Negroes in the community and that they interfere to stop even innocent beginning of Negro group activity."[61]

The reasoning which we are now following, it may be well to state, is not Myrdal's; we are merely culling those conclusions which the data seem to compel the author to make but which he ordinarily surrounds with some mysterious argument about caste.

From one point of view the masters did not have so great a need for racial antagonism during slavery. Black workers could be exploited in comparative peace; the formal law was on the side of the slave owner. As Myrdal observes: "Exploitation of Negro labor was, perhaps, a less embarrassing *moral conflict* to the ante-bellum planter than to his peer today. . . Today the exploitation is, to a considerable degree, dependent upon the availability of extralegal devices of various kinds."[62] Obviously, among these extralegal devices are race prejudice, discrimination, and violence – especially lynching and the threat of lynching. "Discrimination against Negroes is . . . . rooted in this tradition of economic exploitation."[63]

Notes

(a) Park's theory of race relations

30. Consider, for instance, the manner in which David L. Cohn, one of the most rabid and effective apologists for racial discrimination in the South, brings Park into his service. Says Cohn: "Let those who would attempt to solve (the race) question by law heed the words of the distinguished sociologist, Dr. Robert E. Park: 'We do not know what we ought to do until we know what we can do; and we certainly should consider what men can do before we pass laws prescribing what they should do.' " See "How the South Feels," *Atlantic Monthly*, January 1944 p.51.

31. For a comprehensive bibliography of Park's writings, see Edna Cooper, "Bibliography of Robert E. Park," *Phylon*, Vol. VI, Winter, 1945, pp. 373-83.

32. Ibid., p. xxi.

33. In his second inaugural address President Lincoln arrived at a similar conclusion when he declared: "It may seem strange that any men should dare to ask a just God's assistance in wringing their bread from the sweat of other men's faces. . ."

34. It is some such idea Alexis de Tocqueville had when he wrote: "The European is to the other races of mankind, what man is to the lower animals; he makes them subservient to his use; and when he cannot subdue, he destroys them." *Democracy in America*, Vol. II, p. 182.

35. Under feudalism there was no opportunity for the development of race prejudice, for the community of interest among vassals, subvassals, and serfs was based upon personal ties; in modern plantation slavery, race prejudice tends to be at a minimum when personal and sympathetic relationships between master and slave achieve a degree of stability in the process of accommodation.

36. *An Appeal to Conscience*, p. 23.

(b) The modern caste school of race relations

1. See the leading hypothesis by W. Lloyd Warner, "American Caste and Class," *American Journal of Sociology*, Vol. XLII, September 1936, pp. 234-37. See also, by the same author, "Social Anthropology and the Modern Community," ibid., Vol. XLVI, May 1941, pp. 785-96; W. Lloyd Warner and W. Allison Davis, "A Comparative Study of American Caste, in *Race Relations and the Race Problem*, pp. 219-40; W. Allison Davis and John Dollard, *Children of Bondage*; W. Lloyd Warner, Buford H. Junker, and Walter A. Adams, *Color and Human Nature*; W. Allison Davis, Burleigh B. Gardner, Mary R. Gardner and W. Lloyd Warner, *Deep South*; John Dollard, *Caste and Class in a Southern Town*; Buell G. Gallagher, *American Caste and the Negro College*; Robert Austin Warren, *New Haven Negroes*; Kingsley Davis, "Intermarriage in Caste Societies," *American Anthropologist*, Vol. 43, September 1941, pp. 376-95; Robert L. Sutherland, *Color Class and Personality*; Edward A. Ross, *New-Age Sociology*; William F. Ogburn and Meyer F. Nimkoff, Sociology; Kimball Young, *Sociology*; Robert L. Sutherland and Julian L. Woodward, *Introductory Sociology*; Stuart A. Queen and Jeanette R. Gruener, *Social Pathology*; Alain Locke and Bernhard J. Stern, *When Peoples Meet*; Wilbert E. Moore and Robin M. Williams, "Stratification in the Ante-Bellum South," *American Sociological Review*, Vol. 7, June 1942, pp. 343-51; Allison Davis, "Caste, Economy, and Violence," *American Journal of Sociology*, Vol. LI, July 1945, pp. 7-15; James Melvin Reinhardt, *Social Psychology*; Guy B. Johnson, "Negro Racial Movements and Leadership in the United States," *American Journal of Sociology*, Vol. 43, July 1937, pp. 57-71; M. F. Ashley Montagu, *Man's Most Dangerous Myyh*, March 1947, pp. 336-42; Paul H. Landis, Social Control; Ina Corinne Brown, *National Survey of the Higher Education of Negroes*, U.S. Office of Education, Misc. No. 6, Vol 1; Verne Wright and Manuel C. Elmer, *General Sociology*; W. Lloyd Warner, Robert J. Havighurst, and Martin B. Loeb, *Who Shall Be Educated*; St. Clair Drake and Horace R. Cayton, *Black Metropolis*; Mozell C. Hill, "A Comparative Analysis of the Social Organization of the All-Negro Society in Oklahoma," *Social Forces*, Vol. 25, 1946, pp. 70-77; and others.

   The counterpart of this group of thinkers is another school which has with equal enthusiasm attempted to explain caste relationship in terms of racial antagonism. See chapter on the origin of caste.

2. W. Lloyd Warner, "American Caste and Class," *American Journal of Sociology*, Vol XLII, p. 234.

3. Ibid, p. 235.

4. Ibid., p. 236. See also *Deep South* by Davis, Gardner, Gardner, and Warner, p. 13

5. "A Comparative Study of American Caste," in *Race Relations and the Race Problem*, Edgar T. Thompson, ed. Observe, incidentally, this editor's own involvement with the ideas of the school; Ibid., p. xiii.

6. Ibid., pp. 229, 230.
7. "Intermarriage in Caste Societies," *American Anthropologist*, Vol. 43, July-September 1941, pp. 376-95.
8. In *Race Relations and the Race Problem*, p. 231.
9. W. Lloyd Warner, Buford H. Junker, Walter A. Adams, *Color and Human Nature*, pp. 11-12.
10. Op. cit., note, p. 387. See also *Deep South*, p.15
11. We should add that sometimes members of the school speak of "the American system of color-caste" with probable implication that the Indian system is not based upon color.

* * *

39. "The view that the relationships of whites and Negroes in the South are systematically ordered and maintained by a caste structure, and that the status of individuals within each of these groups is further determined by a system of social classes existing within each color-caste, was the creation of Warner." Davis and Dollard, *Children of Bondage*, p. xvi. "The presence of caste and class structures in the society of the deep South was reported upon first by a member of our research group. . . " Davis, Gardner, Gardner, and Warner, *Deep South*, p. 5. "An original interpretation of class and caste distinctions in the United States, providing a useful frame of reference for an appreciation of caste phenomena in this country." Ogburn and Nimkoff, *Sociology*, p. 343.
40. Charles Sumner, *The Question of Caste*, William I. Thomas, "The Psychology of Race Prejudice," *American Journal of Sociology*, Vol. XI, March 1904, pp. 593-611. As early as 1828 Governor William B. Giles of Virginia referred repeatedly to the free Negroes as a "caste of colored population." See John H. Russell, *The Free Negro in Virginia*, p. 165.
41. Among the best of them are C. H. Cooley, *Social Process*, p. 279, and *Social Organization*, pp. 209-28, Park and Burgess, *Introduction to the Science of Sociology*, pp 205-06, 722.
42. See, for example, *The Peoples of India*, p. 263, and *Census of India*, 1901.
43. Reuter, *The Mulatto in the United States*, p. 360; Johnson, "Caste and Class in an American Industry," *American Journal of Sociology*, Vol. XLII, July 1936, pp. 55-65.
44. *American Minority Peoples*, pp. 580-85. See also R. E. Park, "Racial Assimilation in Secondary Groups," op. cit., p. 73.
45. *Following the Color Line*, p. 65.
46. Ibid., p. 218.
47. Ibid., p. 300.
48. It is true that sometimes members of the modern caste school have referred to race relations as "*color*-caste." But, so far as we know, they have never shown in what way "*color*-caste" is different from caste. In fact, some of the early theories on the origin of caste have sought to identify caste with racial antogonism. Therefore, the substitution of the term "color-caste" for caste does not seem to have relieved the fundamental confusion.
49. Ibid., p. 31.
50. Davis, Gardner, Gardner and Warner, op. cit., pp. 7-8.
51. As a typical example of this, see Davis and others, op. cit., pp. 15-136 and 228-539. Consider, in illustration, the weighty significance and originality with which the following commonplace is introduced: "The critical fact is that a much larger proportion of all *Negroes*

are lower class than is the class than is the case with *whites. This is where caste comes to bear*. It puts the overwhelming majority of Negroes in the lowest class group, and keeps them there." (Italics added.) Davis and Dollard, op. cit., p.65. This quotation also illustrates the mystical way in which real problems have been explained away.

52. See R. E. Park in the introduction to Bertram W. Doyle, *The Etiquette of Race Relations*, and Charles S. Johnson, *Growing Up in the Black Belt*. But observe Johnson's relapse. In speaking of Negro-white relationship in the United States he says: "A racial or caste division of labor is one type of adjustment growing out of economic conflict between racial groups." In *Sociological Foundations of Education*, Joseph S. Roucek, ed., p. 423; also in *Patterns of Negro Segregation*, pp. xvi *passim*. Professor Park has been toying with the idea. For instance, Dr. Donald Pierson gives him credit approvingly for the following simple and somewhat inadequate scheme. "In a caste system," Pierson writes, "the racial lines may run thus:

White
Race Lines Mixed-blood
Black

Negroes in Brazil, p. 337. For a similar diagram by Park, see "The Basis of Race Prejudice," *The Annals*, Vol. CXXXX, November 1928, p. 20. See also the preceding chapter.

(c) An American Dilemma

1. Gunnar Myrdal, *An American Dilemma*. Although this is a work of considerable scholarly collaboration, we shall, in this discussion of it, assume that it is entirely by Dr. Myrdal.
2. Herbert Aptheker would disagree heartily with this, for he has published a small book devoted entirely to a criticism of Myrdal's factual data and of their interpretation. See *The Negro People in America*.
3. Op. cit., p. li.
4. Myrdal conceives of this problem – that is to say of race relations in the United States – as "primarily a moral issue of conflicting valuations" and of his "investigation

32. Ibid., p. 693.
33. Ibid., p. 669.
34. Ibid., p. 668.
35. Ibid., pp. 676-77.
36. Ibid., p. 669.
37. Ibid., p. 71.
38. Ibid., p. 690. (Italics added.)
39. Ibid., p. 669.
40. Ibid., p. 689.
41. Ibid., p. 66.
42. Ibid., p. 79. See W. Cunningham, *The Growth of English Industry and Commerce*, Vol. I. pp. 556-557, for a review of this tendency among sixteenth-century English moralists to explain social problems by attributing them to human sinfulness.

43. Probably we should mention here another deplorable achievement of Myrdal's – his developed capacity for obscuring the basis of racial antagonism. Consider in illustration the following paragraph:

    "Though the popular theory of color caste turns out to be a rationalization, this does not destroy it. For among the forces in the minds of the white people are certainly not only economic interests (if these were the only ones, the popular theory would be utterly demolished), but also sexual urges, inhibitions, and jealousies, and social fears and cravings for prestige and security. When they come under the scrutiny of scientific research, both the sexual and the social complexes take on unexpected designs. We shall then also get a clue to understanding the remarkable tendency of this presumably biological doctrine, that it refers only to legal marriage and to relations between Negro men and white women, but not to extra-marital sex relations between white men and Negro women." Ibid., p. 59.

    This excerpt is not exceptional; it characterizes the writing. Its meaning is probably this: "The theory of color caste is a rationalization. Besides the economic interests upon which this rationalization is based, we should take into account certain appetites and instinctual drives common to all human beings." The conclusion in the last sentence is incorrect. It is contrary to both the logic of race relations and the data as recorded in the literature including some of the earliest court records on white-man, Negro-woman sex relations. The deplorable fact about this writing is not so much that it is obscure as that it seeks to maneuver the reader into accepting the rationalization as the real reason for racial antagonism. We could hardly emphasize too much that "sexual urges, inhibitions," and so on, traits common to Negroes as well as, whites, cannot explain why certain whites dominate Negroes. Moreover, the author does not show that anyone has ever argued that the mere fact that a rationalization is recognized for what it is destroys it. This, obviously, is a straw man set up to cover the author's obsession with abstractions.

44. Ibid., p. 75.

45. Ibid., p. 101 (Italics added.)

46. Ibid., p. 69. In almost identical terms André Siegfried interprets the racial situation: "In the wealthy families some of the old-time sentimentality still survives from the slave days, but the 'poor white' sees in the Negro nothing but a brutal competitor who is trying to rob him of his job. His hatred is unrelenting, merciless, and mingled with fear. To understand the South, we must realize that the lower we descend in the social scale, the more violent the hatred of the Negro." *America Comes of Age*, p. 97. See also Edwin R. Embree, *Brown America*, p. 201.

47. Op. cit., p. 597. This social illusion concerning the naturalness of racial antagonism between Negroes and poor whites, a mirage ordinarily perpetuated by the white ruling class, is deeply embedded in the literature. For instance, Professor Louis Wirth declares with finality: "It has been repeatedly found by students of Negro white relations in the South that the so-called white aristocracy shows less racial prejudice than do the 'poor whites' whose own position is relatively insecure and who must compete with Negroes for jobs, for property, for social position, and for power. Only those who themselves are insecure feel impelled to press their claims for superiority over others." See "Race and Public Policy," *The Scientific Monthly*, April 1944, p. 304.

    Now, we may ask, why should competition be more natural than consolidation in the struggle for wealth and position? Why should insecurity lead more naturally to division than to a closing of ranks? Suppose the Negro and the white proletariat of the South decide to come together and unite for increasing power in their struggle for economic position, what are the sources of opposing power – disorganizing power – that will be immediately brought into action? Wirth might just as well argue that the antagonism and open conflicts which ordinarily develop between union strikers and scabs are caused by a feeling of insecurity among the scabs. In the end this argument must be put into that category of vacuus universals which explain nothing, for who in this world does not feel insecure? And if it is a matter of the degree of insecurity, then we should expect Negroes to take the initiative in interracial aggression since they are the most insecure. In the theoretical discussion of race relations "human nature" or the behavior of human beings as such should be taken for granted.

Sometimes thought is effectively cancalized by such apparently objective statements by social scientists as the following: "A standard saying among the southern common folks is that we ought to treat the Negro as we did the Indian: kill him if he doesn't behave and, if not, isolate him and give him what we want to." Howard W. Odum, "Problem and Methodology in an American Dilemma," *Social Forces*, Vol. 23, October 1944, p. 98. Clearly the implication here is that the Southern aristocrats and their university professors are the protectors of the Negroes against the pent-up visciousness of the "southern common folks" – a complete perverson of reality.

48. Ibid., p. 598. In another context he recognizes that "there had been plenty of racial competition before the Civil War. White artisans had often vociferously protested against the use of Negroes for skilled work in the crafts. But as long as the politically most powerful group of whites had a vested interest in Negro mechanics, the protesting was of little avail." Ibid., p. 281.

49. Ibid., p. 286. In the South African situation Lord Olivier makes a similar observation: "When the capitalist employer comes to the scene, making disciminations as to the labor forces he must employ for particular work in order to make his profits, which is the law of his activity to do, then, and not till then, antagonism is introduced between the newly-created wage-working proletarian white and native – who, in regard to the qualifications which properly determine wage contracts, are on exactly the same footing." *The Anatomy of African Misery*, p. 135.

50. Op. cit., p. 57.

51. Hinton R. Helper, the renegade Southerner who never bit his tongue in his criticism of the white ruling class of the South and who, however, never concealed his prejudices against the Negroes, spoke more than a grain of truth when he described the position of the poor whites. It is essentially applicable to present-day conditions. "Nothwithstanding the fact that the white non-slaveholders of the South are in the majority as five to one, they have never yet had any part or lot in framing the laws under which they live . . . The lords of the lash are not absolute masters of the blacks . . . but they are also the oracles and arbiters of all the non-slaveholding whites, whose freedom is merely nominal and whose unparalleled illiteracy and degradation is purposely and fiendishly perpetuated. How little the 'poor white trash,' the great majority of the Southern people, know of the real conditions of the country is indeed sadly astonishing . . . It is expected that the stupid and sequacious masses, the white victims of slavery, will believe and, as a general thing, they do believe, whatever the slaveholders tell them; and thus it is that they are cajoled into the notion that they are the freest, happiest, and most intelligent people in the world, and are taught to look with prejudice and disapprobation upon every new principle or progressive movement." *The Impending Crisis*, pp. 42-44 *passim*.

52. Op. cit., p. 453.

53. Ibid. p. 455.

54. Ibid., p. 466.
55. This statement is made advisedly. The following unreal conflict between status and ideals may indicate further the nebulous level at which the theoretical part of this study is sometimes pitched: "The American Creed represents the national conscience. The Negro is a 'problem' to the average American partly because of a palpable conflict between the status actually him and those ideals." Ibid., p. 23.
56. Ibid., p. 456.
57. Ibid., p 593.
58. Ibid. p. 596.
59. Ibid., p. 721.
60. Ibid., p. 727.
61. bid., p. 459.
62. Ibid., p. 220 (Italics added.)
63. Ibid., p. 208.

The Tenth Anniversary of the Report of the Kerner Commission

12. The Tenth Anniversary of the Report of the Kerner Commission

On the tenth anniversary of the publication of the Report of the Kerner Commission, The New York Times *published a series of articles assessing how far the situation of black Americans had changed in the decade, and black and white perceptions of this change.*

Decade After Kerner Report: Division of Races Persists

> *"Our nation is moving toward two societies, one black, one white – separate and unequal." – THE NATIONAL ADVISORY COMMISSION ON CIVIL DISORDERS, FEB. 29, 1968.*

The division between white and black Americans still exists; and the prospects of healing the rift may be more dismal today than they were 10 years ago, when that warning was issued by the Presidential panel known as the Kerner commission.

As a whole, the nation's 25 million blacks have gained enormously in the last decade, but many students of the nation's racial struggles as well as black and white community leaders throughout the country see a bleak future for the millions remaining in the urban ghettos.

Outside the ghettos, most whites are even more insulated from the slums than they were in 1968. And the blacks who have left in substantial numbers for better lives elsewhere are, for the most part, engrossed in middle-class concerns and no longer active in the cause of those left behind.

Many urban blacks, perhaps 30 percent, have worked their way into the middle class and have moved to the suburbs or to better housing within the cities. Some of those still dependent on public assistance have received substantial increases in real income through rent subsidies, a liberalized food stamp plan, an expanded welfare system and other benefits enacted since 1968.

But chronically high unemployment in black neighborhoods has raised fears that the nation may have acquired a permanent underclass, people who are wards of the Government living out unproductive lives under conditions that most Americans, if they think about them at all, consider unacceptable.

Former Mayor John V. Lindsay of New York City, who was vice chairman of the commission, believes that separation between races and among blacks themselves is a problem so difficult to resolve politically that the Federal Government can approach it only obliquely, not head on.

"They would have to be almost too brave to bear the pain," he said in a telephone interview.

The number of black elected officials has increased dramatically, as has the education level of blacks. From the sterile downtown office buildings that still serve as the nerve centers of commerce in most cities, it is a salt-and-pepper work force that pours into the streets at 5 p.m. Blacks are more visible on television and in sports. In a number of ways, it is an integrated society.

But the places that experienced urban riots in the 1960's have, with a few exceptions, changed little, and the conditions of poverty have spread in most cities.

Ten years ago, the South Bronx was in deep trouble: today, it is in ruins.

Stable neighborhoods in 1968 – the northwest section of St. Louis, for example–are now undergoing housing abandonment.

Scars of the riots are still visible in Washington, Detroit, Newark and other cities. In most of them, blight has been even more devastating than the rioting.

The troubled areas include desolate expanses of New York, Newark, Chicago, Washington, Philadelphia, Cleveland, Detroit, St. Louis, Gary and Buffalo; the sprawling slums of Los Angeles, Houston and Memphis; crumbling old neighborhoods of New Orleans, and hundreds of other central city and suburban areas.

A composite of them would be a land of several thousand square miles, of ruble-strewn streets and vacant blocks, abandoned stores, stripped-down hulks of automobiles, bleak and compacted public and private housing projects, battered school buildings, old men with glazed eyes.

Residential boundaries for blacks have expanded, but not through the metropolitan-wide integration that the commission recommended. Blacks have migrated outward along well-defined corridors – the middle class leaving first for safer neighborhoods and better schools, with the poor "tailgating" them.

How It Happened

On July 27, 1967, when President Johnson announced the appointment of a blue-ribbon panel to investigate the causes of the riots, Detroit was in flames and under Army occupation. Much of Newark was in ruins, and in that month alone 40 cities from Buffalo to San Francisco had been beset by burning, looting and warring the police.

The 11 commission members Mr. Johnson chose were all known as moderates. Gov. Otto Kerner of Illinois was the chairman. Only two members – Roy Wilkins, director of the National Association for the Advancement of Colored People, and Senator Edward W. Brooke, Republican of Massachusetts - were black.

The others, in addition to Mr. Lindsay, were Senator Fred R. Harris, Democrat of Oklahoma; Representatives James C. Corman, Democrat of California, and William M. McCulloch, Republican of Ohio; I.W. Abel, president of the United Steel workers of America; Charles B. Thornton, chairman of Litton Industries Inc.; Katherine Graham Peden, Kentucky's Commissioner of Commerce, and Police Chief Herbert Jenkins of Atlanta.

A large staff, headed by David Ginsburg, a Washington lawyer, was drawn from the liberal establishment that had supported the civil rights movement, which was then at its peak, remaking the social order of the South.

The commission's report was published before the snows had melted in some of the Northern ghettos. The report, which was hotly debated but unanimously voted, found that the riots were a form of social protest against harsh and degrading conditions forced on blacks, and that white racism was largely to blame:

"What white Americans have never fully understood, but what the Negro can never forget, is that white society is deeply implicated in the ghetto," the report said. "White institutions created it, white institutions maintain it and white society condones it."

The report said the nation had three choices: a continuation of its existing policies, the enrichment of the ghetto while abandoning integration, or "combining ghetto enrichment with programs designed to encourage integration of a substantial number of Negroes into the society outside the ghetto."

To avoid a segregated, unequal society, the report added, the third choice would have to be adopted. The commission submitted a long, costly list of recommendations, ranging from civil rights initiatives to the rebuilding of neighborhoods, to implement such a program.

The voluminous report became a best seller, just under 2 million copies at last count. White liberals huddled in suburbs and cities across the country to discuss what they could do.

But the chill of reaction was not long in setting in. President Johnson, peeved at the commission for not pointing out what he had done for blacks, treated it coolly and let it lie.

The conclusion about white racism was condemned, for a variety of reasons, by a wide spectrum of leaders, ranging from Richard M. Nixon, then on the Presidential campaign trail in New Hampshire, to Bayard Rustin, the black civil rights leader. Mr. Lindsay, among others, now agrees that the conclusion, while valid, needlessly aroused opposition to what the commission was trying to accomplish.

While the controversy raged, the Rev. Dr. Martin Luther King Jr. was assassinated on April 4, 1968, setting off an even worse wave of riots.

From 1965 to 1969, when the disorders began to taper off, about 250 persons were killed, 12,000 injured and 83,000 arrested. Property damage totaled several hundred million dollars, according to some estimates.

The riots eventually stopped as the police became more sophisticated and learned how to nip them in the bud and as local black leaders, seeing the enormous damage that had ensued, called for an end to that form of social protest.

Meanwhile, national attention shifted to protests against the Vietnam War and riots on college campuses. Mr Nixon was elected President, and his Administration began a policy of increasing aid to the cities but allowing local officials to decide how to use it.

Skepticism grew about the effectiveness of Government programs, a number of which had become corrupted by those appointed to run them. And civil rights laws intended to bring some blacks into the white suburbs were enforced laxly or not at all. The ghettos remained and festered.

The Picture Now

A check by The New York Times of representative cities and interviews with scores of people involved shows the following comparisons from 1968 to 1978:

Population: Although the situation in each city varies, there are now fewer people in larger areas that could be described as ghettos, except in Southern cities were the integration of blacks is still taking place. In central St. Louis, for example, children returning from school one day last week picked their way past hundreds of abandoned houses to their homes. Ten years ago, those empty buildings were a bustling neighborhood.

Employment: The unemployment rate for all blacks has doubled over the 10-year period, and has been hovering recently at around 14 percent. In the ghettos it is much higher – 40 to 50 percent among black youths in many cities.

As factories have moved out and the economy has become more concentrated in technology and services, there are fewer opportunities in the manufacturing jobs that once provided the first step into the job market for the urban poor.

Education: There is a consensus that central city schools have declined in quality even as teachers' salaries have risen. In most cities, the ghetto schools are virtually all black or Hispanic as integration efforts have faltered.

Housing: Tens of thousands of deteriorated but structurally sound housing units have been abandoned. Some of the abandoned buildings were erected since 1968 in areas designated as "model cities" by the Federal Government. Rehabilitation and new construction have not kept up with the need in most areas. In New Orleans, there is a waiting list of 10,000 for units of dreary public housing. Blacks there are doubling up in shacks as whites line up old buildings for renovation.

Crime: While the police statistics that measure serious crime are seldom dependable, there appears to have been an increase over the 10-year period. Typically, in New York, there were 304,000 felony complaints in 1966, as against 552,000 in 1976. While New York and most other cities have reported some decline in the past year or so, it is believed to reflect a decline in the number of young, who commit most of the crime, rather than better control over lawlessness.

Federal Aid: While the ghettos have remained unchanged, or have worsened, Federal aid to cities has increased enormously. In 1976, direct Federal aid to St. Louis made up only 1 percent of the general revenue. This year, Federal aid is expected to constitute 54 percent.

Newark will have gone from less than 2 percent to 55, Buffalo from 2 percent to 69, Cleveland from 8 percent to 58. Even Tulsa, Okla., a city not high on the Government's crisis index, is dependent on the Federal Government for about one-half of its total budget.

The money has been such a windfall that Richard P. Nathan of the Brookings Institution recently told Congress that only a handful of cities, New York included, now have a fiscal crisis. But, with few exceptions, the money has gone largely to supplant other sources of revenue rather than to enrich the ghetto or other declining areas.

J. Herbes

The New York Times, 26 February 1978

Poll Indicates More Tolerance, Less Hope

Ten years after black youths ravaged many a Northern inner city, the whites who still inhabit those cities are more tolerant racially than they were before, far more likely to accept black neighbors and black friends for their children. They feel that blacks are making good progress and they seem to find little real urgency in the black situation.

This perception of urban America, however, is not widely shared by black citizens.

The anger and smoldering resentment that fueled the riots seem to have receded, but so has optimism among blacks. If anything, they say they find the racial barriers to jobs, good housing and other necessities even higher than they were before. Nearly half today say they believe that whites do not care whether they get a better break. In sum, a sense of neglect, resignation, perhaps futility, seems to prevail among urban blacks.

This widened gulf between black and white perceptions of racial realities in 1978 became apparent in a new survey conducted by The New York Times and CBS News. The survey was meant to replicate, as closely as possible, a similar study of racial attitudes conducted in the winter of 1968 by the University of Michigan for the Kerner commission.

The new study was based on telephone interviews with 489 whites and 374 blacks in 25 large Northeastern and Middle Western cities. About one of every five surveyed was a New Yorker. Because of demographic changes in those cities in the last decade and differences in the ways the two surveys were conducted, some caution is needed in making strict comparisons.

The commission declared in 1968 that Americans would need "new attitudes, new understanding, and above all, new will" to avoid future racial discord. The evidence in the new survey suggests strongly that there are indeed new attitudes about race relations and new understanding among whites, but perhaps not the new will to take the bitter medicine the remedies may require.

Whites and blacks have long held divergent perceptions of racial prejudice and injustices; the events of the last decade appear to have done little to diminish the differences.

Whites are far more likely now to say that blacks should be able to "live wherever they can afford to." Six of 10 said that a decade ago and nearly nine out of 10 today. The proportion saying that they would mind "not at all" if a black family of similar social class moved in next door has risen dramatically, from 46 to 66 percent. The reality, as seen by blacks, is different. While more than two-thirds of them say they would prefer a fully integrated neighborhood, only a fifth live in such areas, and two-thirds live in all or mostly black sections.

Whites are largely convinced that things have markedly improved for blacks since the 60's; black are not. Two-thirds of all whites today say that blacks have made "a lot of progress" in getting rid of racial discrimination in the last 10 or 15 years. Less than half of the blacks agree with that; a majority, 51 percent, say there has not been "much real change." A decade ago by contrast, two-thirds of the blacks in the Michigan study said there had been a lot of progress in the 10 to 15 years before the riots.

The increased pessimism of blacks has not, however, been translated into greater hostility toward or suspicion of whites.

They give credit to whites generally for more sensitive and tolerant attitudes on race. Asked how many whites in their city "dislike" blacks, 39 percent of the blacks surveyed this year say "many" or "almost all" do, down from 57 percent a decade ago. Over half now say "only a few" whites dislike their fellow black citizens.

This feeling seems to mirror changes in white attitudes. A third of all whites interviewed in 1968 asserted that whites "have a right to keep blacks out of their neighborhoods if they want to." Today only one in 20 own up to such feelings.

The blacks seem to sense neither hostility nor encouragement from whites. They are less likely than before to feel whites want to see blacks get a "better break," or want to "keep blacks down." Rather, they are more likely now (44 percent as compared with 33 percent in 1968) to say whites "don't care one way or the other."

To some extent the responses may be affected by the fact that the survey covered only residents of cities, not suburbs, meaning that many prosperous whites and blacks who have migrated to the suburbs in recent years were excluded. Blacks with higher income were found to be more likely than others to report experiencing bias personally and to be pessimistic about racial progress.

The 1968 study found that age explained many of the differences in attitudes within the black community. The younger persons interviewed were more militant and dissatisfied with their lot than older blacks. Today those age differences seem to be smoothed out, perhaps a result of the fading of militant black leaders from the national scene and a greater emphasis on economic gains by the black leadership.

Among whites, however, considerable generational differences remain. Younger whites are still far more likely to be aware of black difficulties than are older.

R. Reinhold

The New York Times, 27 February 1978

Attitudes to Race Relations

The lack of unanimity on almost any aspect of the tangled relationship between the races was a significant finding in an informal survey in a number of cities where racial strife in the mid-1960's led to violence and hatred. Gone was anything approaching black solidarity on basic issues, or even on assessments of social, economic and political progress.

Virulent racism was expressed by members of both races, but most of those interviewed indicated that extremists, both black and white, had less influence today than they did 10 years ago when the National Advisory Commission on Civil Disorders issued its report.

But above anything else, the survey suggested that, rather than the two separate societies predicted by the Kerner commission, three separate societies have emerged: white, poor black and middle-class black.

Attitudes within these three segments vary widely, but judging by the survey the majority views may be summarized in the following ways:

White America: A decade of changing racial patterns, economic setbacks and other pressures has seen the eclipse of active white support for accelerated black social progress. While most whites do not want to turn back the clock, it is becoming an accepted maxim that rapid black advancement on a broad scale can only be achieved through "reverse discrimination" and white sacrifices. "Black progress now should be the product of black sweat and not white handouts," a building contractor in Miami told an interviewer.

Middle-Class Black America: This segment of society expanded greatly as those with natural gifts, luck or training took advantage of the opportunities that the civil rights movement gave blacks. Their upward mobility has been in the classic American mold, concerned chiefly with material accumulation. "Young black middle-class college kids don't have a social conscience today the way they did back in the 60's," observed John Lewis, a black who was appointed a top administrator in the ACTION program by the Carter Administration.

Poor Black America: The growth of the middle class had the effect of moving many with talent and leadership potential out of the ghetto, leaving it more bereft and powerless than before. The mass of black people mired in poverty describe the bleakness of ghetto conditions – crime, drugs, bad housing, fatherless homes, poor schooling and unemployment – but a surprising number continue to talk hopefully, if not completely confidently, about chances of improvement in the future. This attitude appears to be more widespread in the South than in Northern cities.

J. Nordheimer

The New York Times, 27 February 1978

Aspects of 1968

The year 1968 was one nobody expected. By the time it was over, not even the 31,770,222 Americans who had just voted Richard M. Nixon into the Presidency were sad to see it go.

In his history of the United States from 1932 to 1972, William Manchester calls it "the year everything went wrong." It was the year that the Rev. Dr. Martin Luther

King Jr. and Senator Robert F. Kennedy were murdered, the Pueblo was captured, the Kerner commission warned that the nation was headed toward “two societies, separate and unequal,” the American Government said it had wrested a victory from the Tet offensive, Columbia University and the streets of Chicago around the Democratic National convention erupted and Spiro T. Agnew was elected Vice President of the United States.

Even from the vantage point of 1978, the only way to understand the events of 1968 fully is to remember the hopes that were leading up toward it. The civil rights movement had been moving apace for more than a decade and had made progress that seemed highly significant. Young people, alarmed by the Vietnam War, had been galvanized into political action. Along with the rioting, there was great intellectual ferment in the black sections of Northern urban communities.

Though it was a time of uncertainty, many Americans who wanted a more just society believed that there was reason for hope.

Nevertheless, for each citizen who saw in the ferment reason for hope, there were others profoundly disturbed by it. Alongside the peace movement, but comingled with it in many respects, there was a youth culture questioning American values with everything from new sexual mores and large-scale use of drugs to desecration of such hallowed symbols as the nation’s flag.

Some young Americans were thrilled by Che Guevara’s vision of “two, three, many Vietnams.” and others, most of them black, were emotionally drawn to the banner of the Black Panther Party, which had emerged the year before, in earnest and with guns, on the streets of Oakland.

President Johnson seemed to be developing a greater and greater obsession with the war, and at the same time he appeared to be less and less able to achieve the peace he said he wanted so fervently. He also appeared less and less interested in the domestic social goals that many thought were his best dreams.

Roughly a month before his last visit Memphis, Dr. King told two Federal officials of his conviction that the civil rights movement had to proceed to economic issues and broaden its base to include all Americans mired in poverty. He planned to bring that poverty to Washington, he said, and put it on the Mall between the Lincoln Memorial and the Washington Monument “for the whole American Government to see the misery from across the nation.”

Just as that conversation was taking place, the Commission on Civil Disorders, appointed by President Johnson after the 1967 Detroit riot and headed by Gov. Otto Kerner of Illinois, issued its report.

The commission concluded that racism was a major malady posing a fundamental threat to American society.

* * *

[The] commissioners felt [relief] after a long struggle, when they achieved a consensus despite the diversity of their views and backgrounds. But they anticipated another obstacle, and their concern turned out to be justified.

"Our second worry was that L.B.J. would view the report as a criticism of him and his policies," Mr. Lindsay said recently.

"We wanted action, but though President Johnson was very gracious when he received the report, he never mentioned it again. It ended up on the shelf."

R. Wilkins

The New York Times, 28 February 1978

Middle-Class Gains Create Tension in Black Community

When it predicted the emergence of two separate societies, the National Advisory Commission on Civil Disorders never foresaw two separate societies within the black community.

In its report 10 years ago, the commission mentioned the black middle class only in passing. "A rapidly enlarging Negro middle class," its report predicted, would not "open up an escape hatch from the ghetto."

That assessment has proved to be erroneous, at least for those blacks who entered the middle class. Indeed, one of the most striking developments in American society in the last decade has been the abandonment of the ghetto by millions of upwardly mobile blacks.

In some cases, they now live side by side, with white families in similar economic circumstances. More often, they have moved to middle-class black neighborhoods, which have expanded in almost every American city. The houses and yards are indistinguishable from those in affluent white communities. And, in many instances, so are the attitudes of the residents.

The result has been tension between two elements of black society, a tension not unlike the kind the commission found between whites and blacks. And many who have followed the developments – and many who have lived them – are deeply troubled.

"There is growing estrangement," said Alfred D. Smith, a social worker who moved from inner city Boston to Newton, an affluent suburb. "The empathy is there, but there's less contact between the middle class and poor blacks."

Many see the new members of the black middle class ignoring their brothers still trapped in poverty, and some even fear class violence among black Americans.

James W. Compton, executive director the Chicago Urban League, noted that "when the lights failed in New York last summer, the fifth largest black business in this country was all but destroyed in a few hours."

"It certainly is a dilemma, and a lot of blacks don't want to even acknowledge there are class differences," said Dr. Alvin F. Poussaint, a psychiatrist and dean of students at the Harvard Medical School.

"But they exist, and they're getting worse. By pretending there are no class distinctions, strategy to deal with the problem can't evolve. Some blacks ignore it because to recognize it would show disunity, they feel. But the strains of the conflict are beginning to show."

Dr. Poussaint said that a decade ago, "middle-class blacks I consulted and met with inevitably asked me what could they do to help their black brothers; now I'm rarely asked." Sociologists and psychologists find middle-class blacks "digging in" for themselves, believing that white Americans are not going to give much more to blacks, while low-income blacks perceive that they are not going to get help from whites or blacks.

Low-income blacks feel that their protests and rioting made possible the gains by the middle class, which is now running from ghetto areas to "live white." Some experts, as well as many members of the middle class, acknowledged that their lifestyle was closer to that of the white middle class than to that of poor blacks.

Various studies have shown that middle-class blacks leave the inner city for the same reasons as middle-class whites: fear of crime, desire for better education for their children and better housing, among other things.

Dr. Leon Chestang, who teaches at the school of social administration of the University of Chicago, termed the widening gap "frightening," and Mr. Compton chided those blacks "who have recently escaped from poverty."

"The rising black middle class, the few who have tasted the better life, is not rising to its full responsibilities. Our sharing is too often casual rather than sacrificial," he remarked in a recent address.

"But, as the gulf between haves and have-nots widens, as the comforts of the well-off stand out in sharpening contrast to the discomforts of the poor, the threat of social disorder and disruption grows."

Mr. Compton warned that if the "black underclass" revolts again, "their rising will be against class as well as race." He added:

"If the black poor take to the streets again and burn and loot because too few people have too much, and too many too little, there will be no safe place on either side of the barricades for middle-class blacks."

On the other hand, William L. Taylor, director of the Center for National Policy Review in Washington, questioned whether higher income blacks had an ultimate obligation to uplift those still in the ghetto.

"It is very wrong to single out the black middle class and say that it has some special responsibility to do what other ethnic groups don't do," he said. "It's the responsibility of us all to help out the have-nots."

Mr. Taylor, former staff director of the United States Commission on Civil Rights, agreed with others, including Dr. Poussaint, who said the black middle class continued to serve the poor through organizations such as the National Association for the Advancement of Colored People and the National Urban League.

Dr. Chestang said that middle-class blacks were often "social intervenors" for poorer blacks – serving as mentors and models, offering guidance and support, "exposing them to things they had no knowledge of."

"Such people are essential to survival," he said, "and now with the gap increasing, social intervenors won't be as available as they used to be to the young poor, who need them more than ever."

There has always been a small but influential black middle class that, in many cases, set itself apart – psychologically, if not physically. Still, it produced the leaders and set the standards and sometimes the taste of the community. Now middle-class enclaves, like Sheppard Park in Washington, "Pill Hill" in Chicago, Laurelton in Queens and Lochmond Estates outside Atlanta, appear at times to represent barriers rather than bridges among blacks.

R. Delaney

The New York Times, 28 February 1978

Black and White Community Statistics

In 1976, black families had a median income of $9,252, an increase of 105 percent over 10 years. In that same year, 30 percent of all black families earned $15,000 or more. A decade ago, only 2 percent were at that level.

But 1976 also saw 31 percent of all black individuals living below the poverty line, as against 42 percent in 1966. And among families headed by women, 36 percent of families in the black community in 1976, the poverty rate was 55 percent. It was 65 percent 10 years earlier.

Those statistics illustrate the two faces of black America today, 10 years after the National Advisory Commission on Civil Disorders issued its report. One group is rapidly acquiring more education, better jobs and higher income; another remains mired in poverty, an unyielding "underclass" with few qualifications and little motivation.

In certain ways, the gap between black and white America has closed substantially. Black female clerical workers, for instance, now earn 99 percent of the average salary for whites. In 1975, 93 percent of all black teenagers were enrolled in high school, a jump of 10 percentage points in 20 years and only one point less than the mark for whites.

In other ways, the gap remains large. The median black family income, $9,252, is still only about 60 percent of the average white family median income, $15,537. Blacks are twice as likely to die of diabetes and seven times as likely to be victims of homicide.

Diminished Political Power

The Kerner commission said that America was moving toward "two societies, one black, one white – separate and unequal." Today, it's probably more accurate to say that America is divided into two classes, one comfortable and one not.

Professor William J. Wilson, a black sociologist at the University of Chicago and author of "The Declining Importance of Race," points out that a generation ago the new "black bourgeoisie" made its money mainly by serving the black community itself. Most of them were doctors, lawyers, undertakers and teachers. Today, middle-class blacks also make money in the white world, as managers in large corporations, for instance, or as skilled union craftsmen.

Prof. Wilson wrote: "It is clearly evident in this connection that many talented and educated blacks are now entering positions of prestige and influence at a rate comparable to or, in some situations, exceeding that of whites with equivalent qualifications. It is equally clear that the back underclass is in a hopeless state of economic stagnation, falling further and further behind the rest of society."

While most black leaders are pleased by the success of the rising middle class, they worry that its distance, intentional or unintentional, from the ghetto has fractured the unity of the black community and thus diminished its political power.

Unemployment

In sketching a demographic portrait of the racial situation today, some of the most important statistics concern jobs.

Unemployment for all groups varies according to the business cycle, but has consistently been twice as high as that for whites. At the end of last year, the jobless rate was 6.3 percent for whites, 13.2 percent for blacks. For white teenagers it was about 15 percent, for black youths about 40 percent.

* * *

Analysts generally agree that a large part of the unemployment problem in the black community is structural, and not easily solved by an upturn in the economy. Many jobs from assembly lines to corner groceries, are leaving the inner cities for the suburbs.

* * *

Another problem is that many black youngsters are unwilling to take menial jobs that might be available. Some black leaders agree with them, but others take a different view.

* * *

Whatever the reasons for black unemployment, younger working blacks are moving steadily into better jobs. In a recent study, the Congressional Budget Office noted that, as of 1974, 32 percent of all black workers held white-collar positions, up from 14 percent in 1959. In the same period, the percentage doing domestic household work had dropped from 15 to 5.

Among better paid workers, the gap between blacks' and whites' income narrows. In 1974, the median income for black male professionals was $11,088, or 82 percent of the figure for whites. For black female professionals the median was $8,376 or 15 percent more than for comparable white women.

Poverty

On the other end of the spectrum, the poverty rate for blacks is generally put at more than three times that for whites, although some economists dispute the computations.

The figures for blacks, they say, do not include illicit or unreported funds that boost the income of some families.

More important, they do not include in-kind benefits such as food stamps, medical care and housing subsidies. If those benefits are counted as income, says the Congressional budget office, the poverty rate for black families is cut in half.

Another key variable in black income is family status. The number of black households headed by women spurted to 35 percent in 1976 as opposed to 11 percent in the white community.

Education

Jobs and income are closely related to education, and it is in this area that blacks have made their biggest strides. In 1973, blacks in their mid-20's had completed an average of almost 12 years of schooling, only one year less than the whites and an increase of four years over blacks in the 50's.

At the same time, many educators feel the quality of education received by blacks lags far behind that of whites. One recent test showed that 92 percent of all white 17 year-year-olds were functionally literate, as opposed to only 58 percent of the blacks.

The number of black college students has more than doubled in the last 10 years, and today blacks make up 10.7 percent of the total college enrollment, only one point below their portion of the school-age population.

Medical Care

Quality of life is difficult to measure statistically, but medical care is one critical benchmark, and here, the litany is familiar: A lot has been accomplished, more needs to be done.

Since Medicare and Medicaid were introduced in the mid-1960's, many blacks have had access to their first decent health care. In the last 10 years, infant mortality rates for blacks have dropped almost in half, but remain far above those for whites. Black life expectancy increased three full years, to age 67, but lagged six years behind the white figures.

In education and in health, blacks have benefitted from huge Federal programs initiated after the turmoil of the mid-60's. For instance, black youngsters received between one-third and one-half of all Federal money allocated to elementary and secondary education, a total of more than $3 billion late last year. In health, blacks account for 36 percent of the drug abuse program.

S.V. Roberts

The New York Times, 28 February 1978

Blacks and Politics

Nowhere is such change more evident than in the political arena. The conventional wisdom among people who have worked on the domestic side of the Federal Government or around the country in race relations is that the Voting Rights Act of 1965 has been the most successful social legislation to come out of Congress in the last 20 years.

There is no question that the progress has been real. One startling example has been the recent courtship of black voters by Senator James O. Eastland of Mississippi, who has spent much of his political life and his considerable power fighting such legislation as the Voting Rights Act. Yet he is being seen now campaigning side by side – and sometimes arm in arm – with Aaron Henry, longtime president of the N.A.A.C.P.'s State Conference of Branches in Mississippi.

Mr. Henry, to the dismay of a number of black spokesmen who have denounced this political alliance, has issued a plea to his friends to give Senator Eastland a chance. The Senator, for his part, seems to welcome an alliance that would have been unimaginable just five years ago and that signals the power of the 400,000 black voters on the Mississippi rolls.

There are other signs of significant change. The Washington-based Joint Center for Political Studies, which will soon celebrate a decade of black political progress, has assembled an impressive array of statistics indicating that there is reason to celebrate. A statement recently issued by the center notes:

"Facts and figures help to tell the story: eight black Congresspersons in 1968, 16 in 1978: one black elected state executive in 1968, four today, including two lieutenant governors. Within 10 years the number of black state senators increased 81 percent, and the number of black state representatives, 74 percent. The number of municipal black officials has tripled in the past 10 years, currently totaling 2,083. In 1970, there were only 48 black mayors in the United States; today there are 163, including the mayors of Los Angeles, Detroit, Washington, D.C., Atlanta, Newark and, as of May, New Orleans."

R. Wilkins

The New York Times, 6 March 1978

Sources: *The New York Times*, 26 February; 27 February; 28 February; 6 March 1978.